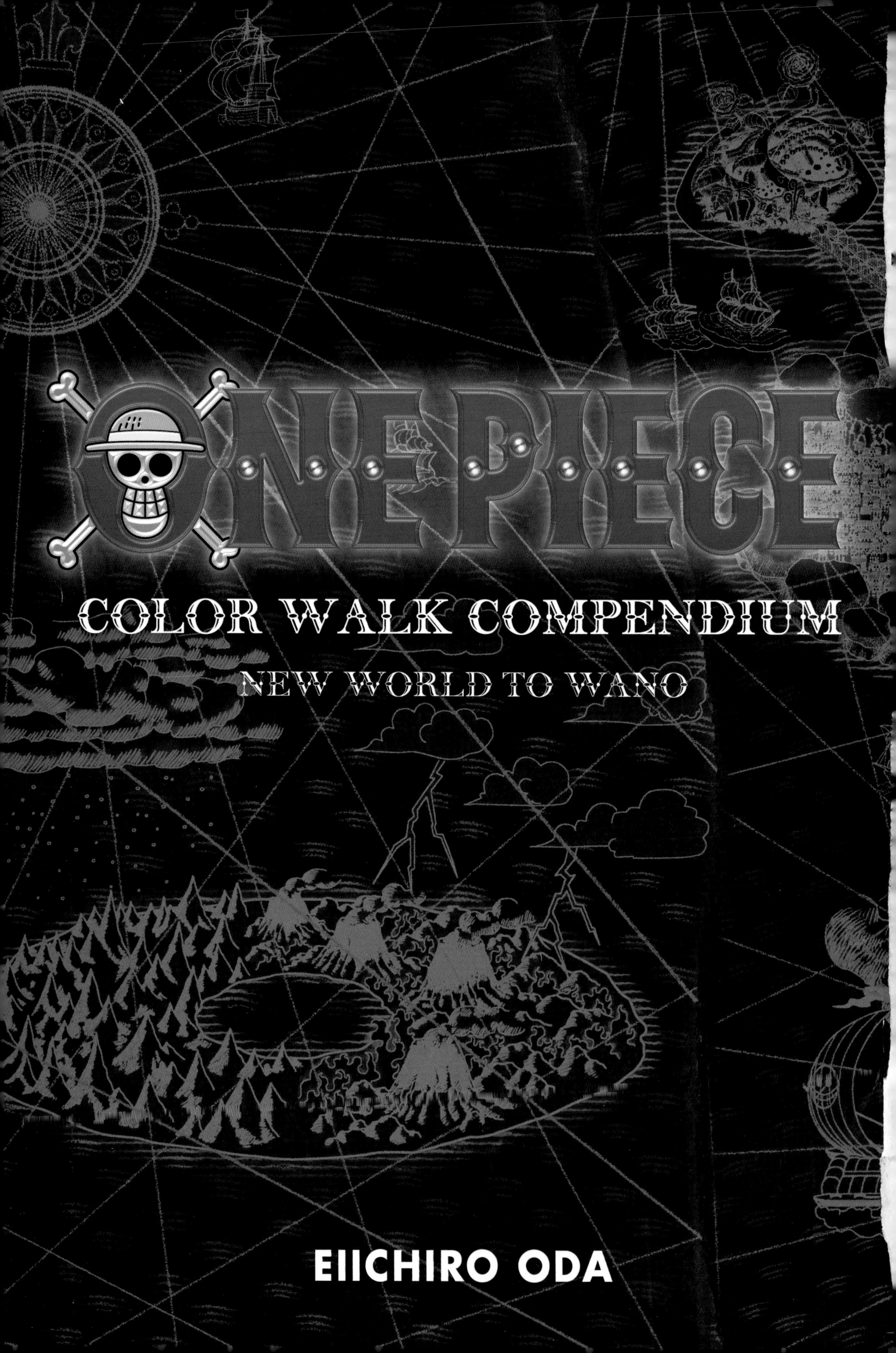

ONE PIECE

COLOR WALK COMPENDIUM

NEW WORLD TO WANO

EIICHIRO ODA

WALK COMPENDIUM

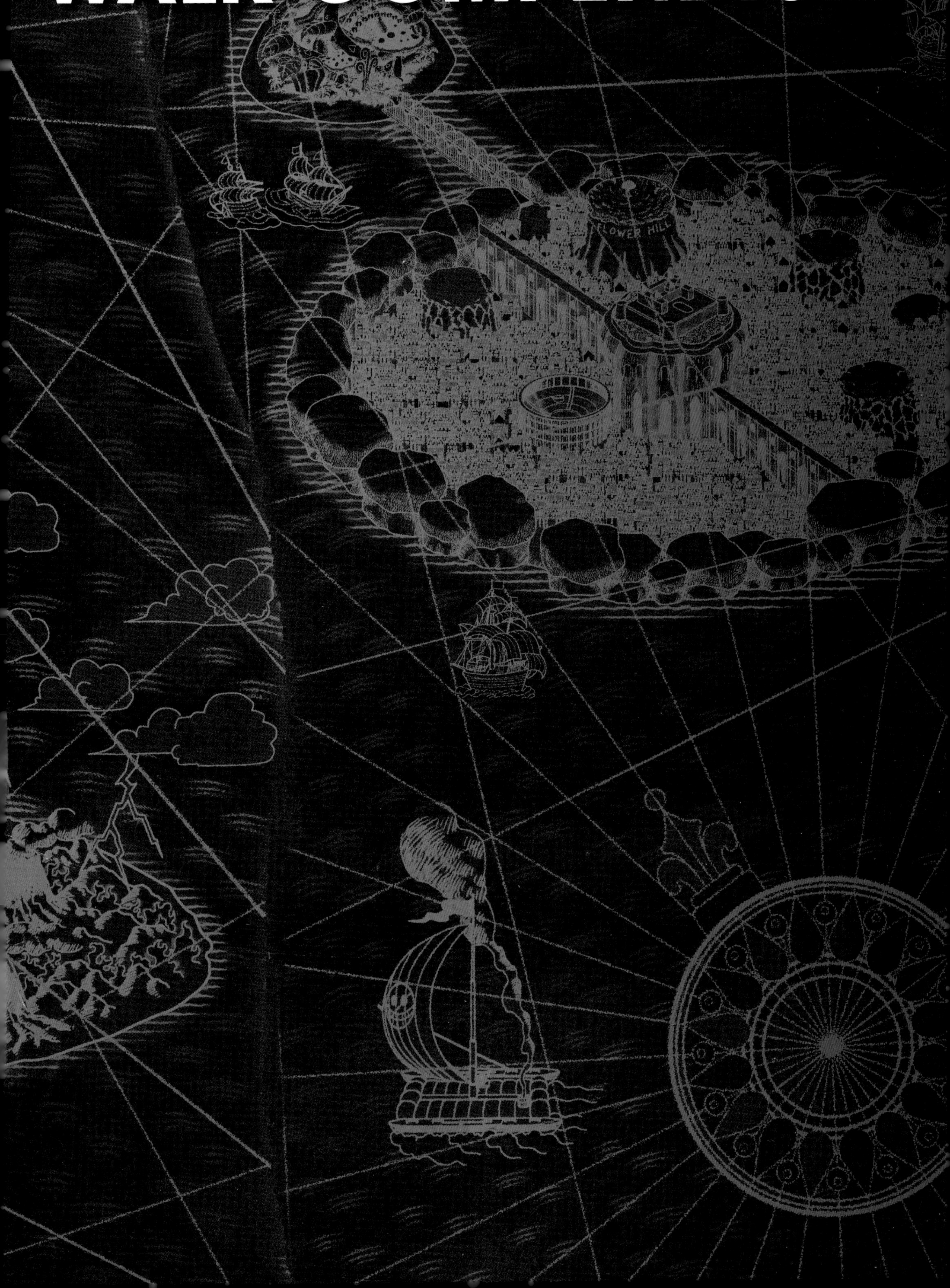
FLOWER HILL

ONE PIECE
NEW WORLD TO WANO

COLOR

TABLE OF CONTENTS

TWO YEARS
LATER...
SAILING DAY
HAS COME
AGAIN!

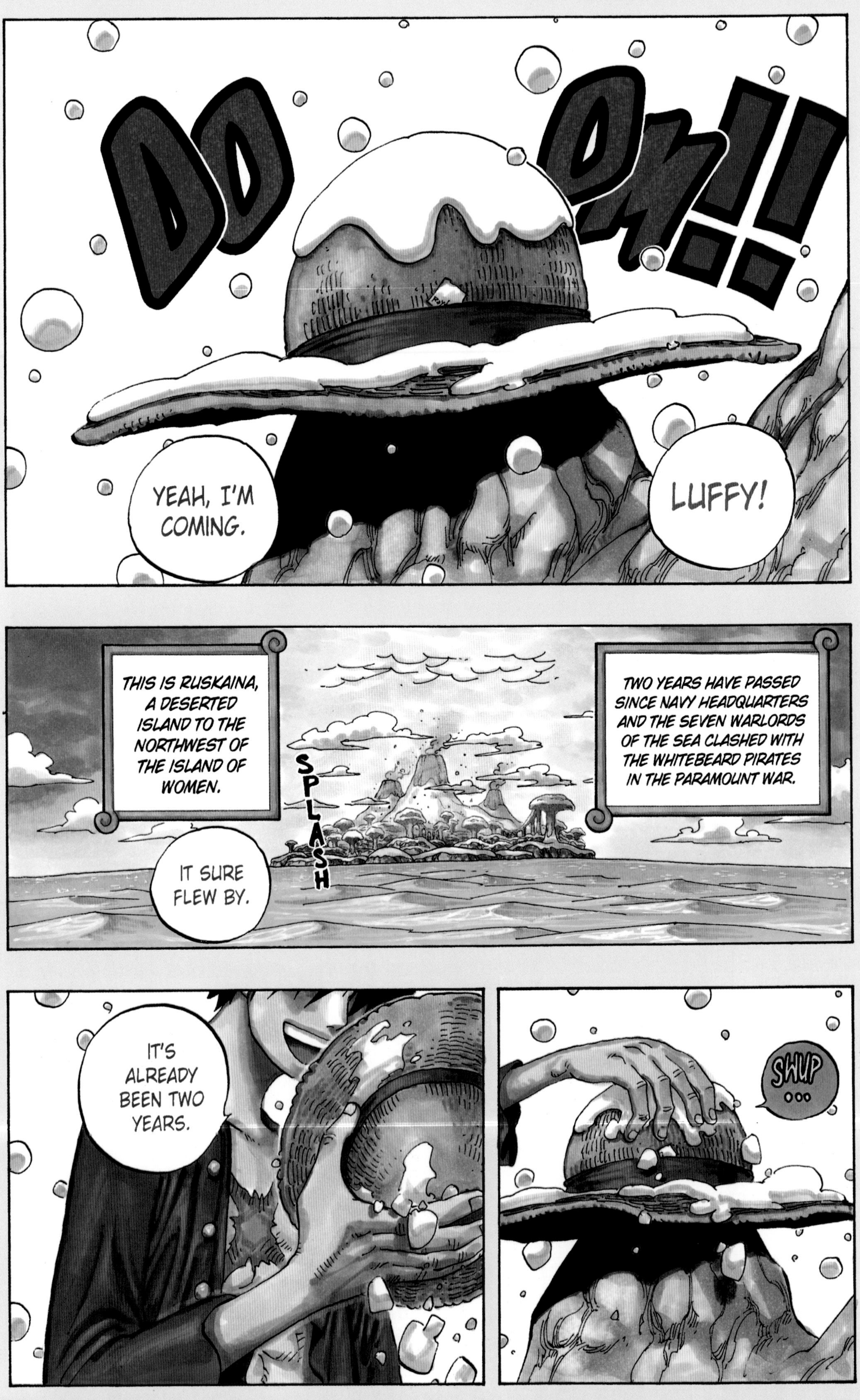
DOOM!!
LUFFY!
YEAH, I'M COMING.
TWO YEARS HAVE PASSED SINCE NAVY HEADQUARTERS AND THE SEVEN WARLORDS OF THE SEA CLASHED WITH THE WHITEBEARD PIRATES IN THE PARAMOUNT WAR.
THIS IS RUSKAINA, A DESERTED ISLAND TO THE NORTHWEST OF THE ISLAND OF WOMEN.
SPLASH
IT SURE FLEW BY.
SWUP ...
IT'S ALREADY BEEN TWO YEARS.

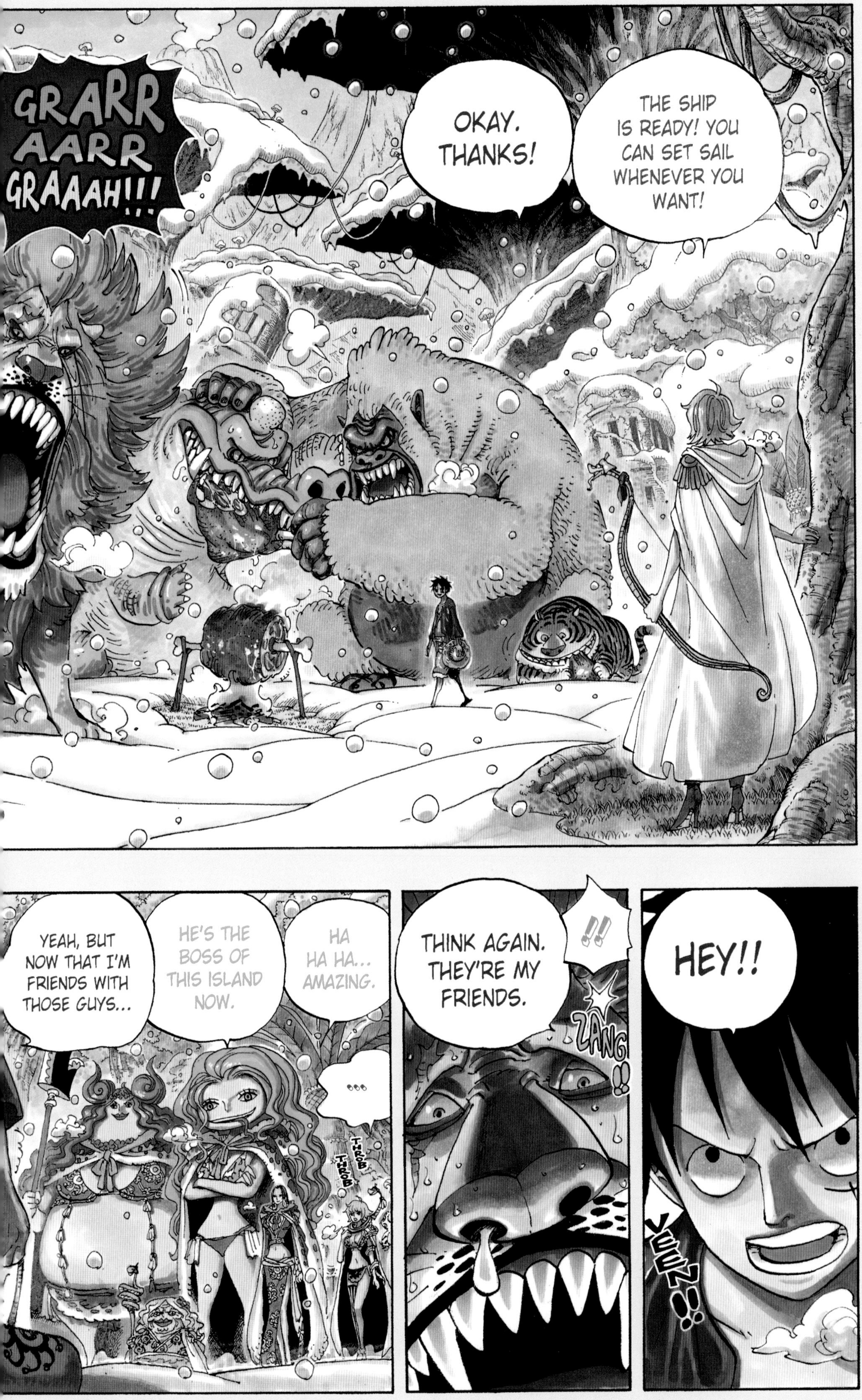
THE SHIP IS READY! YOU CAN SET SAIL WHENEVER YOU WANT!
OKAY. THANKS!
GRARR AARR GRAAAH!!!
HEY!!
VEEN!!
!!
THINK AGAIN. THEY'RE MY FRIENDS.
ZANG!!
...
THROB THROB
HA HA HA... AMAZING.
HE'S THE BOSS OF THIS ISLAND NOW.
YEAH, BUT NOW THAT I'M FRIENDS WITH THOSE GUYS...

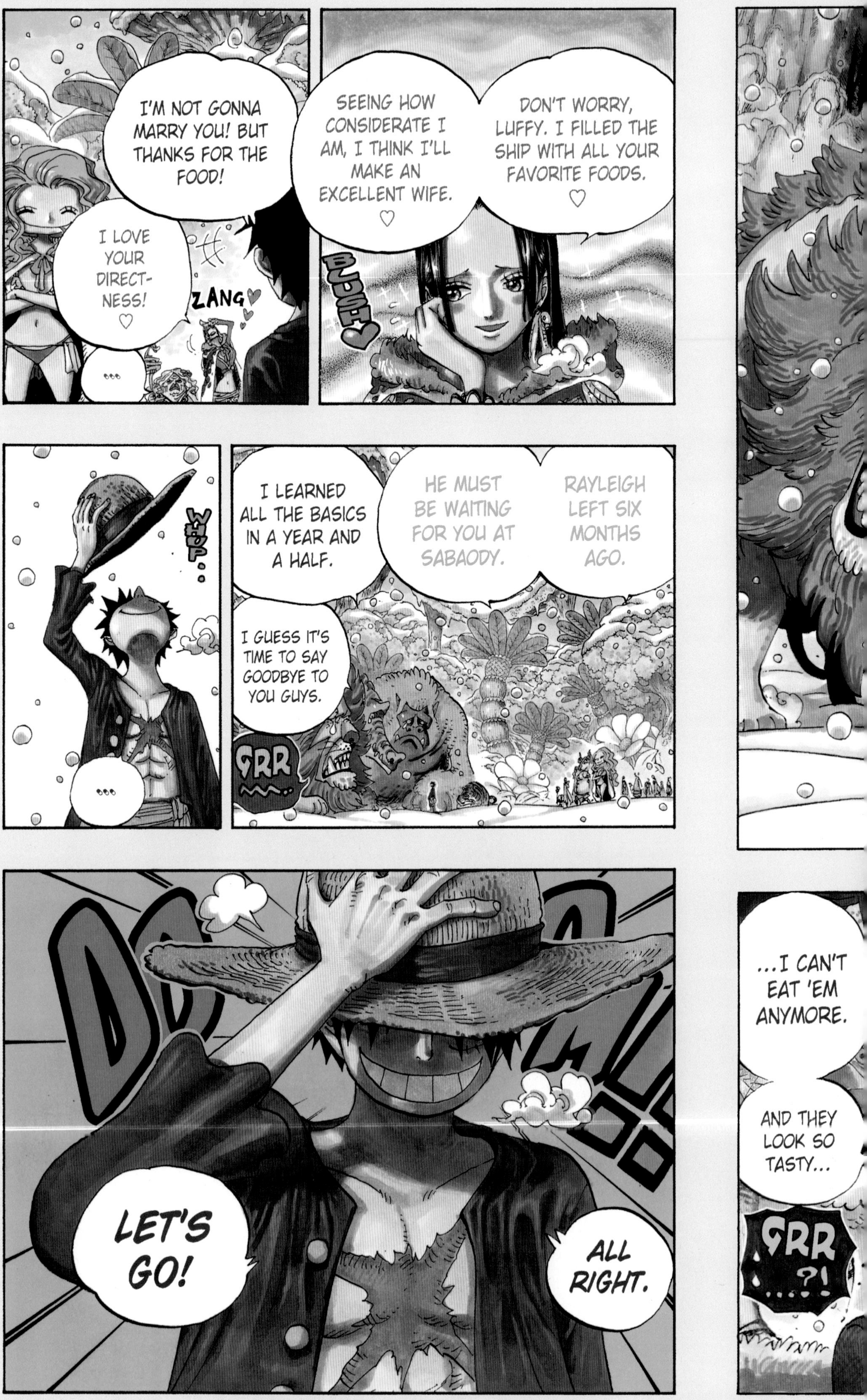
DON'T WORRY, LUFFY. I FILLED THE SHIP WITH ALL YOUR FAVORITE FOODS. ♡
SEEING HOW CONSIDERATE I AM, I THINK I'LL MAKE AN EXCELLENT WIFE. ♡
BLUSH
I'M NOT GONNA MARRY YOU! BUT THANKS FOR THE FOOD!
I LOVE YOUR DIRECT-NESS! ♡
ZANG
...
RAYLEIGH LEFT SIX MONTHS AGO.
HE MUST BE WAITING FOR YOU AT SABAODY.
I LEARNED ALL THE BASICS IN A YEAR AND A HALF.
I GUESS IT'S TIME TO SAY GOODBYE TO YOU GUYS.
GRR
WHUP
...
...I CAN'T EAT 'EM ANYMORE.
AND THEY LOOK SO TASTY...
GRR
?!
ALL RIGHT.
LET'S GO!

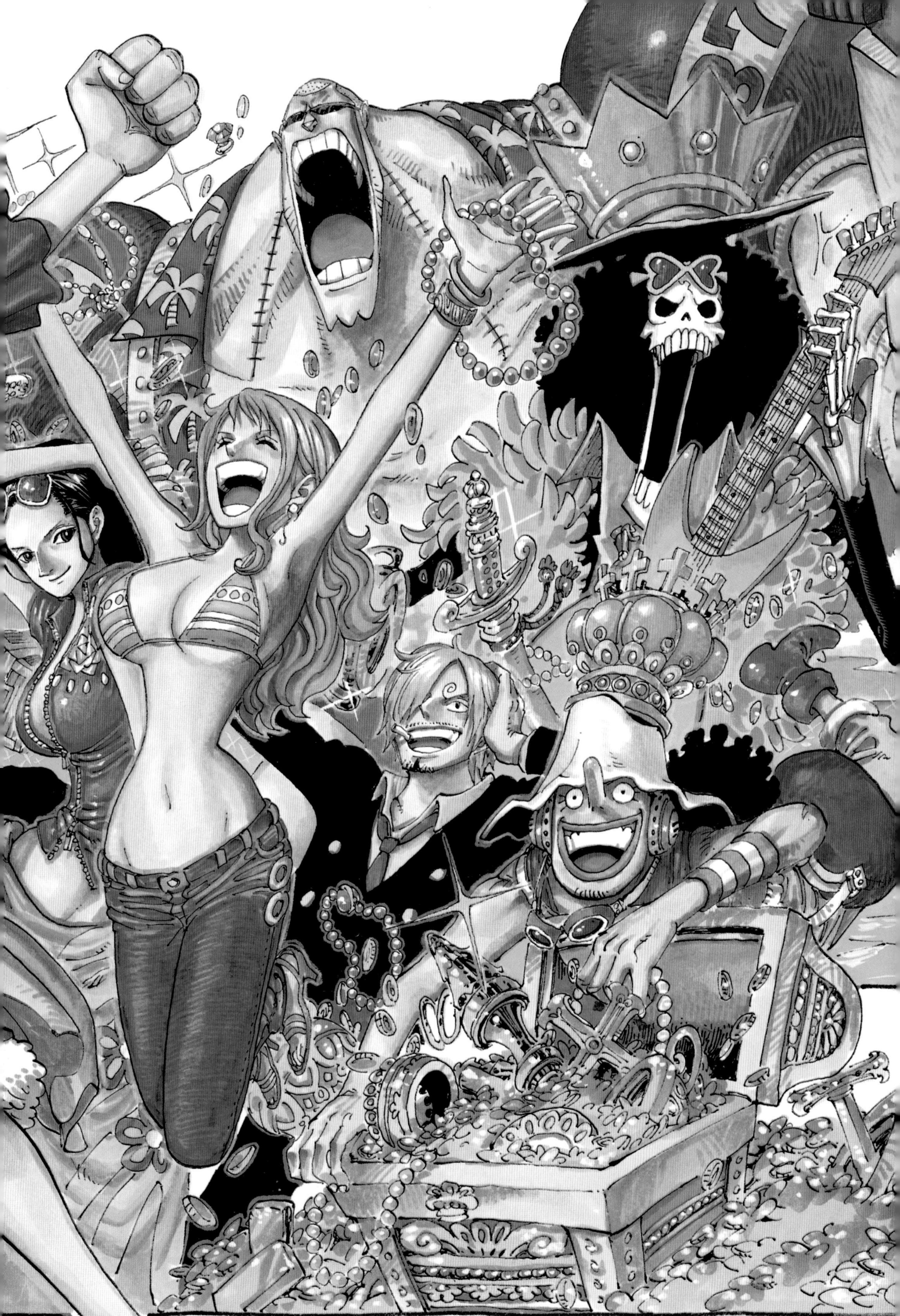

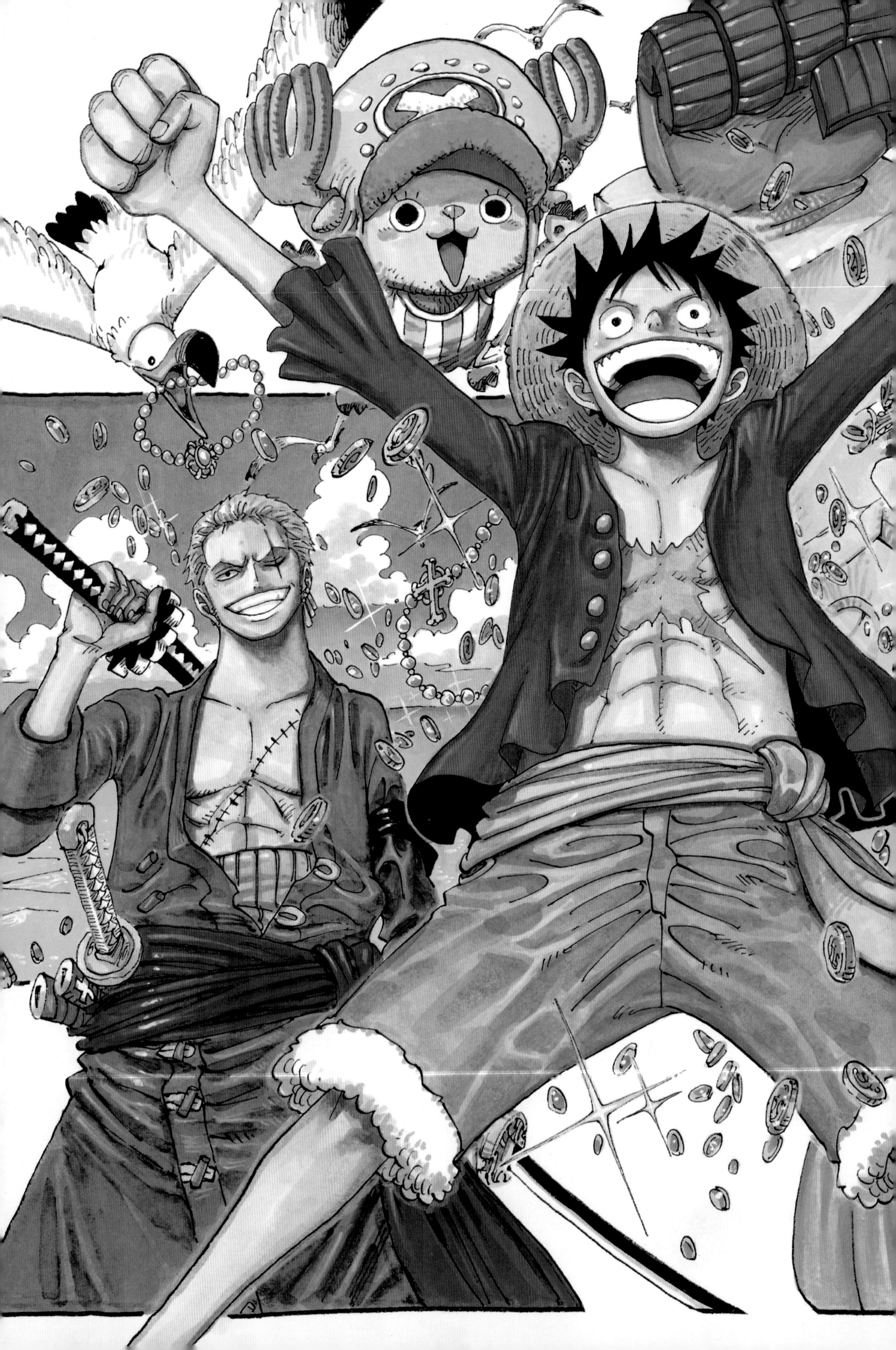

2010

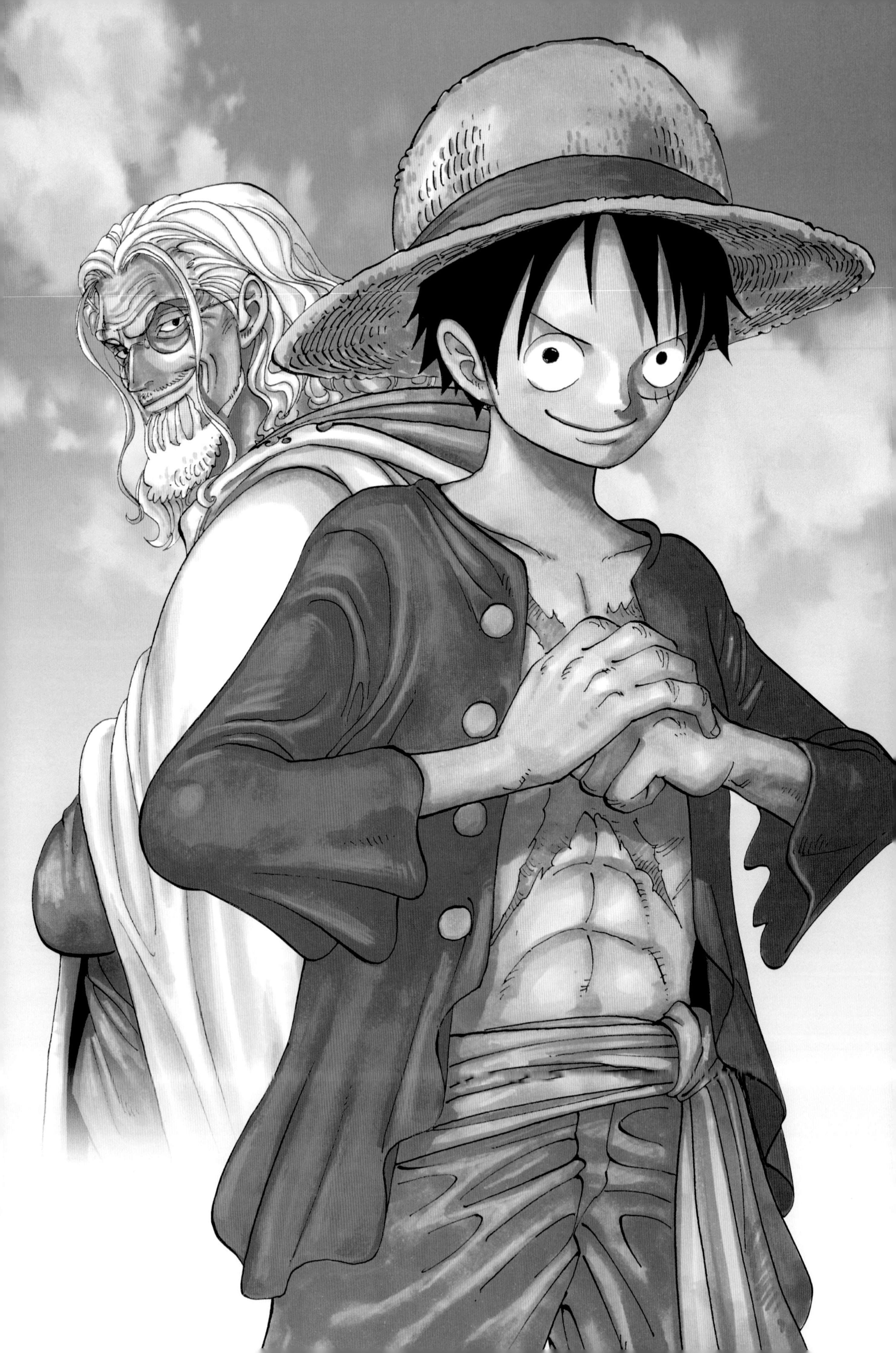

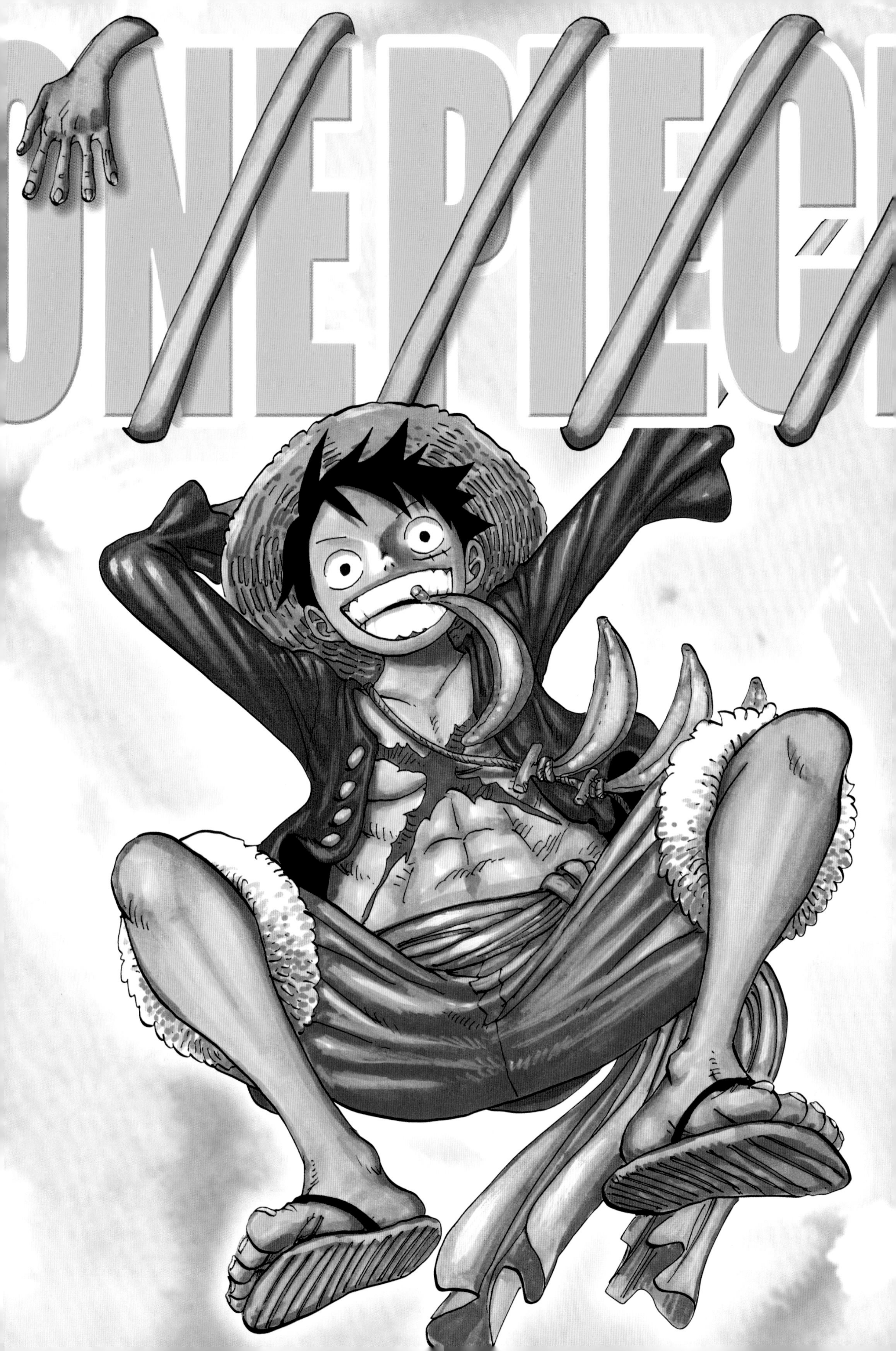

 Comments P.8–9

We shot past the years Luffy and the crew spent training. Now we're meeting up to resume the adventure two years later. A new act begins! I hope this one was familiar for you. I depicted Luffy's growth by composing this piece with the same structure as the spread from chapter 1.

Comments P.20–21

If fish-men and humans lived together on the seafloor, what culture would result? Luffy and the gang are taking the Fish Bus on the Water Road to the Mermaid Beach.

Comments P.24–25

I drew this one when I was obsessed with collecting Dominique Gault's miniature-town buildings. There's just something nice about a balloon seller, isn't there?

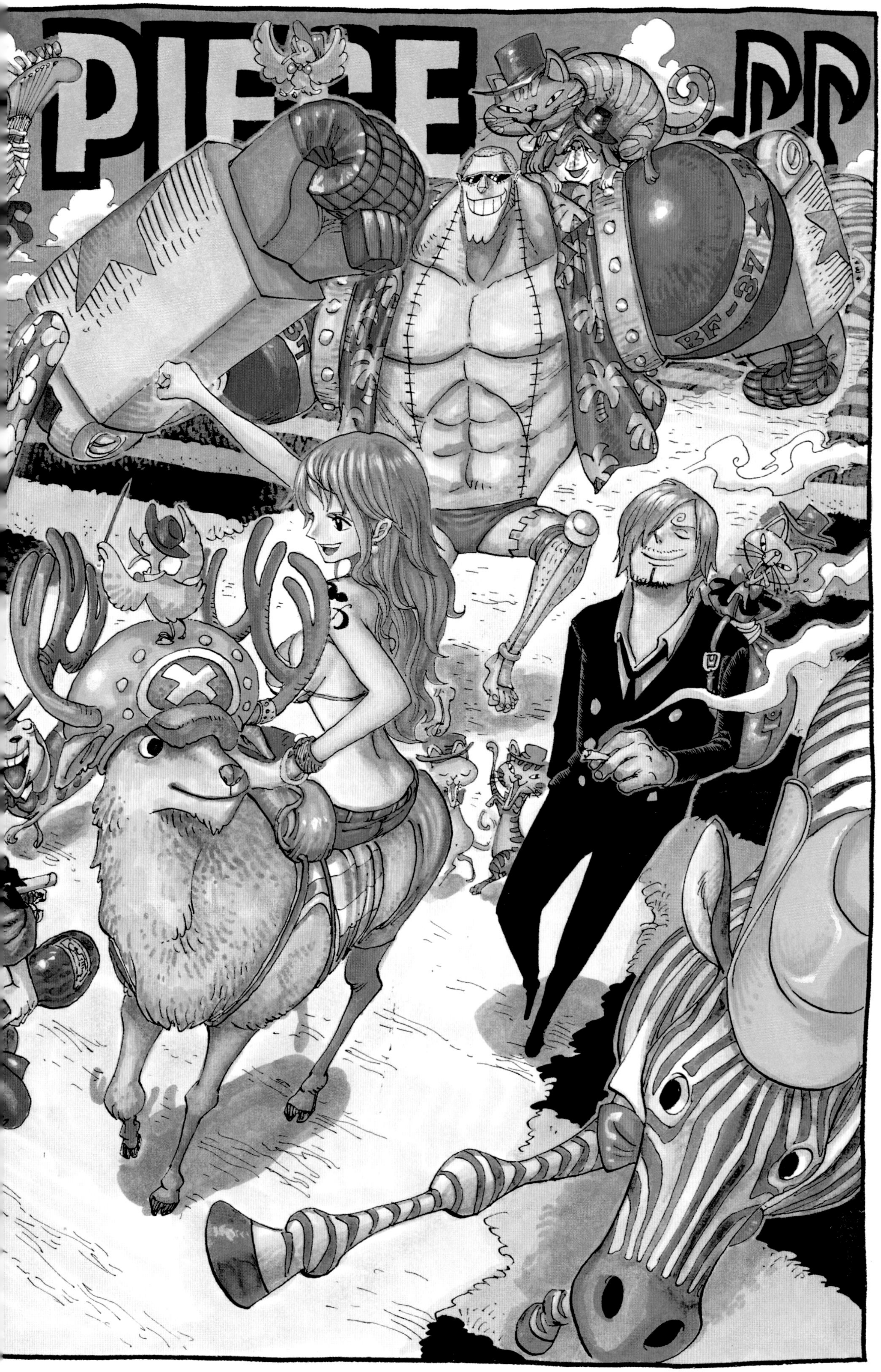
PIECE
BF-37

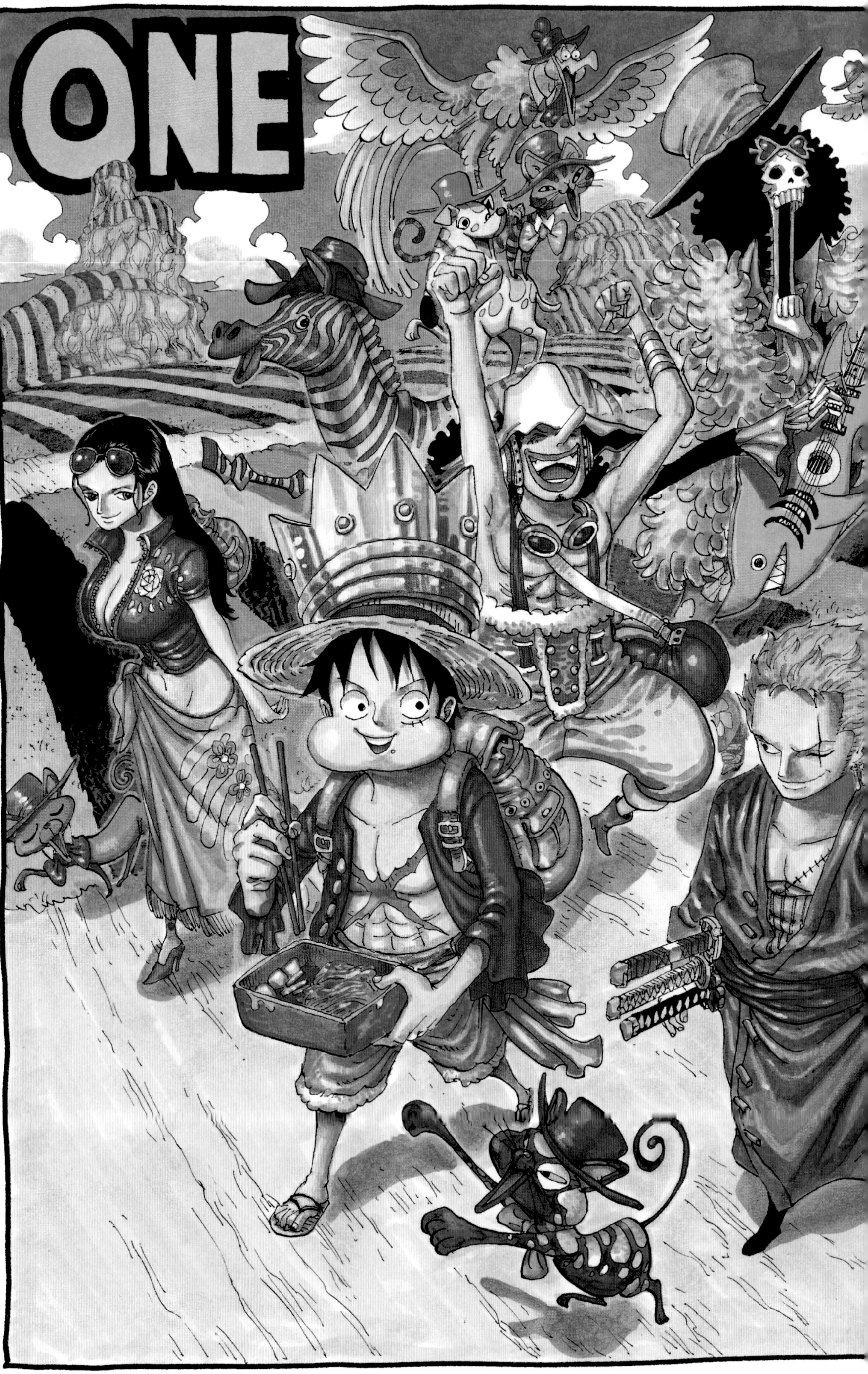
ONE

2011

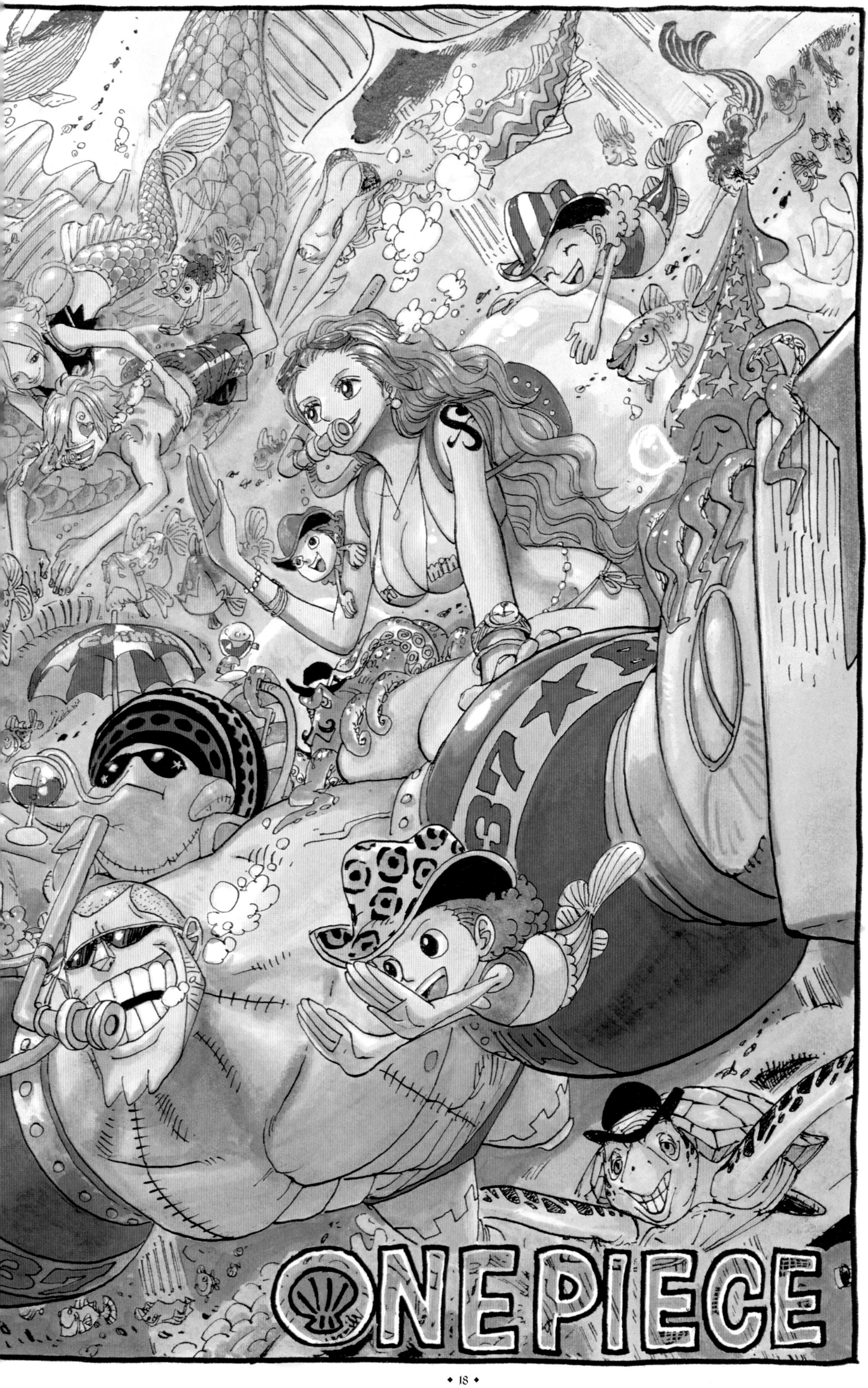
ONE PIECE

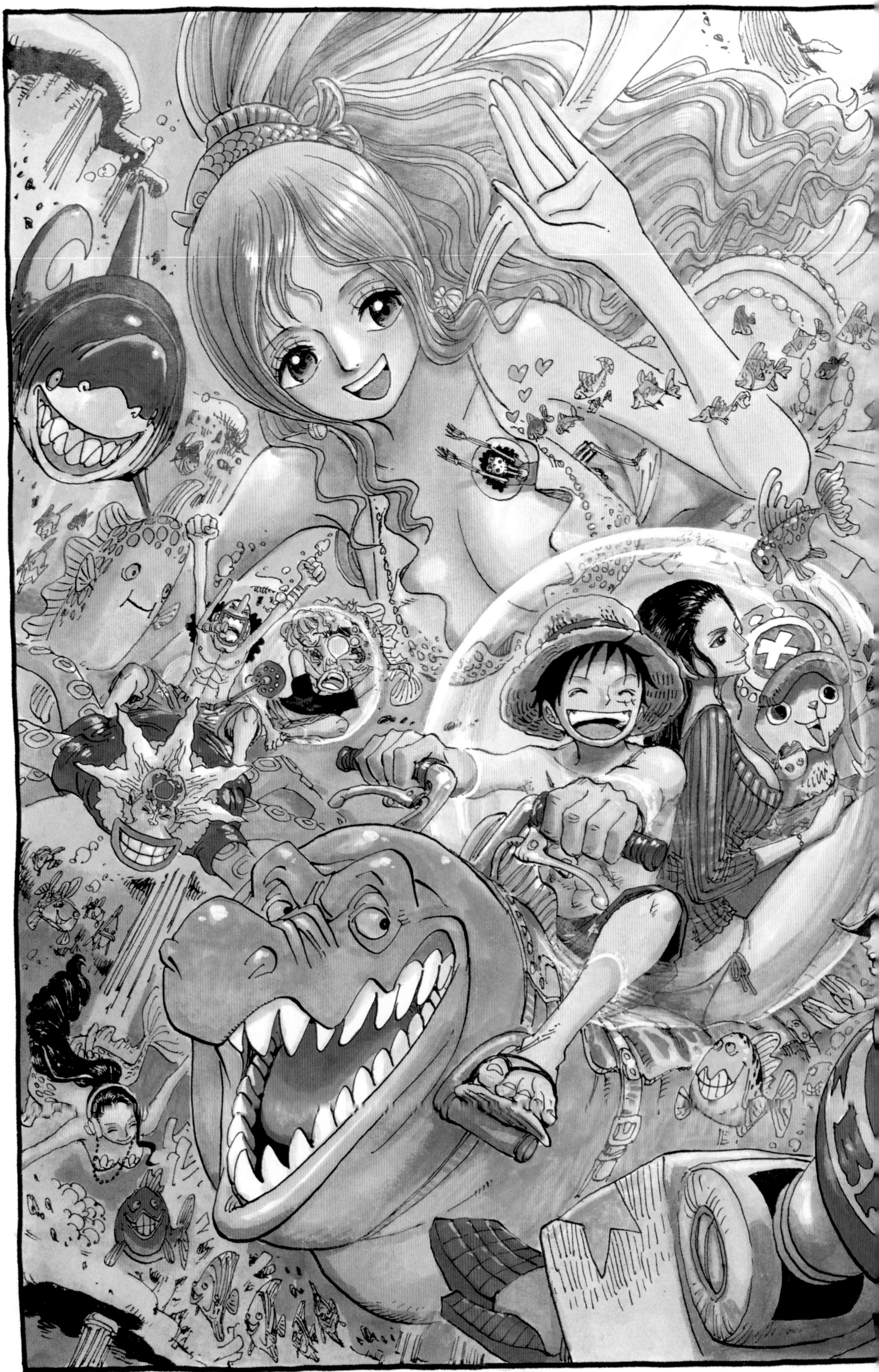

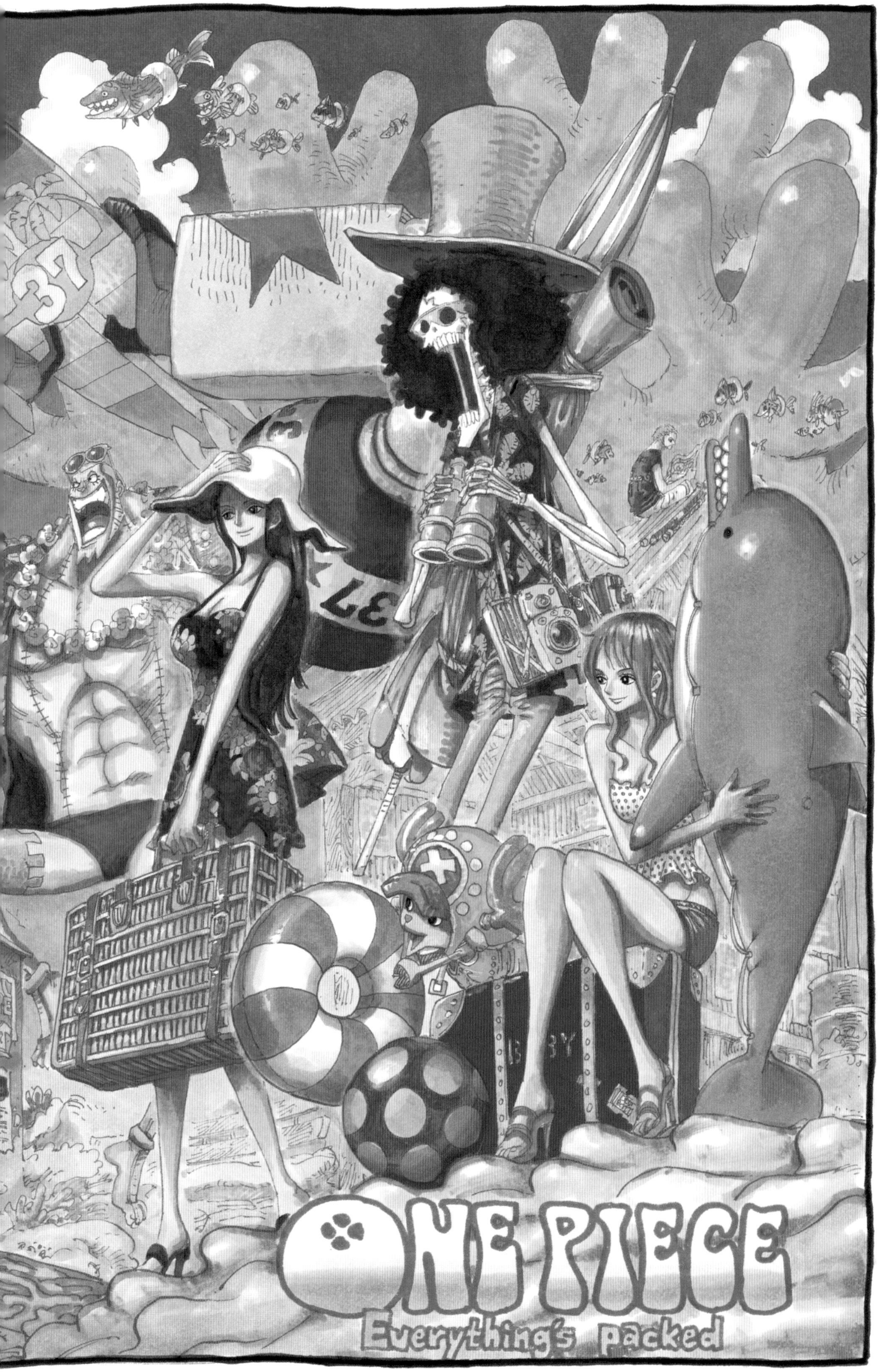
ONE PIECE
Everything's packed

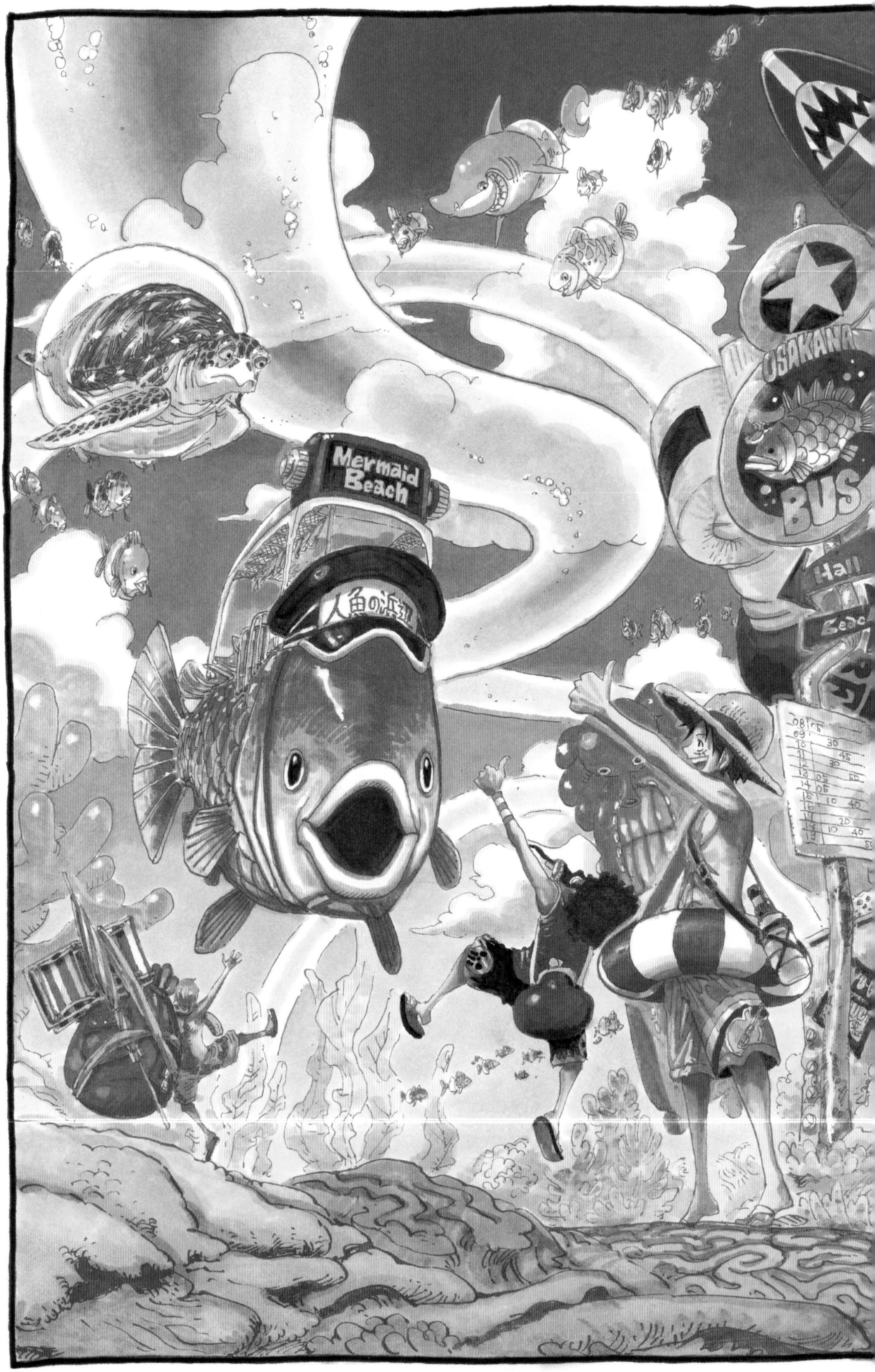
Mermaid Beach
人魚の浜辺
OSAKANA
BUS
Hall

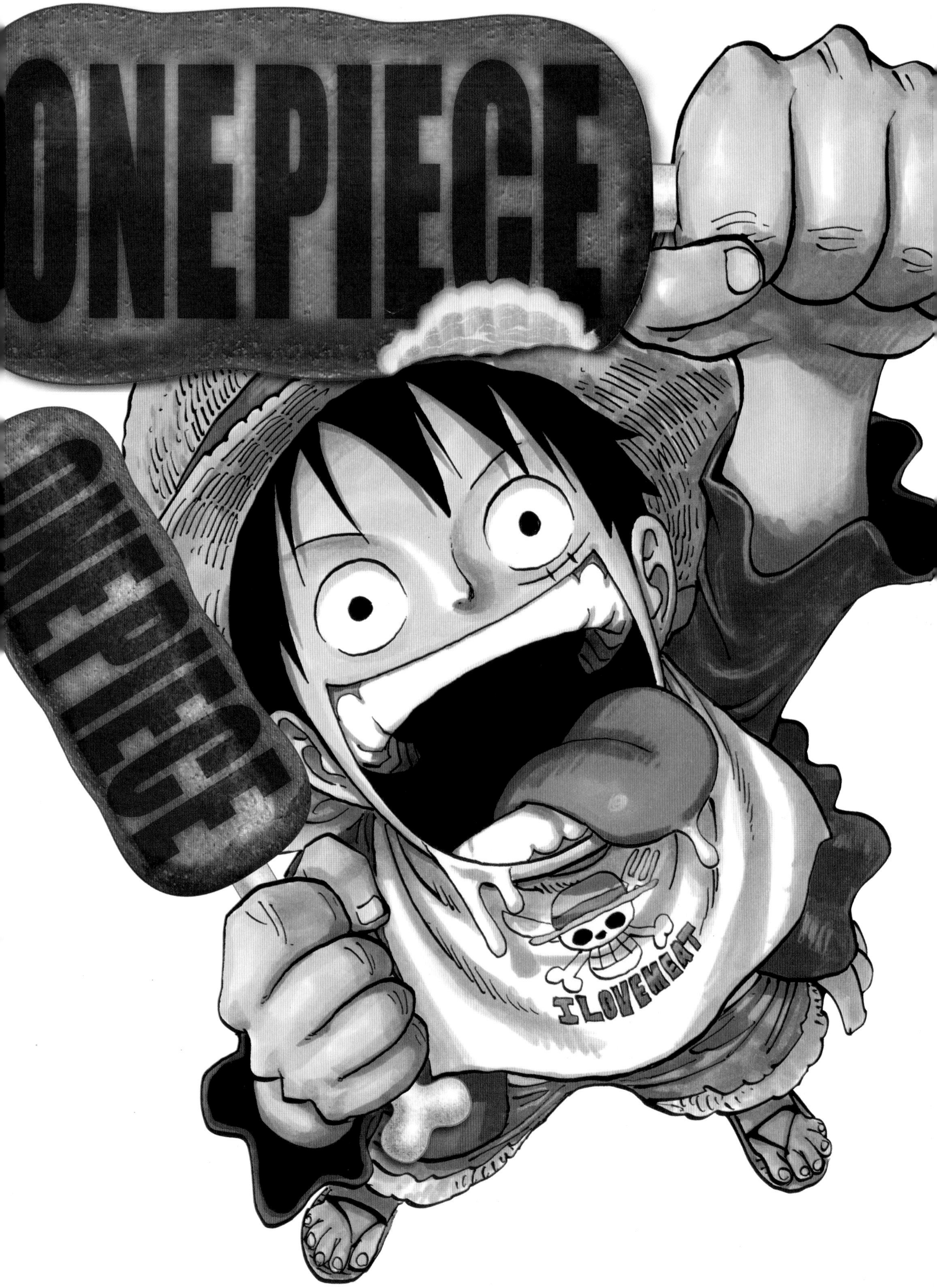
ONE PIECE
I LOVE MEAT

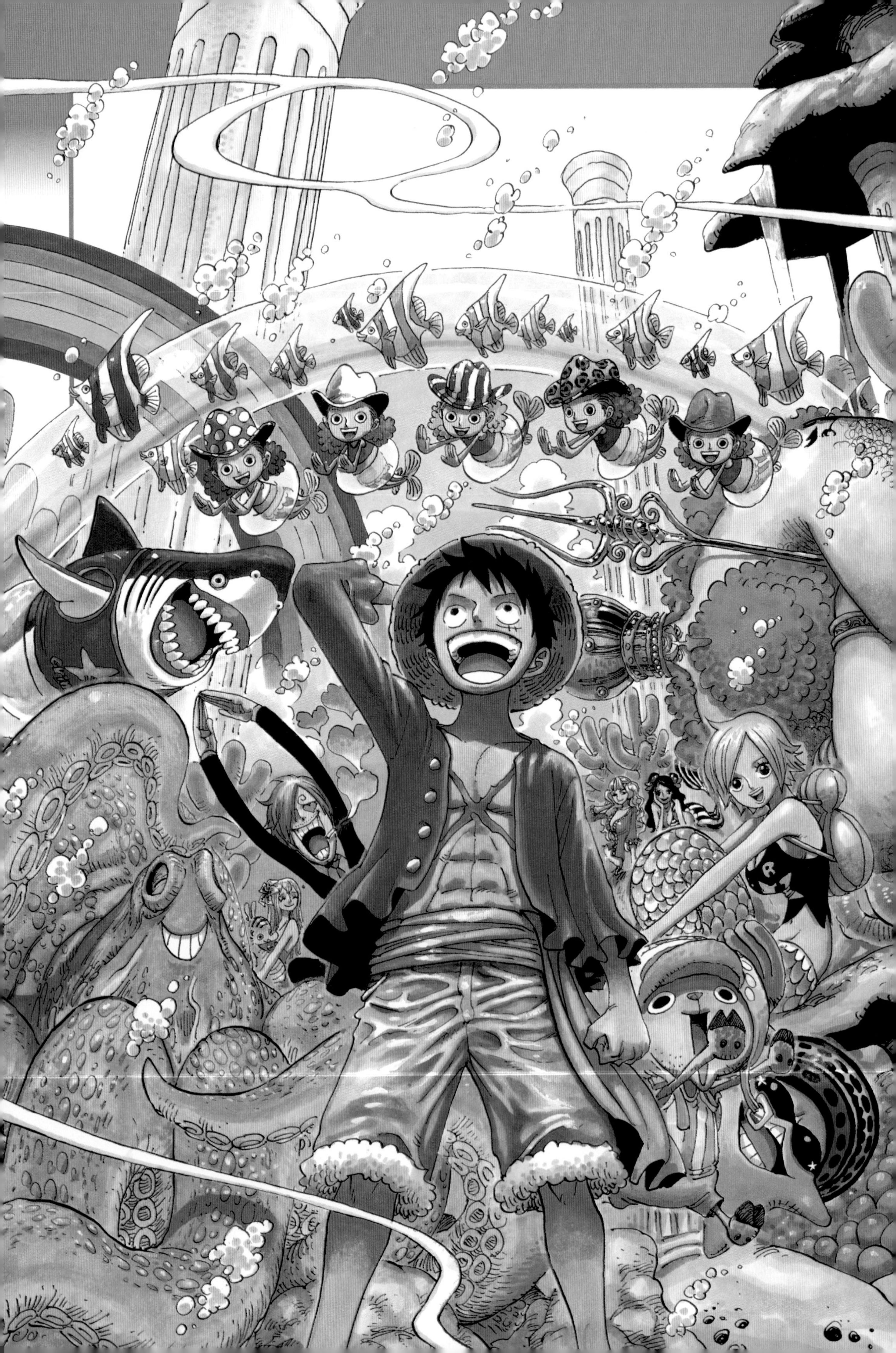

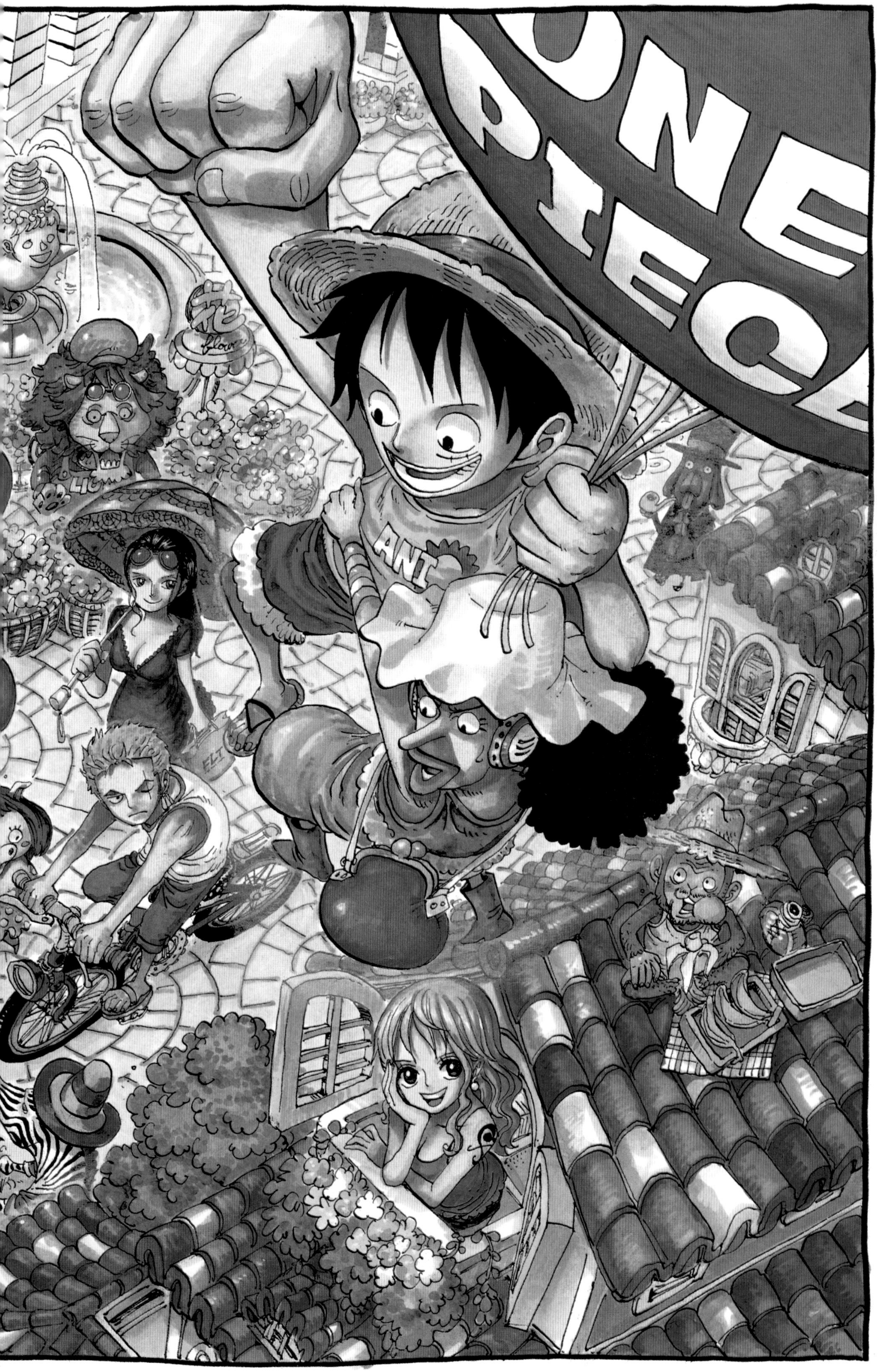
ONE
ANT

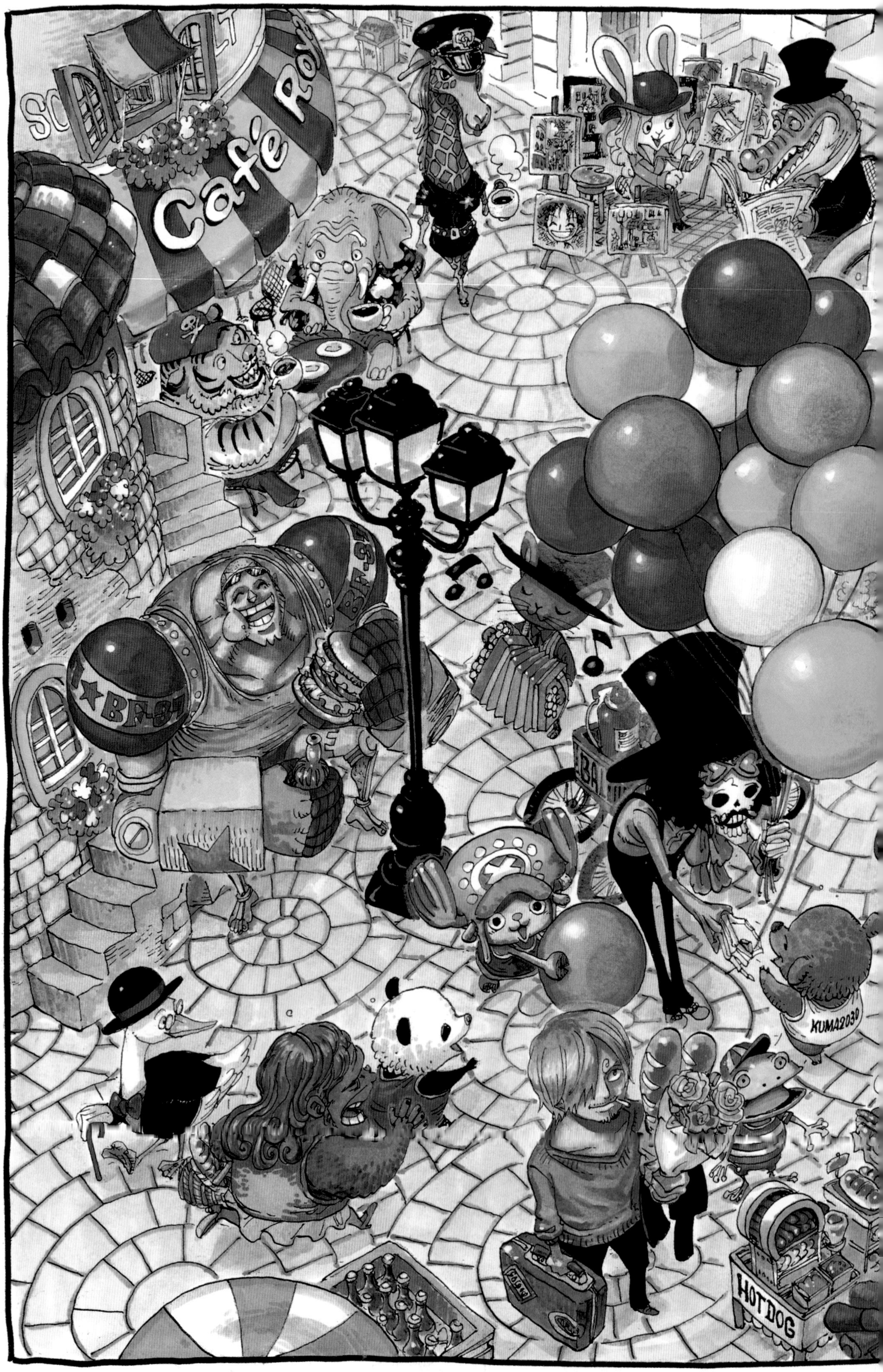
Café
BF-37
KUMA2030
HOT DOG

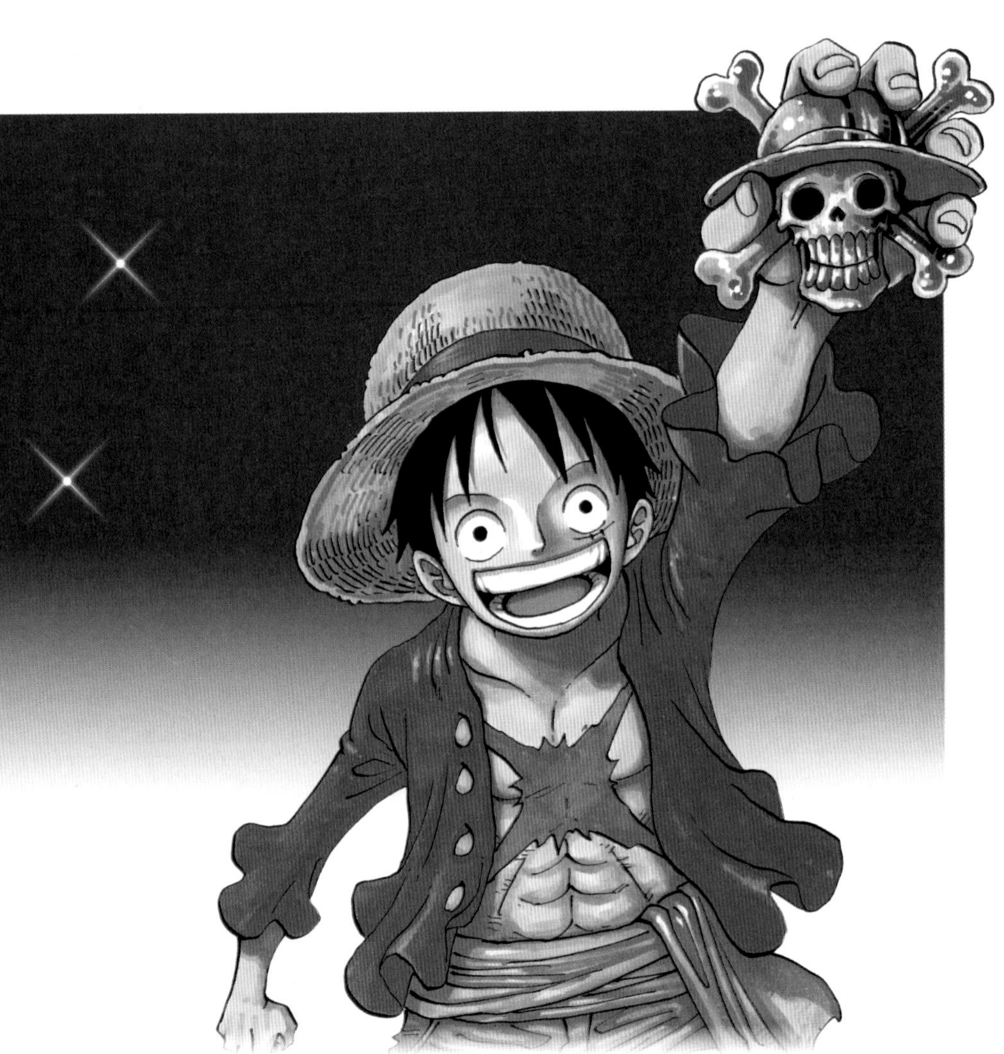

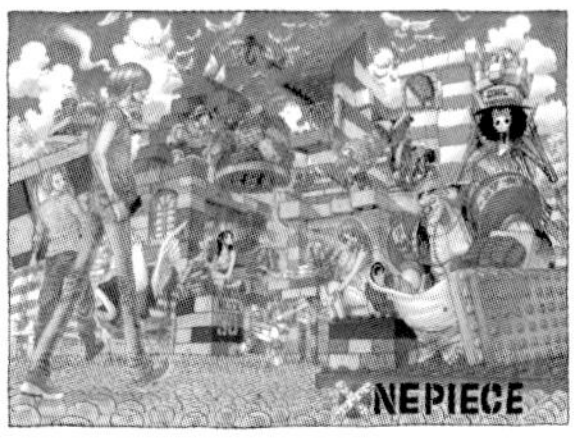

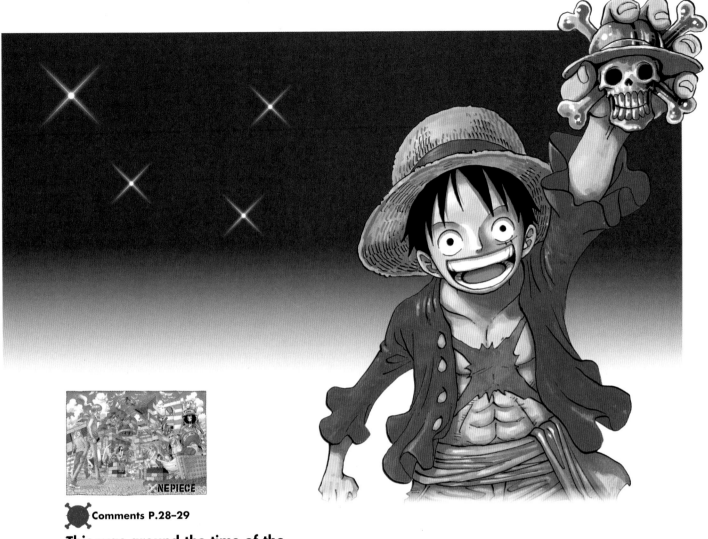

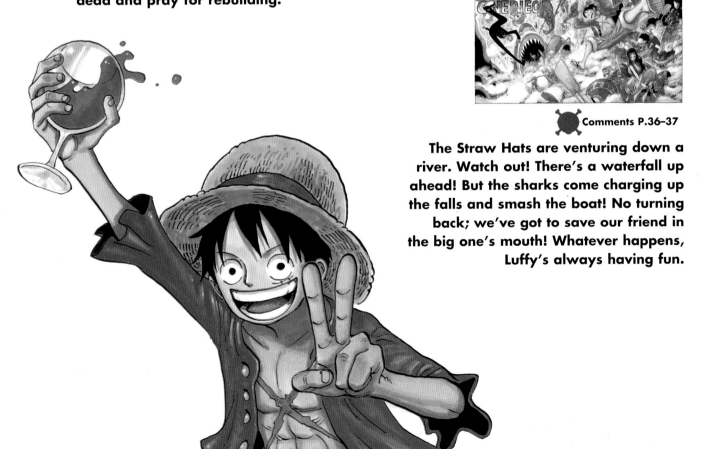

Comments P.28–29

This was around the time of the terrible earthquake in eastern Japan. I drew it hoping to remember the dead and pray for rebuilding.

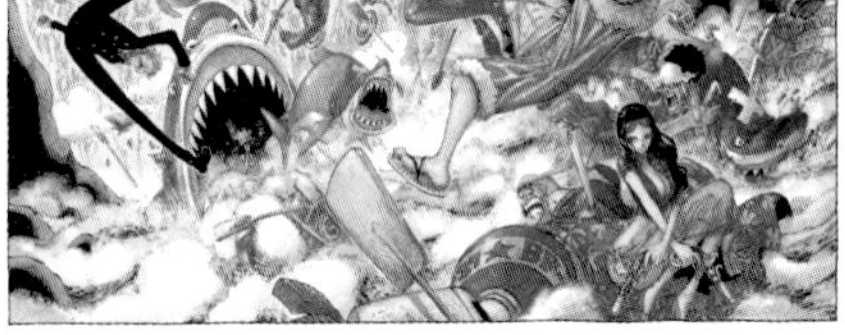

Comments P.36–37

The Straw Hats are venturing down a river. Watch out! There's a waterfall up ahead! But the sharks come charging up the falls and smash the boat! No turning back; we've got to save our friend in the big one's mouth! Whatever happens, Luffy's always having fun.

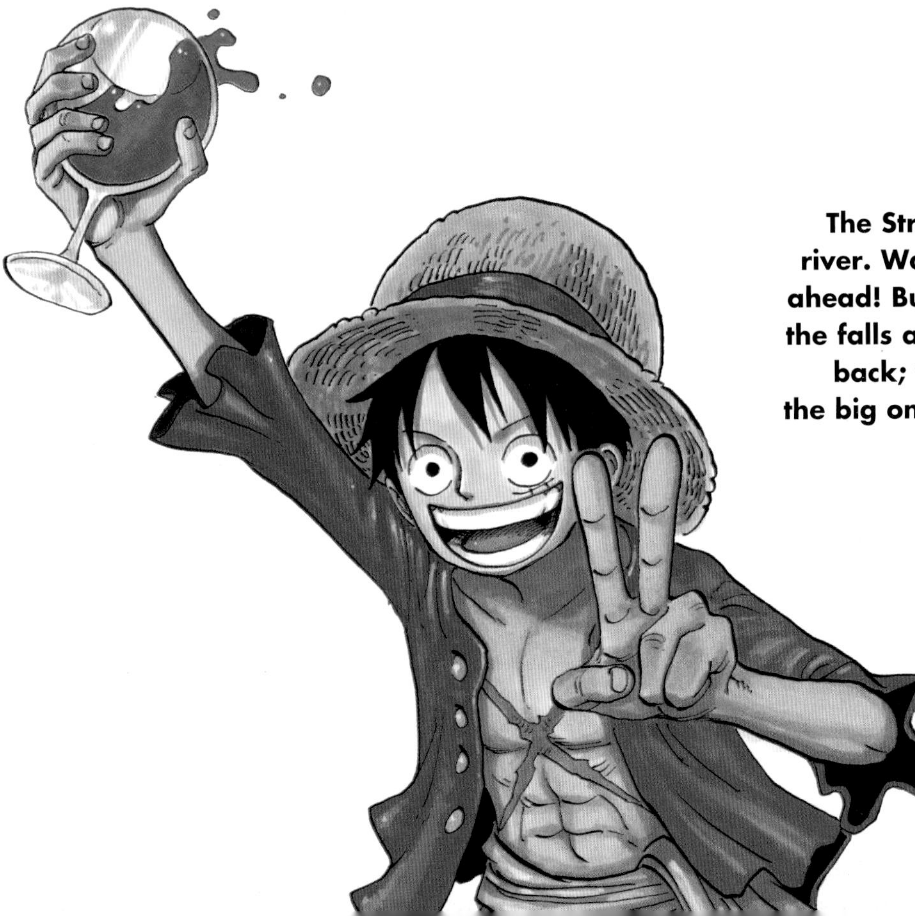

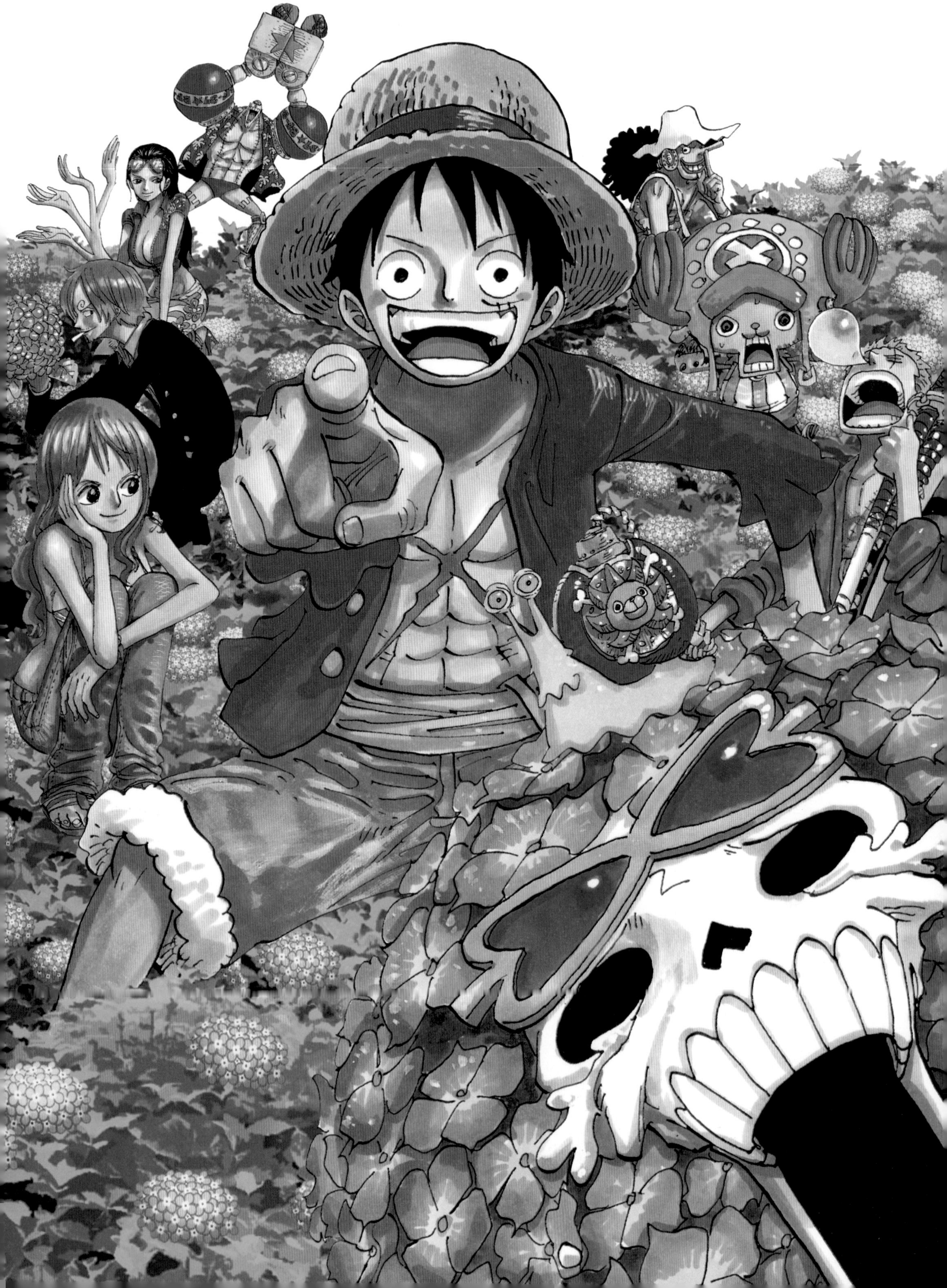

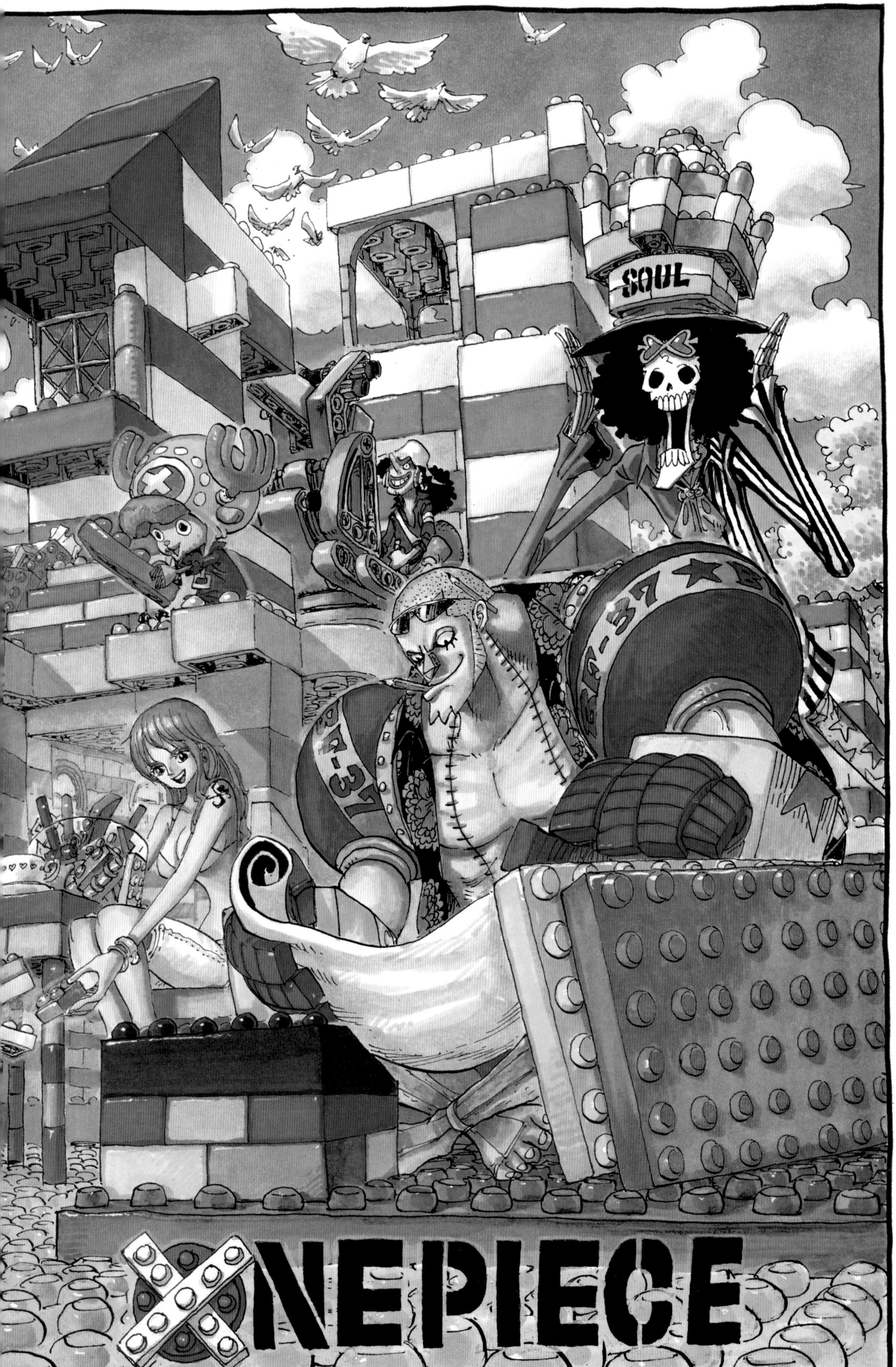
SOUL
BF-37
BF-37
NEPIECE

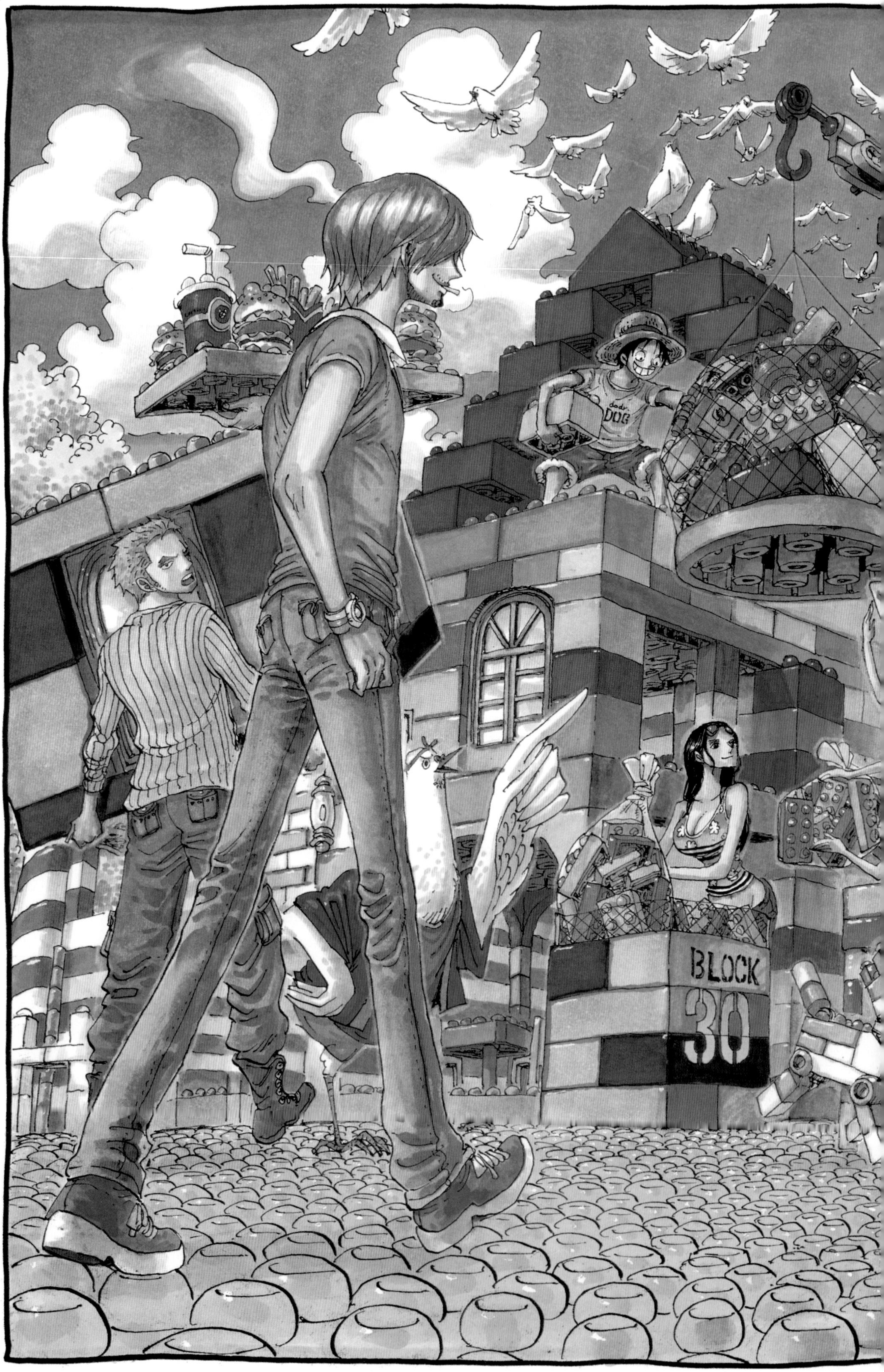
BLOCK
30

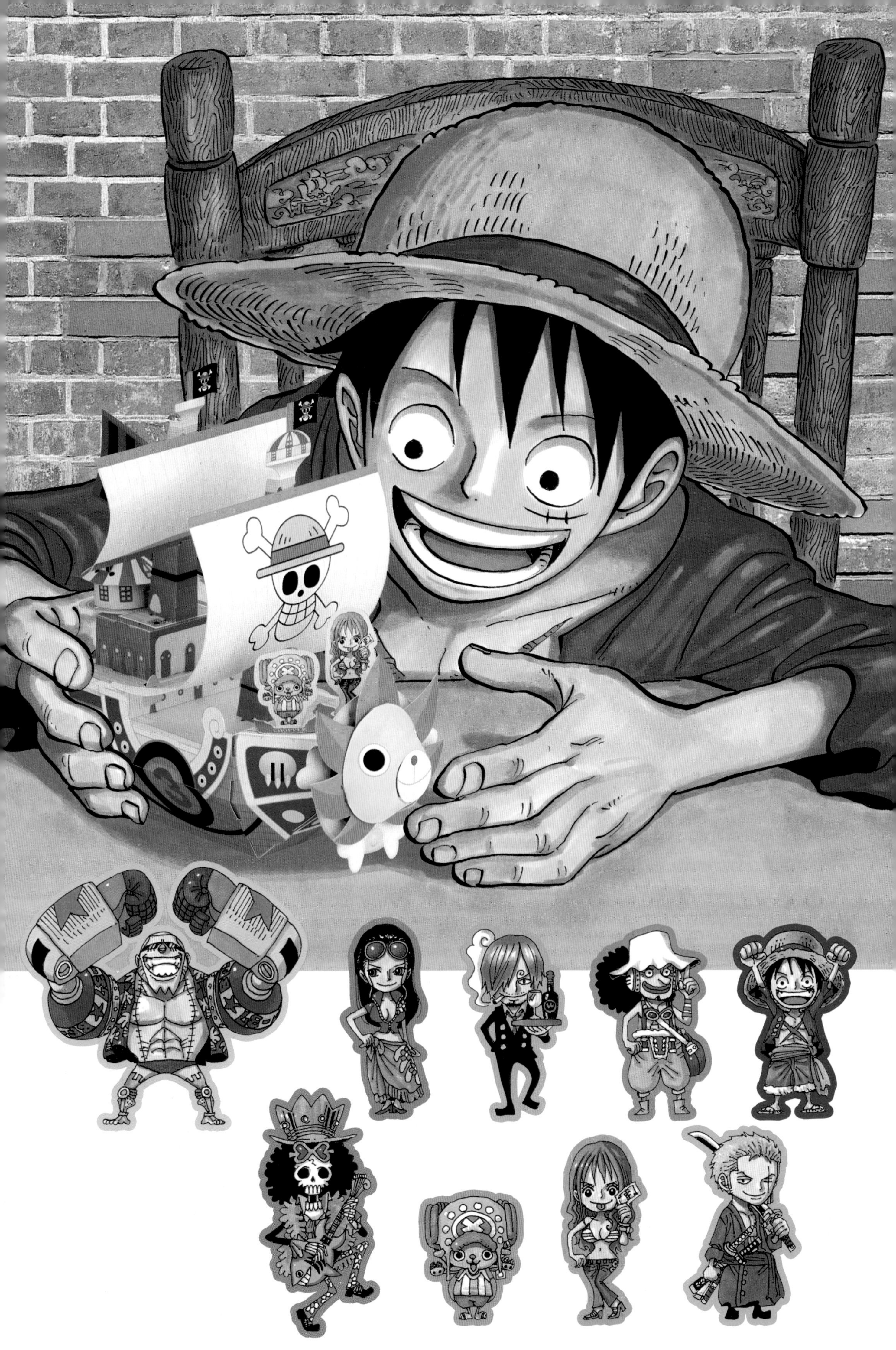

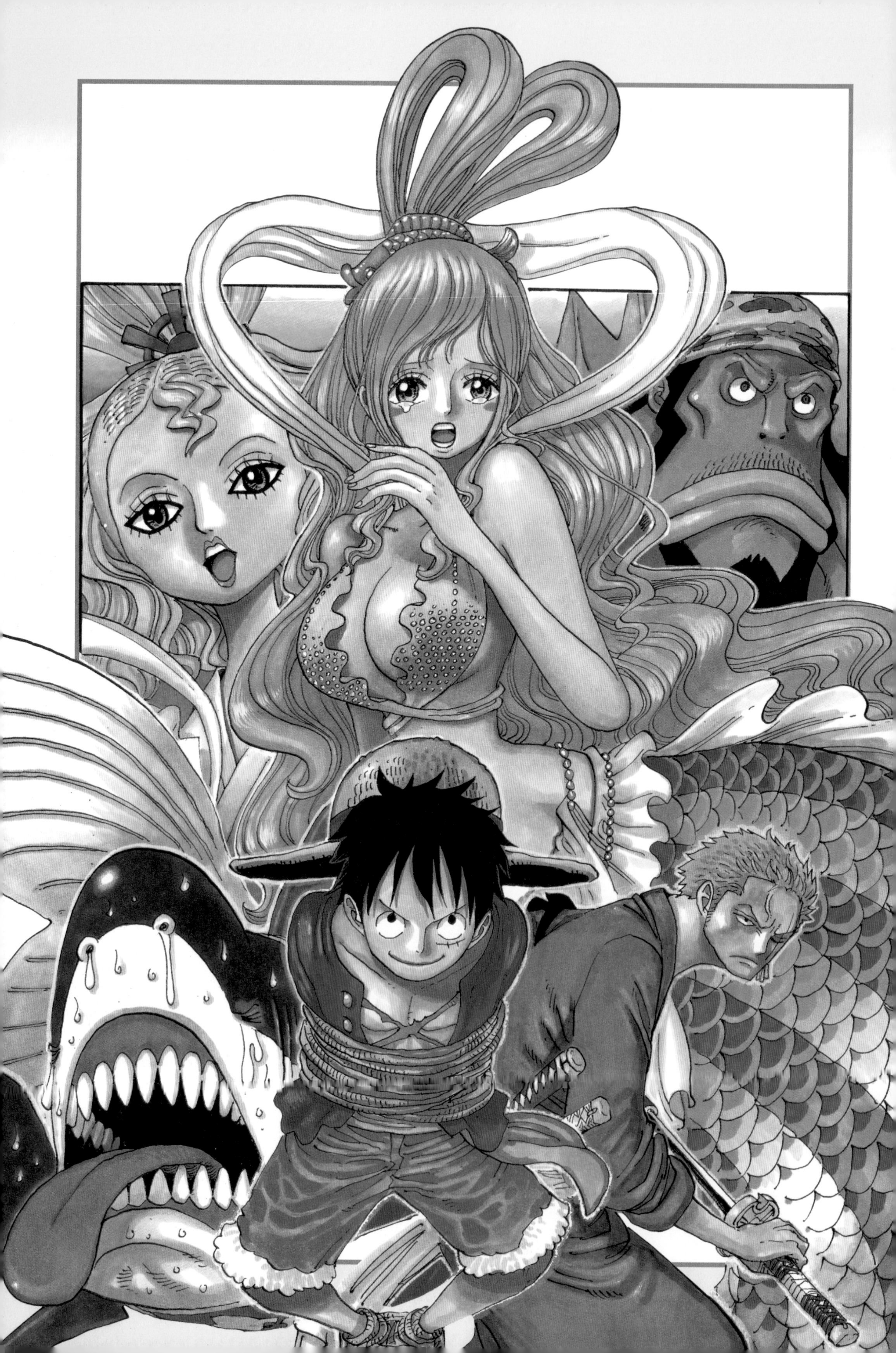

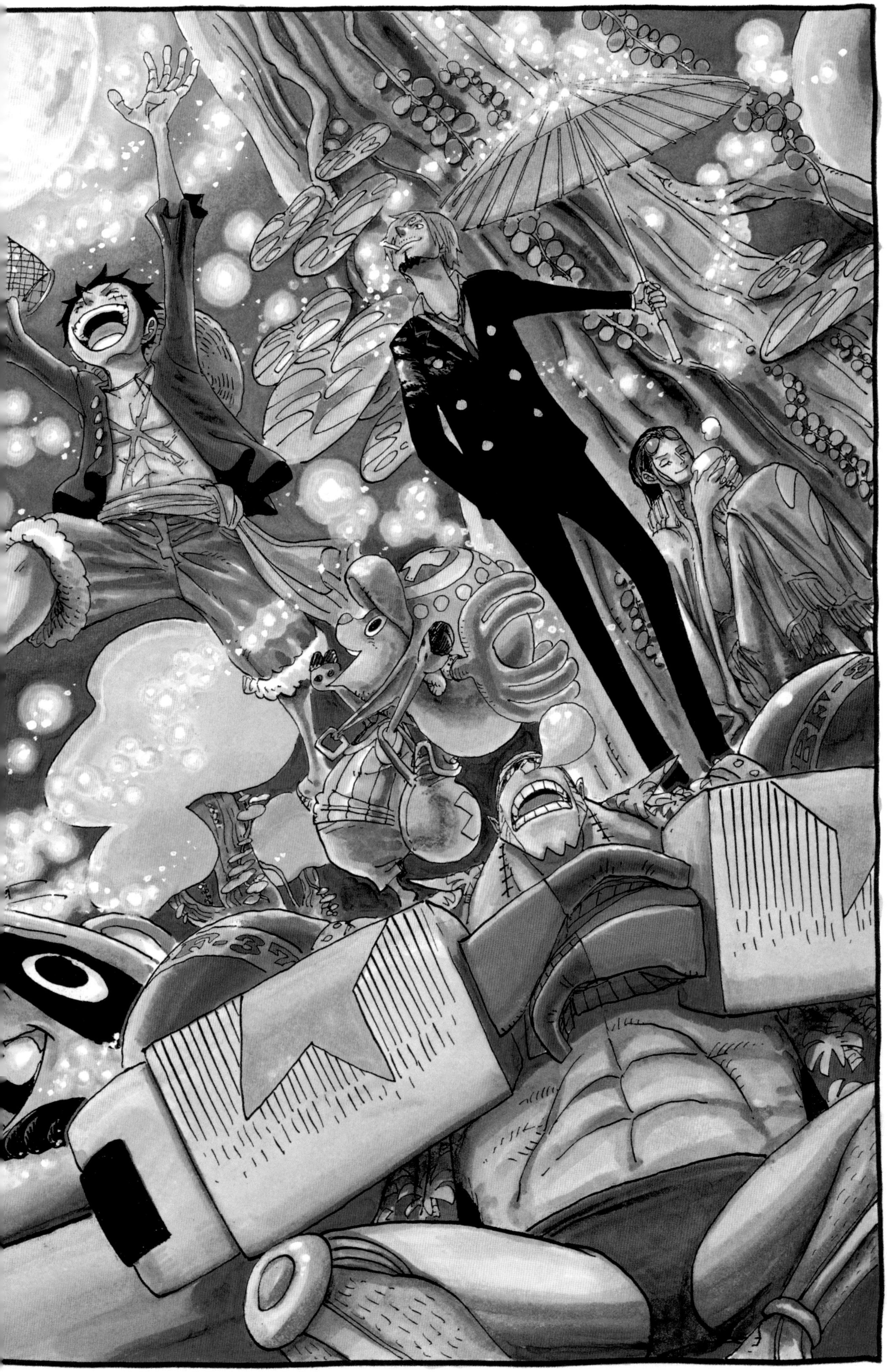

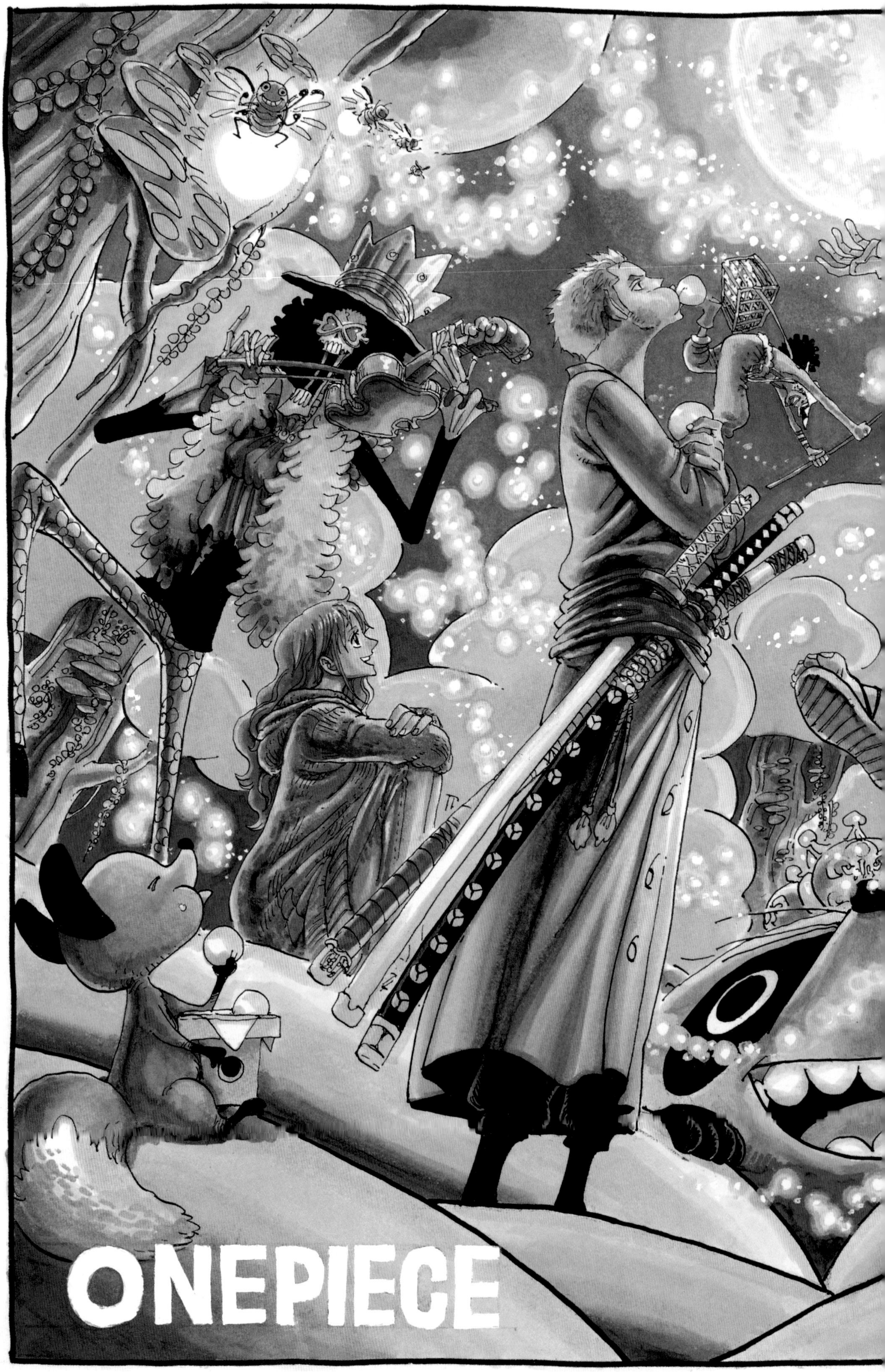
ONEPIECE

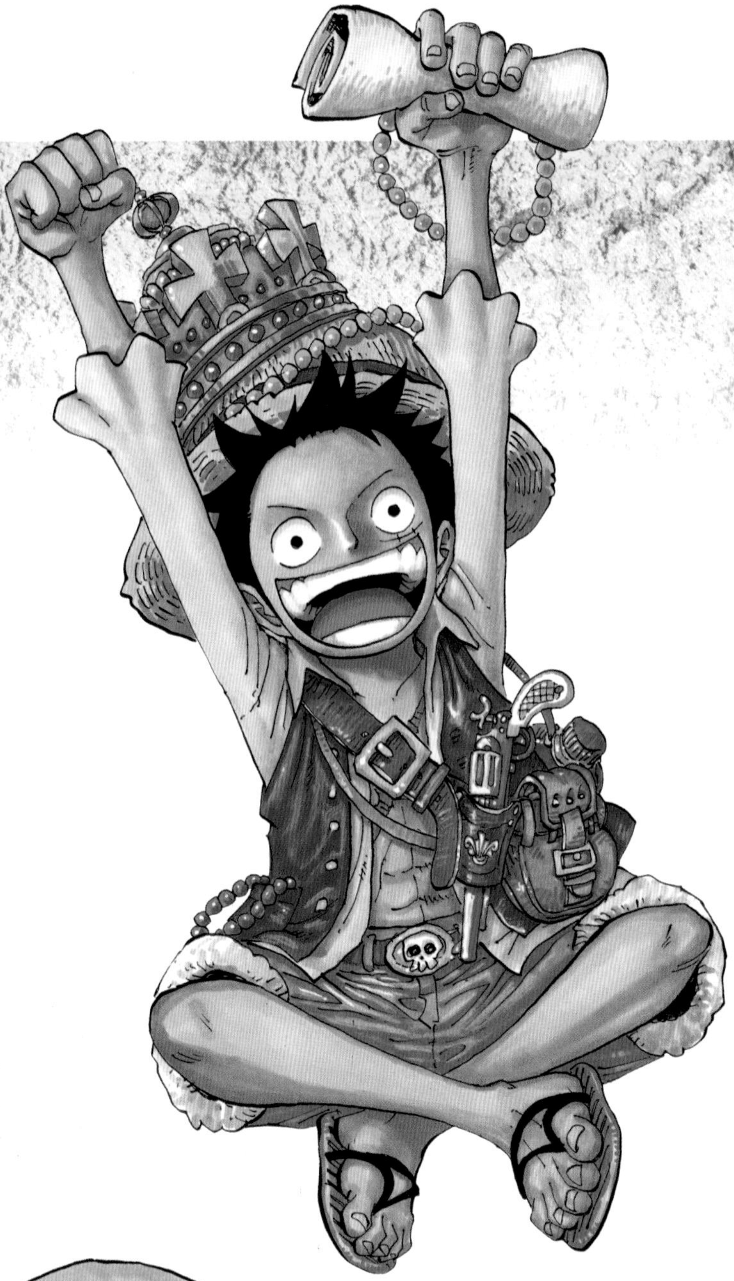

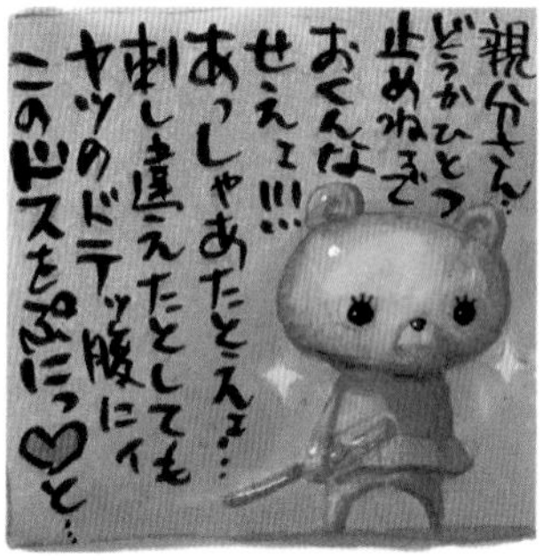
親分さん…
どうかひとつ止めねぇでおくんなせぇェ!!!
あっしゃあたとえェ…刺し違えたとしてもヤツのドテッ腹にイこのドスをぶにっ♡と…

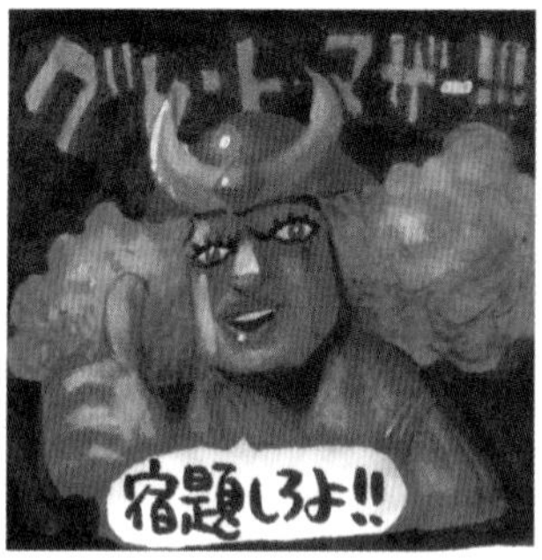
グレート・マザー!!!
宿題しろよ!!

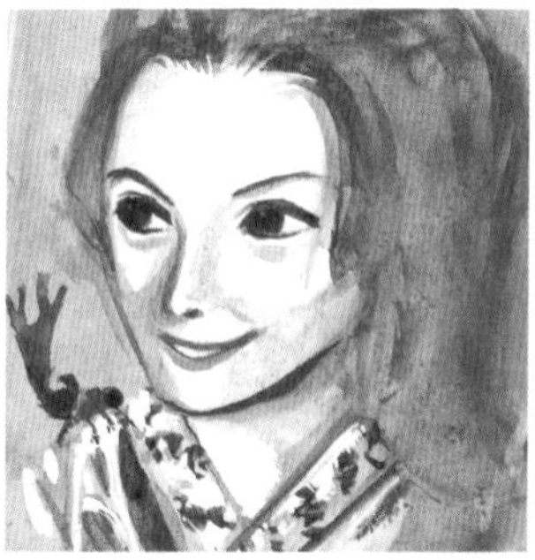

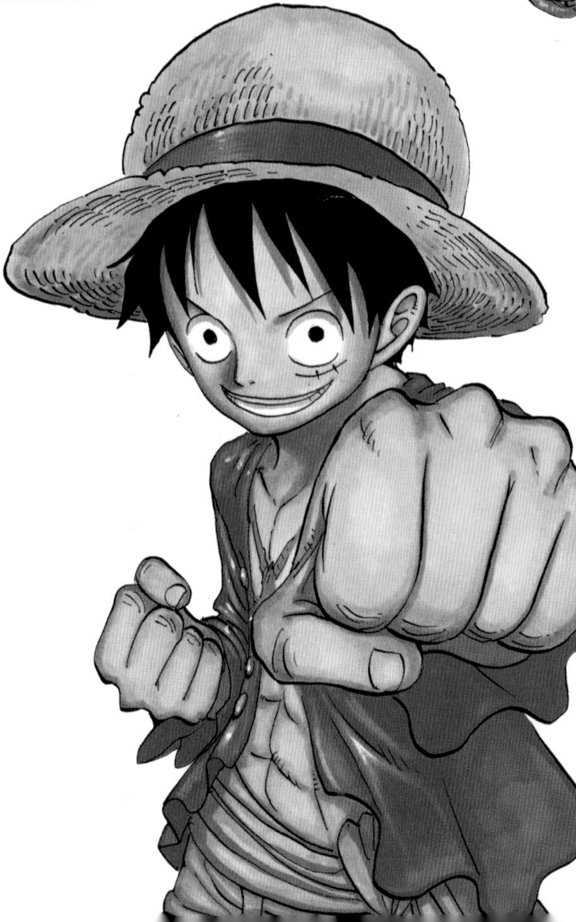

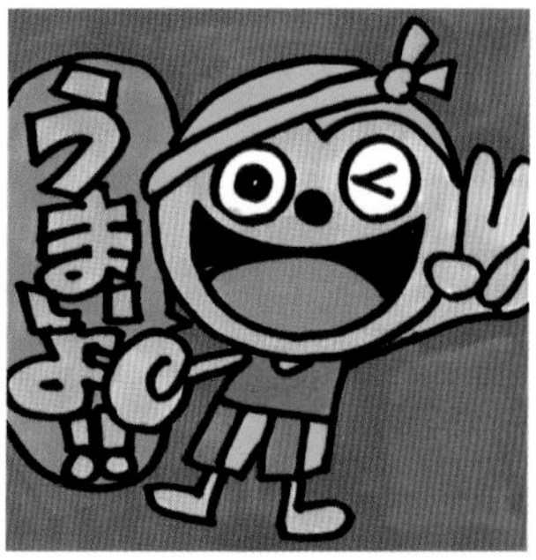
うまいよ!!

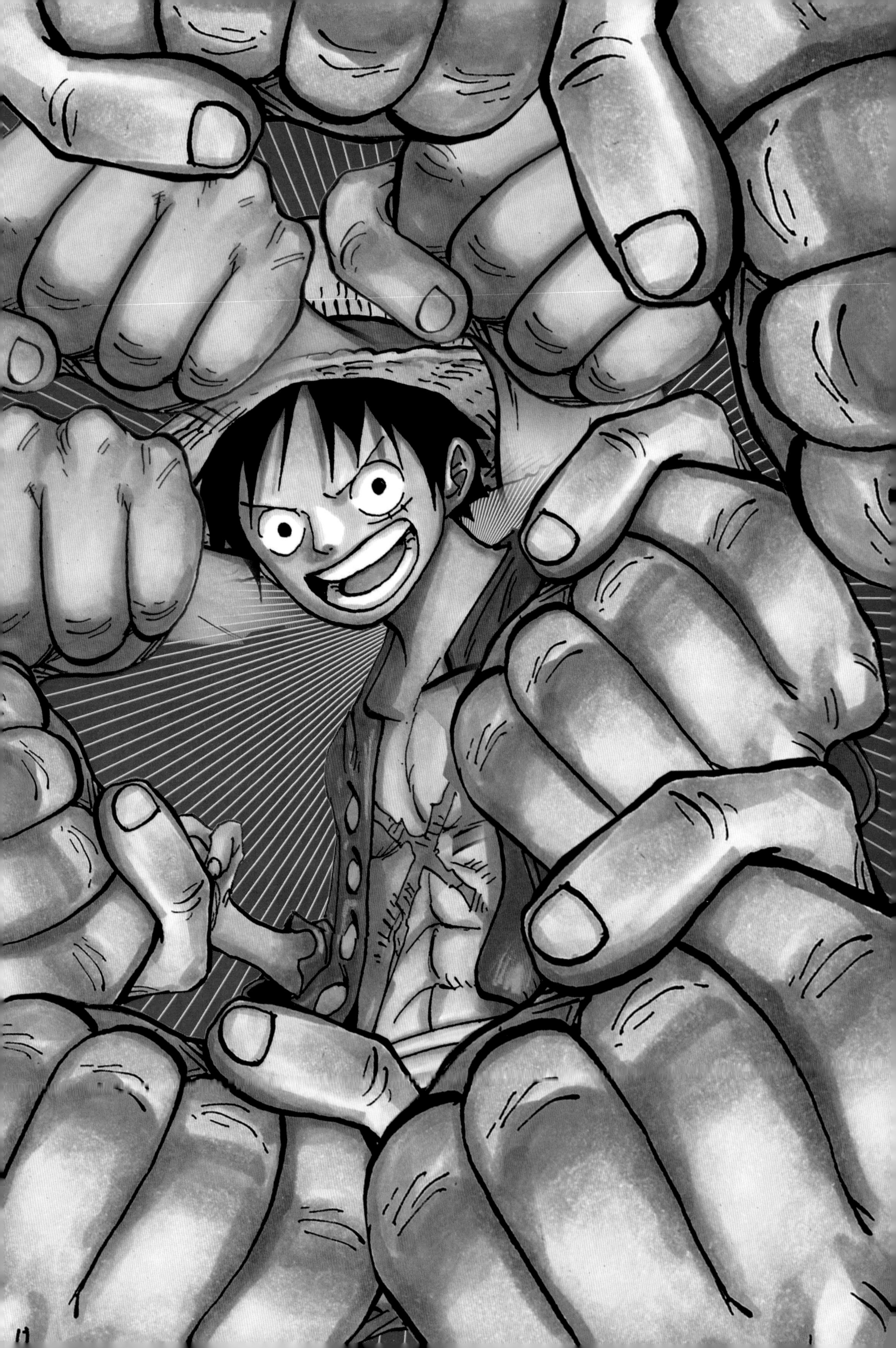

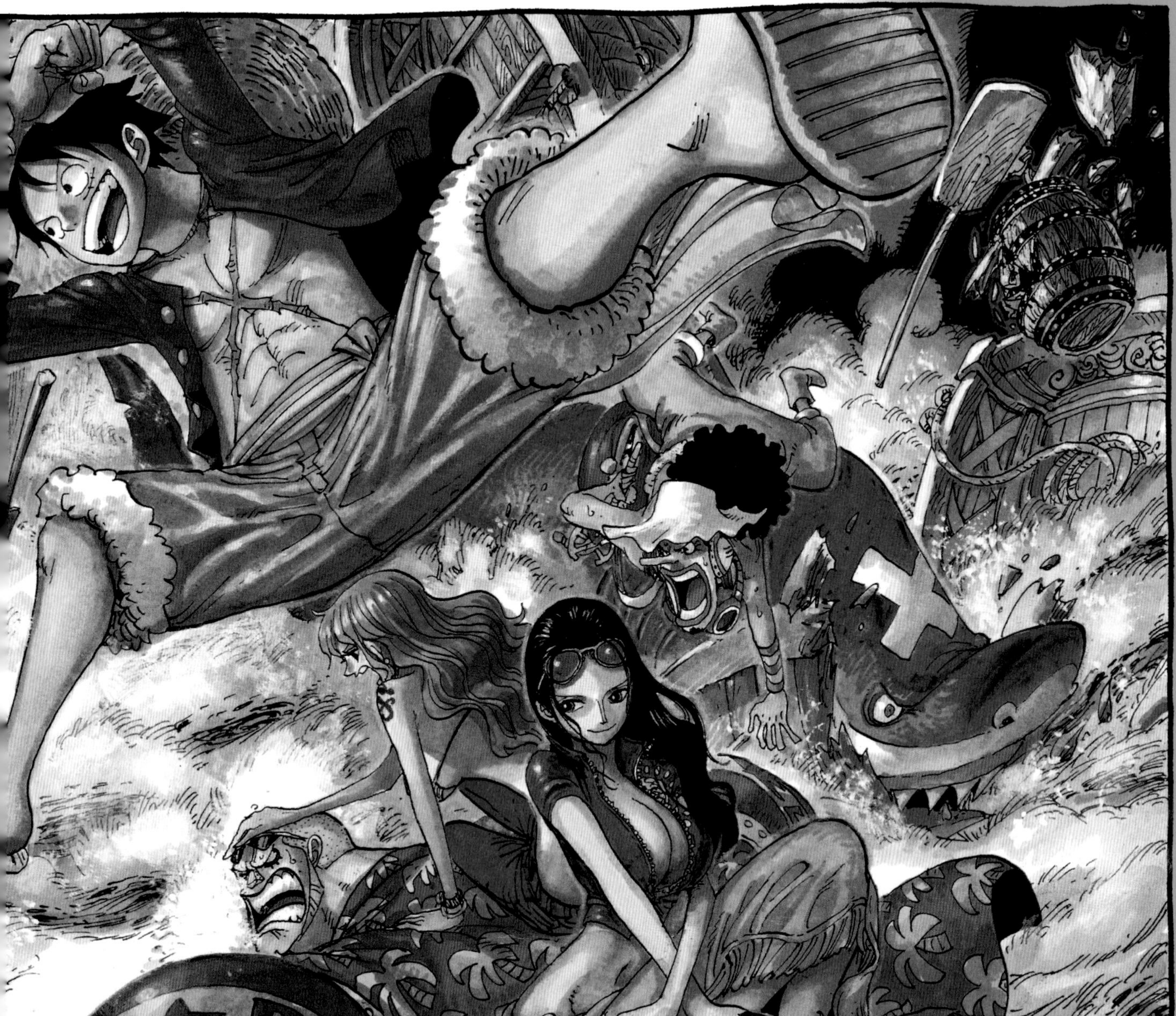
37★BF.

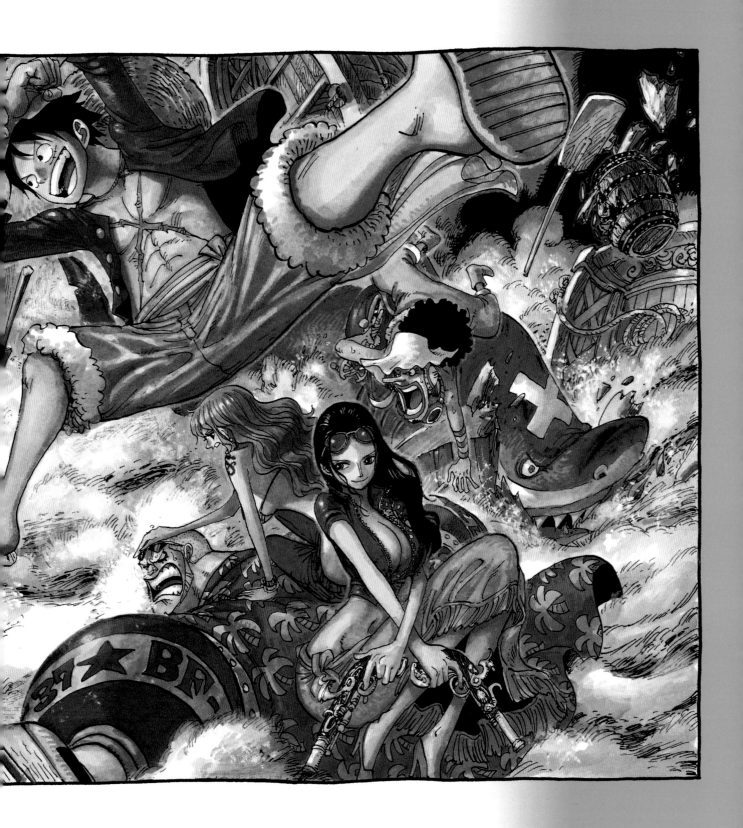

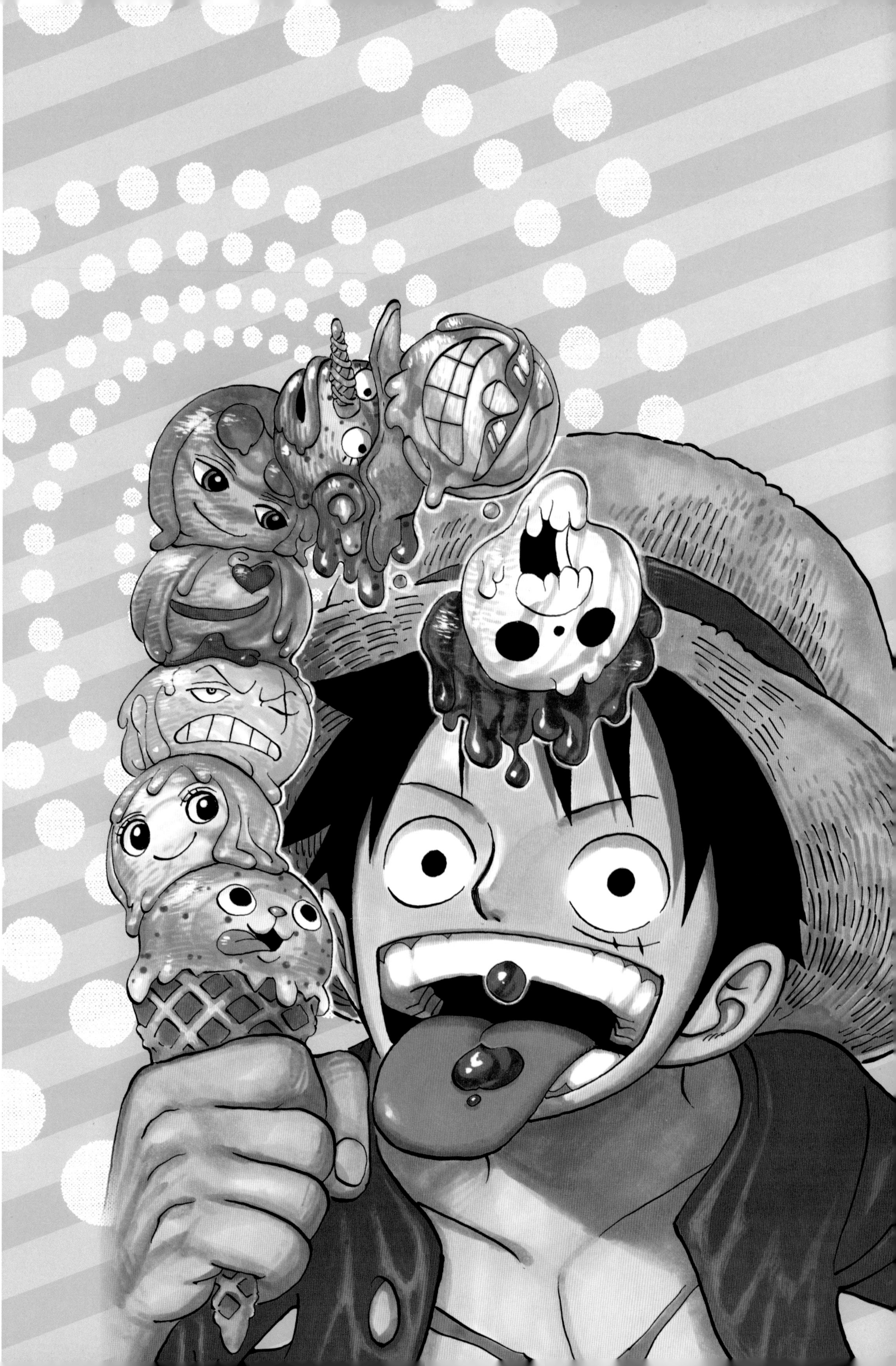

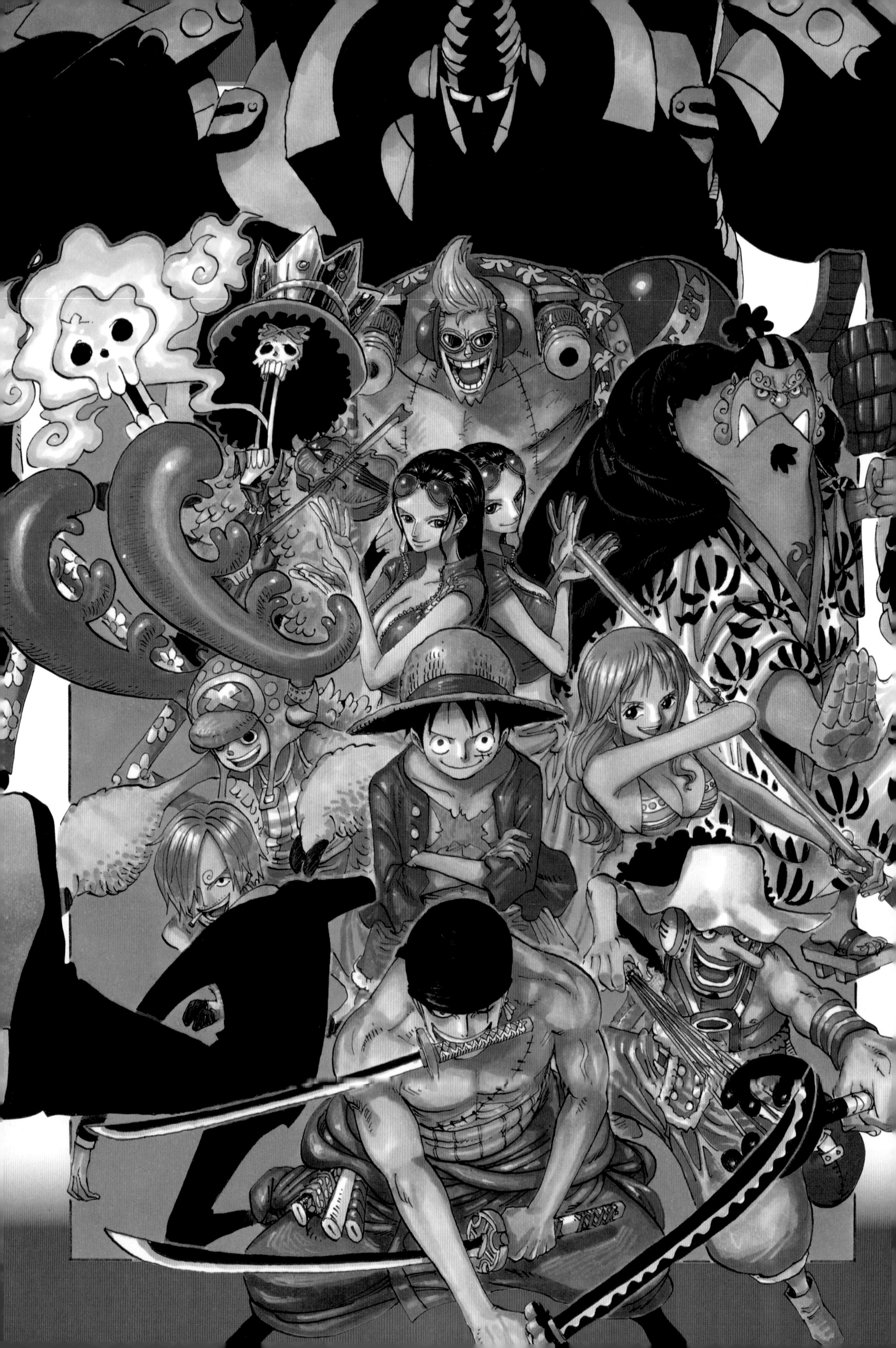

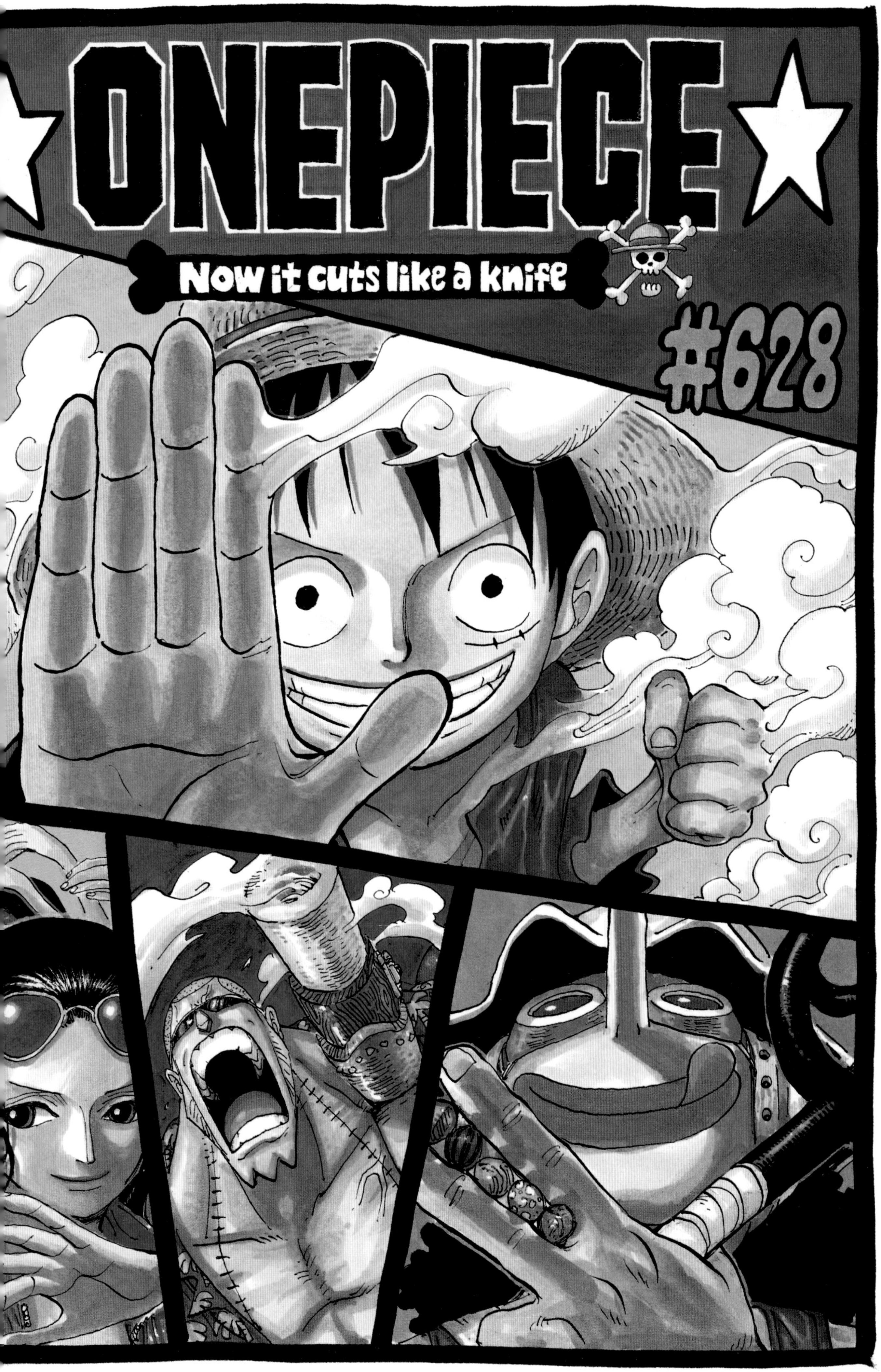
ONEPIECE
Now it cuts like a knife
#628

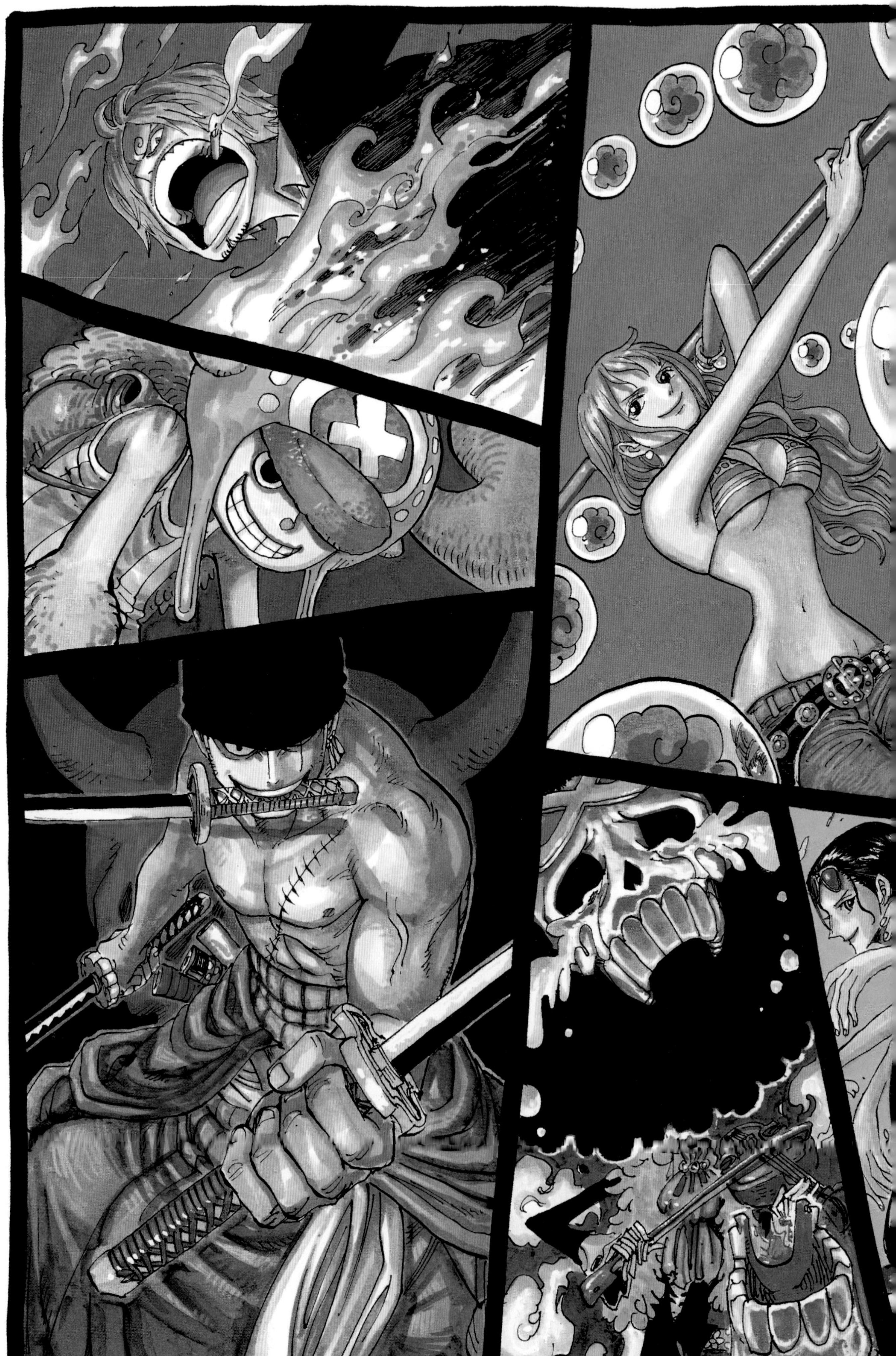

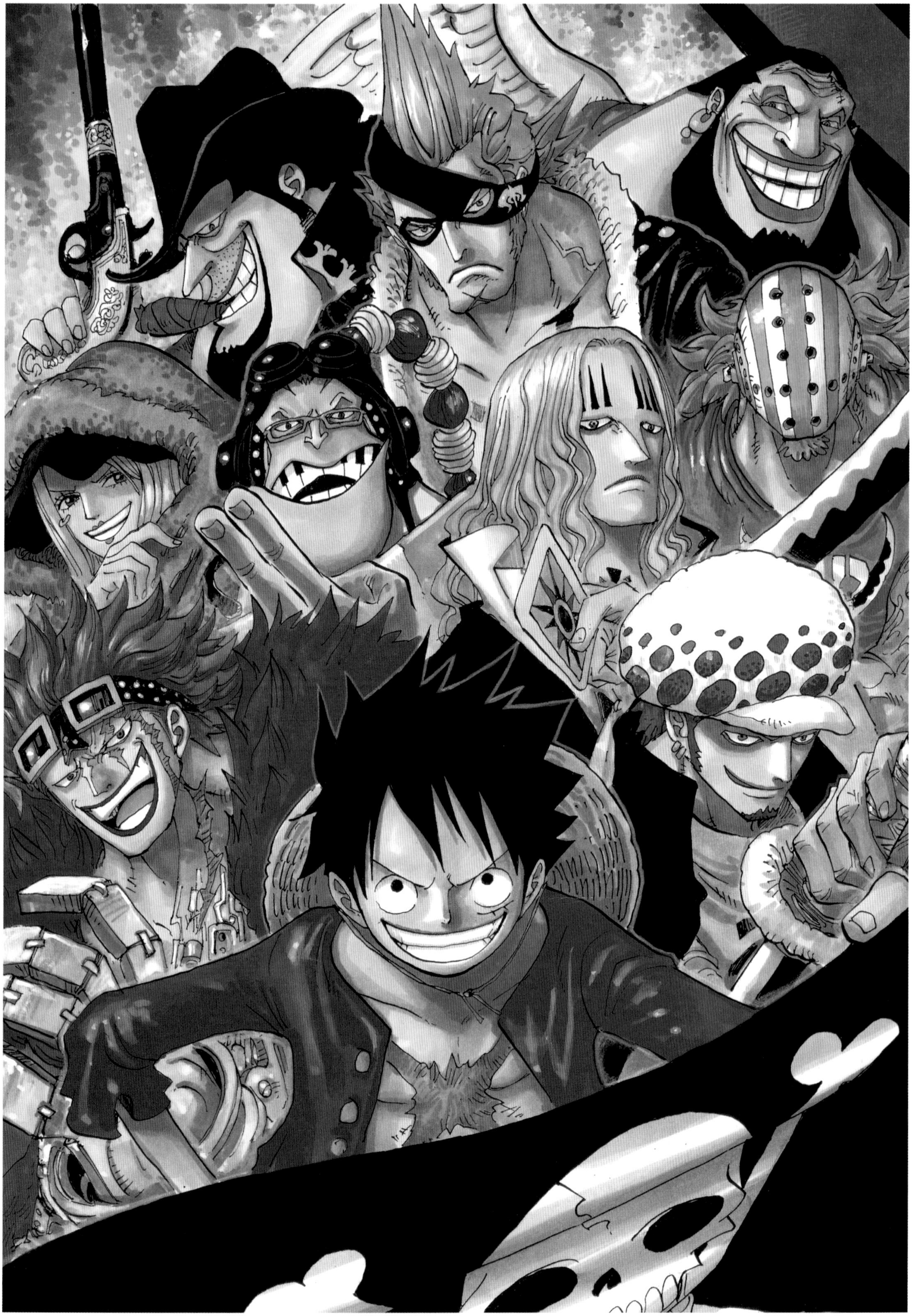

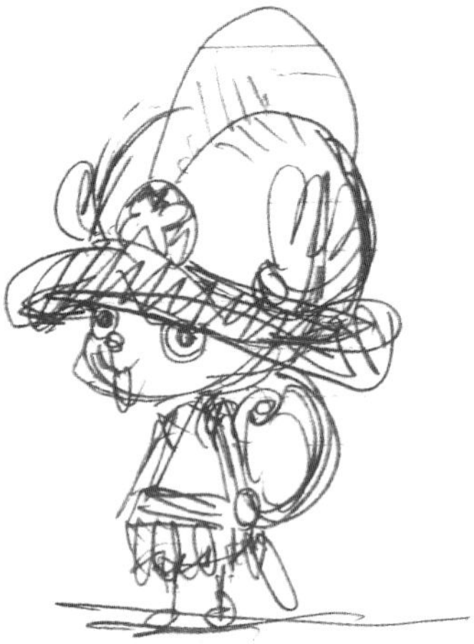

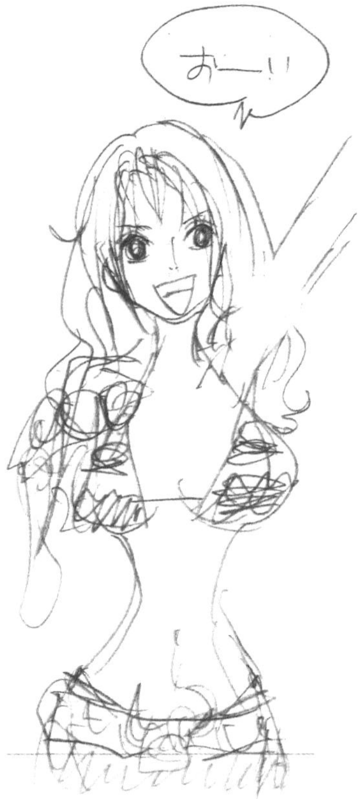
おー!!

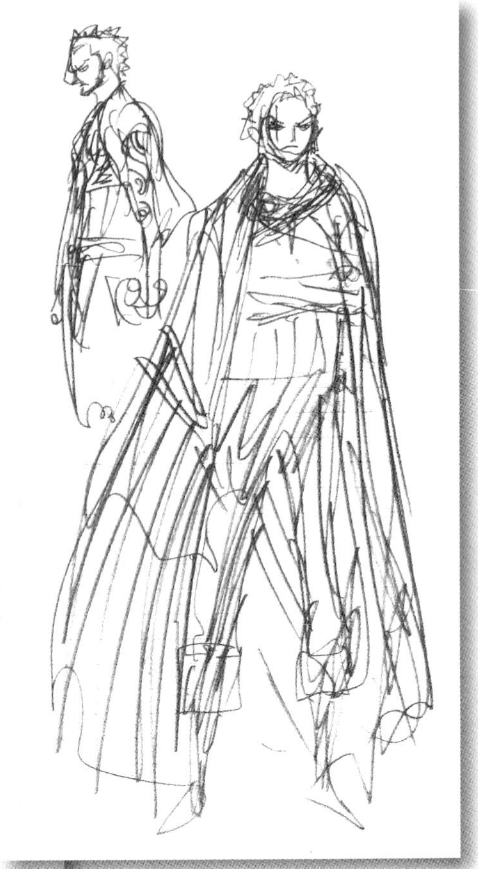

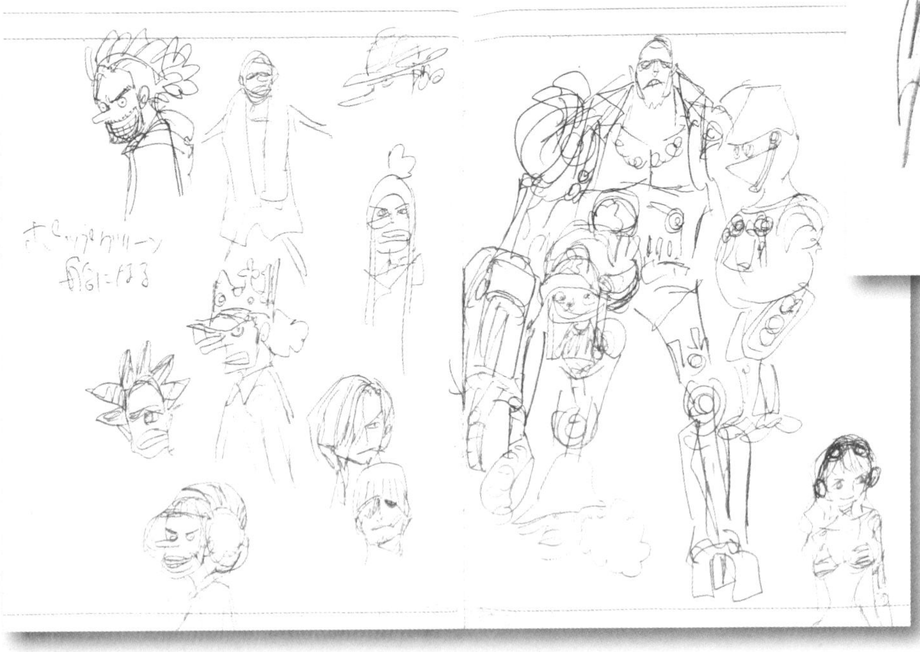
ポップグリーン
船になる

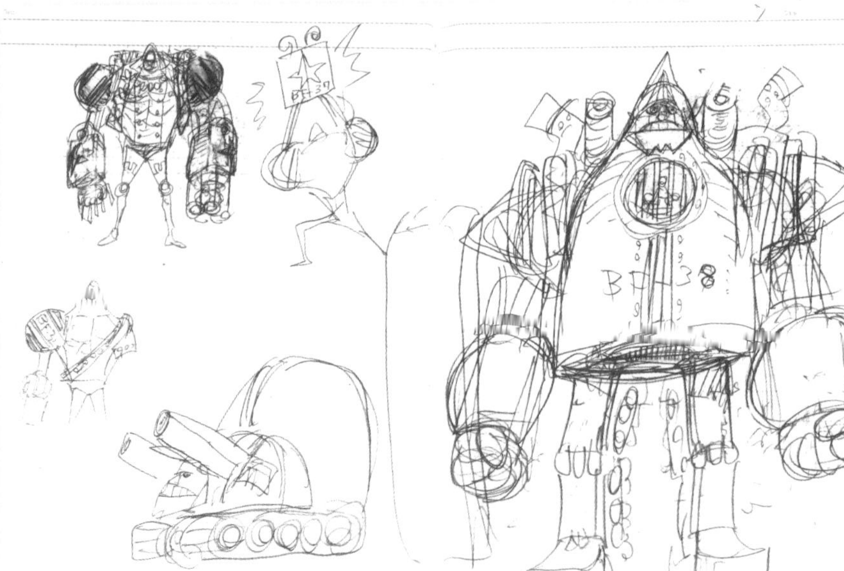

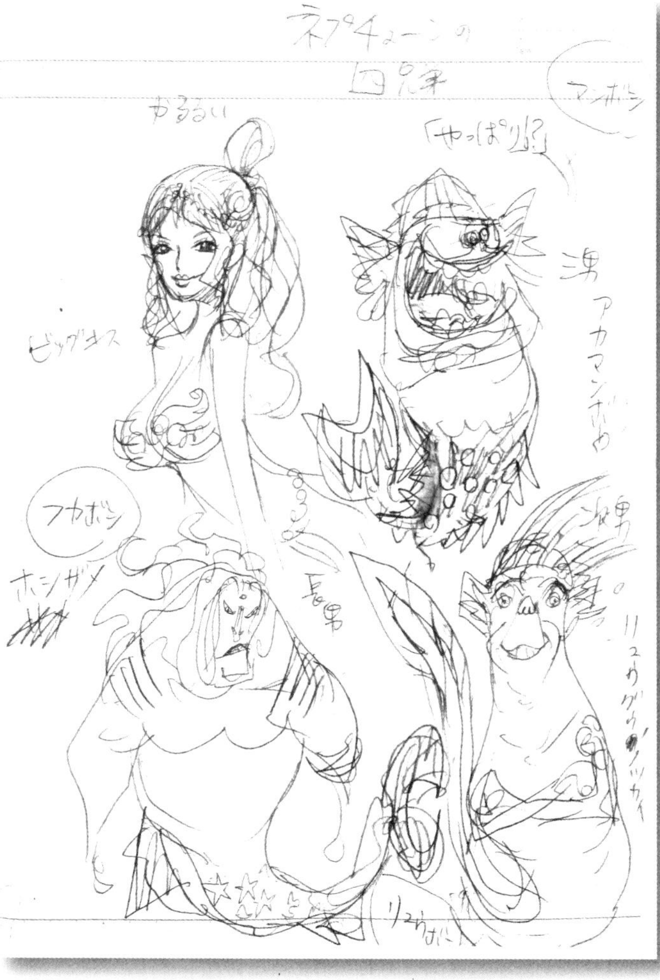
「やっぱり!?」
フカボシ
ホシザメ
長男

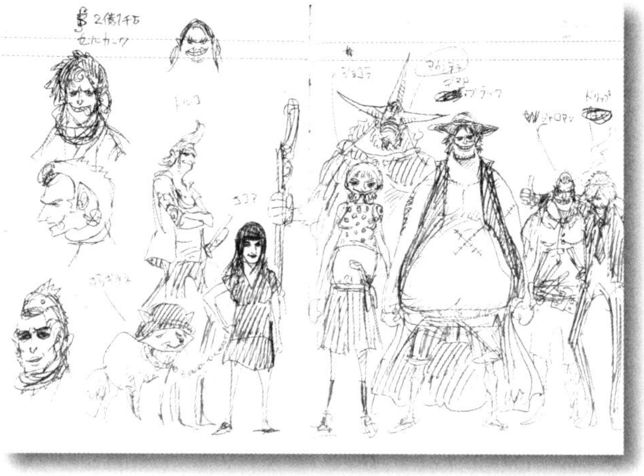

IMAGINATION

姫

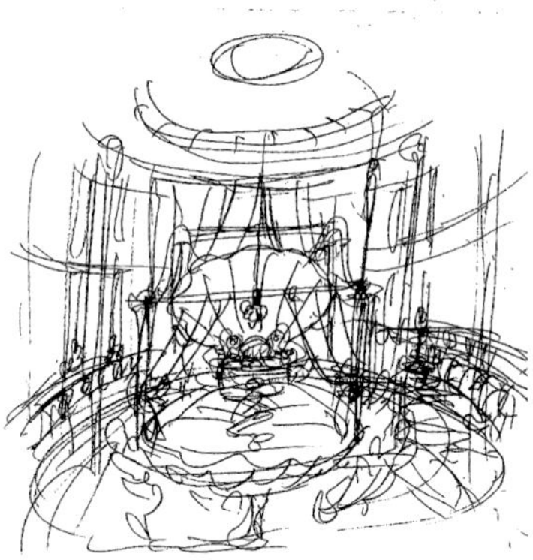

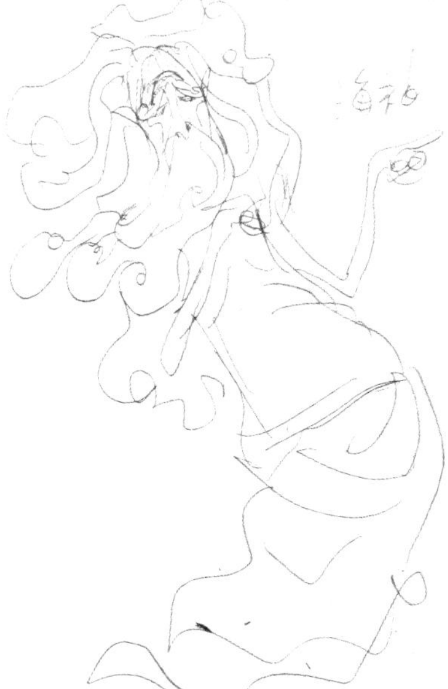

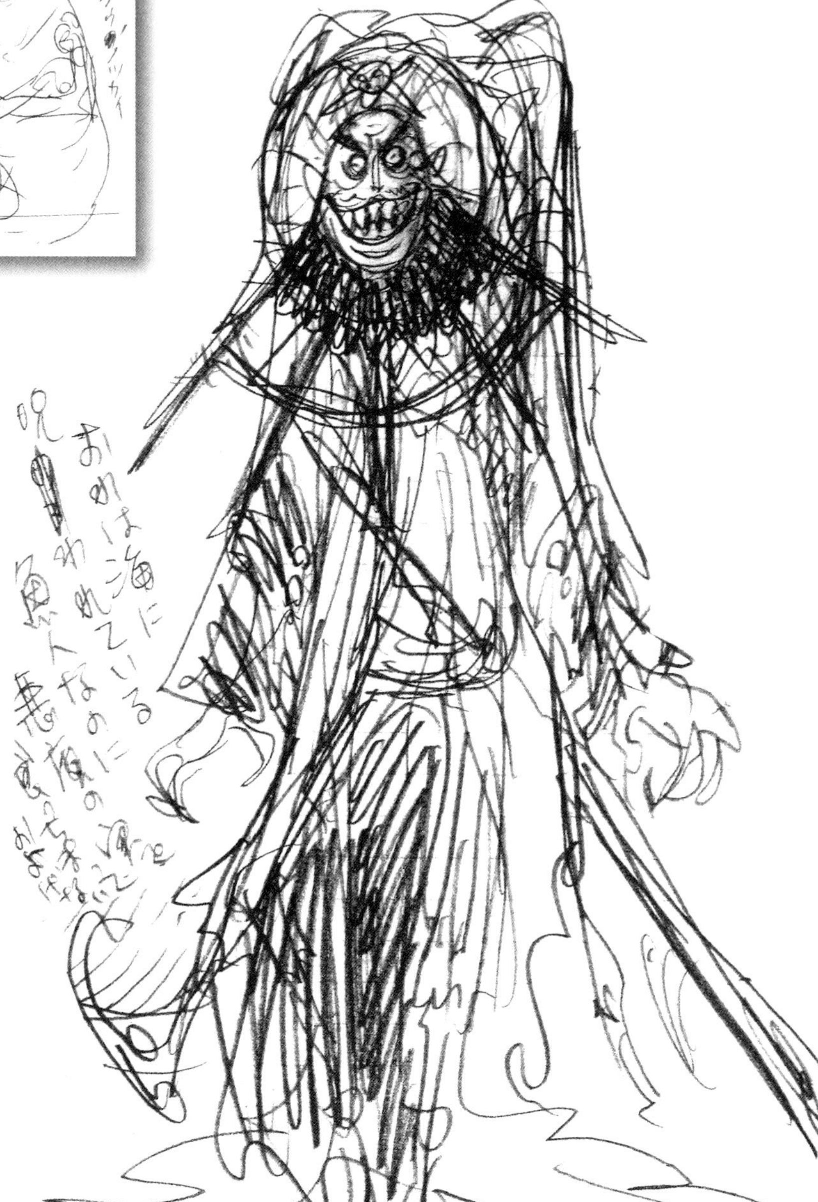
おれは海に
呪われている
魚人なのに

Flying Dutchman

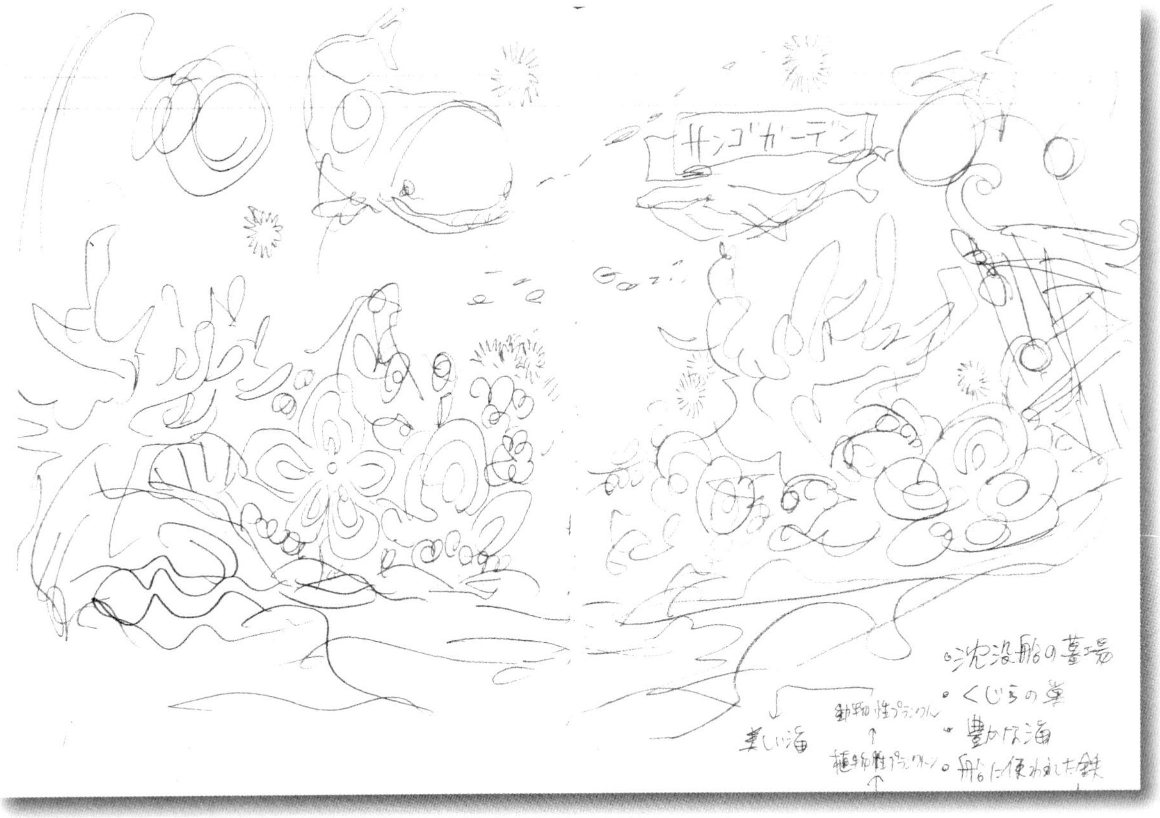
サンゴガーデン
美しい海
動物性プランクトン
植物性プランクトン
・沈没船の墓場
・くじらの巣
・豊かな海
・船に使われた鉄

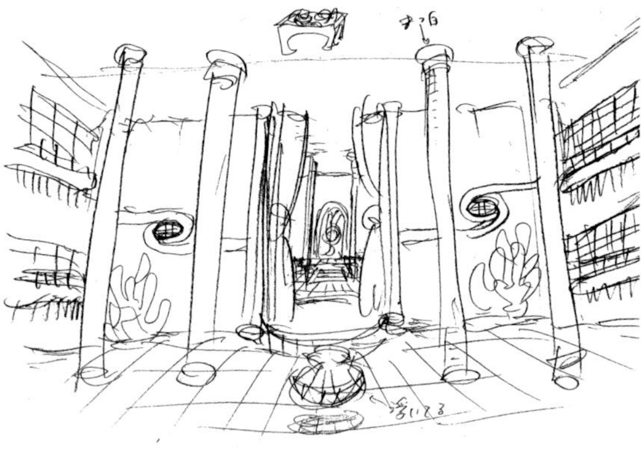

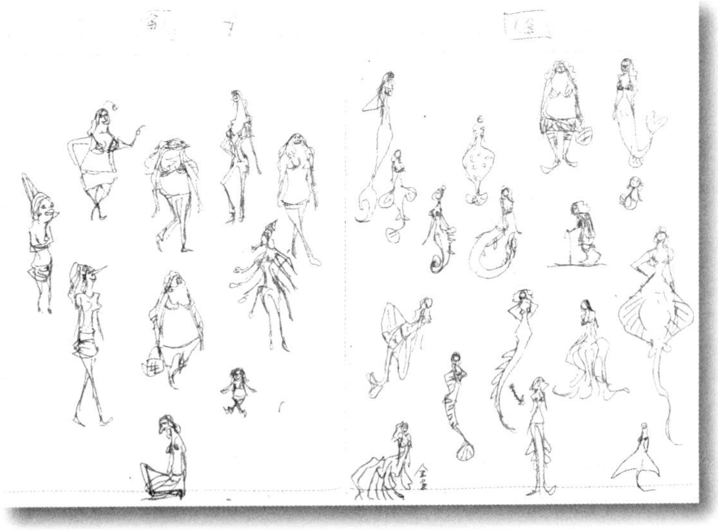

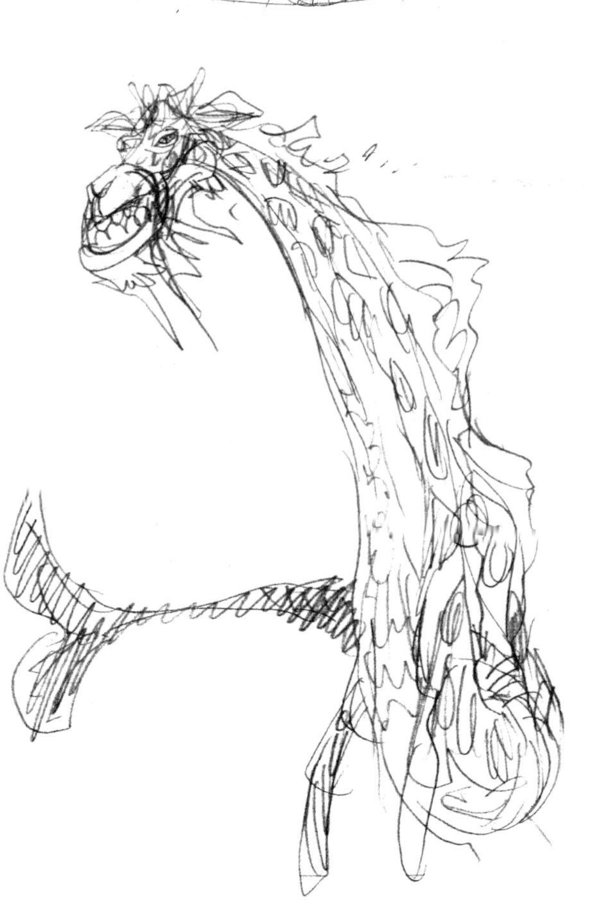

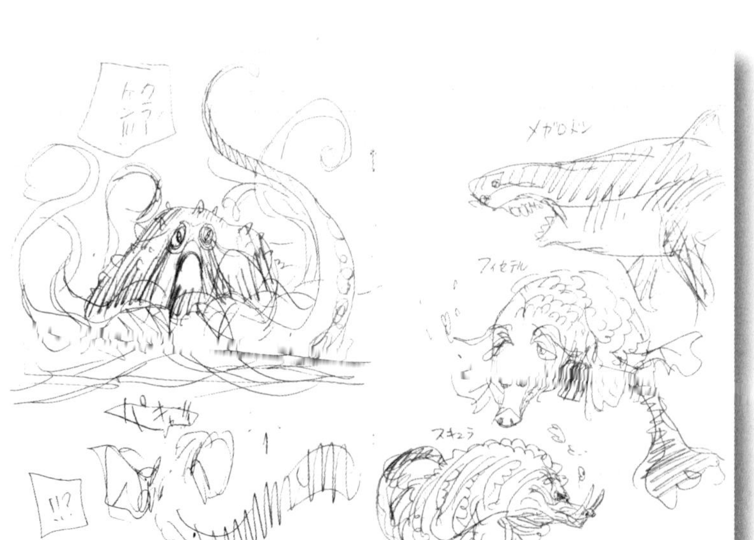
メガロドン
フィセテル

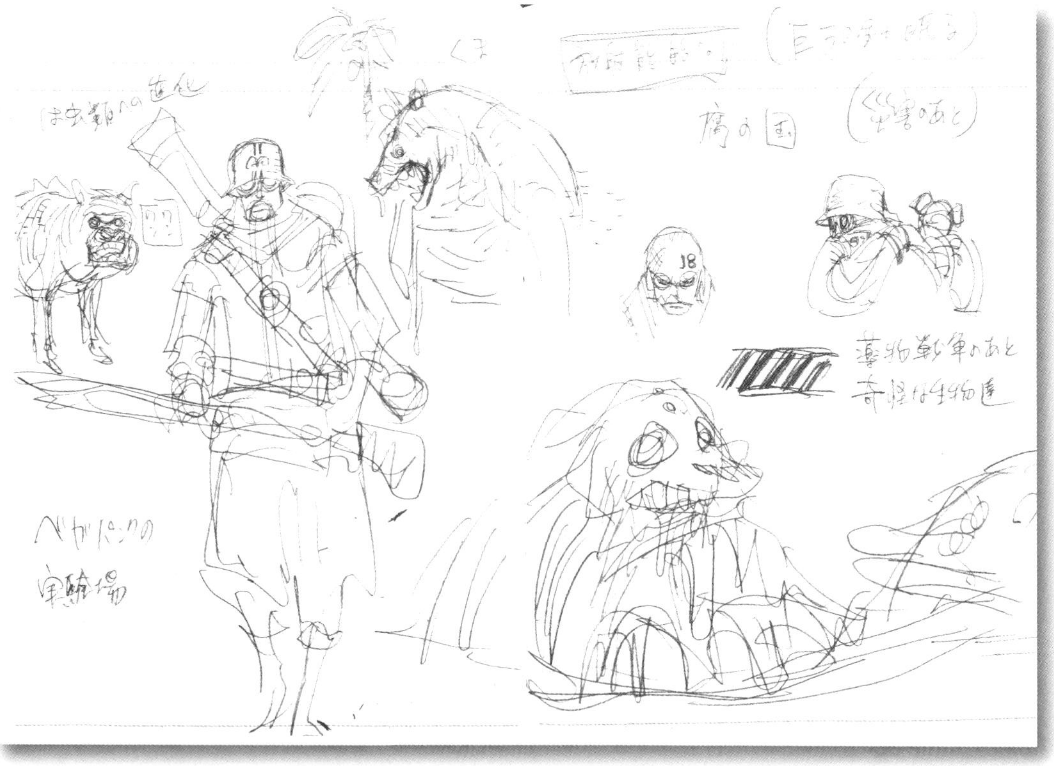
腐の国
ベガパンクの実験場
薬物戦争のあと
奇怪な生物達
18

IMAGINATION

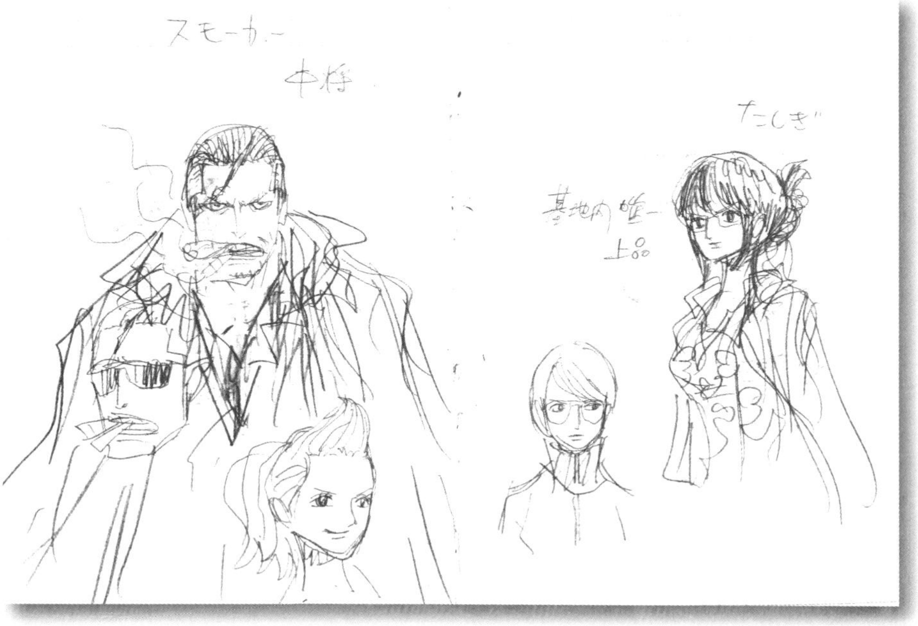
スモーカー
中将
たしぎ
上品

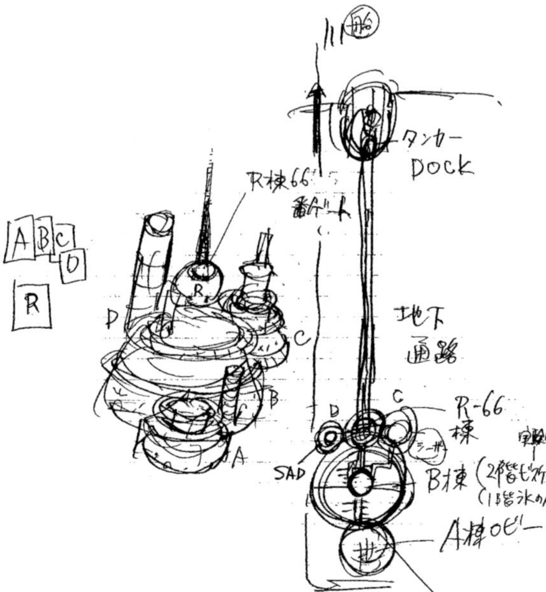
A
B
C
D
R
タンカー
DOCK
R棟66
地下
通路
R-66
棟
SAD
B棟
A棟ロビー
たしぎの一件

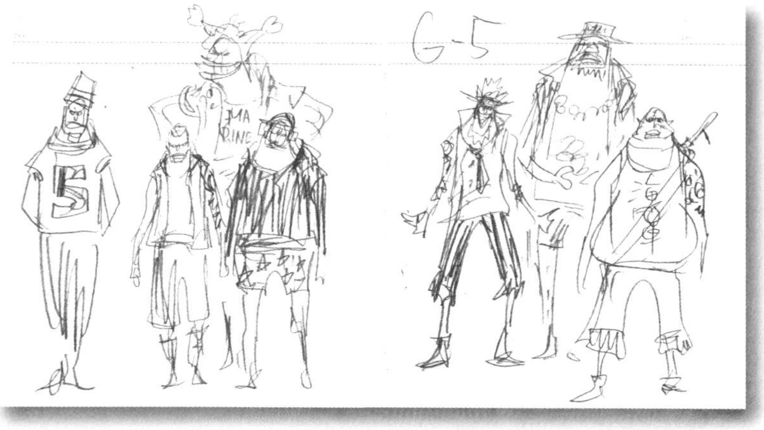
G-5
5

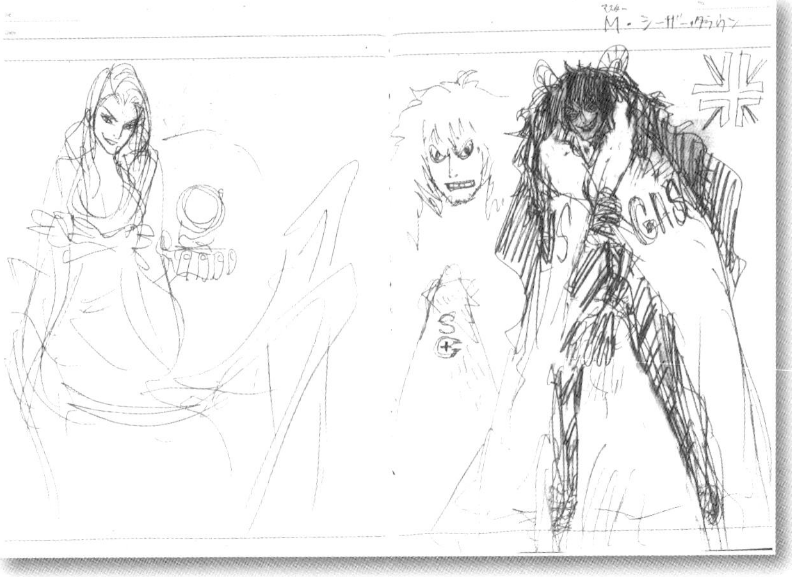
M・シーザー・クラウン
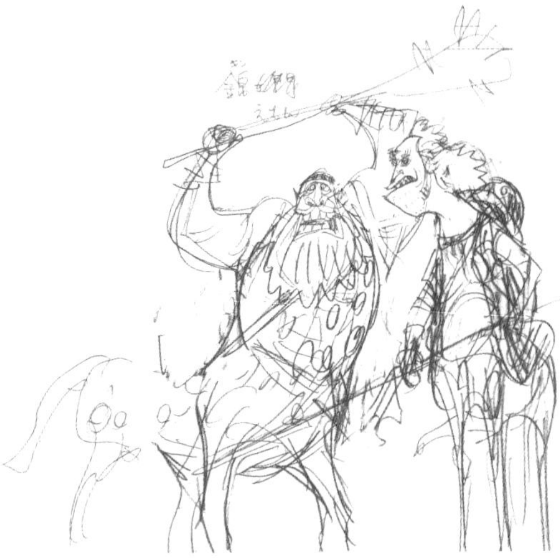
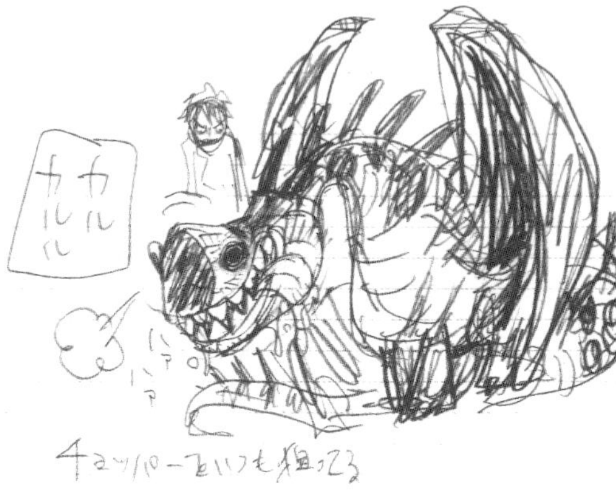
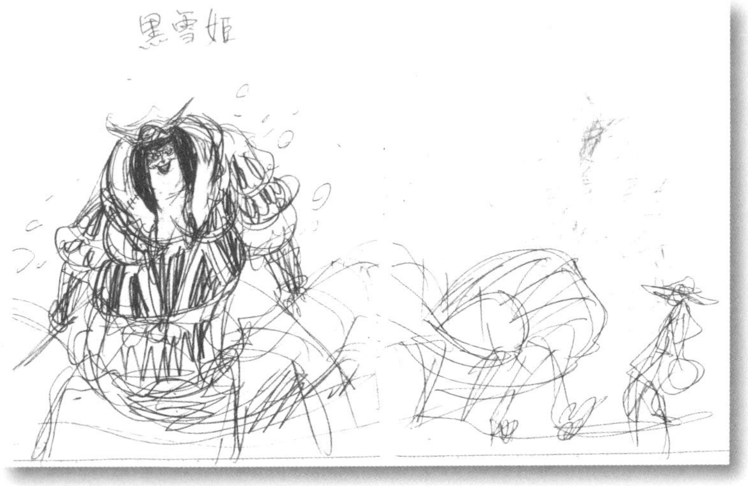
黒雪姫
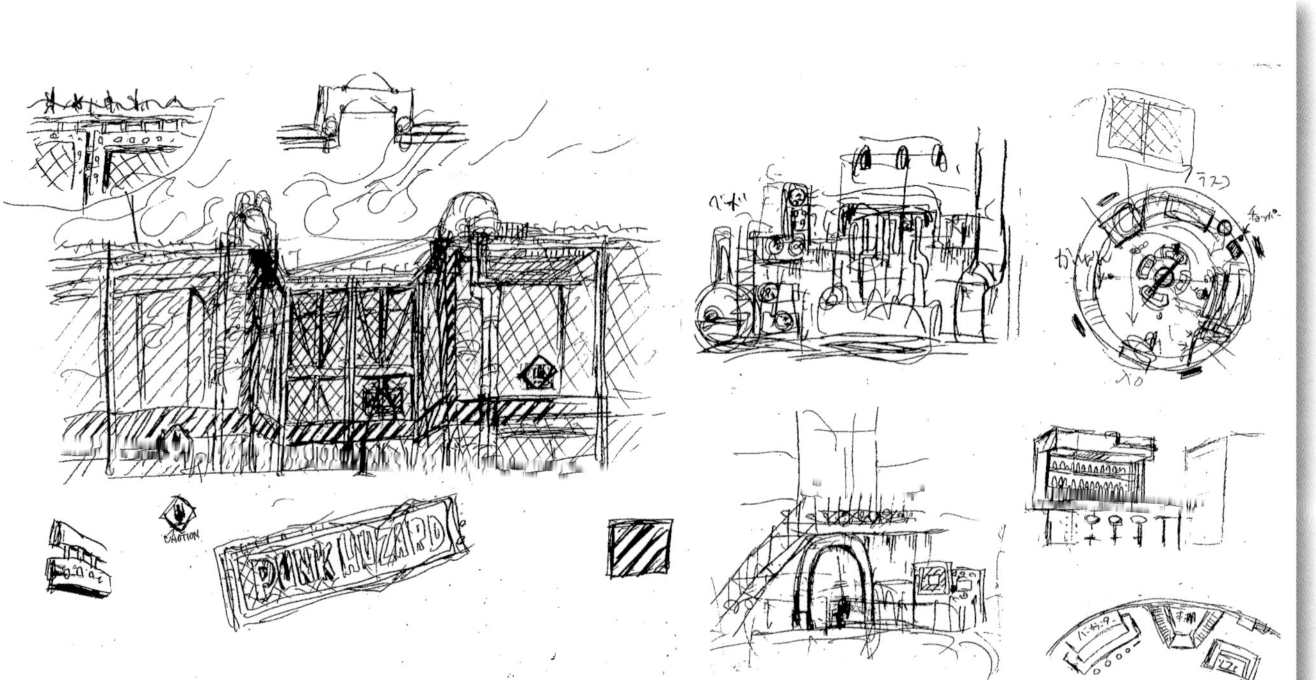
CAUTION
PUNK HAZARD

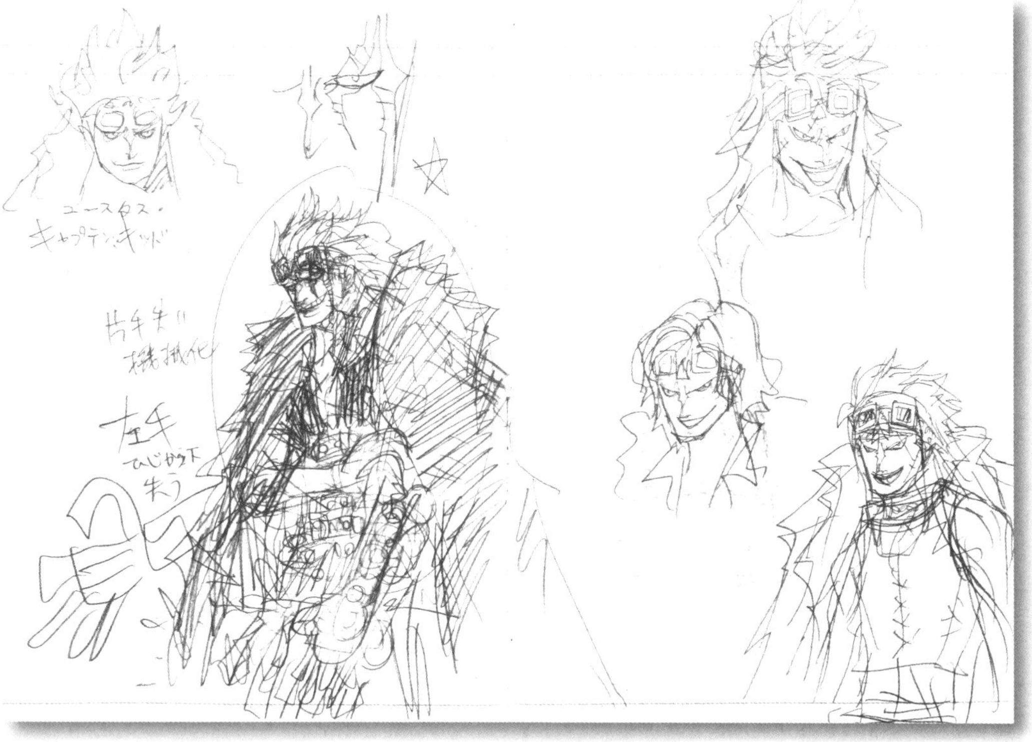
ユースタス・
キャプテン・キッド
片手失い
機械化
左手
ひじから下
失う

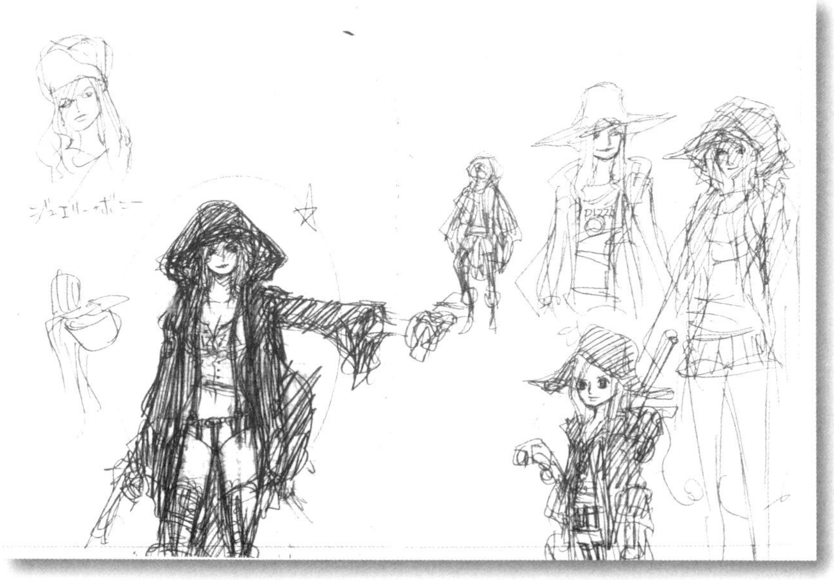
ジュエリー・ボニー

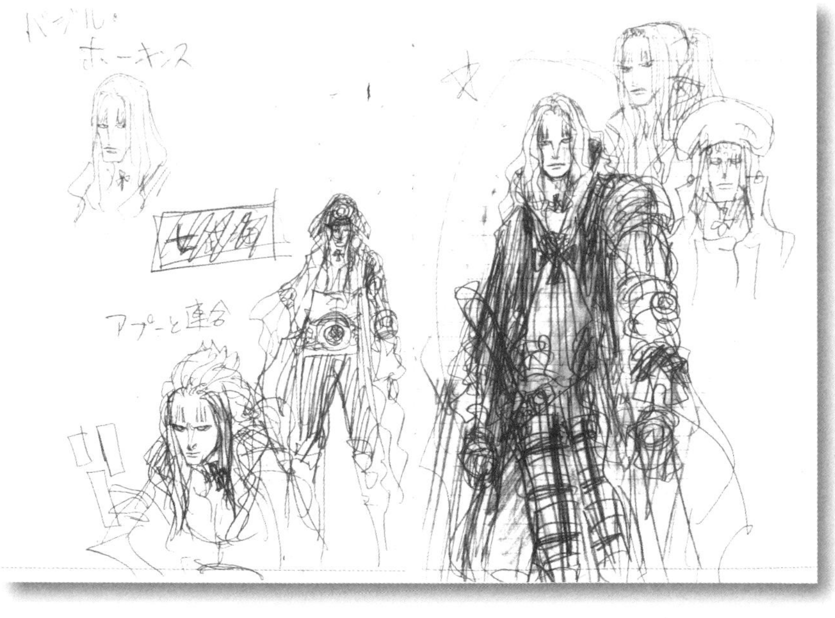
バジル・
ホーキンス
アプーと連合

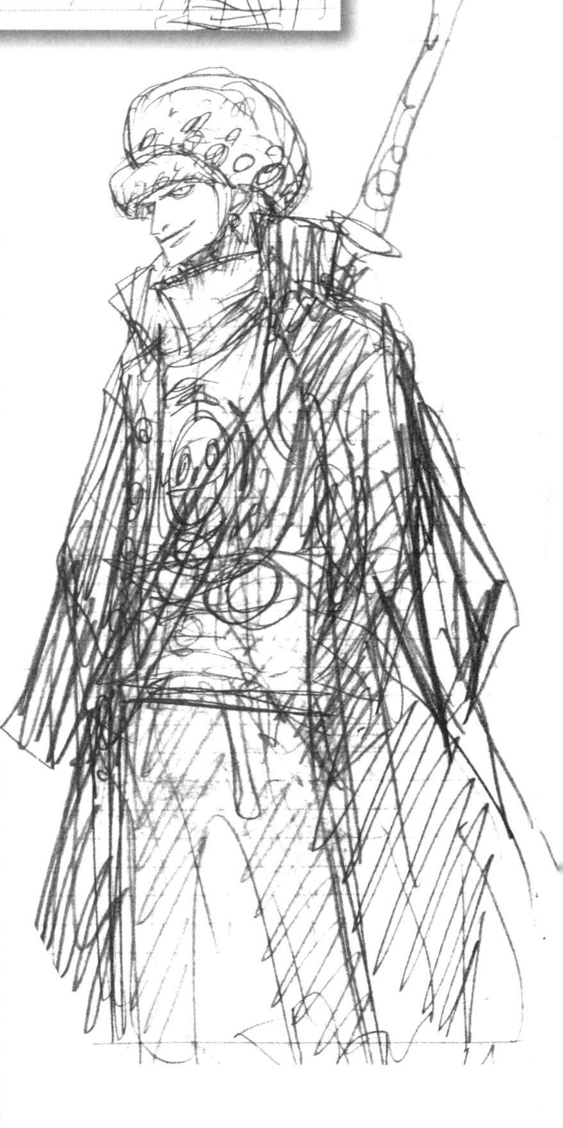

IMAGINATION

2012

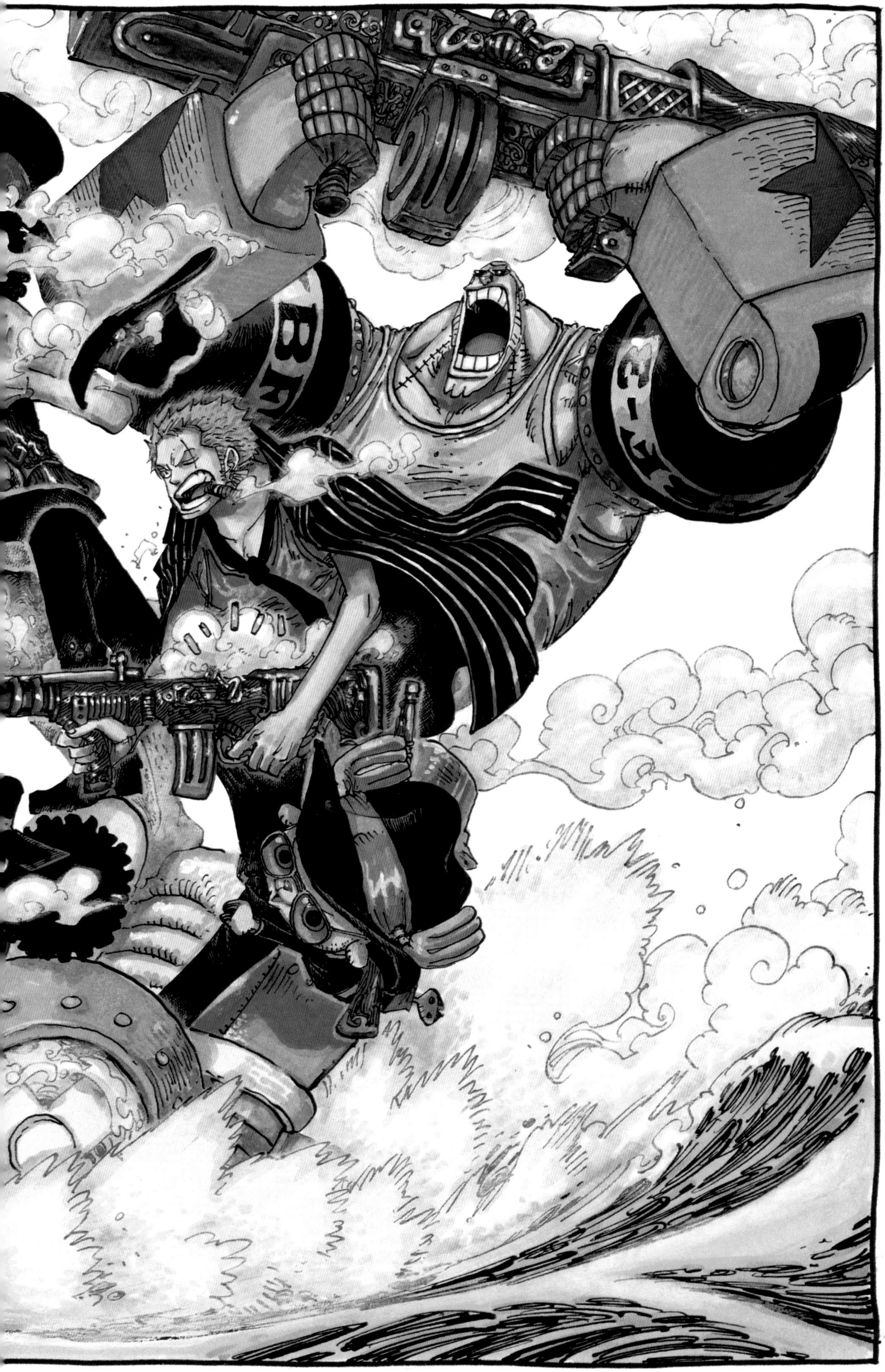

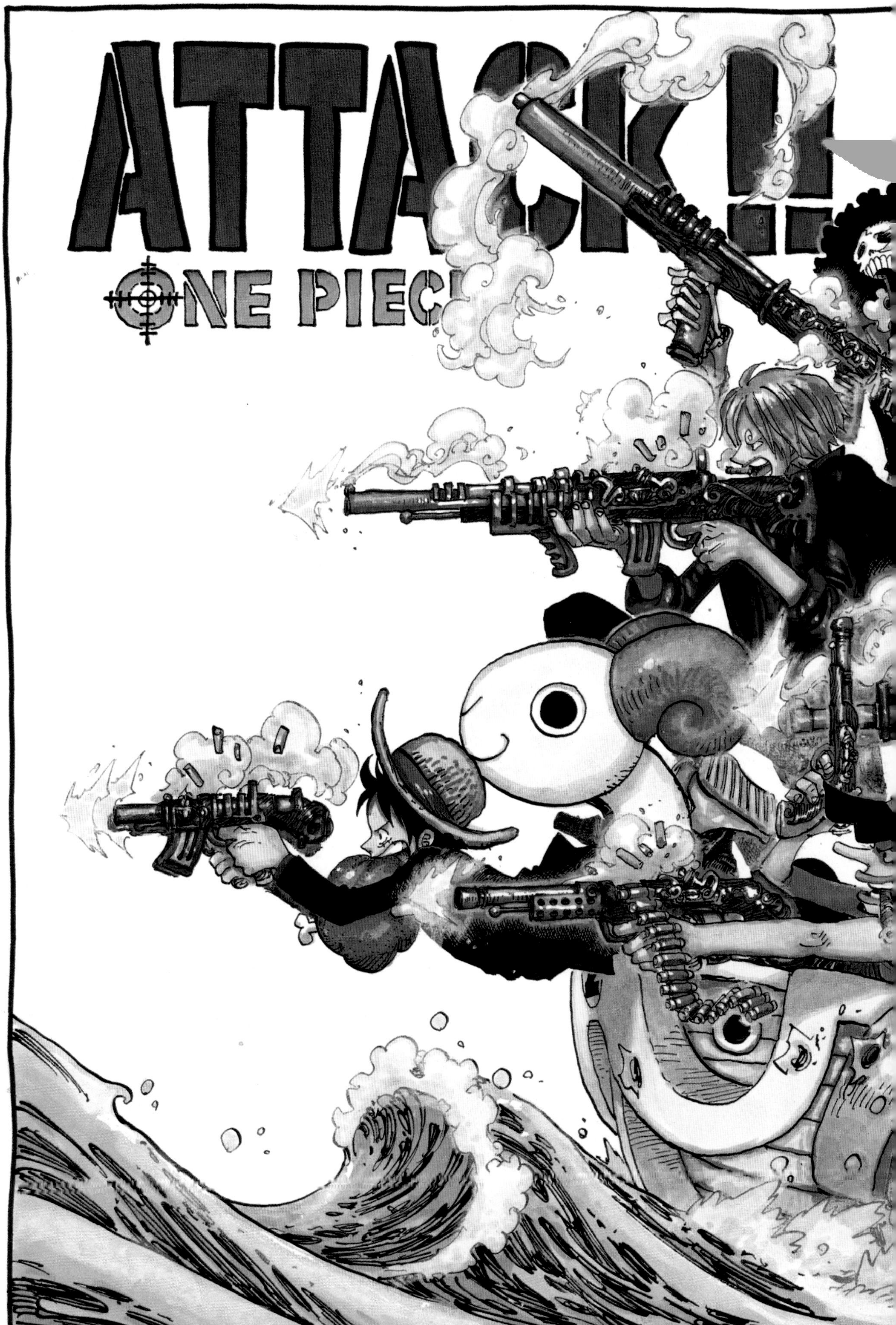
ATTACK!!
ONE PIEC

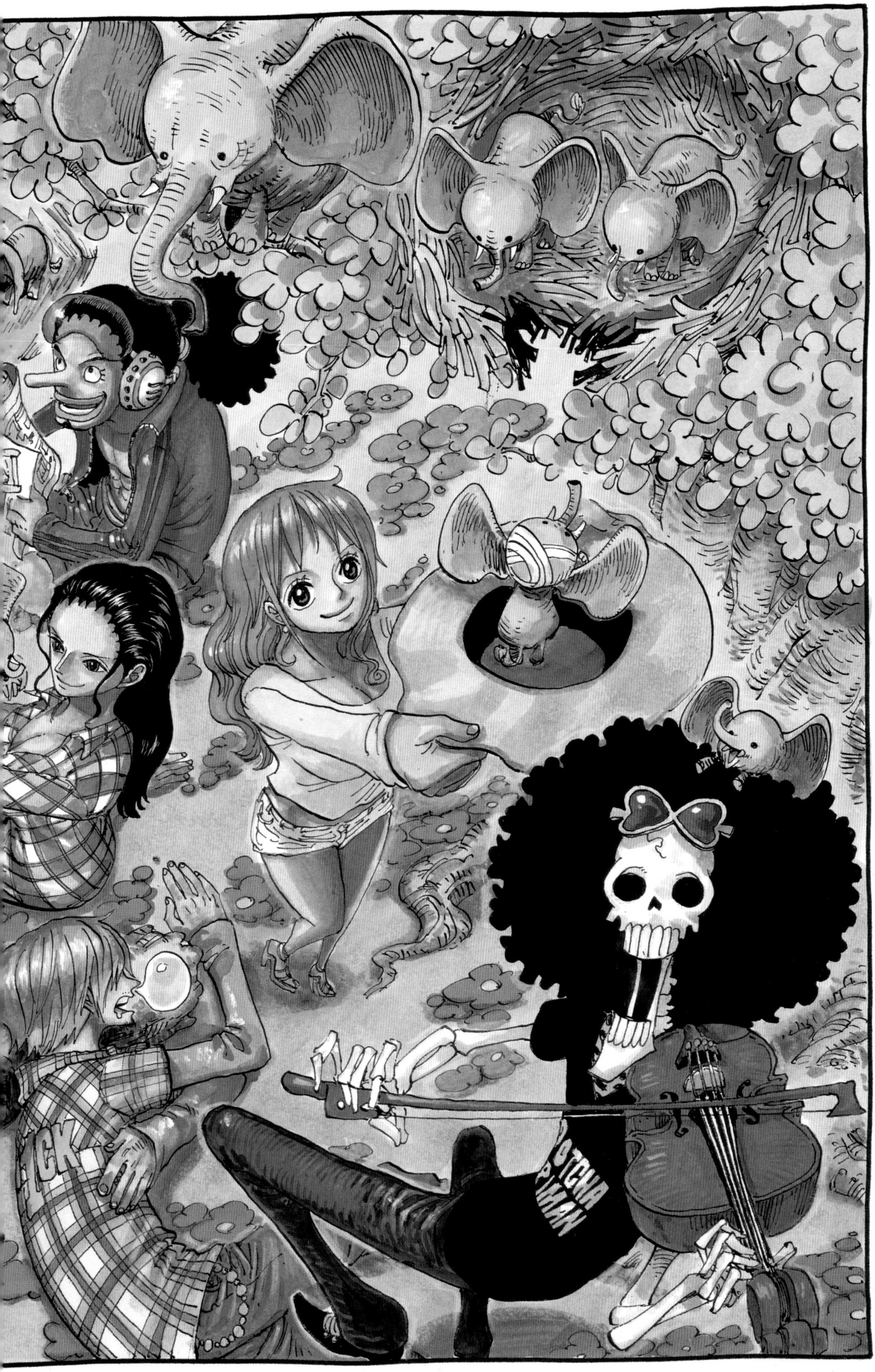

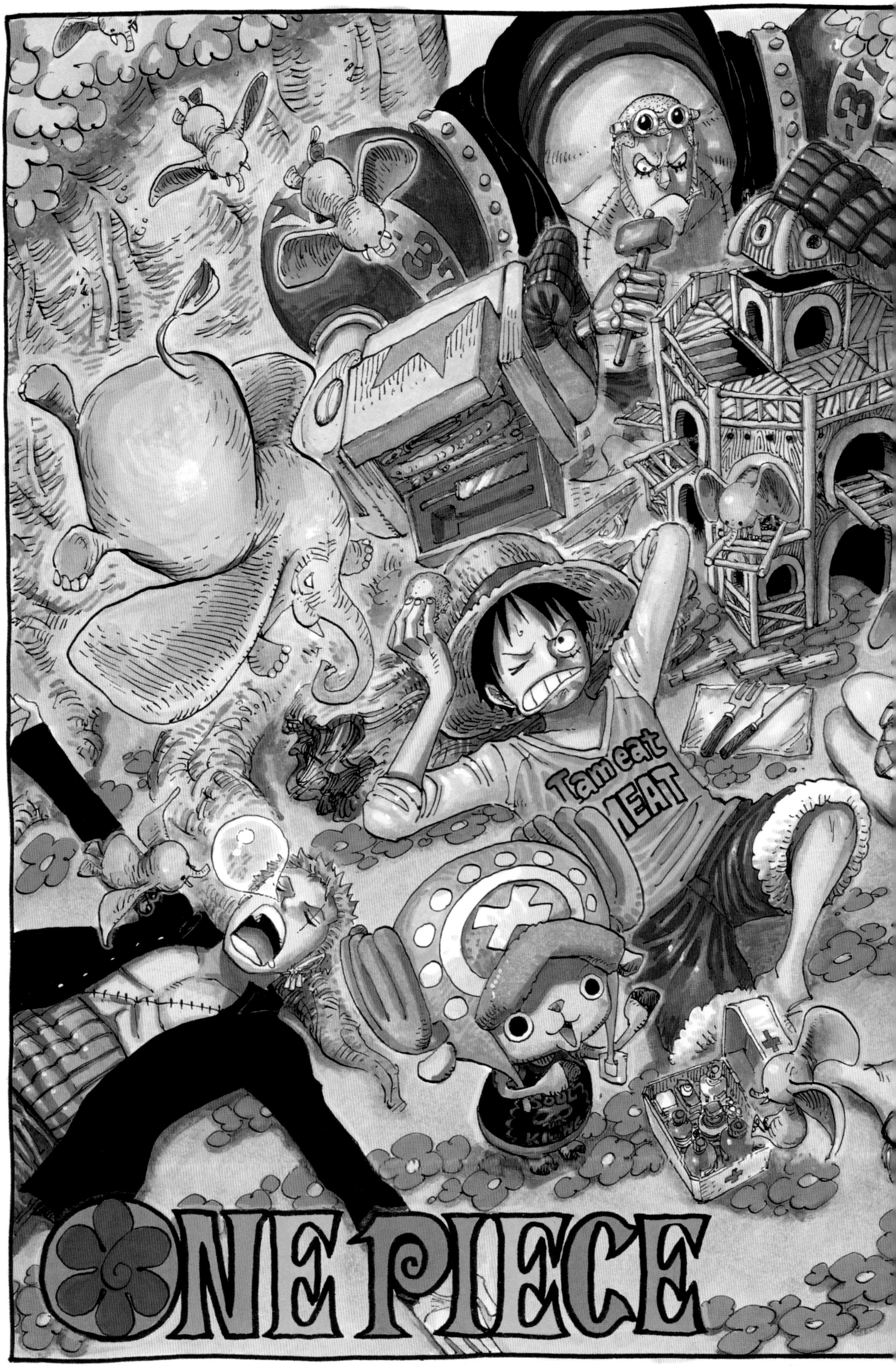
ONE PIECE
Tam eat
MEAT

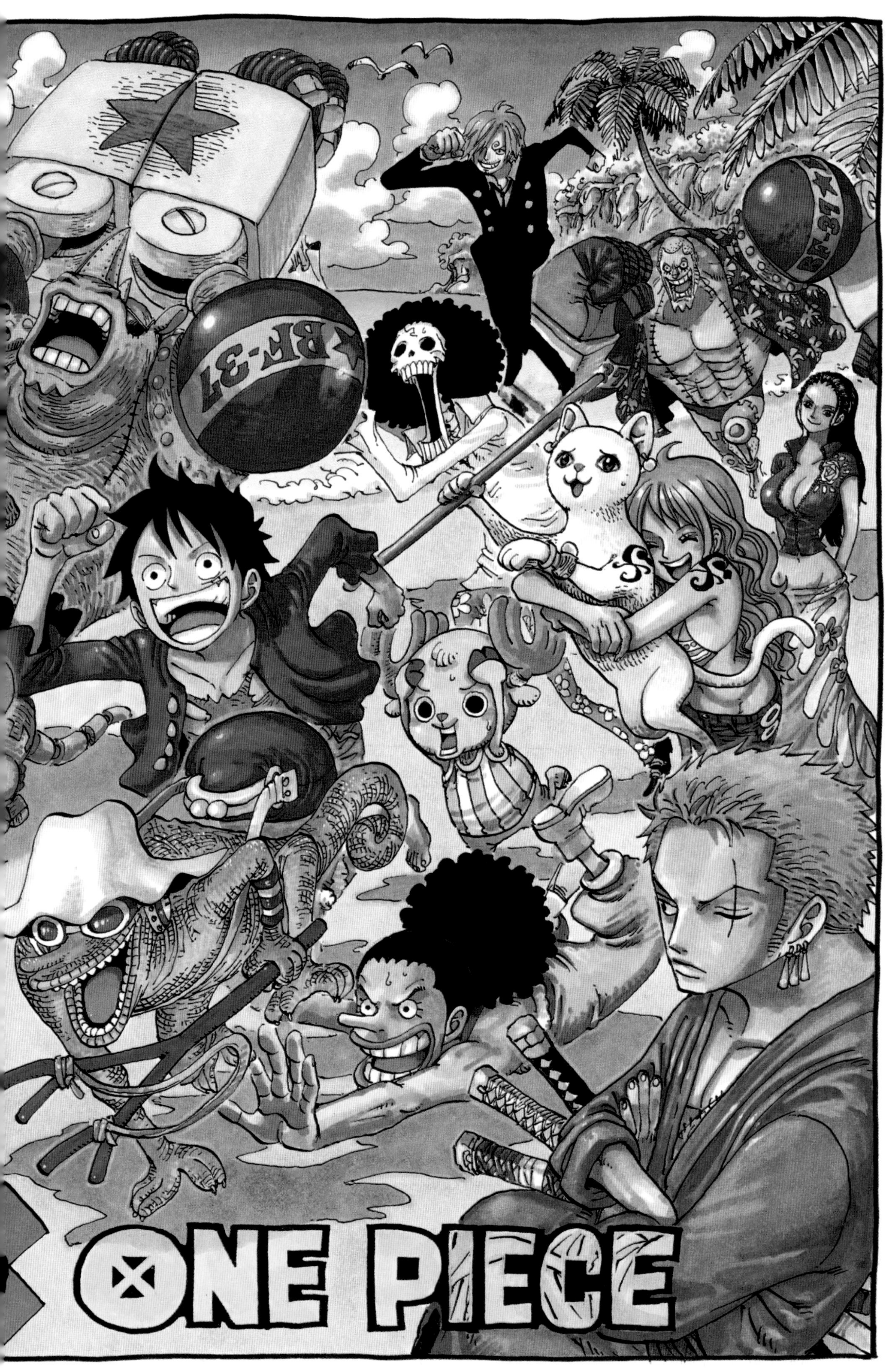
ONE PIECE
BF-37
BF-37

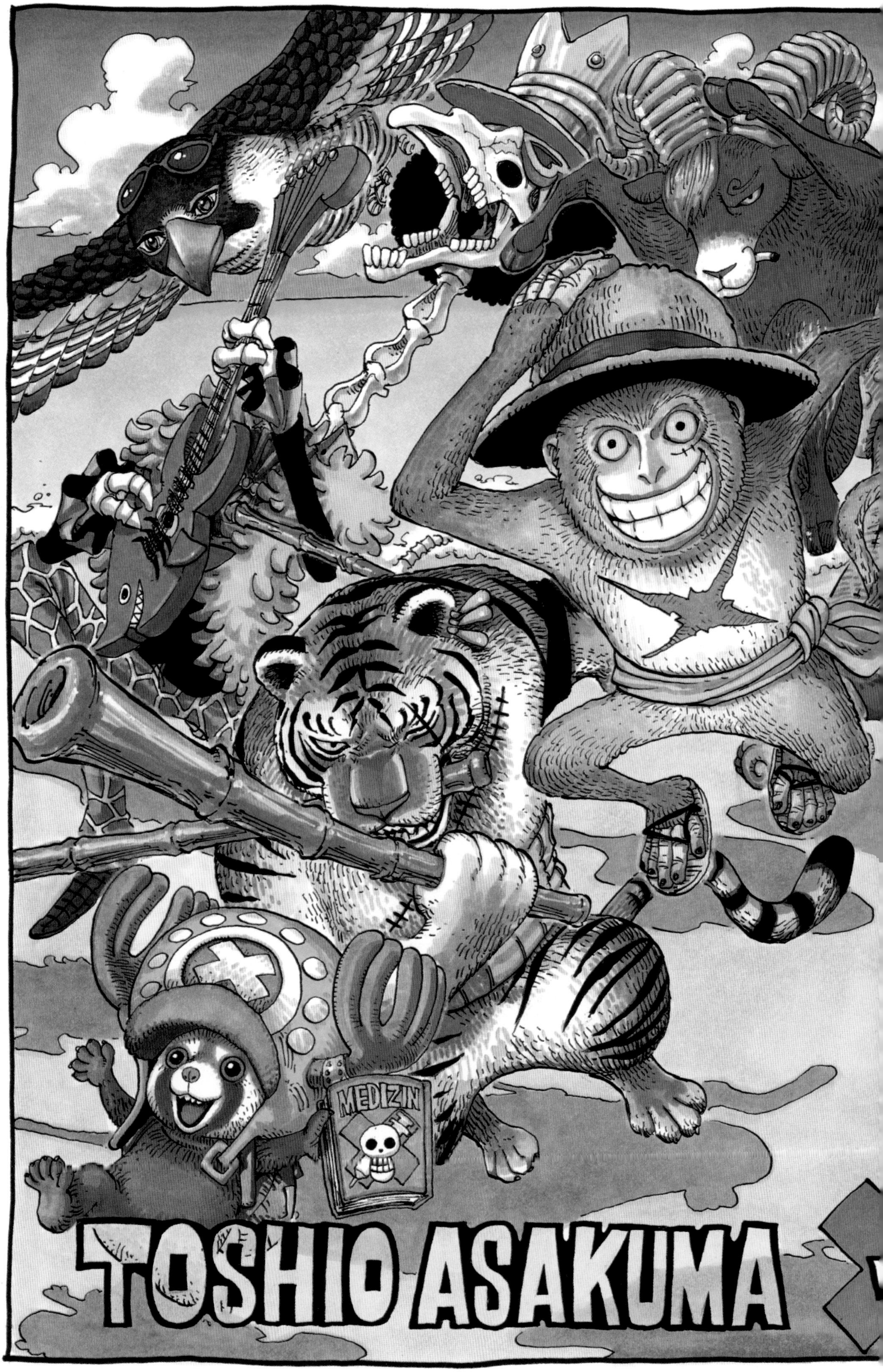
MEDIZIN
TOSHIO ASAKUMA

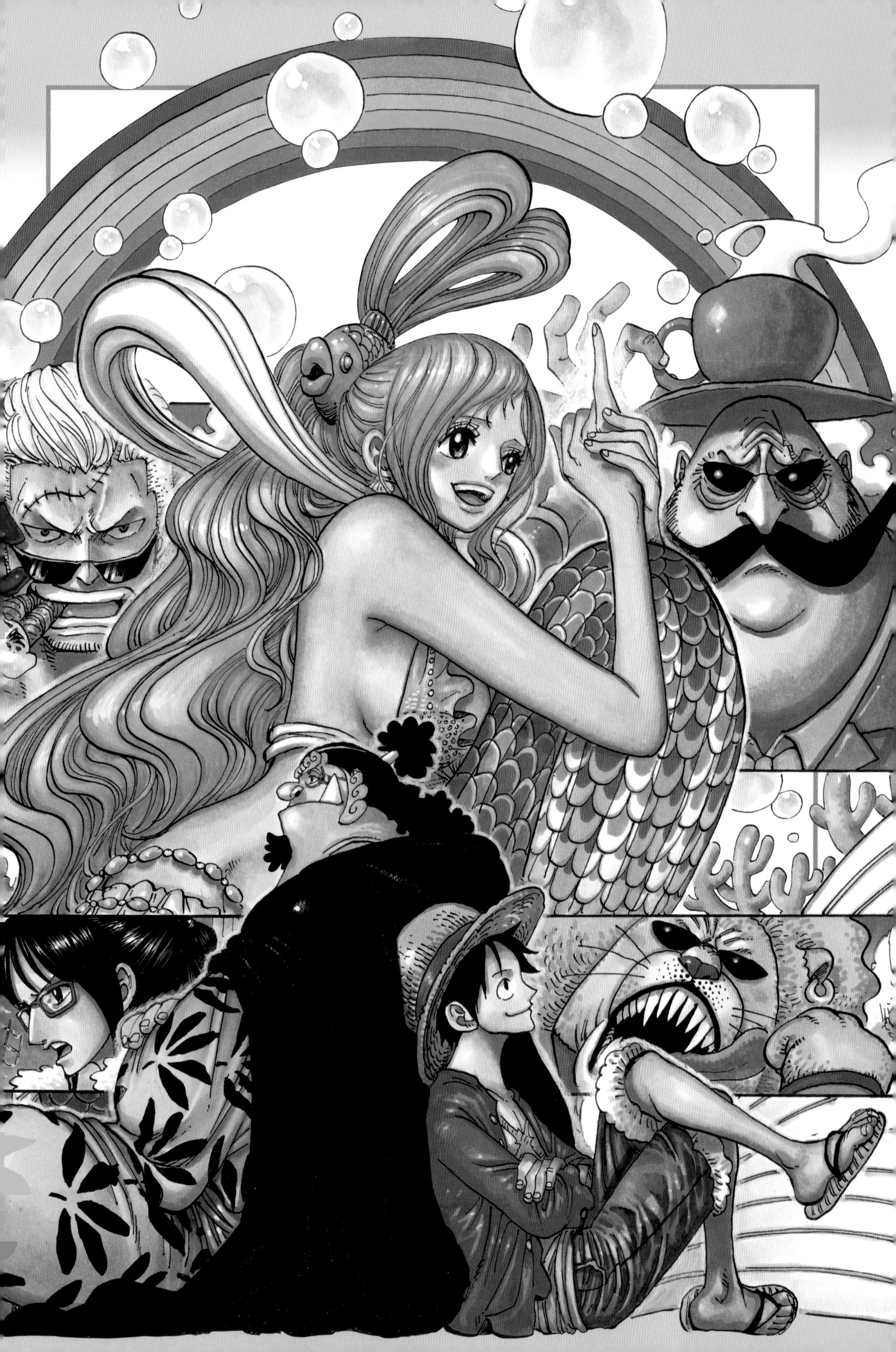

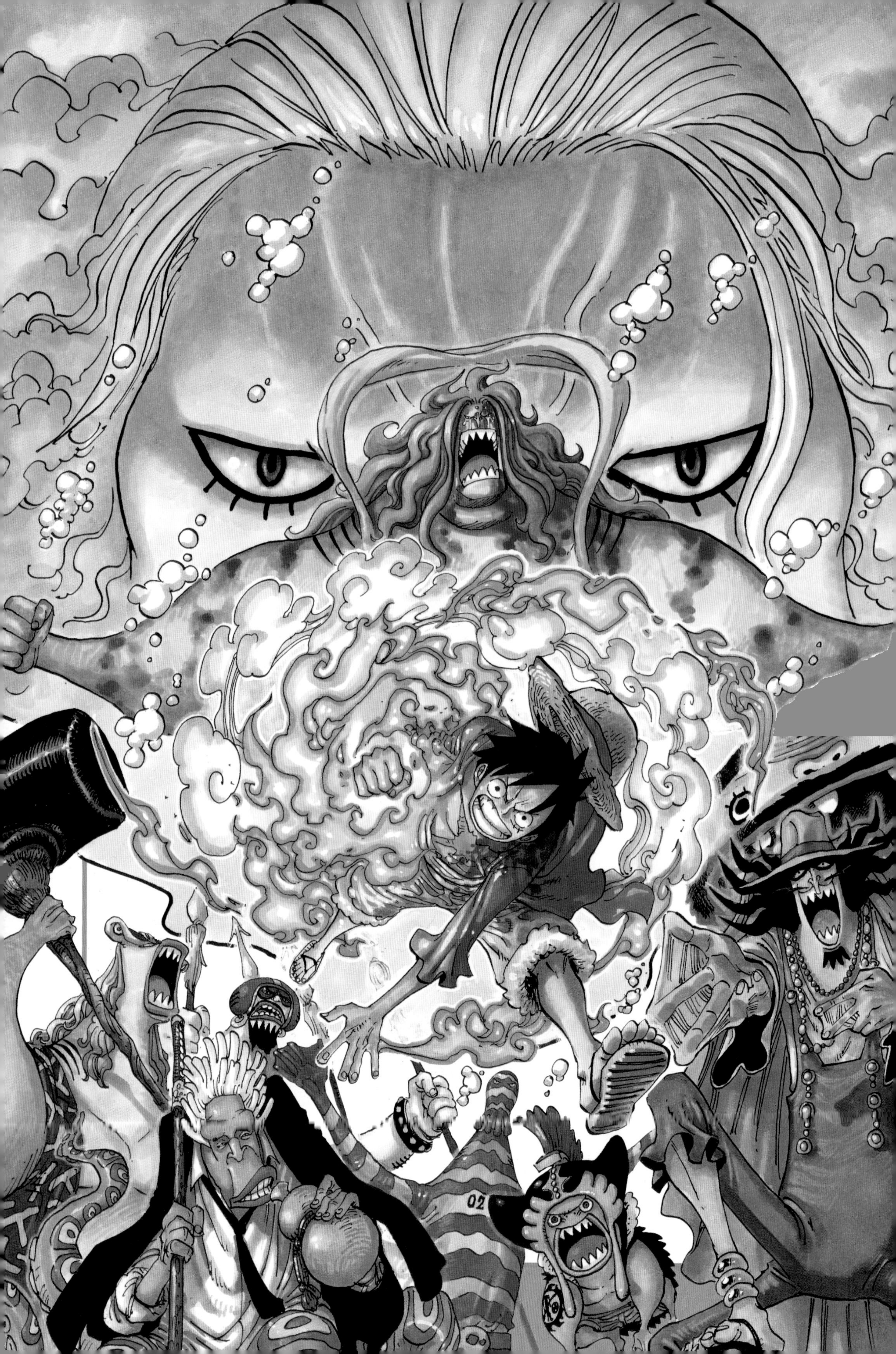
02

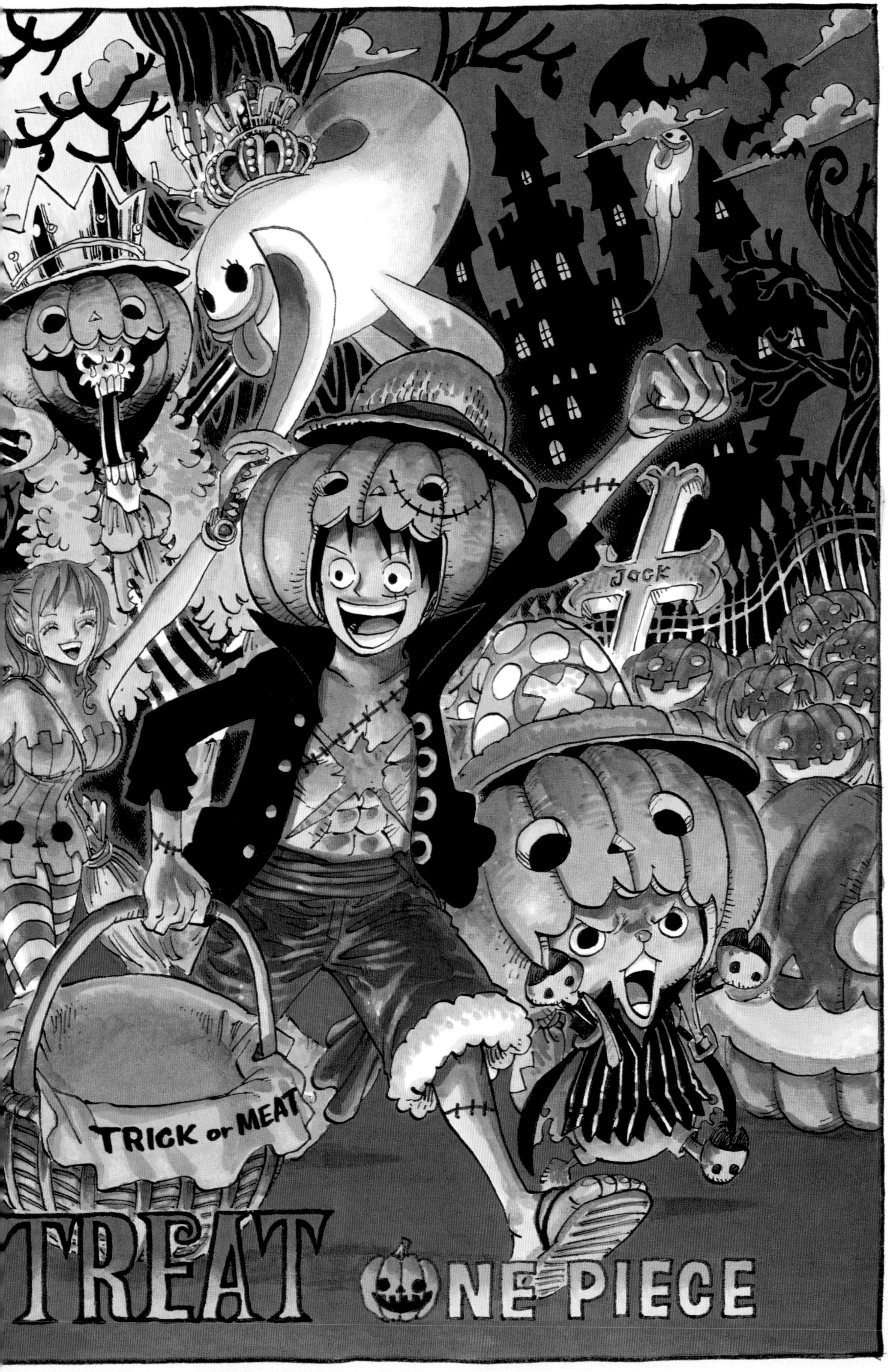
JACK
TRICK or MEAT
TREAT
ONE PIECE

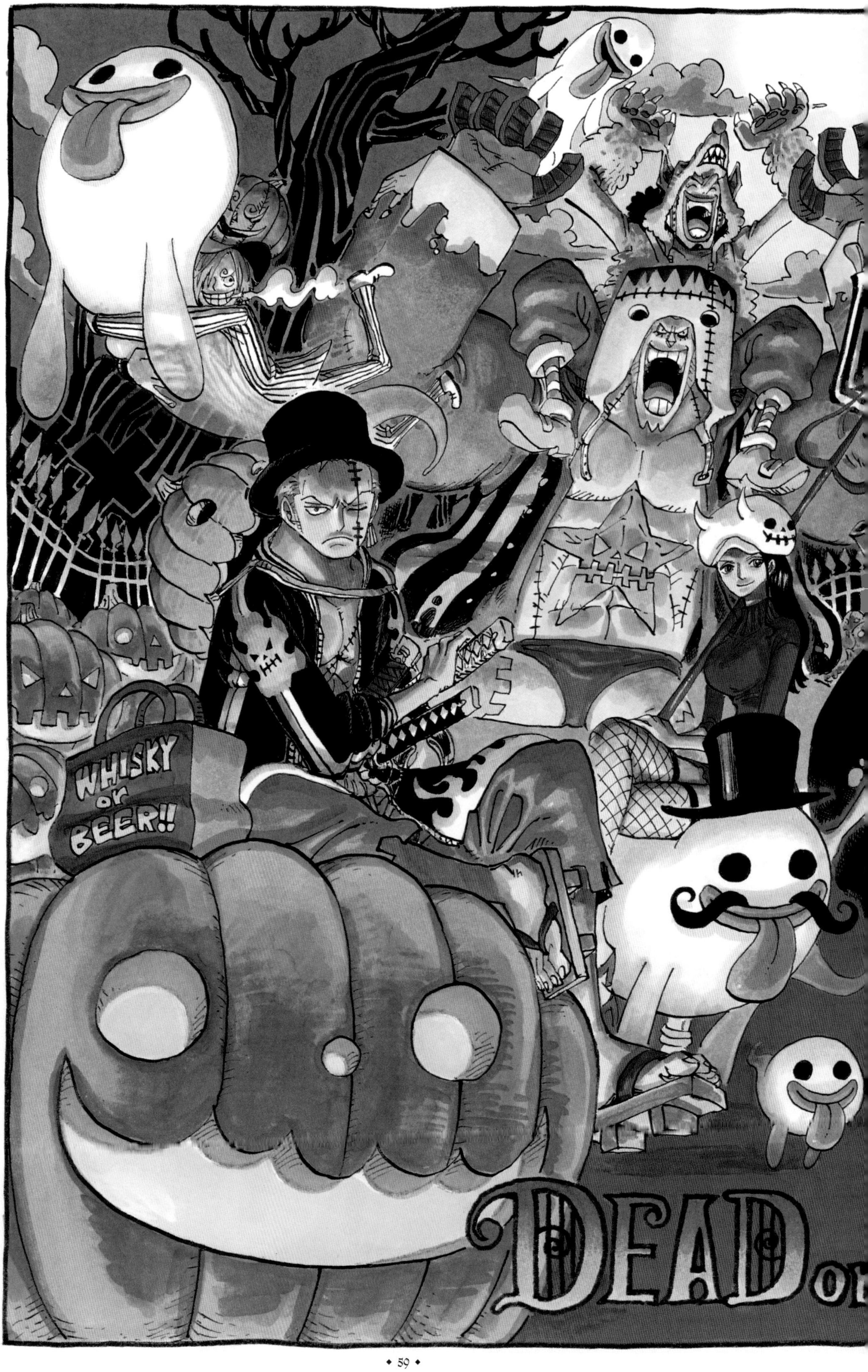
WHISKY or BEER!!
DEAD or

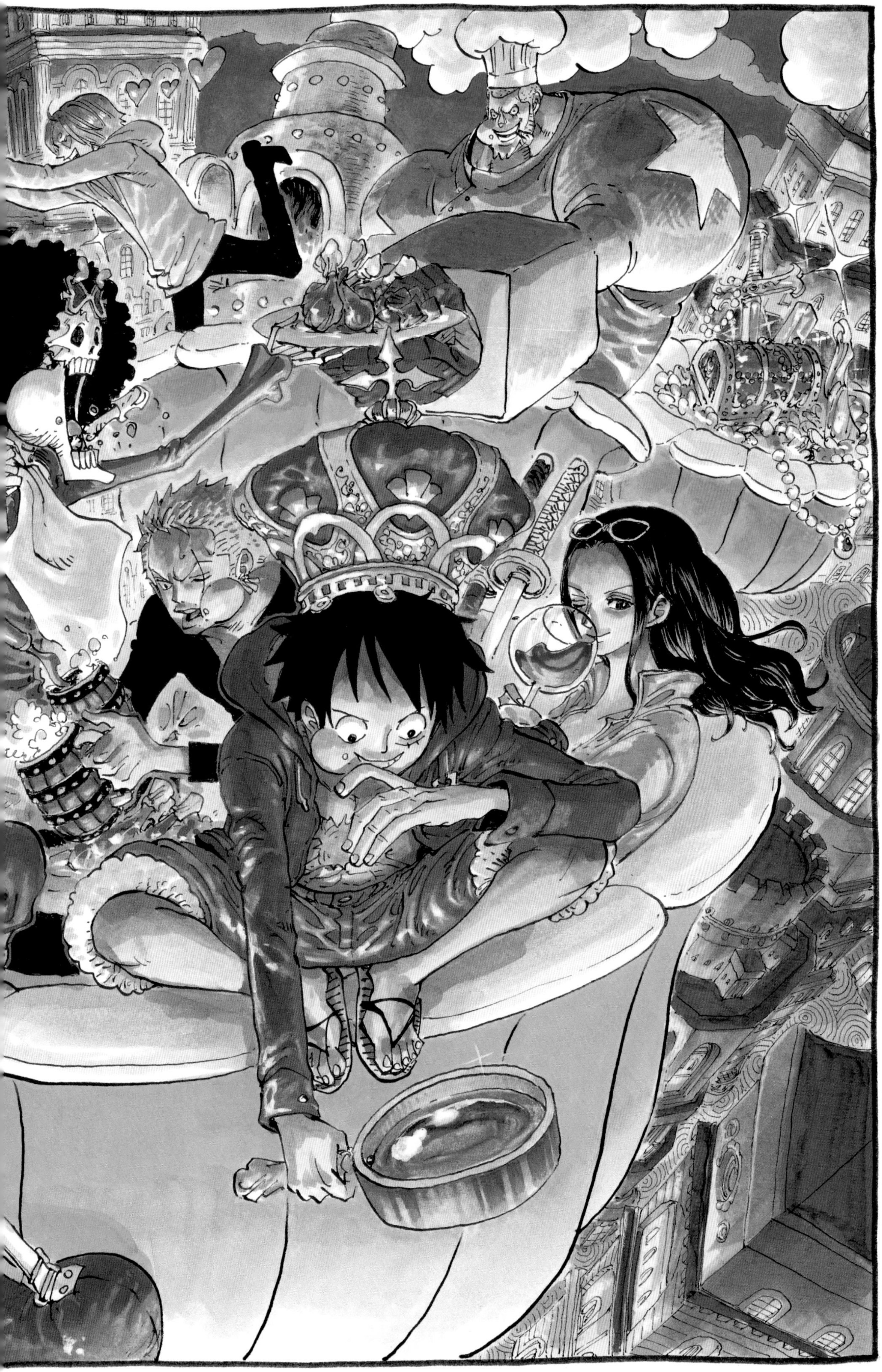

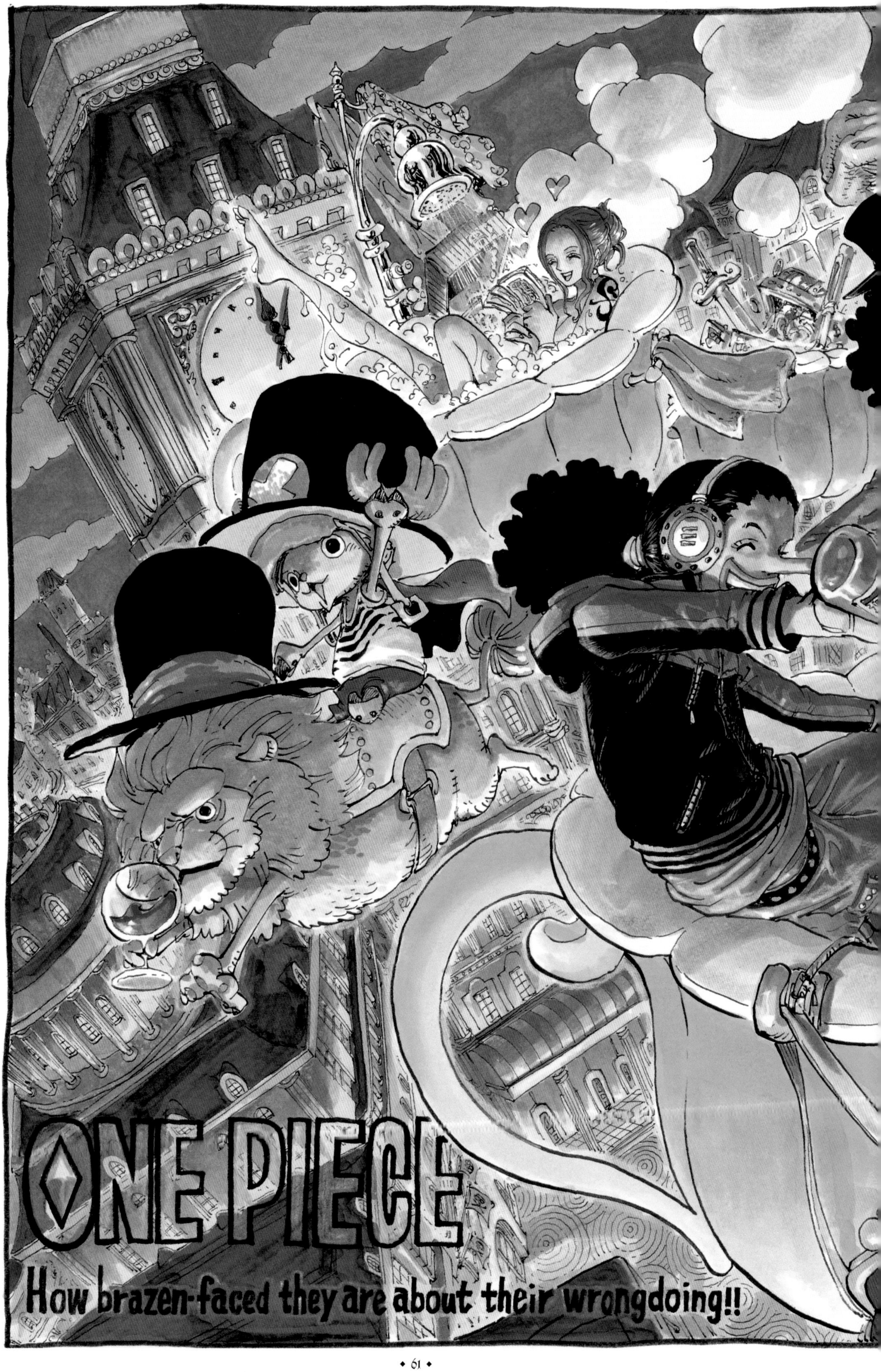
ONE PIECE
How brazen-faced they are about their wrongdoing!!

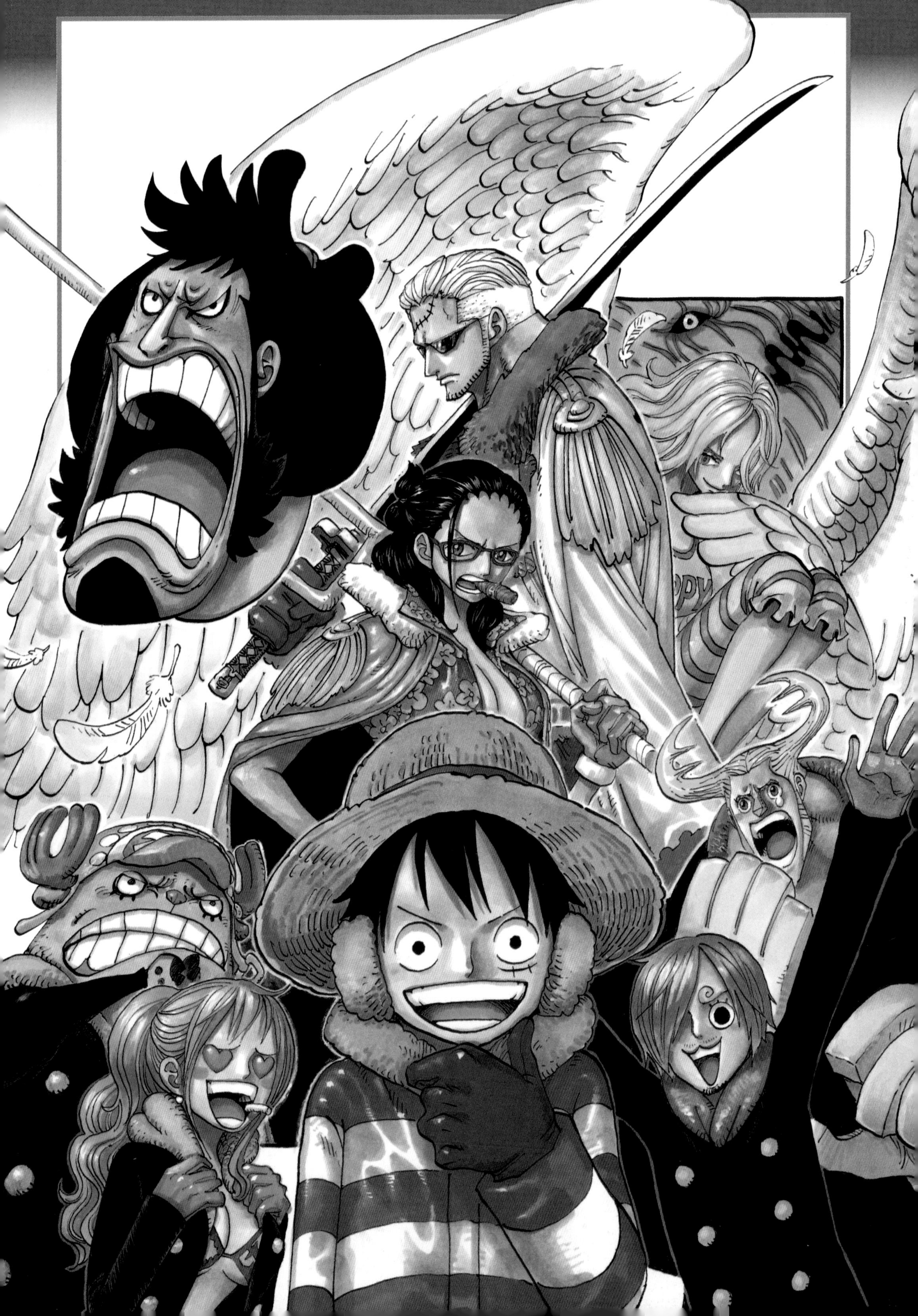

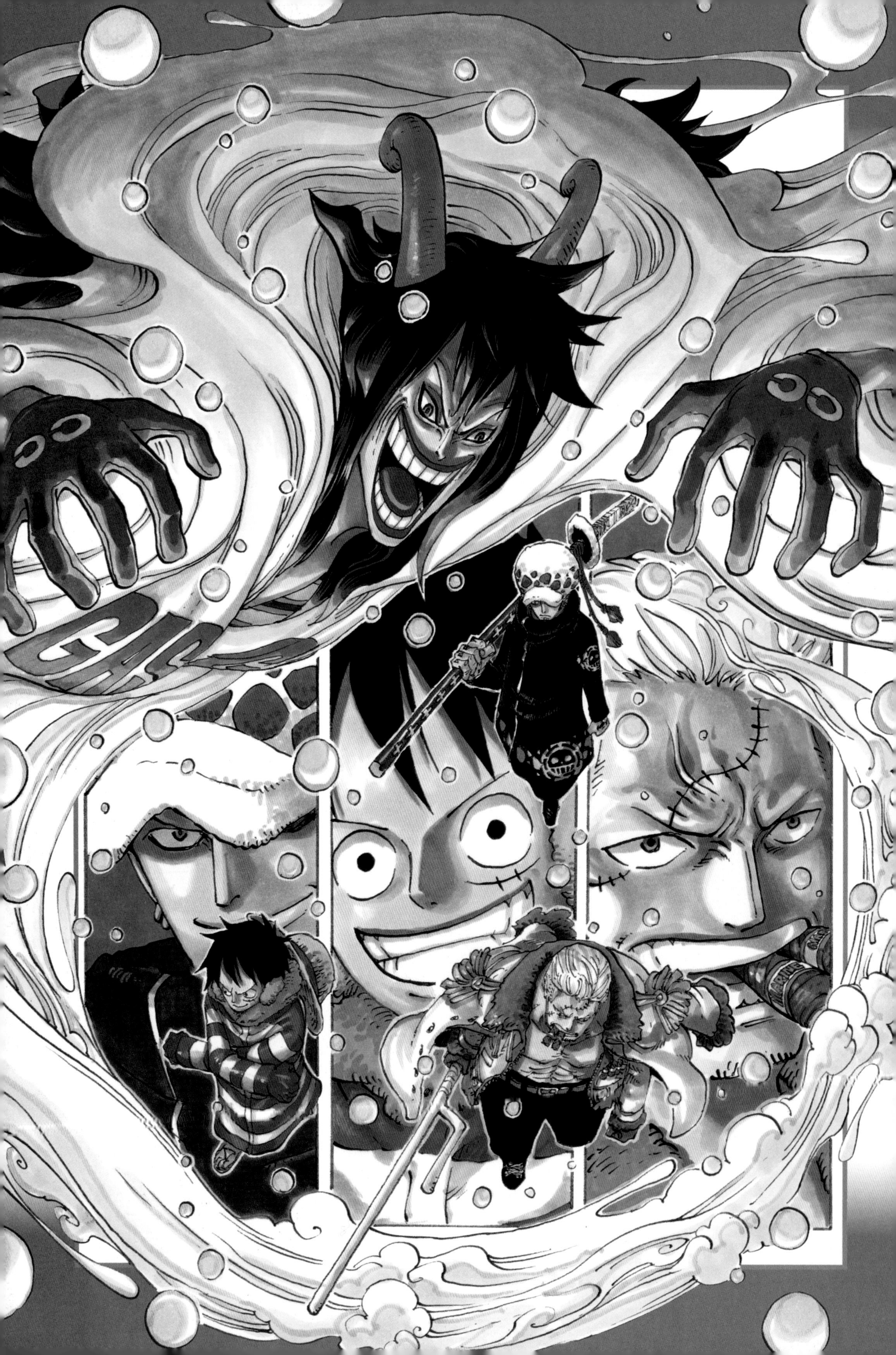

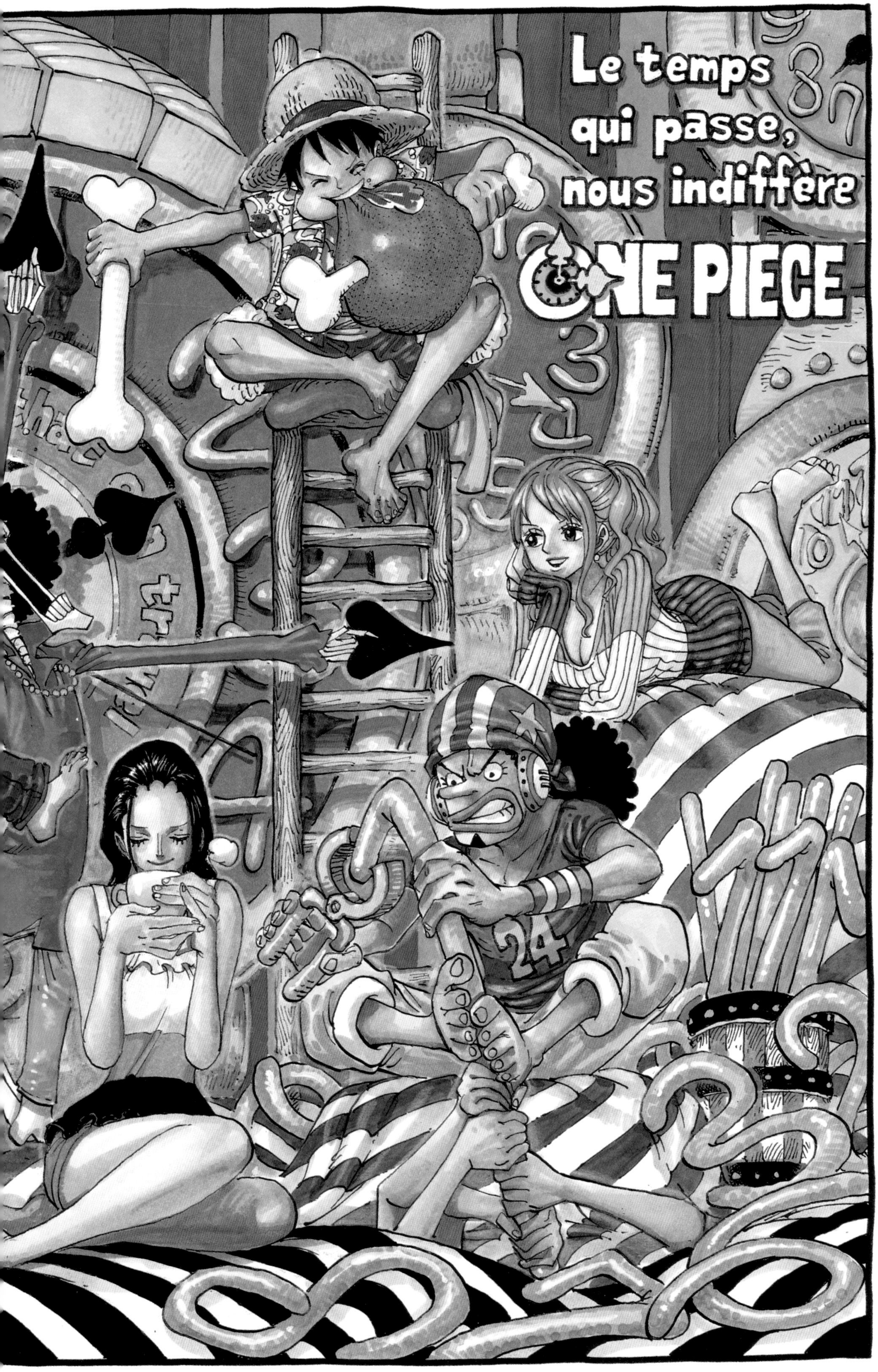
Le temps qui passe, nous indiffère
ONE PIECE

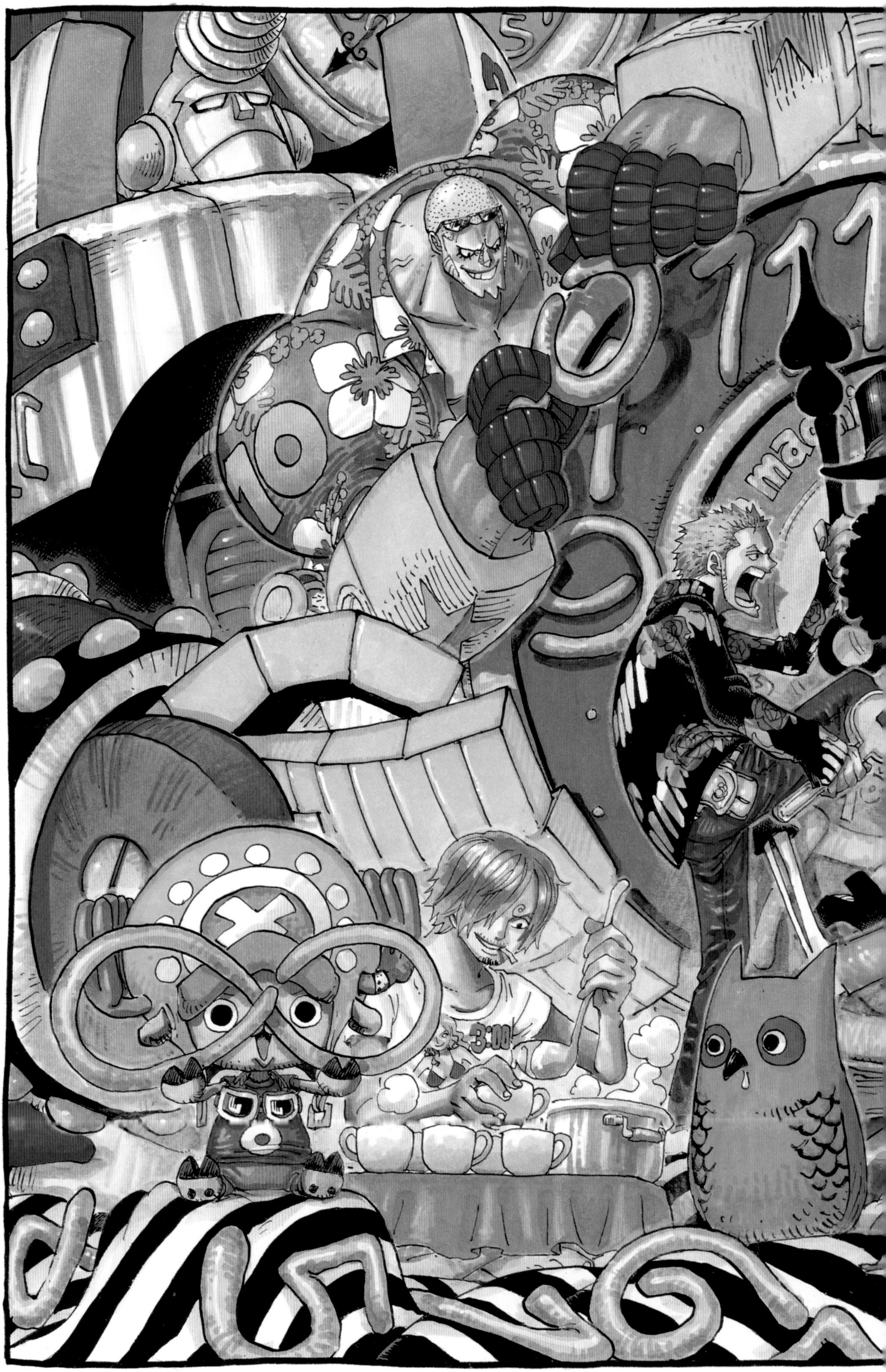

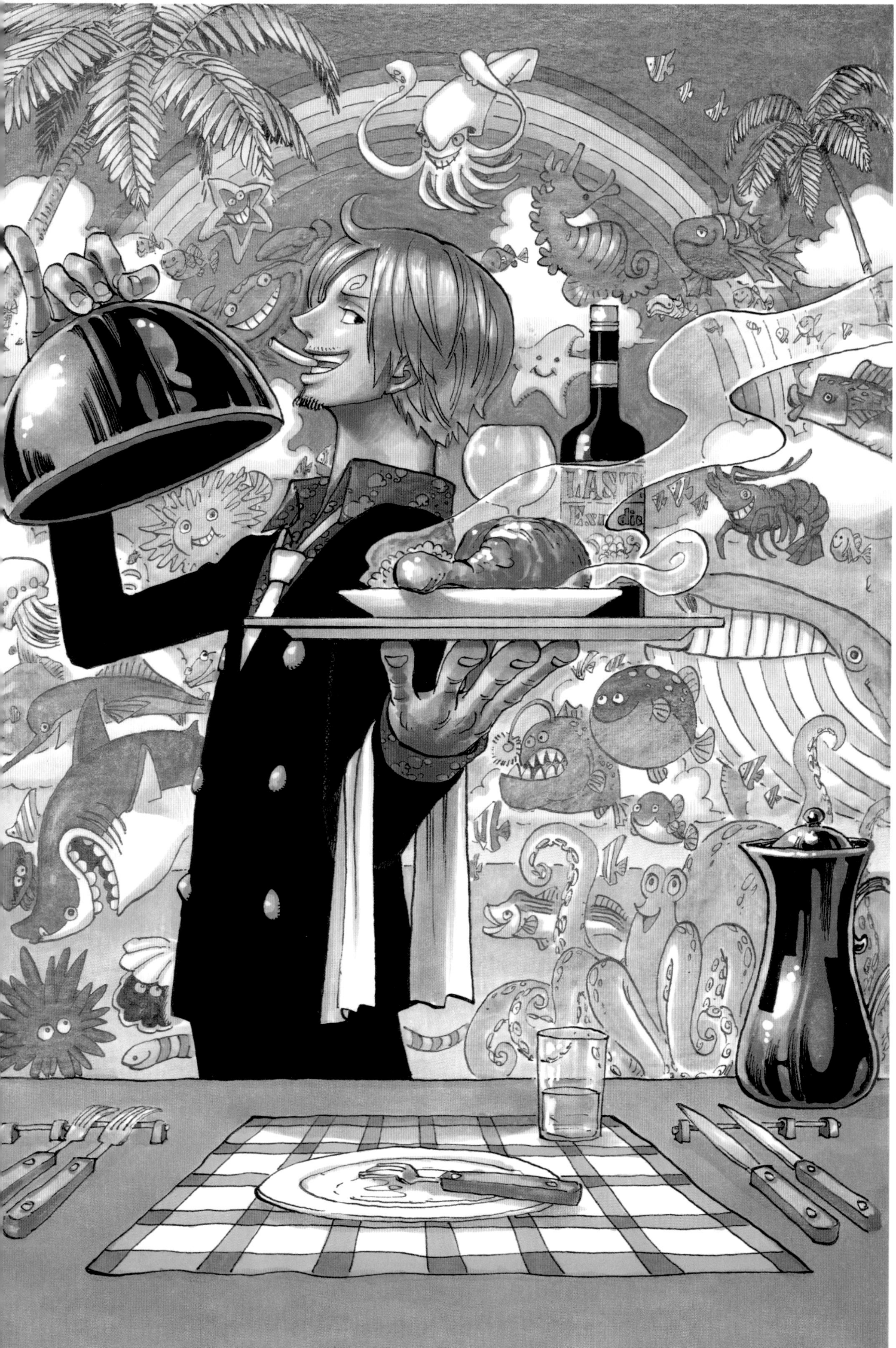

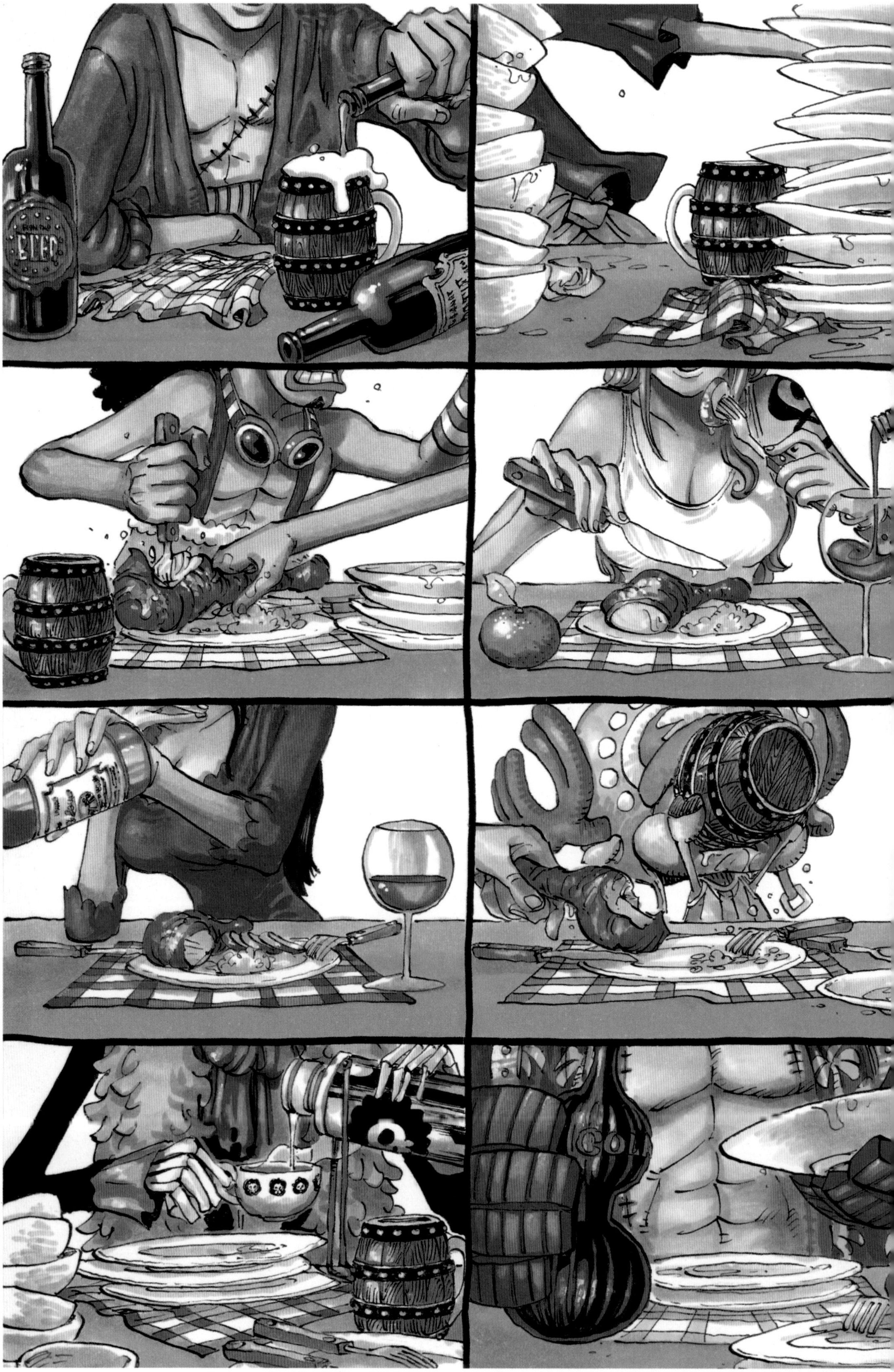

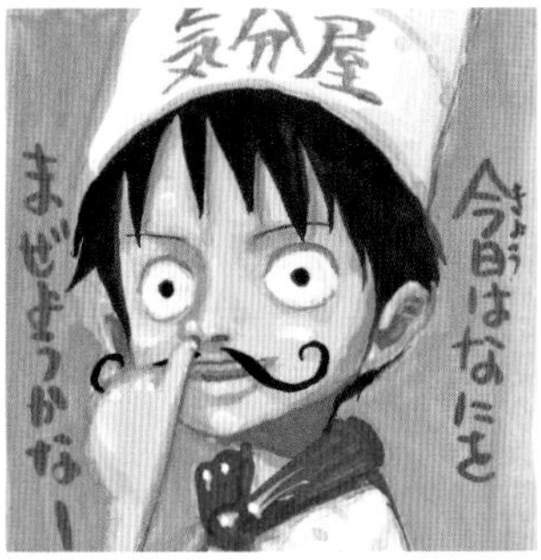
気分屋
今日はなにを
まぜようかなー
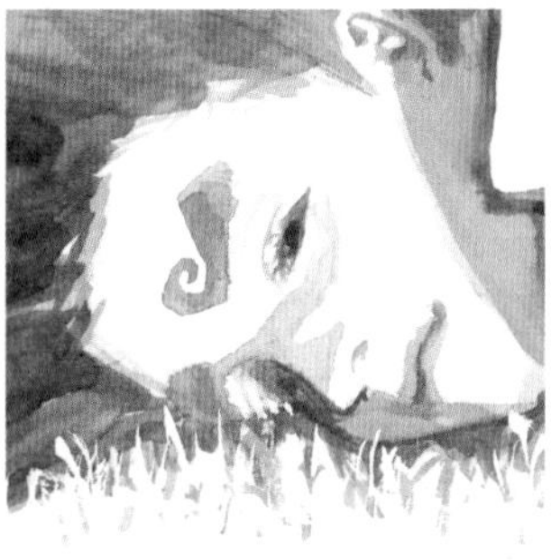
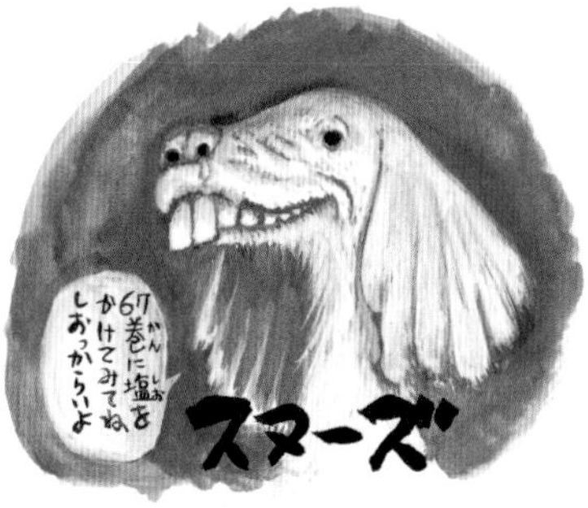
67巻に塩をかけてみてね、しおっからいよ
スヌーズ
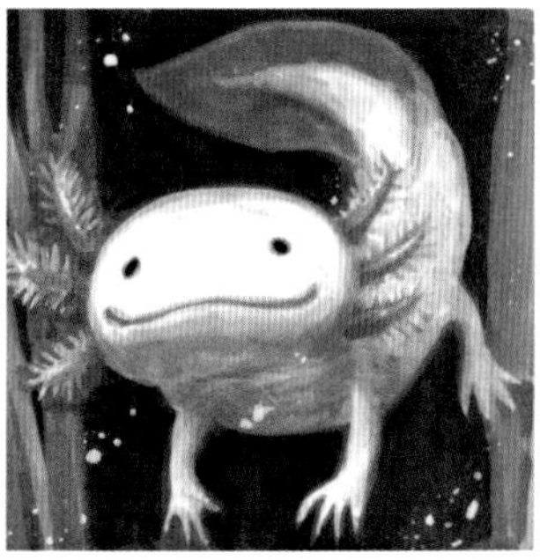
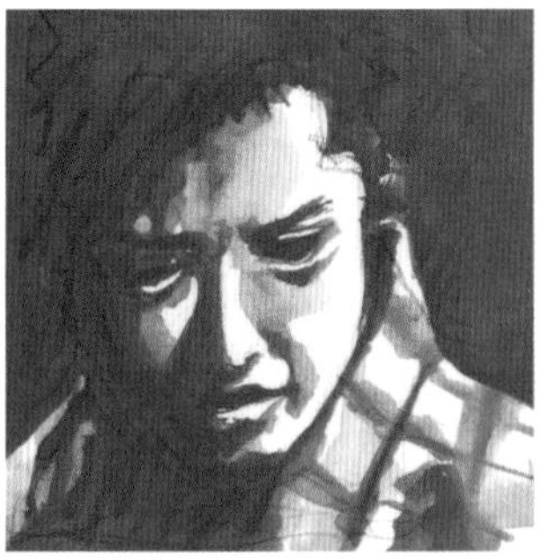
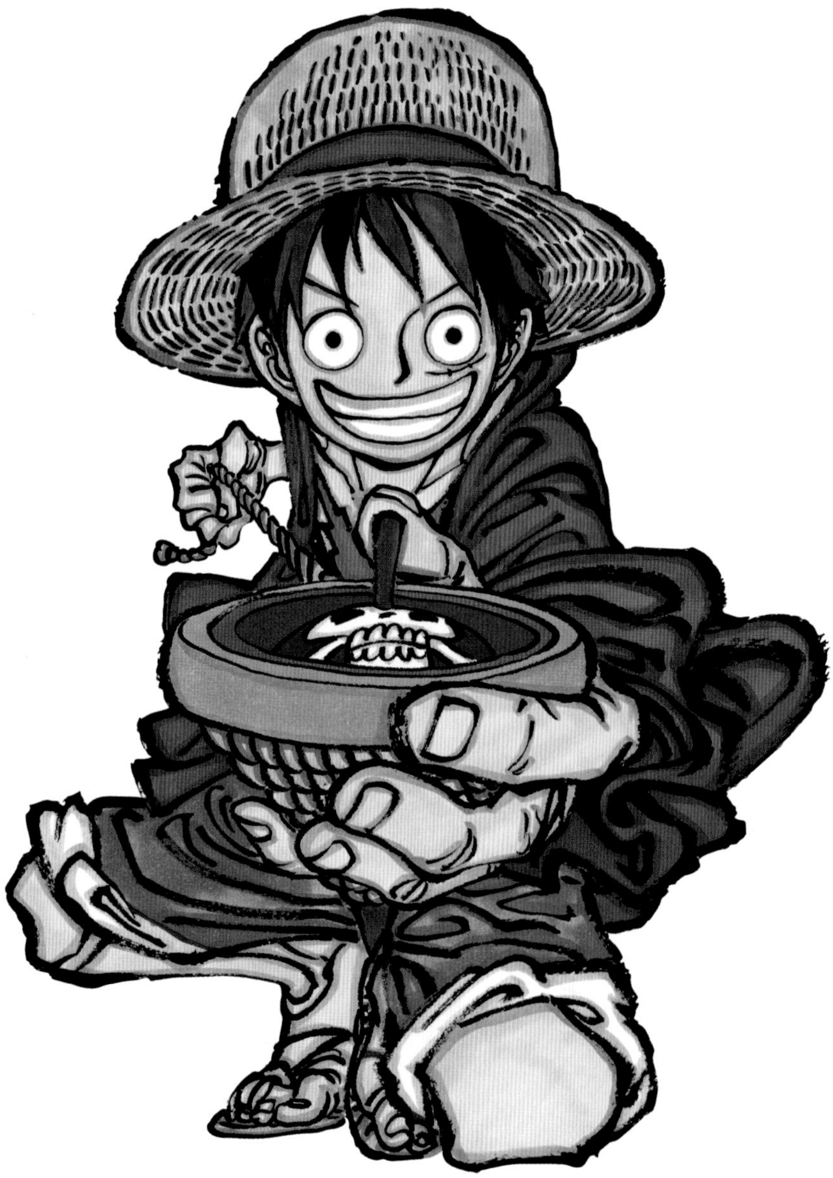

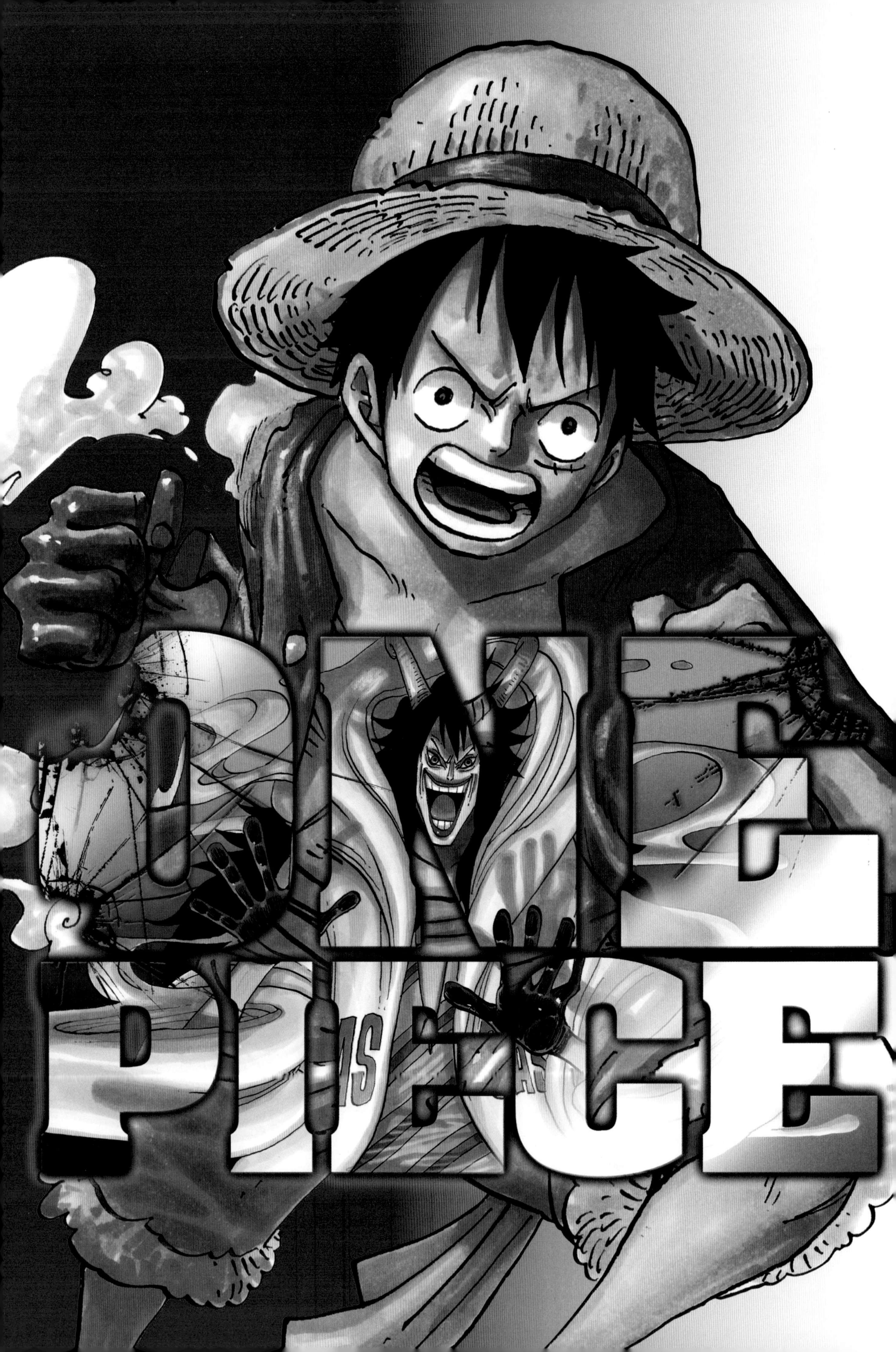
ONE
PIECE

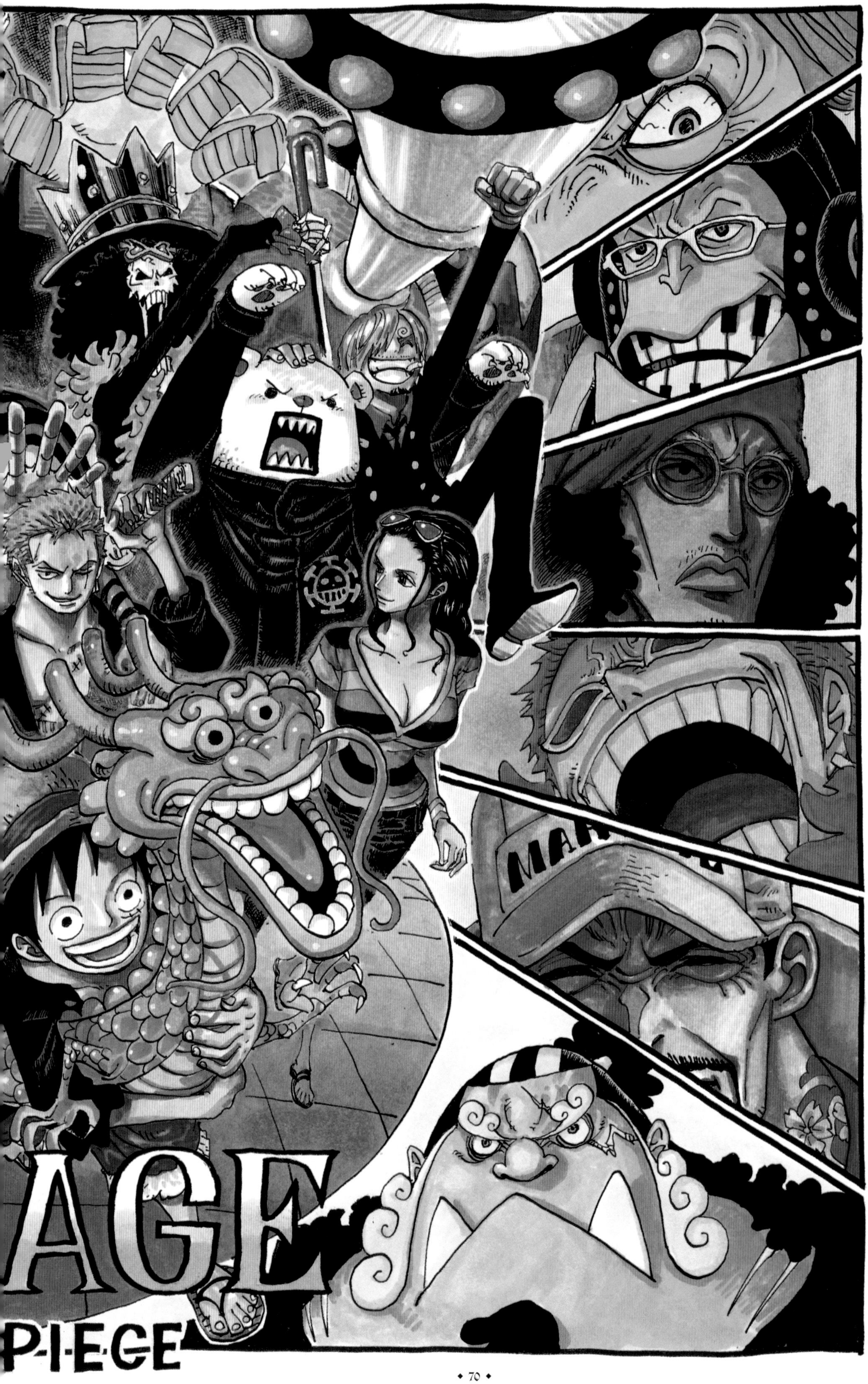
AGE
P·I·E·C·E

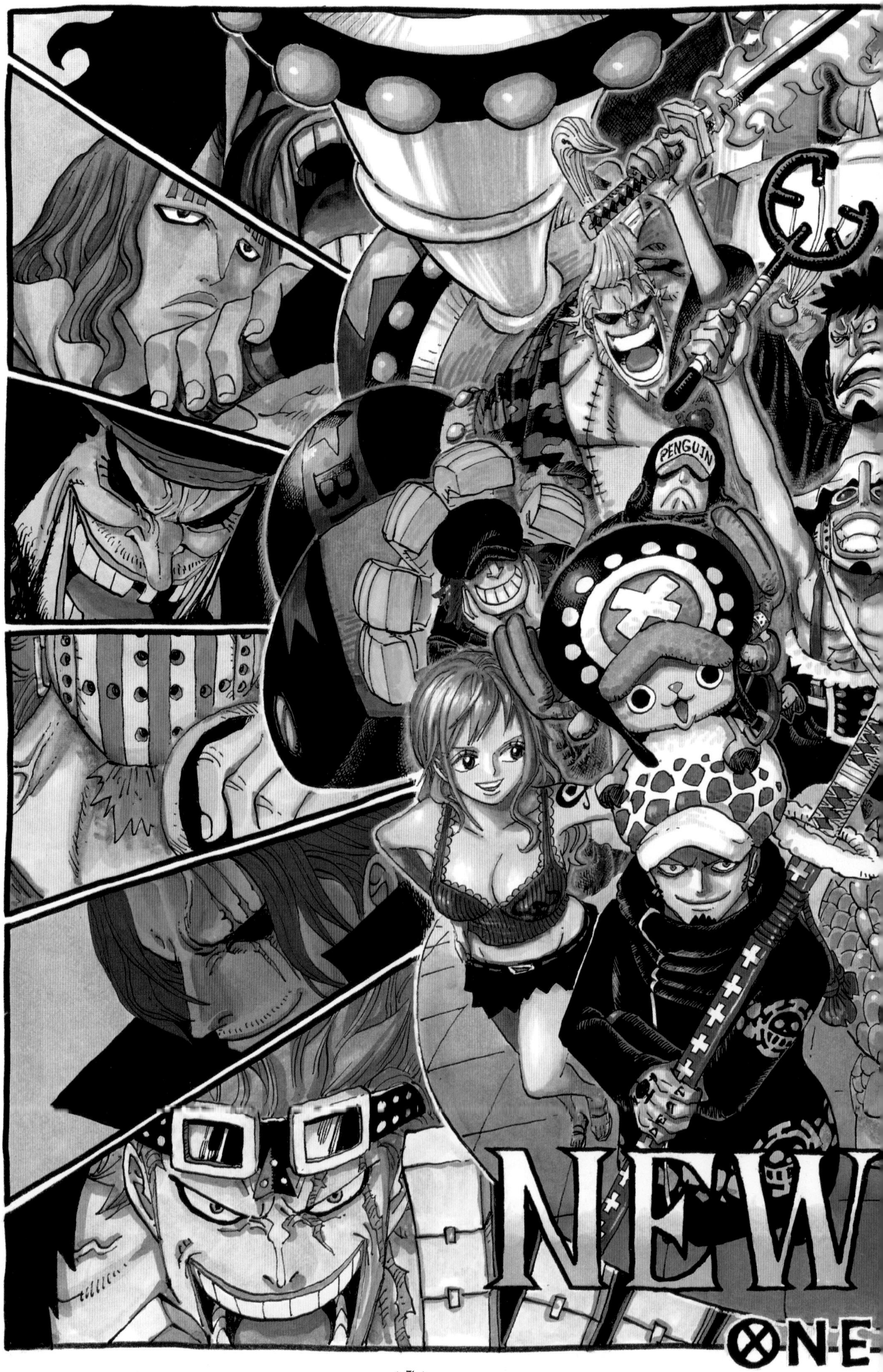
PENGUIN
NEW
ONE

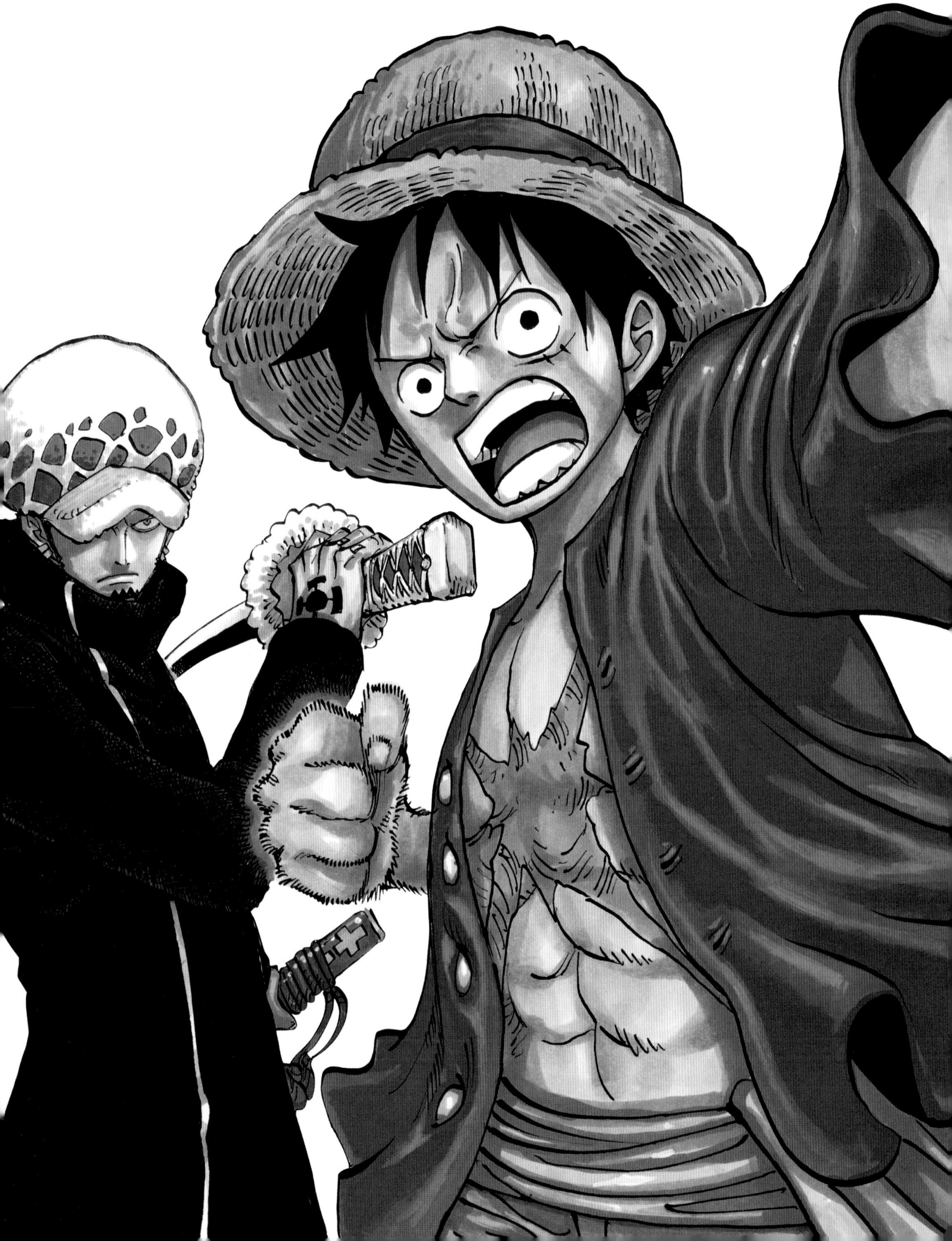

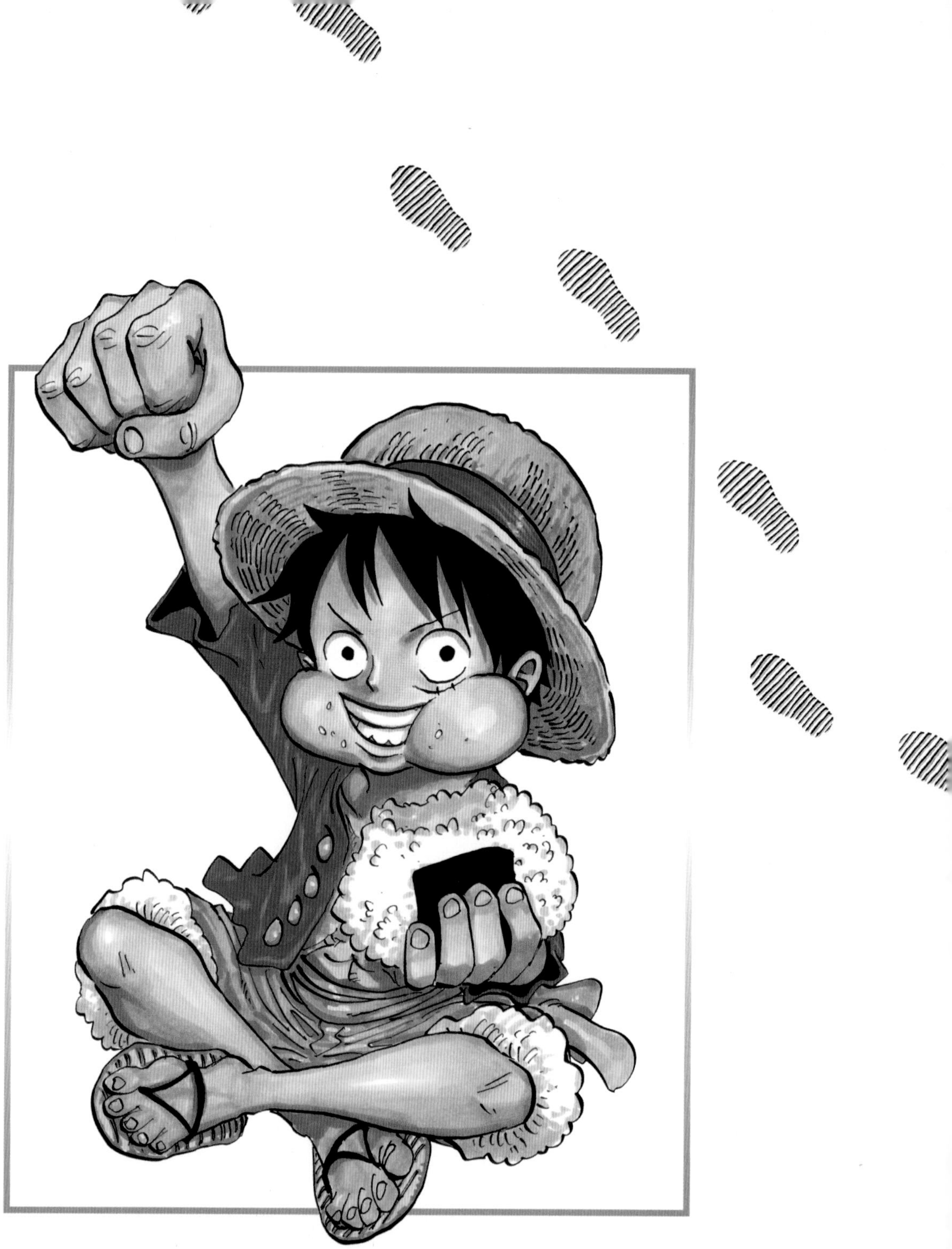

2013

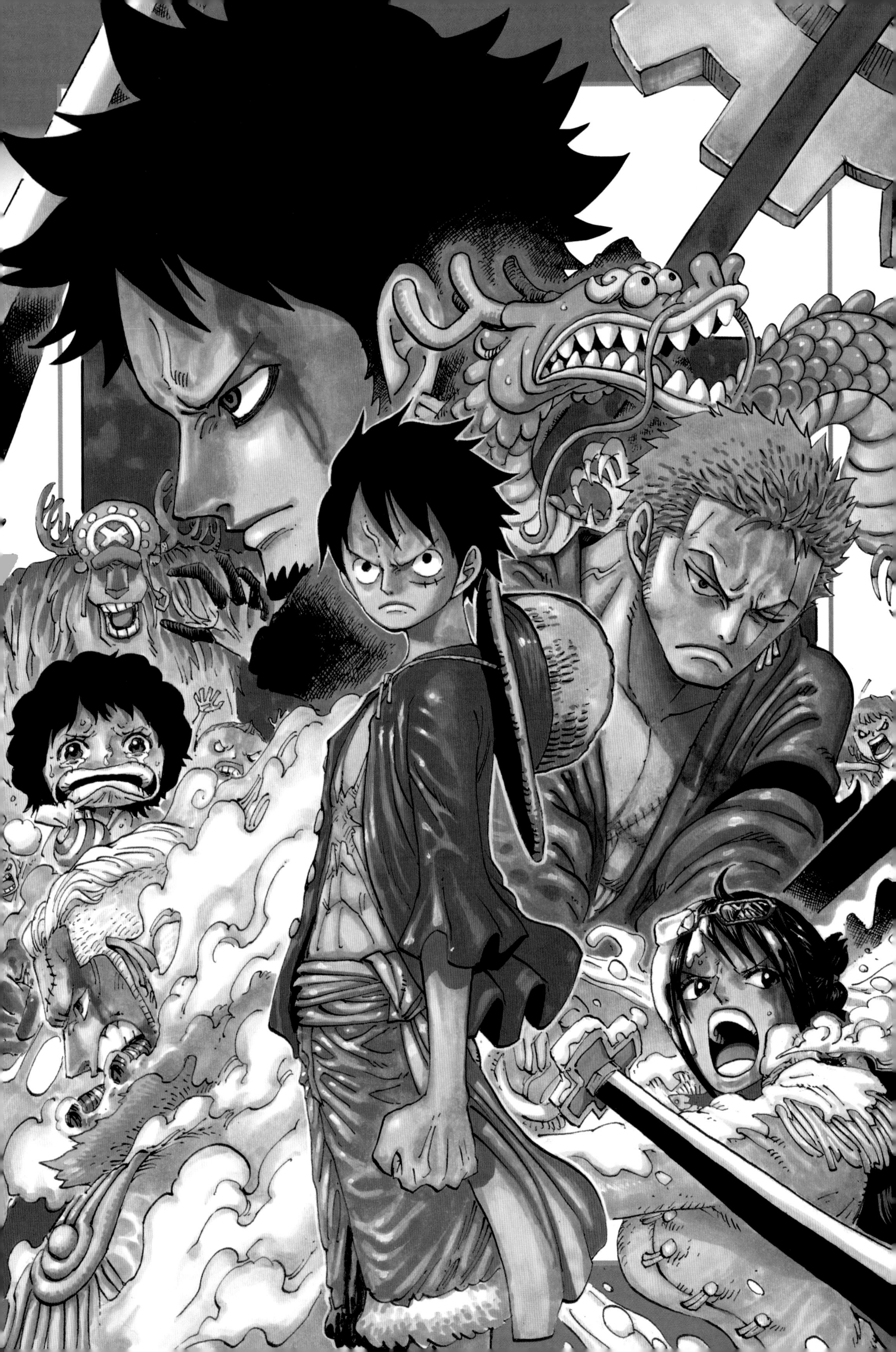

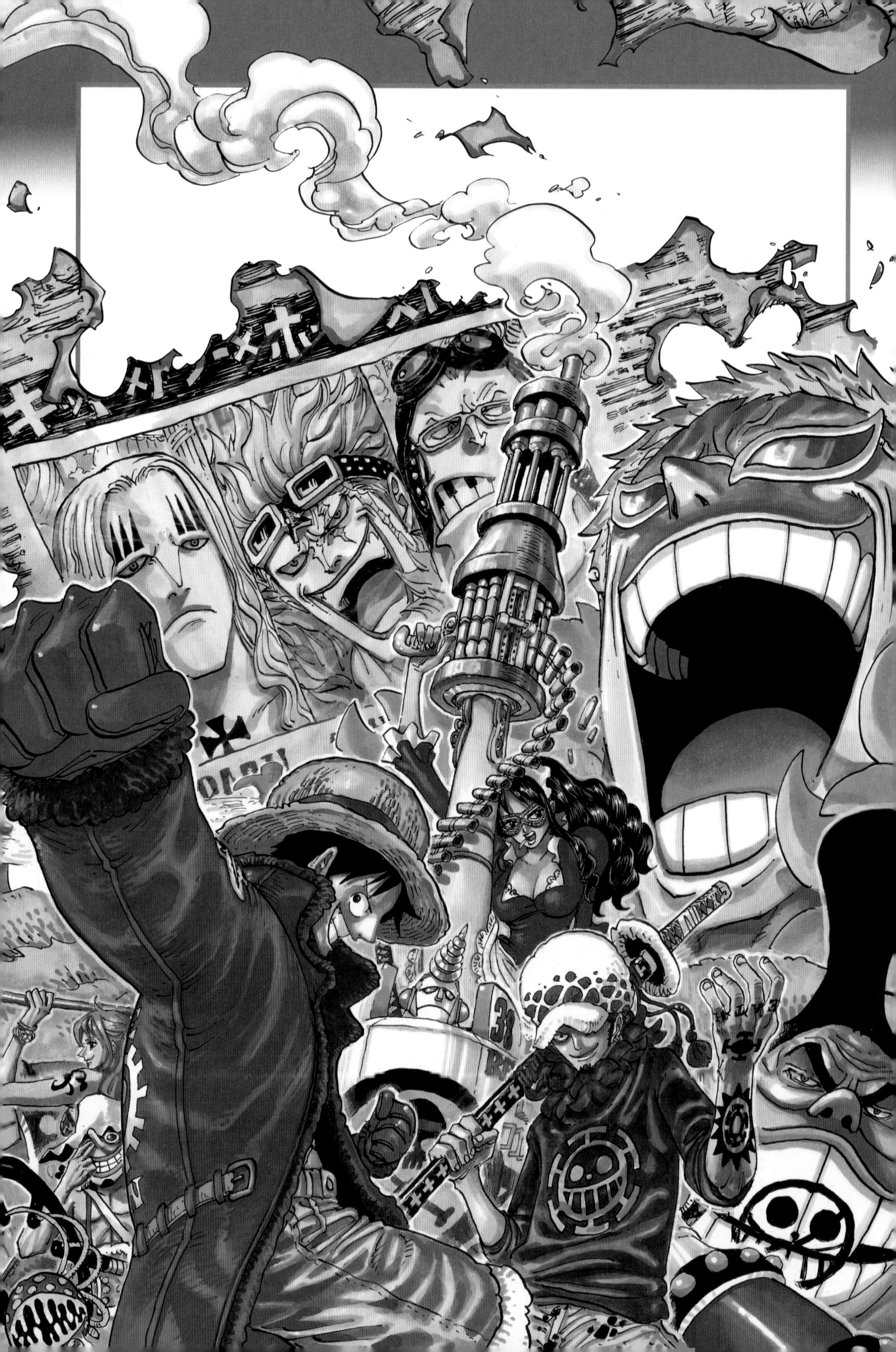

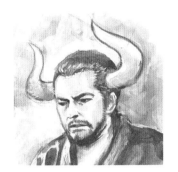

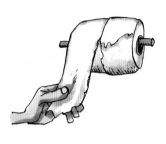

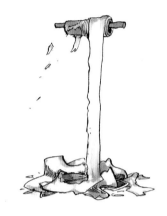

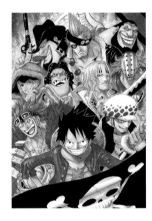

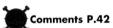

Comments P.42

This piece was a reader's request. I didn't look before I leapt on this one! I hadn't considered the designs of the Worst Generation after the two-year time skip! But I decided, "That's okay. I'll just draw them all together!" And so I did.

TOSHIO ASAKUMA vs ONE PIECE

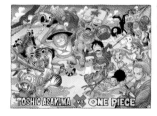

Comments P.54–55

Toshio Asakuma's chilled-out animal figures are just the best. I was already a fan, and my wish came true when we got to do a collaboration. A bunch of animals are passing themselves off as the Straw Hats! This was very exciting for me.

ONE PIECE

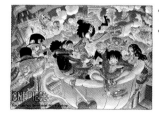

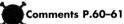

Comments P.60–61

A major metropolis has been pillaged! The city is all abuzz! The sirens are howling and the police are running about, but it's all for naught. The thieves are toasting to their successful getaway in the sky above.

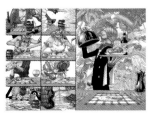

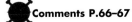

Comments P.66–67

Believe it or not, Sanji put out a book called *One Piece: Pirate Recipes*. He's the star, so the rest of the crew can't show their faces! The glimpses of them are all very much in character.

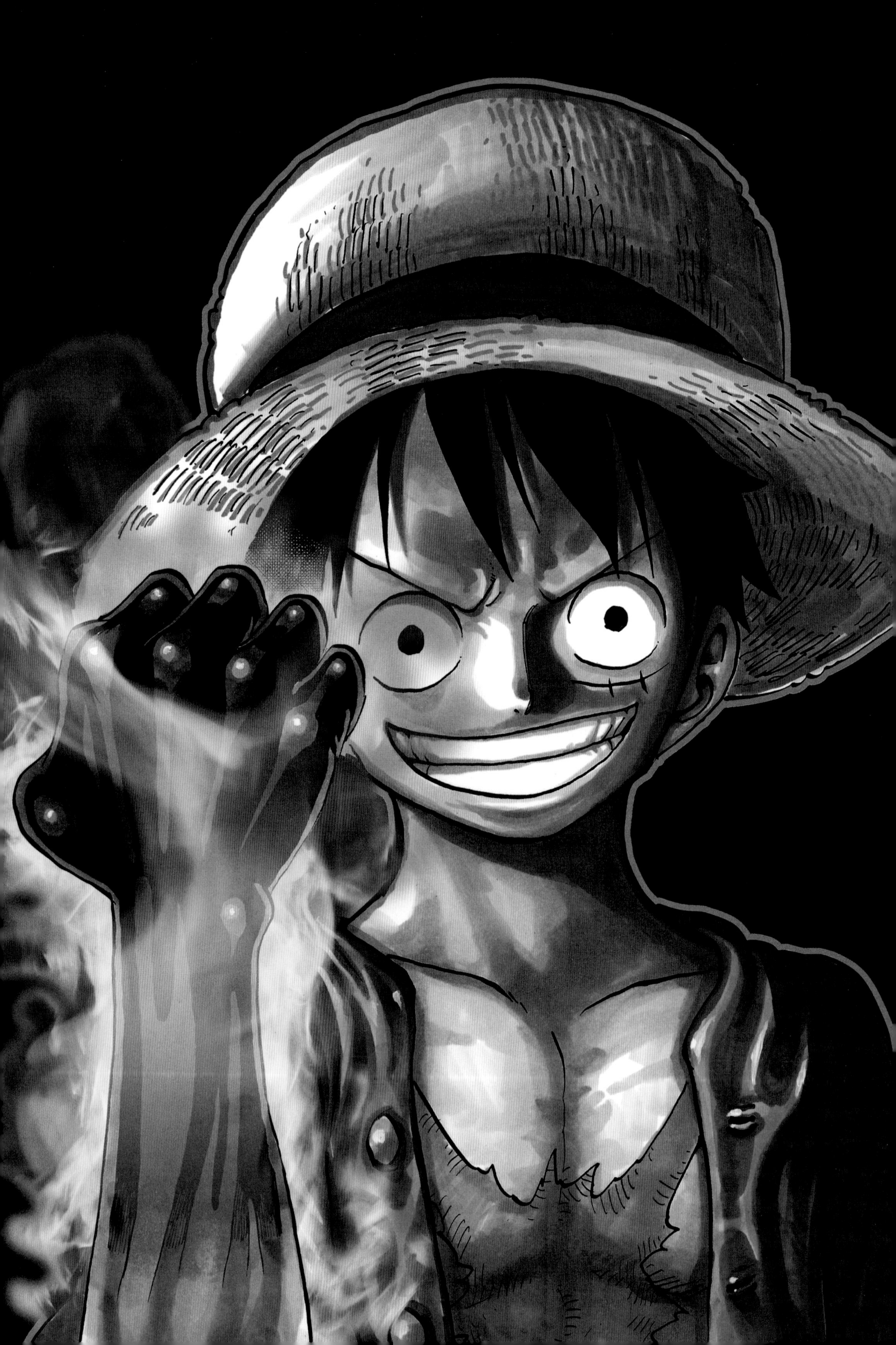

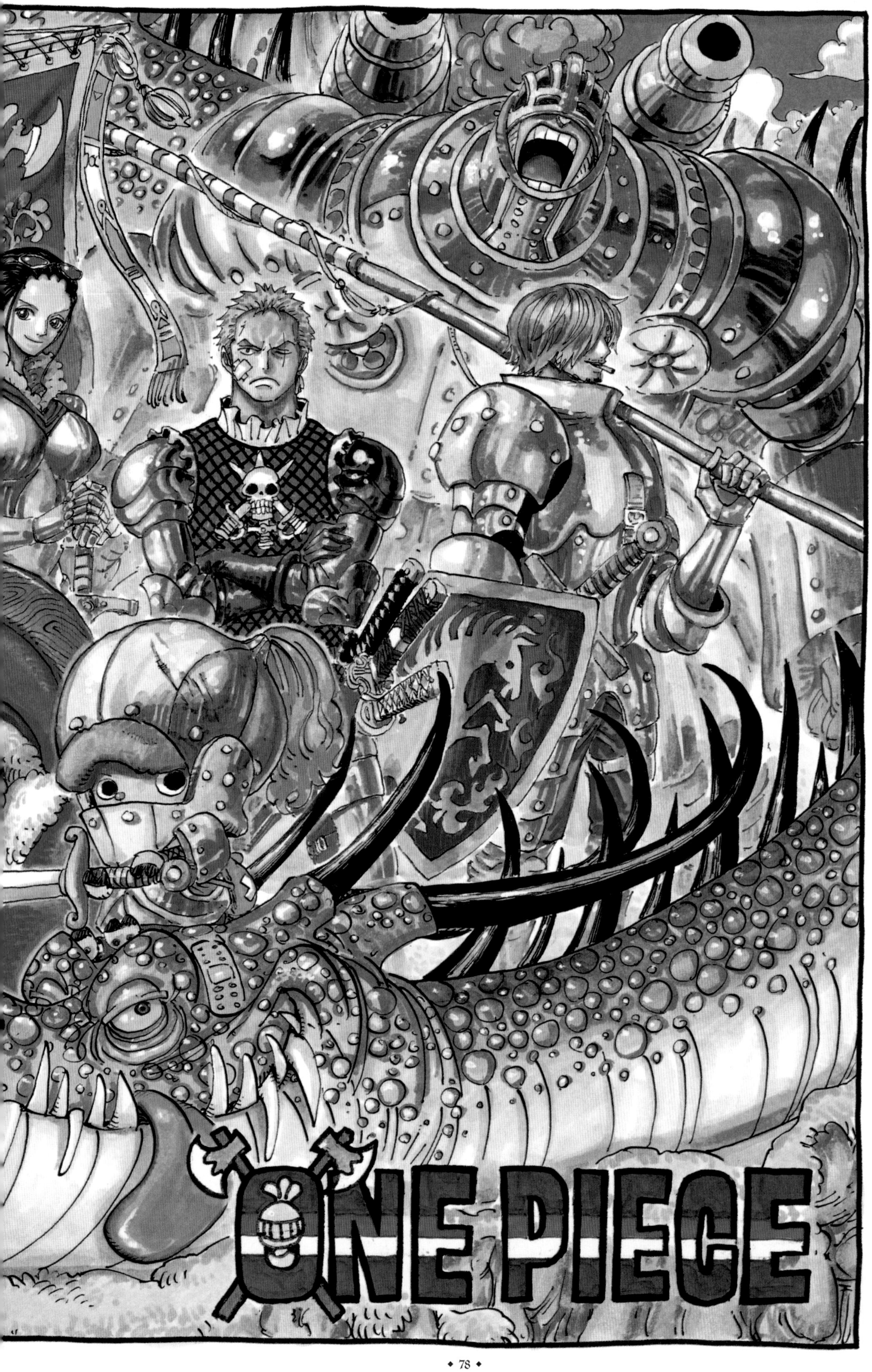
ONE PIECE

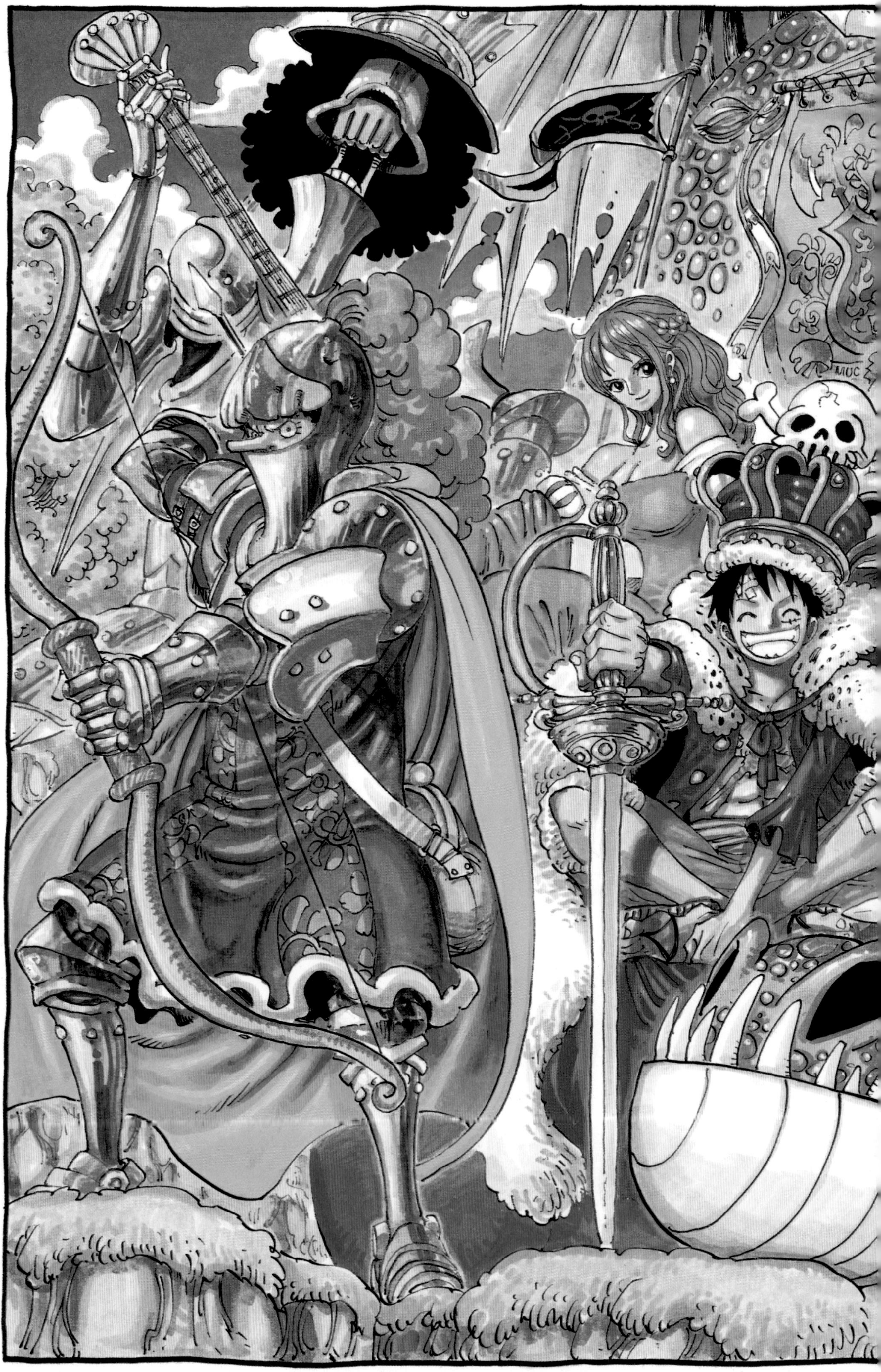

ONEPIECE

MOVIE

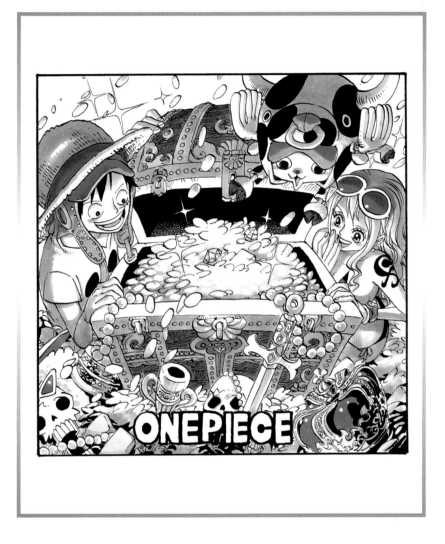

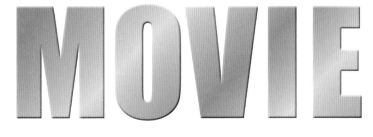

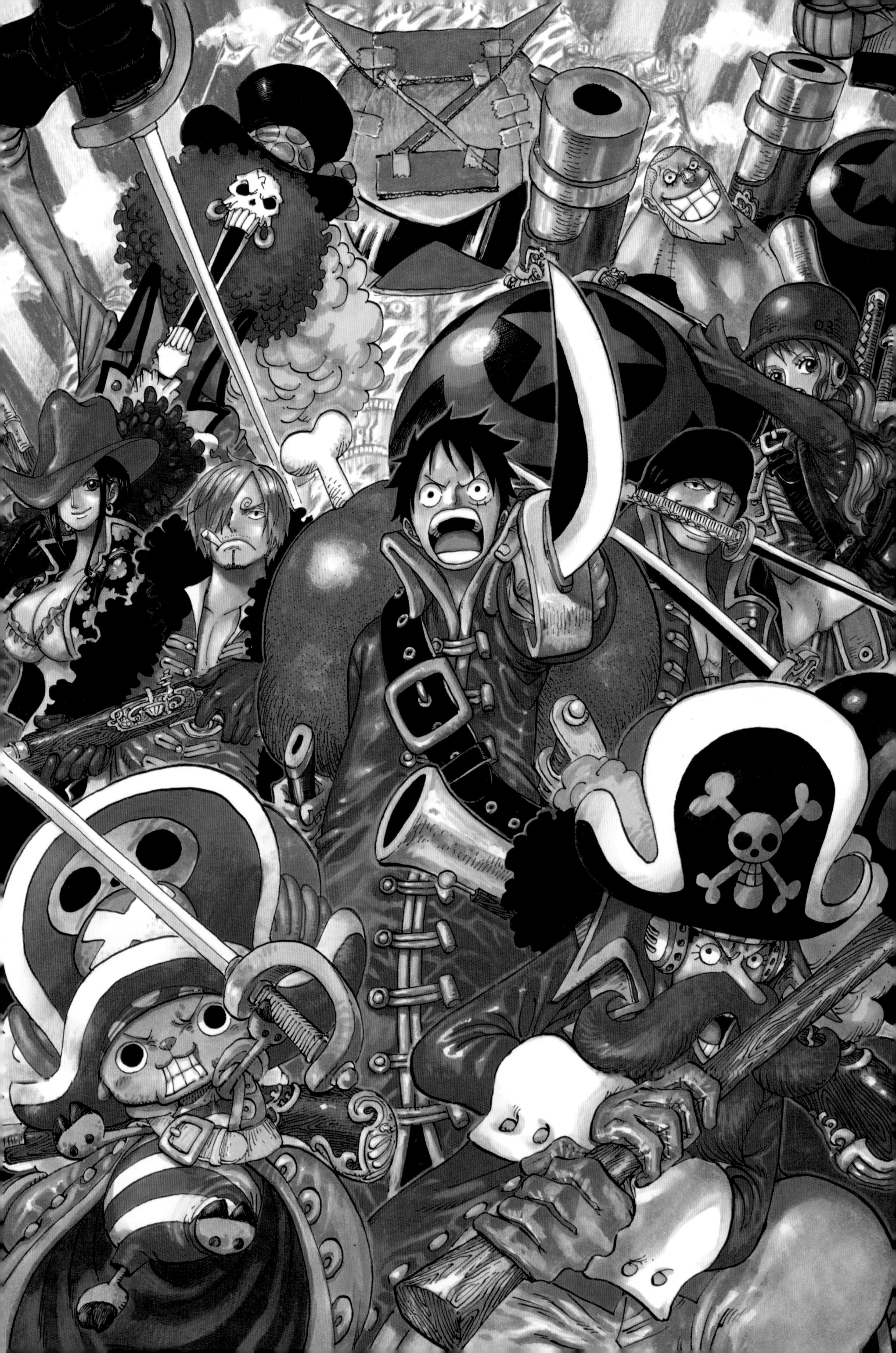

START!
+1
NEPIECE FILM
すごろく冒険島
-1
GOAL!!
+1
+1
+1
-1

NEW AGE
ONE PIECE

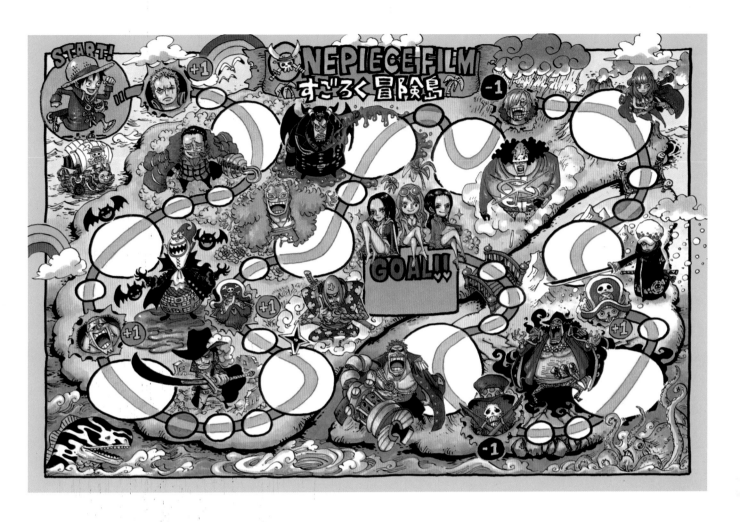

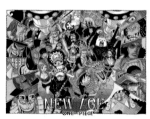

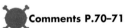

Comments P.70–71

The new generation are teaming up in the New World! If you don't want to fight, get out now while you can!

ONE PIECE

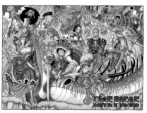

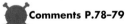

Comments P.78–79

A fierce dragon attacks the countryside. But a wandering band of knights brings it down.
Leader: "Hey! Give us all your food in return!!"
Mystery Woman: "And all your treasure too!!"

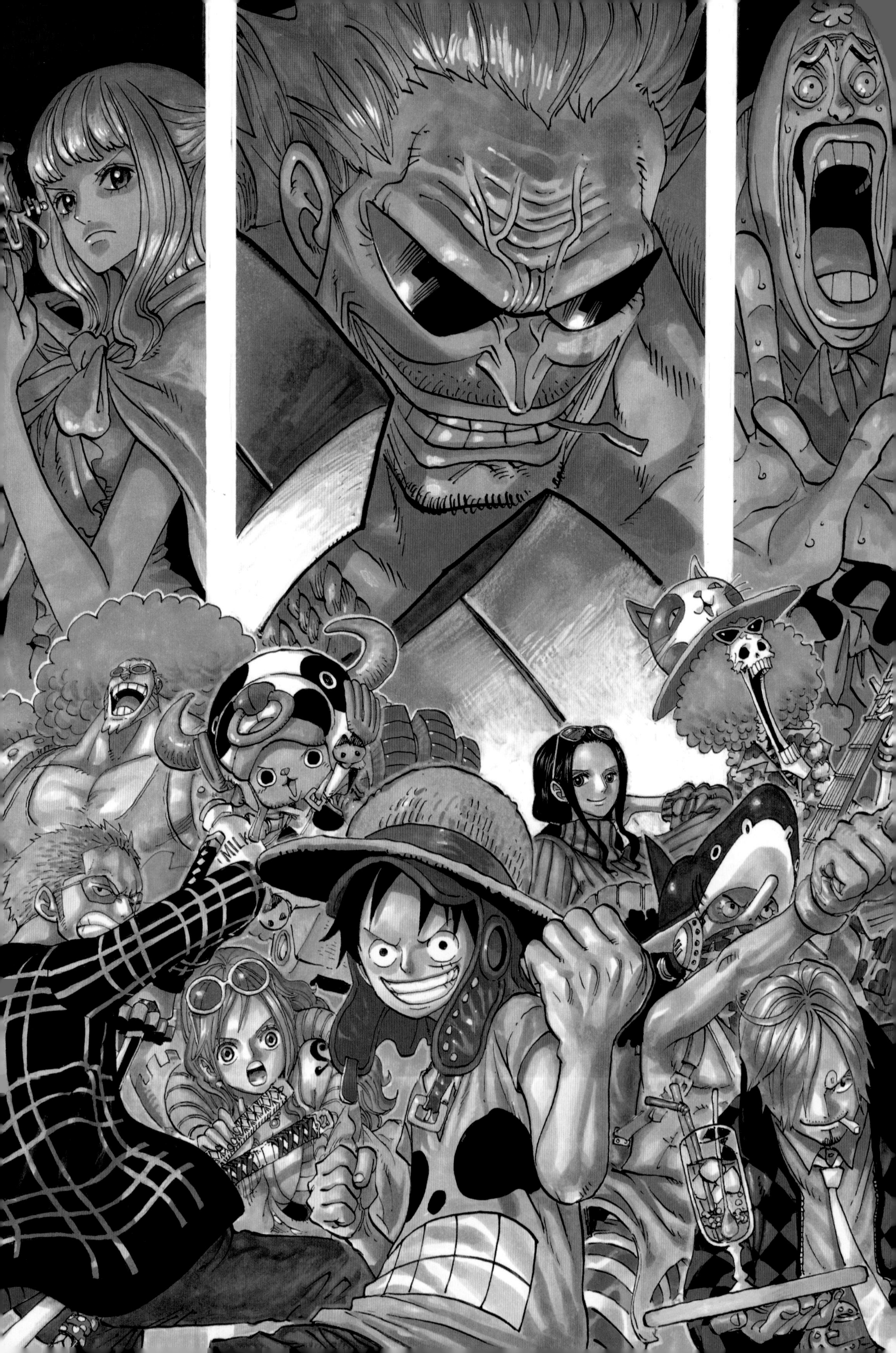
MILK

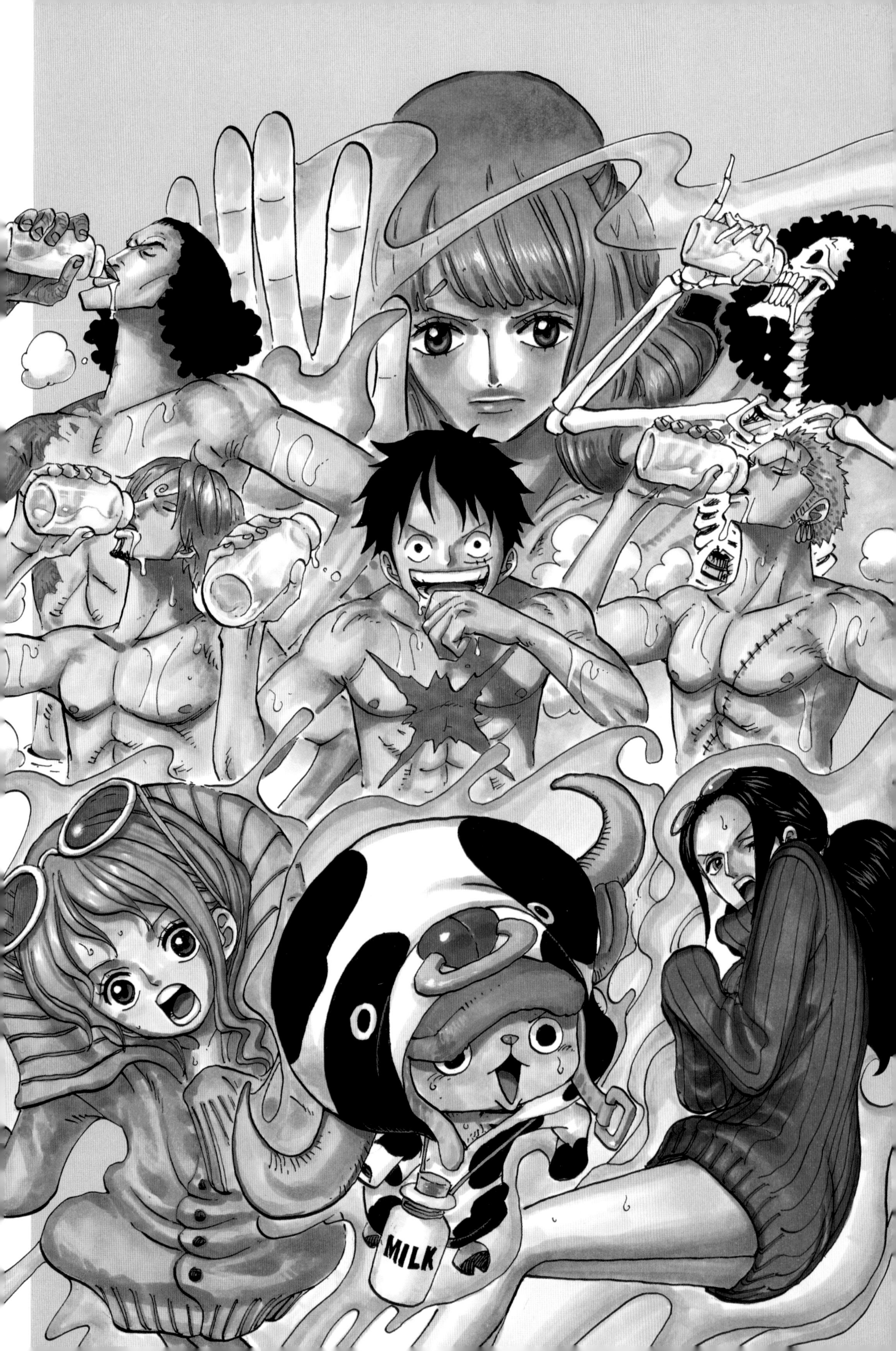
MILK

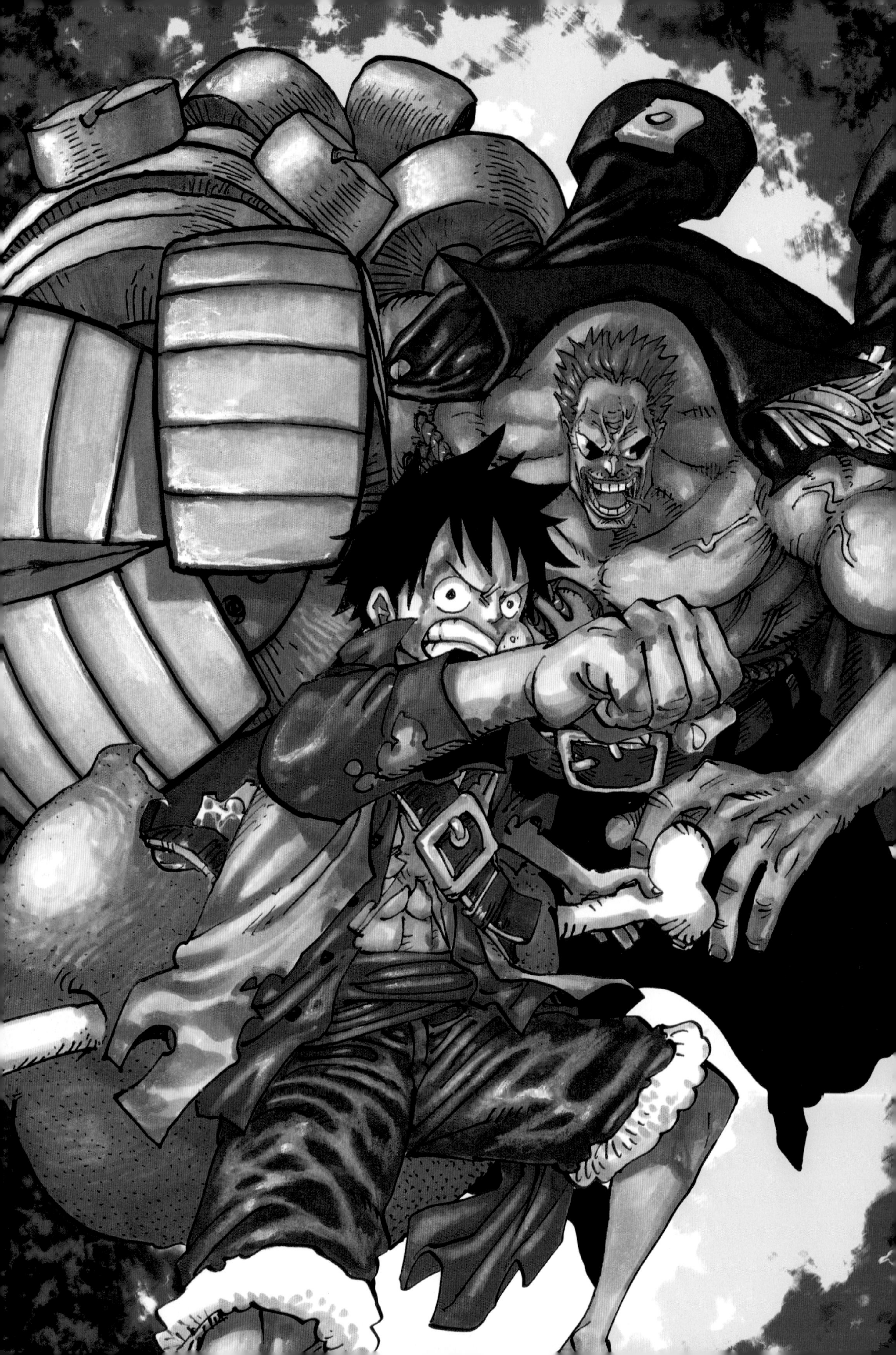

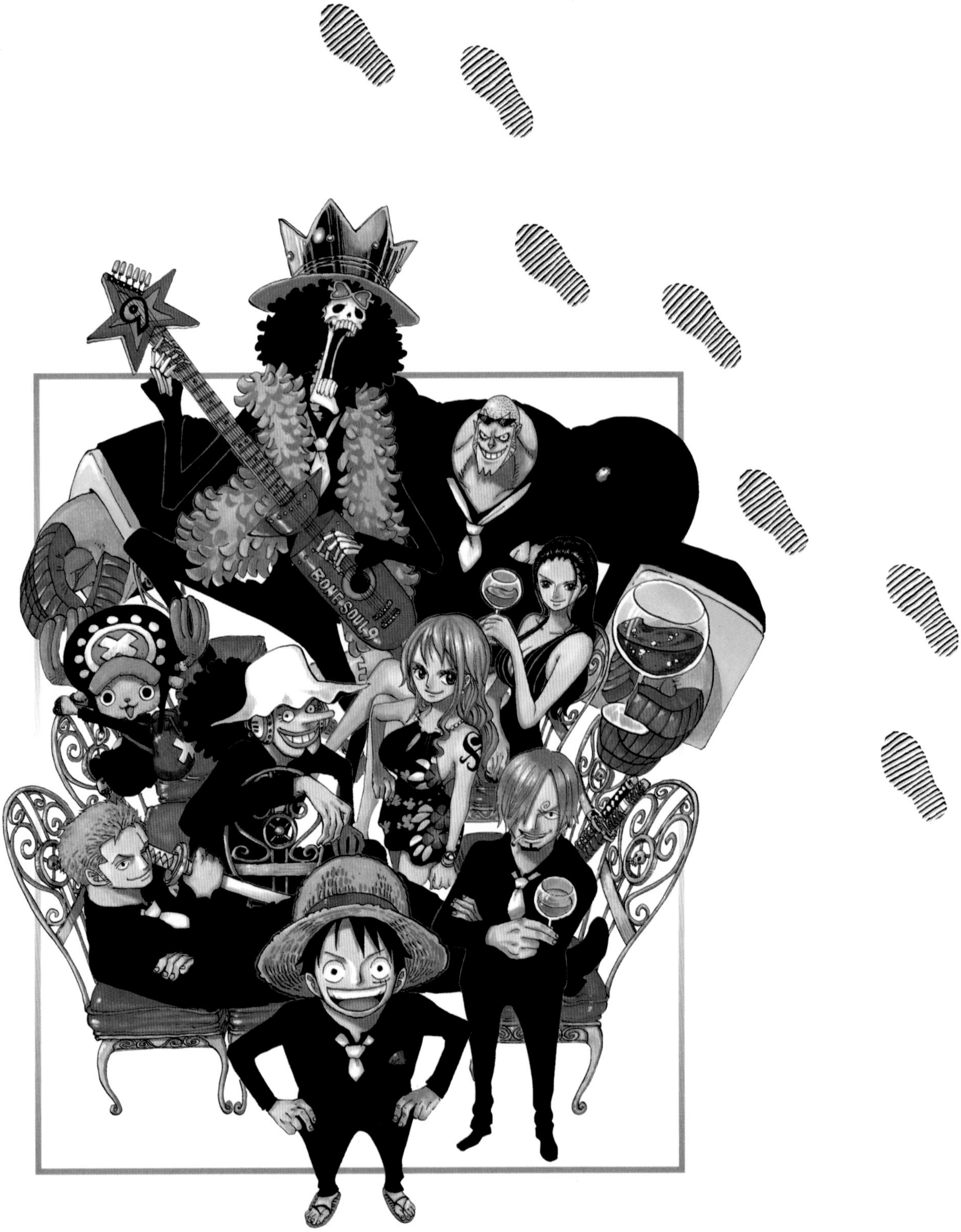
BONE SOUL9

EXHIBITION

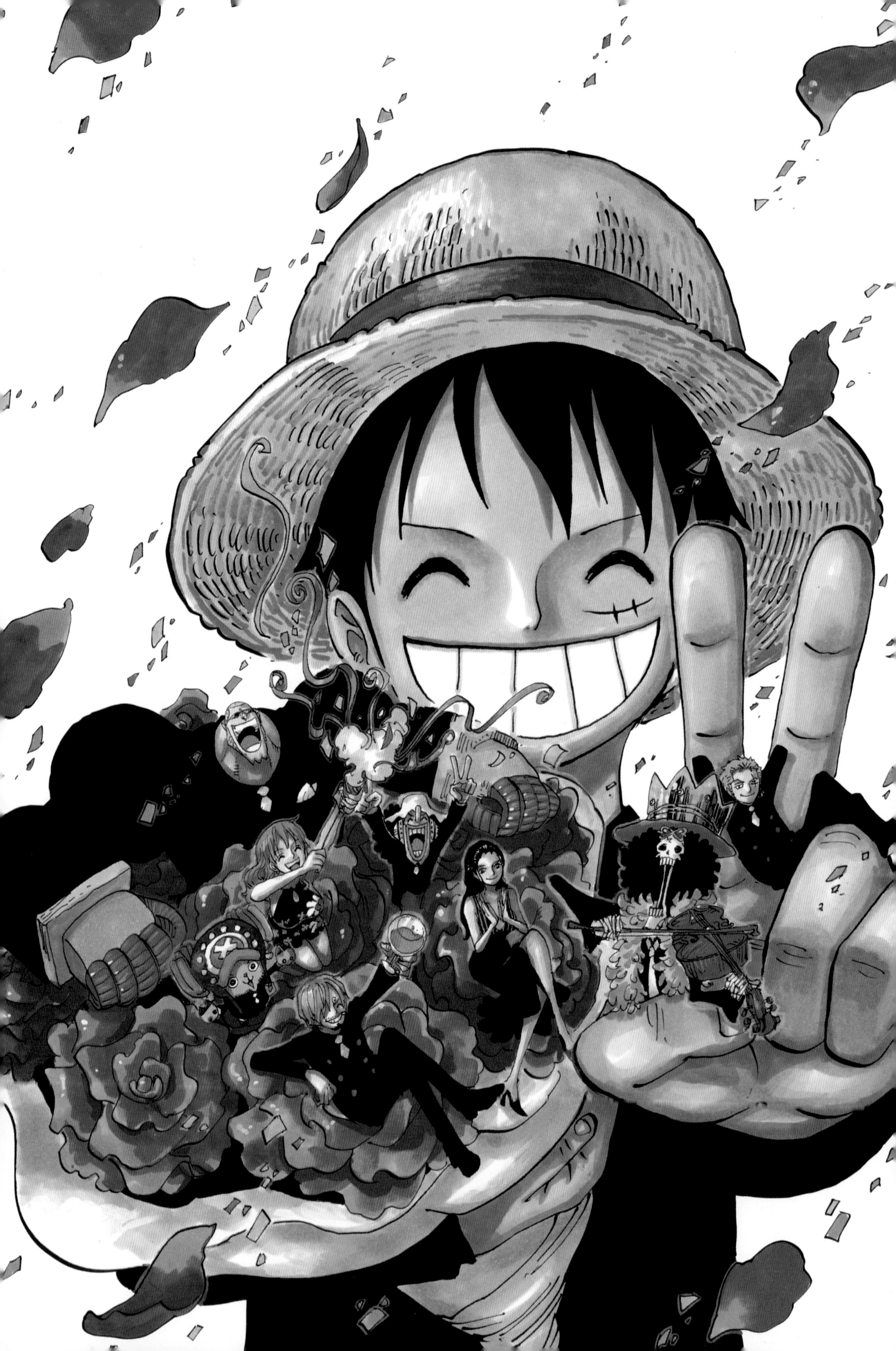

Comments P.90–91

It looks normal in this art book, but the
original piece was drawn at four times
this size, in fact. It was for an exhibit
called *One Piece Ten*. This was very
fulfilling to make.

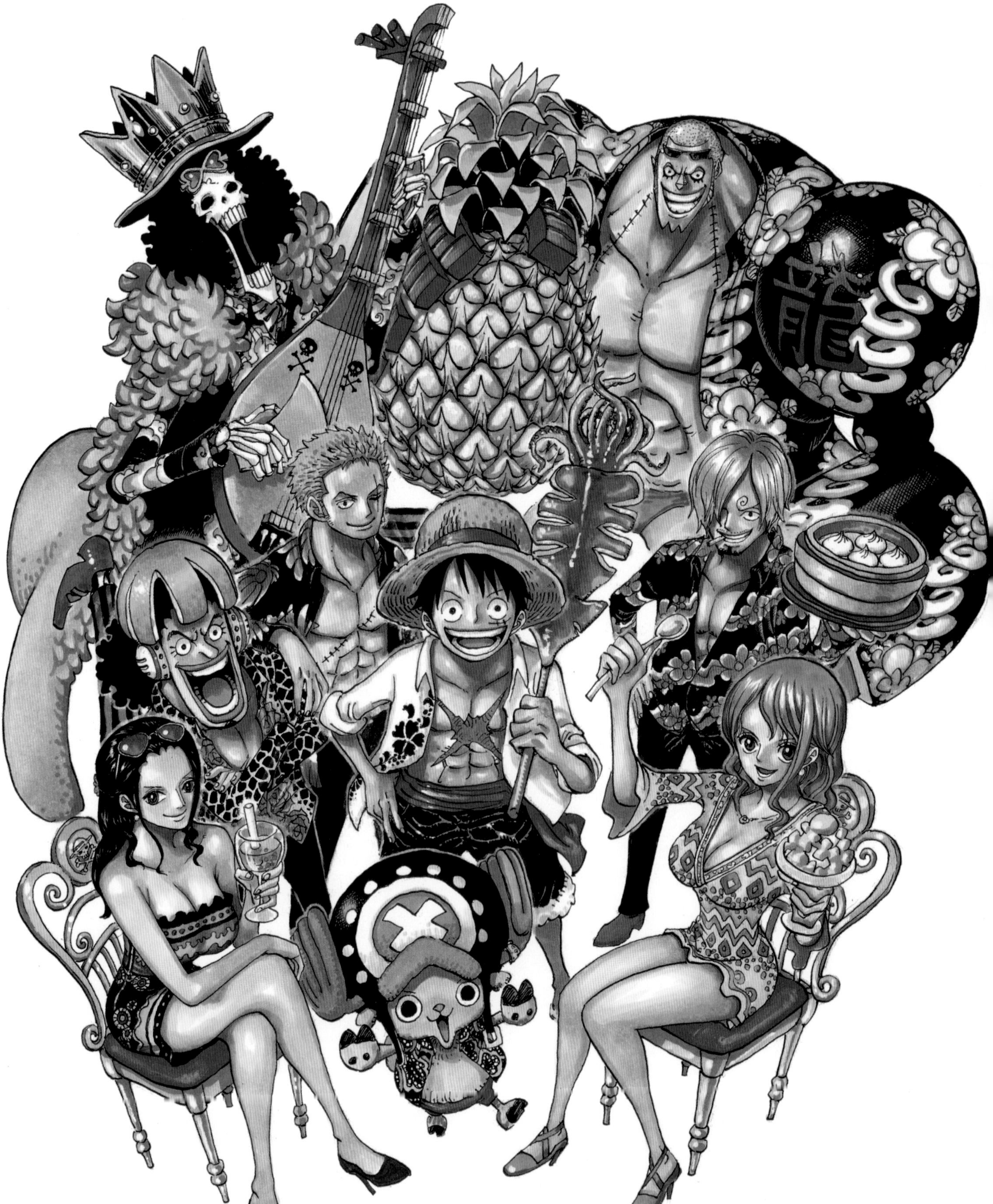
龍

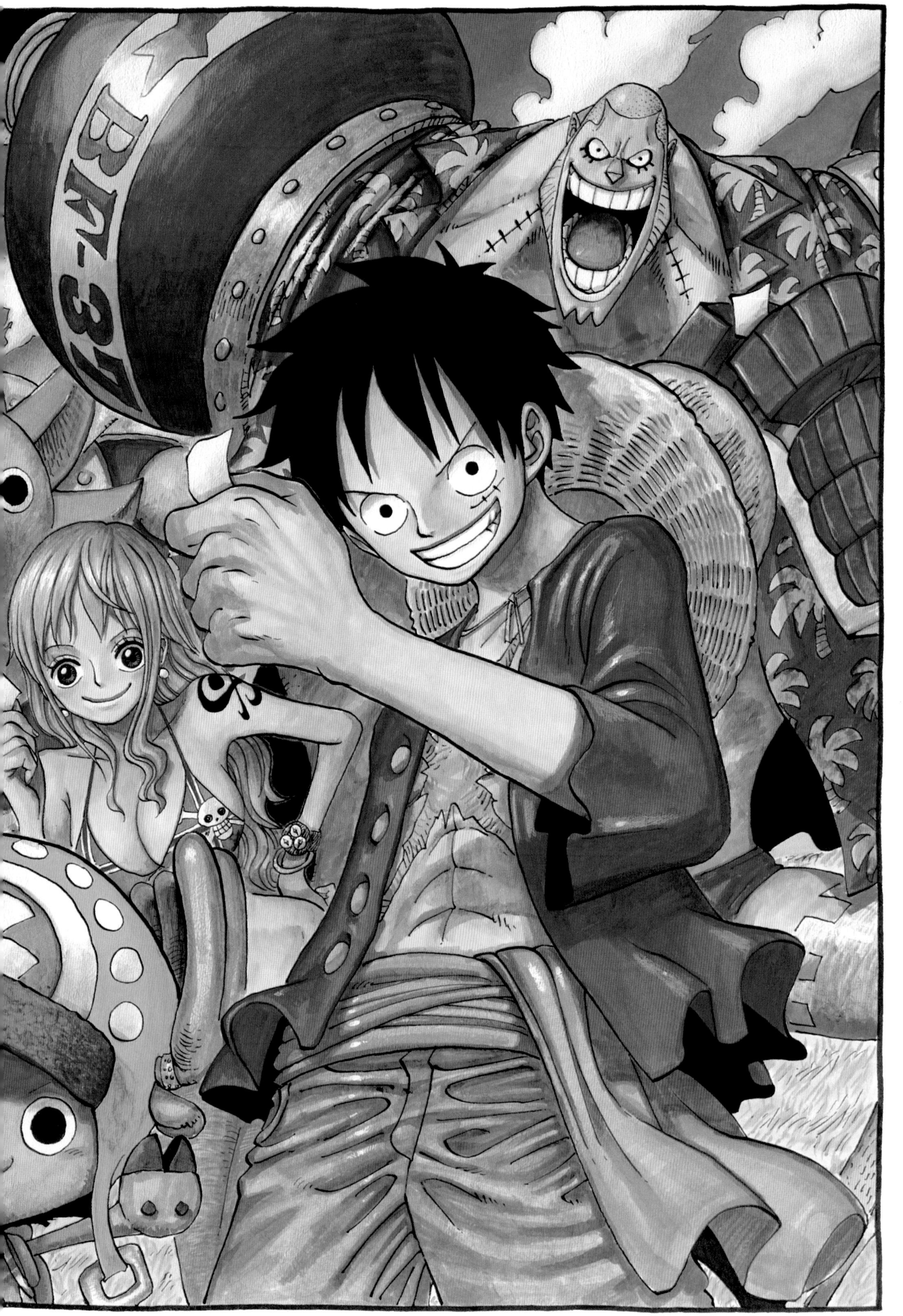
BR-37

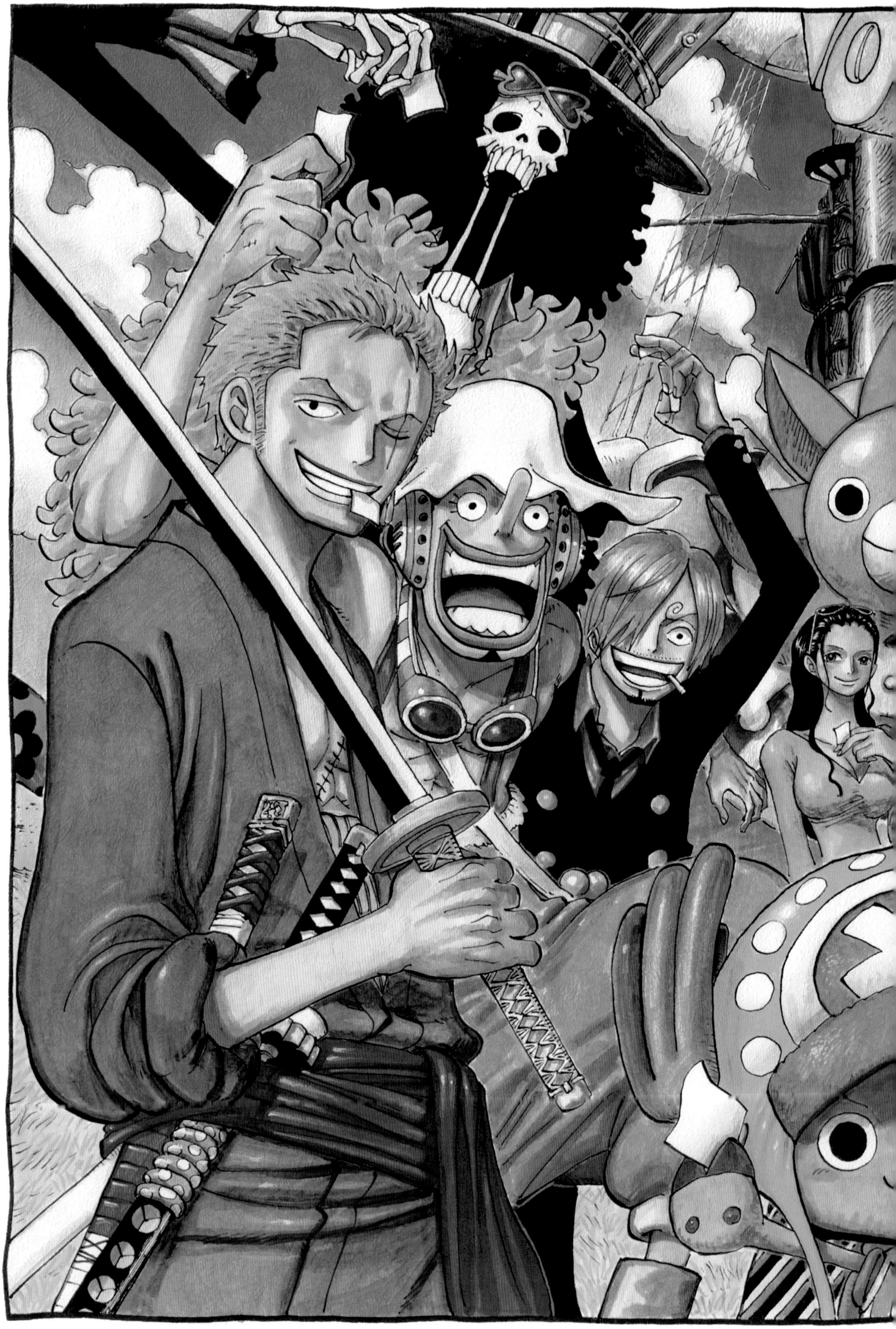

COLLABORATION

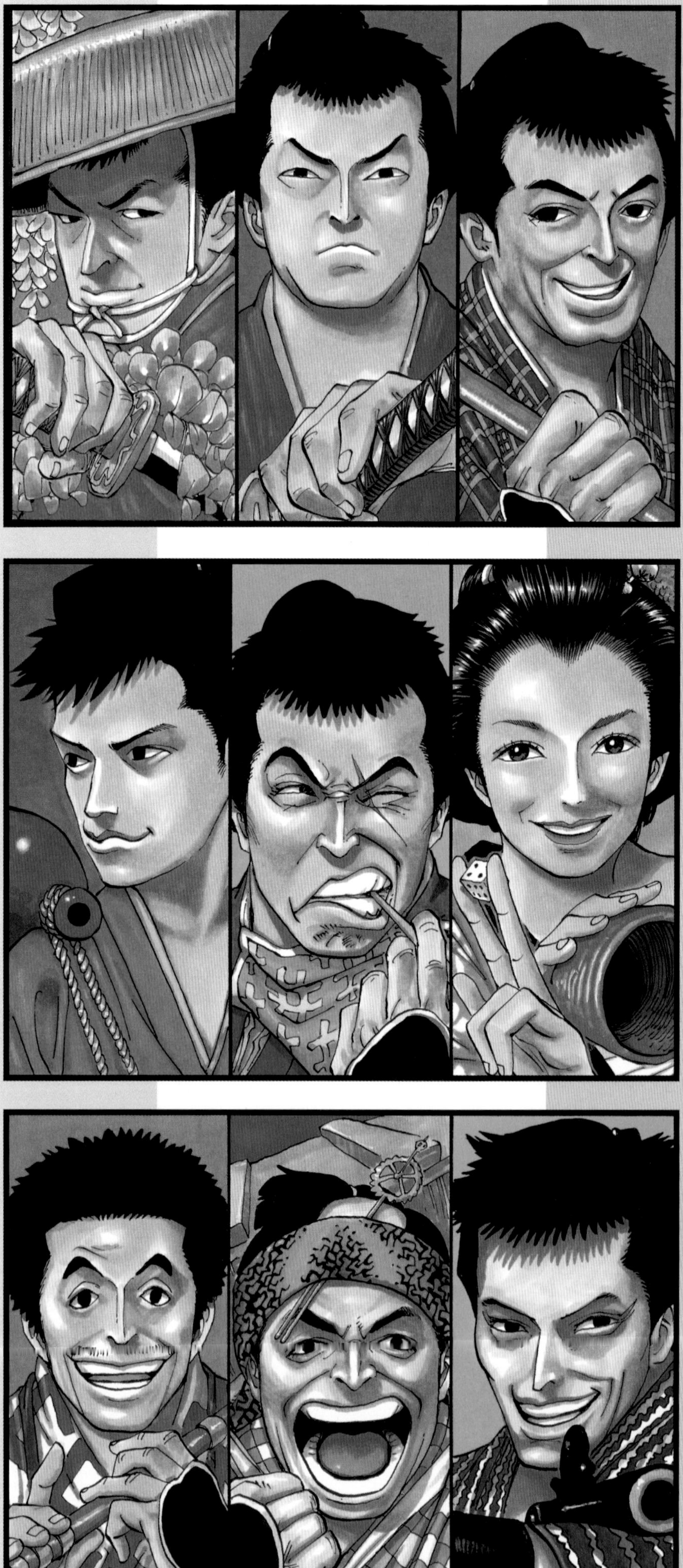

2

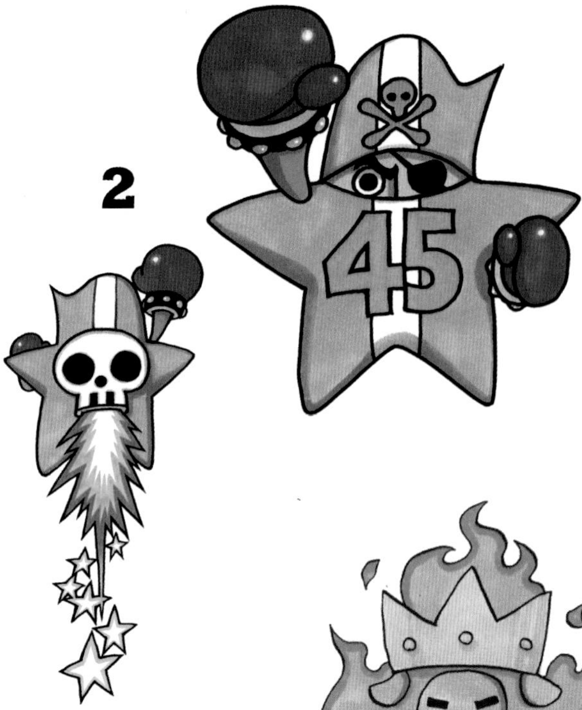
45

3

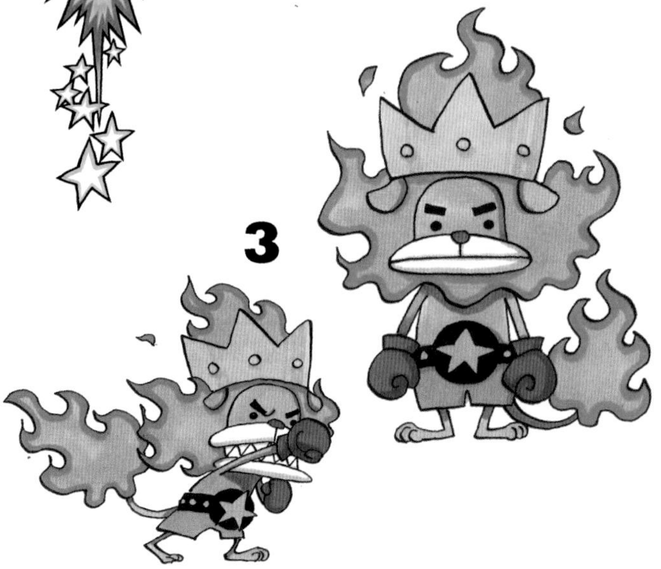

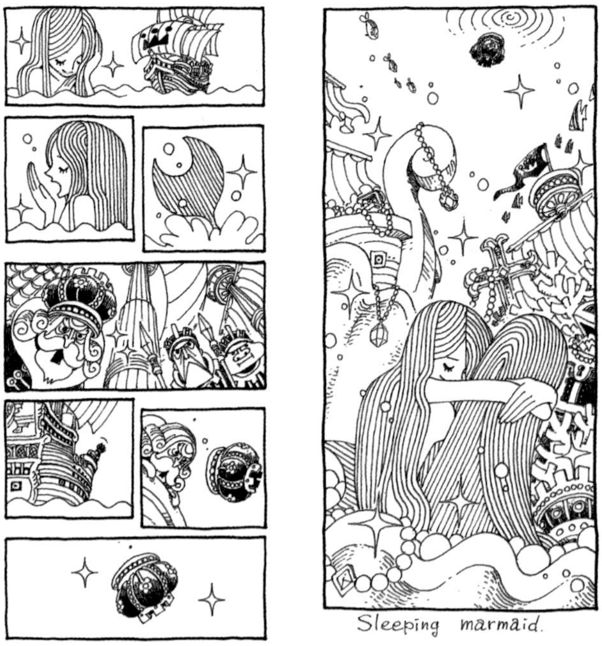
Sleeping marmaid.

1

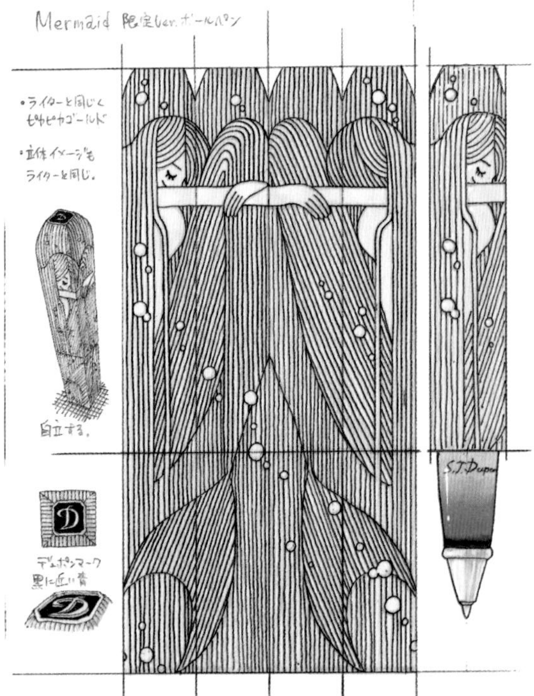
Mermaid 限定ver. ボールペン
・ライターと同じく
・立体イメージも
ライターと同じ。
自立する。
デュポンマーク
黒に近い青
S.T.Dupont

(P.93) An illustration for a DVD box set of the *Jirocho Sangoku-shi* movies, designed in collaboration with Studio Ghibli's Toshio Suzuki. *Mr. Suzuki drew the title calligraphy

(P.94) 1. Package illustration and rough sketch of S. T. Dupont's *Sleeping Mermaid Collection* pen and lighter

2. *Weekly Shonen Jump* 45th Anniversary Mascot Character "Jutter" design

3. *Saikyo Jump* Mascot Character "Pharaon"

4. Bookmark illustration for bookstore-centric disaster relief fund "Wish Mark"

(P.95) Illustration of *Wingman* for Masakazu Katsura's 30th anniversary art book

(P.96–97) All advertisements for *One Piece*'s 300 million copies sold celebration project: "Crossing Japan! OPJ47 Cruise newspaper hijack!" Advertisements ran in newspapers in all forty-seven prefectures of Japan between November 1 and 20, 2013. Also appeared in the *New York Times* on November 21 and Taiwan's *China Times* on November 22. This campaign received the 2014 Japan Newspaper Advertisement Award.

(P.98) A dream collaboration of Luffy and the actor Takuya Kimura for *Takuya Kimura x Men's Non-No Endless.*

4

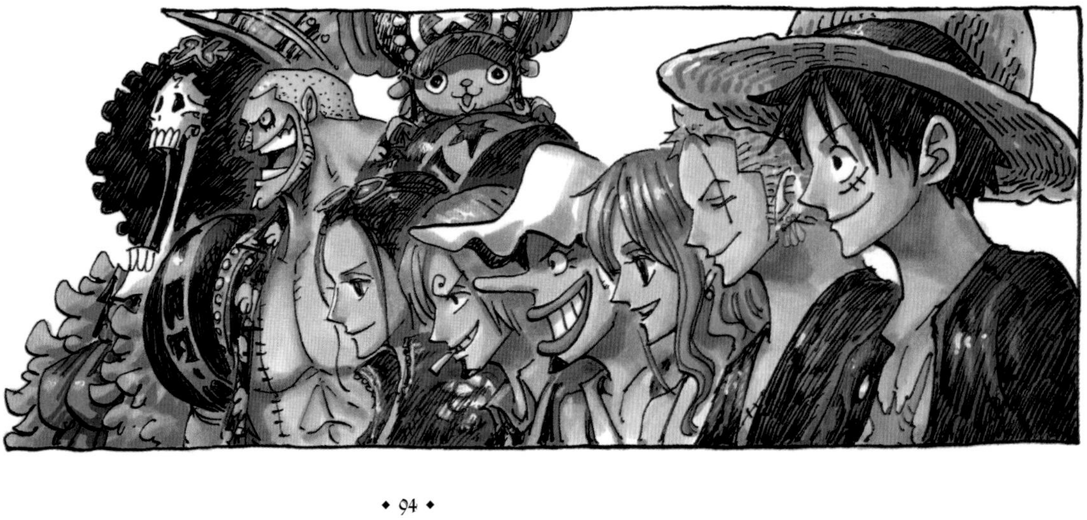

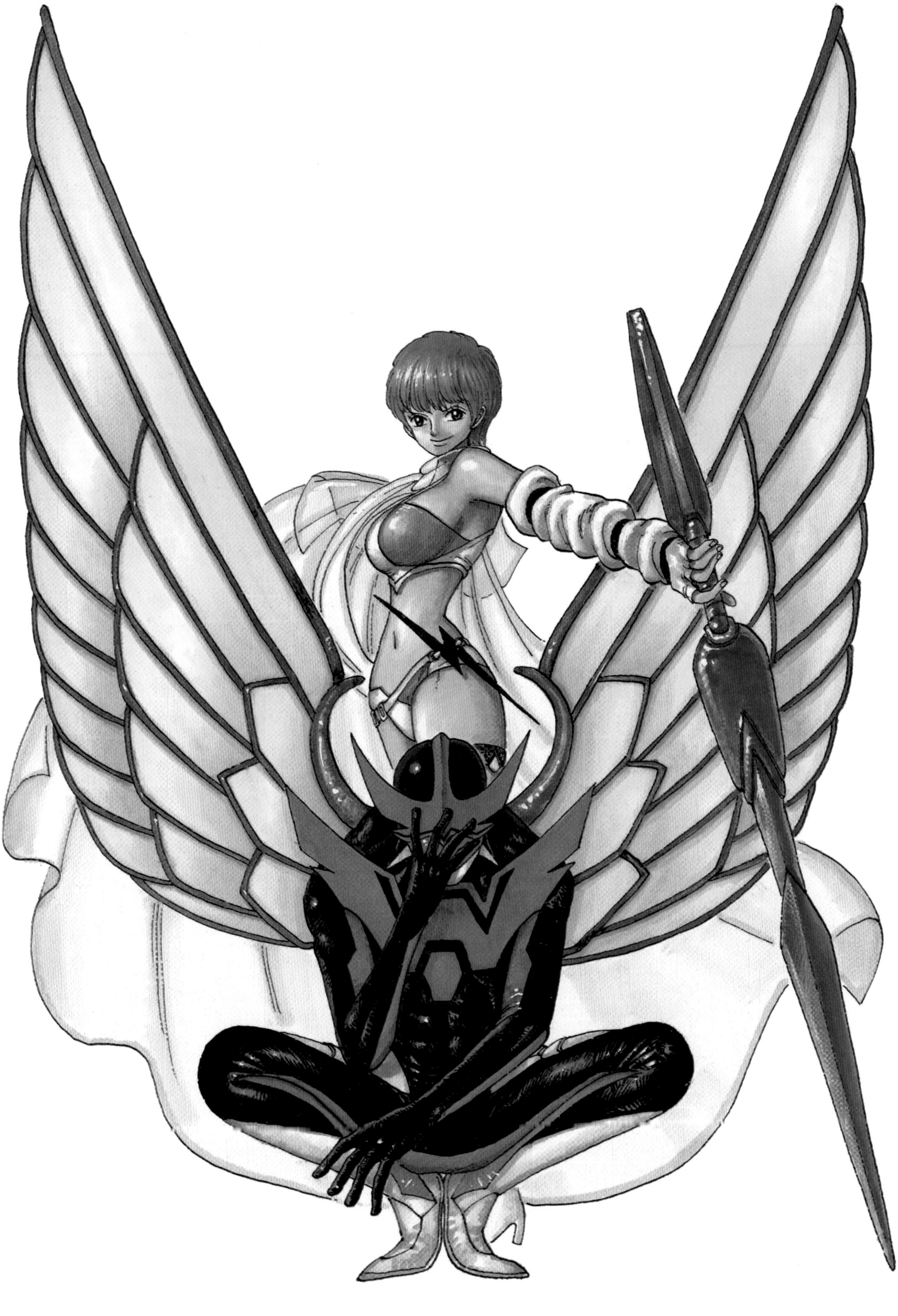

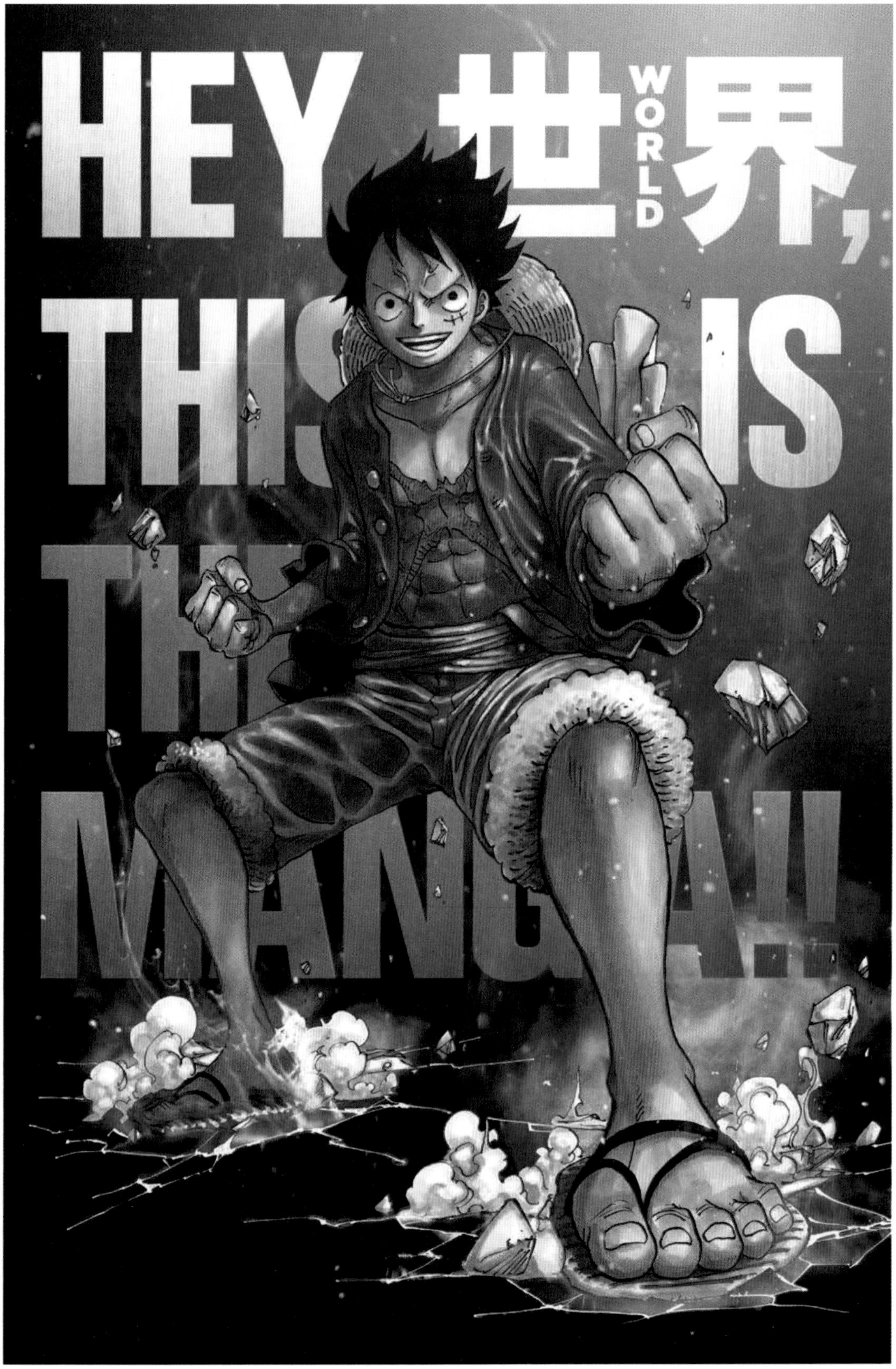
HEY 世界,
WORLD
THIS IS
MANGA!!

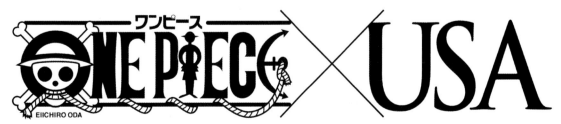

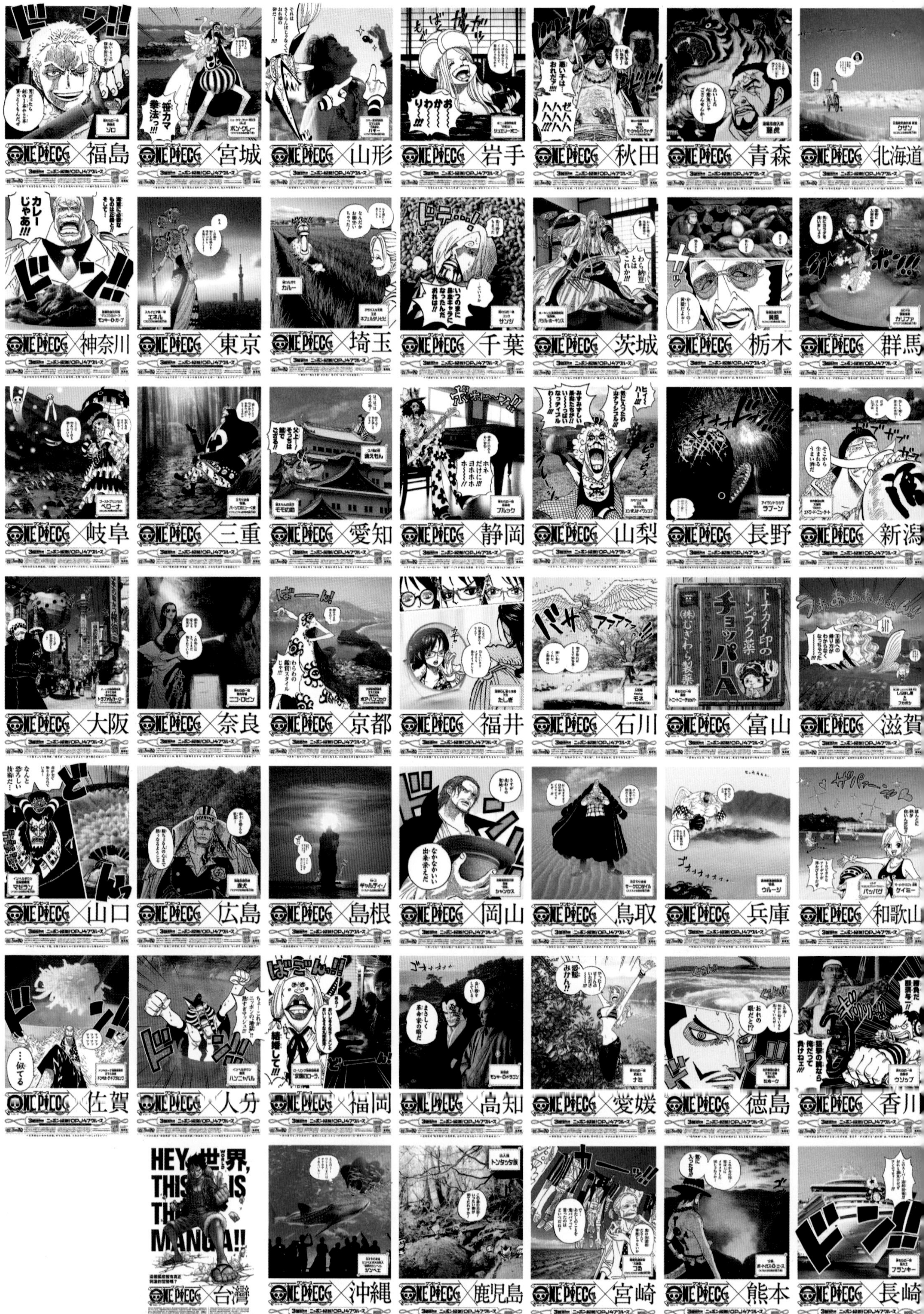
ONE PIECE×北海道
ONE PIECE×青森
ONE PIECE×秋田
ONE PIECE×岩手
ONE PIECE×山形
ONE PIECE×宮城
ONE PIECE×福島
ONE PIECE×群馬
ONE PIECE×栃木
ONE PIECE×茨城
ONE PIECE×千葉
ONE PIECE×埼玉
ONE PIECE×東京
ONE PIECE×神奈川
ONE PIECE×新潟
ONE PIECE×長野
ONE PIECE×山梨
ONE PIECE×静岡
ONE PIECE×愛知
ONE PIECE×三重
ONE PIECE×岐阜
ONE PIECE×滋賀
ONE PIECE×富山
ONE PIECE×石川
ONE PIECE×福井
ONE PIECE×京都
ONE PIECE×奈良
ONE PIECE×大阪
ONE PIECE×和歌山
ONE PIECE×兵庫
ONE PIECE×鳥取
ONE PIECE×岡山
ONE PIECE×島根
ONE PIECE×広島
ONE PIECE×山口
ONE PIECE×香川
ONE PIECE×徳島
ONE PIECE×愛媛
ONE PIECE×高知
ONE PIECE×福岡
ONE PIECE×大分
ONE PIECE×佐賀
ONE PIECE×長崎
ONE PIECE×熊本
ONE PIECE×宮崎
ONE PIECE×鹿児島
ONE PIECE×沖縄
HEY 世界, THIS IS THE MANGA!!
ONE PIECE×台灣
ONE PIECE展台灣,正式決定!!

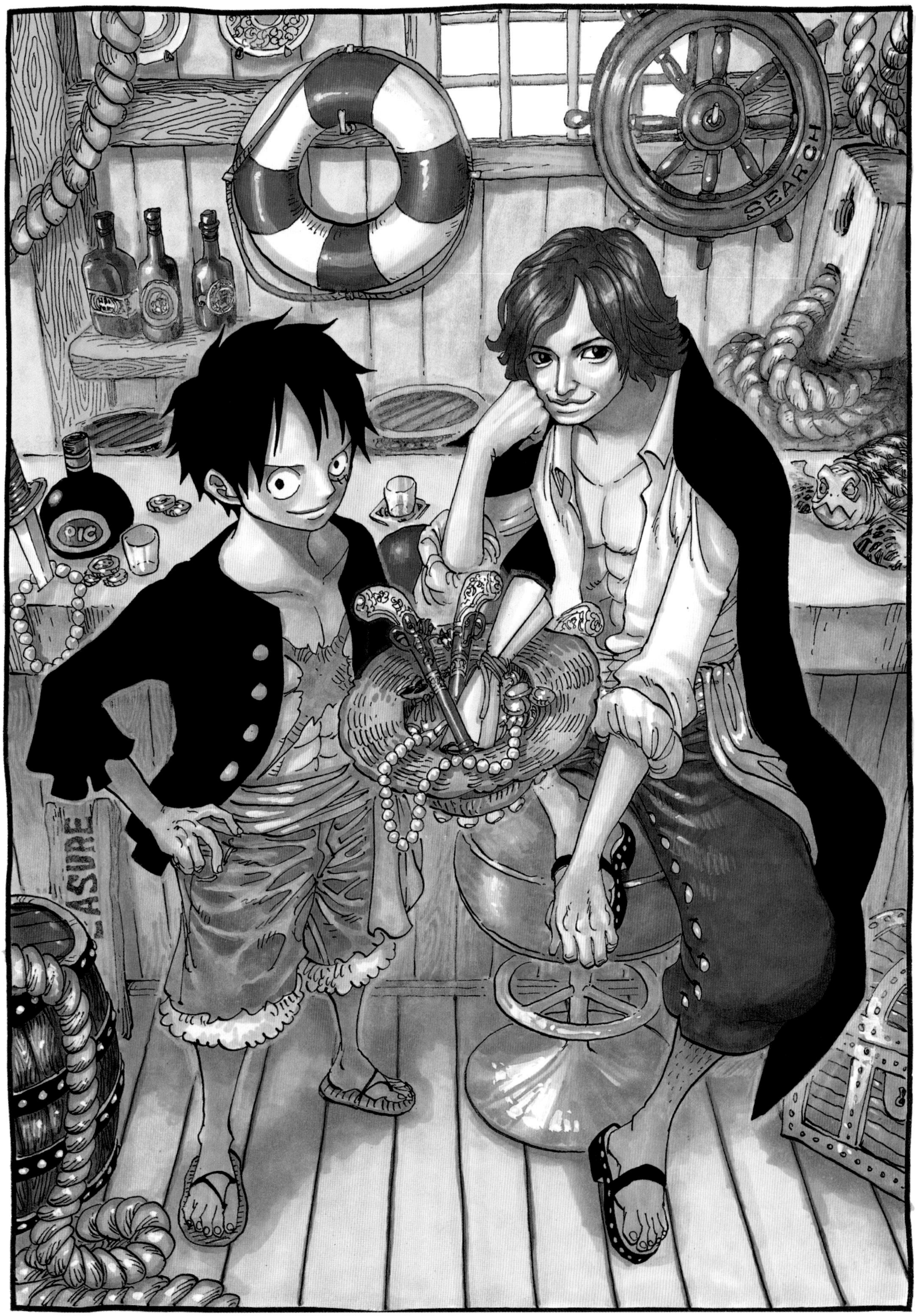
SEARCH
ASURE

AUTHOR'S COMMENT
2010 ~ 2013

When there's a fight going on, and one side says, "I win!" but the other doesn't budge, insisting, "No, I haven't lost," then the fight isn't over. But if one side says, "That's it, I've lost!" then the winner is automatically crowned.

The relationships between apprentices and teachers is kind of similar in the manga world today. Just because you worked as someone's assistant doesn't make you their apprentice. It's the moment that the assistant calls the artist "Sensei" that you are teacher and apprentice.

I have three teachers, and each one has taught me valuable lessons that make me who I am today. An apprentice is an eternal loser. For all of my life, I will never match my teachers.

This is my seventh collection of color illustrations. Thank you for all of your support!!

Eiichiro Oda

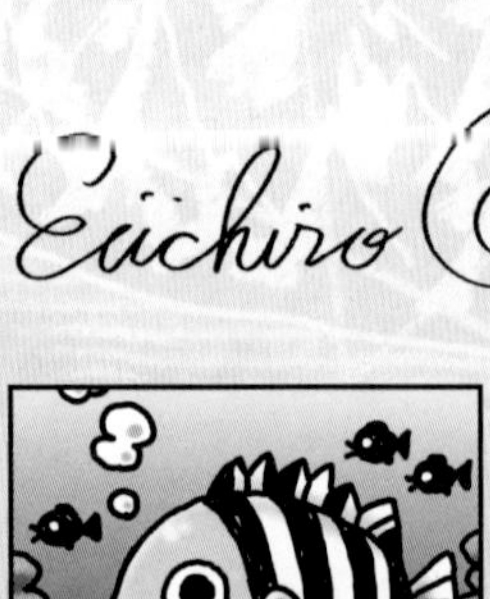

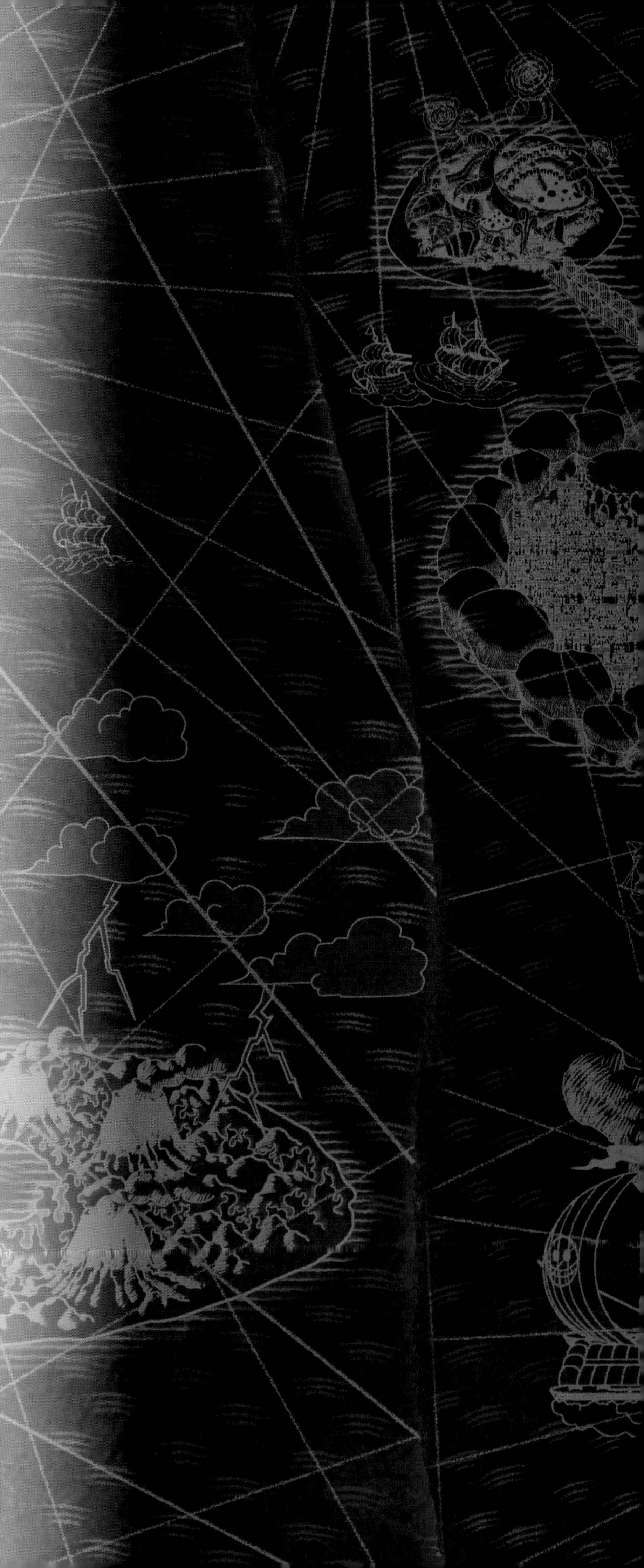

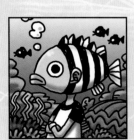

TOWARD

THE END OF THE

GRAND LINE,

ADVENTURE

CONTINUES!

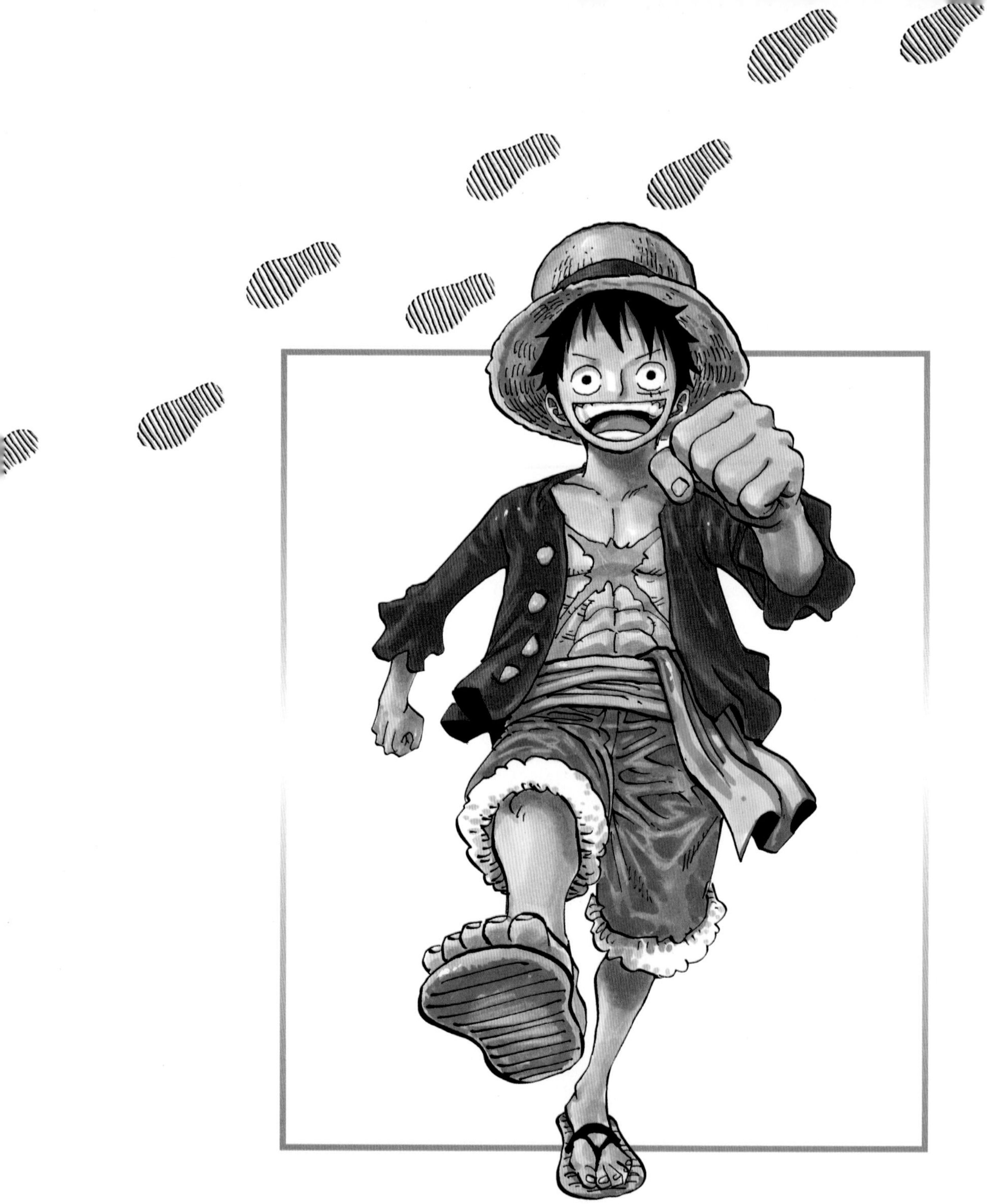

2013

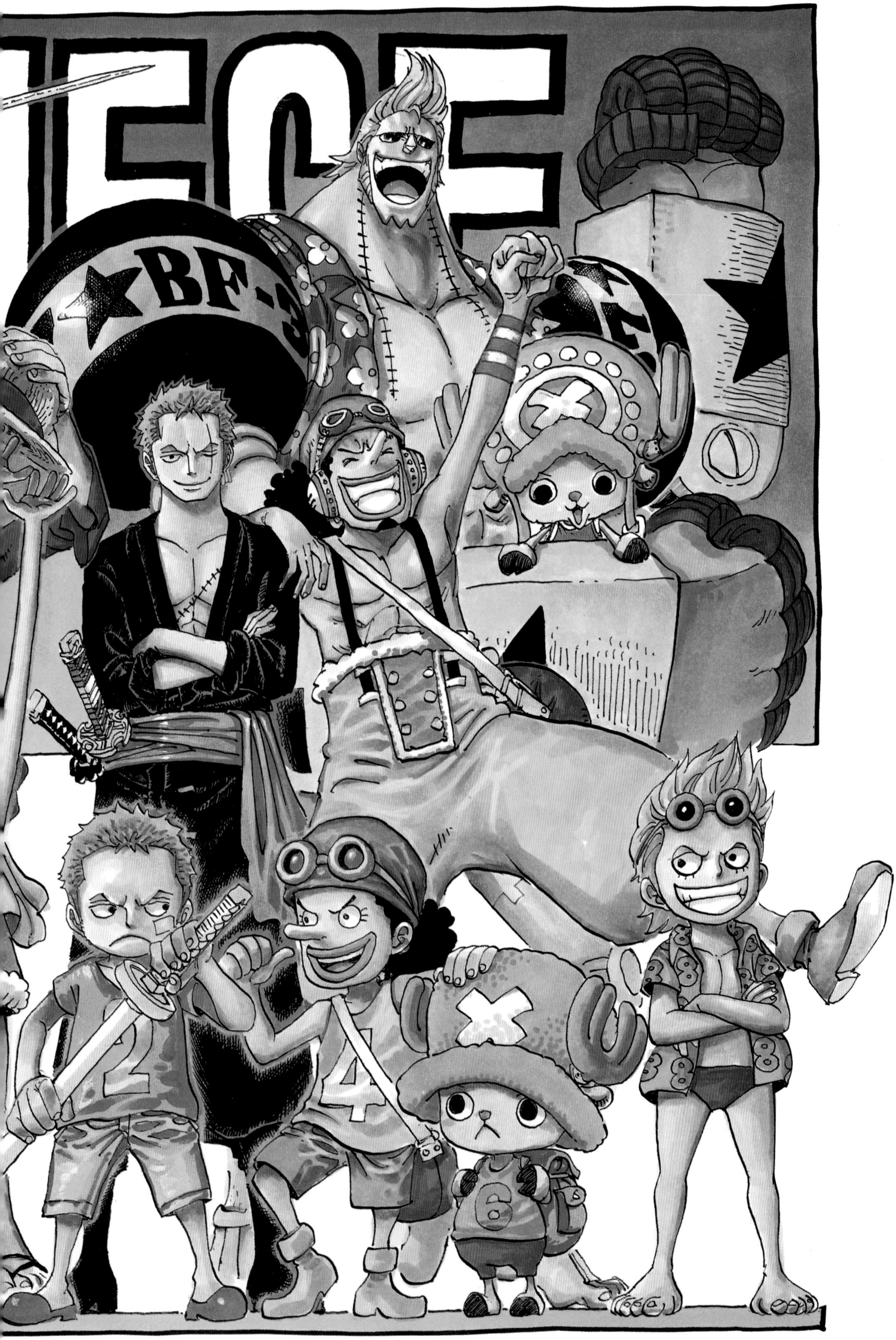

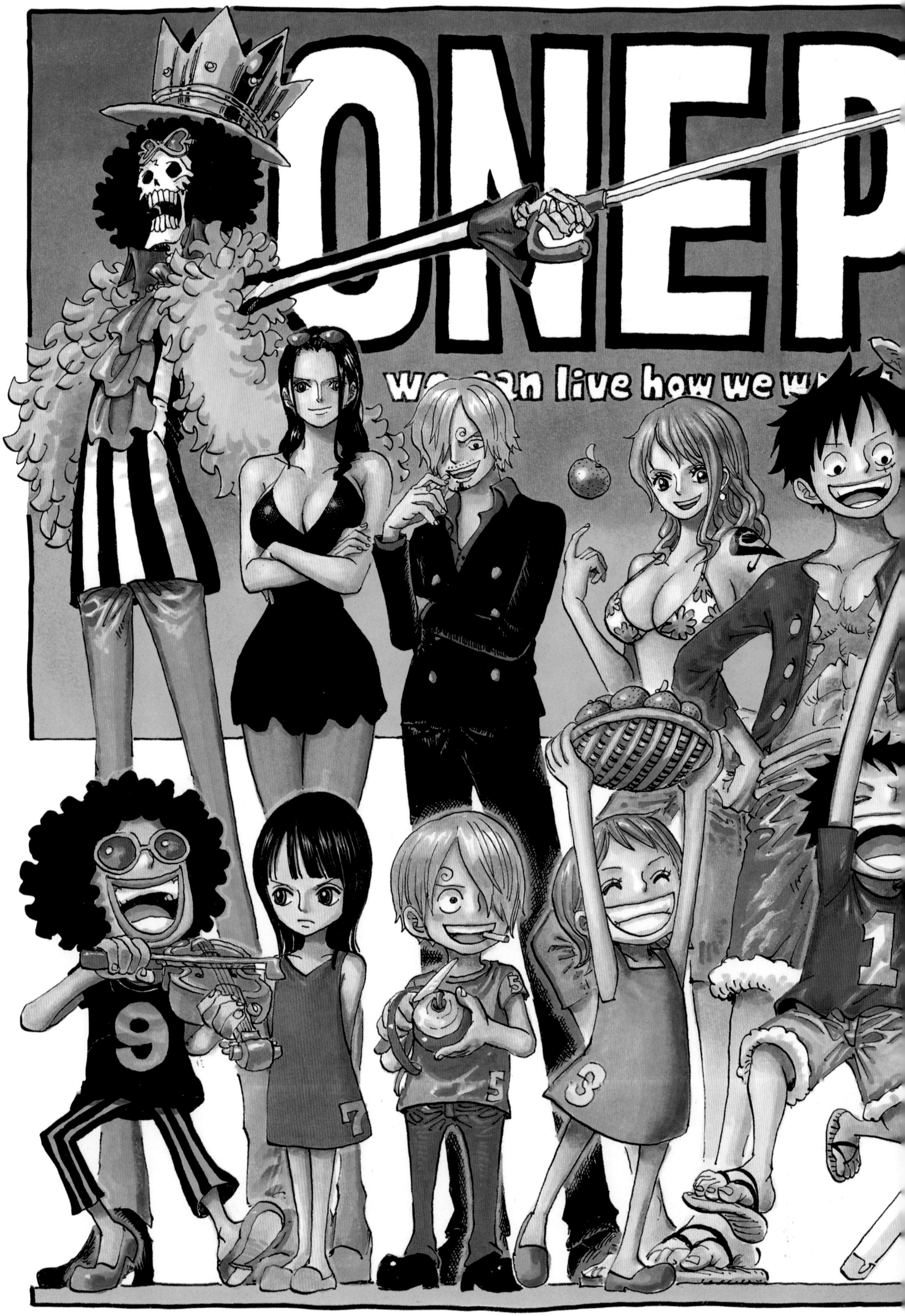
ONEP
live how we

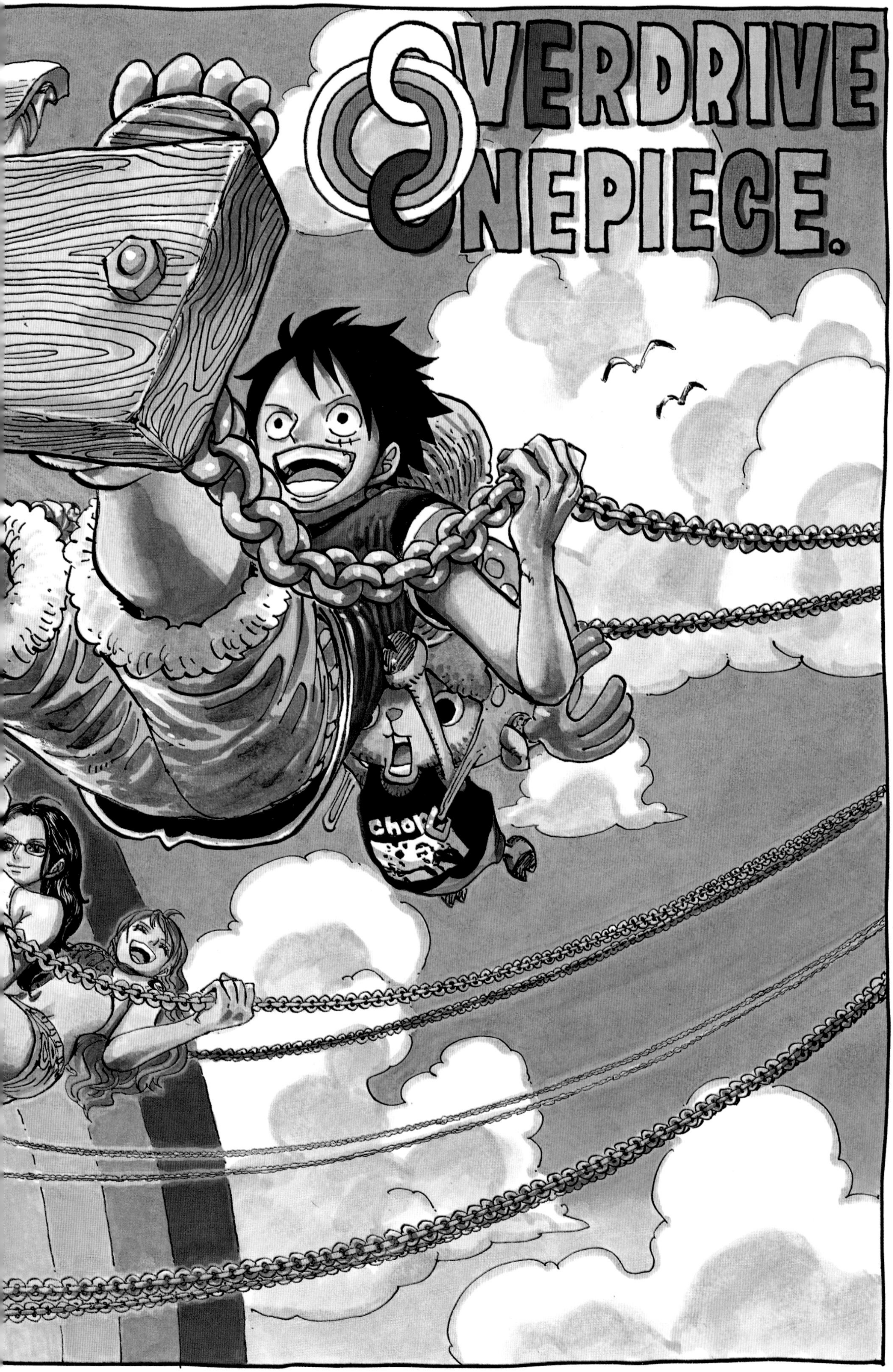
OVERDRIVE
ONEPIECE.
chop

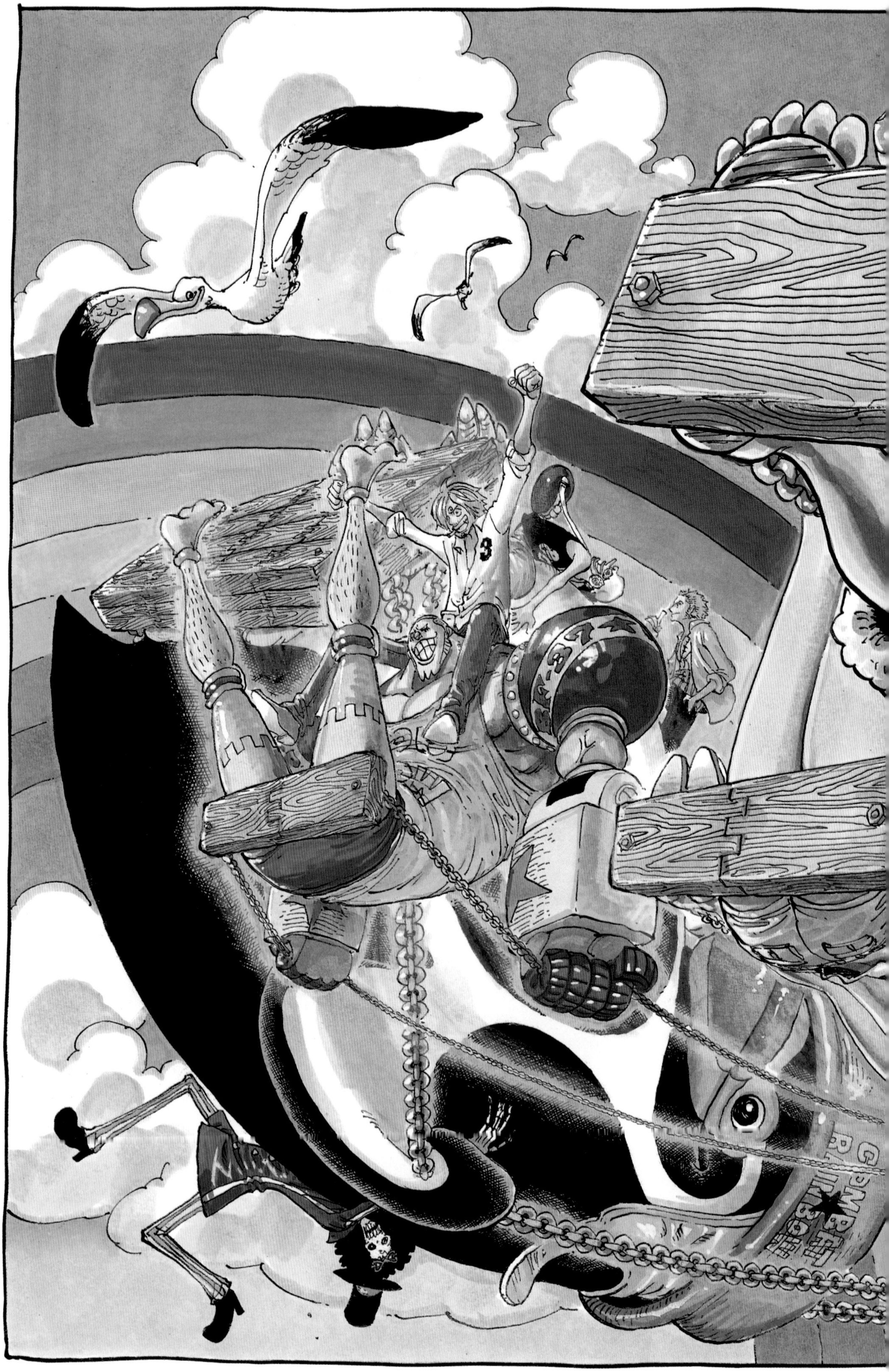

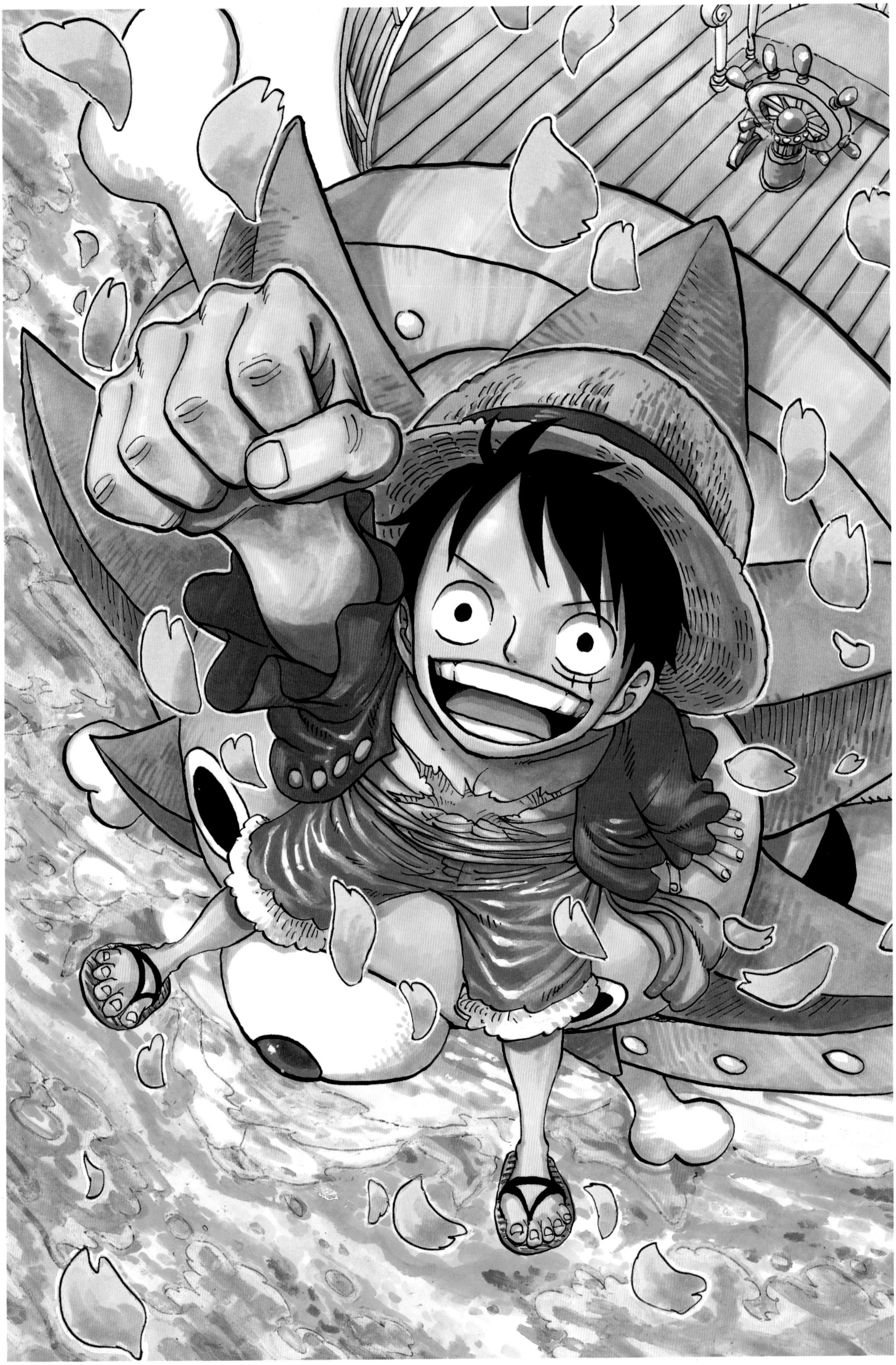

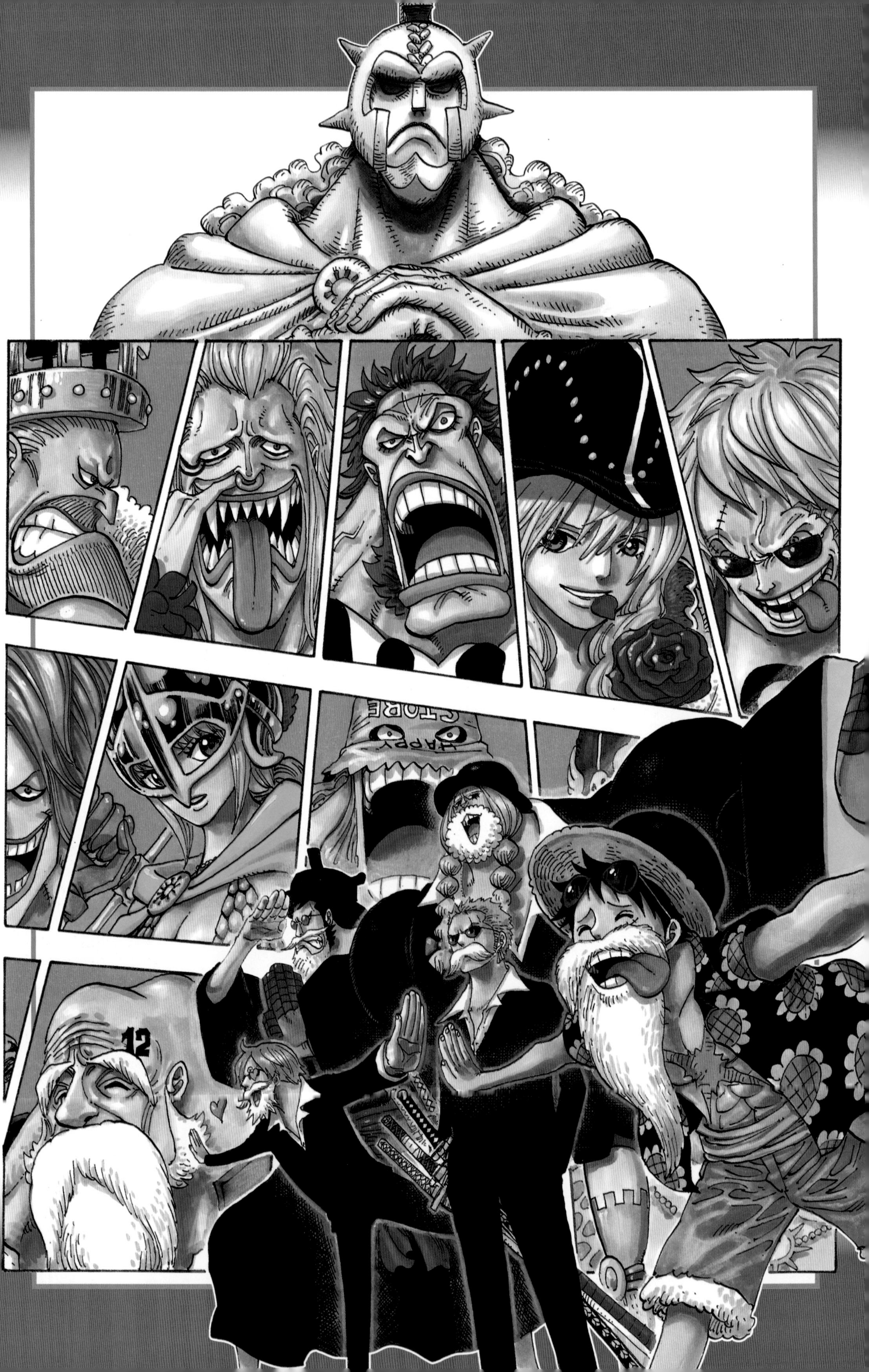

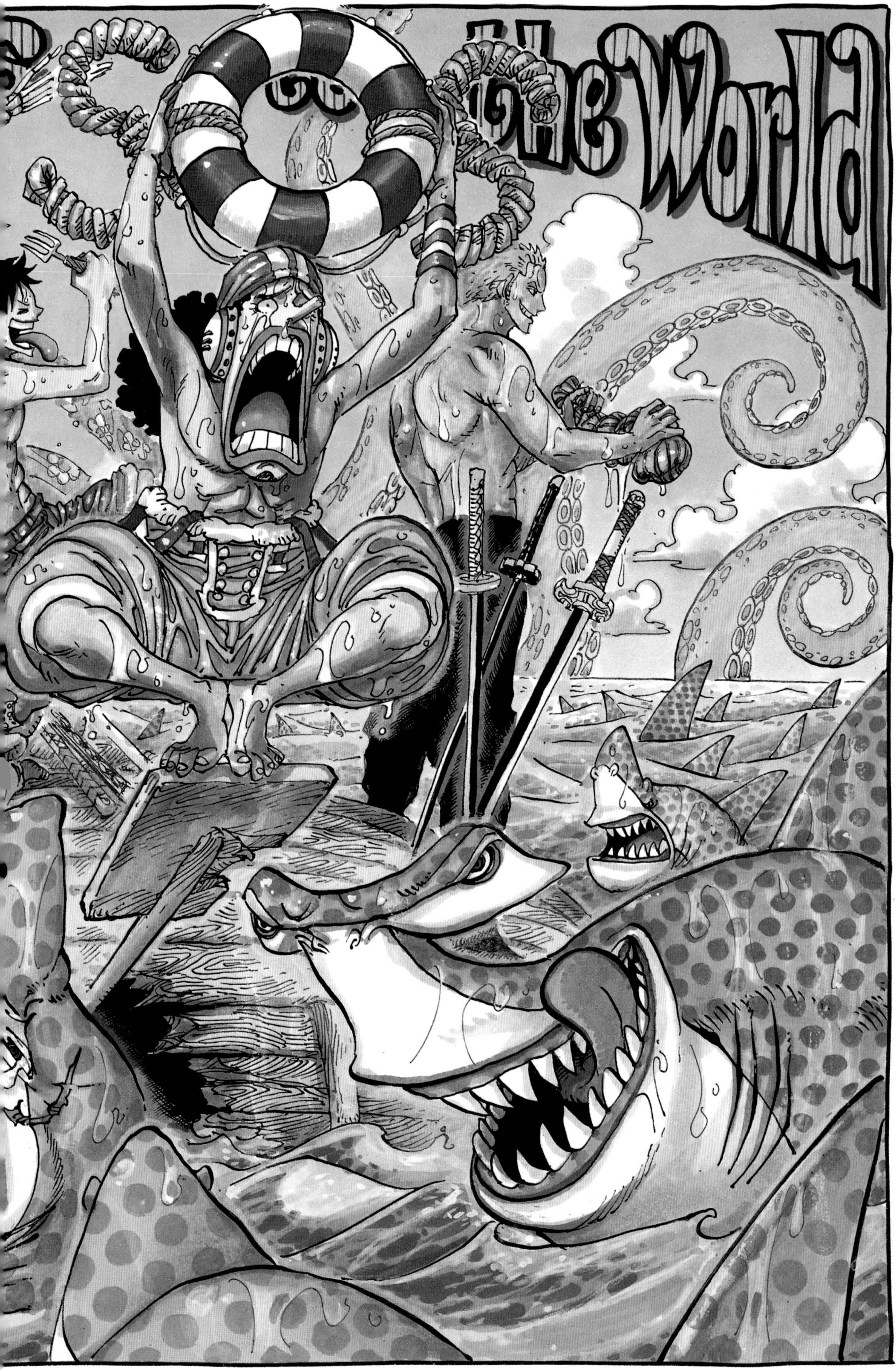

the World

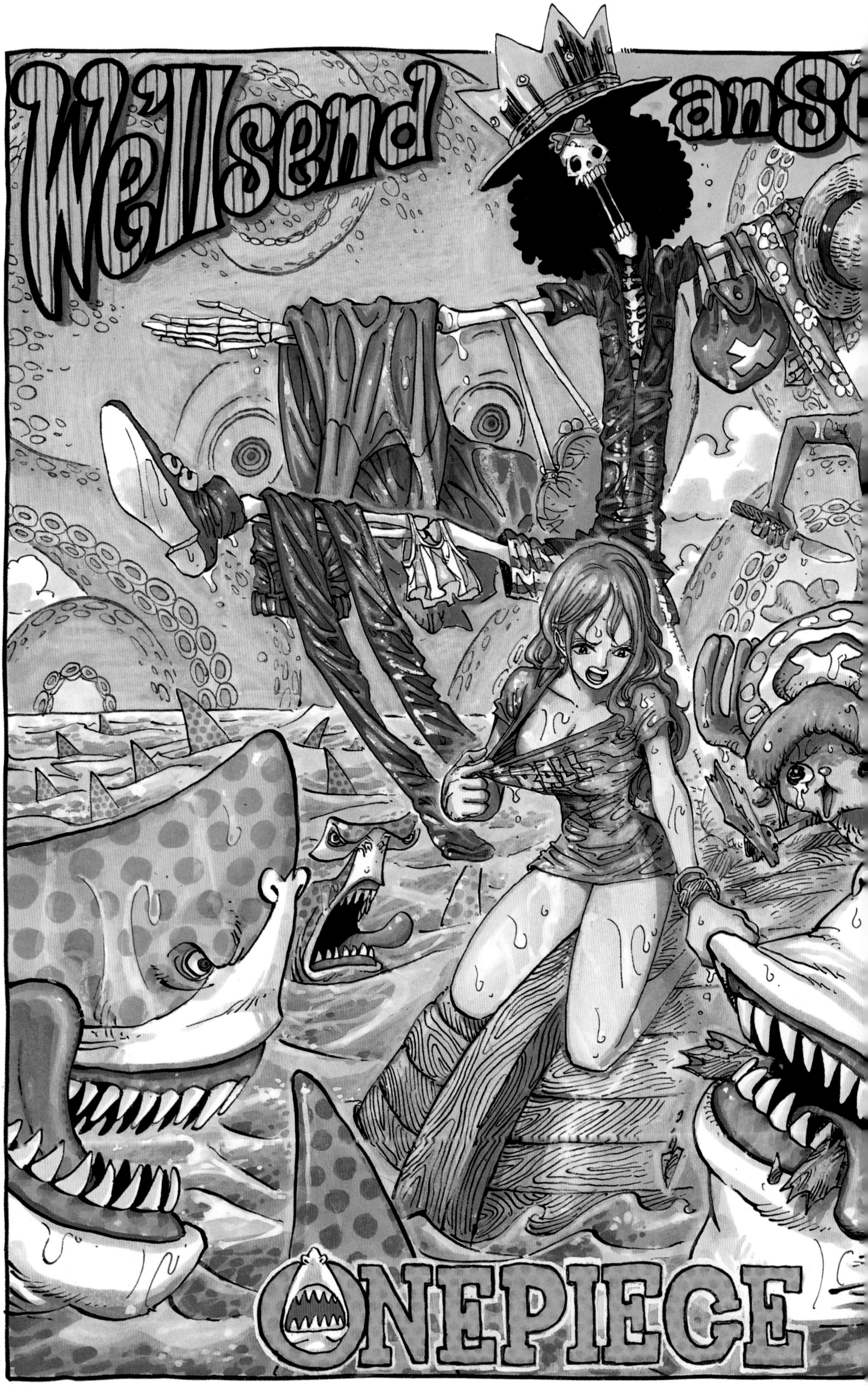
We'll send
ONE PIECE

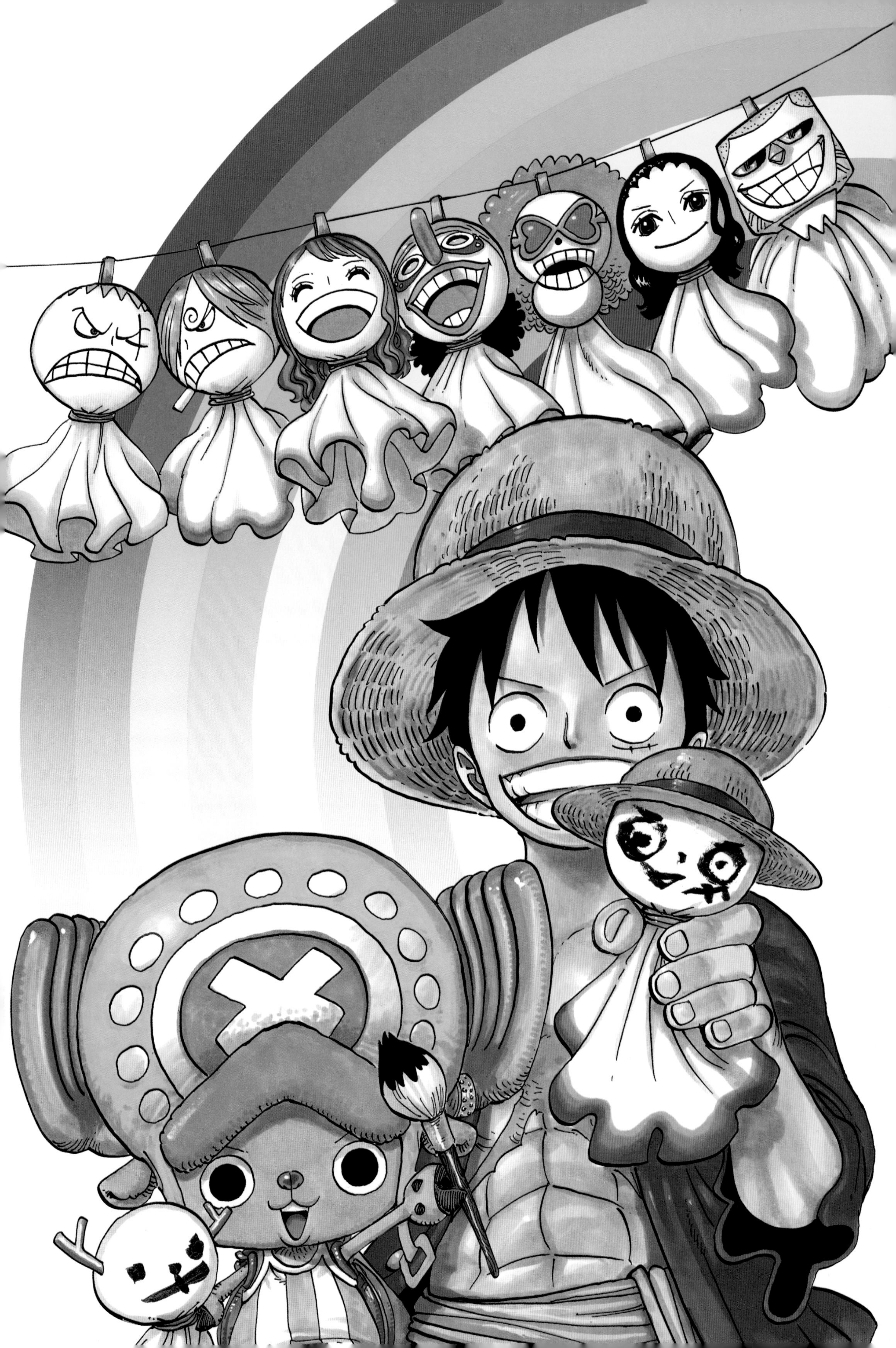

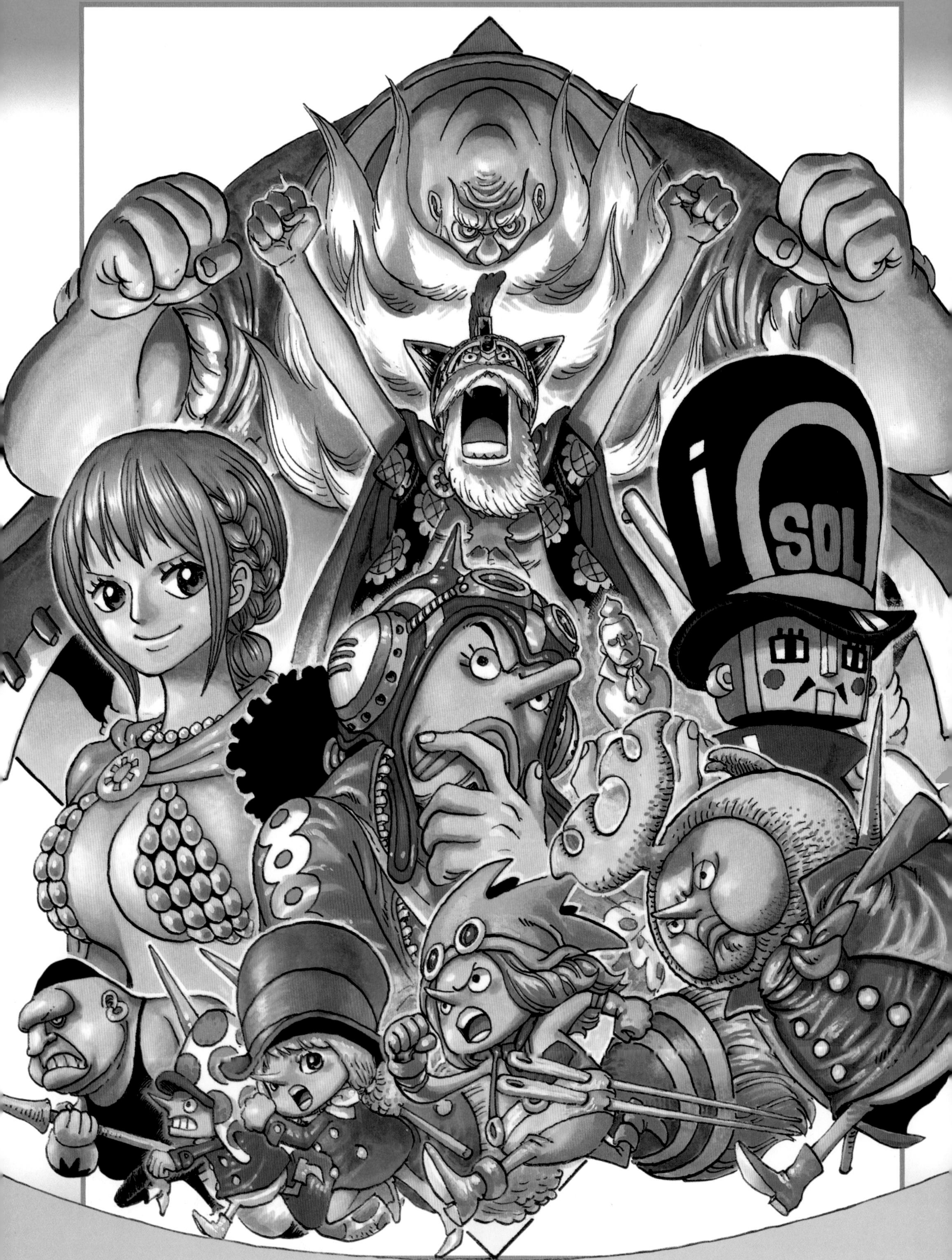
SOL

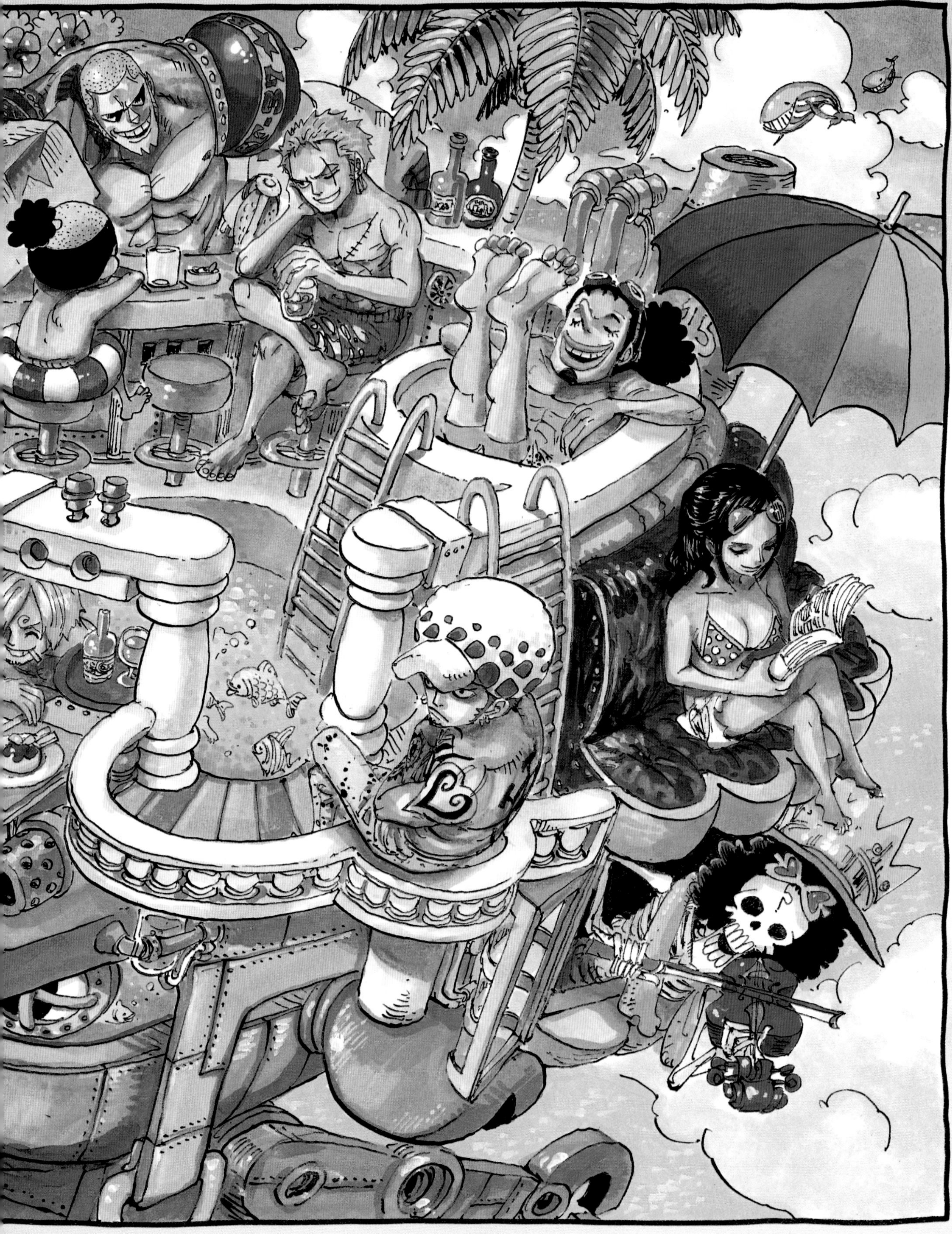

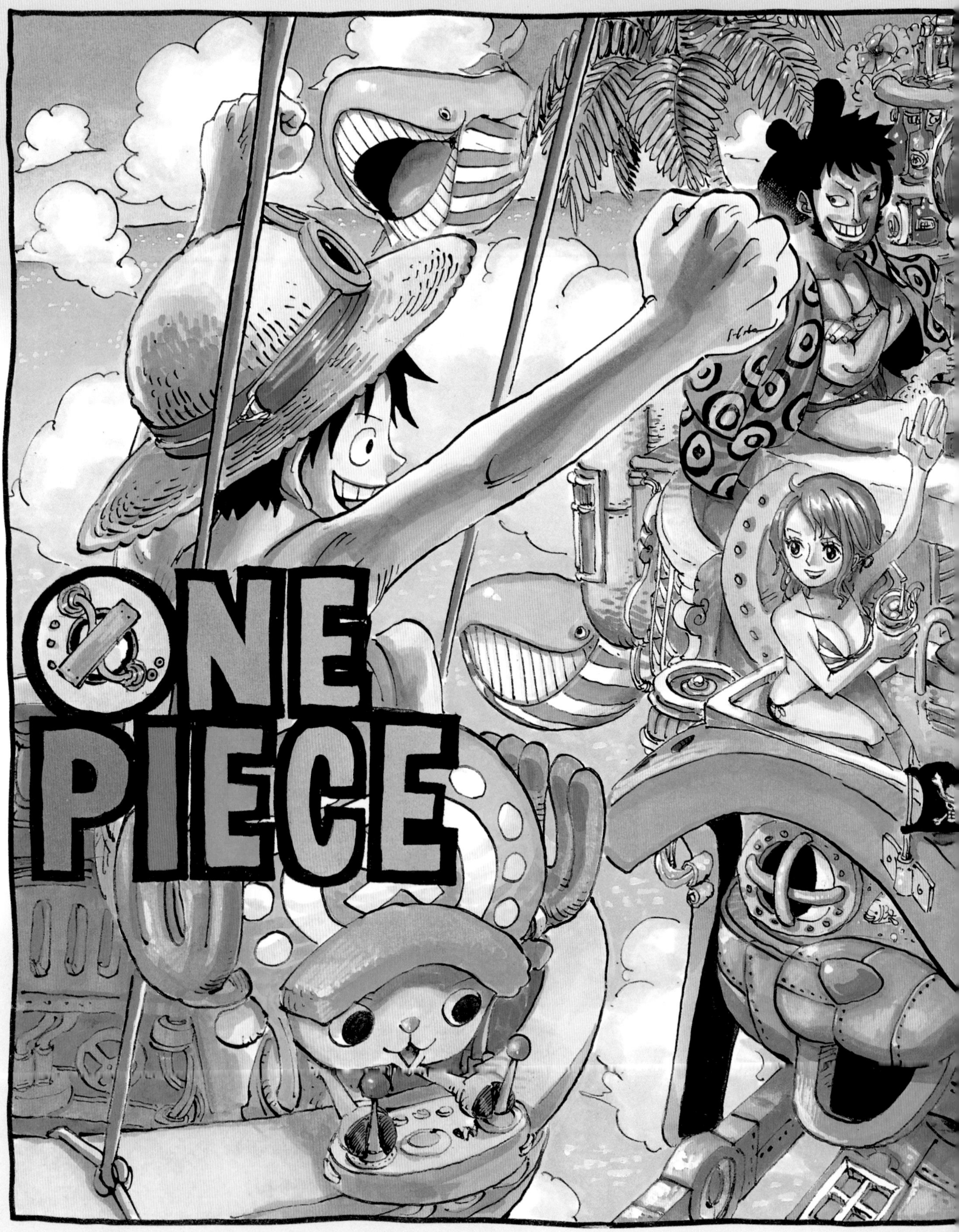
ONE
PIECE

300 MILLION COPIES!
THANKS, EVERYBODY!!

LET'S SLIP INTO ALL THE HOUSES AFTER SANTA...
...AND MAKE OFF WITH THE PRESENTS HE LEFT BEHIND!!
NICE PLAN, CAPTAIN!!
HEH HEH HEH, THERE WE GO.
THIEF!! THIEF!! GIVE BACK THE CHICKEN AND CAKE!!!
WHAT?! BUT I DIDN'T TOUCH ANY OF YOUR FOOD!!

ONE PIECE

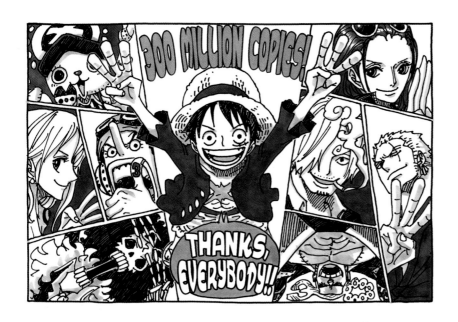

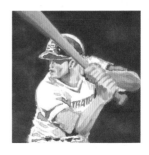

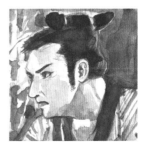

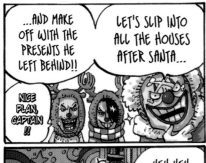

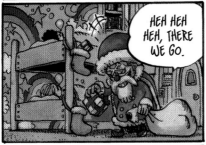

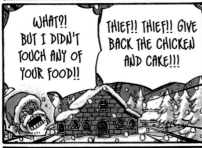

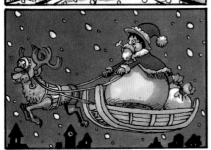

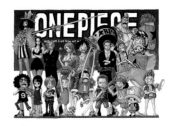

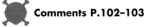

Comments P.102–103

Osugi, my editor at the time, asked me to do this idea for a color spread. Drawing it summoned a lot of feelings in me. We've come so far together.

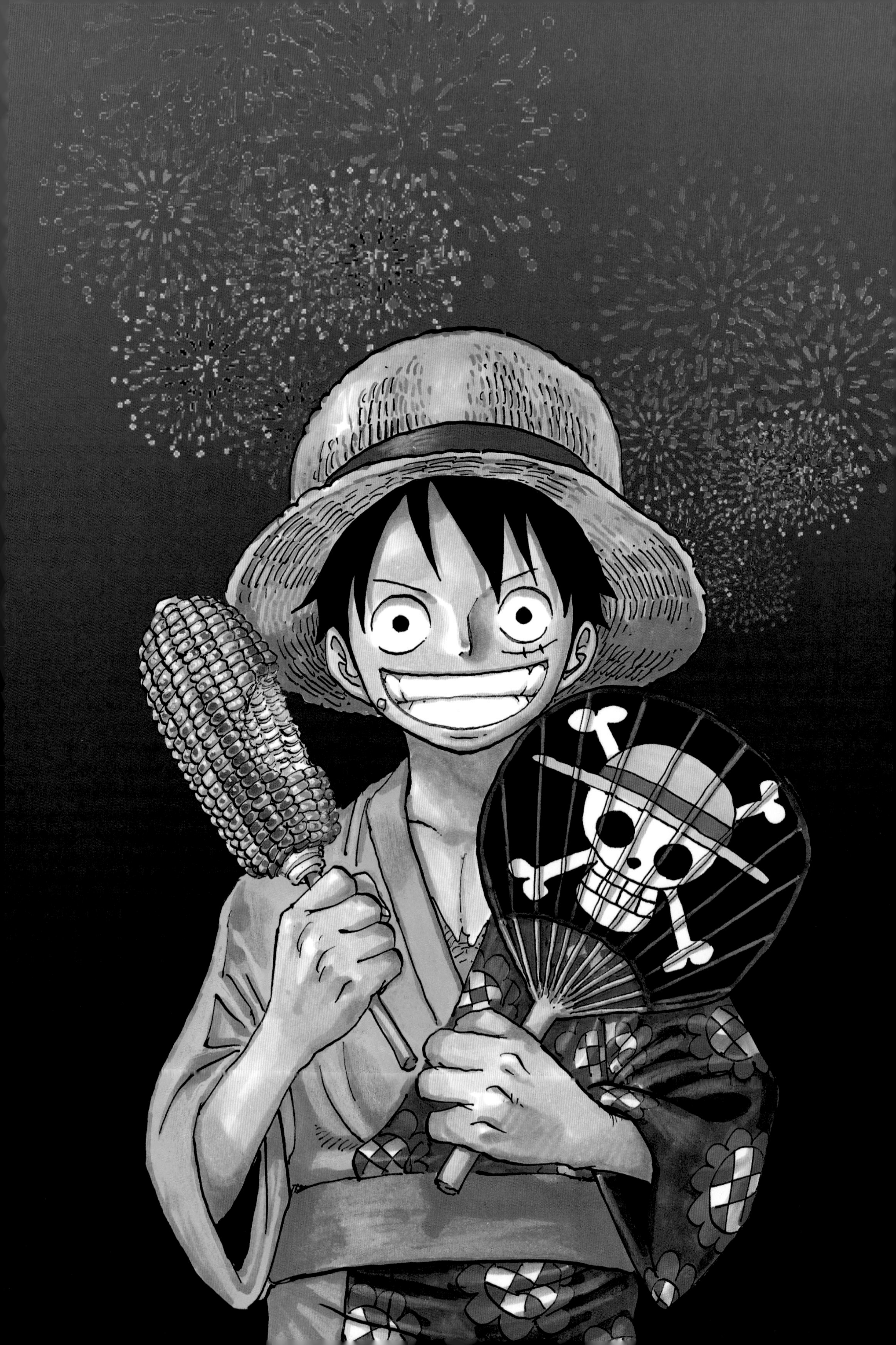

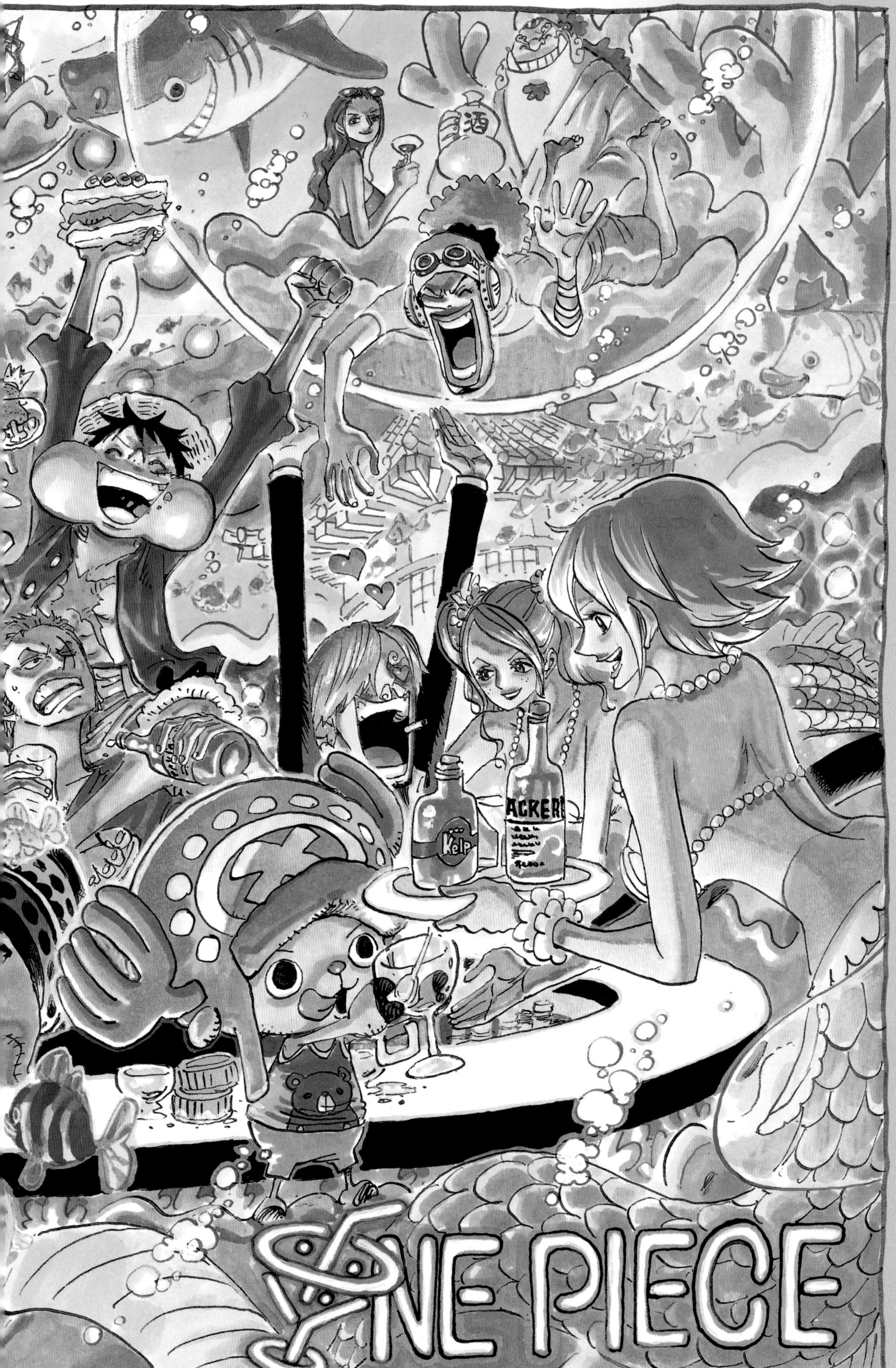
酒
Kelp
ONE PIECE

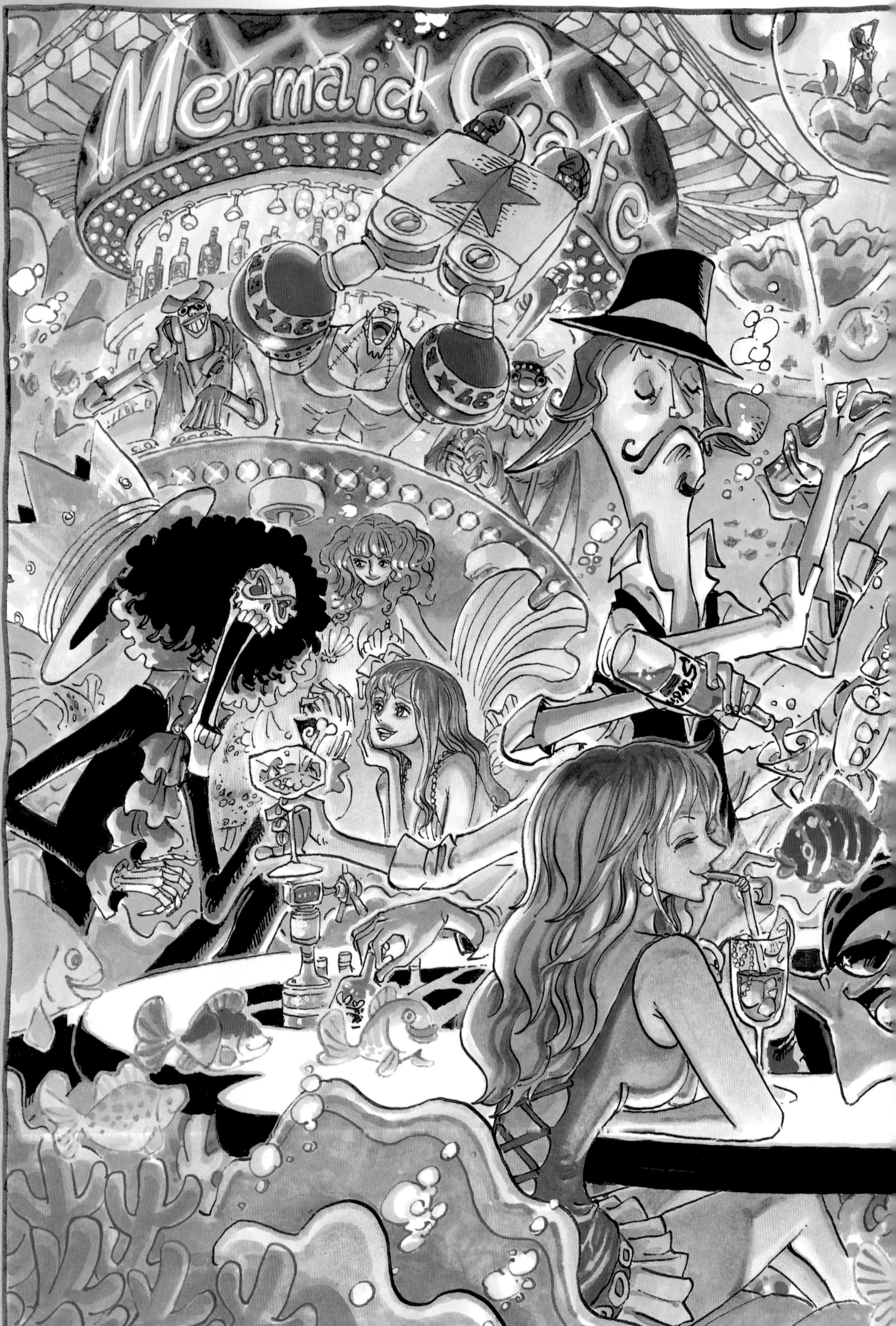
Mermaid Cafe

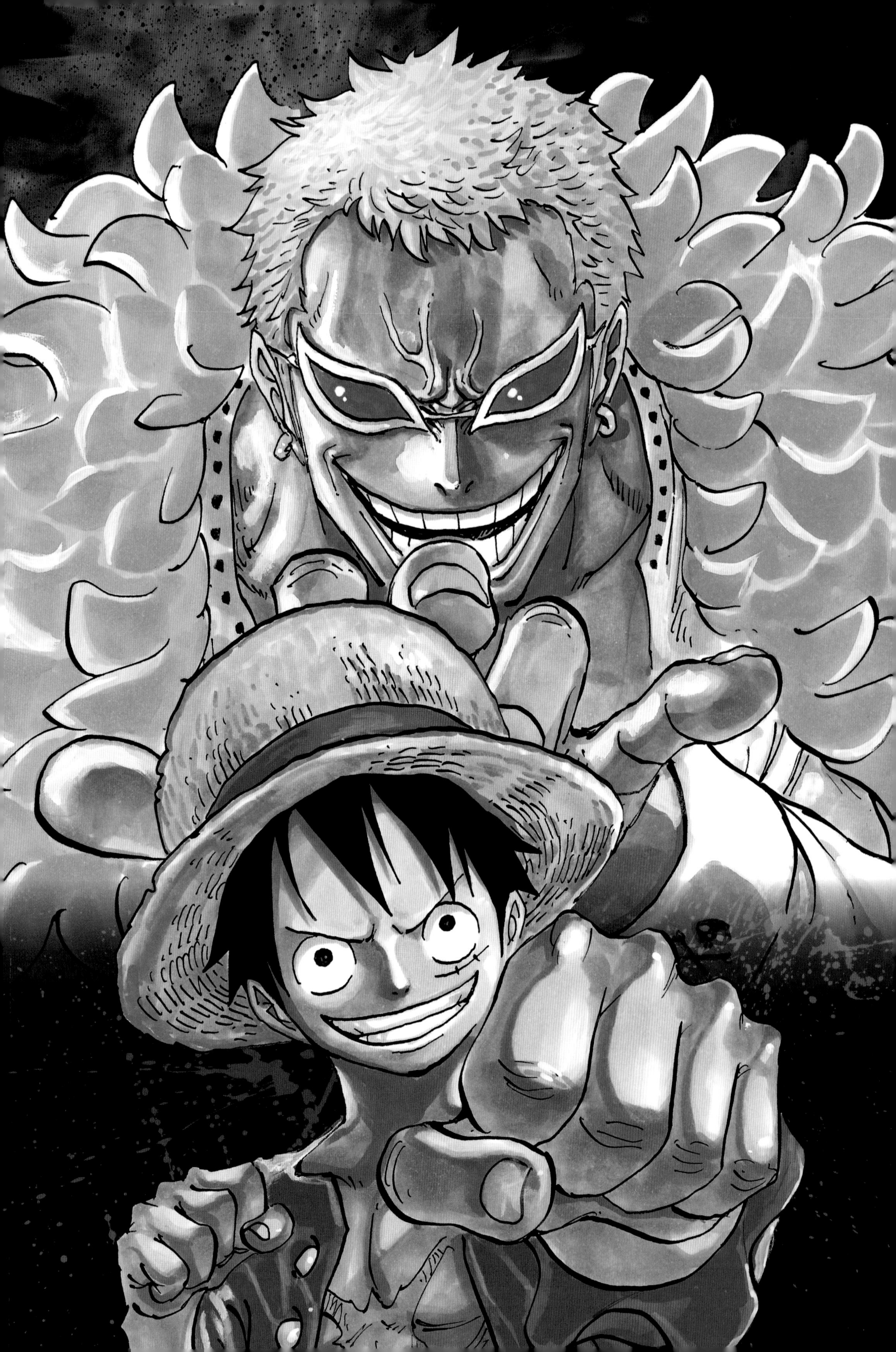

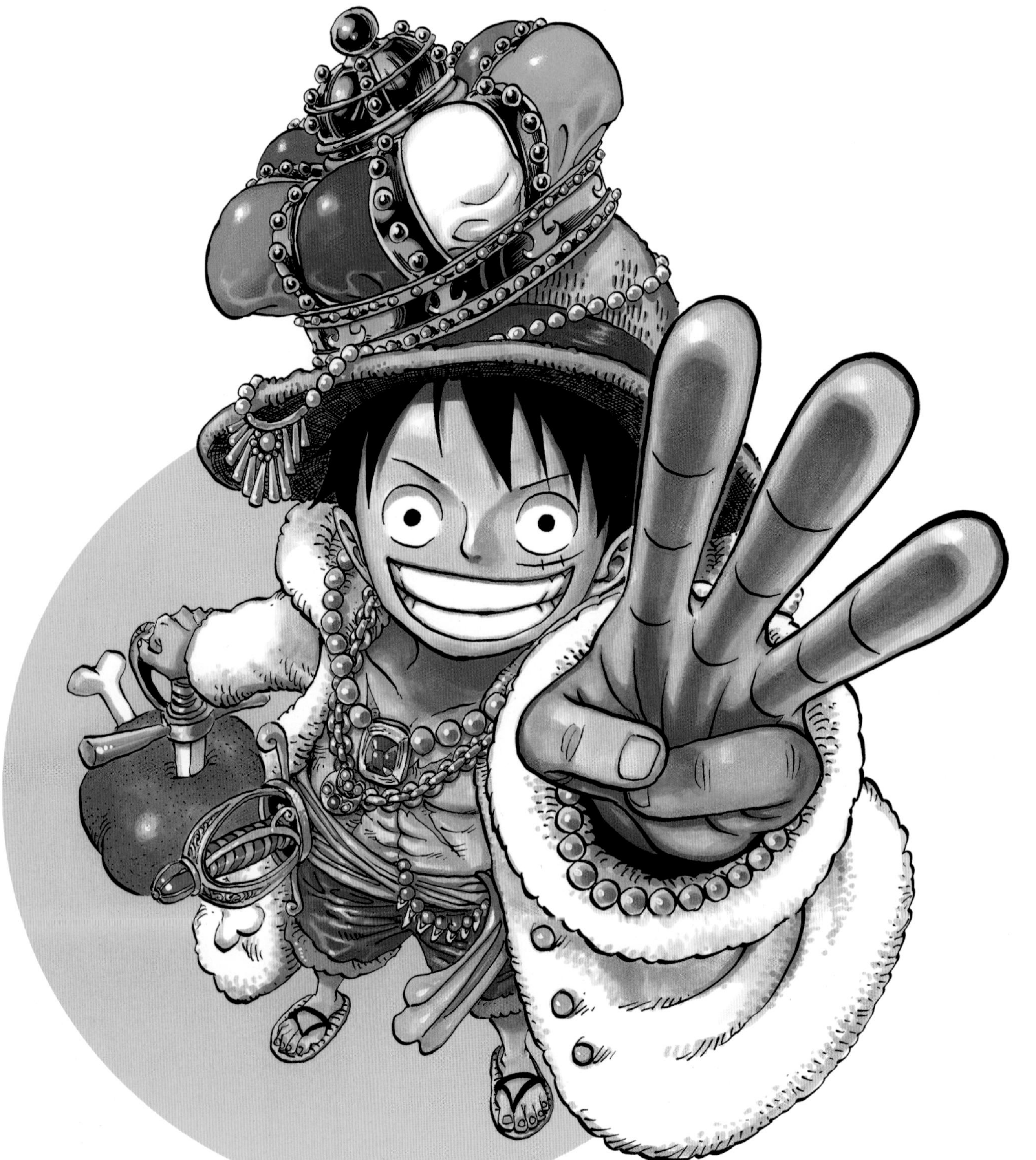

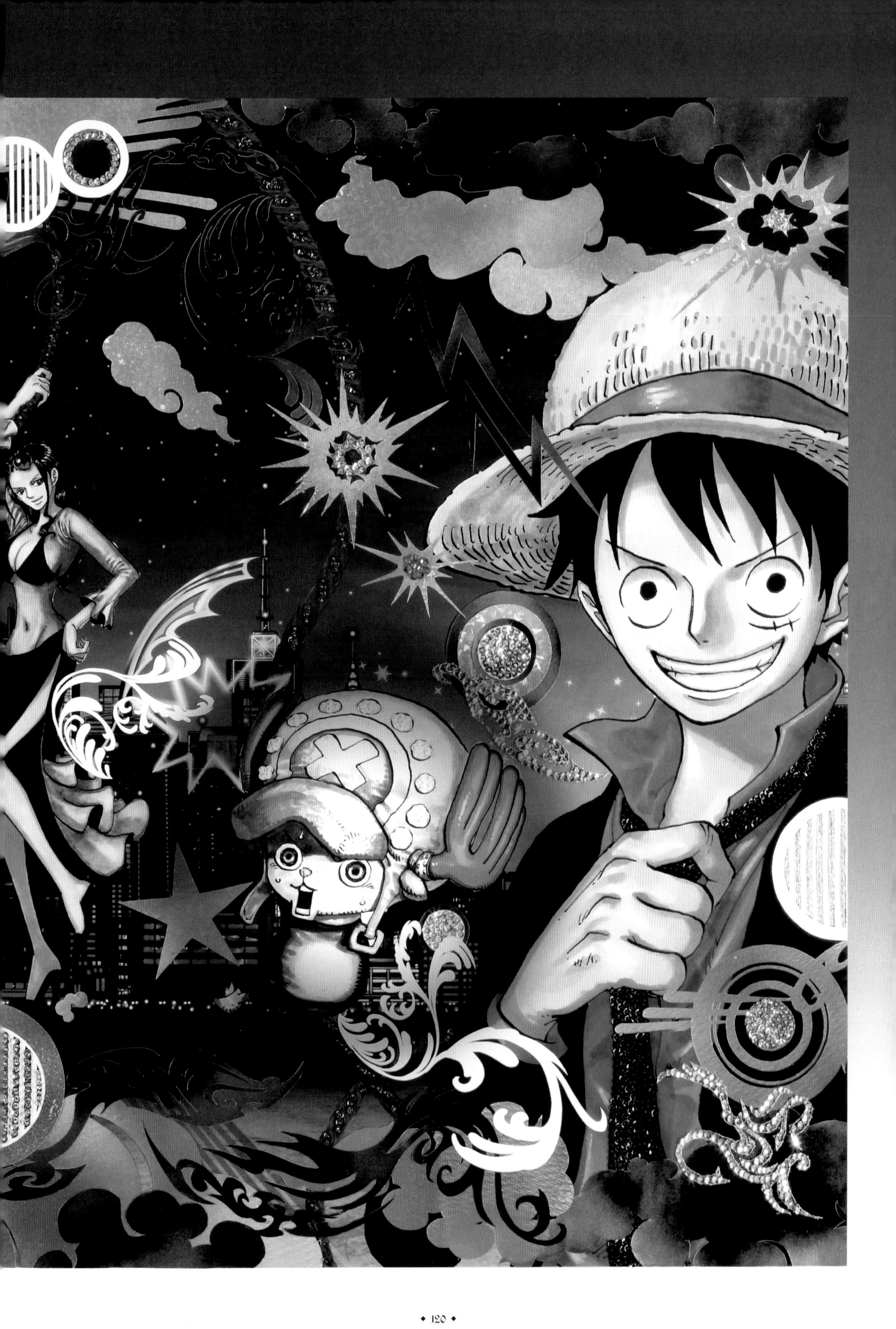

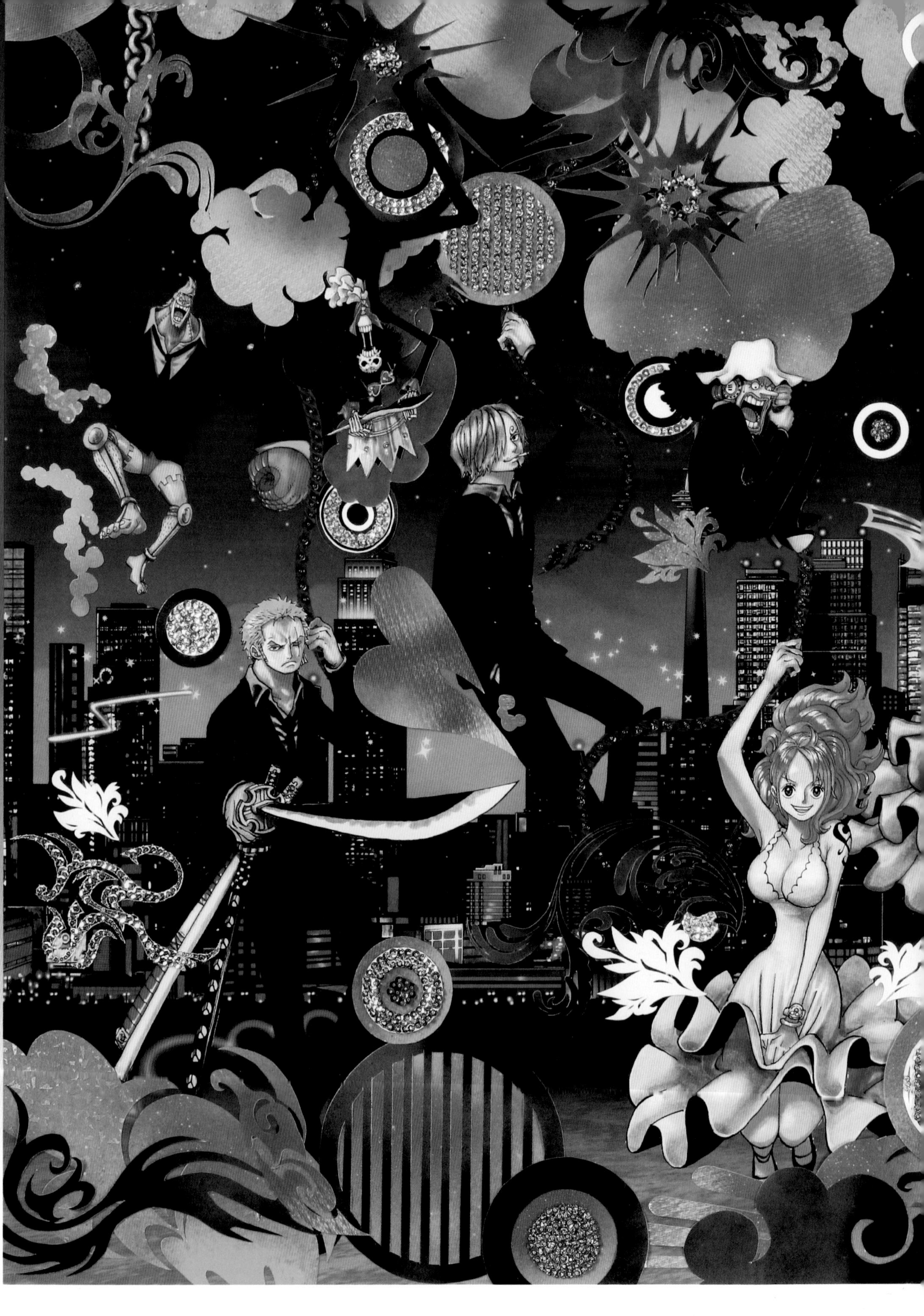

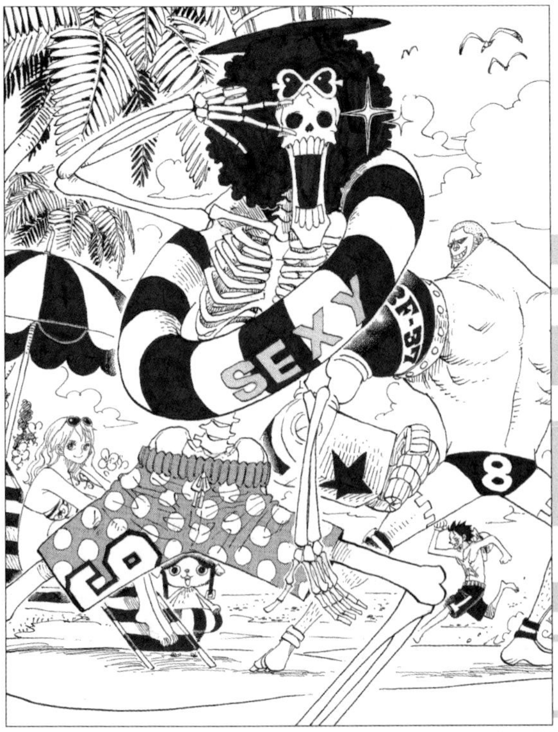
SEXY
BF-37

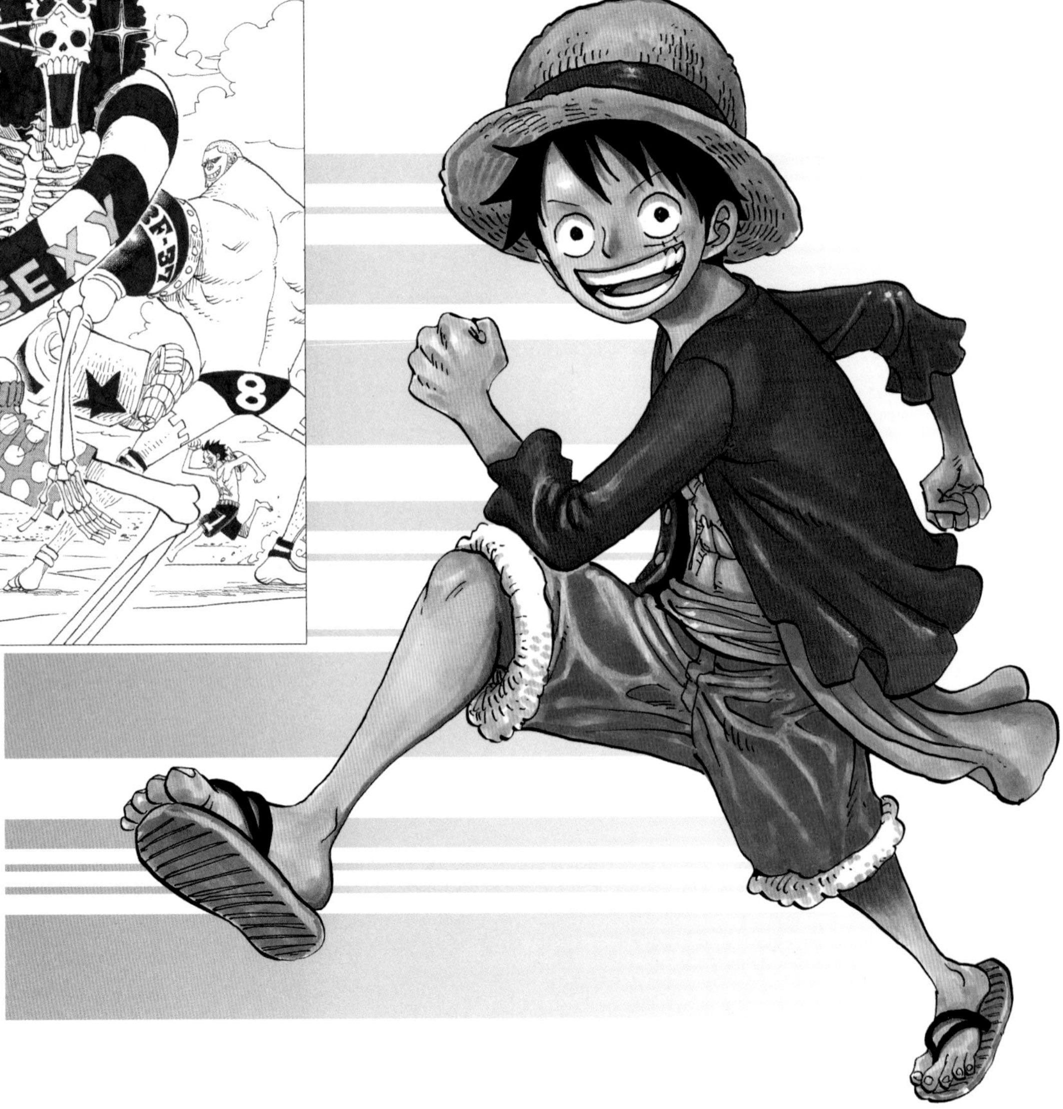

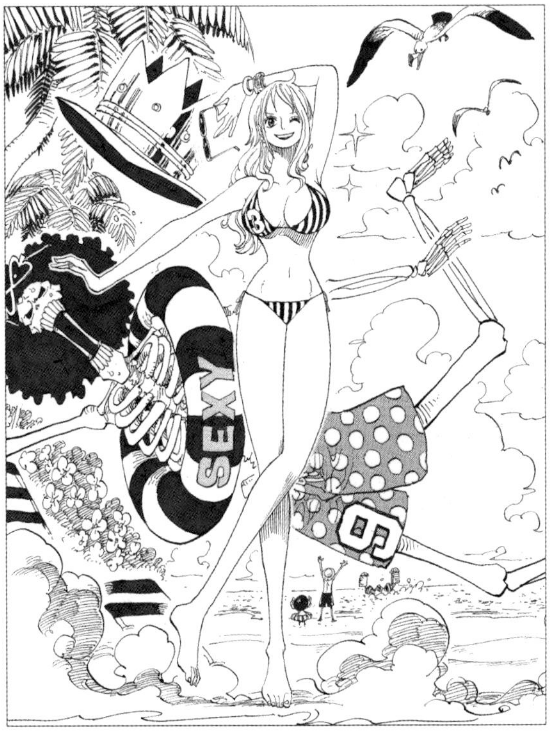
SEXY

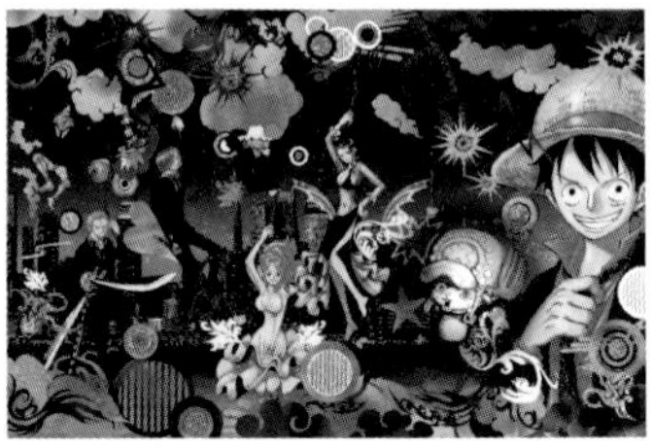

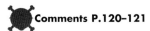

Comments P.120–121

This piece was a collaboration with an artist named Asami Kiyokawa, who adds physical decoration to photographs. She made the Straw Hats very striking and fashionable. This is the kind of art that a guy like me could never come up with!

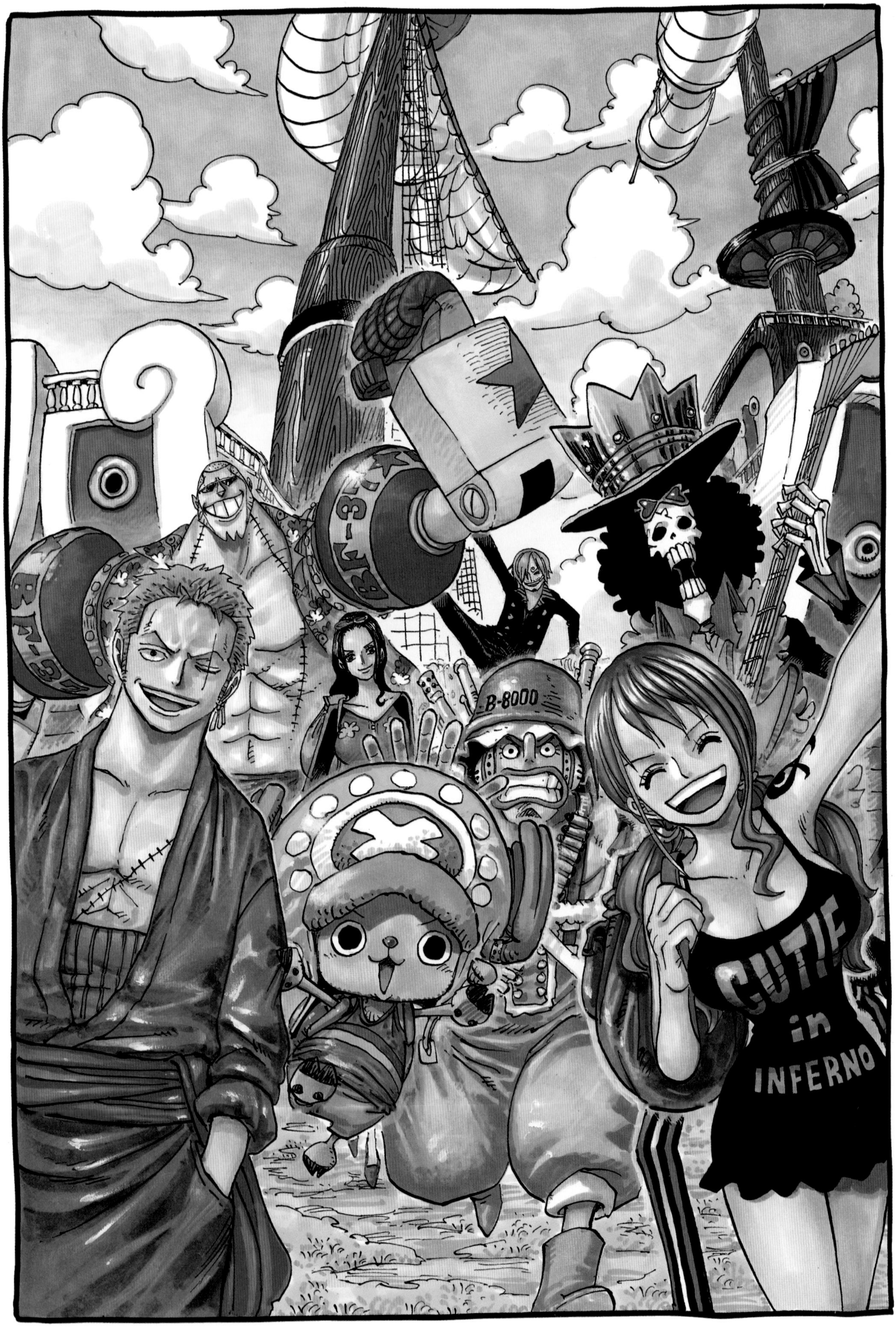

B-8000
CUTIE
in
INFERNO

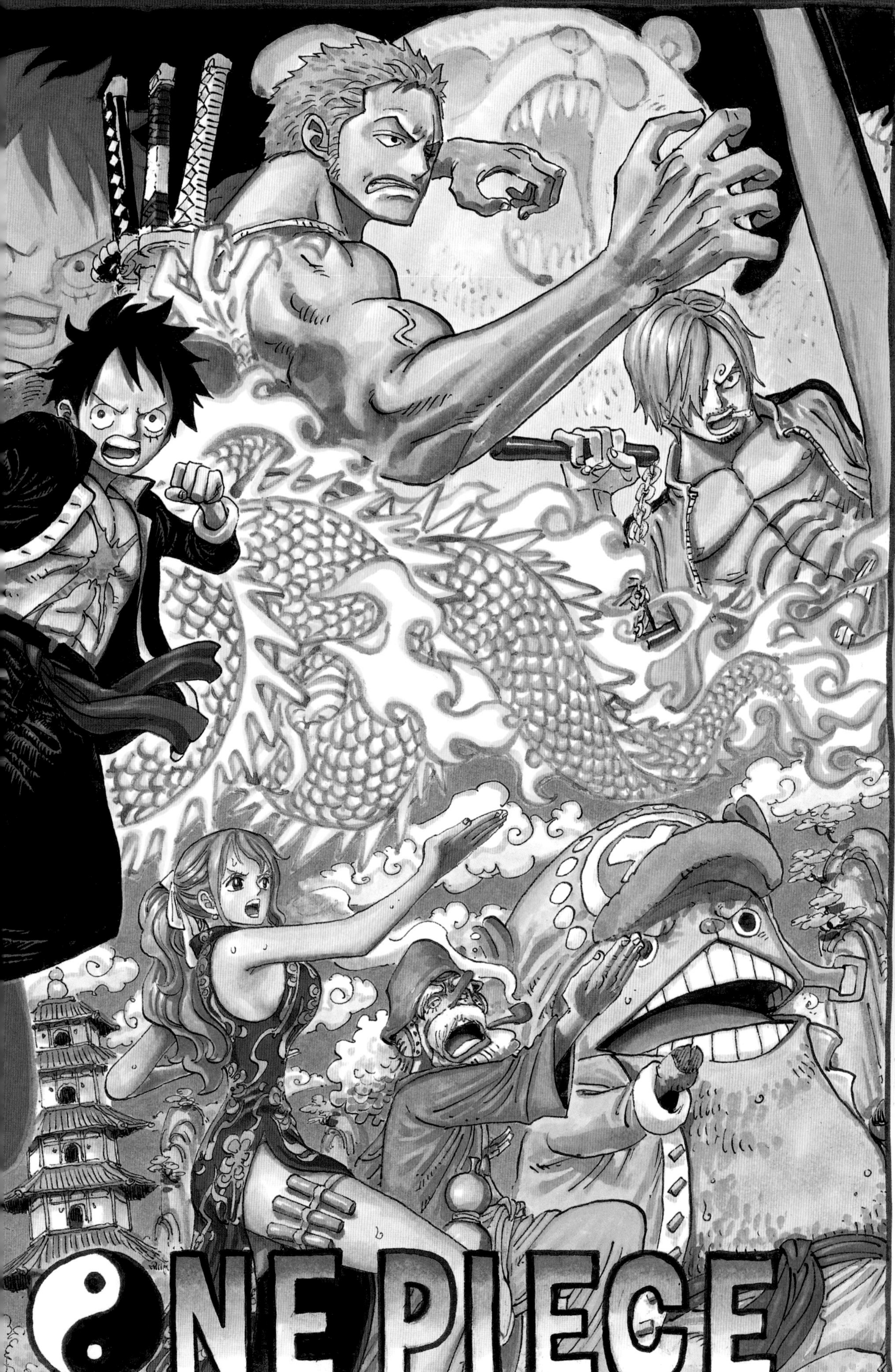
ONE PIECE

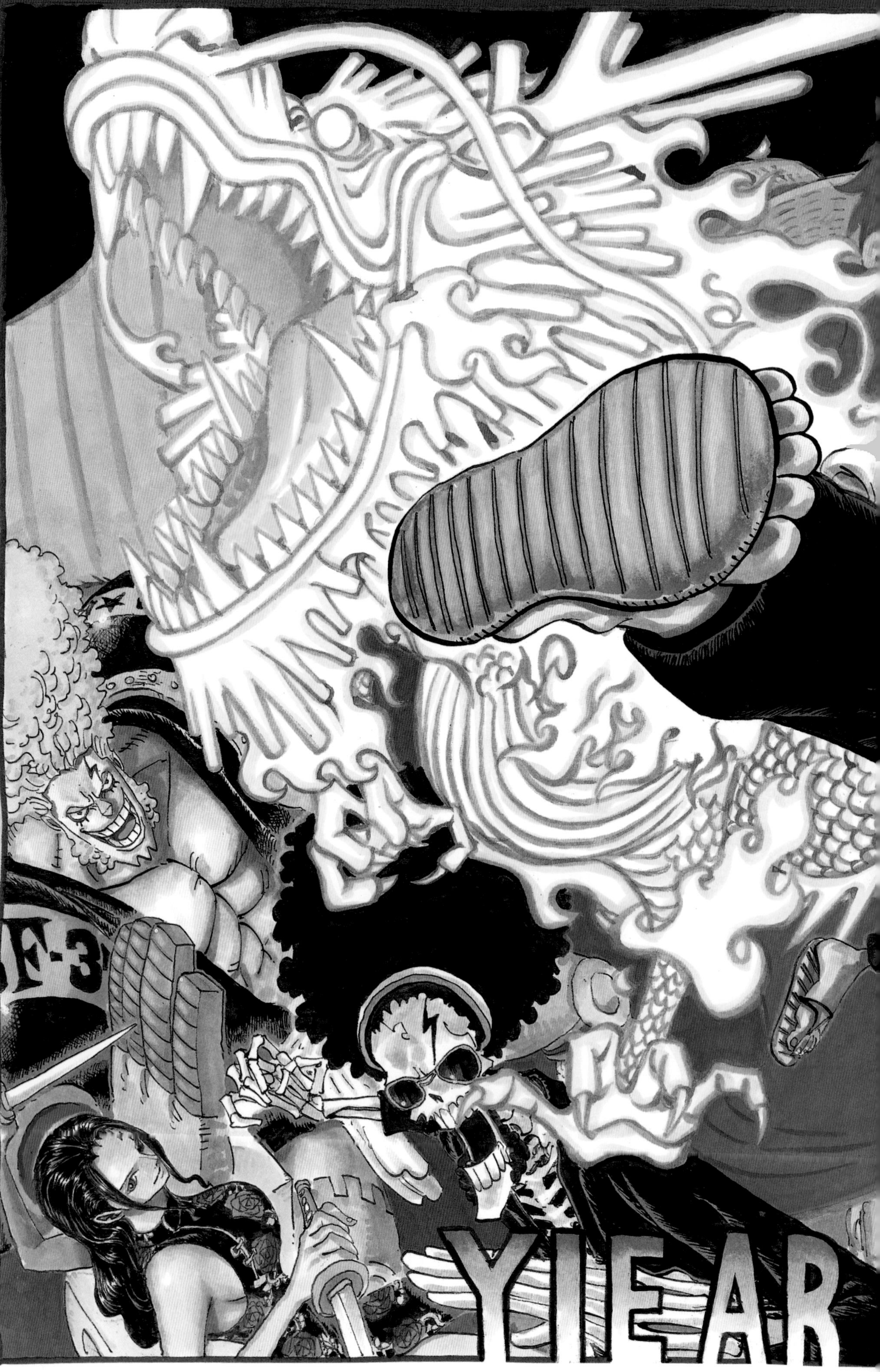
YIEAR

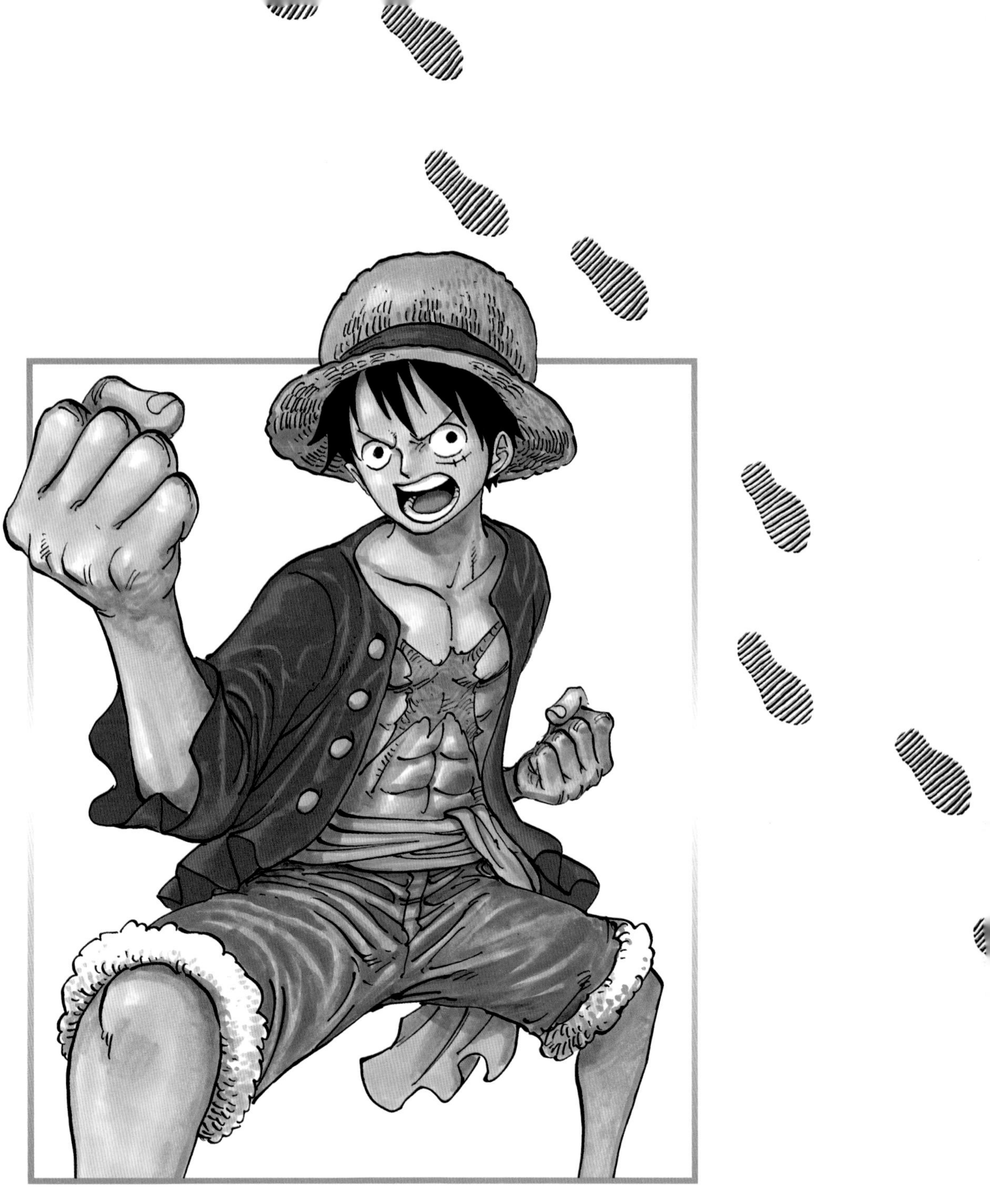

2014

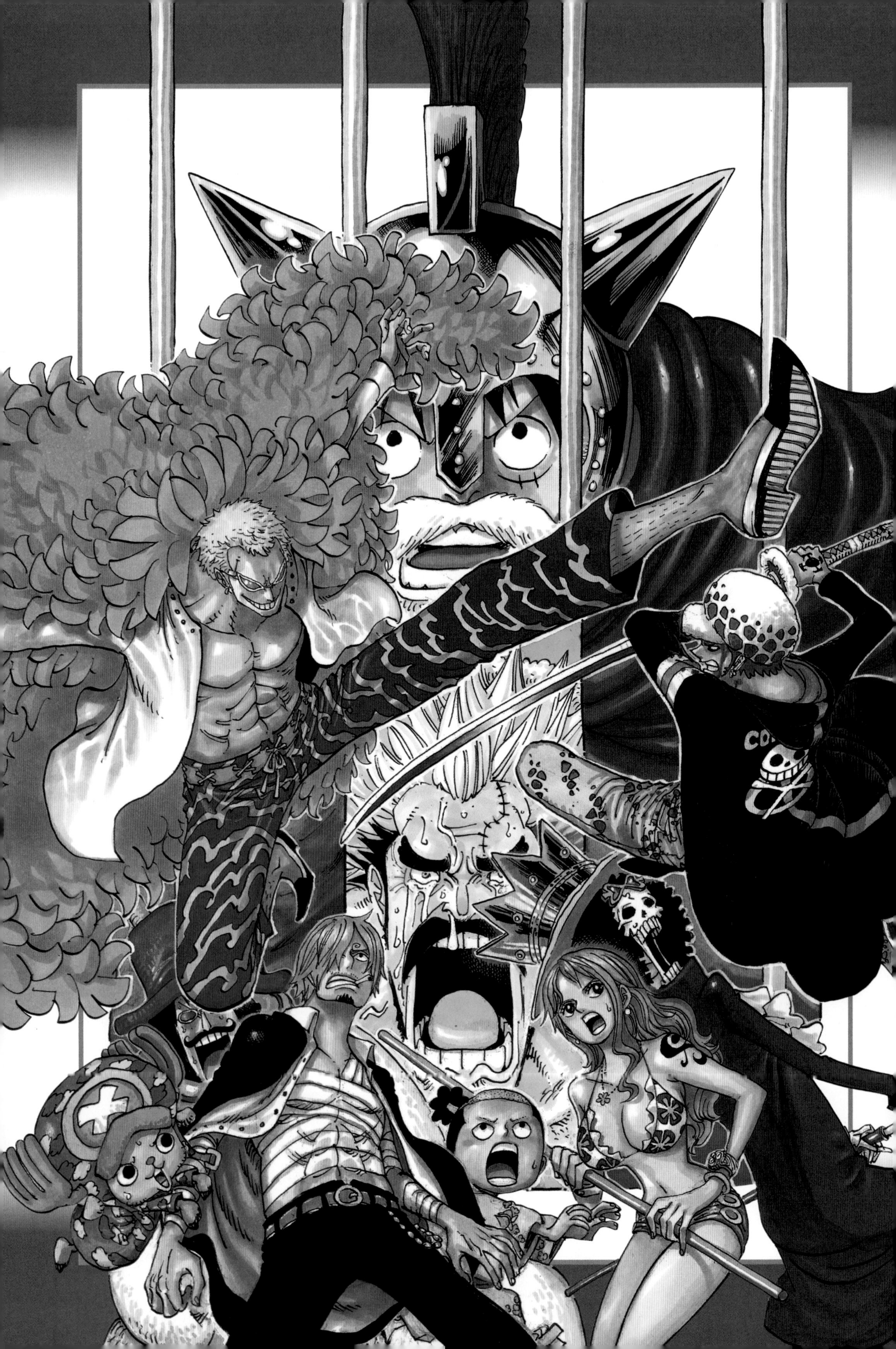

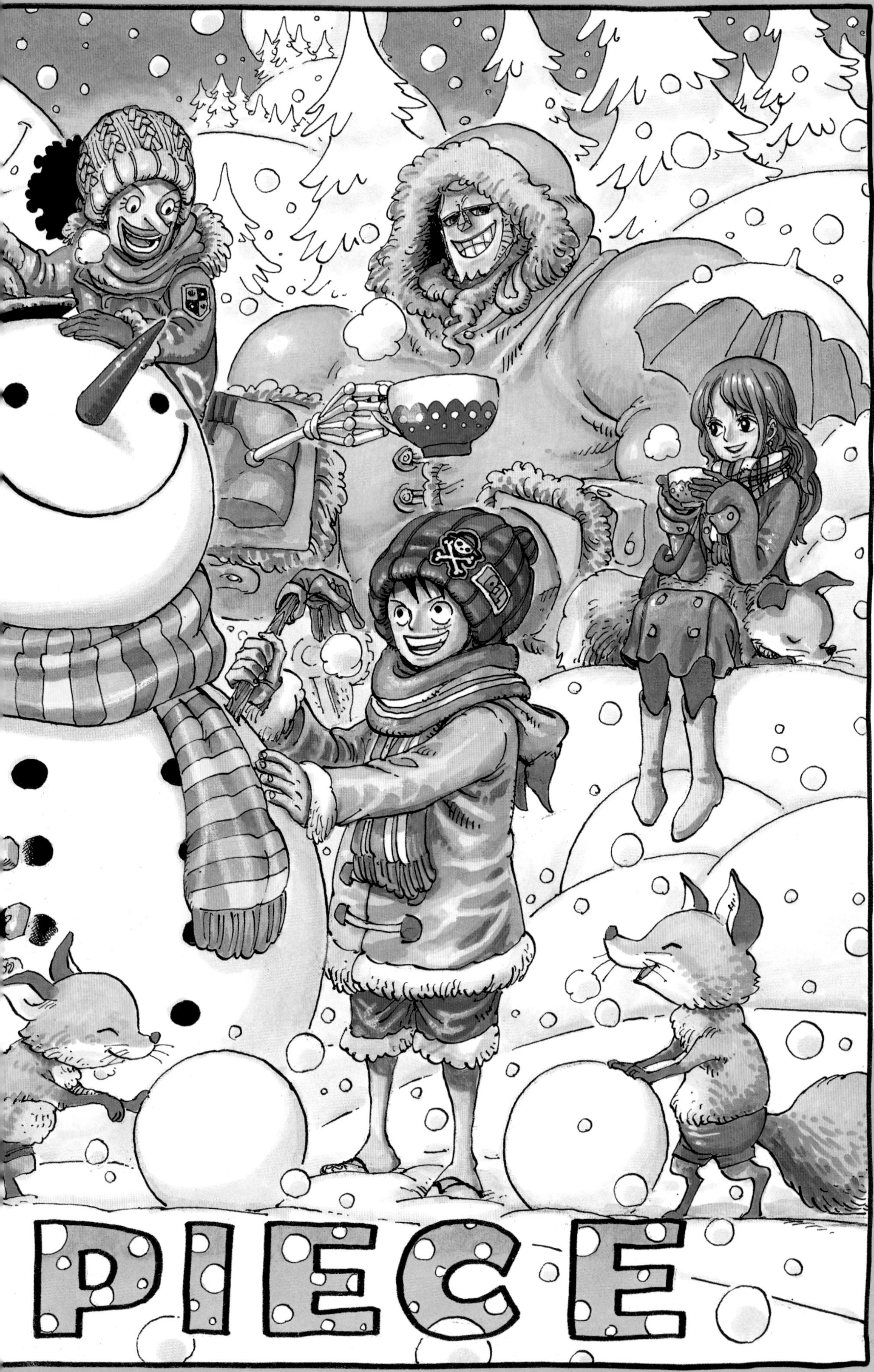
PIECE

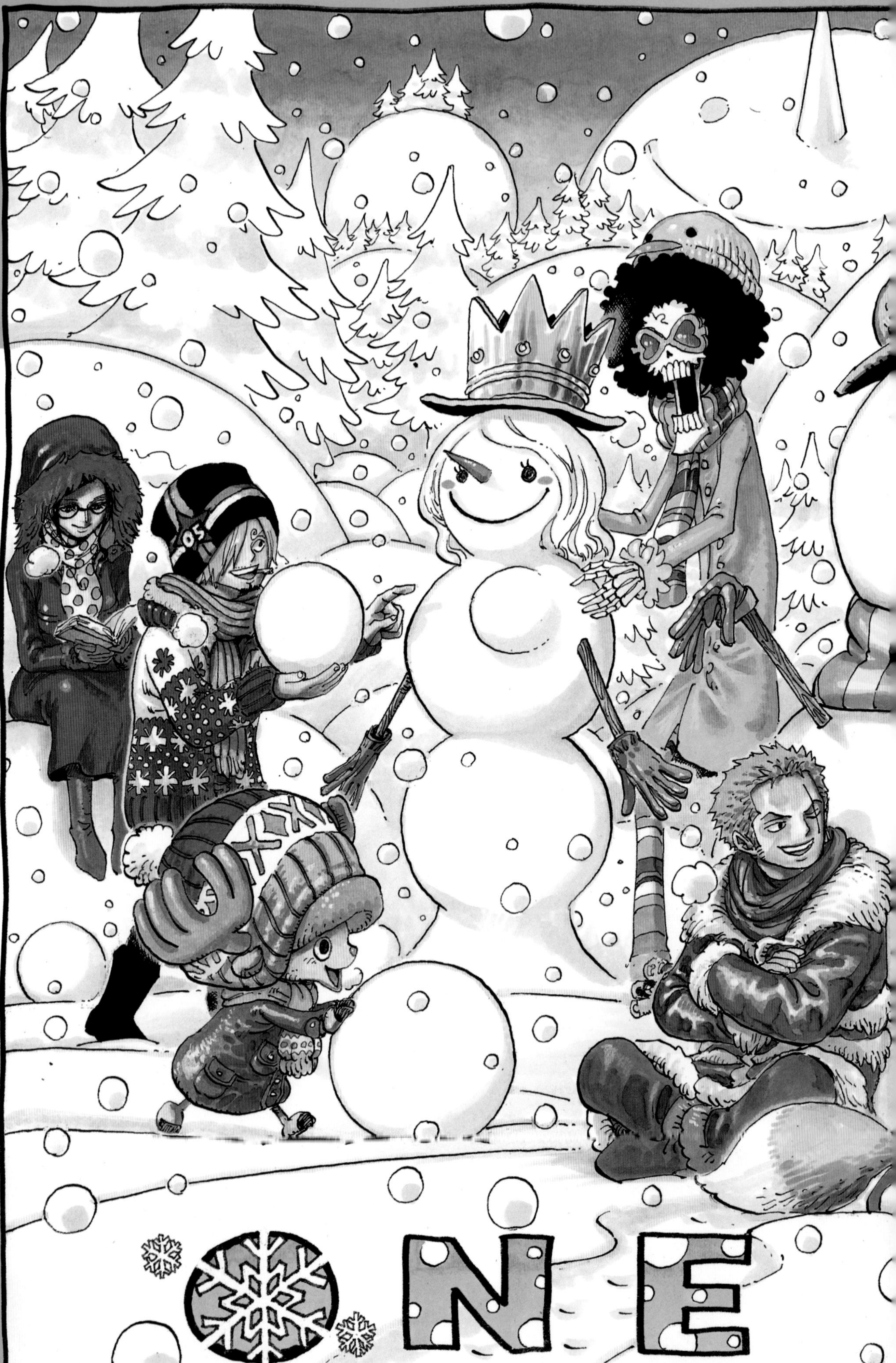
ONE

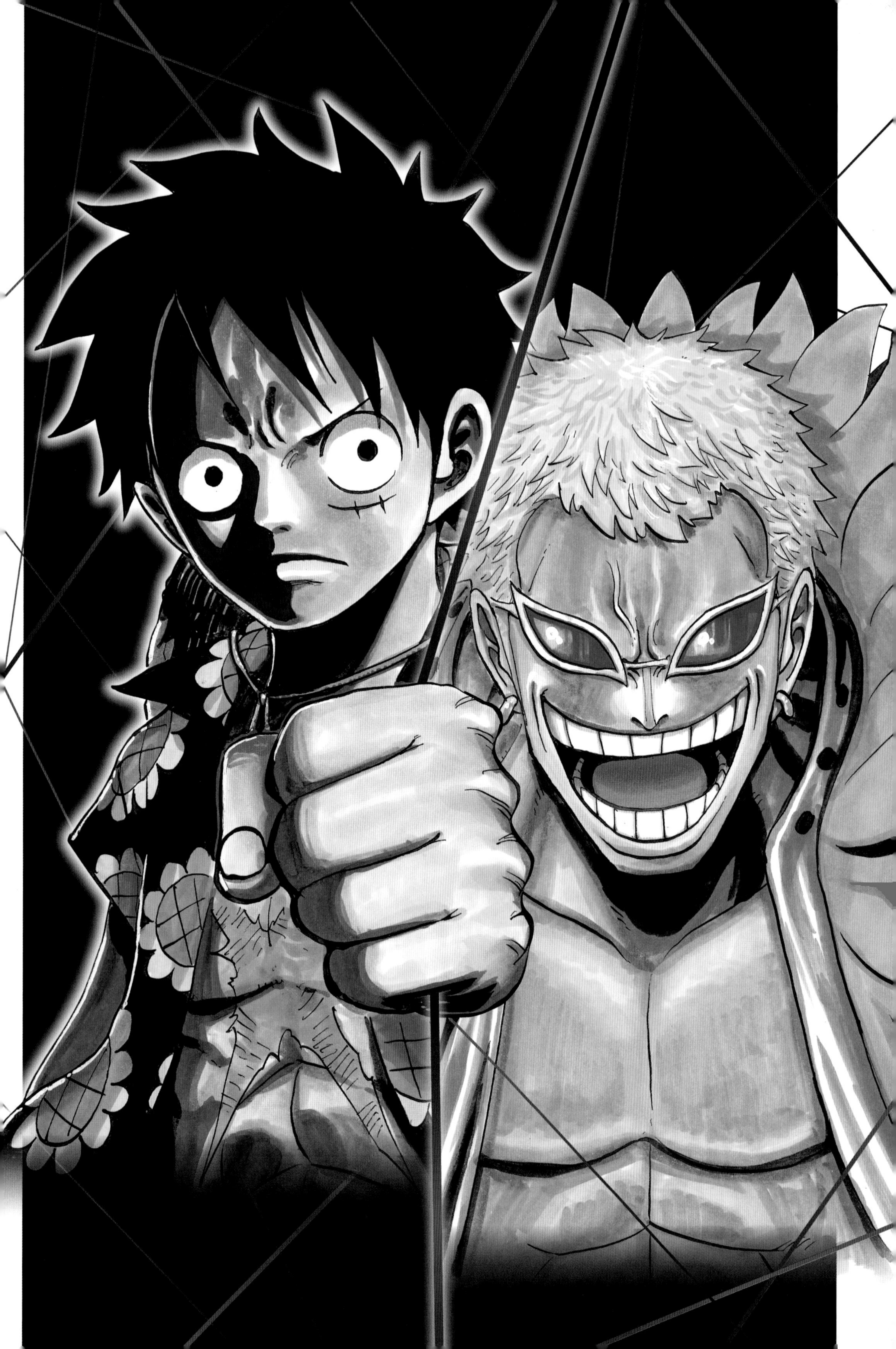

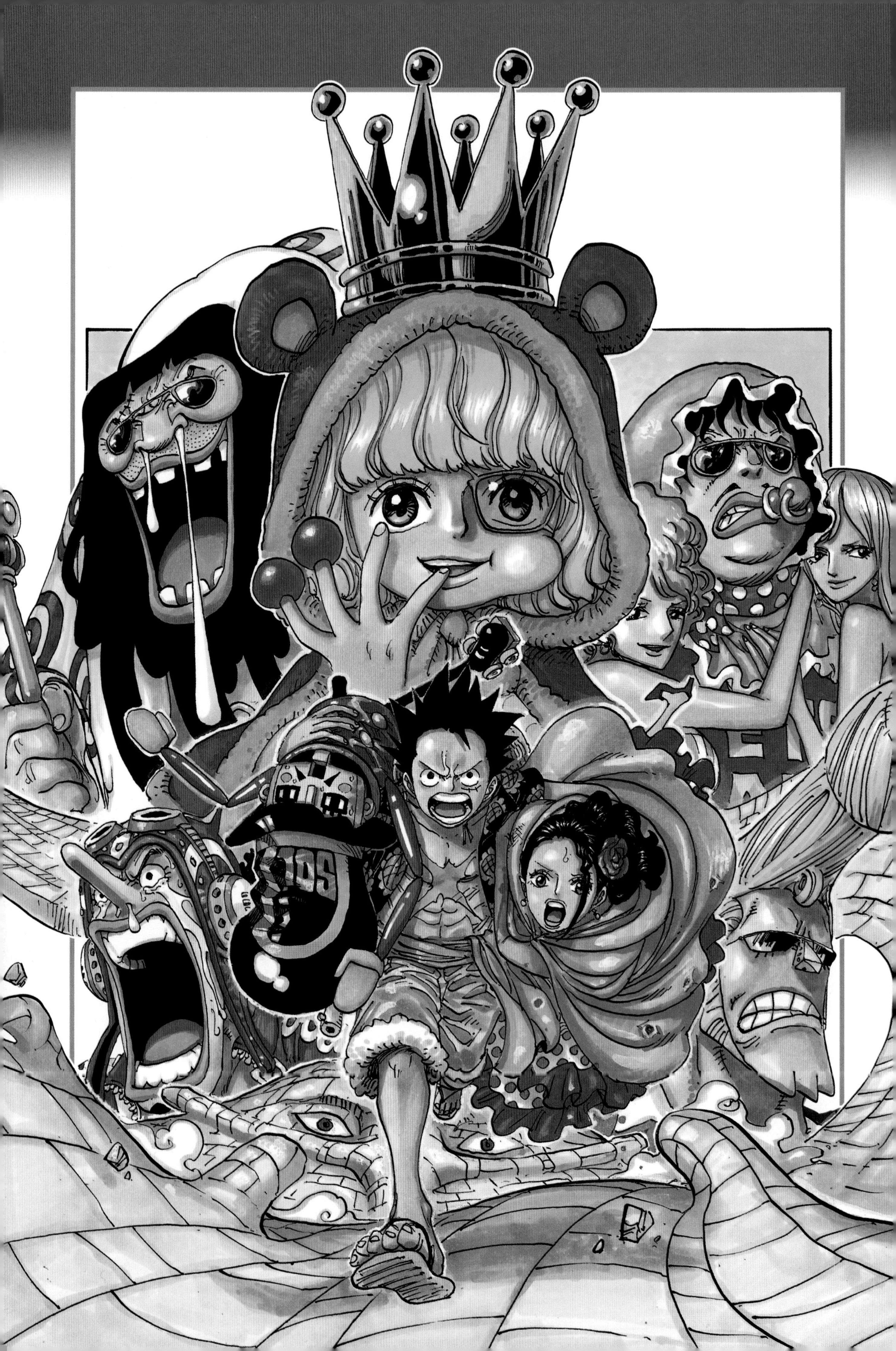

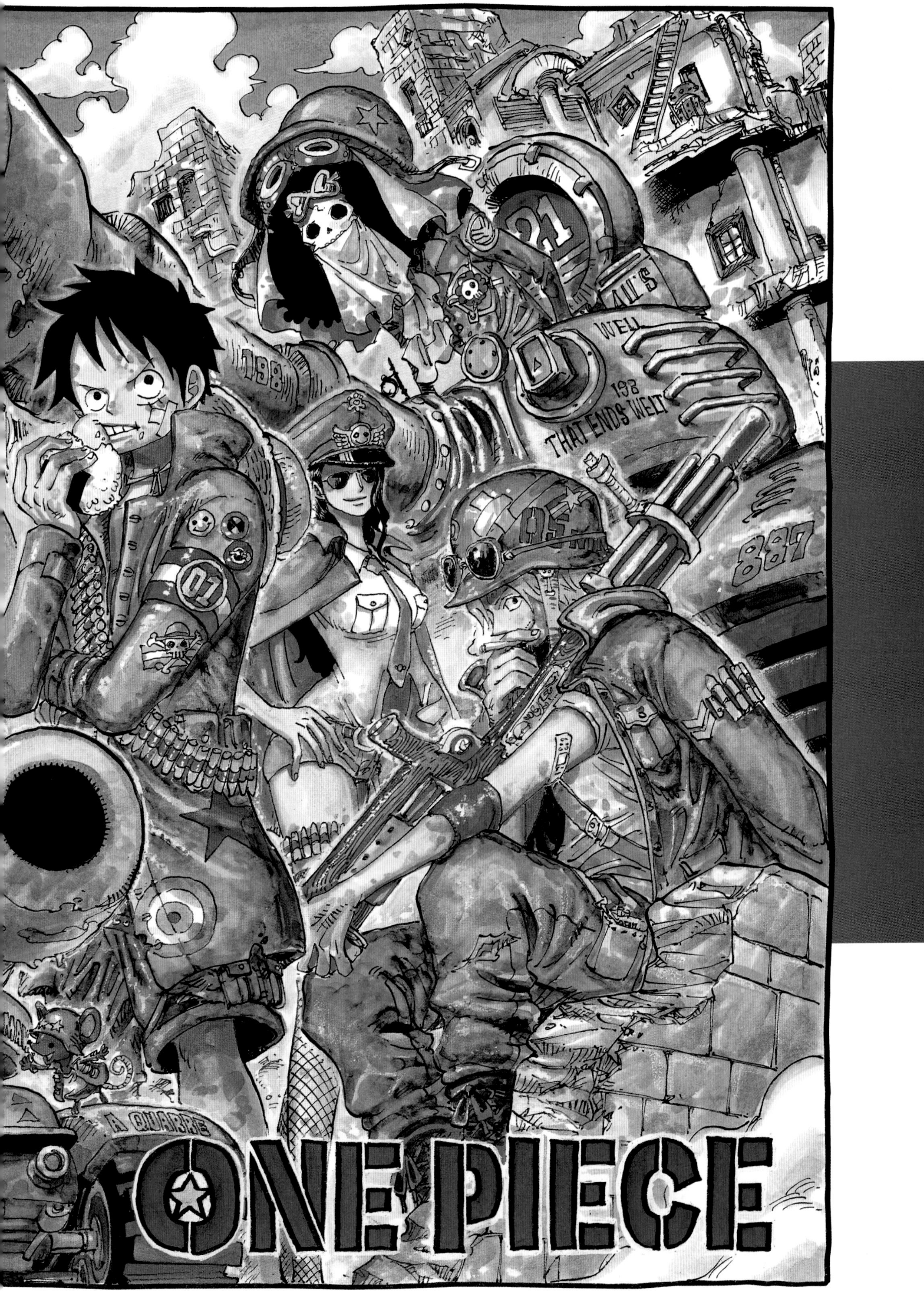
ONE PIECE

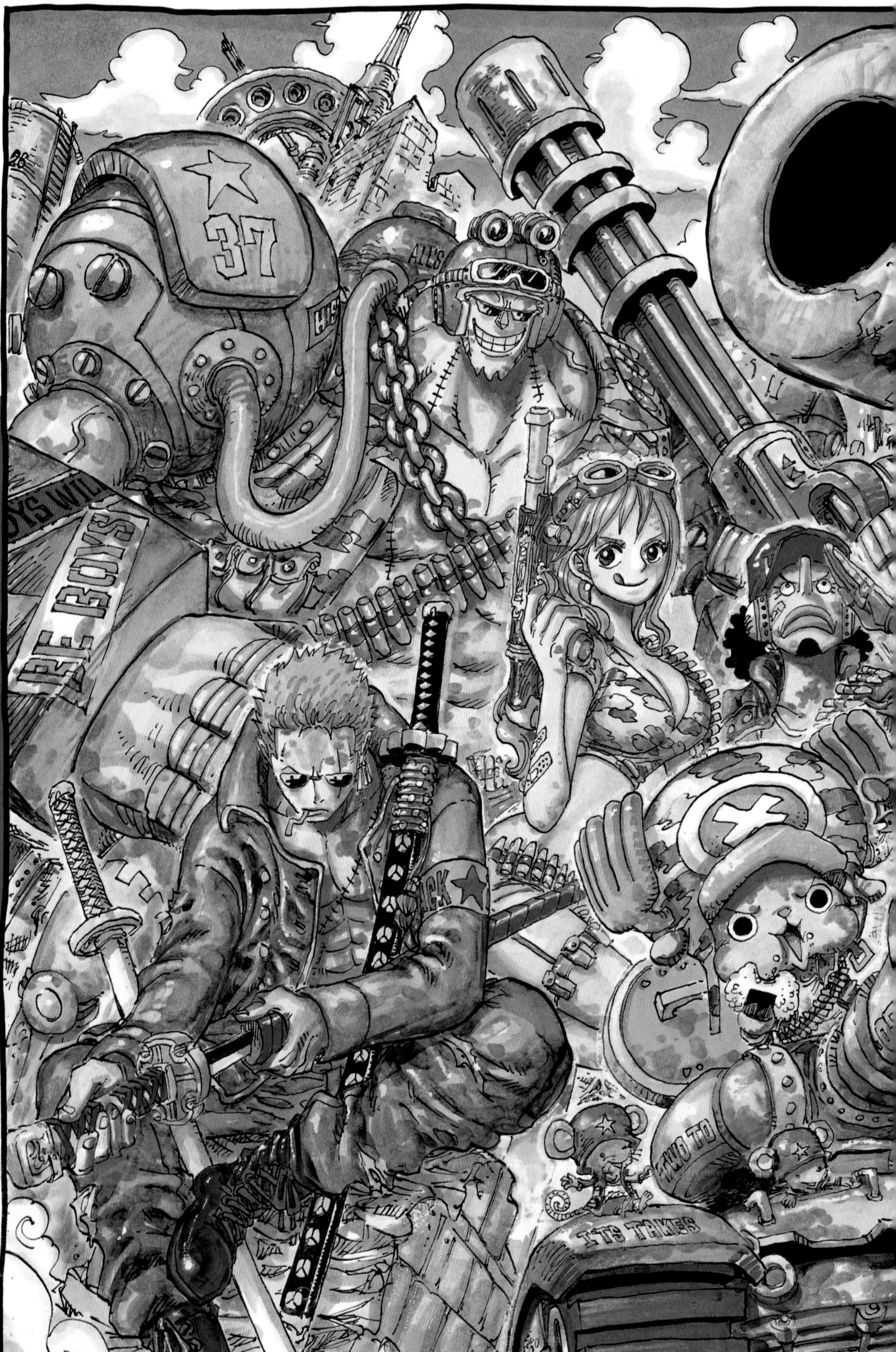
37
TWO TO
IT'S TAKES

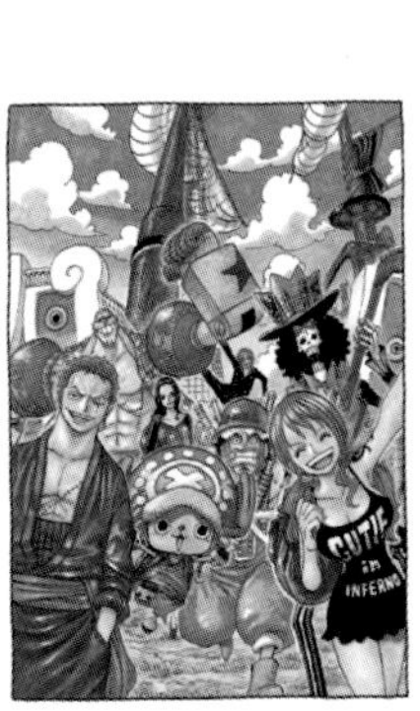

Comments P.123

This was on the cover of a special spin-off of *Jump*. My policy is that Luffy should only grace the cover of *Weekly Shonen Jump*. My editor, who is aware of this, said, "Draw the rest of the Straw Hats except for Luffy, then." Isn't that cheating? Ha ha. I did it anyway. This is Luffy's view looking at the gang.

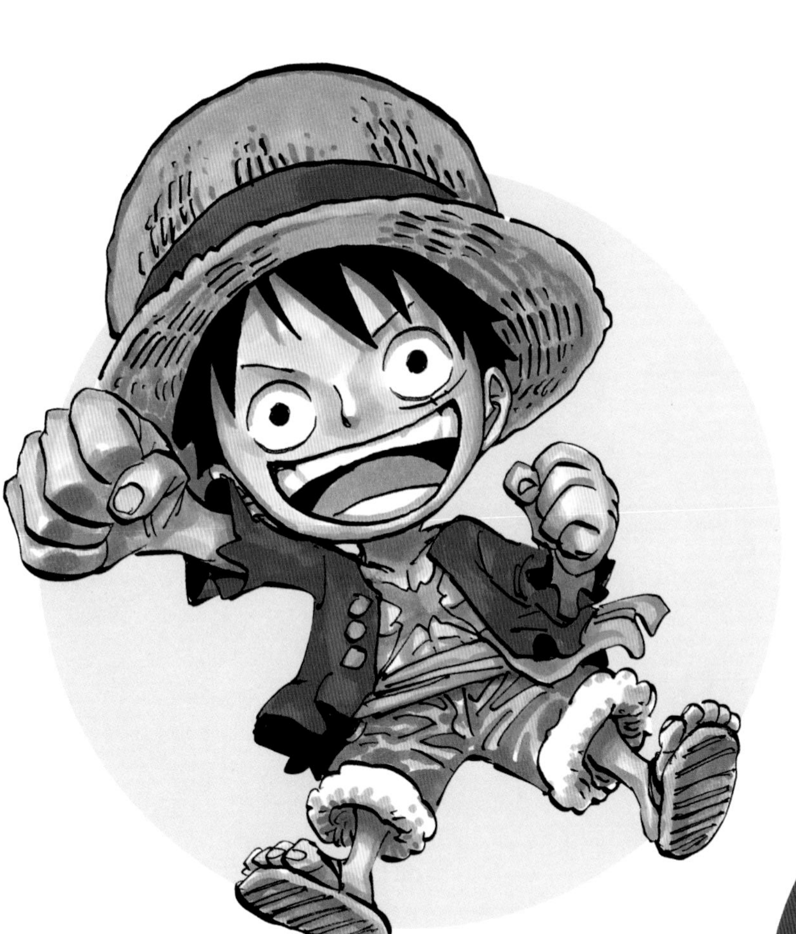

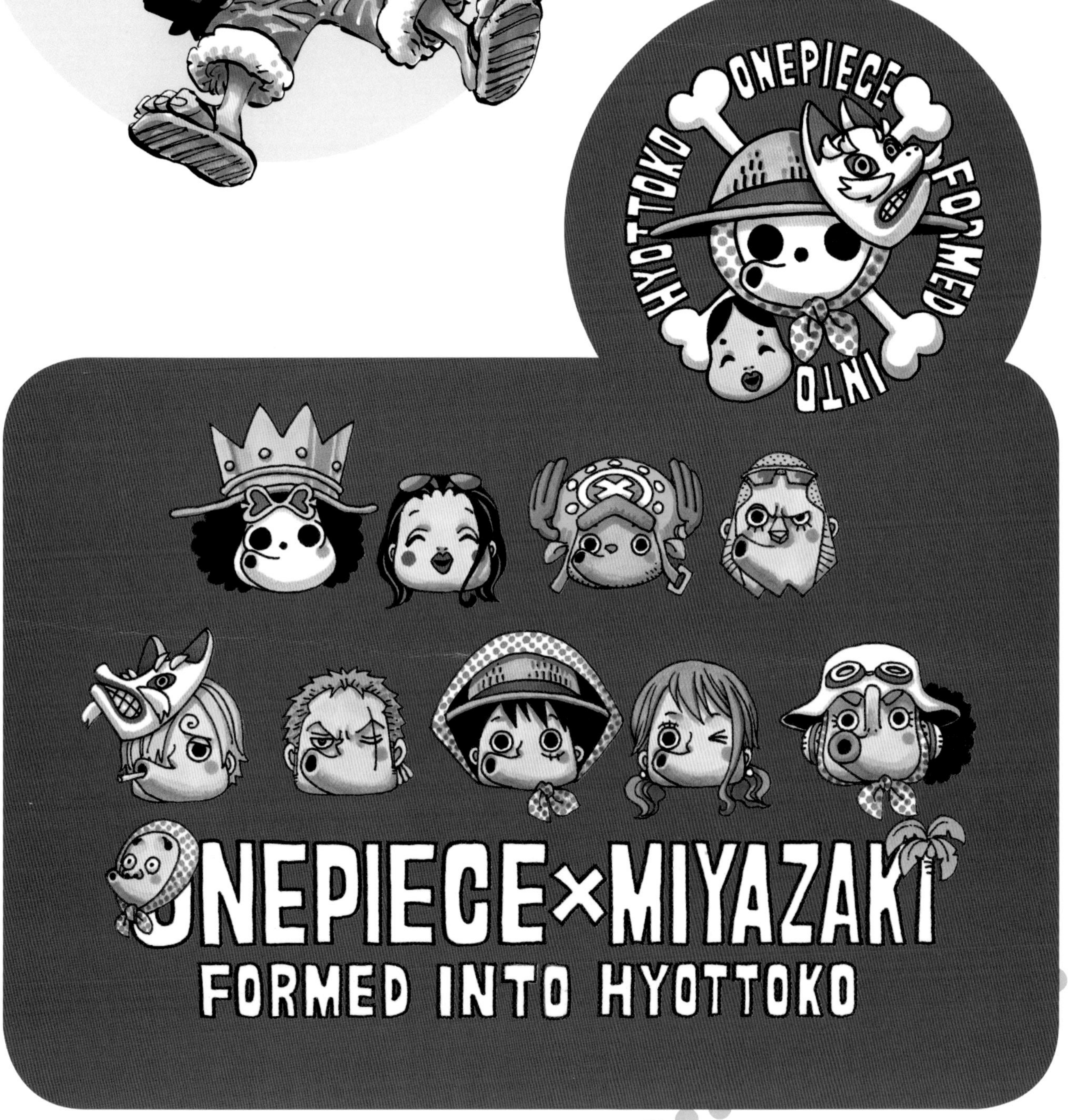
ONEPIECE
FORMED INTO
HYOTTOKO
ONEPIECE×MIYAZAKI
FORMED INTO HYOTTOKO

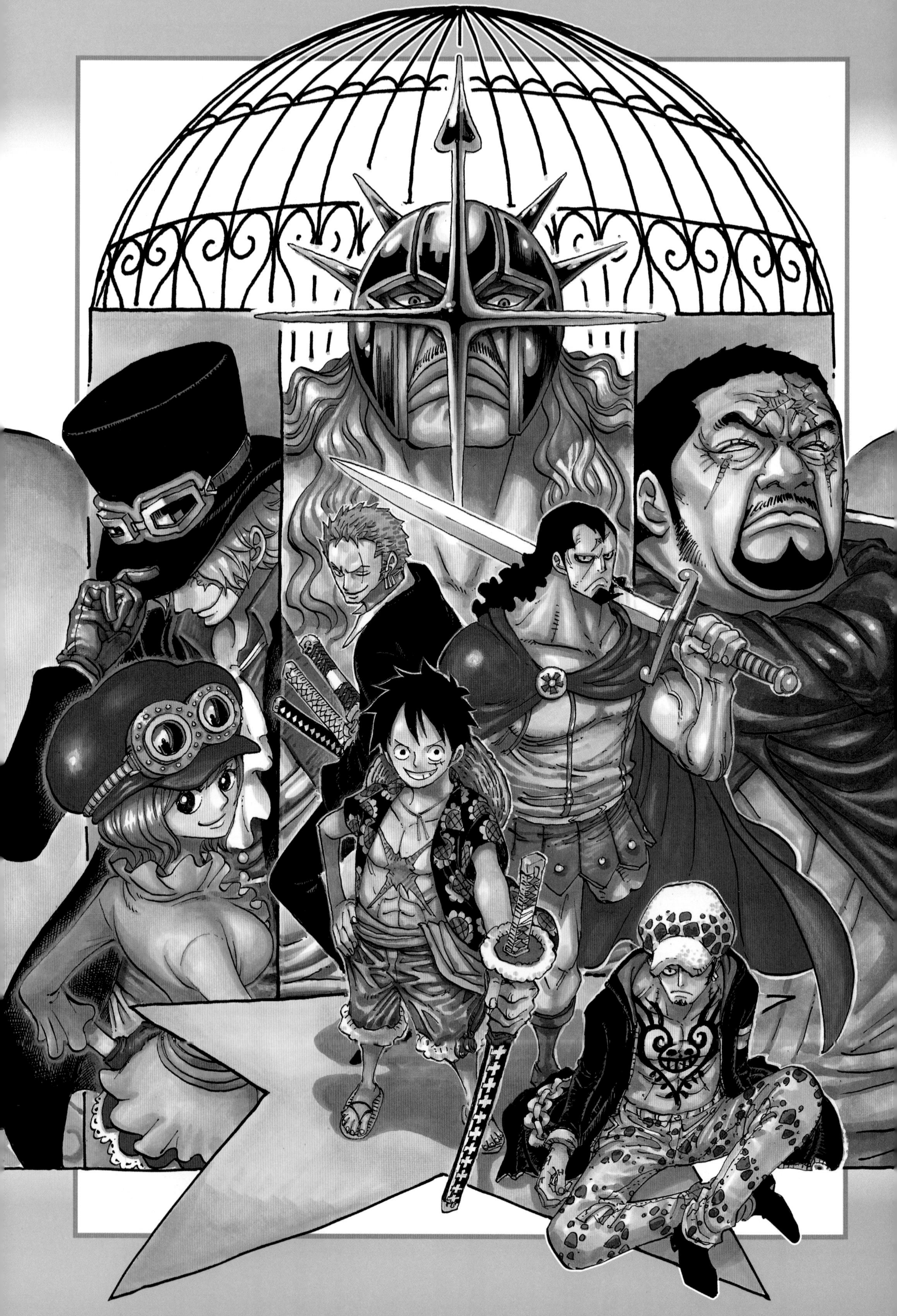

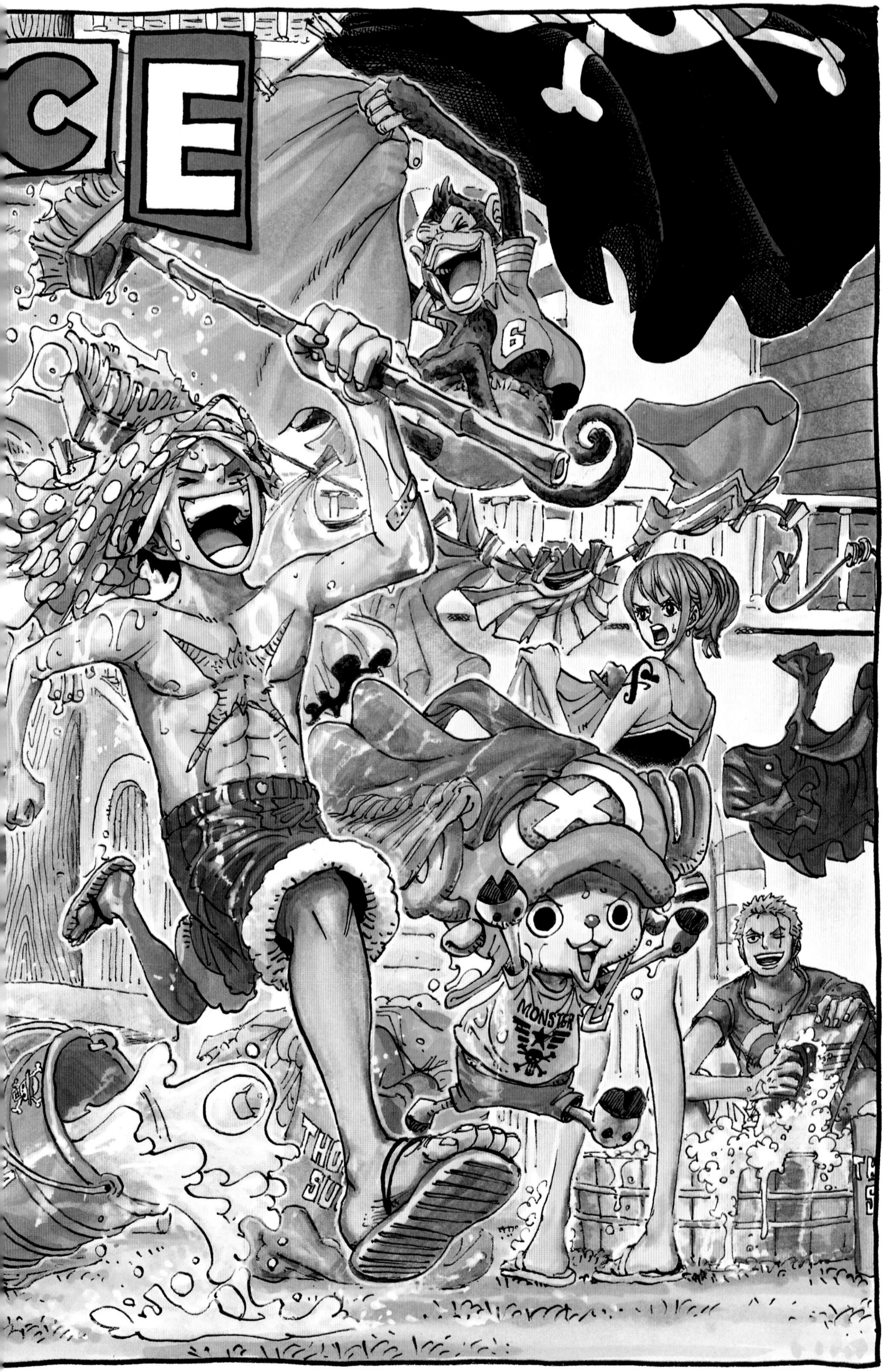
CE
MONSTER

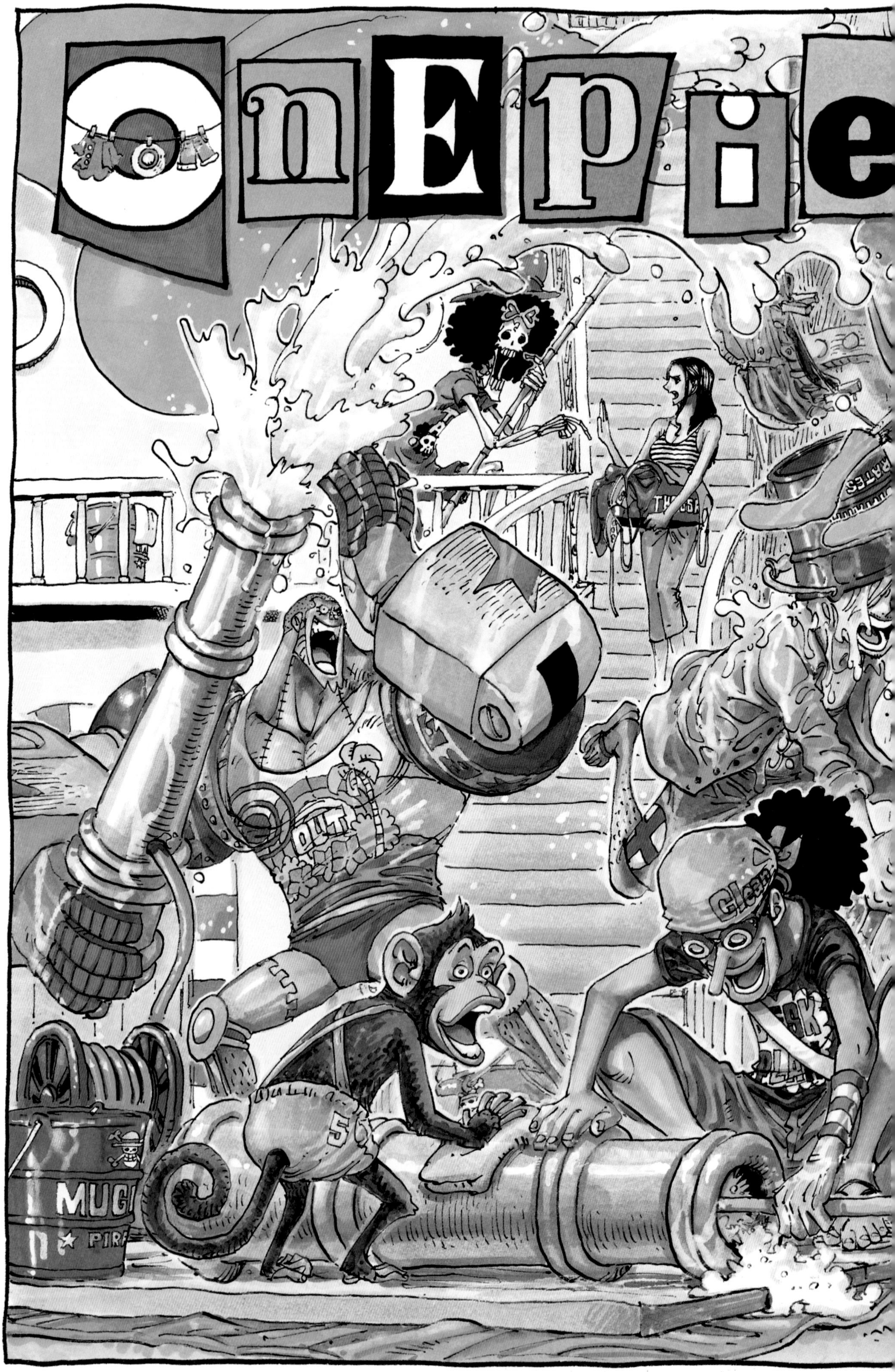
OnEPie
OUT
MUG
PIRA

BEWARE OF THE BEAR PIRATES!

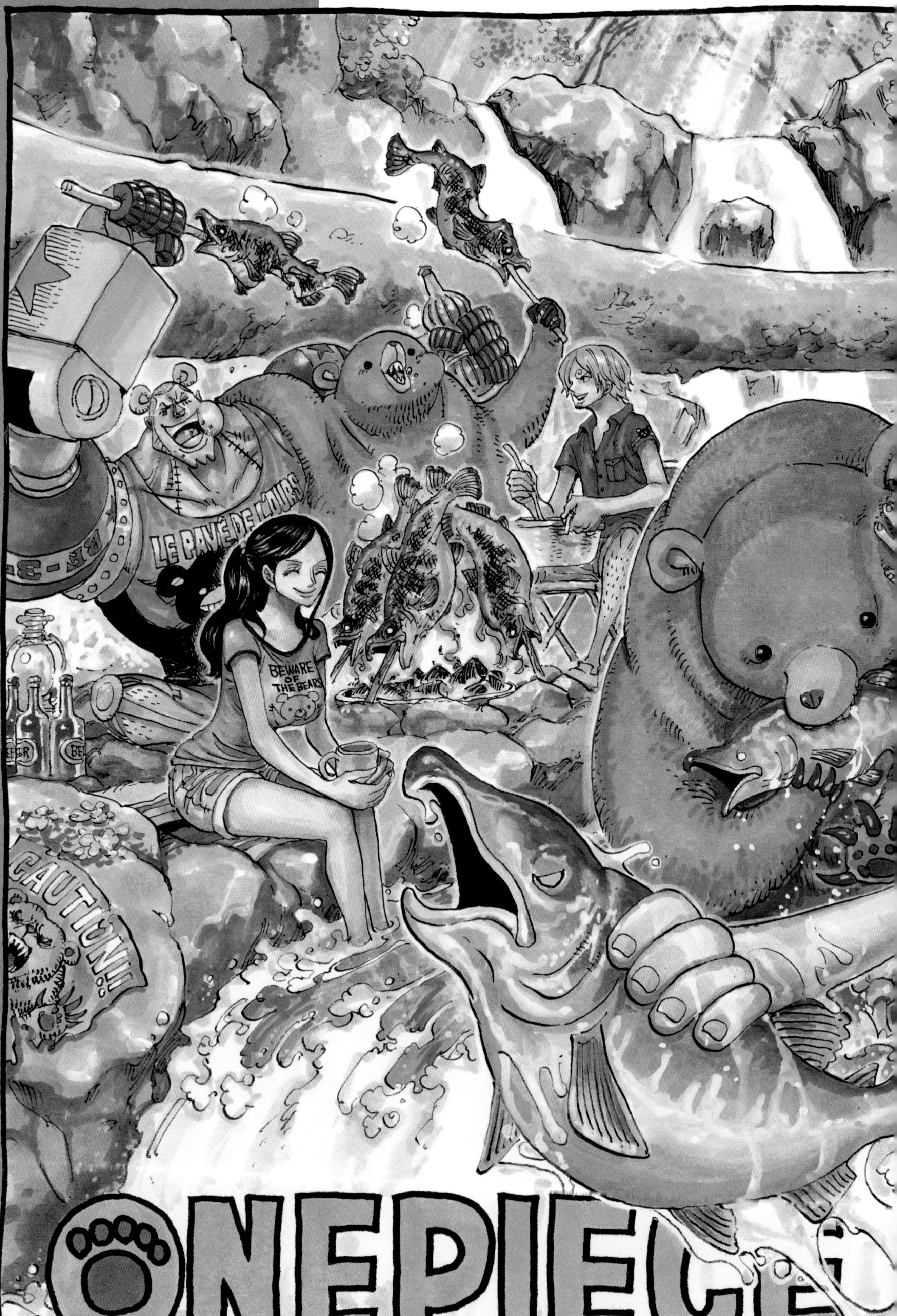
LE PAVÉ DE L'OURS
BEWARE OF THE BEARS
CAUTION!!
ONEPIECE

Comments P.124–125

When I was a kid, kung fu movies were all the rage. I'm guessing either Zolo or Sanji get killed by the evil Franky Army, so Luffy has to learn new kung fu from Master Usopp, then get revenge with his new Fire Dragon Kick!!

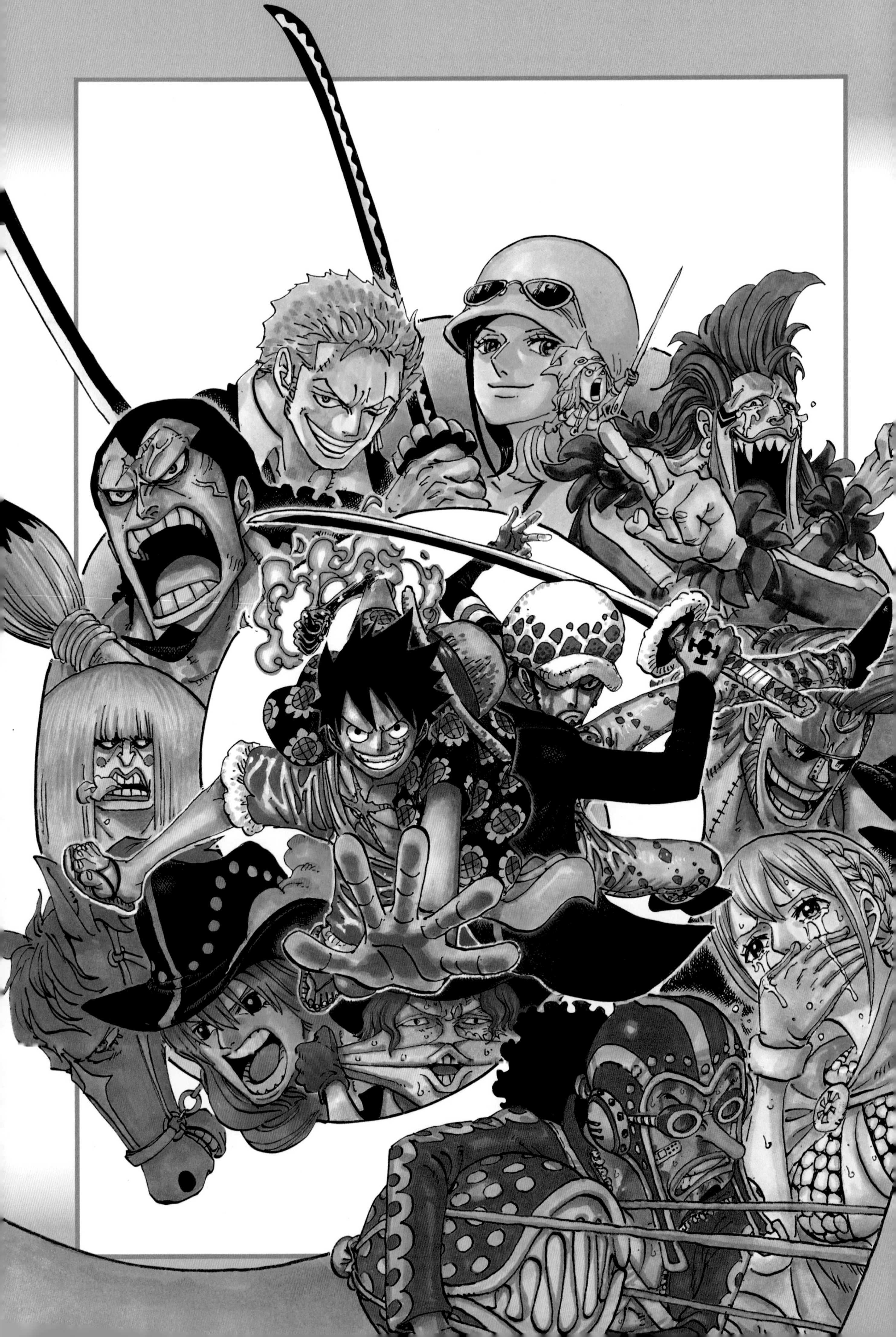

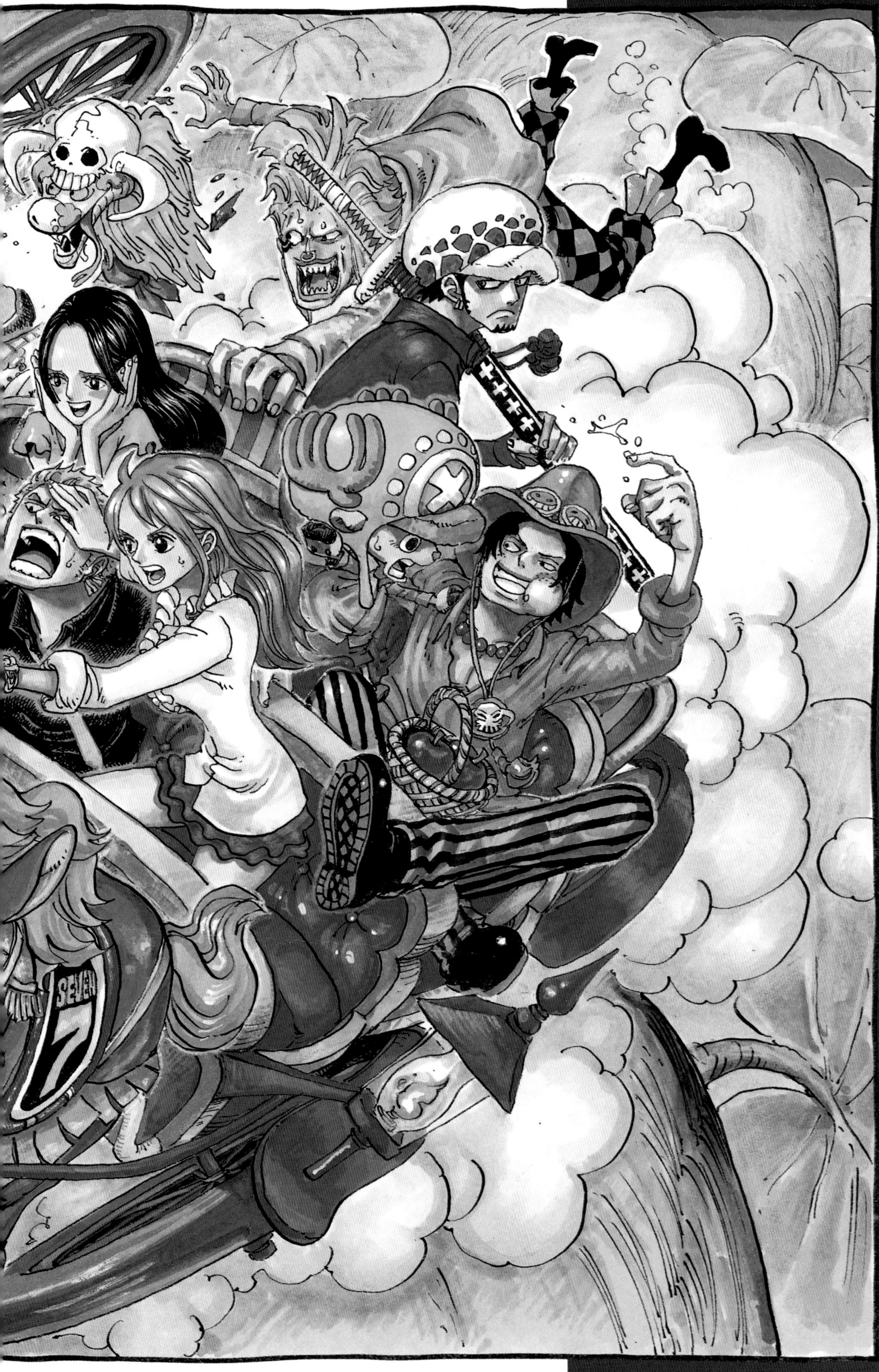
SEVEN
7

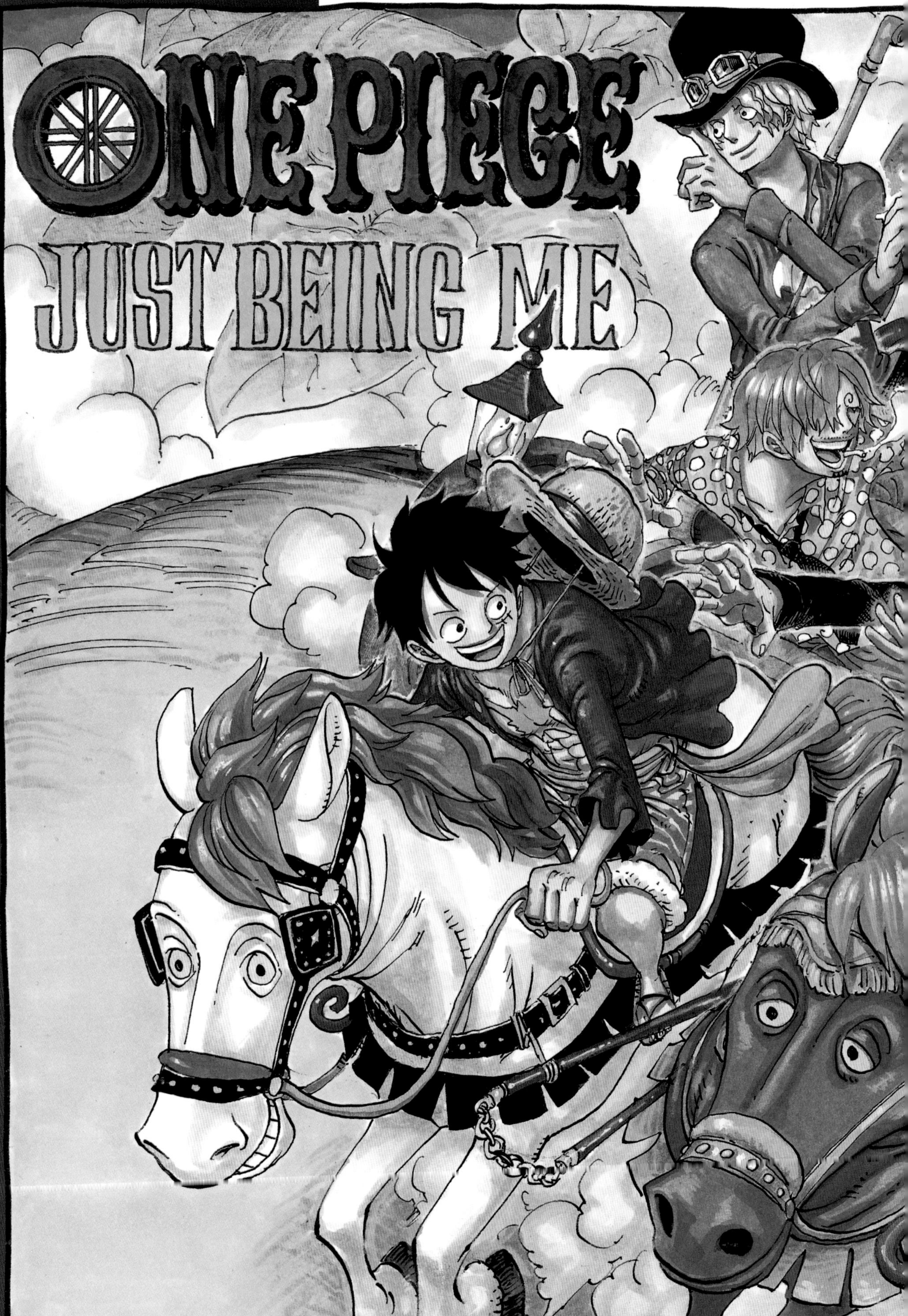
ONE PIECE
JUST BEING ME

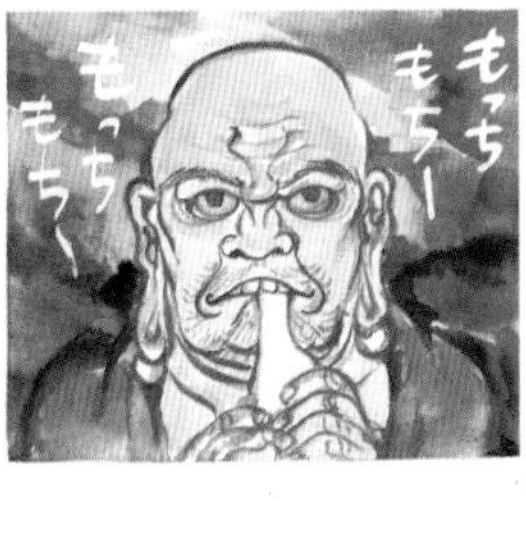
もっち
もちー
もっち
もち〜
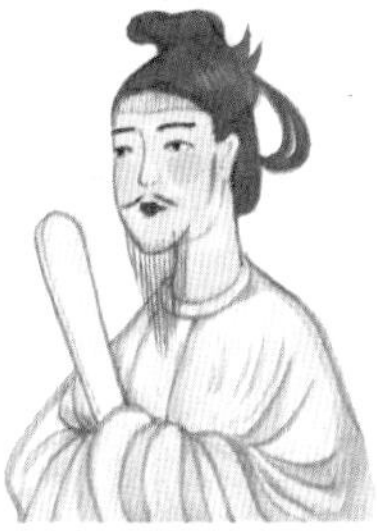
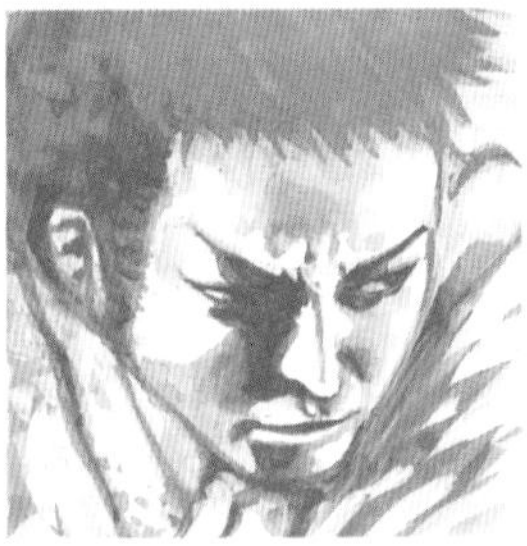
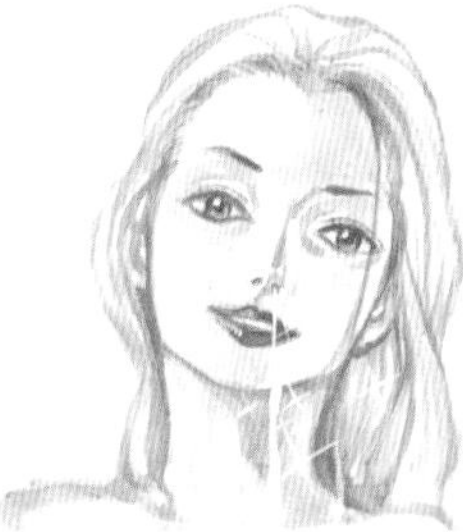
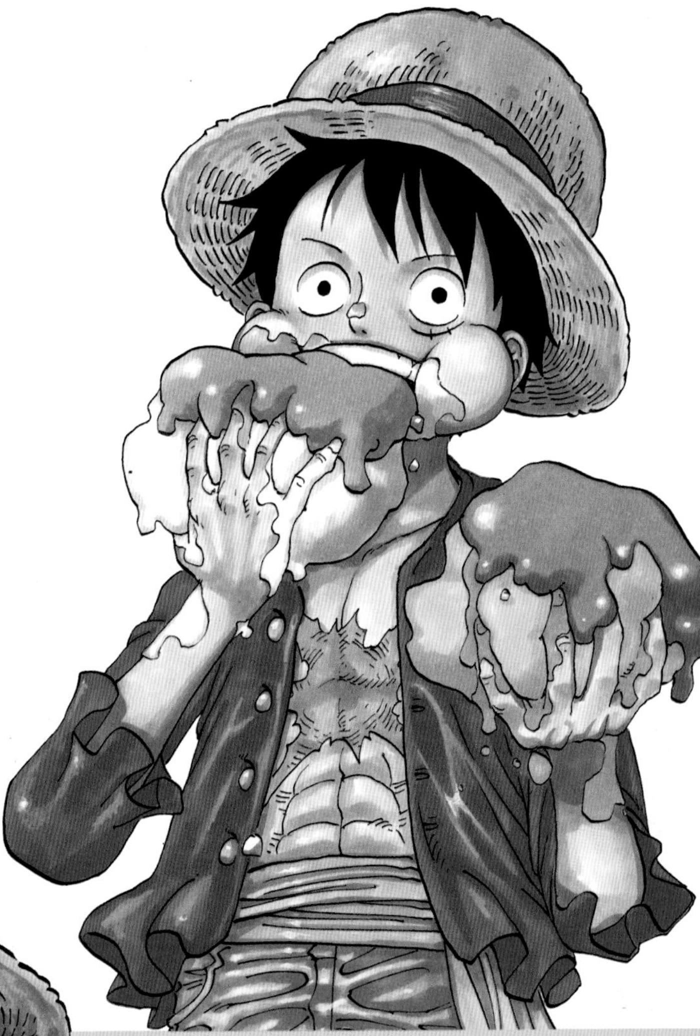
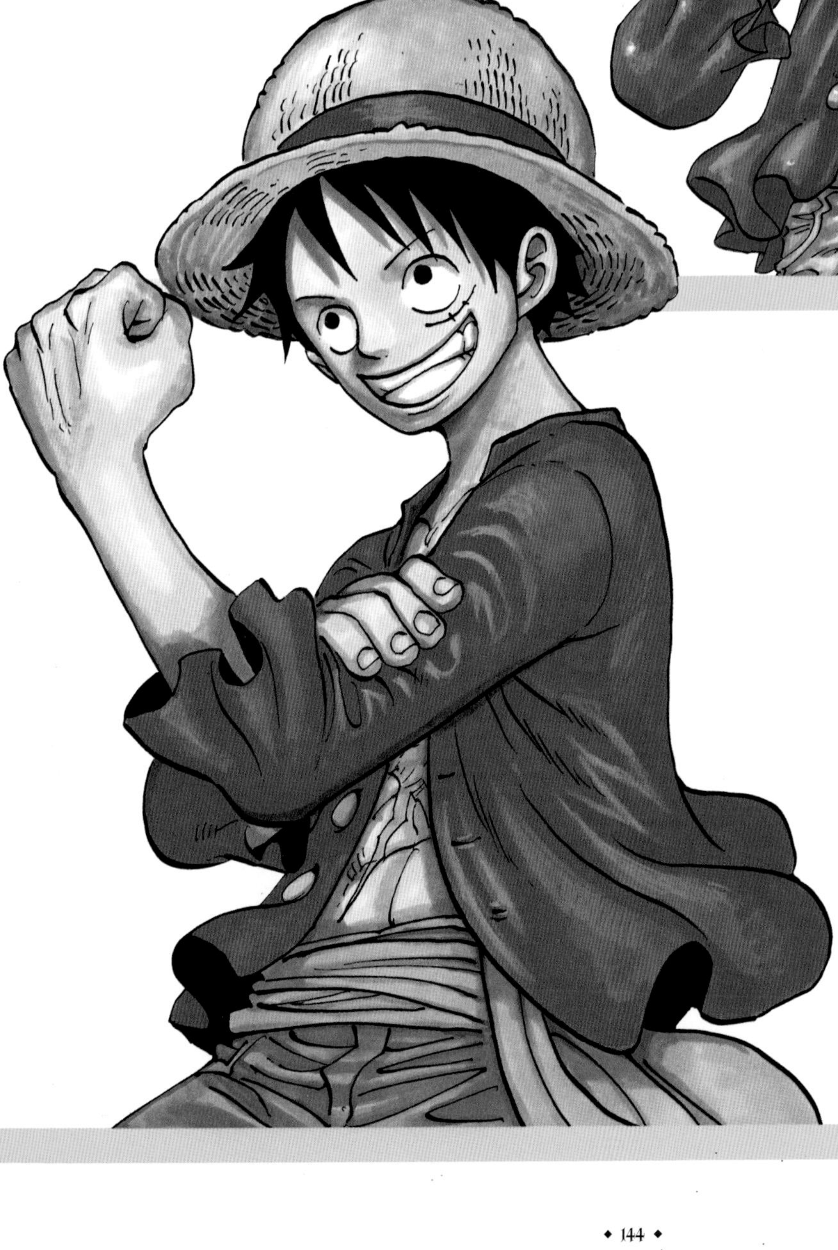

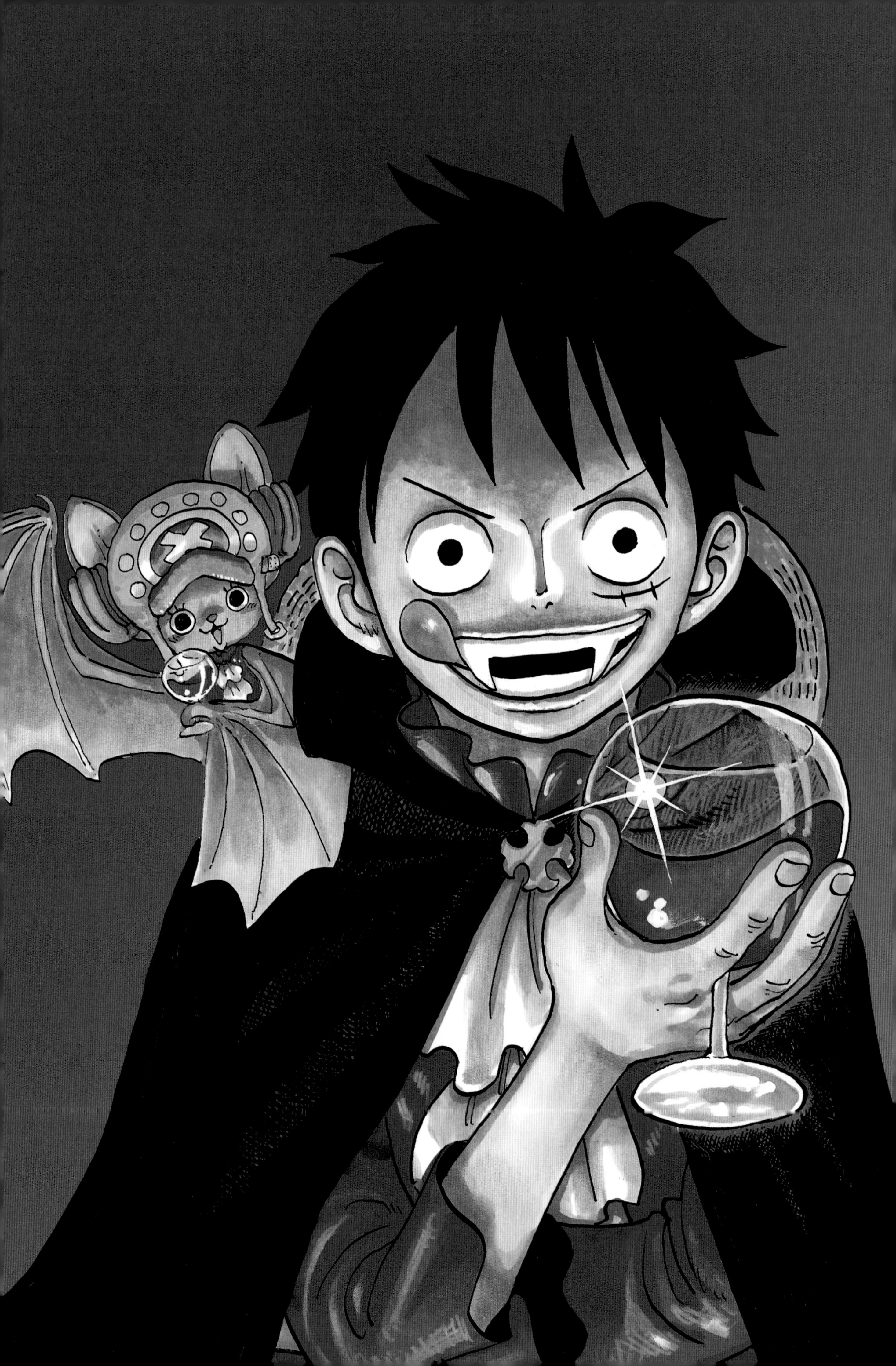

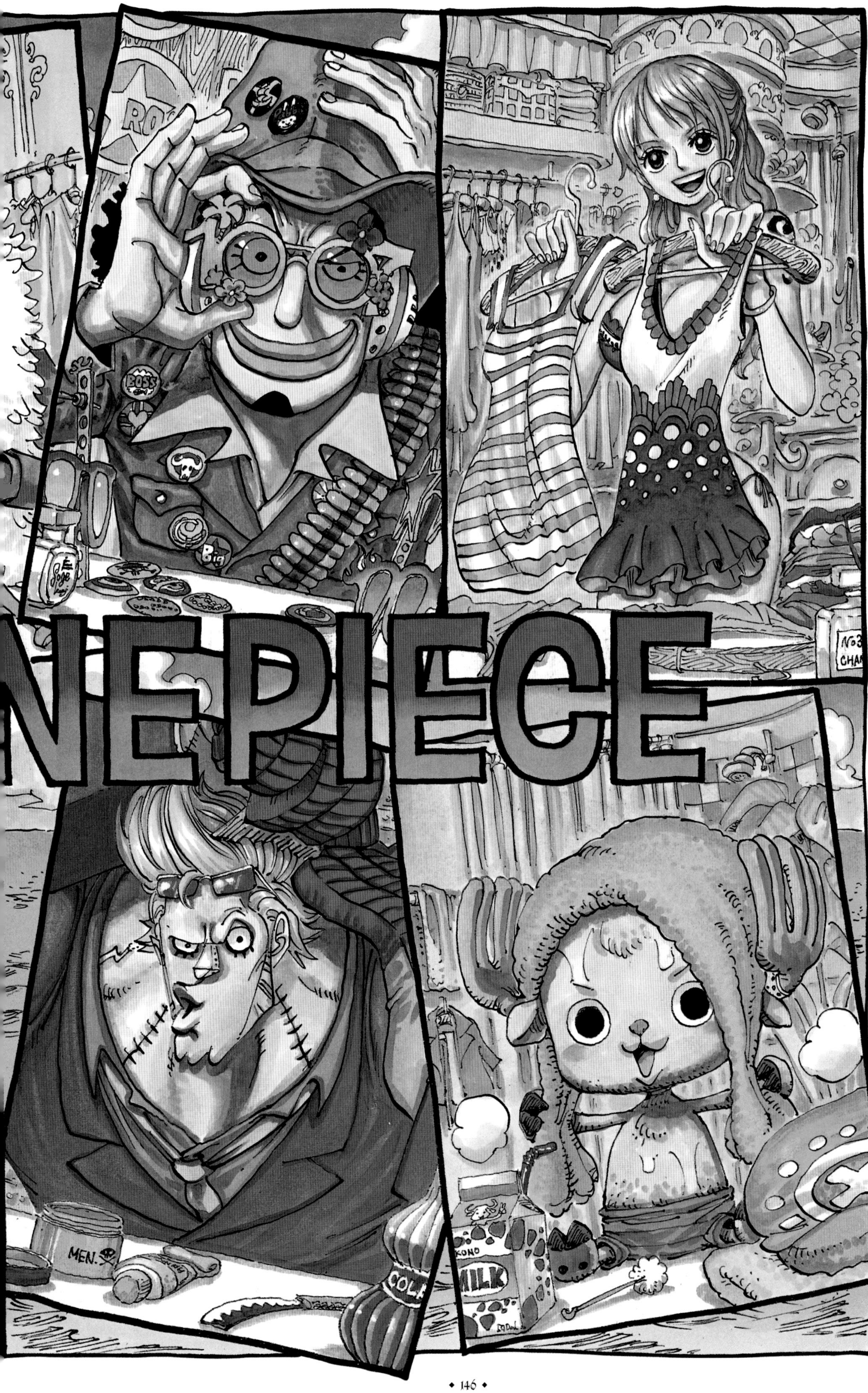

NEPIECE
BOSS
Big
MEN.
COLA
MILK

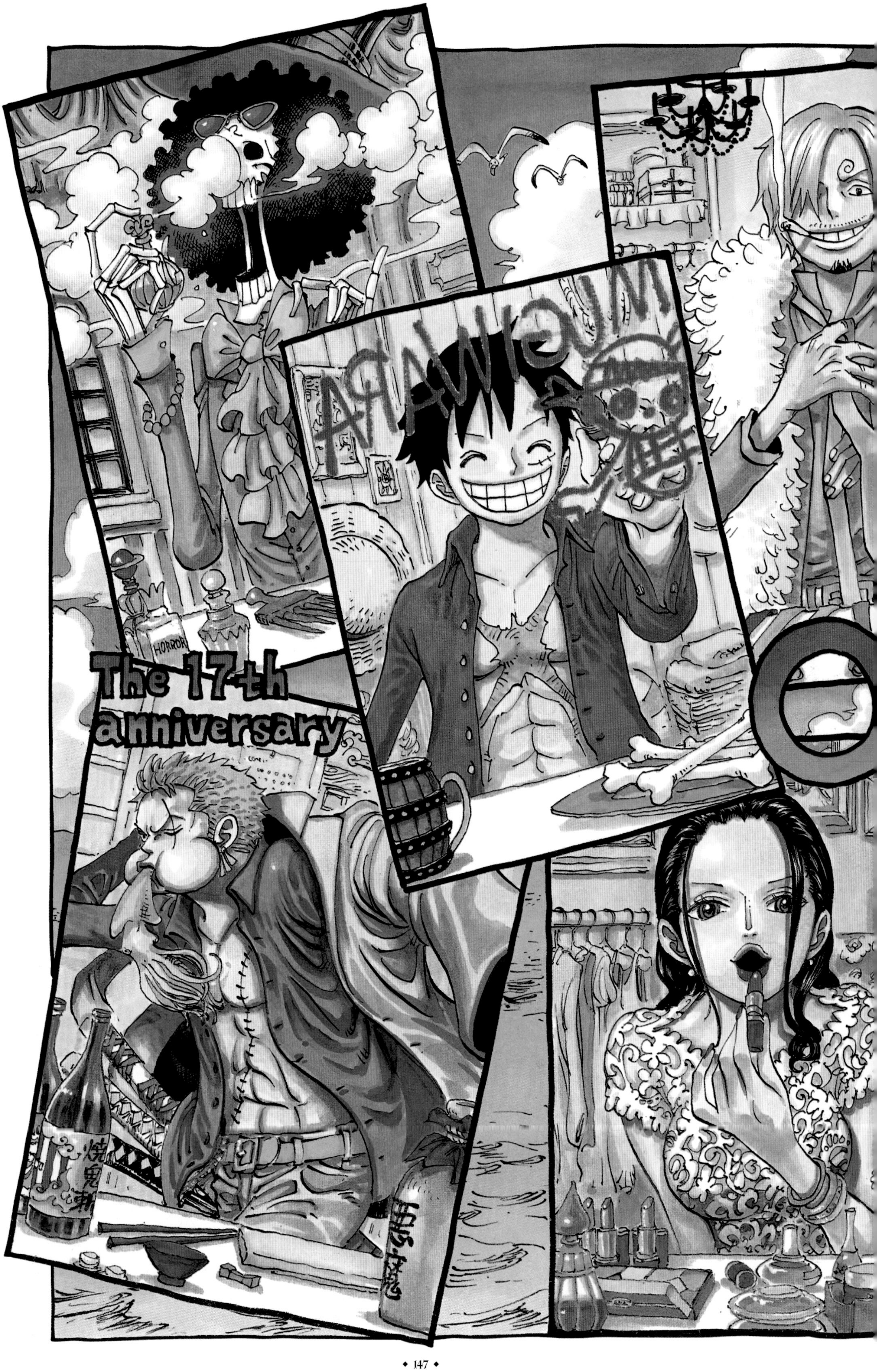
The 17th anniversary
MUGIWARA
HORROR

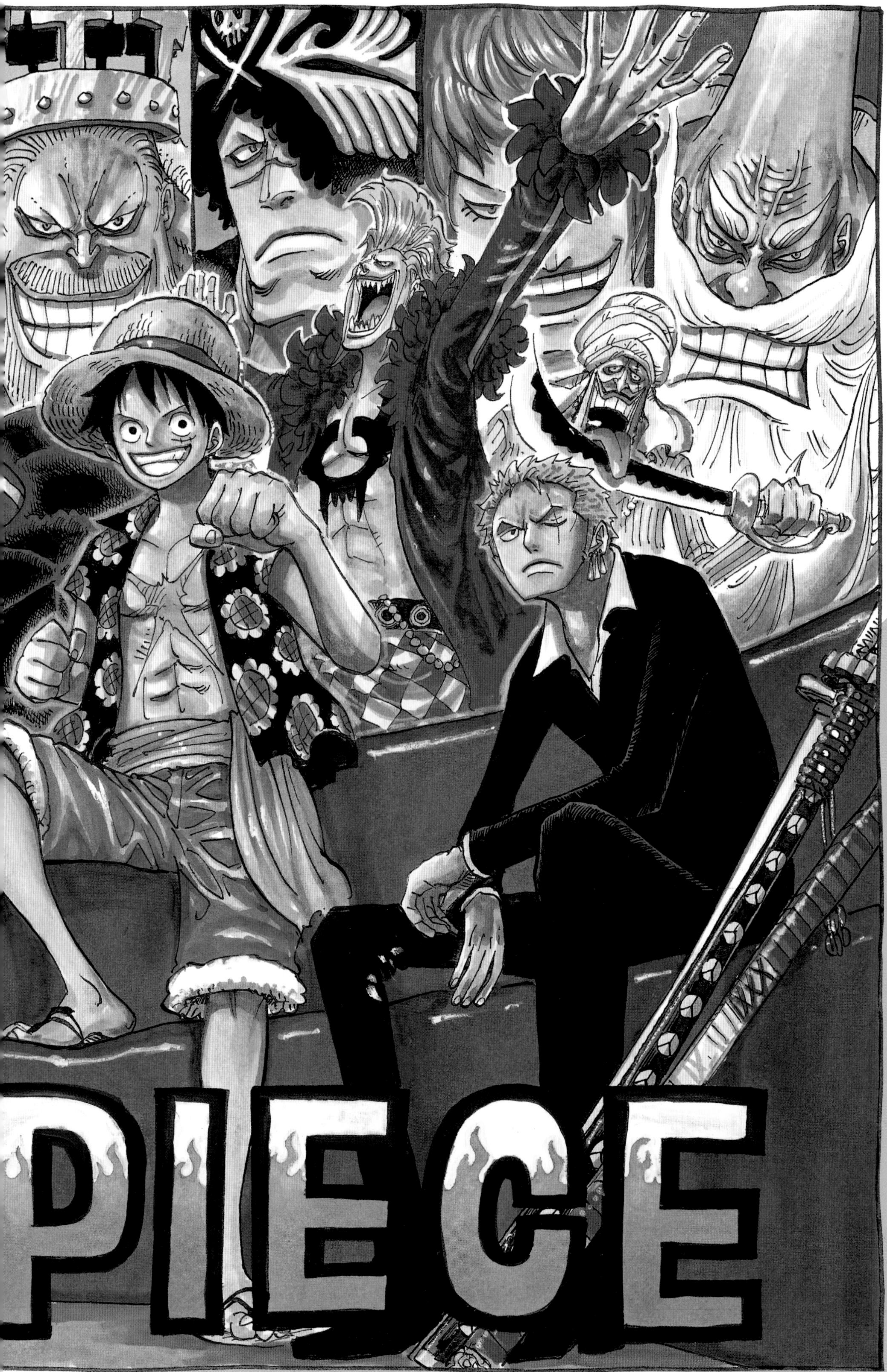
PIECE

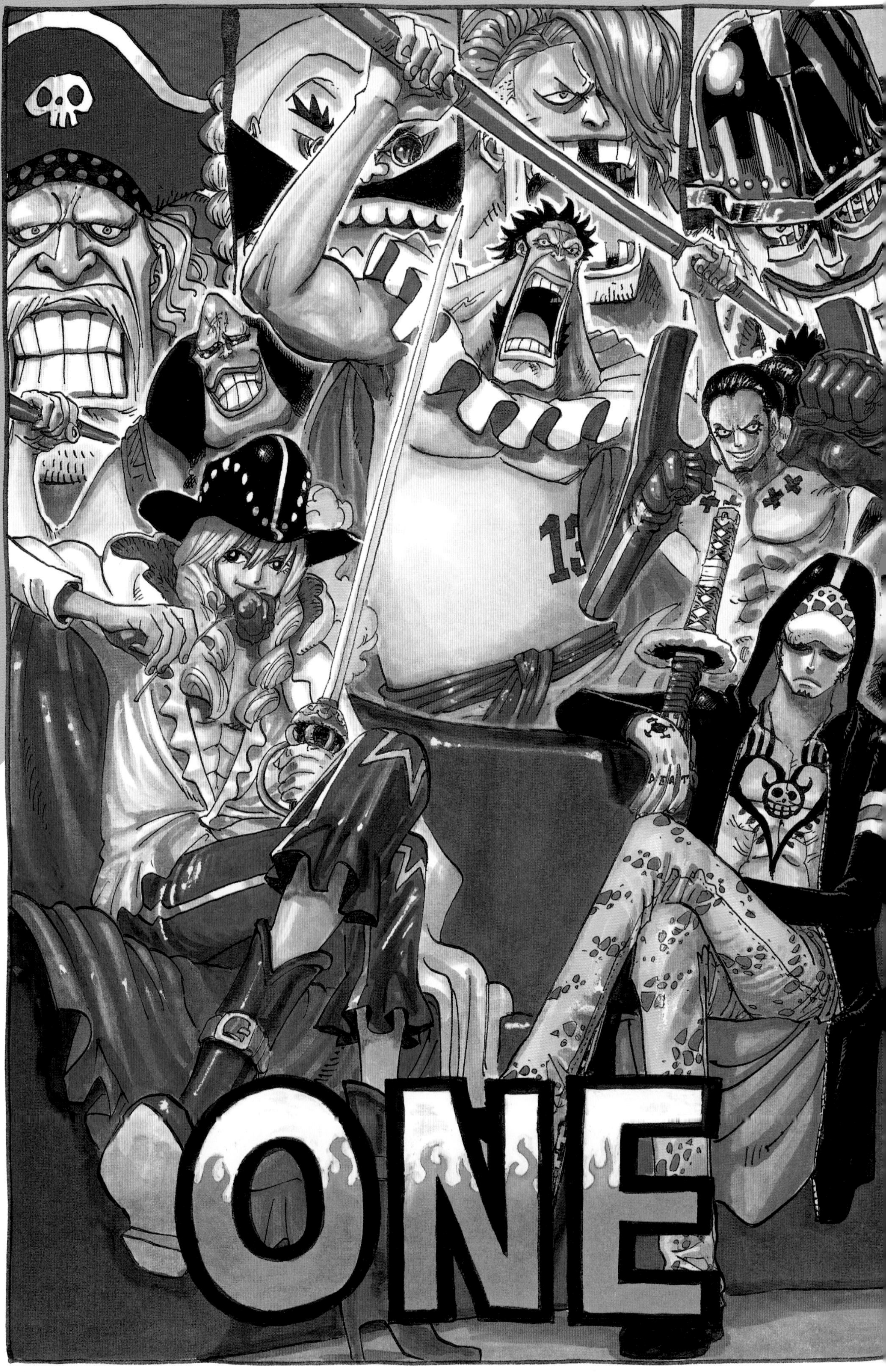
ONE
13

COLLABORATION

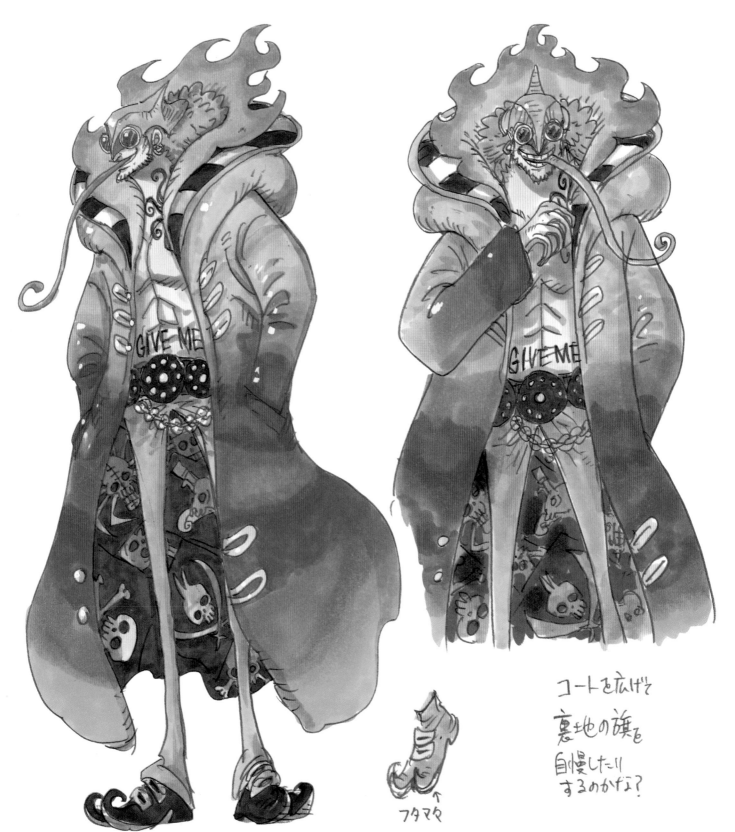

フタマタ

コートを広げて
裏地の旗を
自慢したり
するのかな？

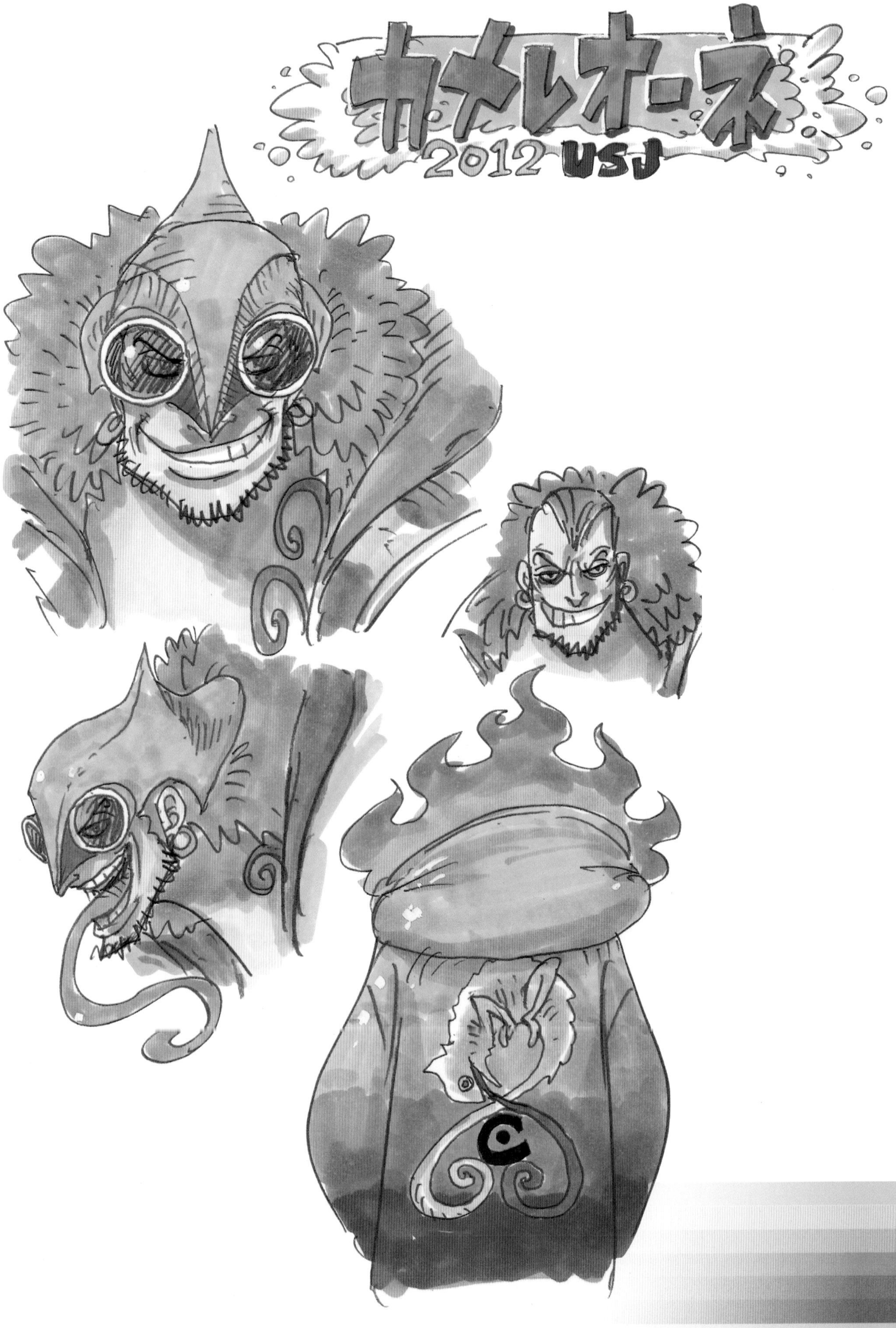
カメレオーネ
2012 USJ

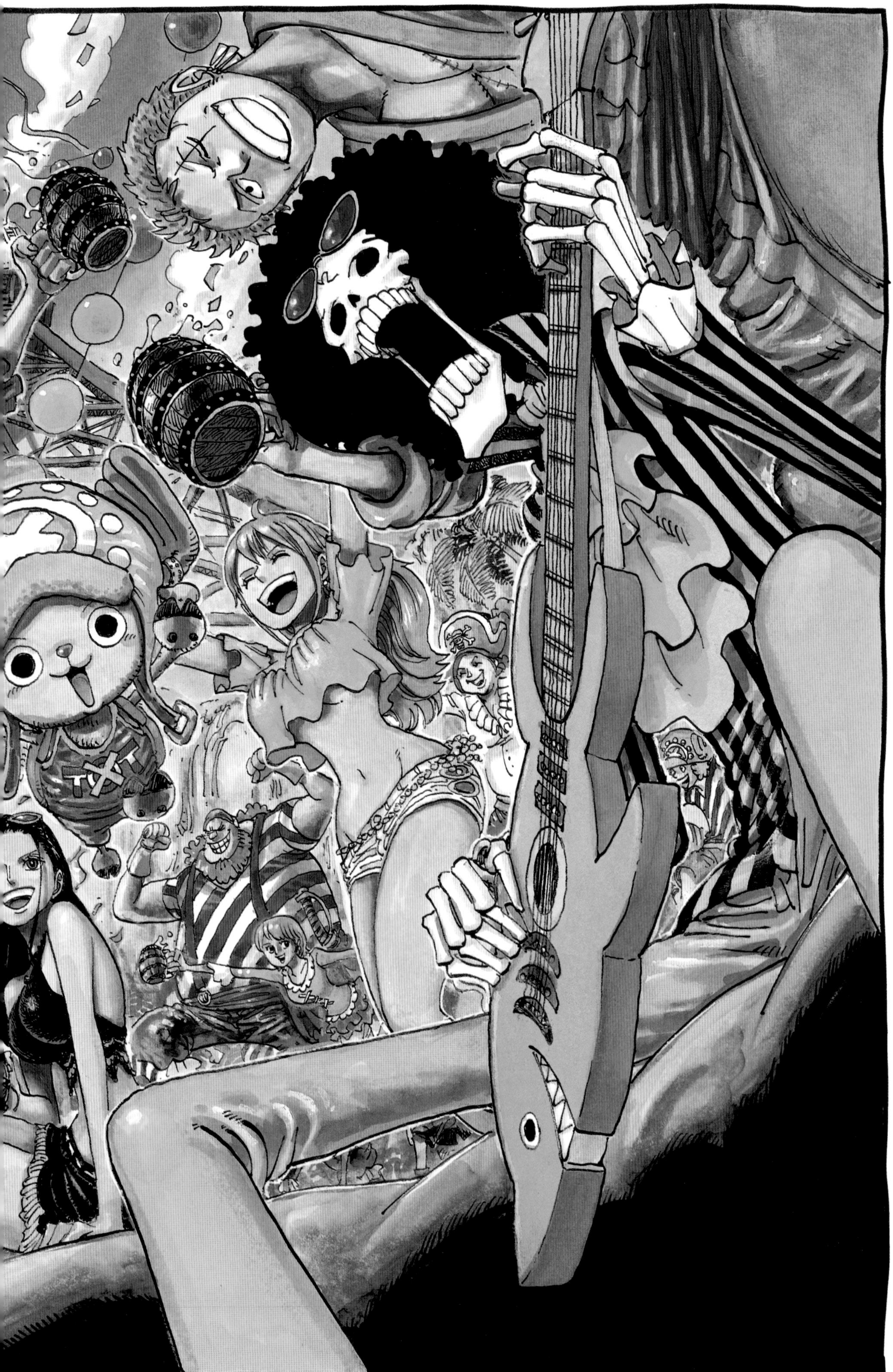

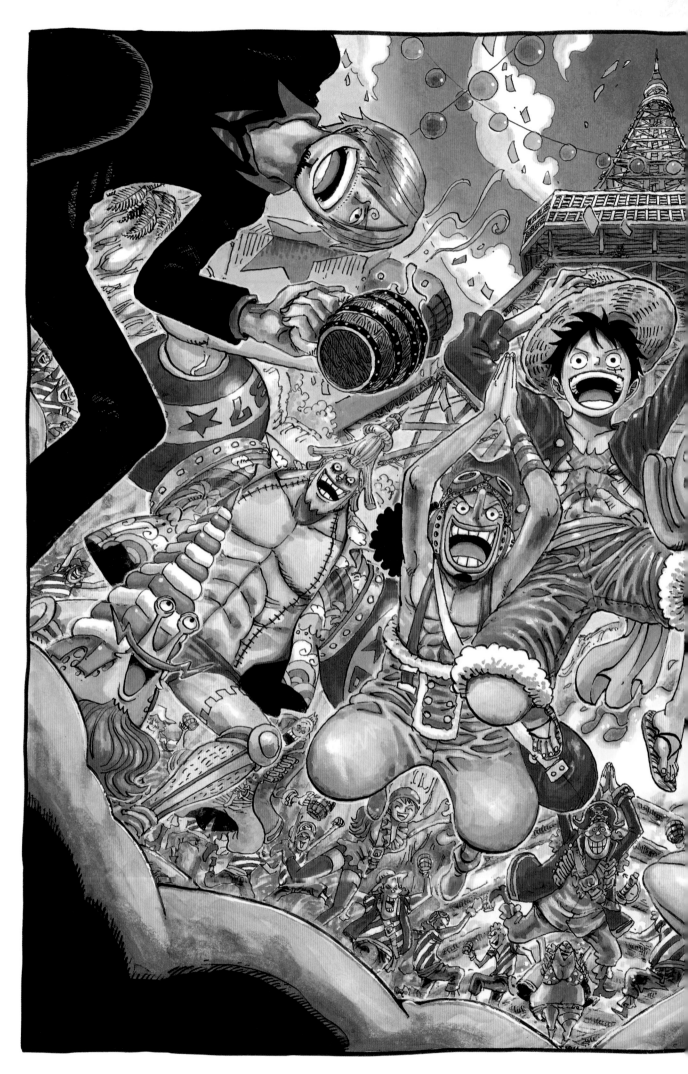

2015

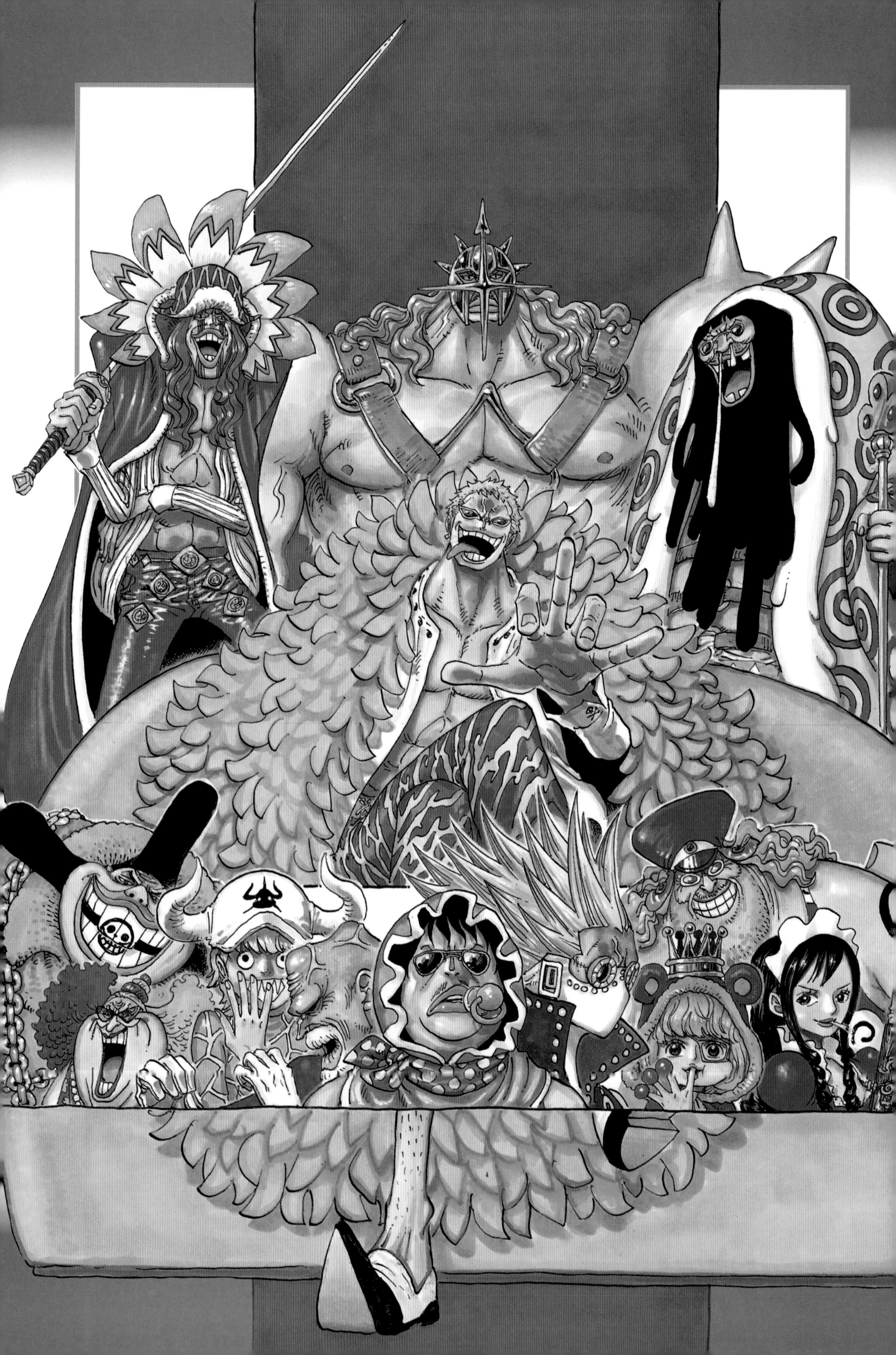

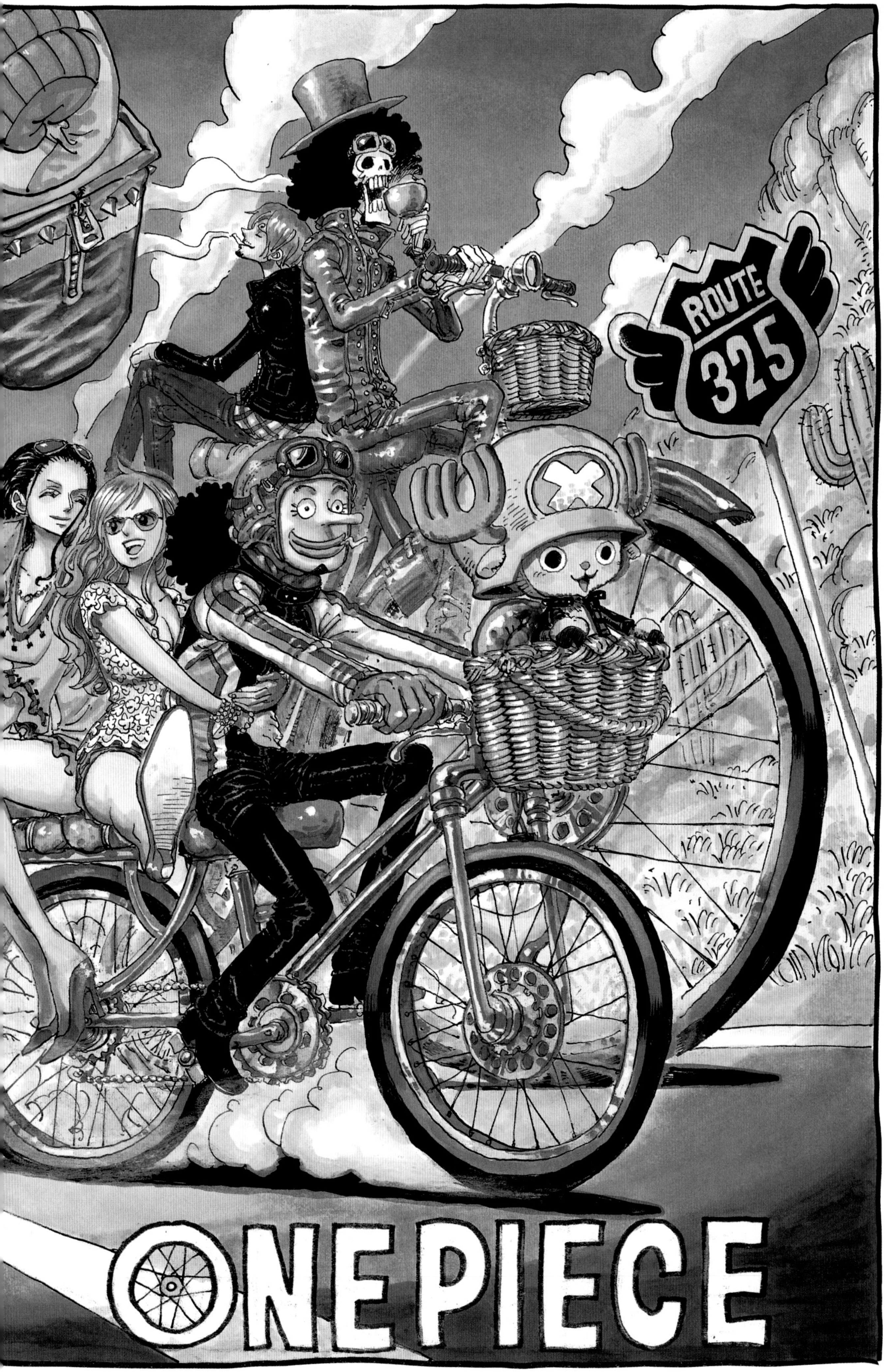
ROUTE
325
ONE PIECE

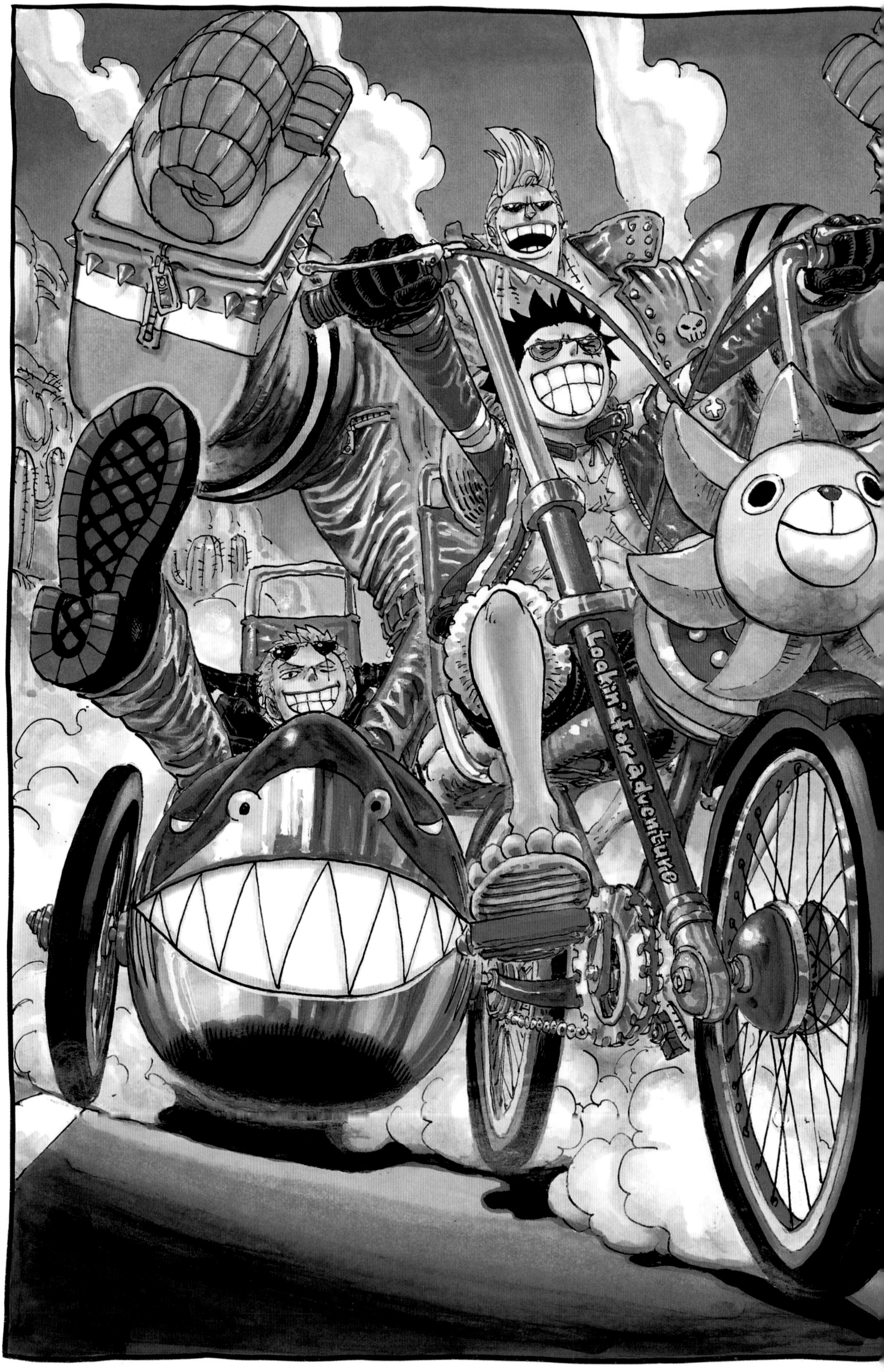
Lookin' for adventure

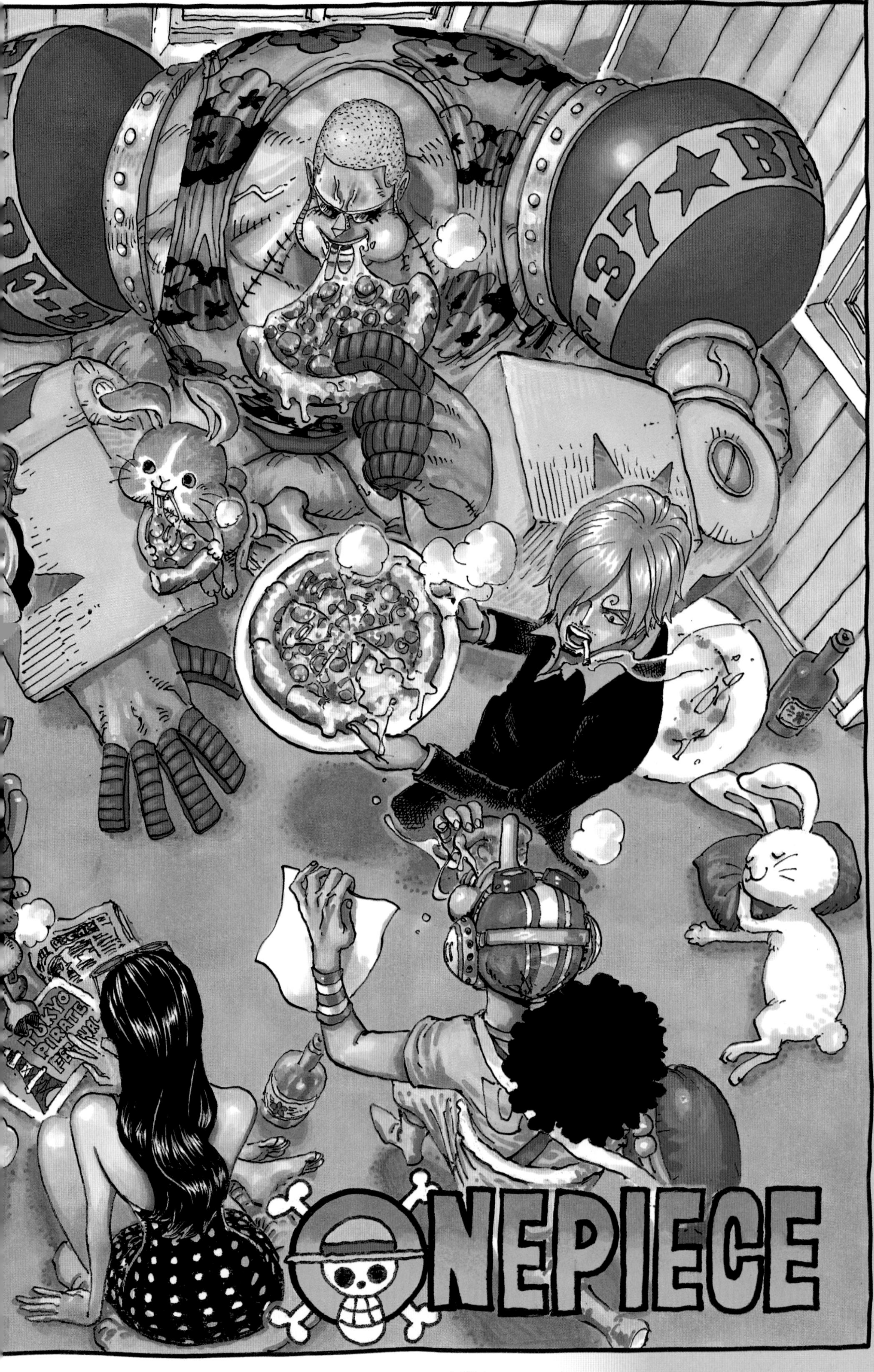
ONE PIECE

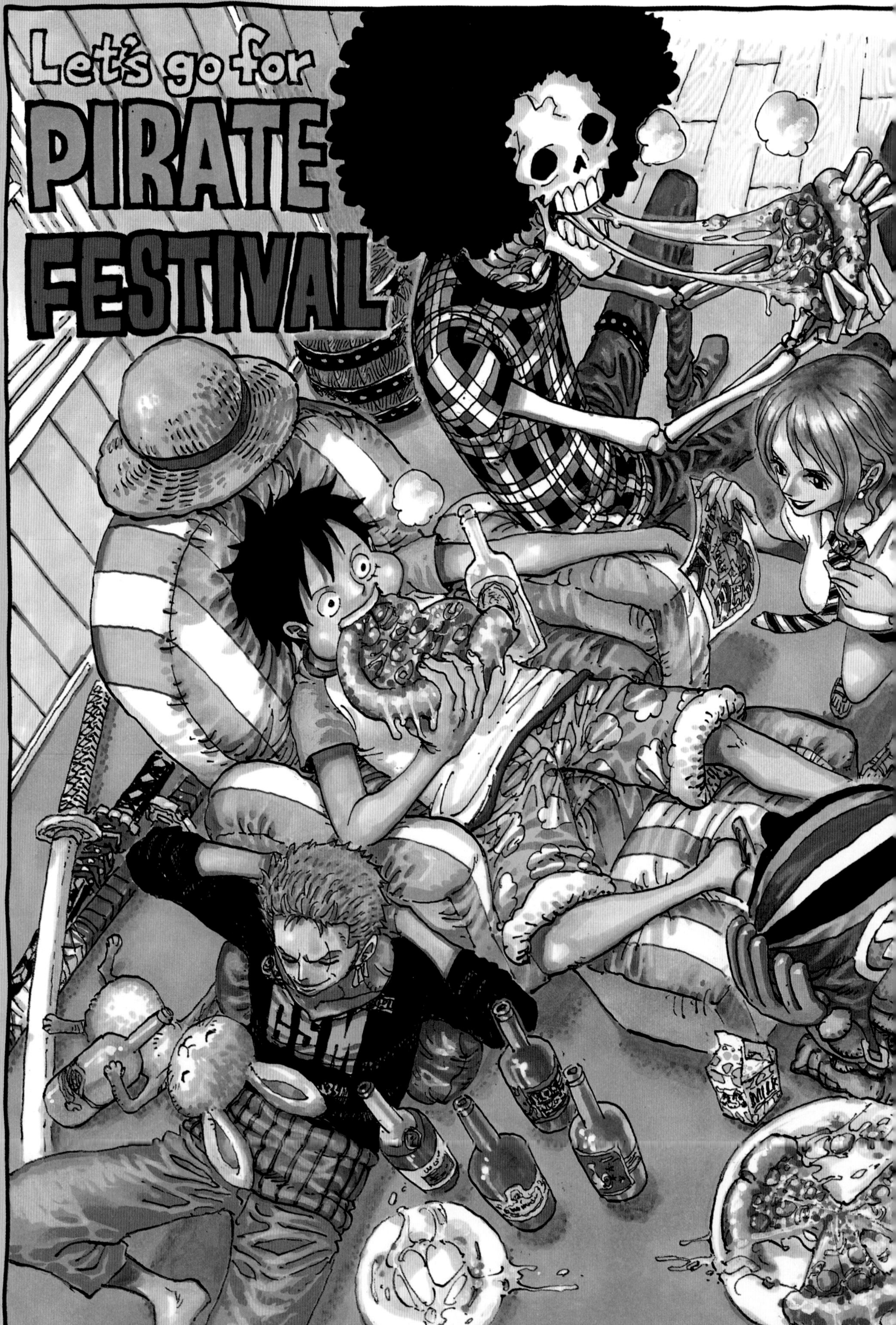
Let's go for
PIRATE
FESTIVAL
MILK

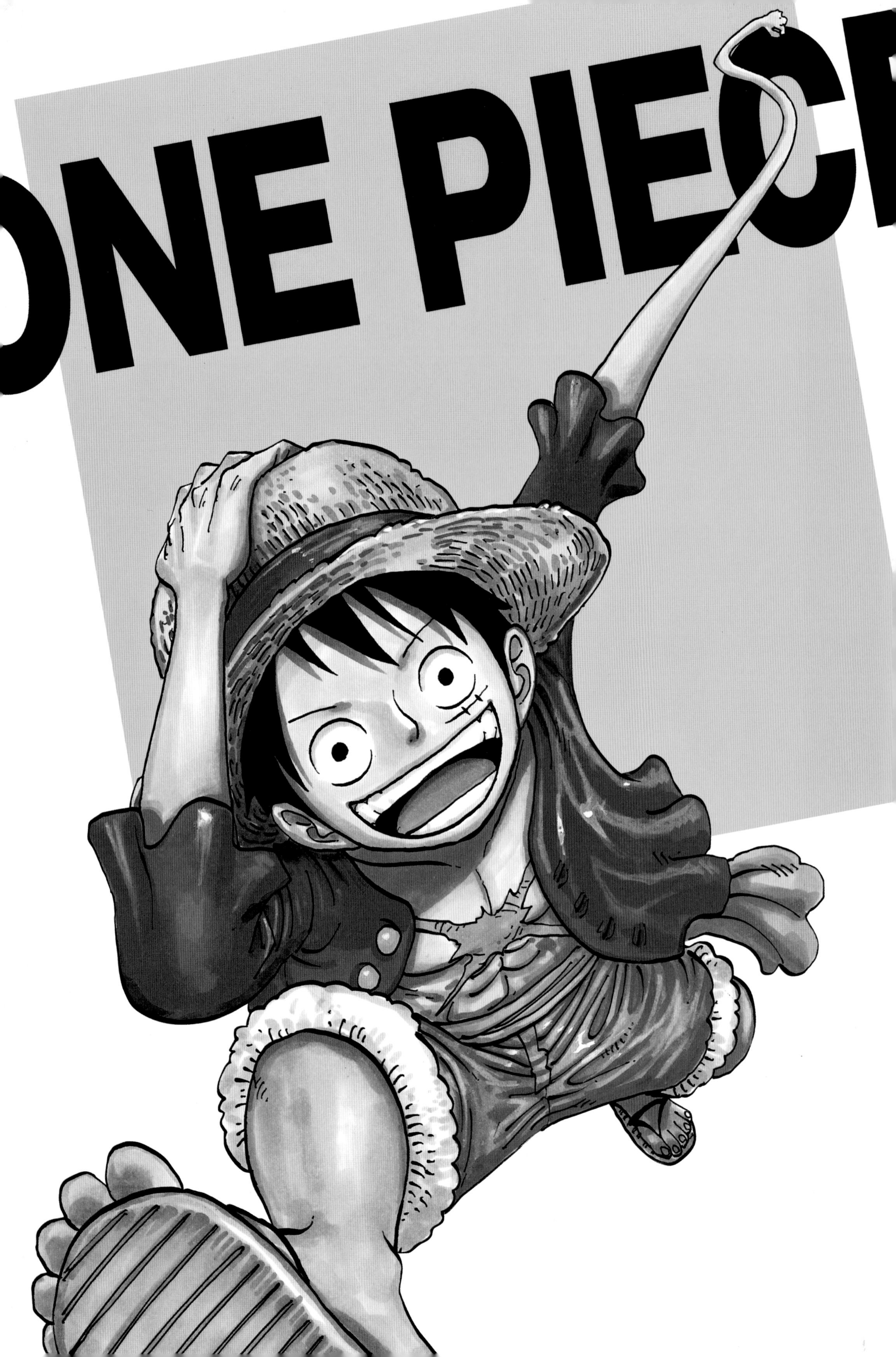
ONE PIECE

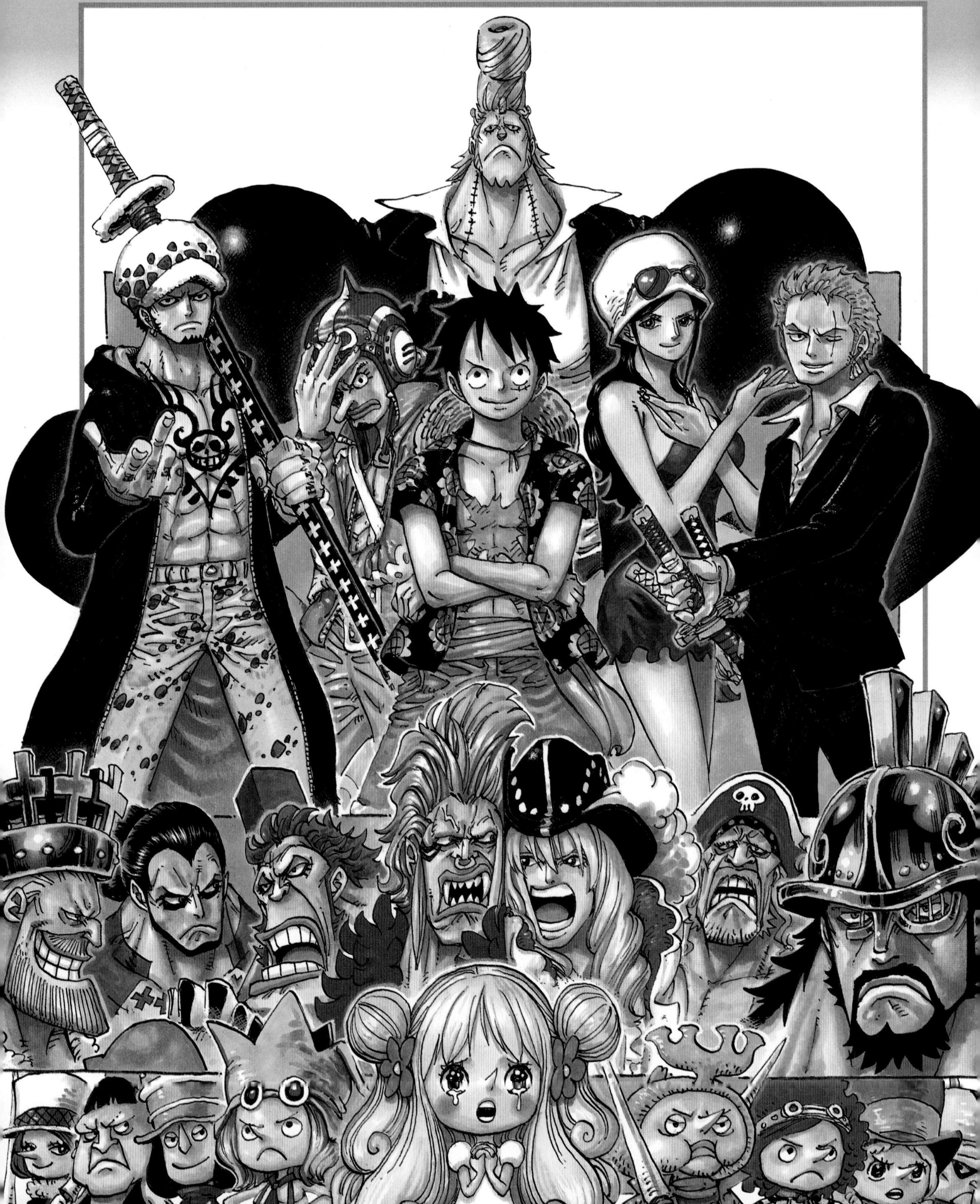

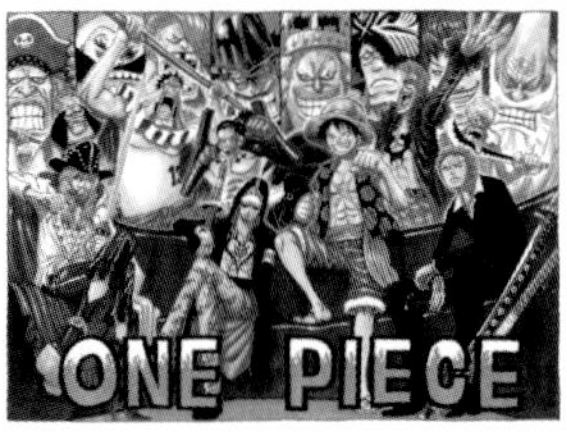
ONE PIECE

Comments P.148–149

This was a piece I did while I was in the hospital recovering from my tonsillectomy. The color of the lights there was different from my studio, so the skin tones feel a bit different. It hasn't taken me so long to do a drawing in years.

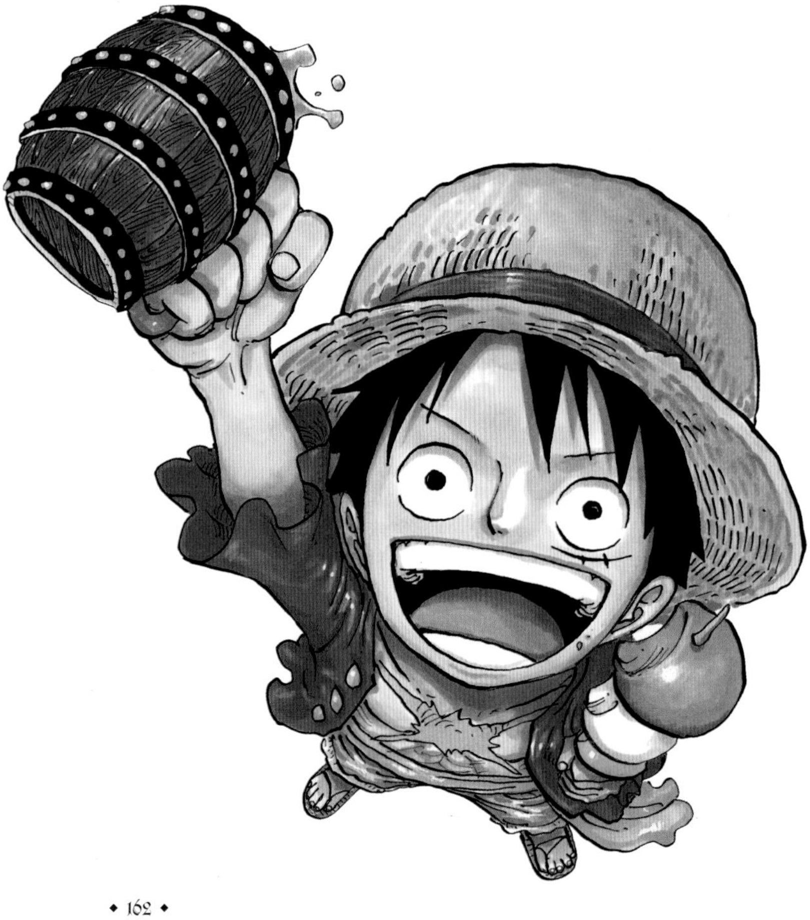

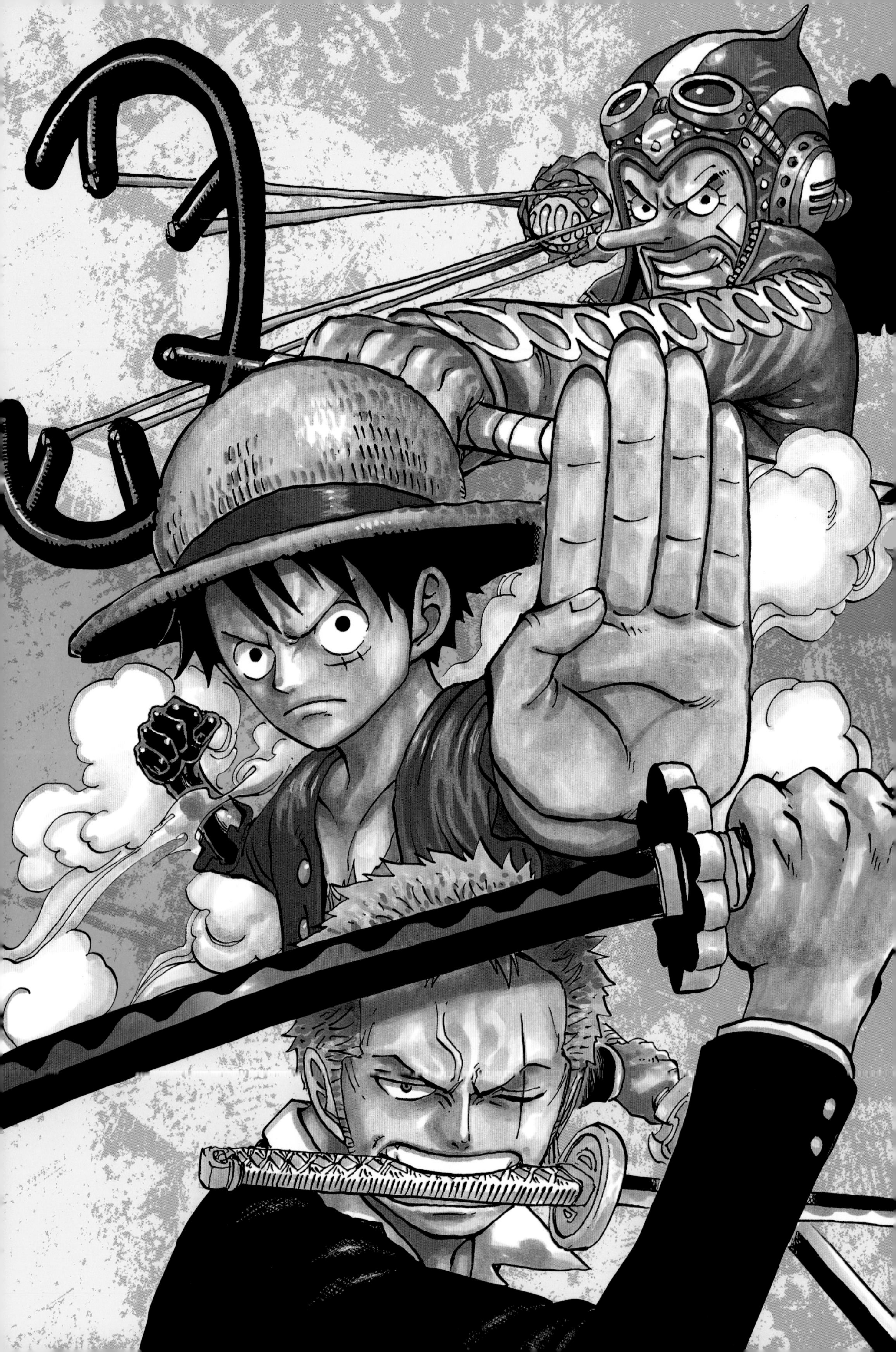

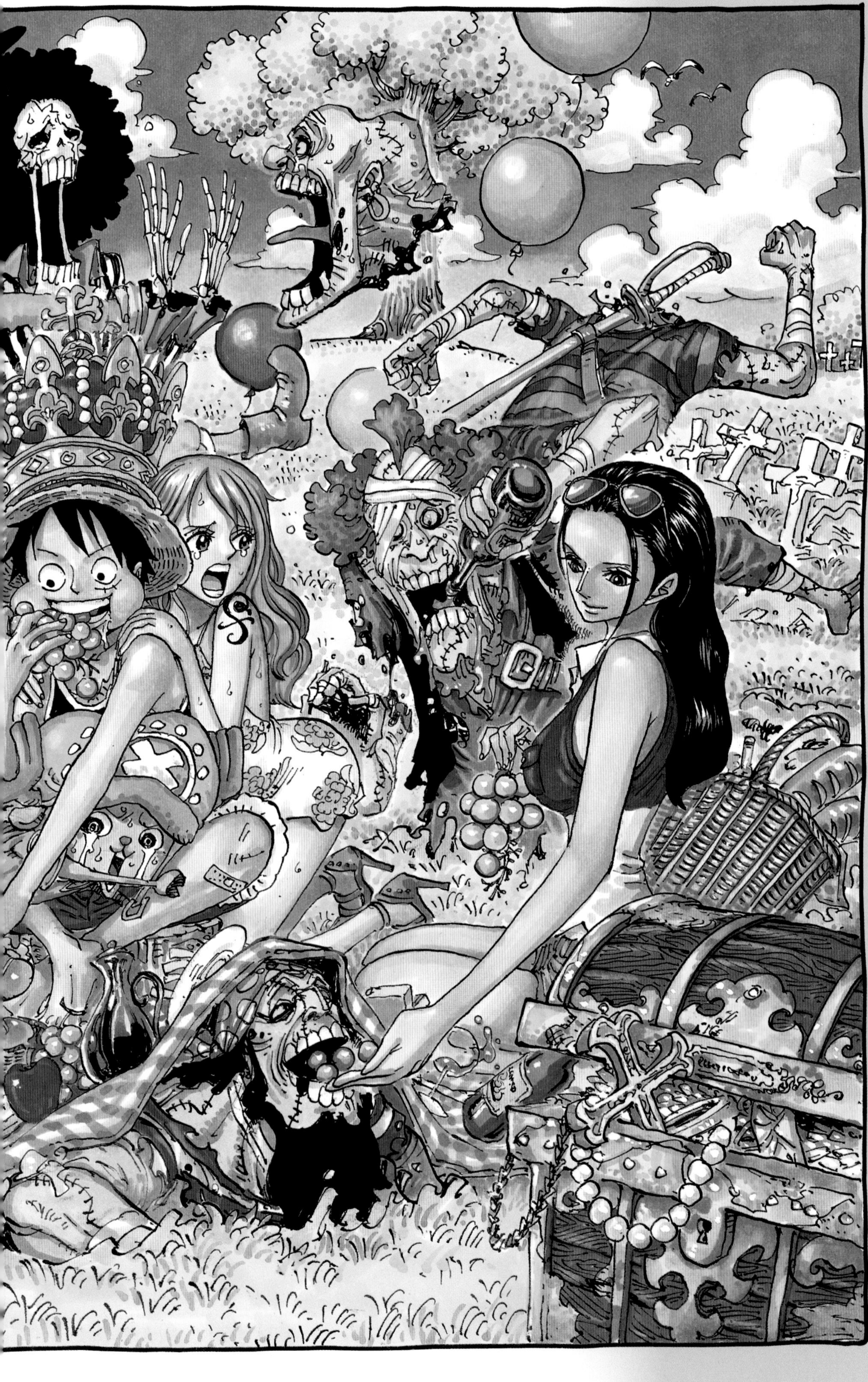

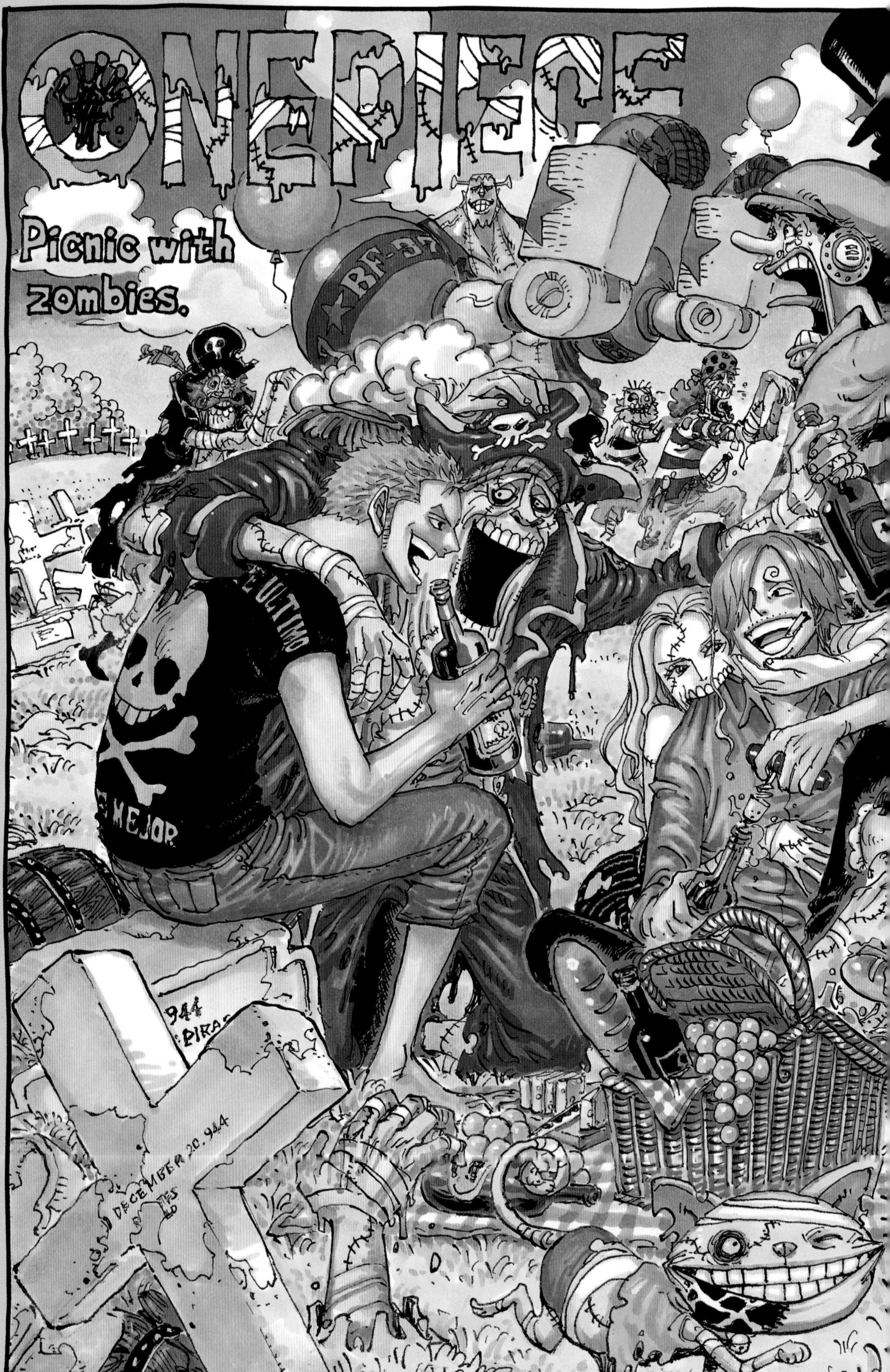
ONE PIECE
Picnic with zombies.
BF-37
EL ULTIMO
EL MEJOR
DECEMBER 20. 944

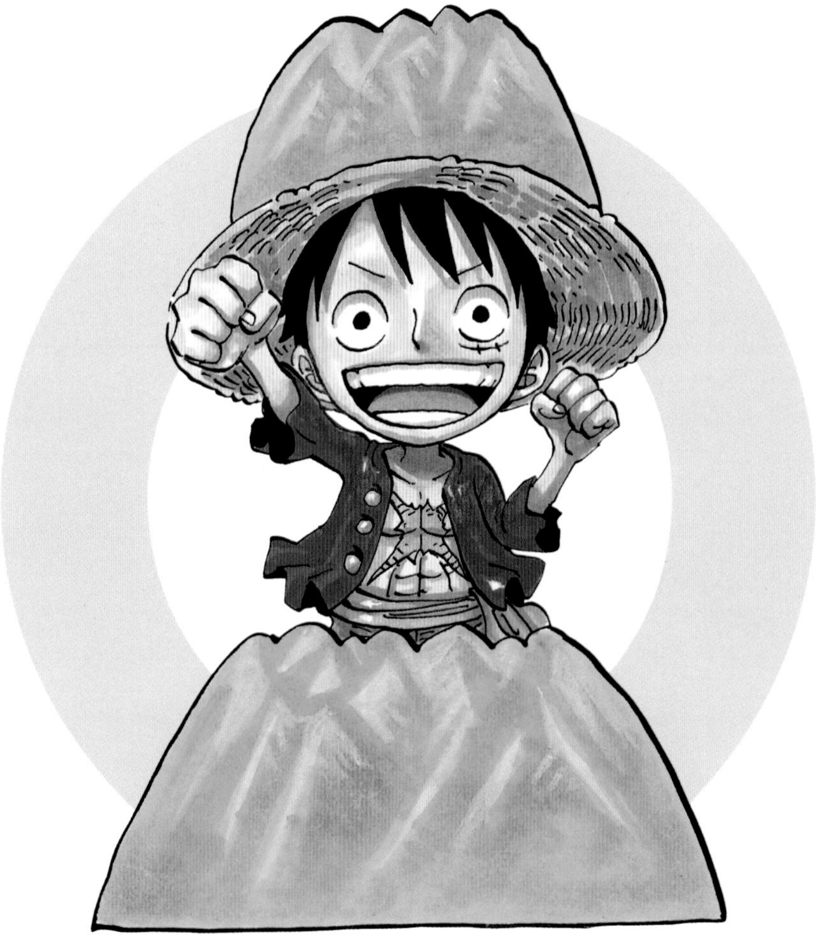

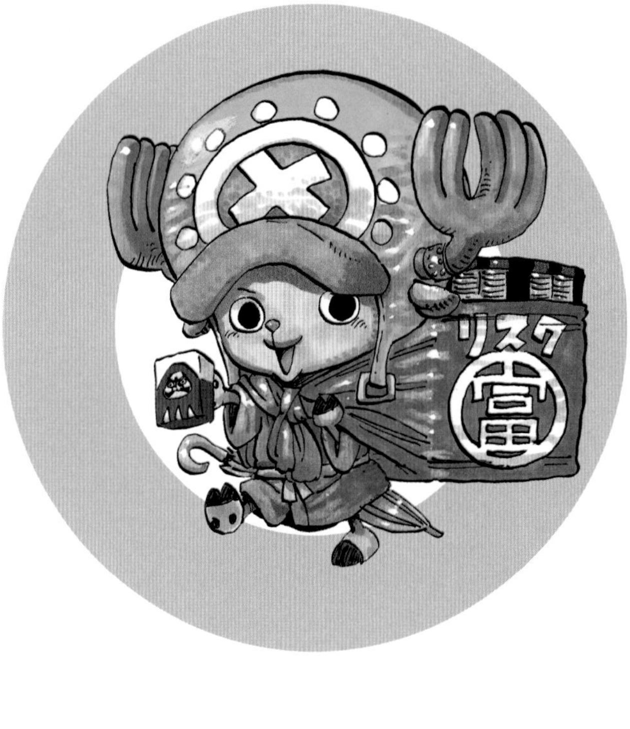
リスク
富

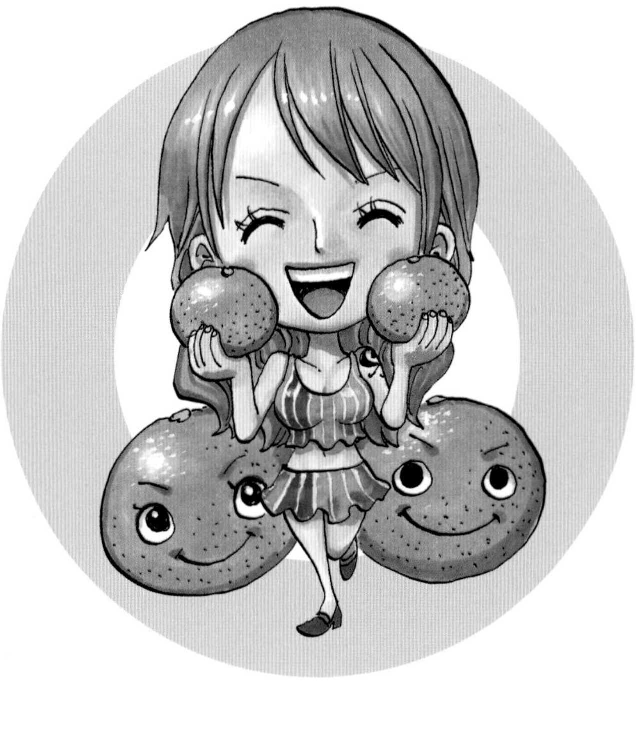

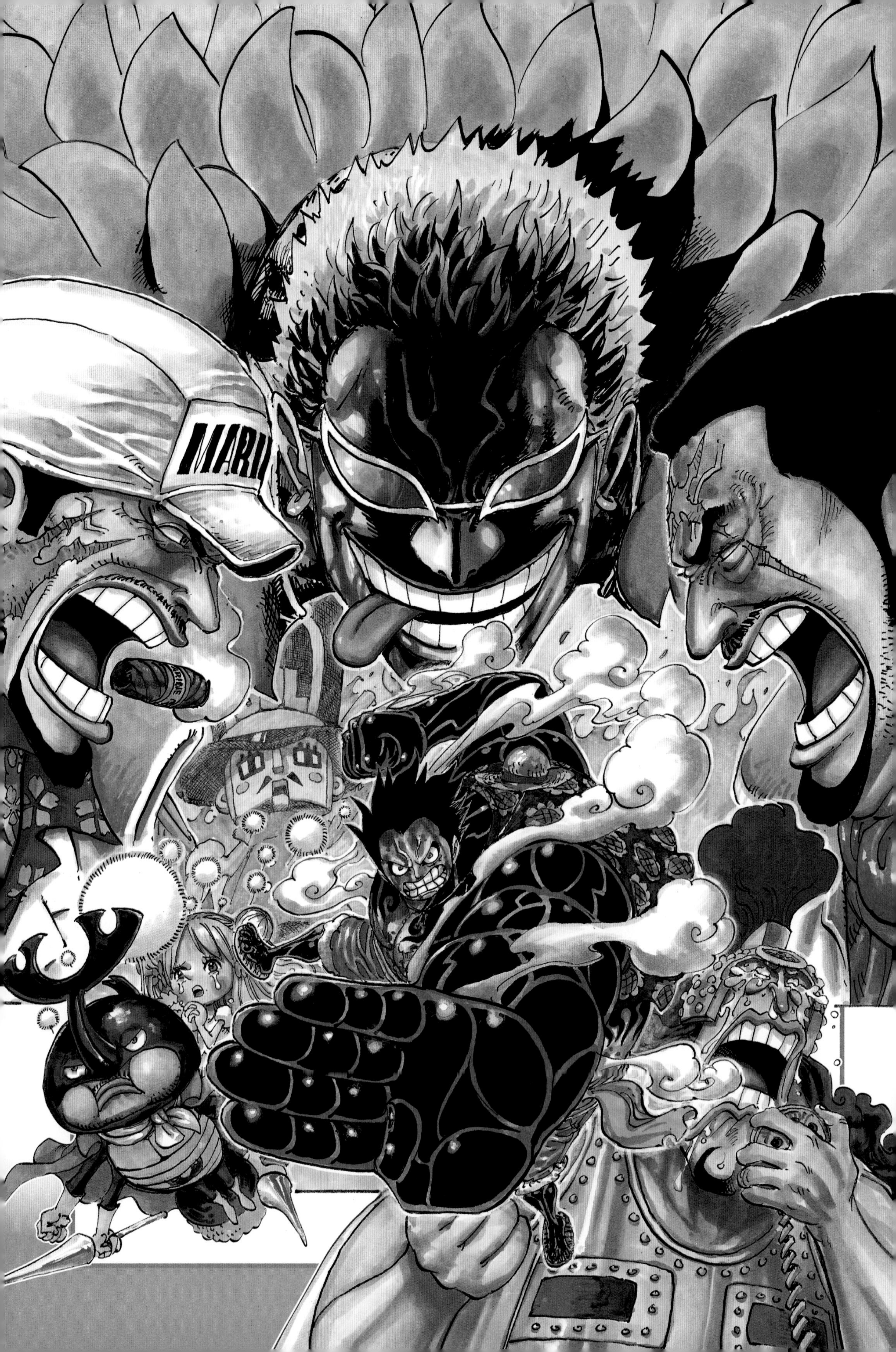

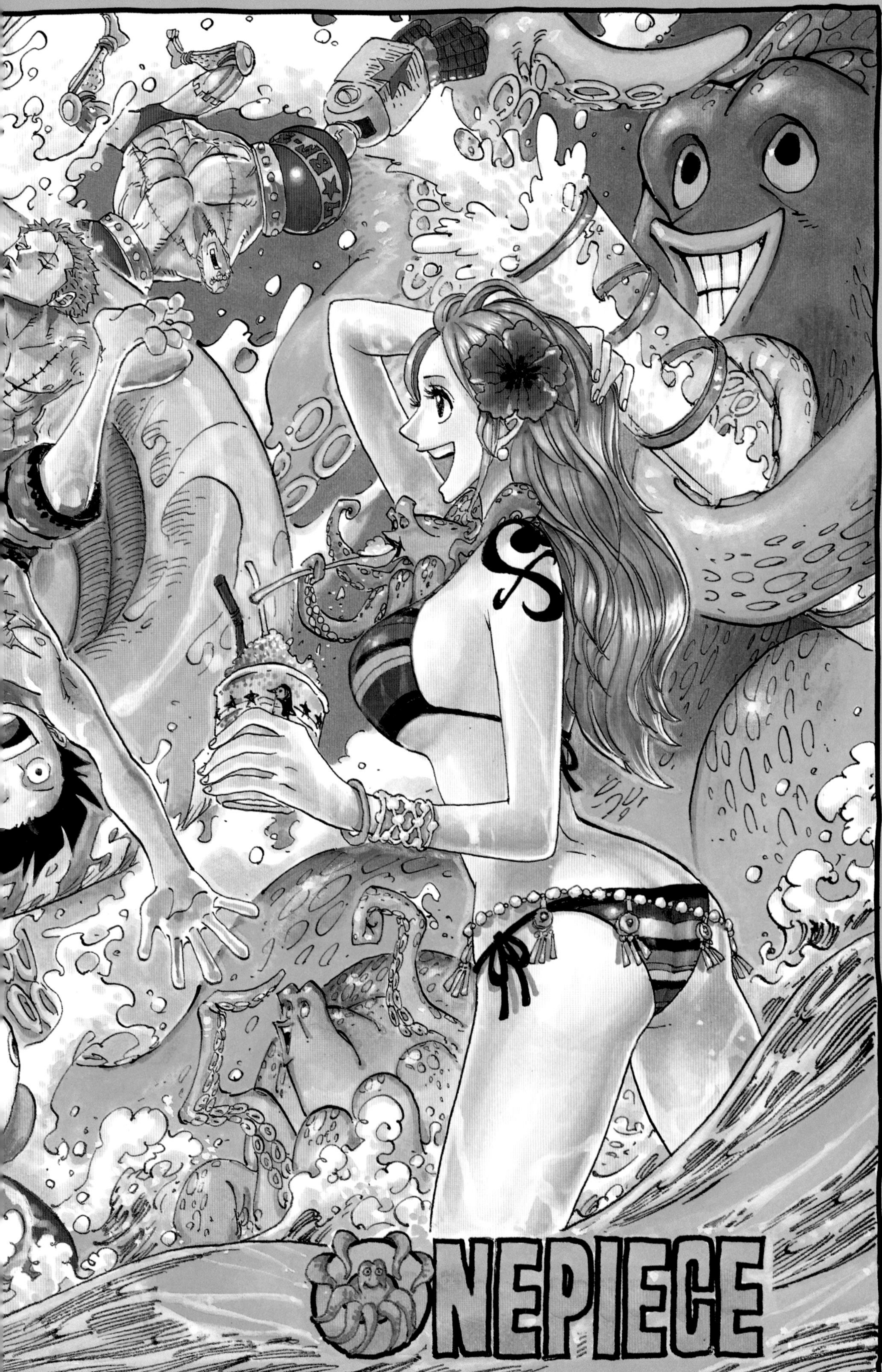
NEPIECE

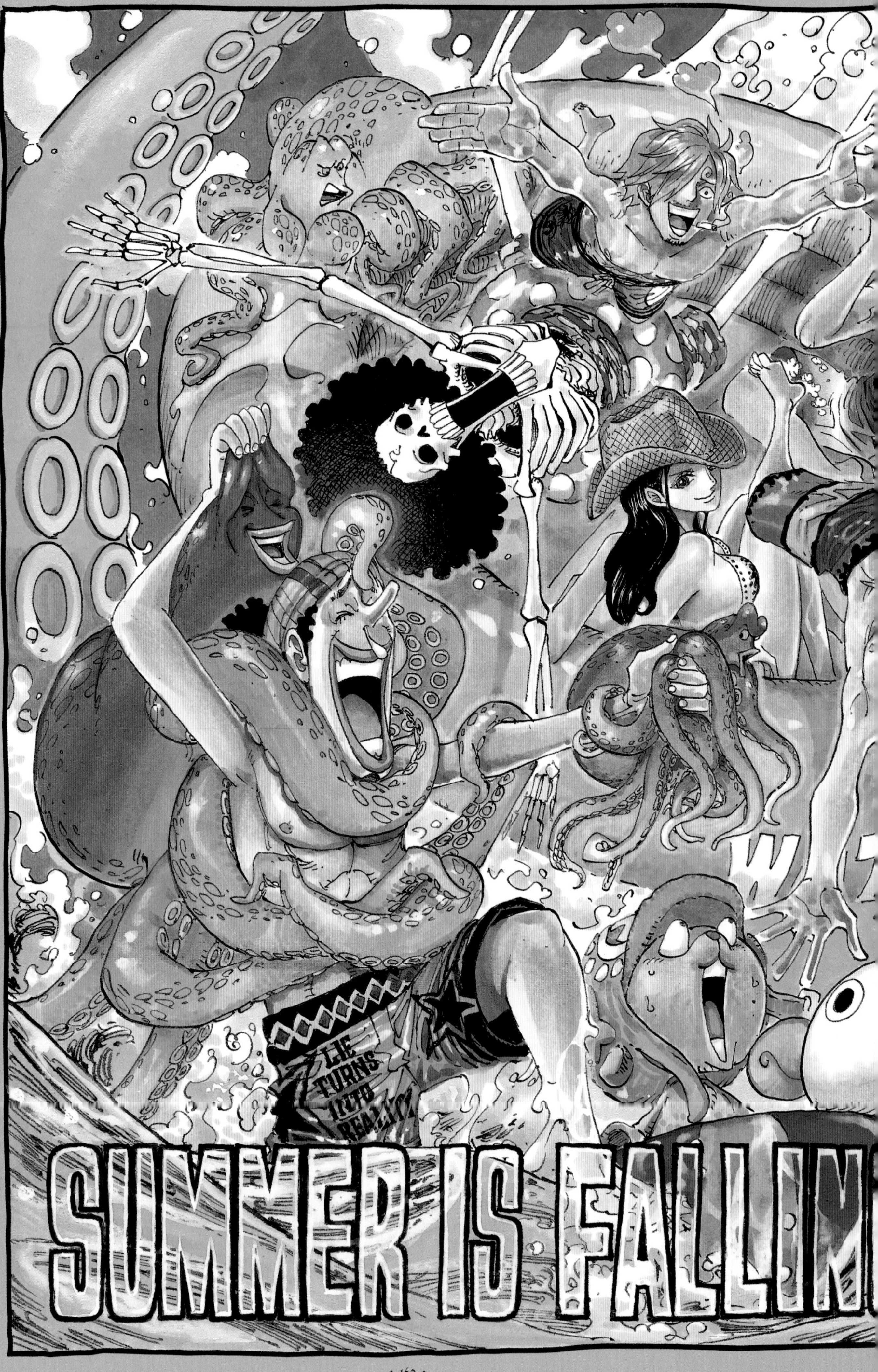
LIE TURNS INTO REALIT
SUMMER IS FALLIN

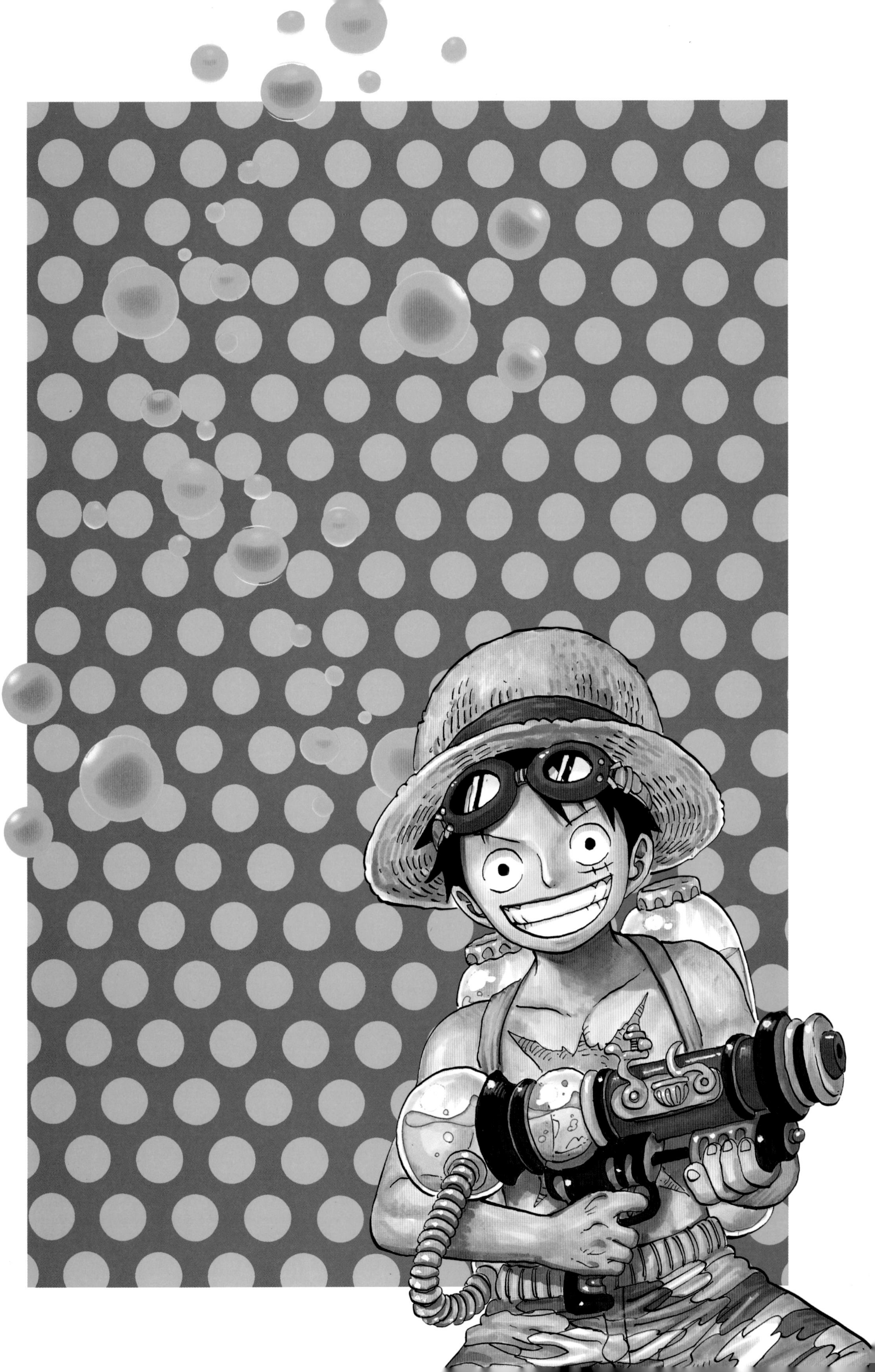

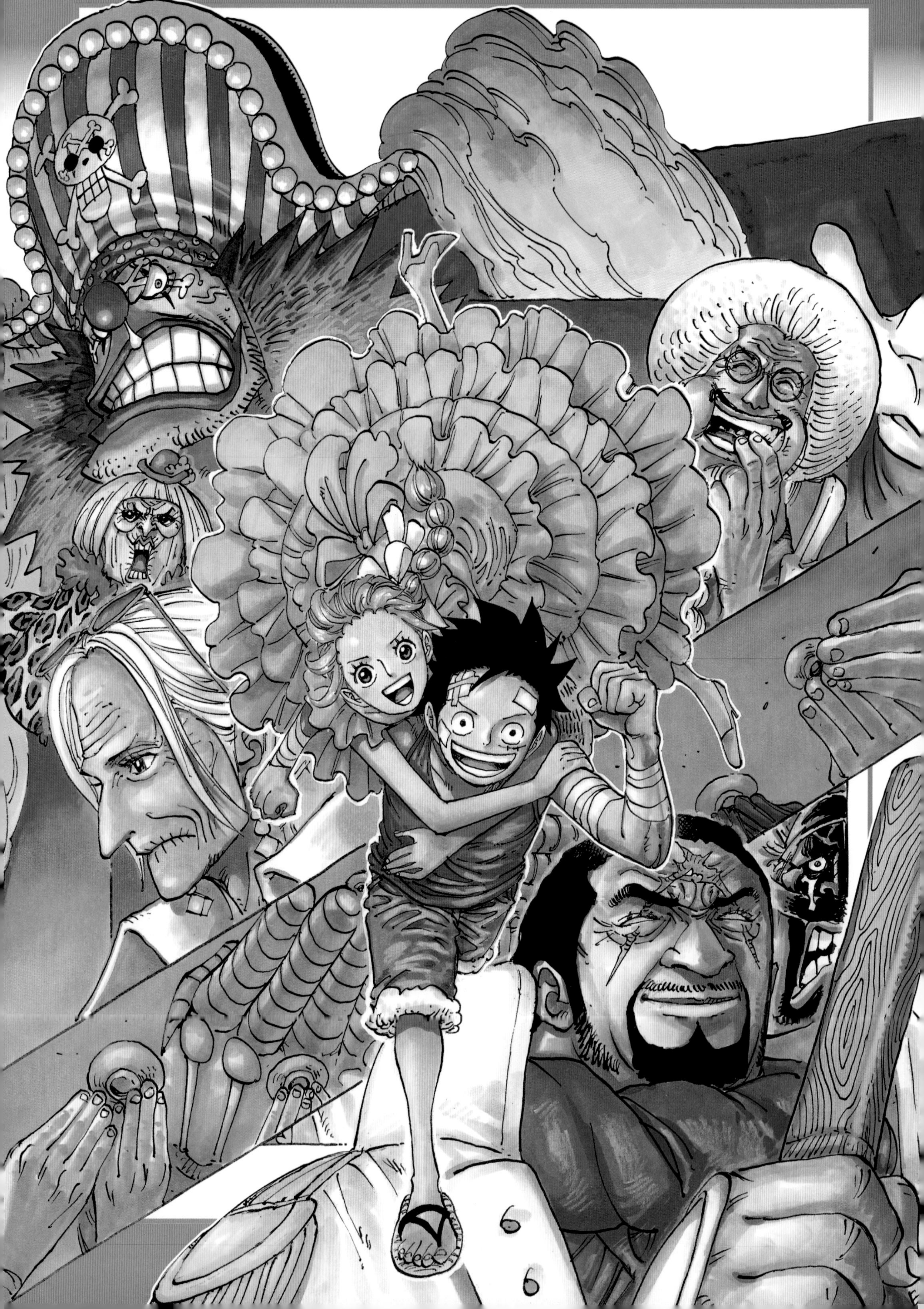

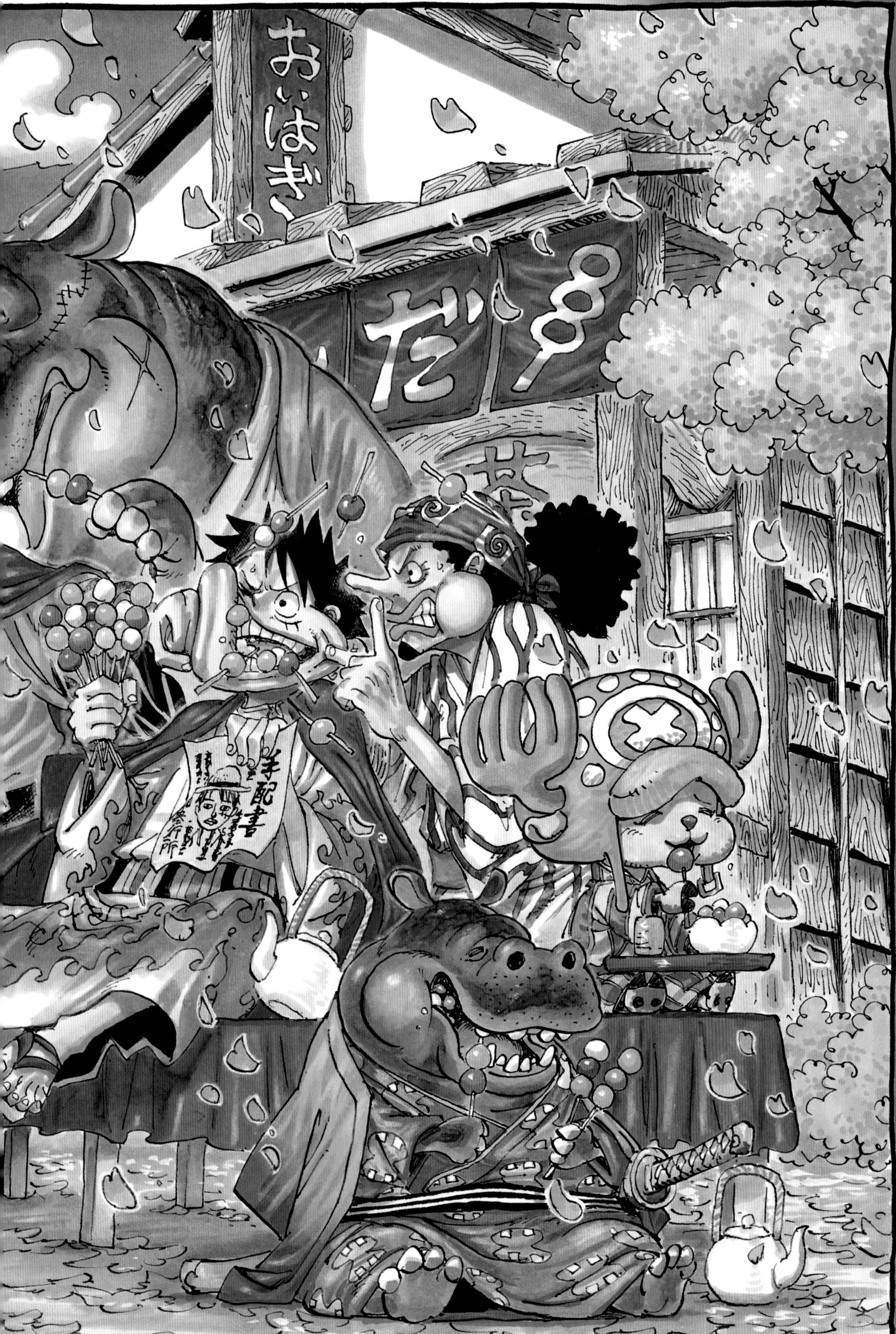
おはぎ
手配書

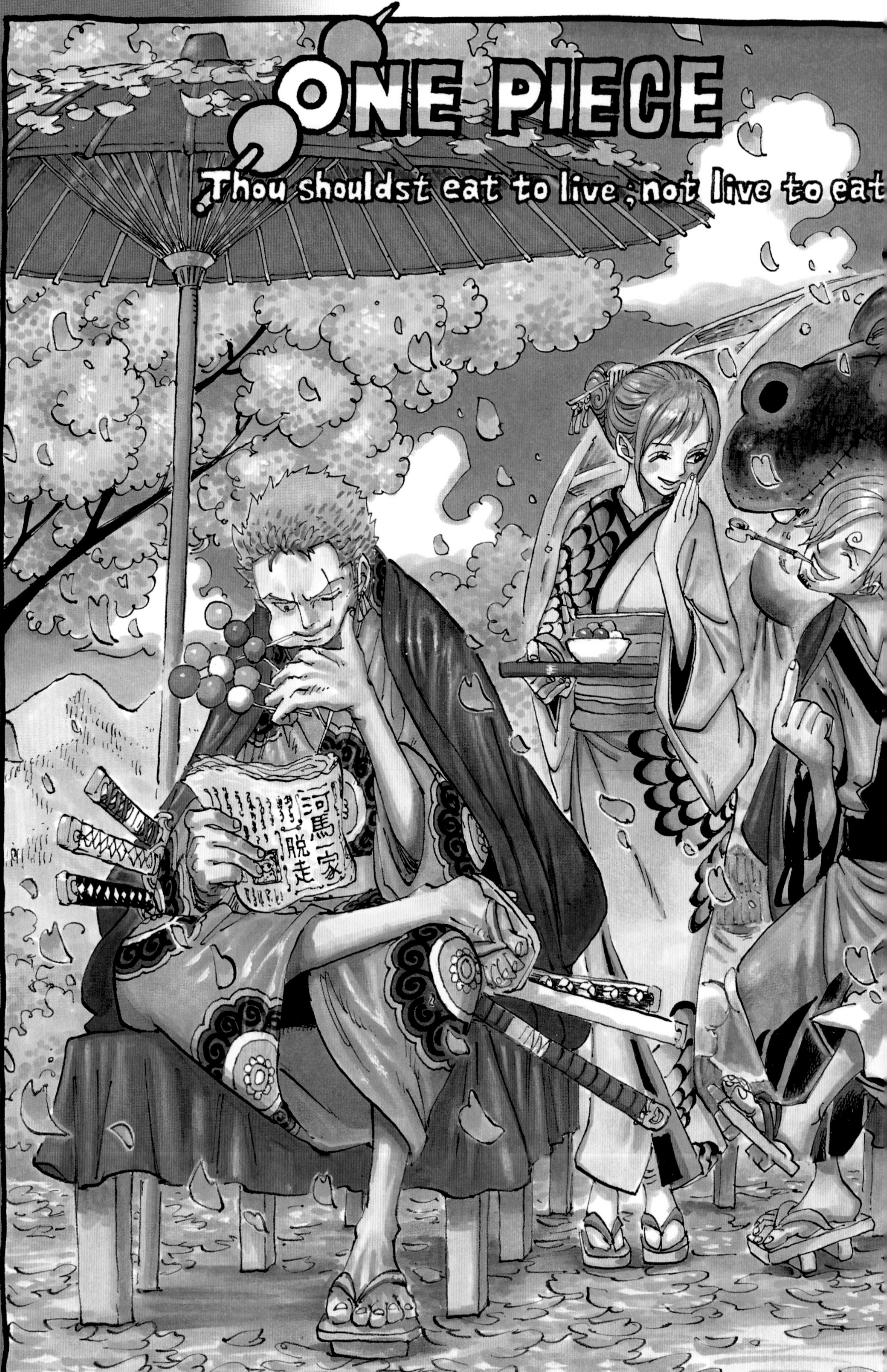
ONE PIECE
Thou shouldst eat to live; not live to eat
河馬一家
脱走

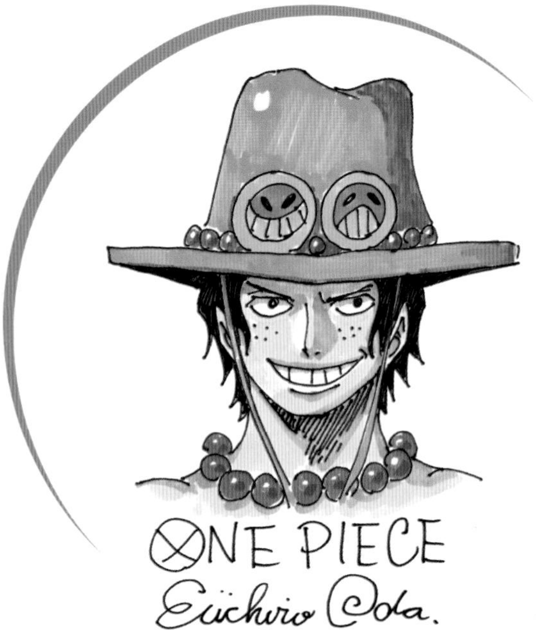
ONE PIECE
Eiichiro Oda.

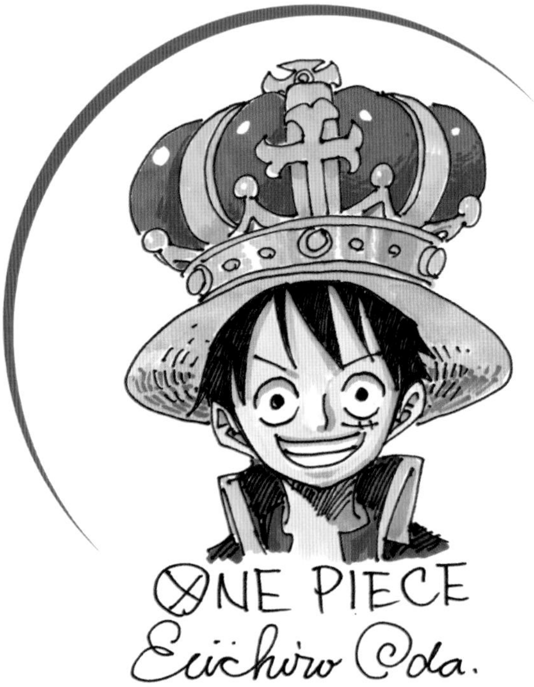
ONE PIECE
Eiichiro Oda.

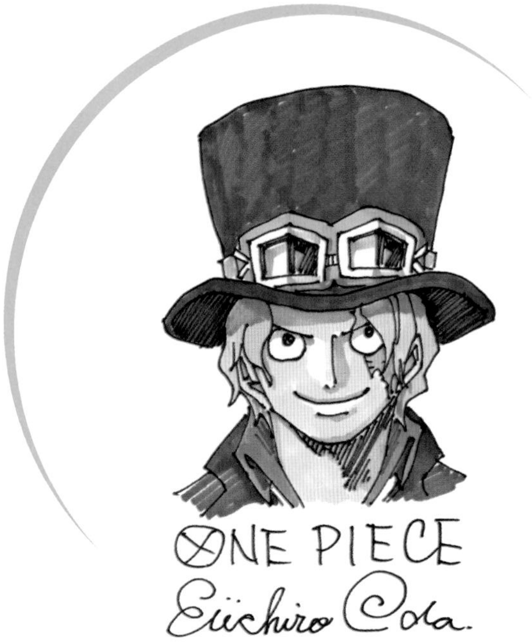
ONE PIECE
Eiichiro Oda.

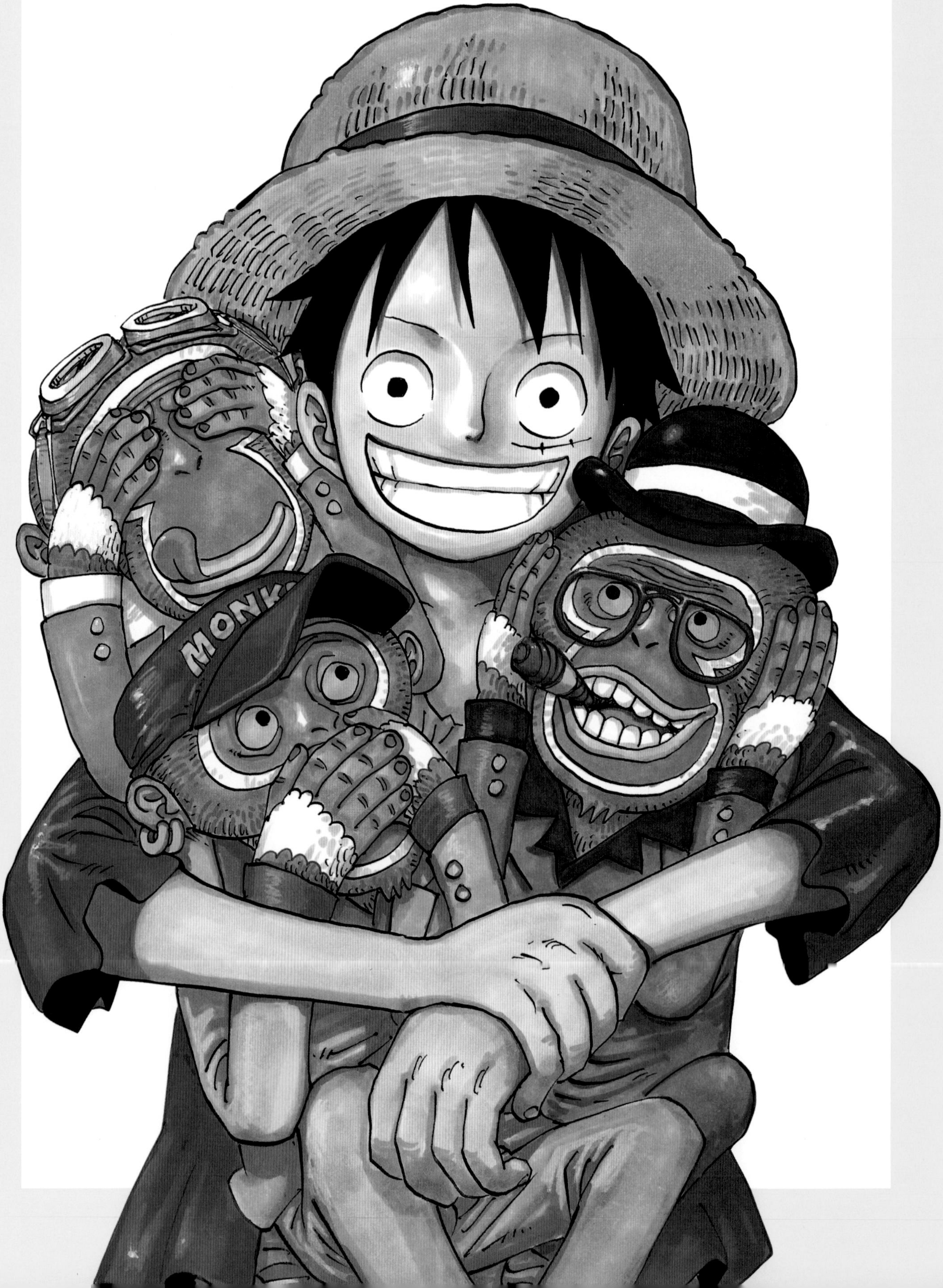

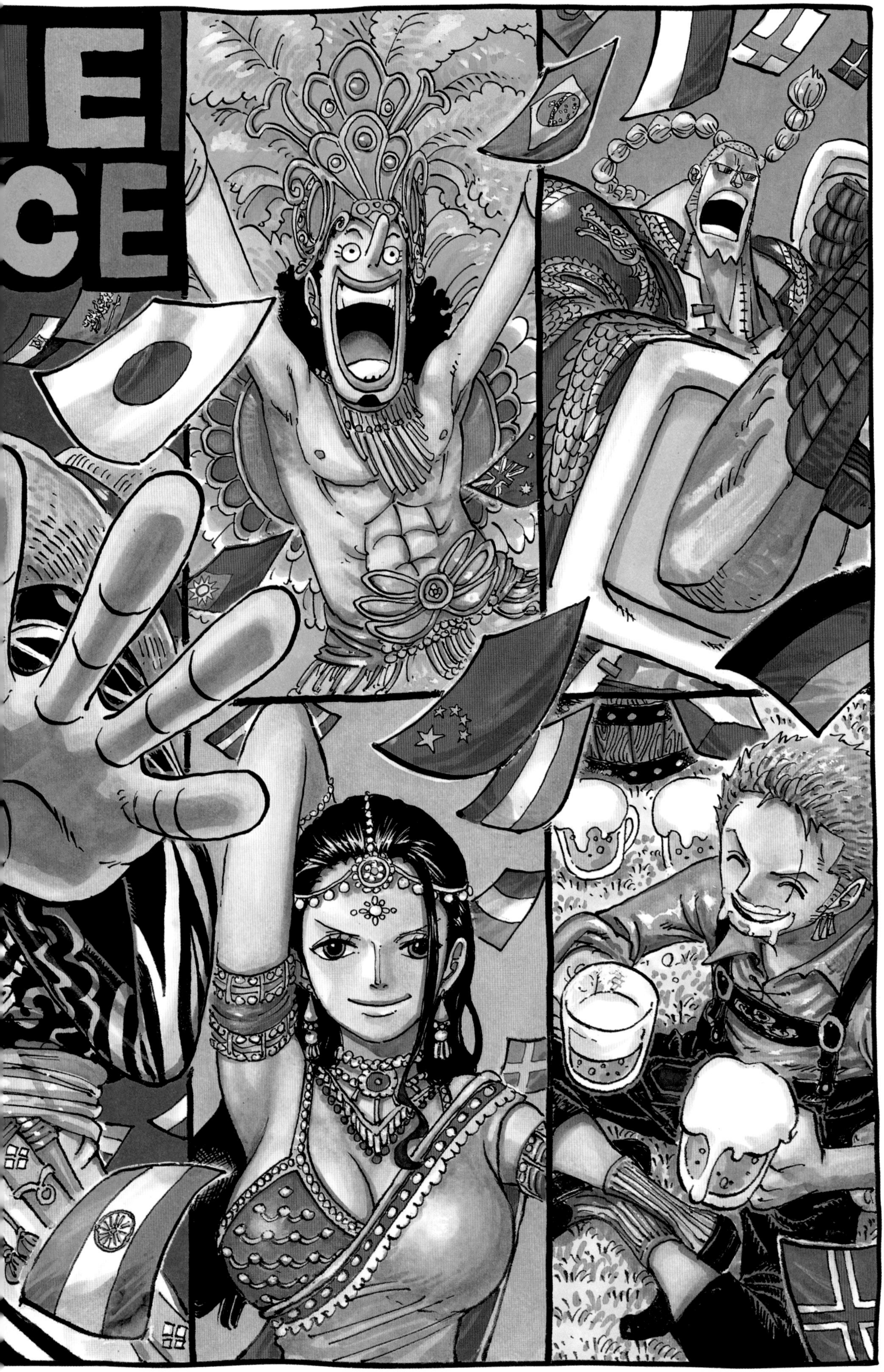

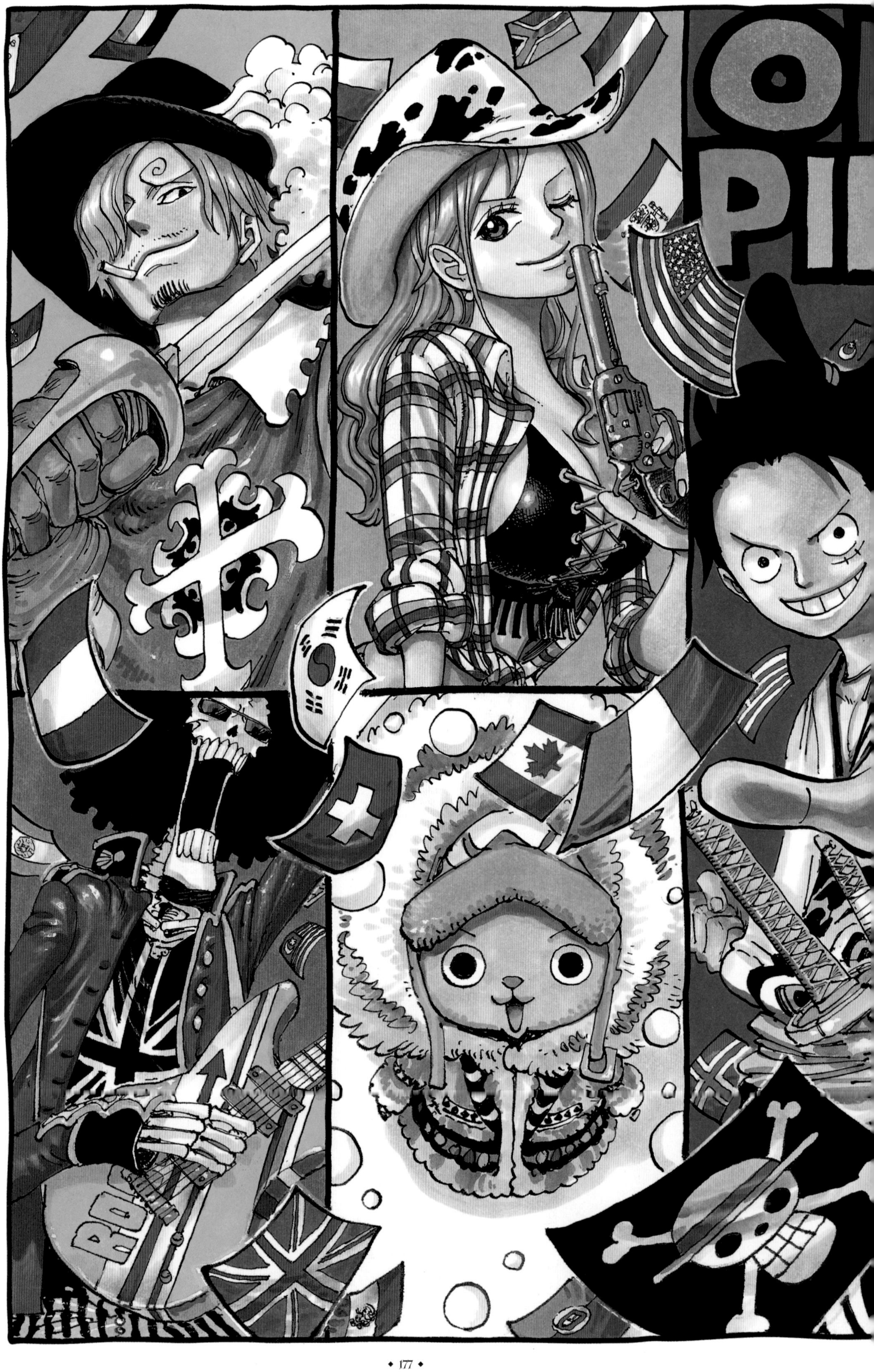

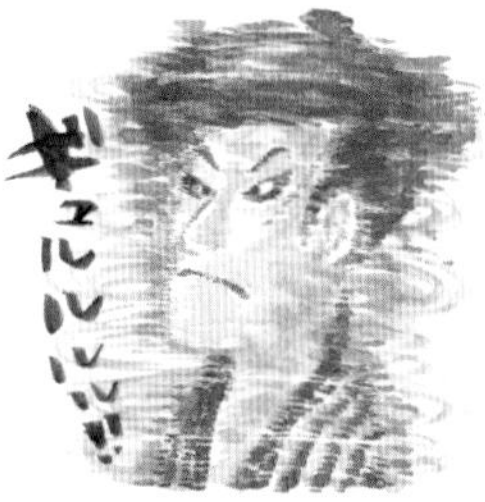

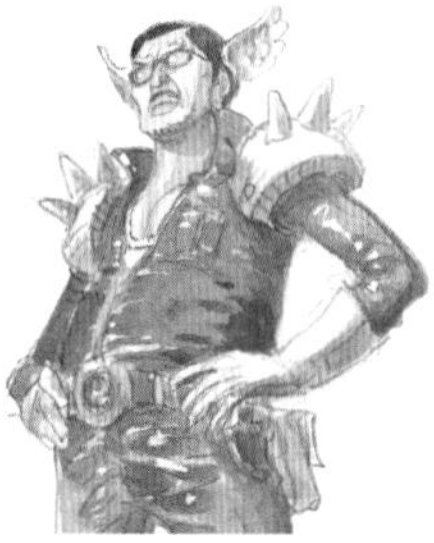

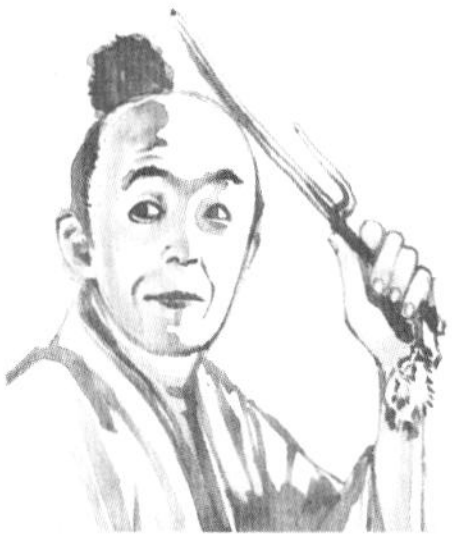

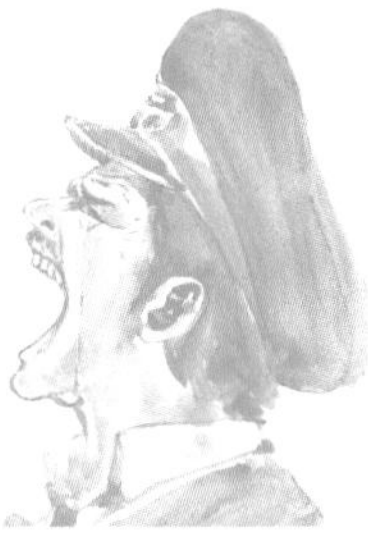

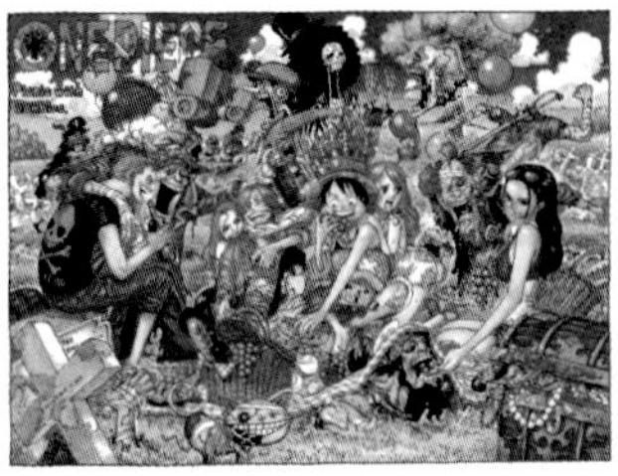

Comments P.164–165

I was really hooked on a zombie TV show when I drew this. You bet I want to draw zombies.

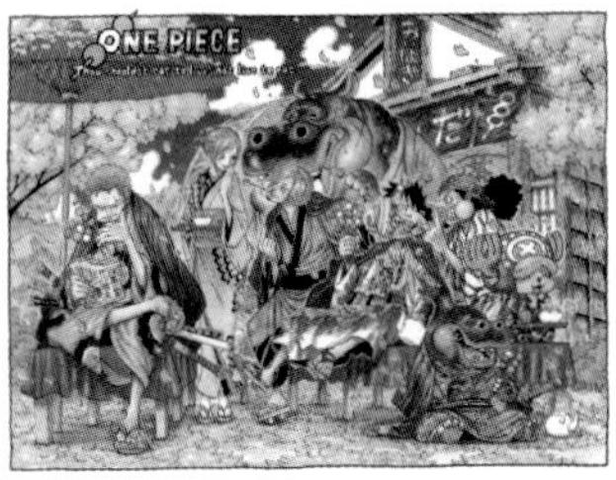
ONE PIECE

Comments P.172–173

Is that *ohagi,* the famous treat of sweet red bean paste with sticky rice, on the sign of this tea house? No, look closer: it says *oihagi,* meaning "bandits." These guys are about to be robbed for all they're worth...by Onami the thief.

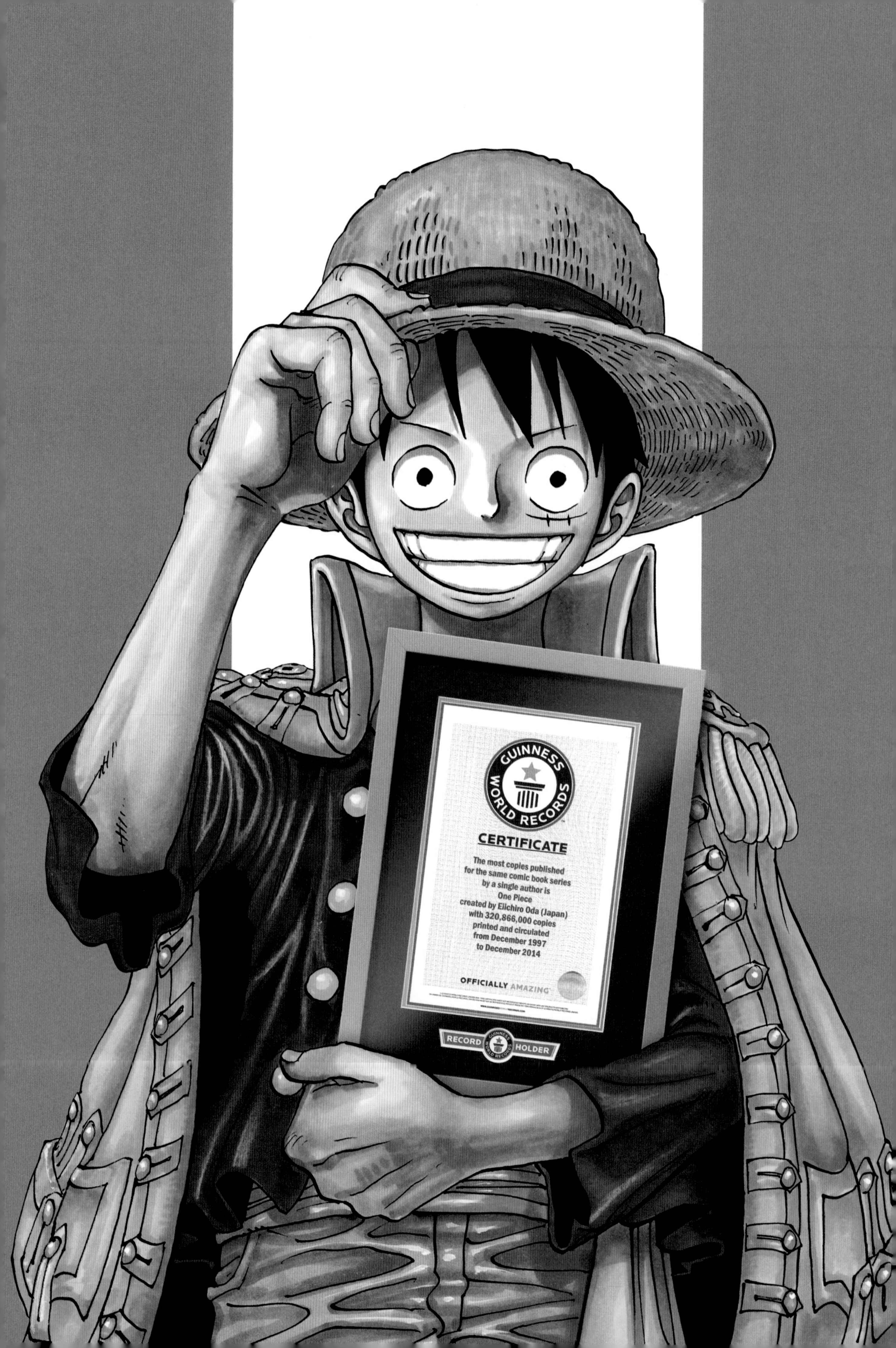
GUINNESS WORLD RECORDS
CERTIFICATE
The most copies published for the same comic book series by a single author is One Piece created by Eiichiro Oda (Japan) with 320,866,000 copies printed and circulated from December 1997 to December 2014
OFFICIALLY AMAZING
RECORD HOLDER

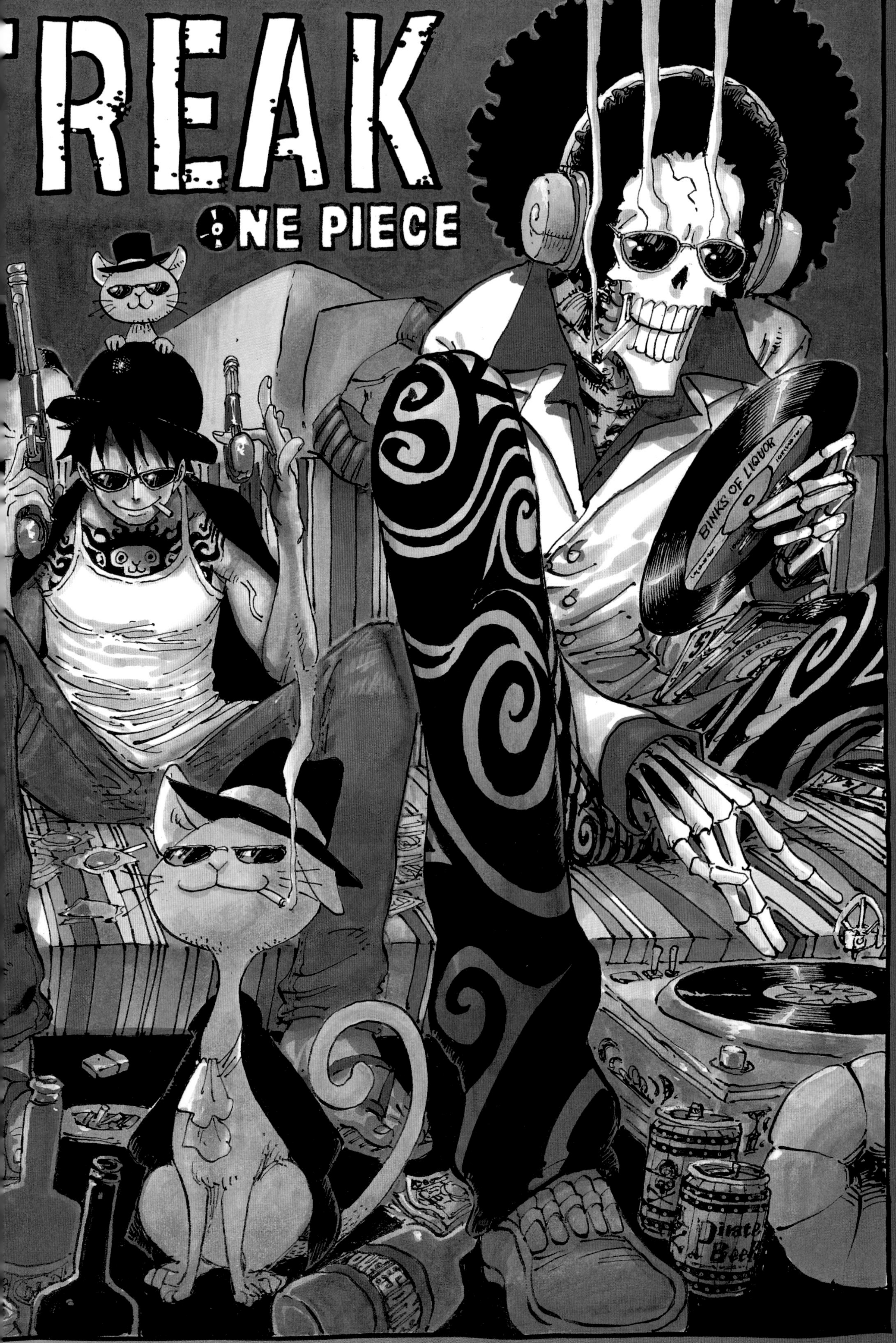
REAK
ONE PIECE
BINKS OF LIQUOR
Pirate
Beer

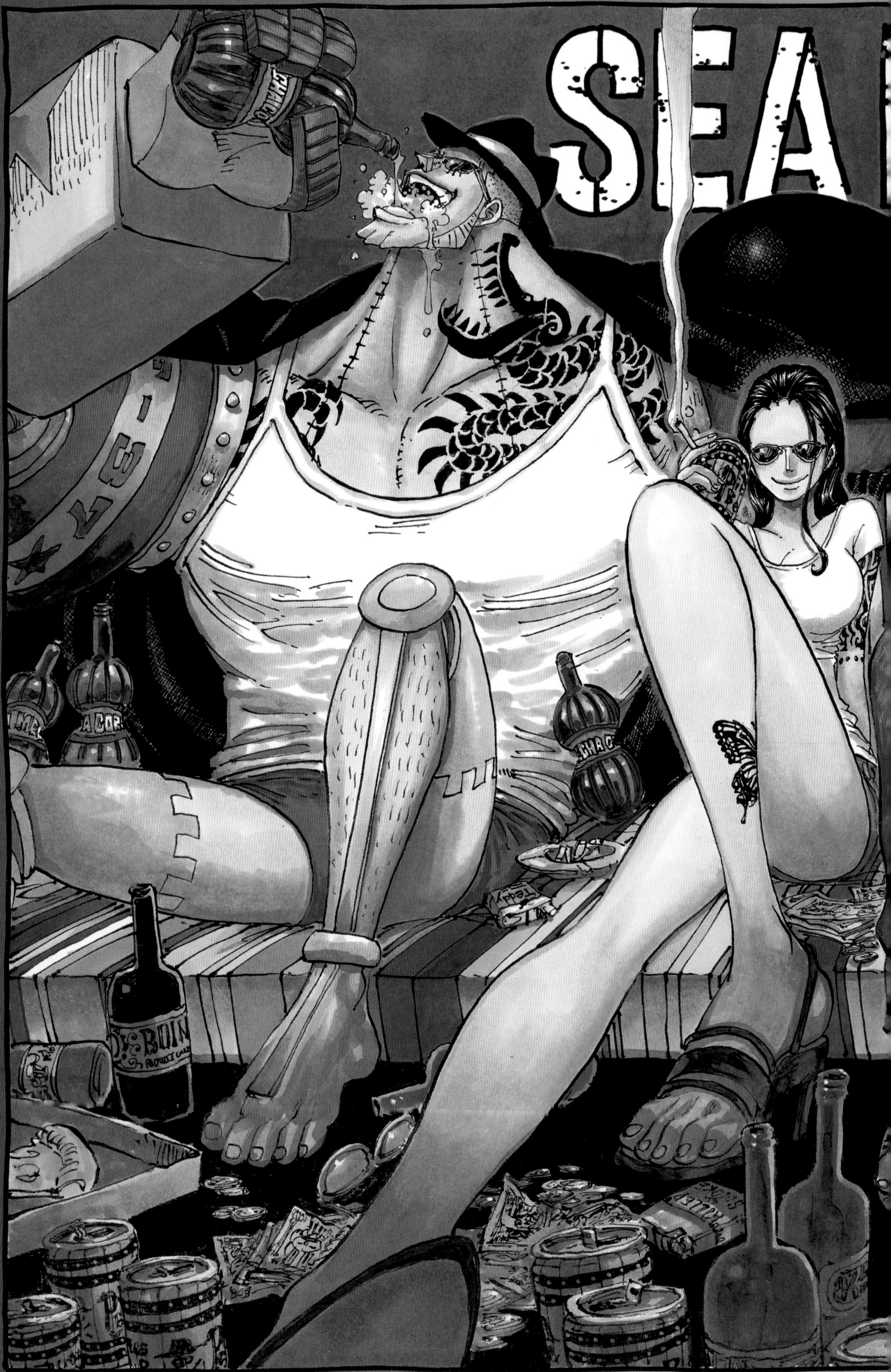
SEA

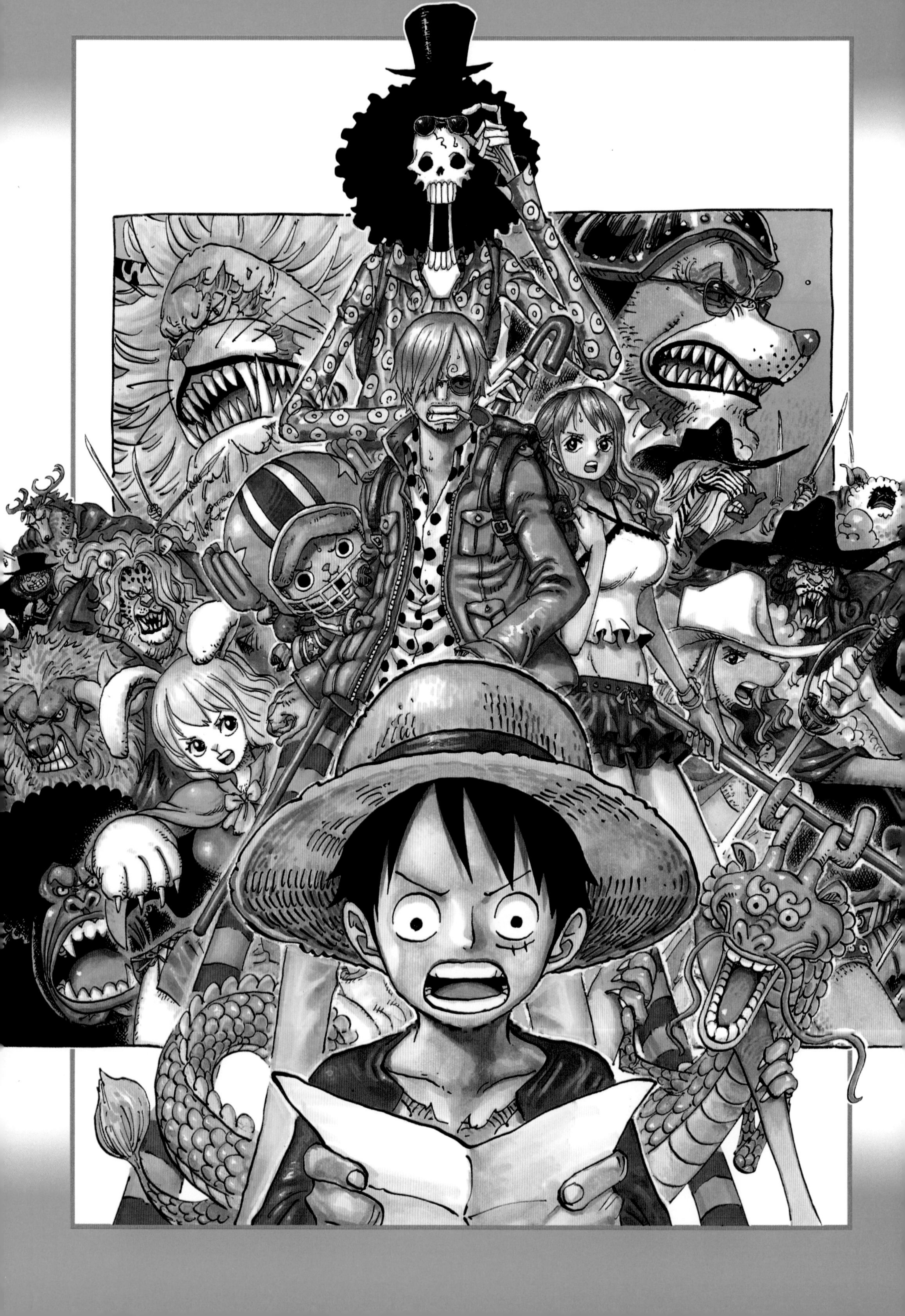

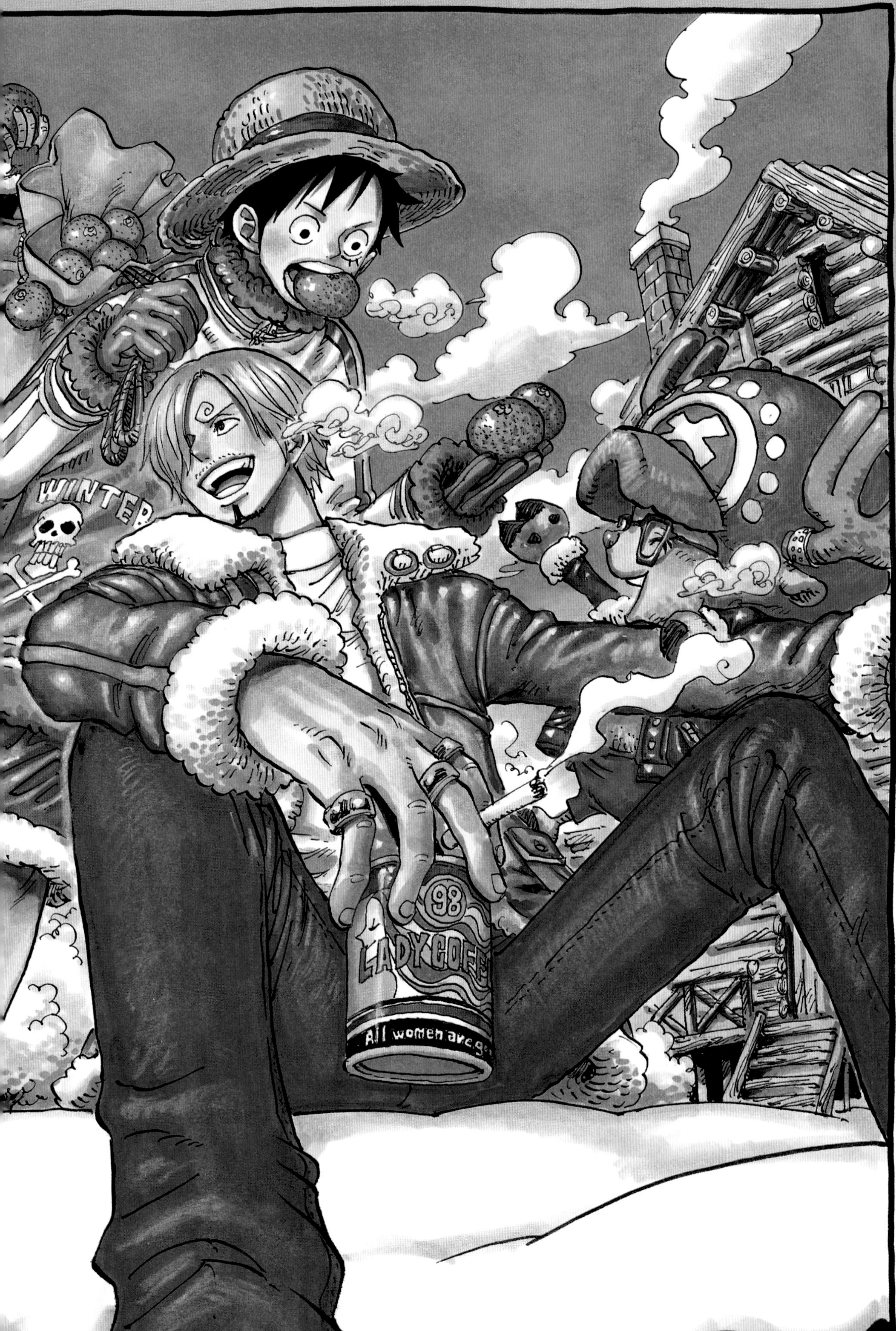
WINTER
98

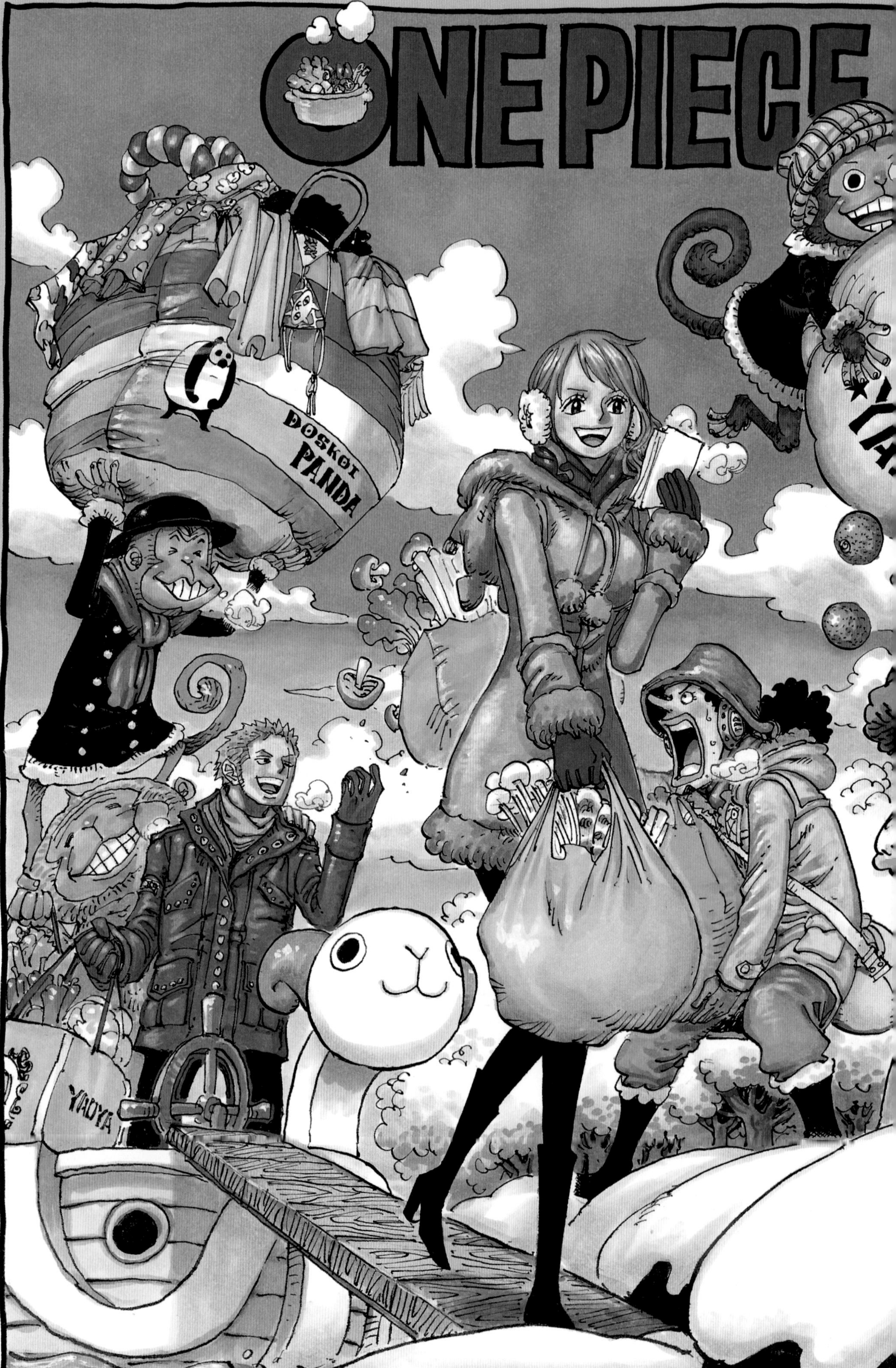
ONE PIECE
DOSKOI PANDA
YAOYA

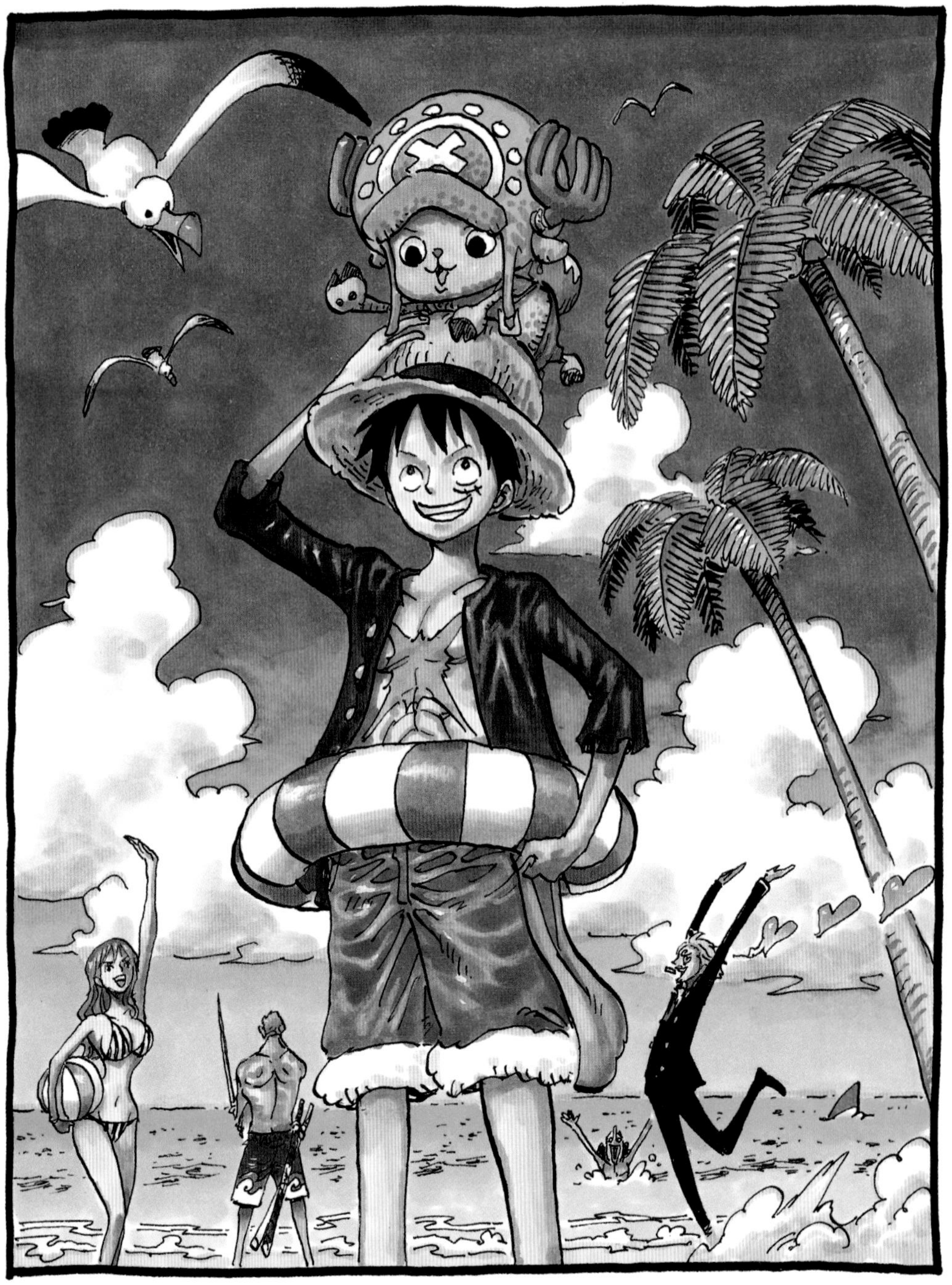

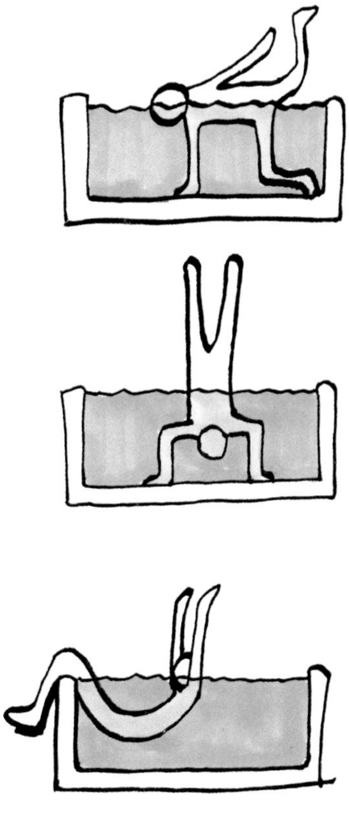

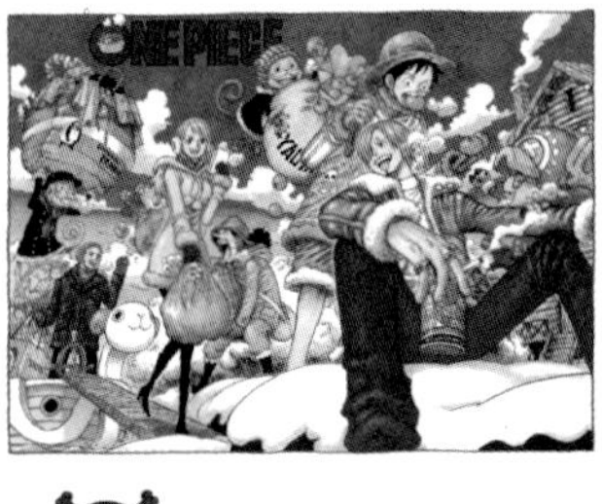

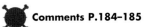

Comments P.184–185

An illustration made during the production of the film *Gold*. If you look at the pile of clothes they bought, it's all the outfits in the movie.

KABUKI

The popular stage show *Super Kabuki II: One Piece* first premiered in October 2015. Here's a batch of kabuki-themed illustrations done for this show!

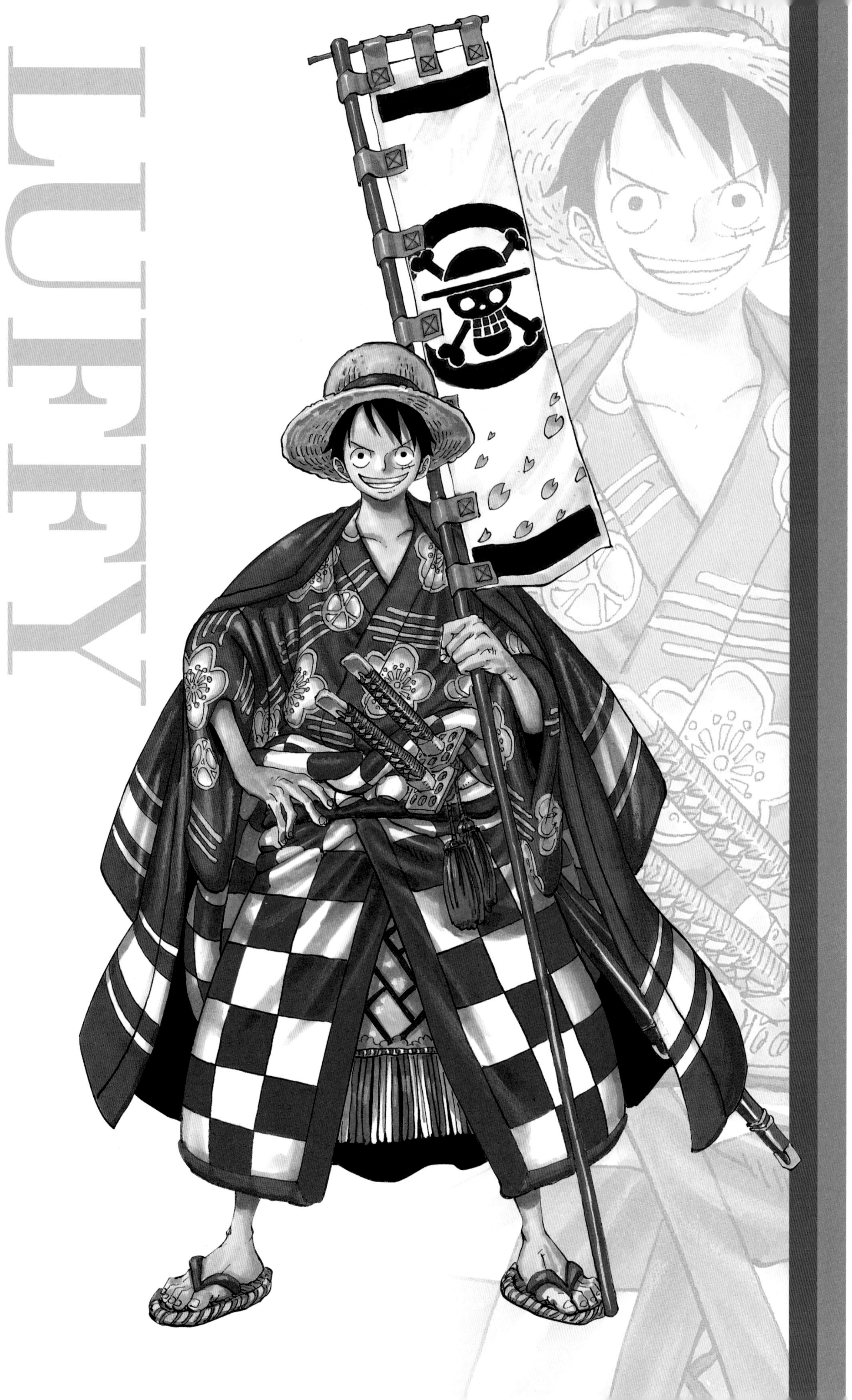
LUFFY

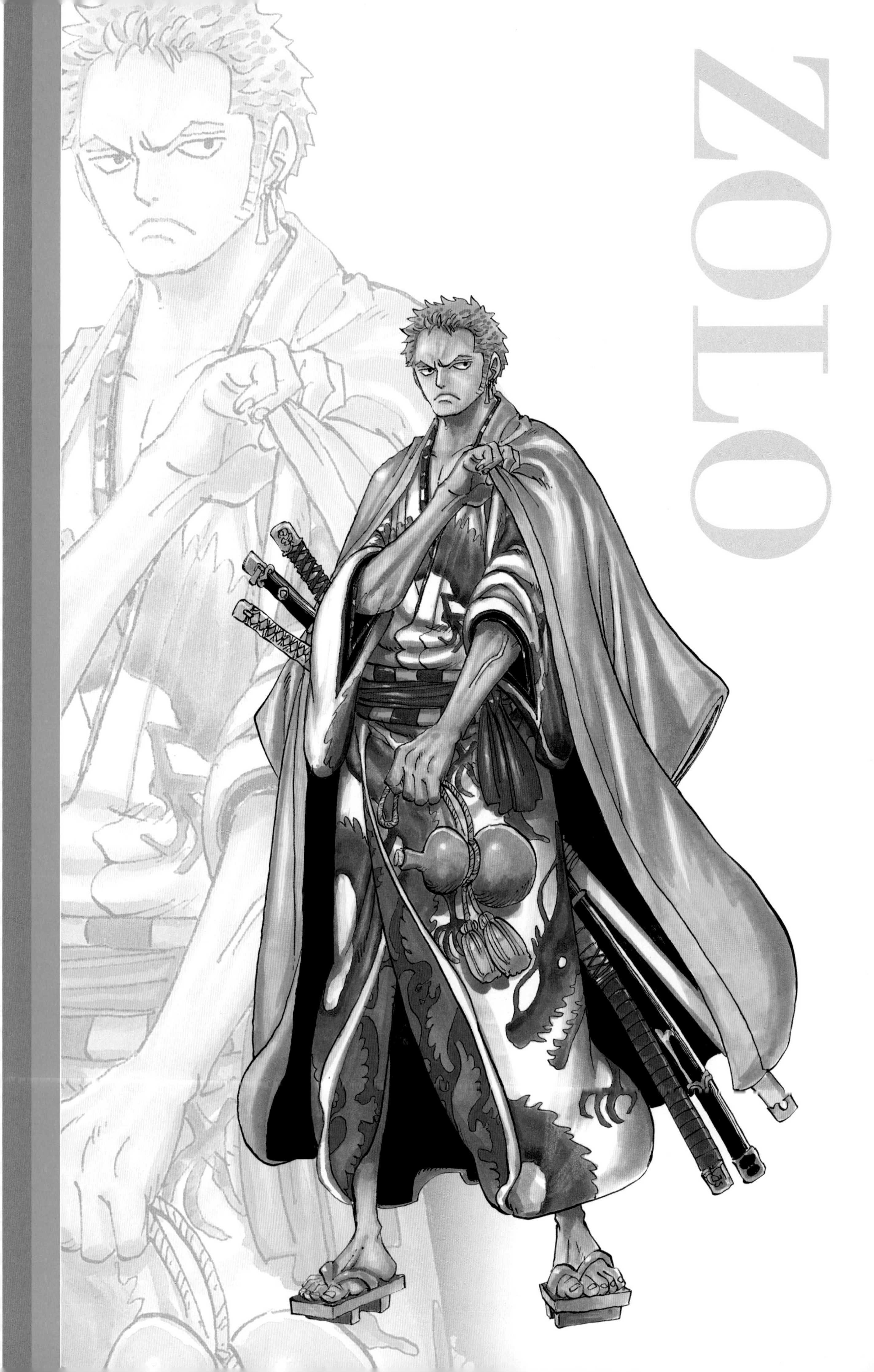
ZOLO

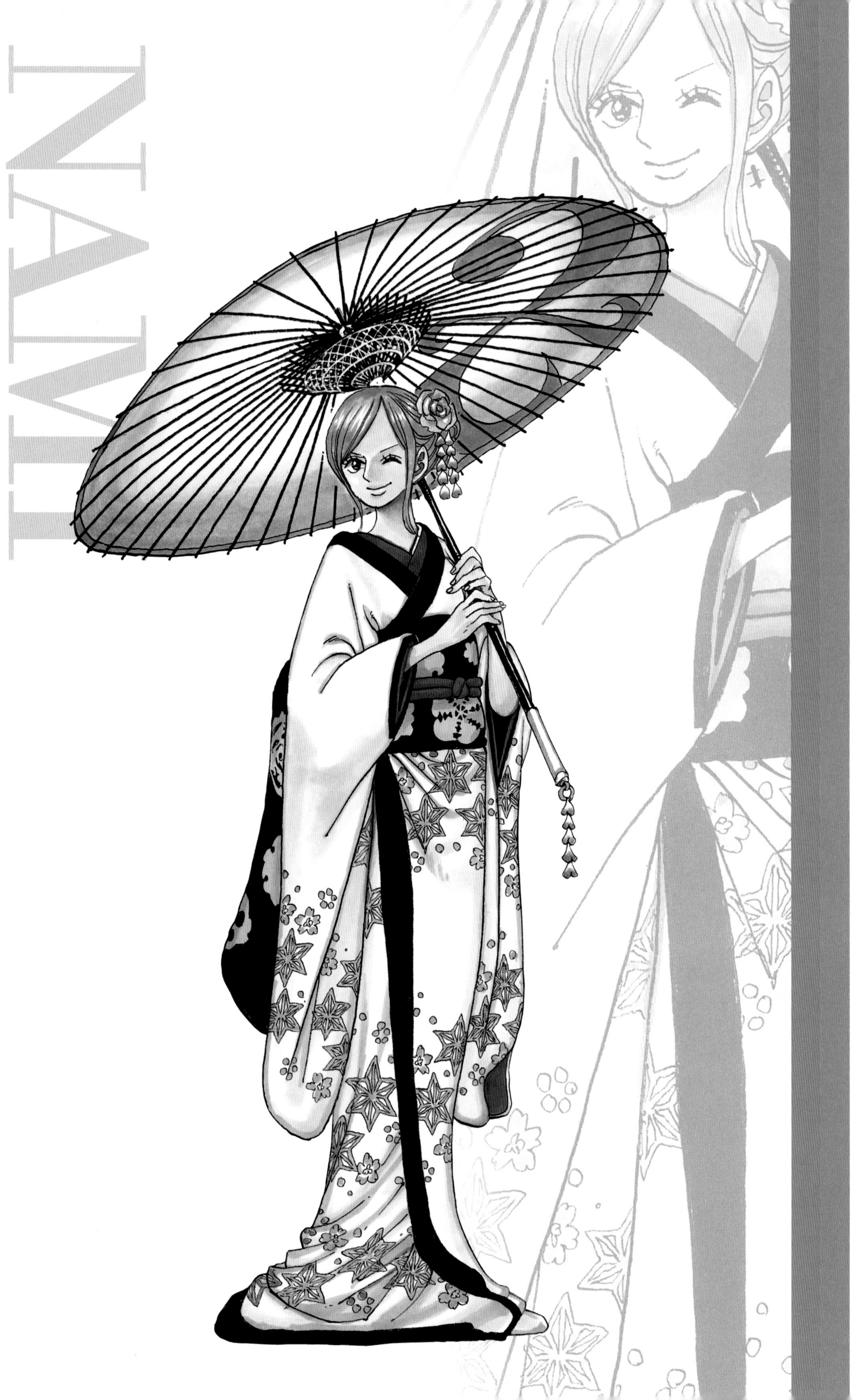
NAMI

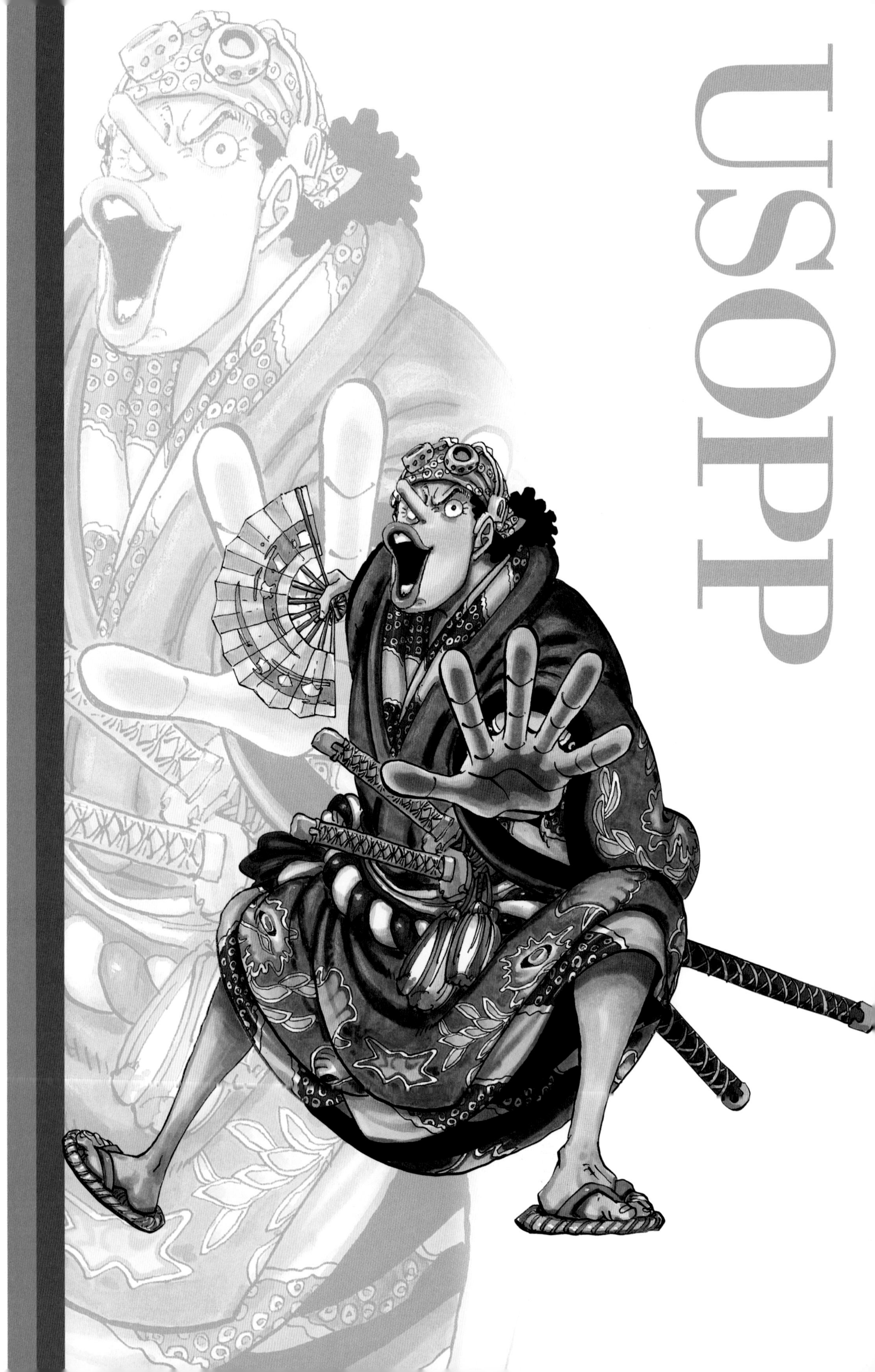
USOPP

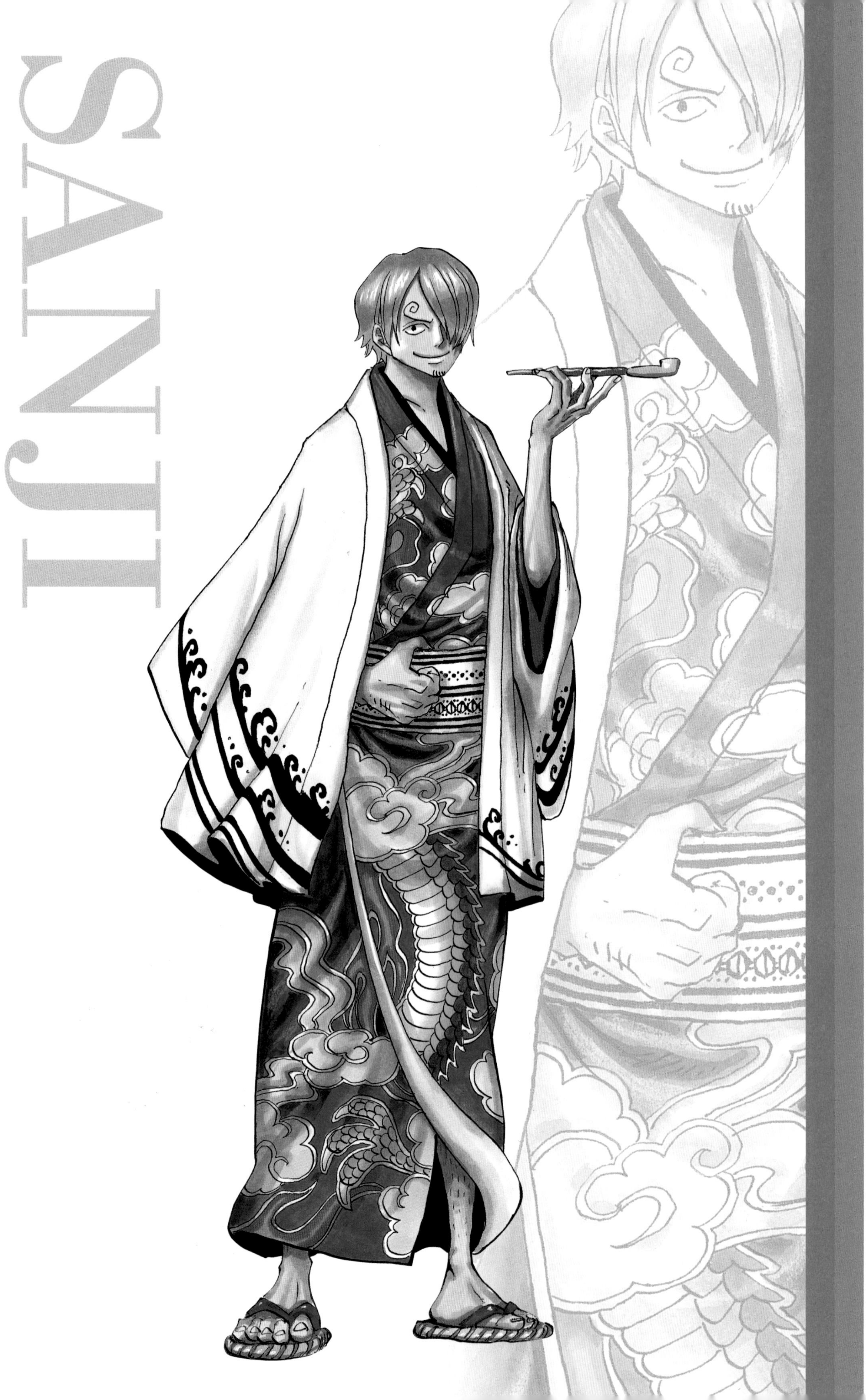
SANJI

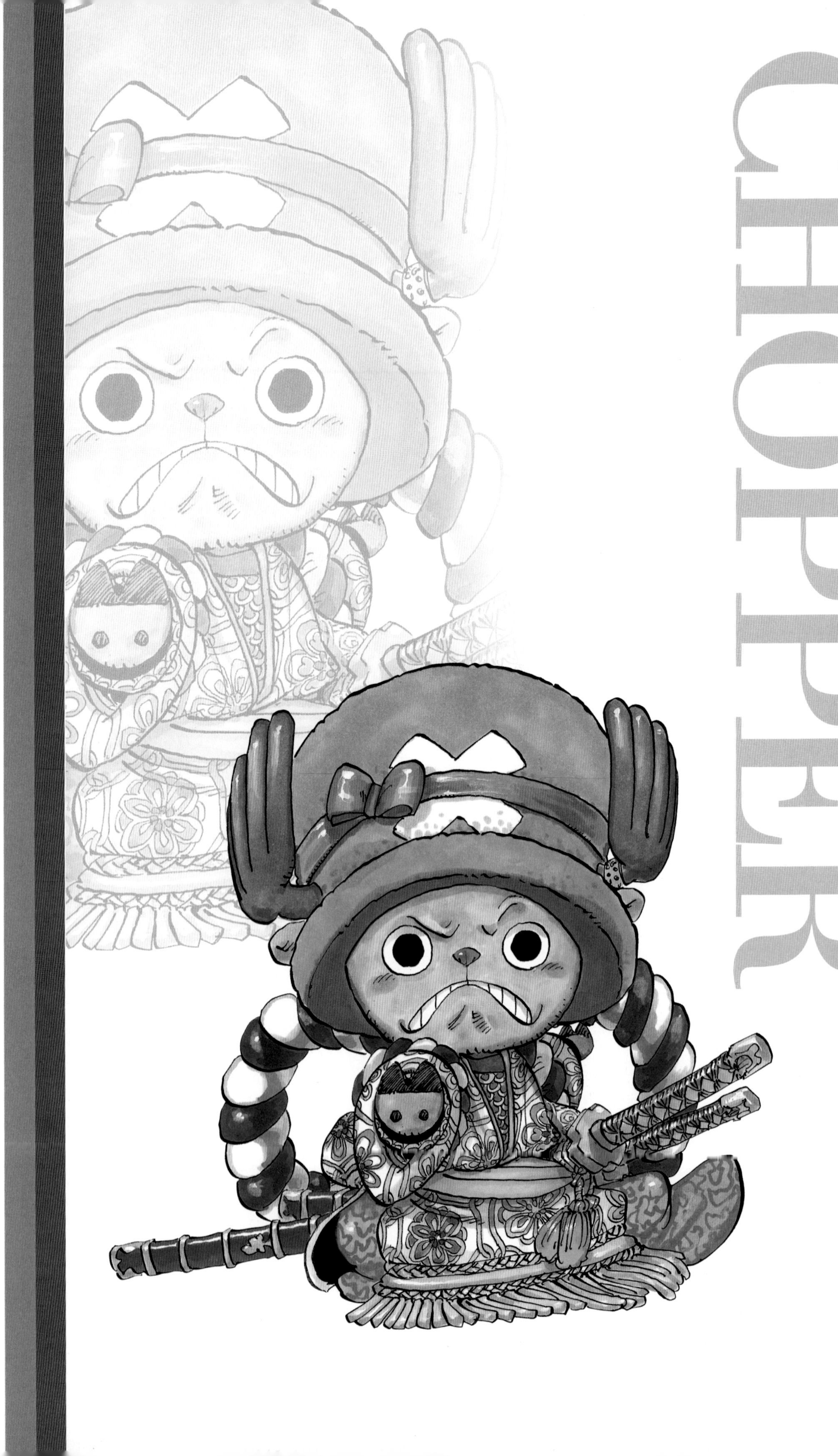
CHOPPER

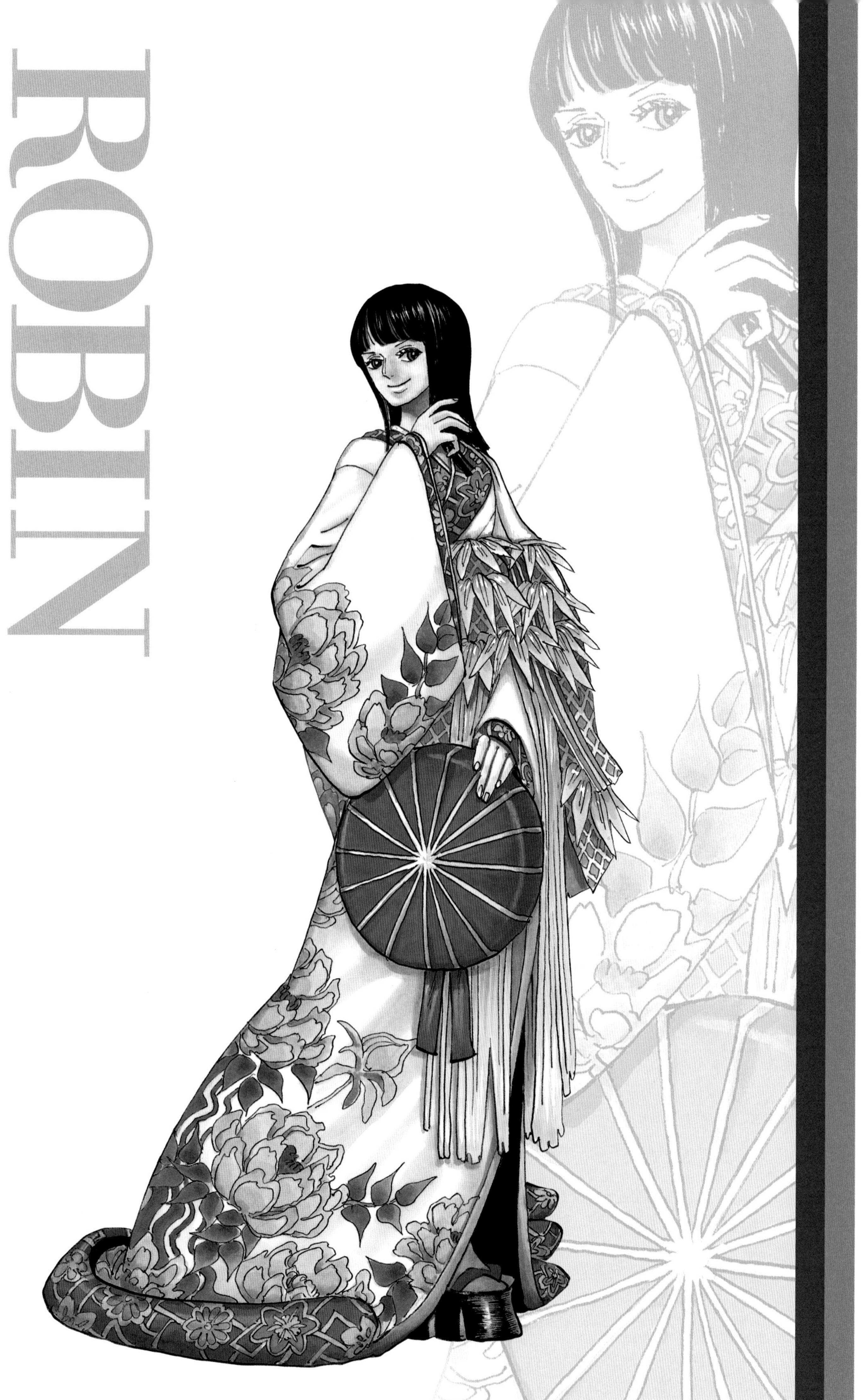
ROBIN

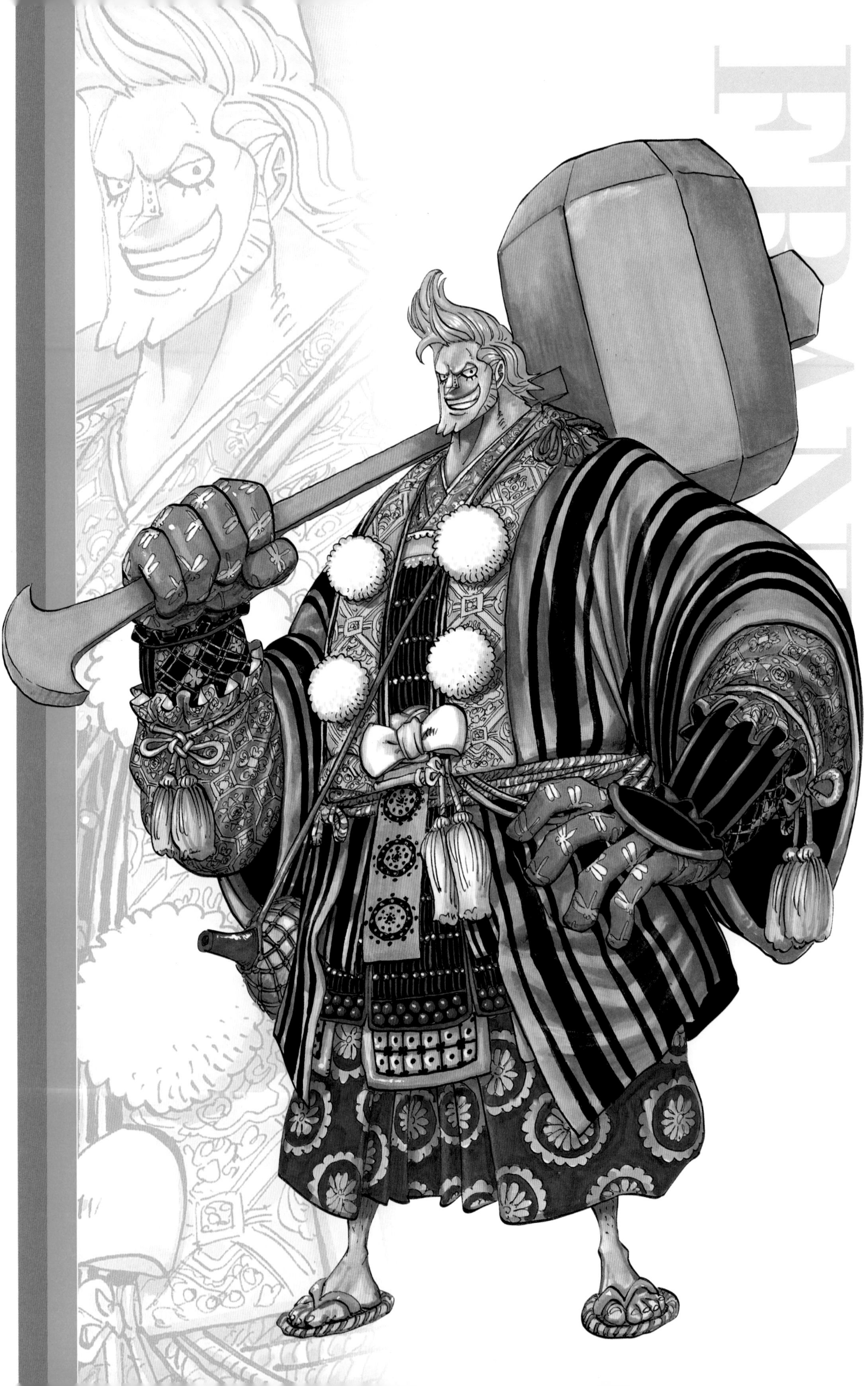

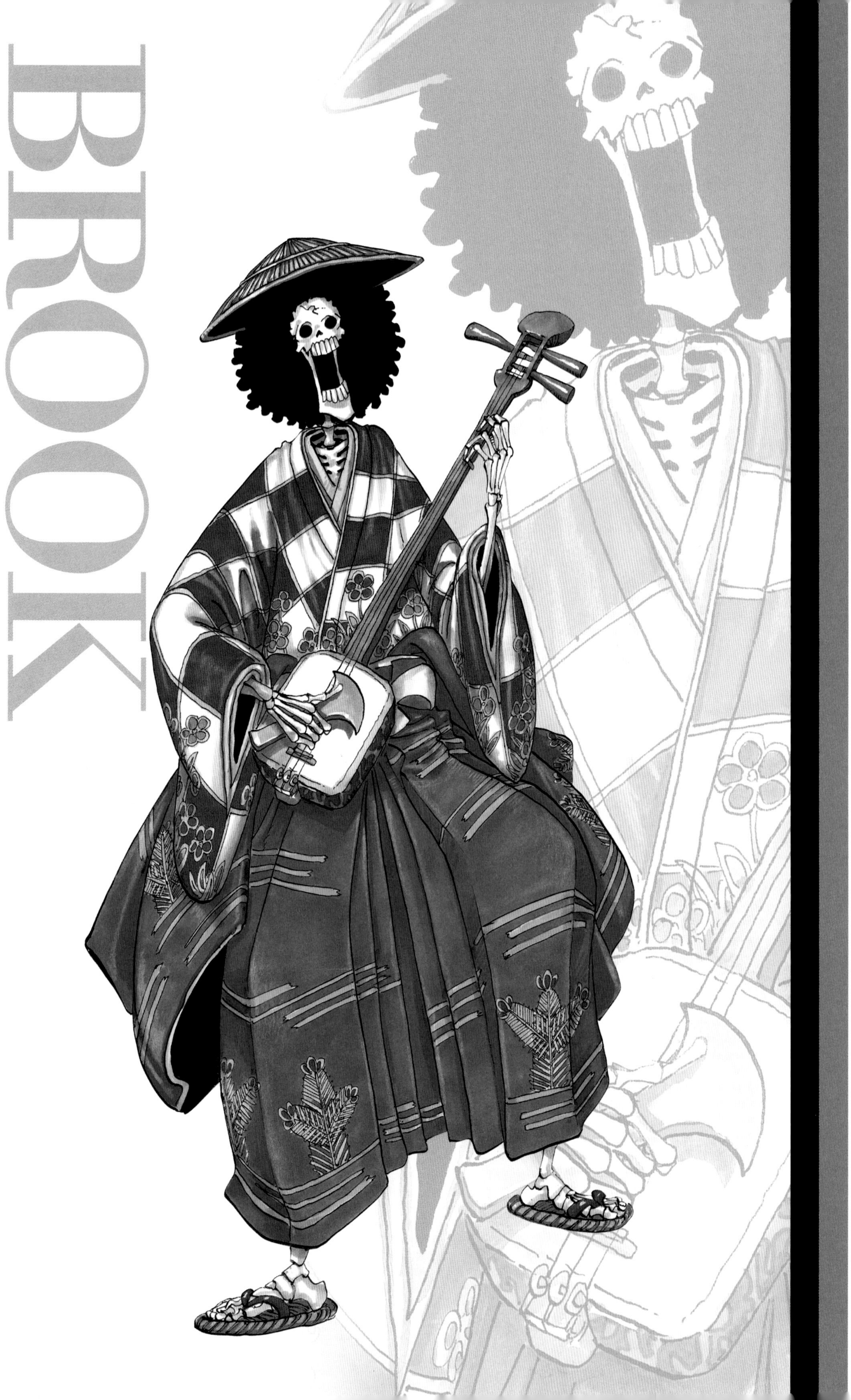
BROOK

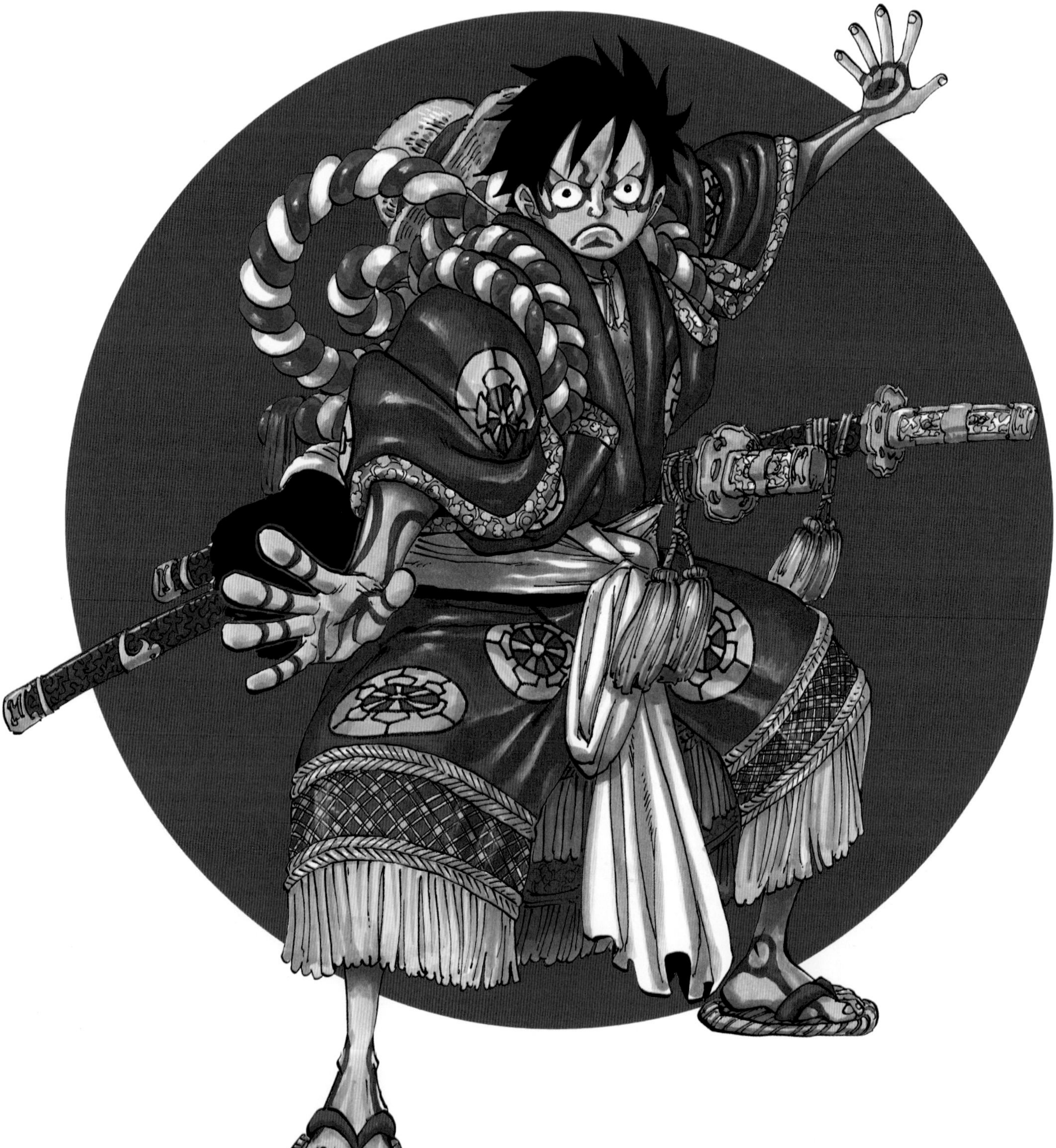

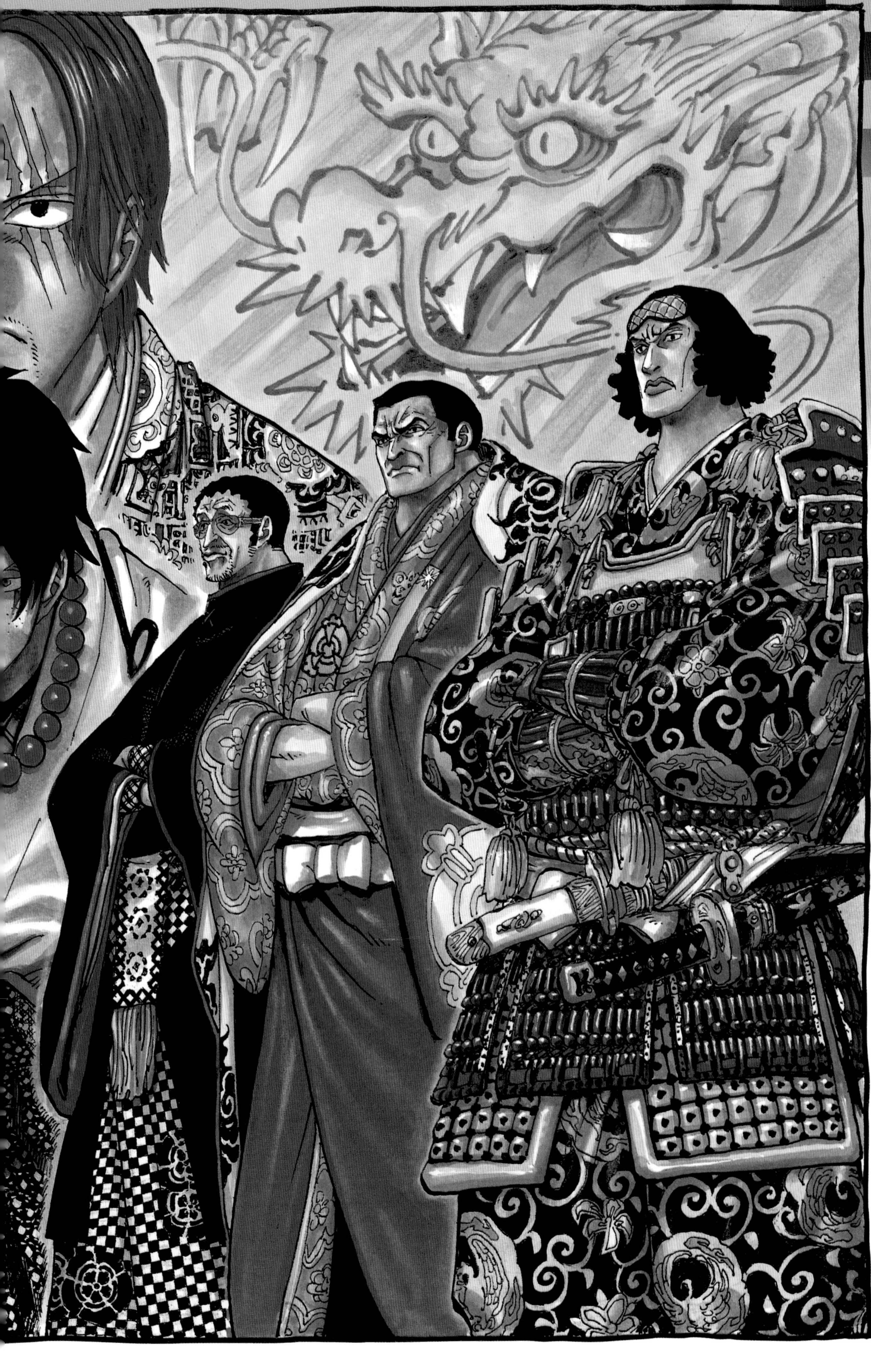

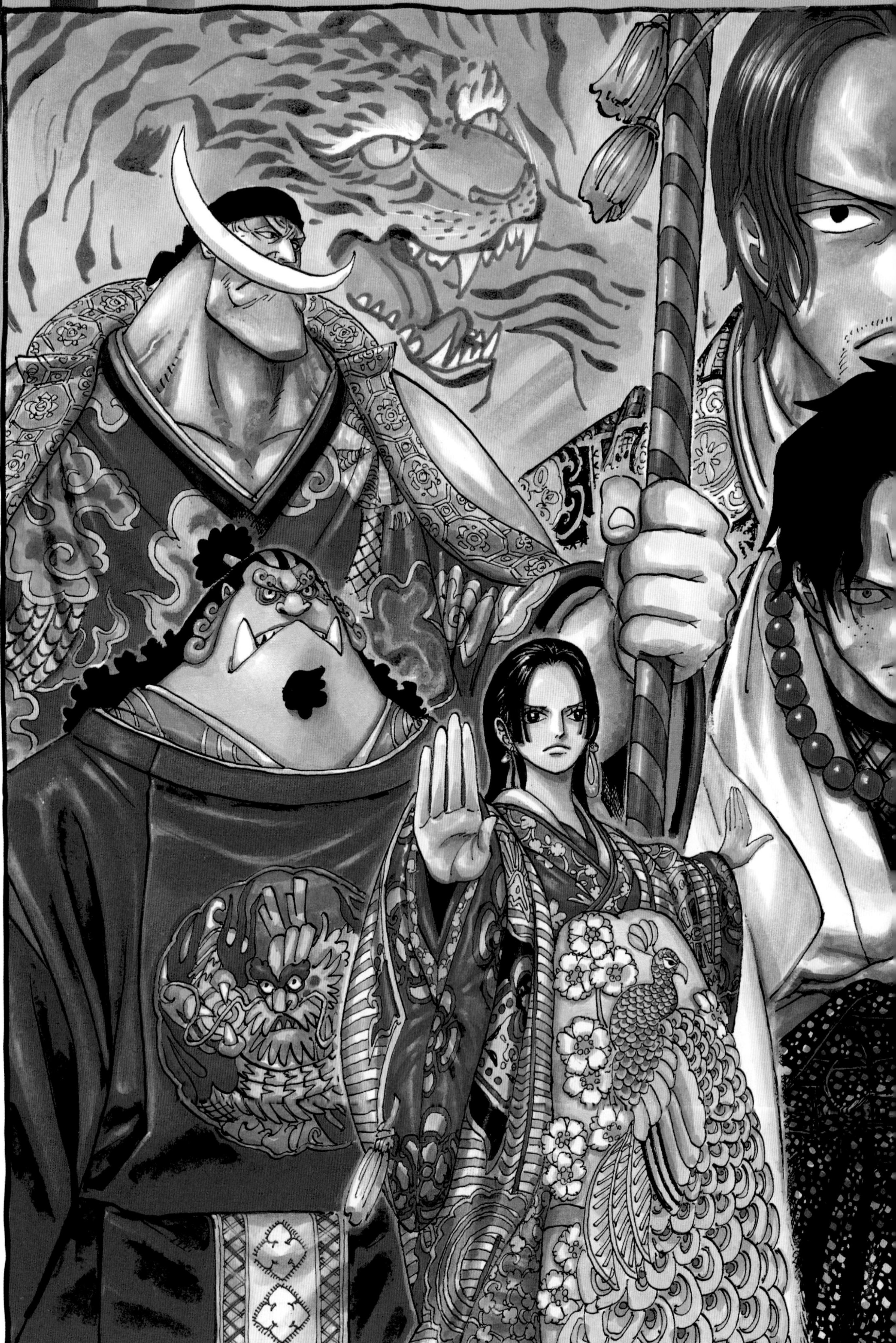

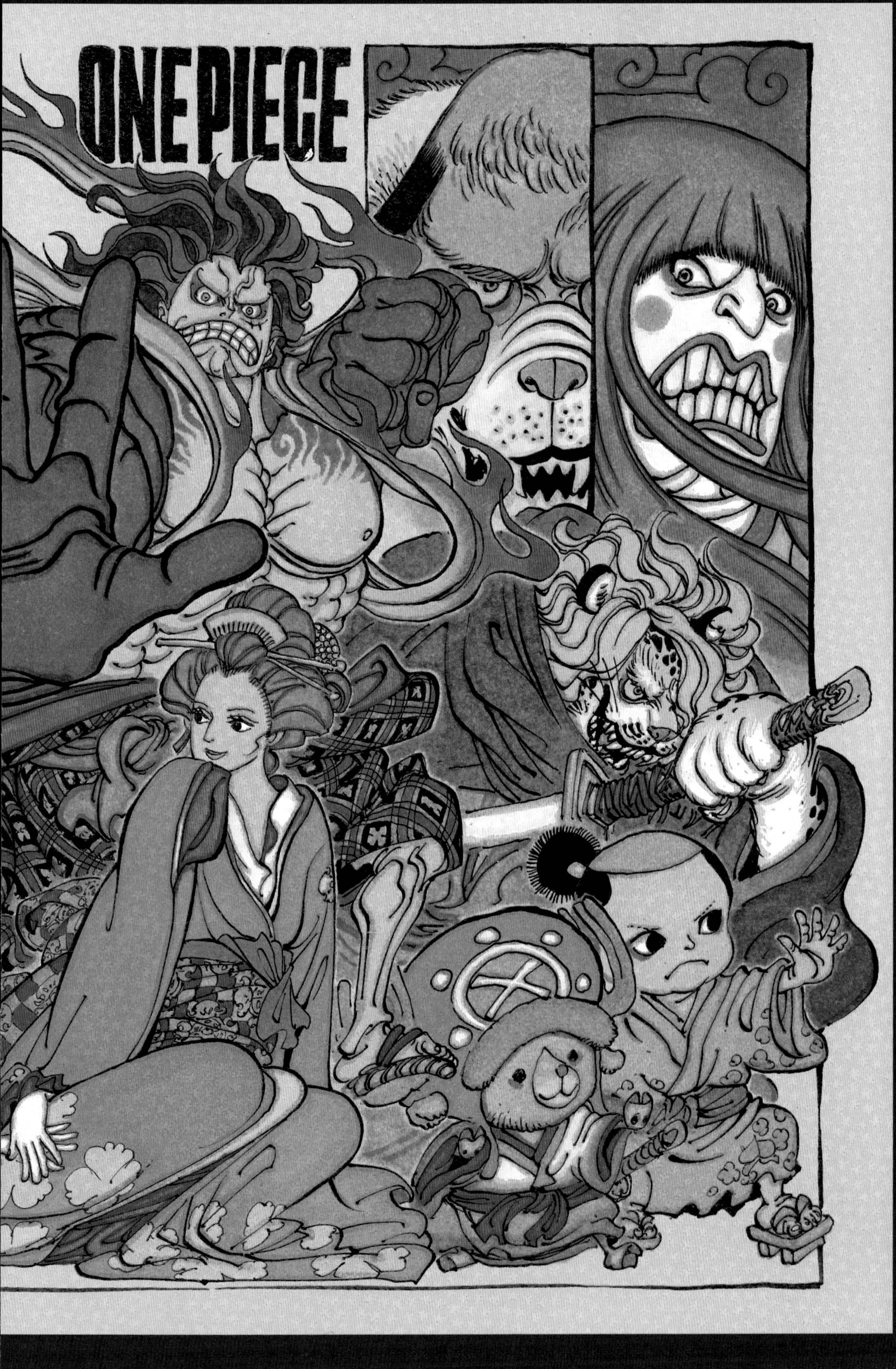
ONE PIECE

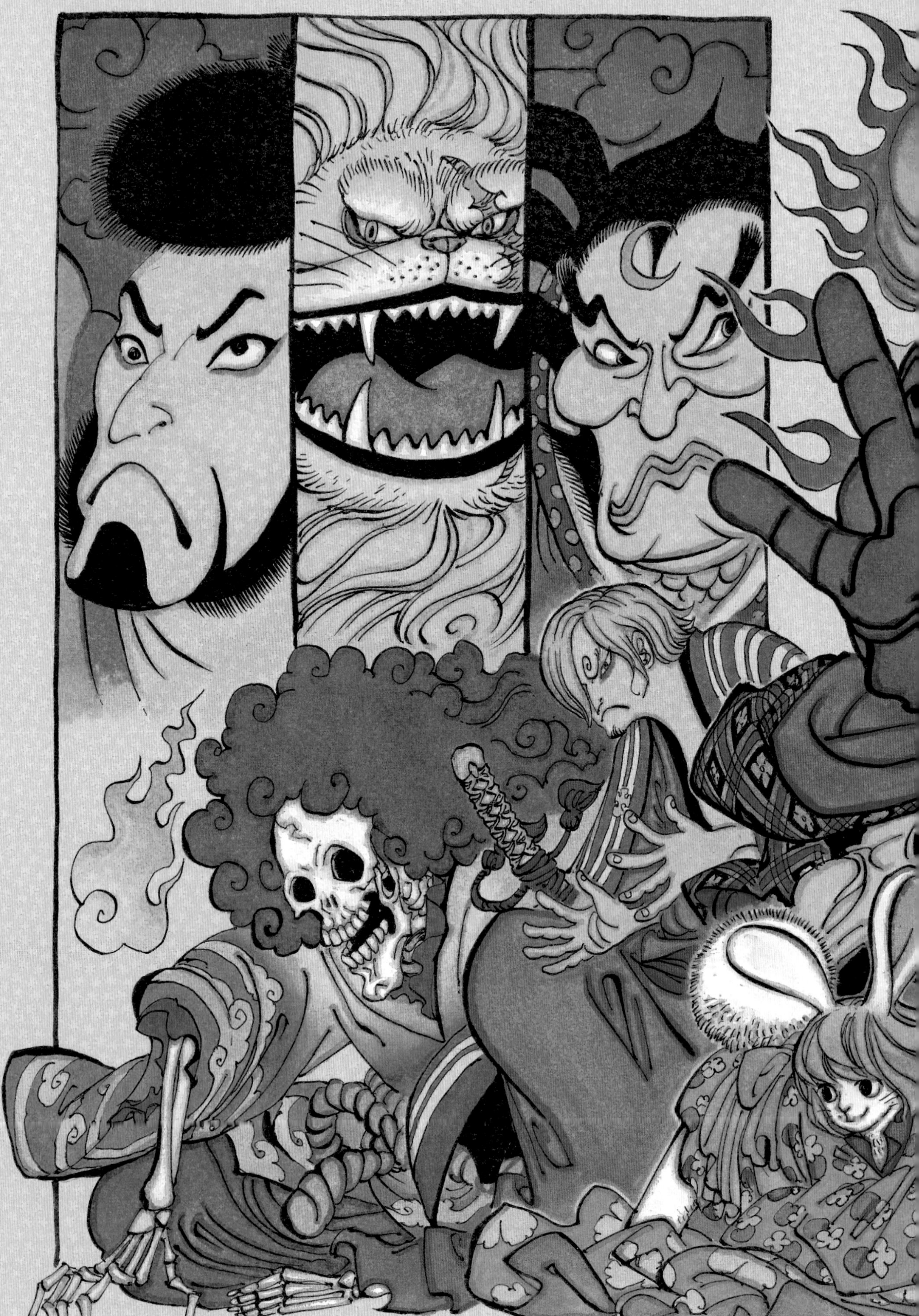

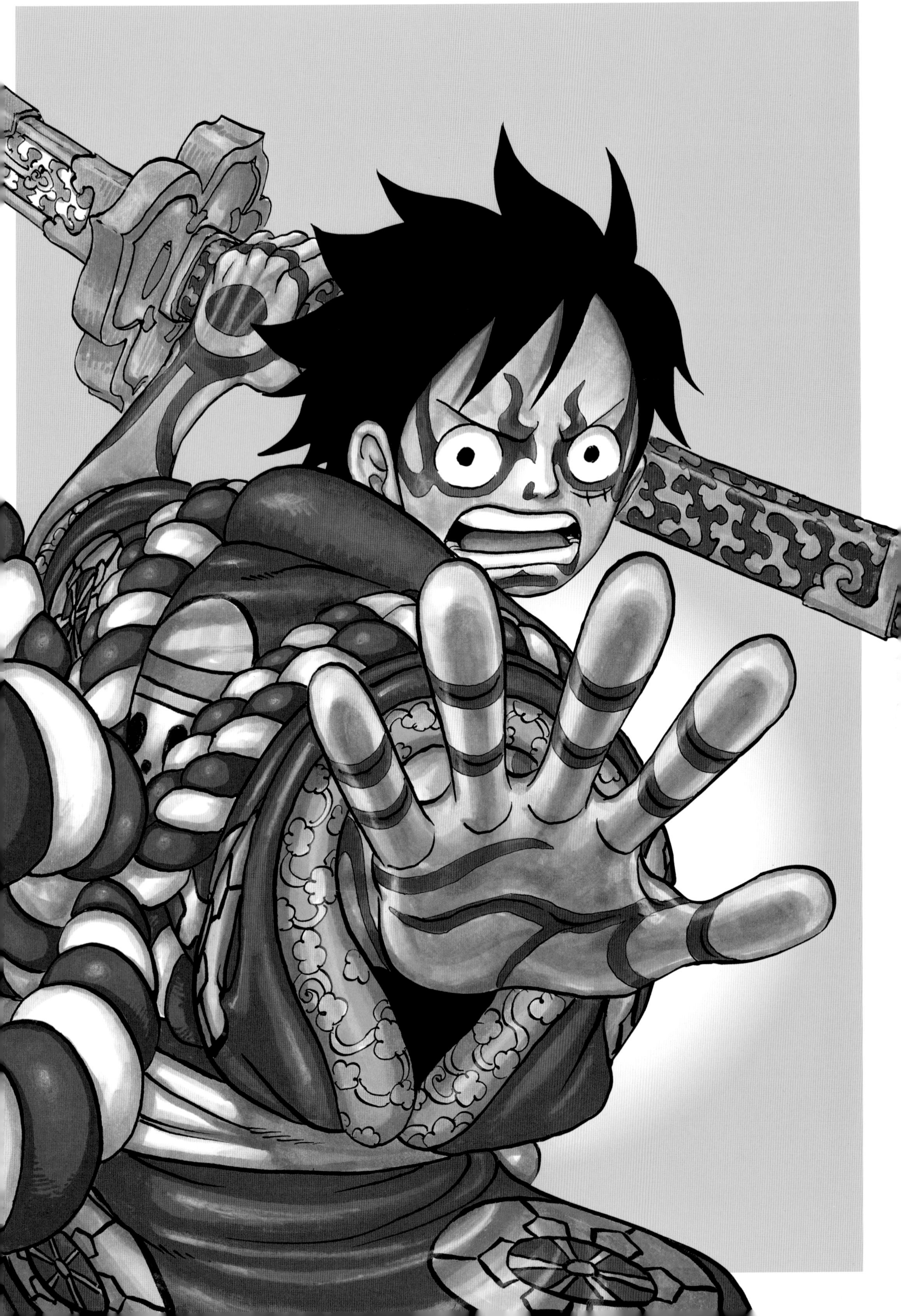

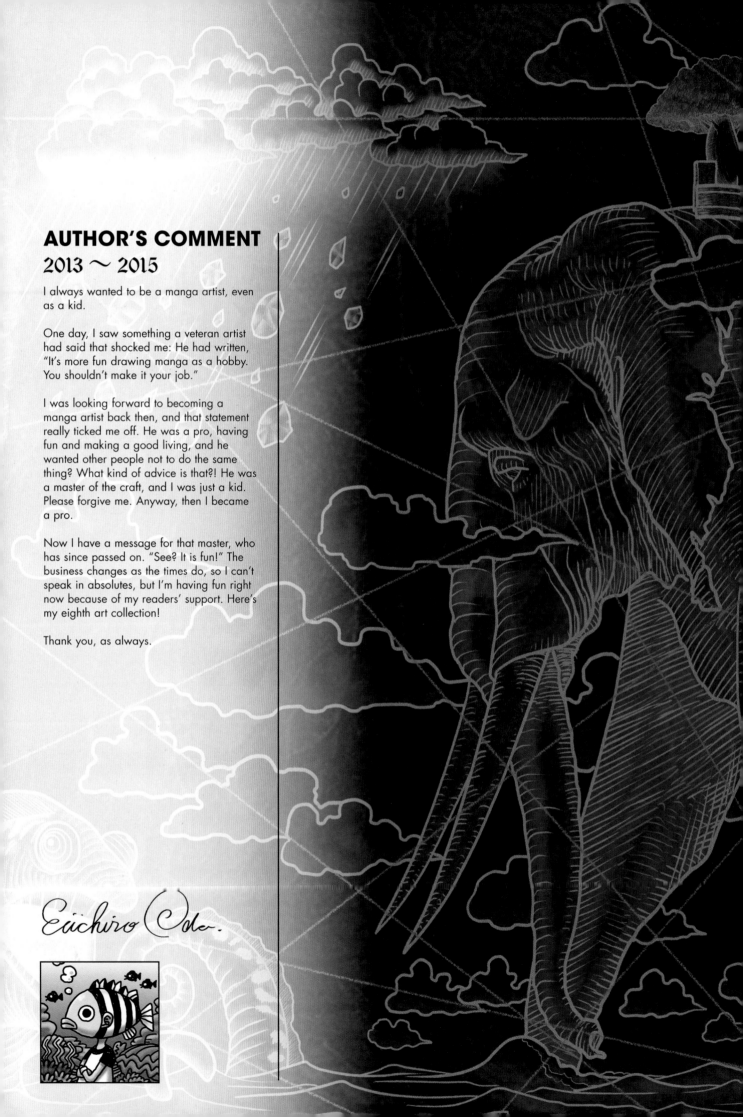

AUTHOR'S COMMENT
2013 ~ 2015

I always wanted to be a manga artist, even as a kid.

One day, I saw something a veteran artist had said that shocked me: He had written, "It's more fun drawing manga as a hobby. You shouldn't make it your job."

I was looking forward to becoming a manga artist back then, and that statement really ticked me off. He was a pro, having fun and making a good living, and he wanted other people not to do the same thing? What kind of advice is that?! He was a master of the craft, and I was just a kid. Please forgive me. Anyway, then I became a pro.

Now I have a message for that master, who has since passed on. "See? It is fun!" The business changes as the times do, so I can't speak in absolutes, but I'm having fun right now because of my readers' support. Here's my eighth art collection!

Thank you, as always.

Eiichiro Oda.

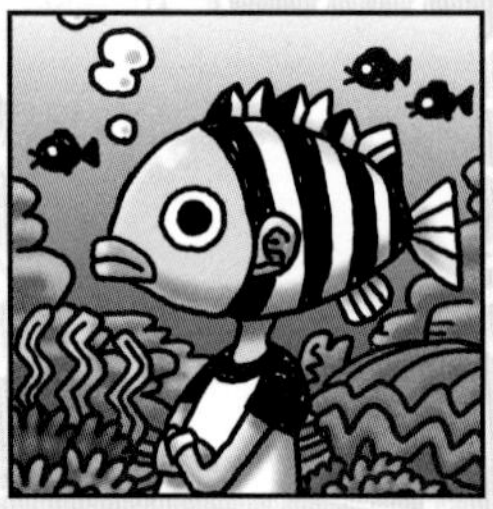

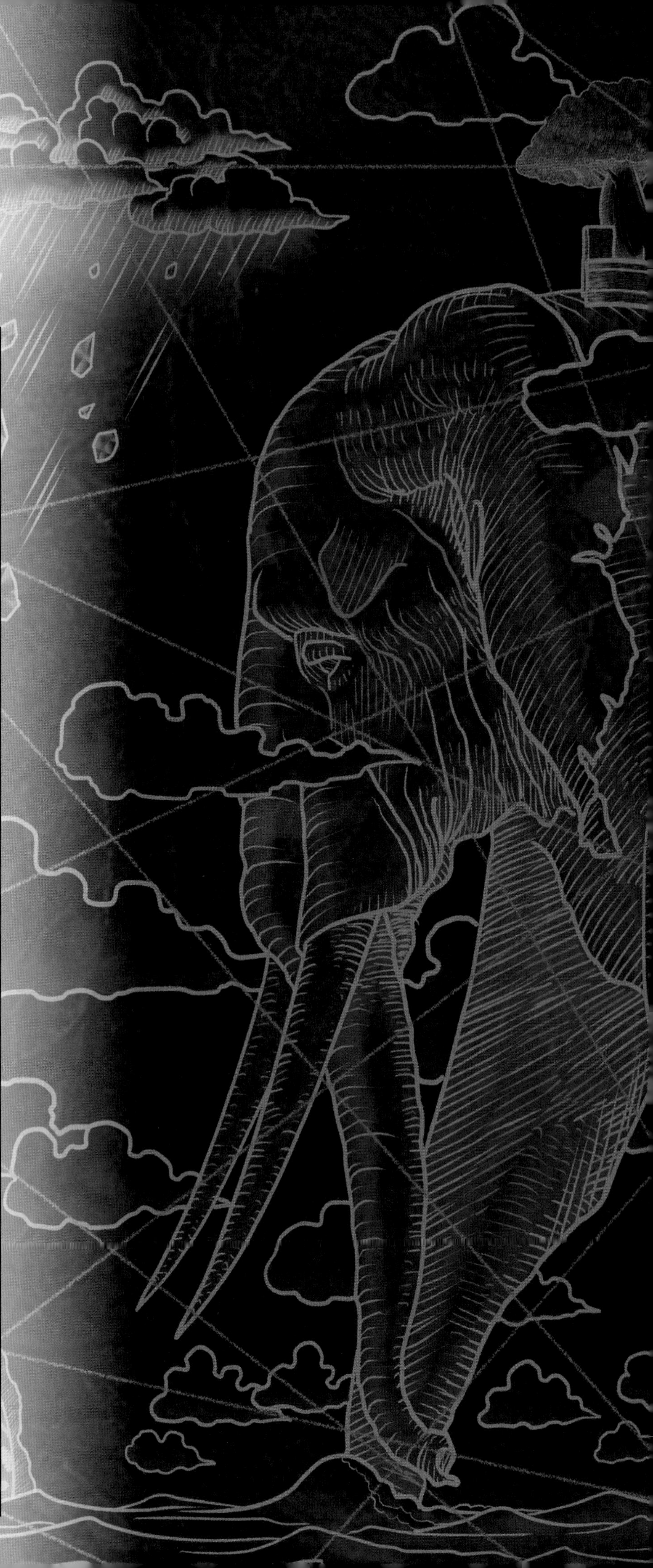

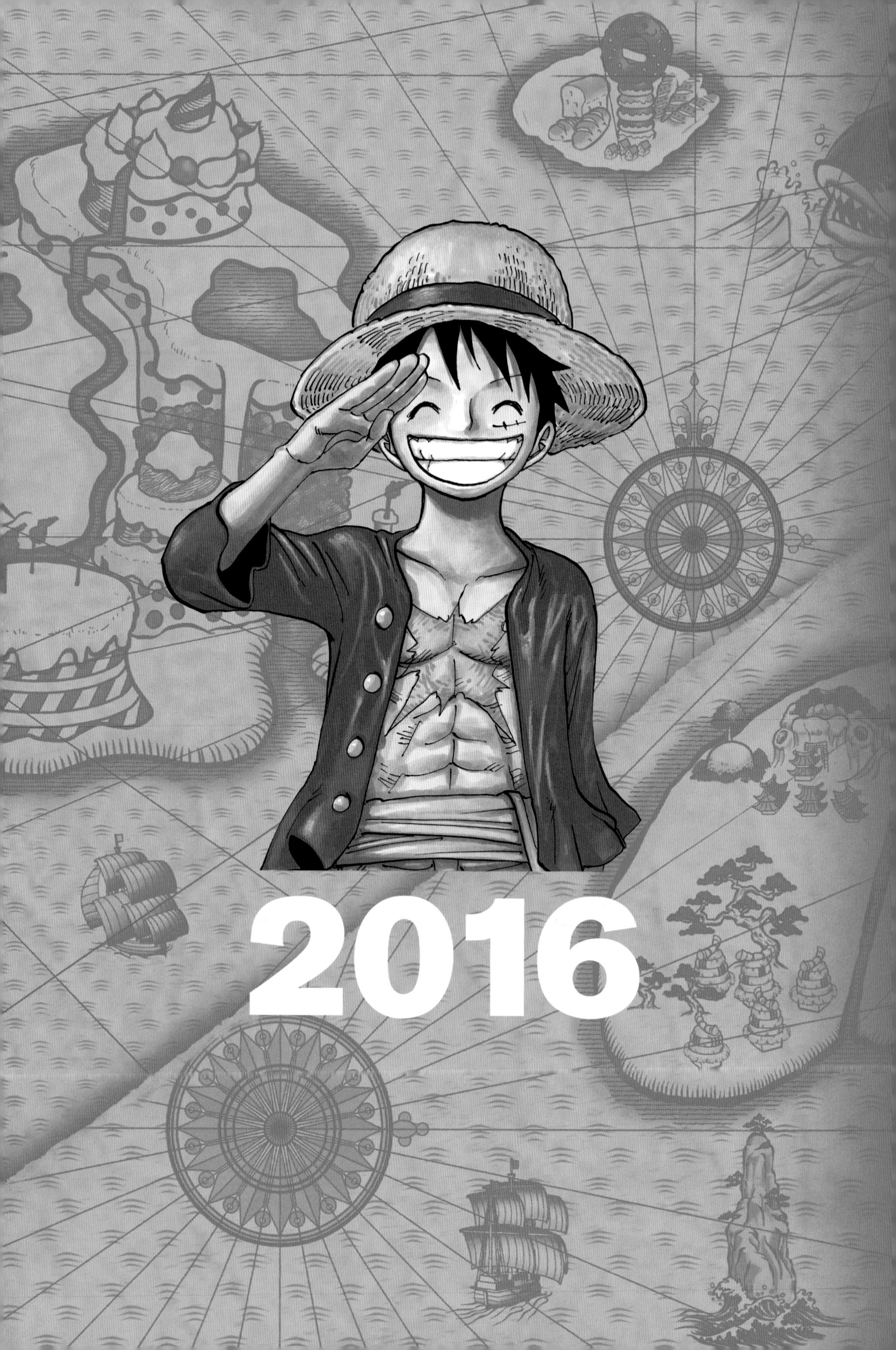
2016

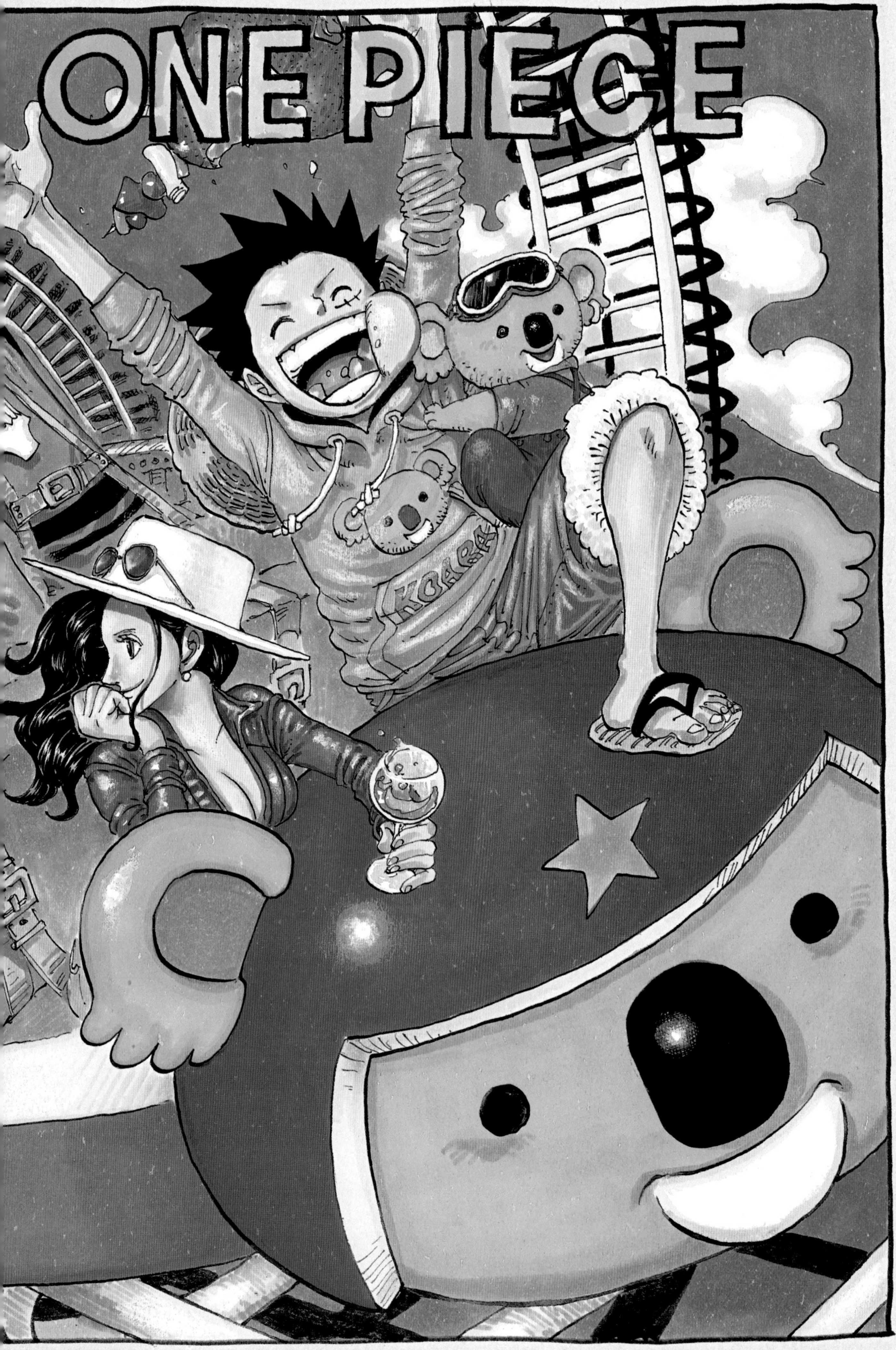
ONE PIECE
KOALA

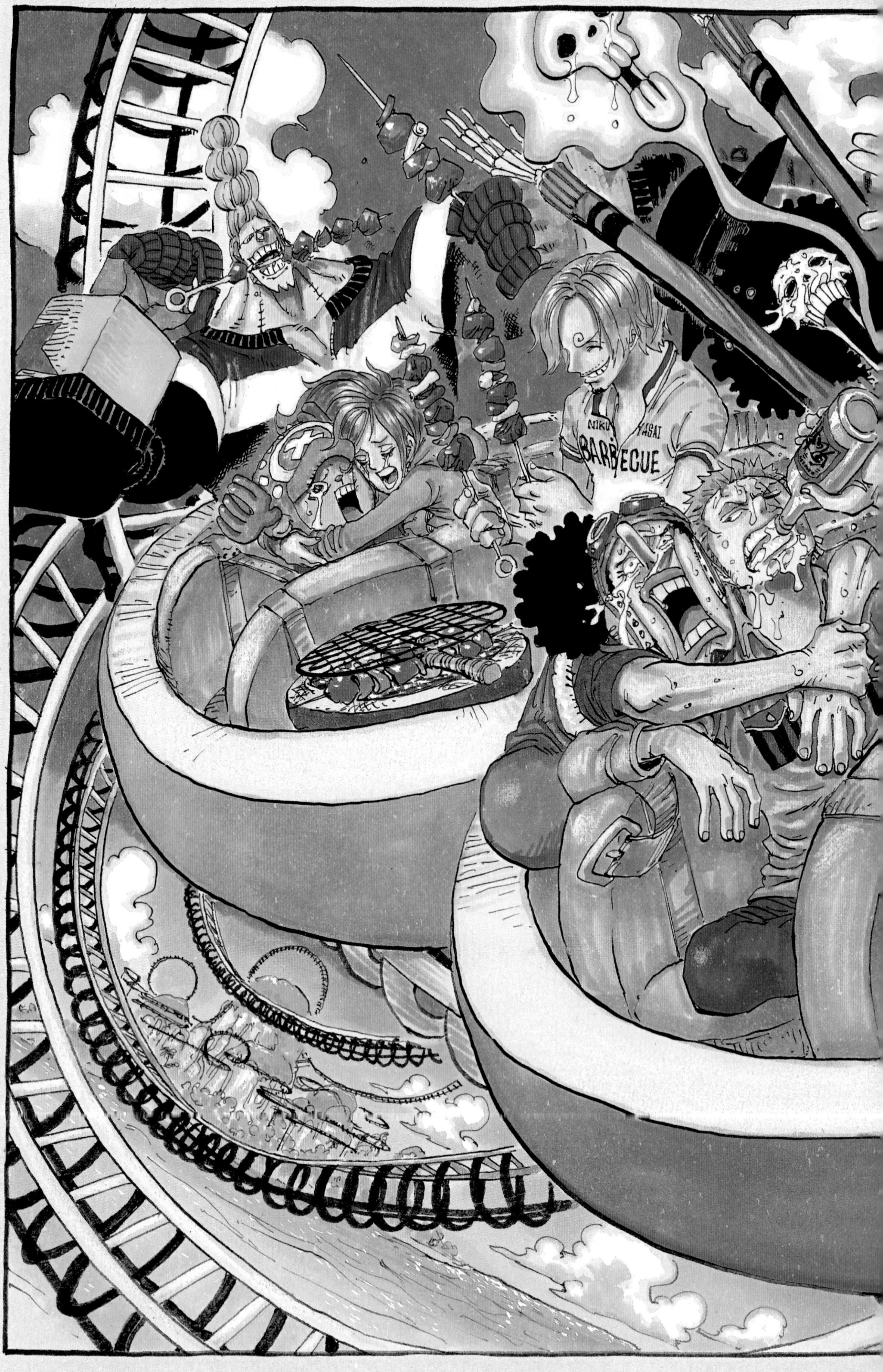
NIKU YASAI
BARBECUE

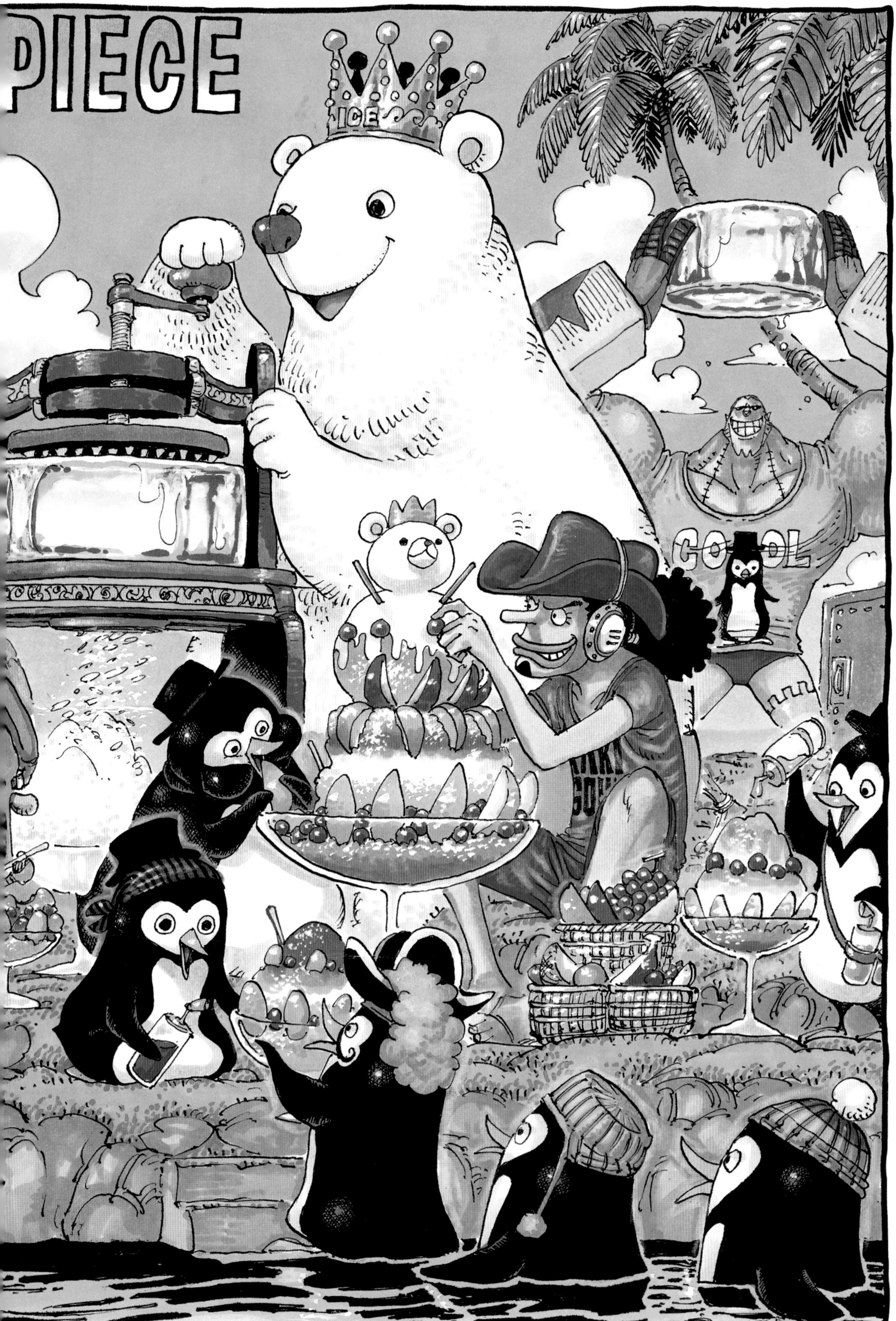
PIECE
ICE
COOL

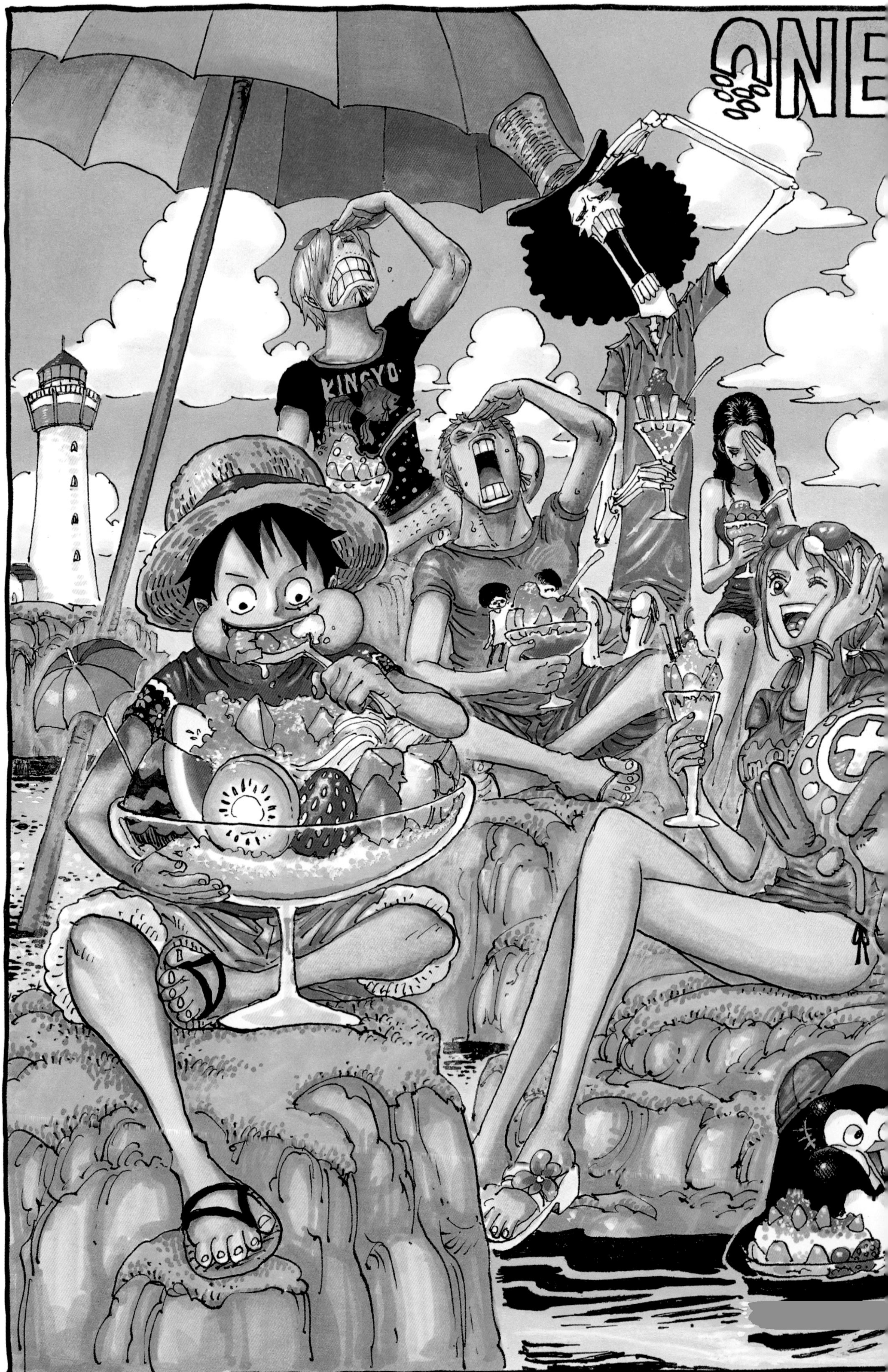
ONE
KINGYO

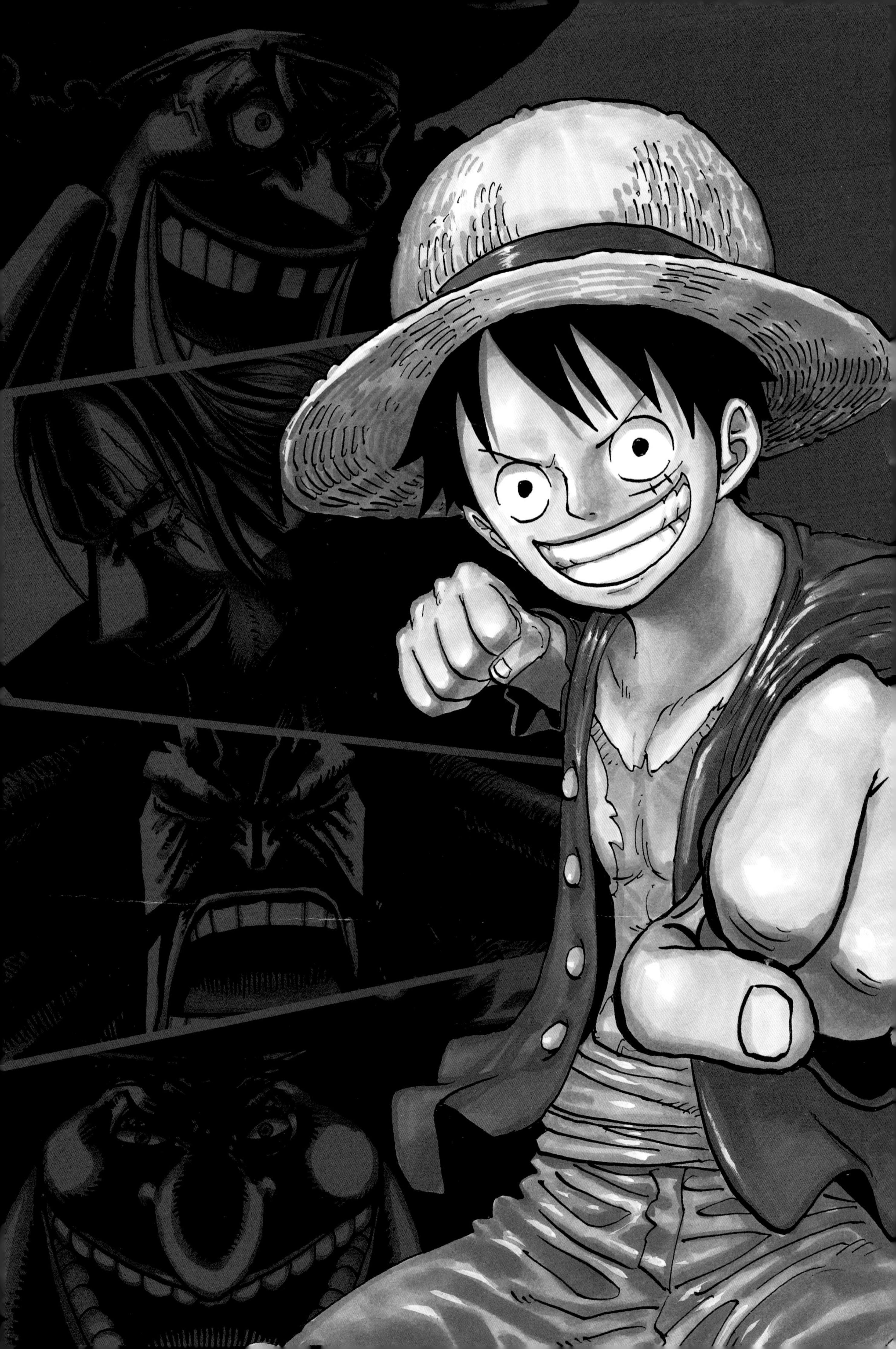

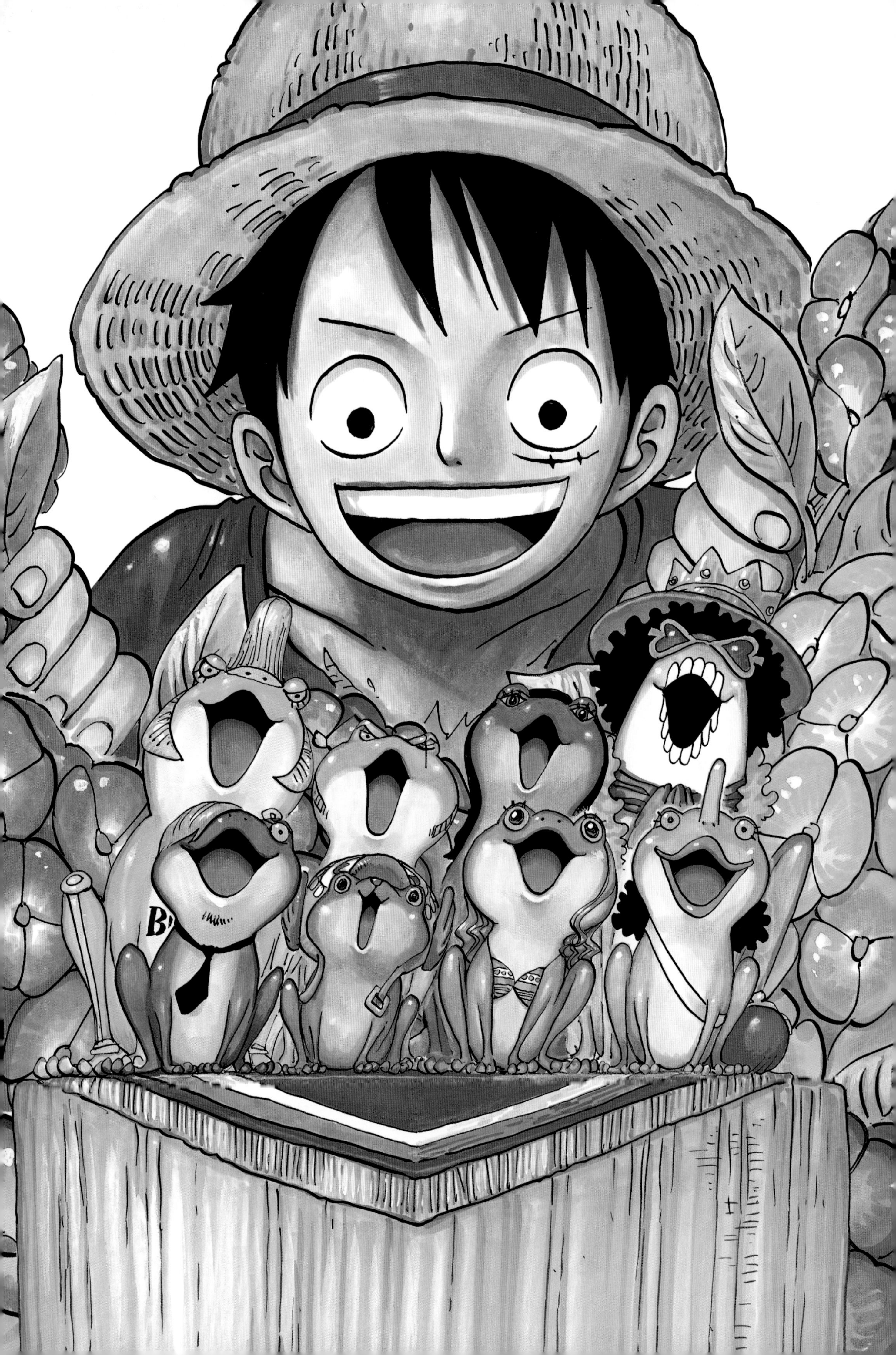

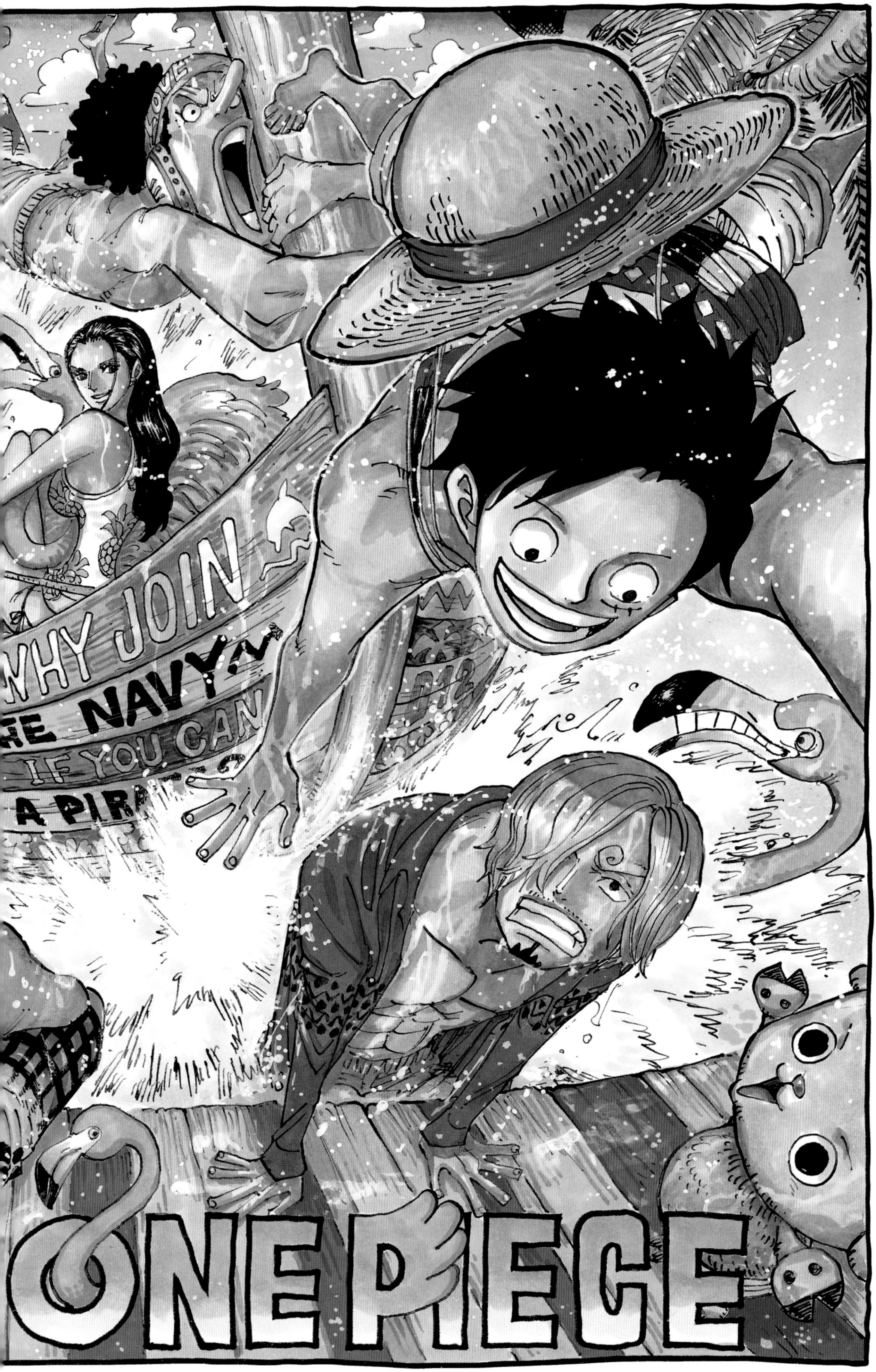

WHY JOIN
THE NAVY
IF YOU CAN
A PIR
ONE PIECE

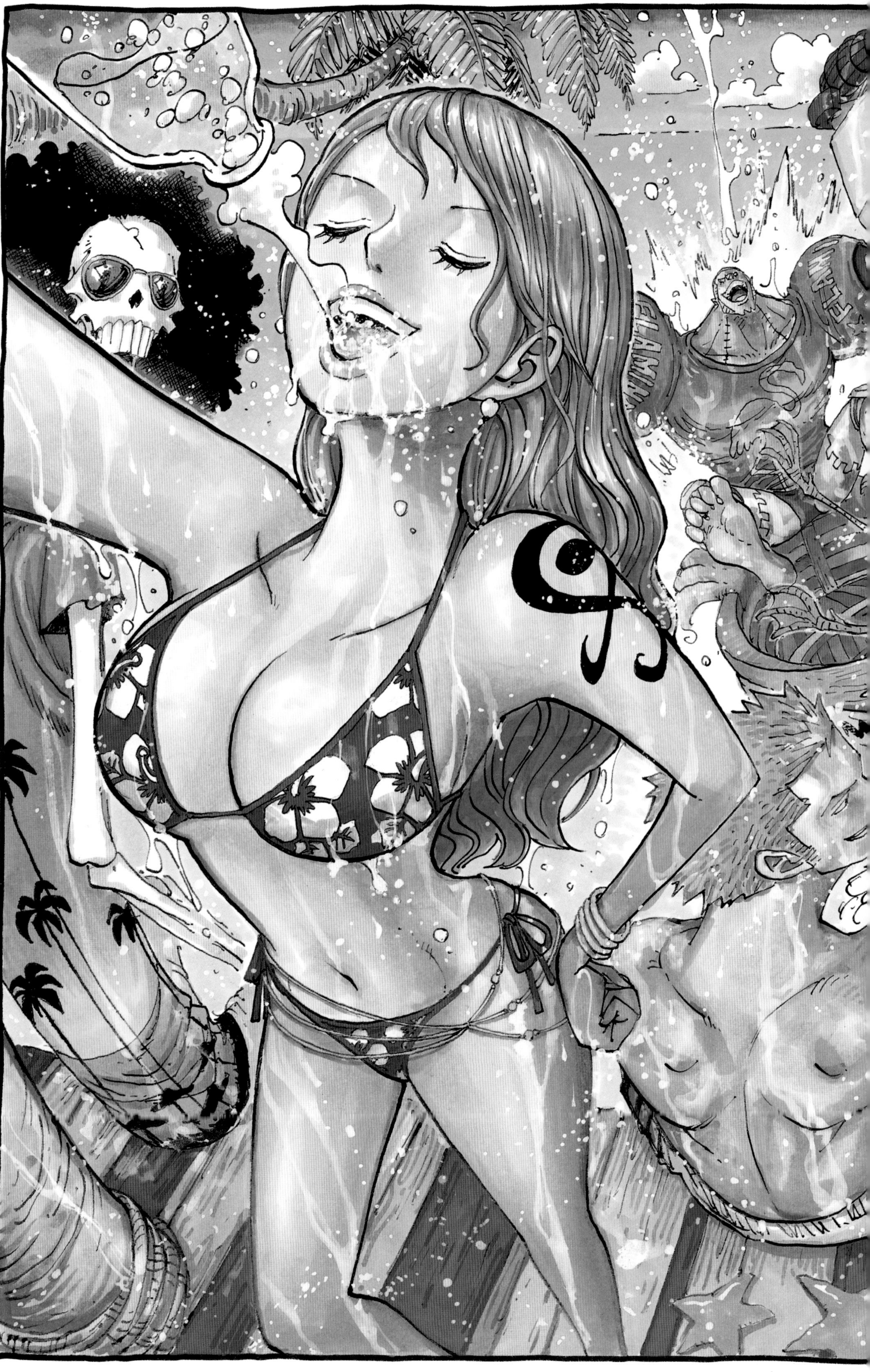

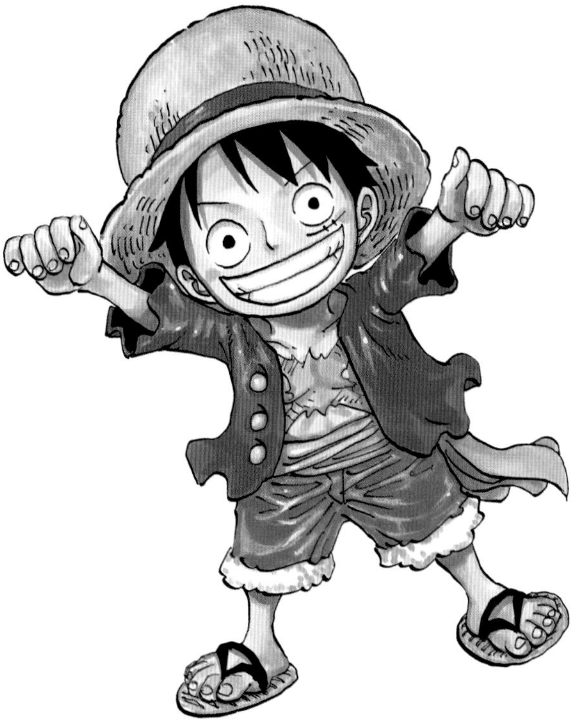

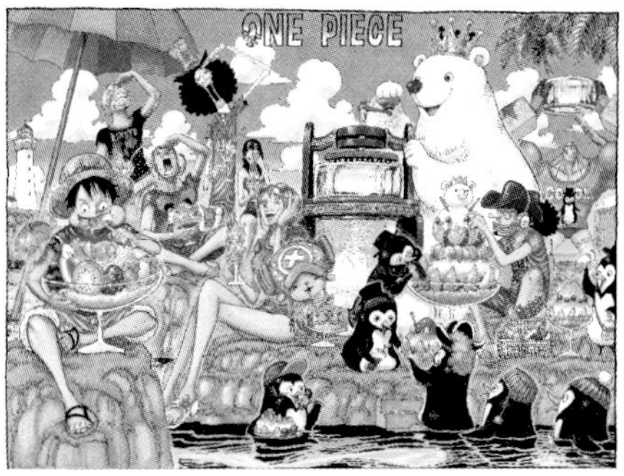
ONE PIECE

Comments P.208–209

There's a kind of shaved ice they sell in Kyushu called "polar bear." It's where a polar bear makes the shaved ice for you, as seen here. Only one of those statements is false.

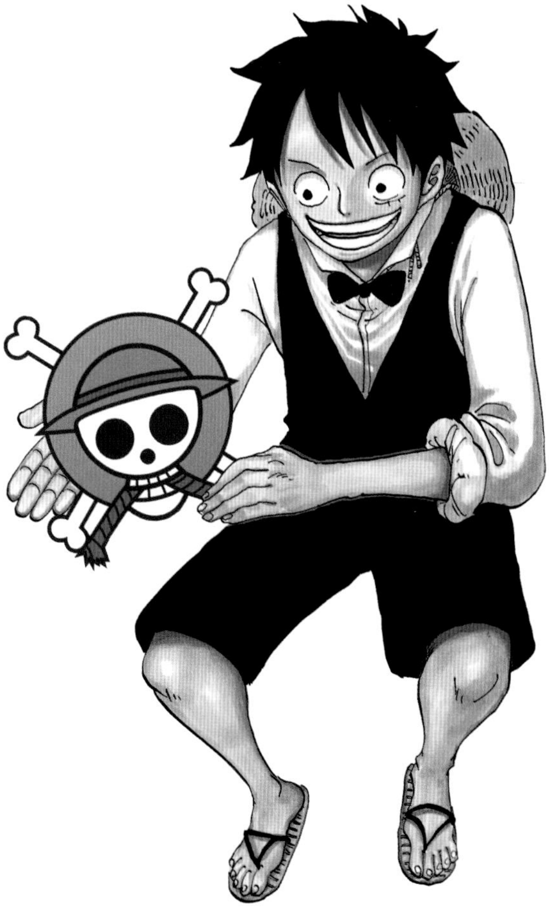

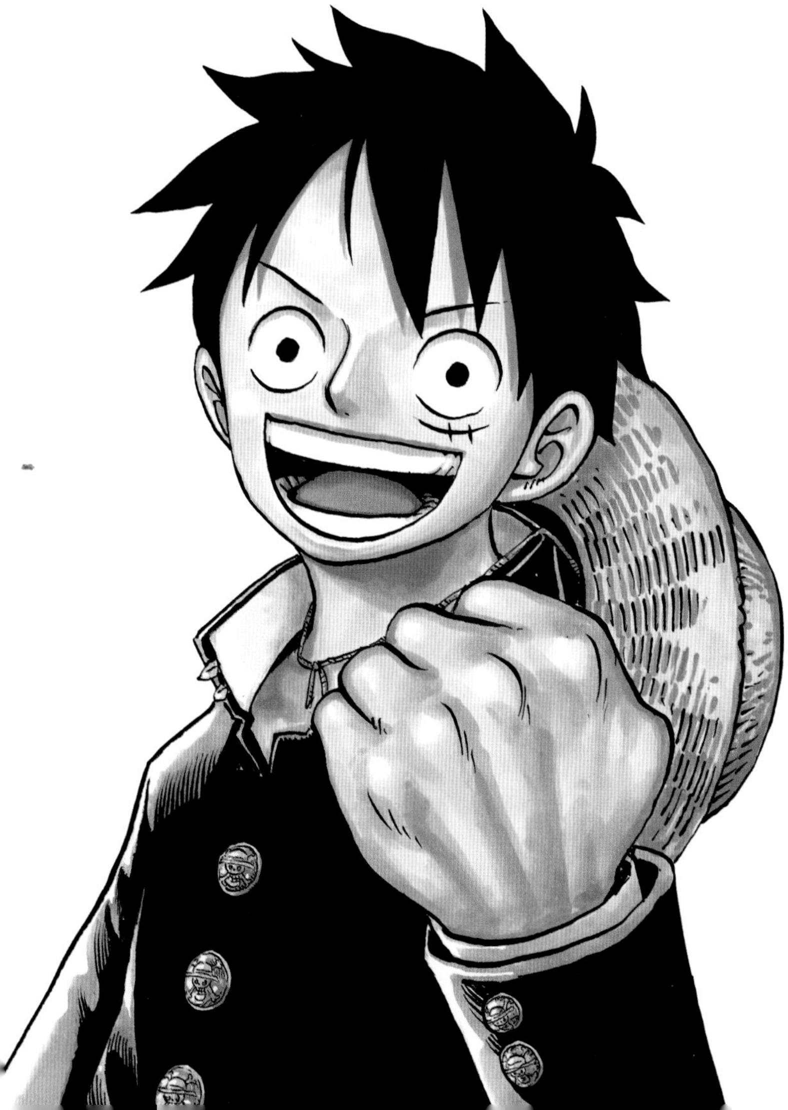

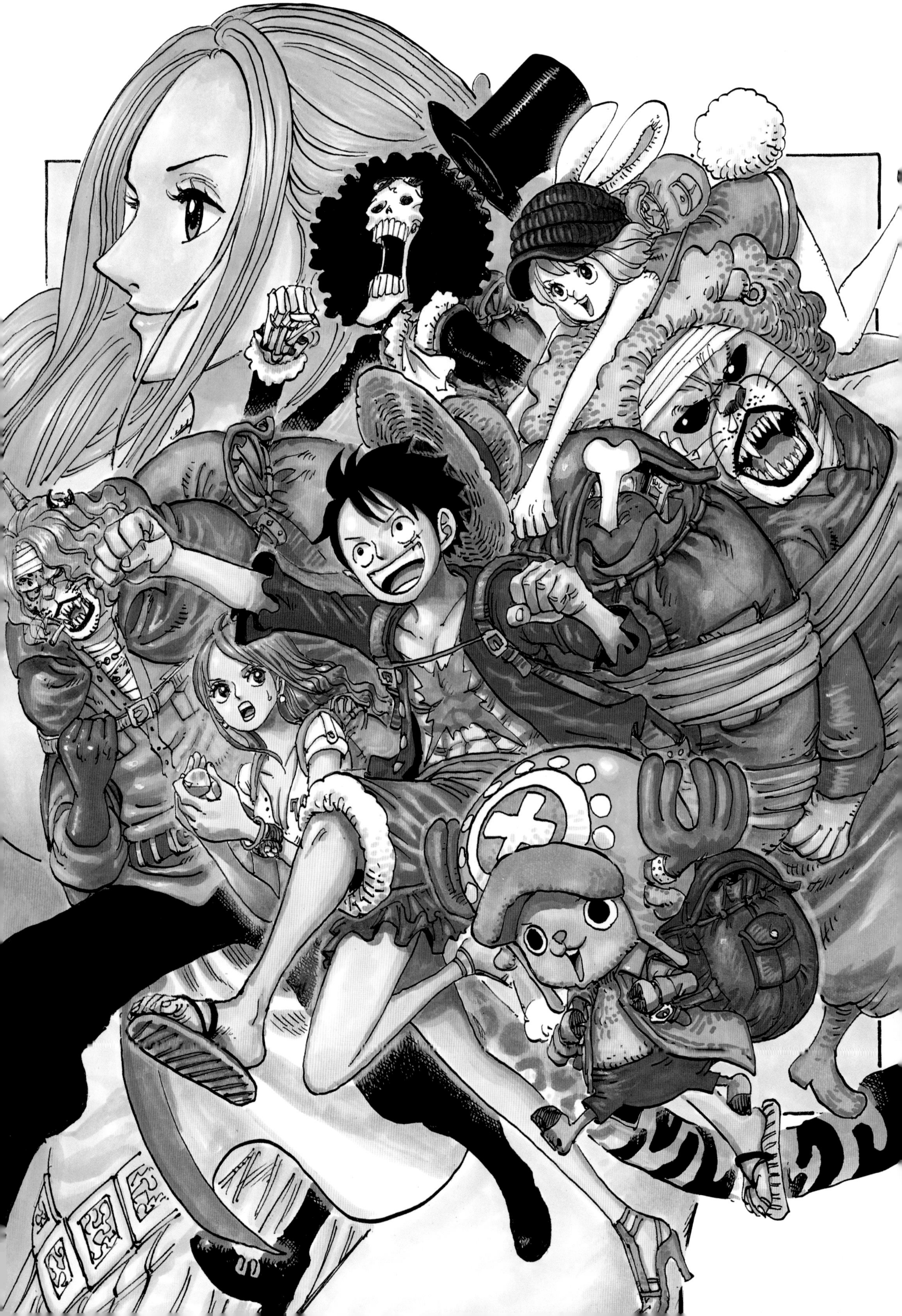

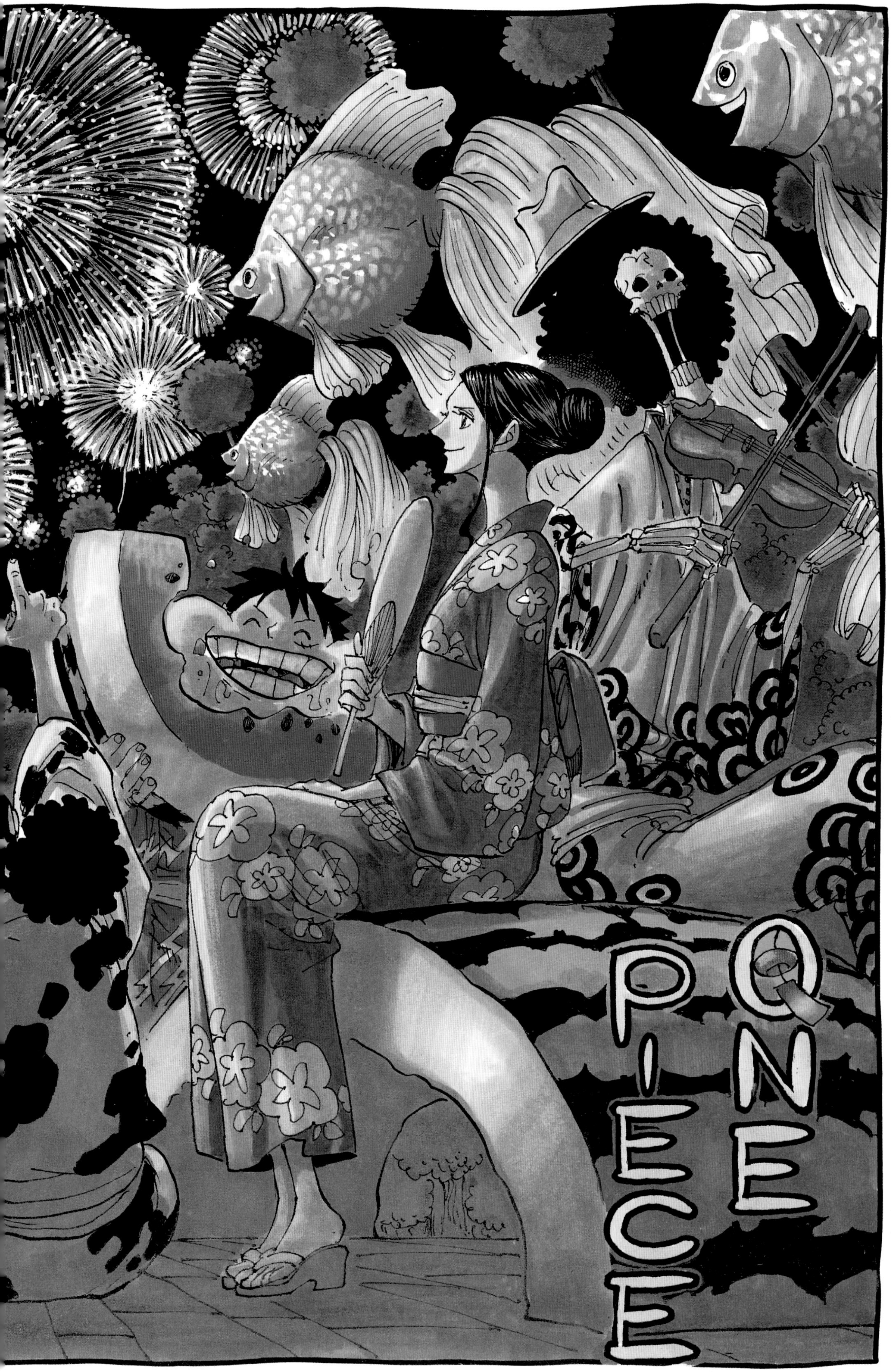
ONE PIECE

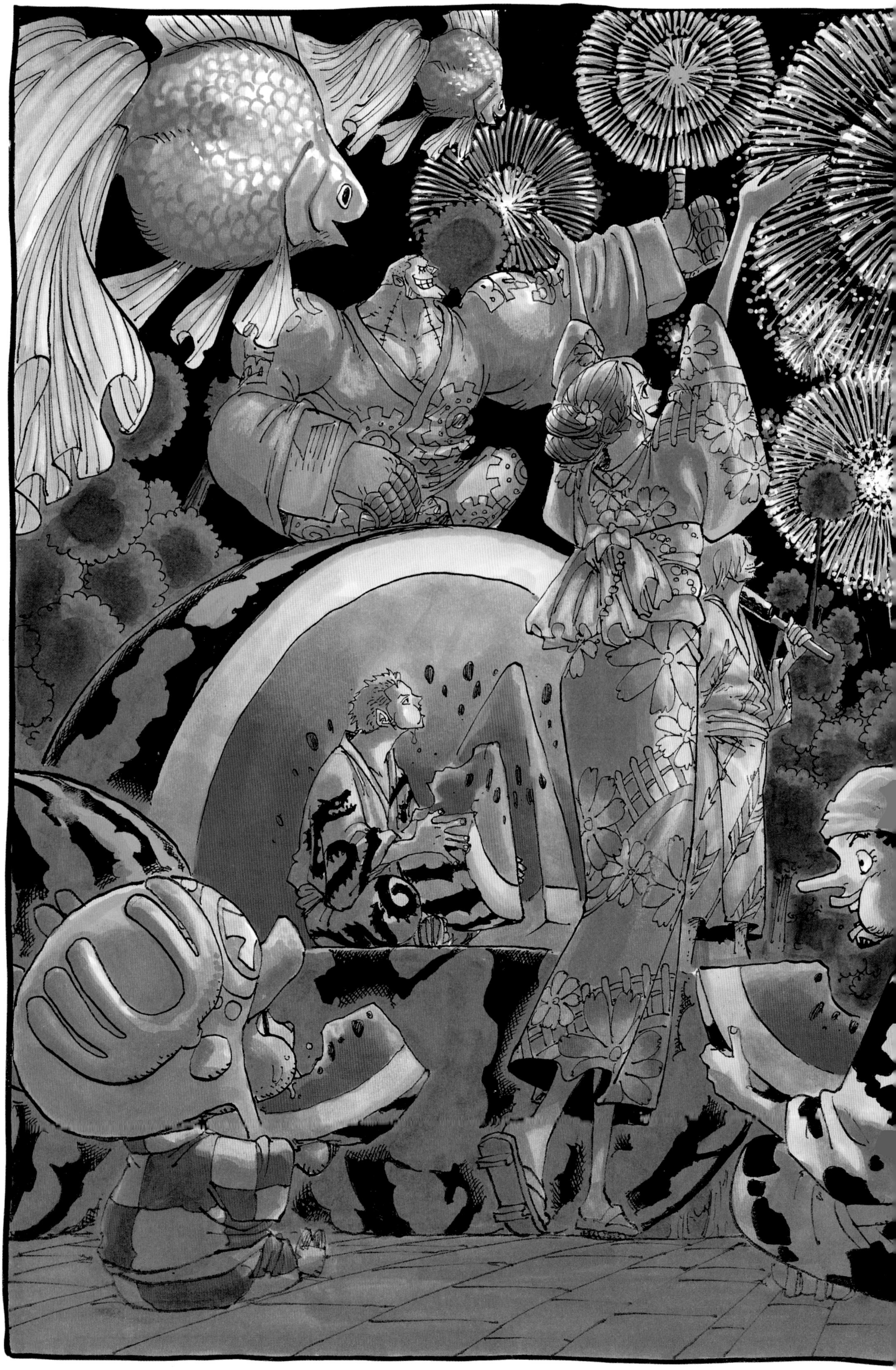

ONE
PIECE

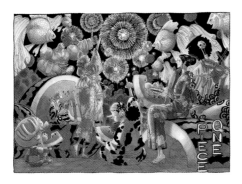

Comments P.216–217

My editor requested an image with fireworks. So I drew a "Japanese summer." I have many fond memories of eating giant watermelon and watching the fireworks with flying goldfish.

ONE PIECE
Oda.
OFFICIAL

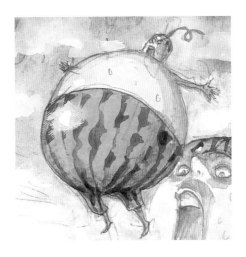

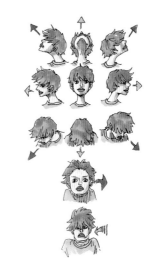

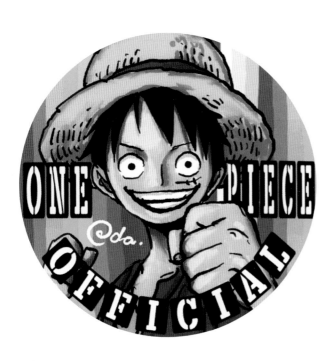

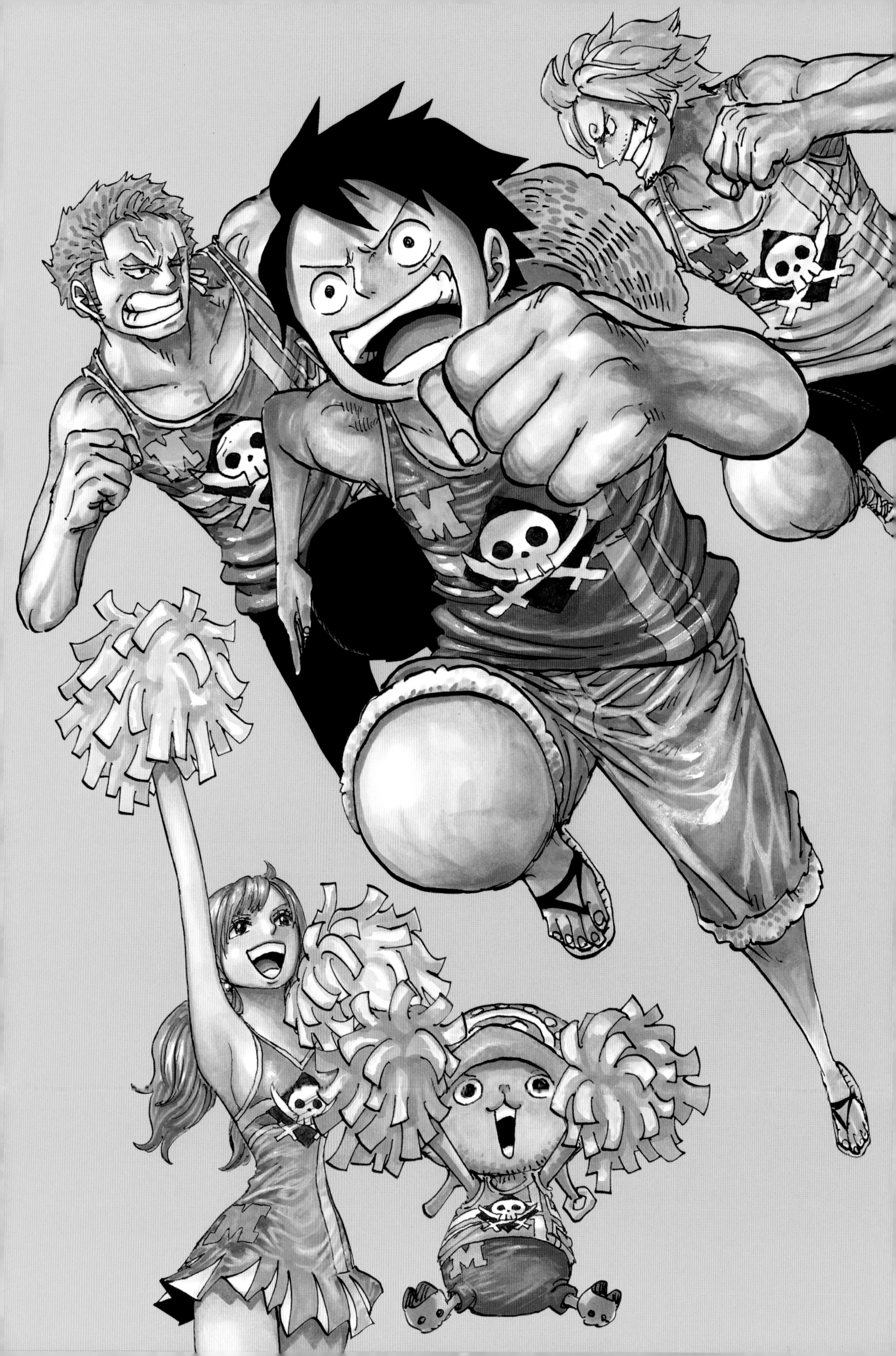

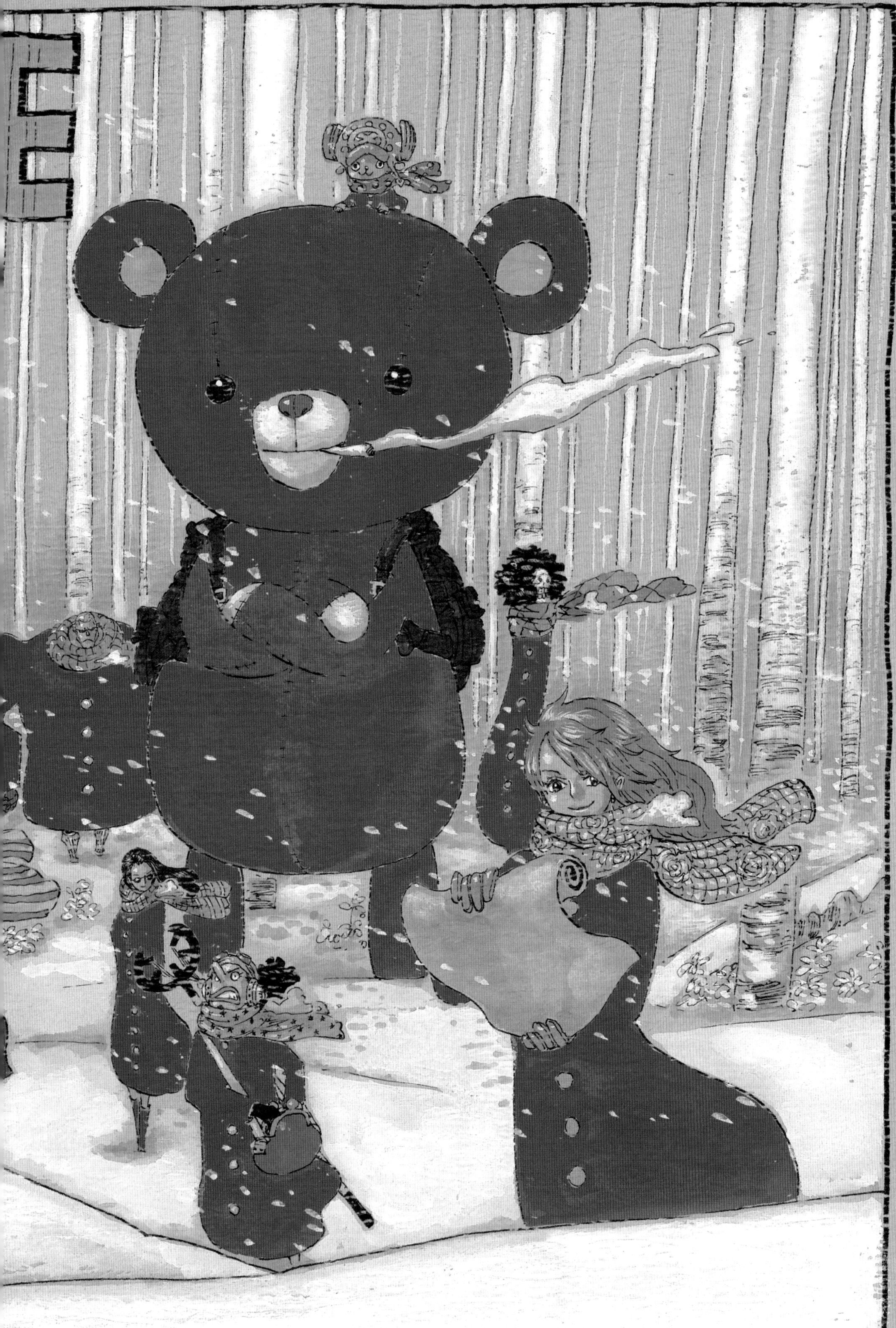

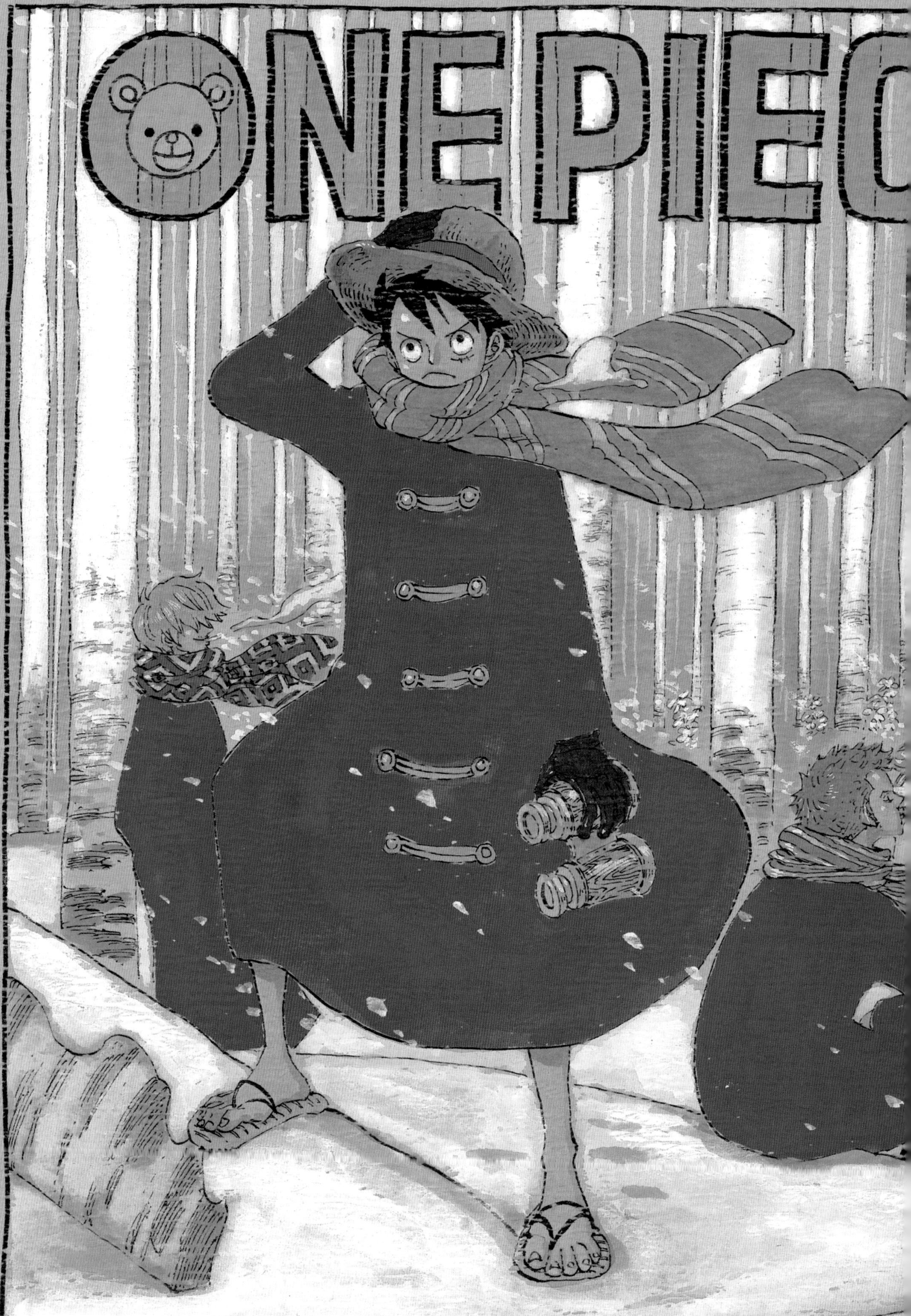
ONEPIEC

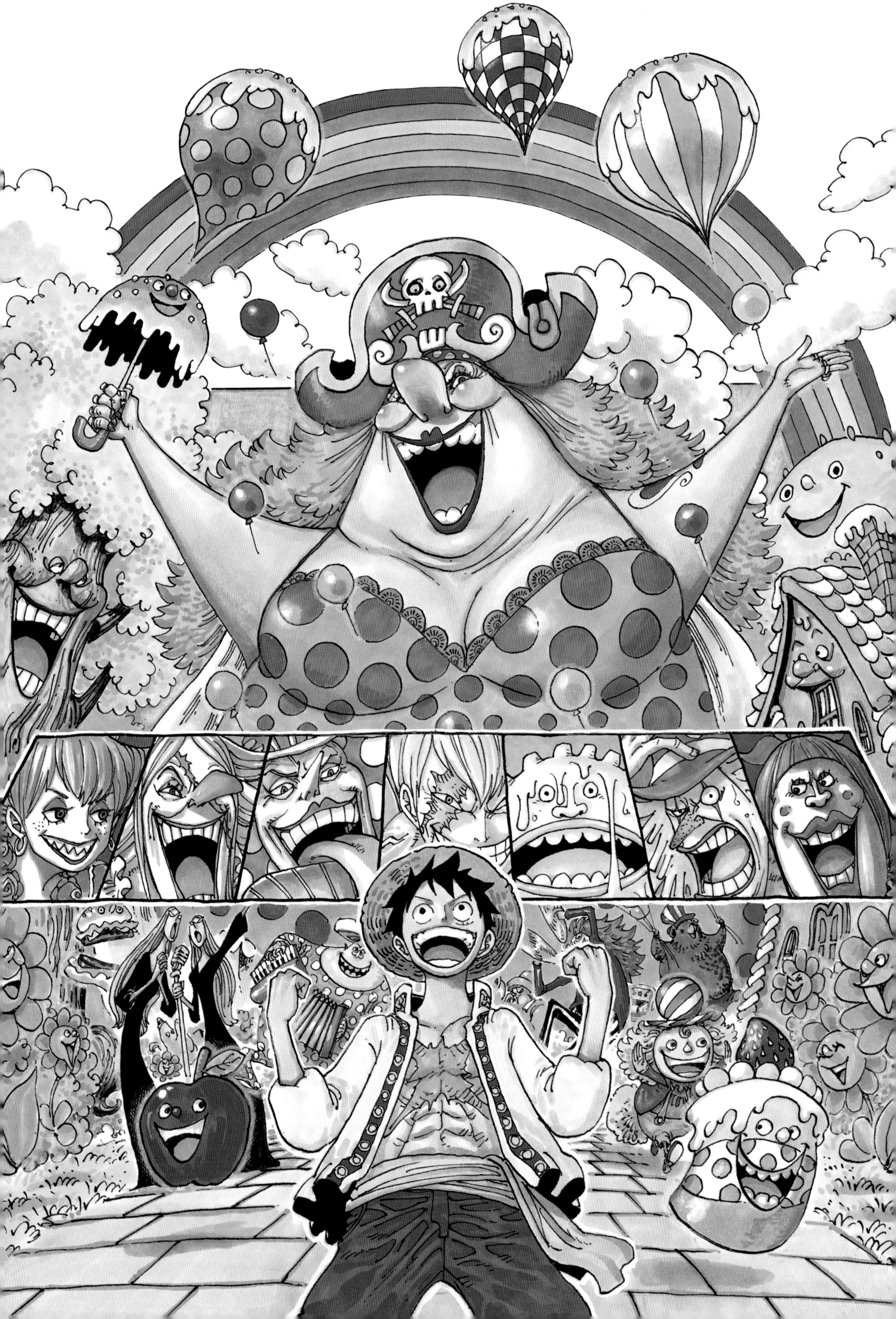

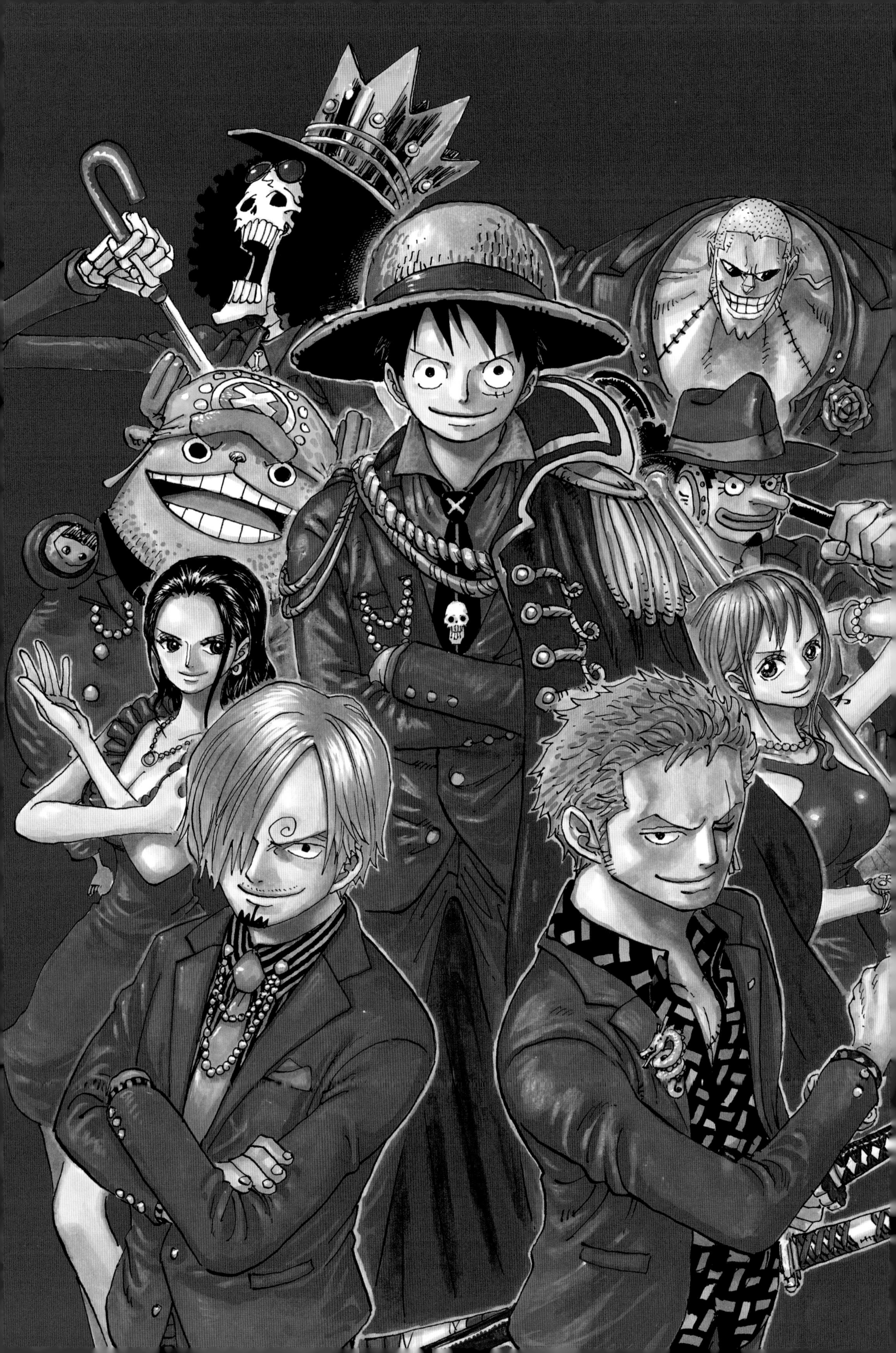

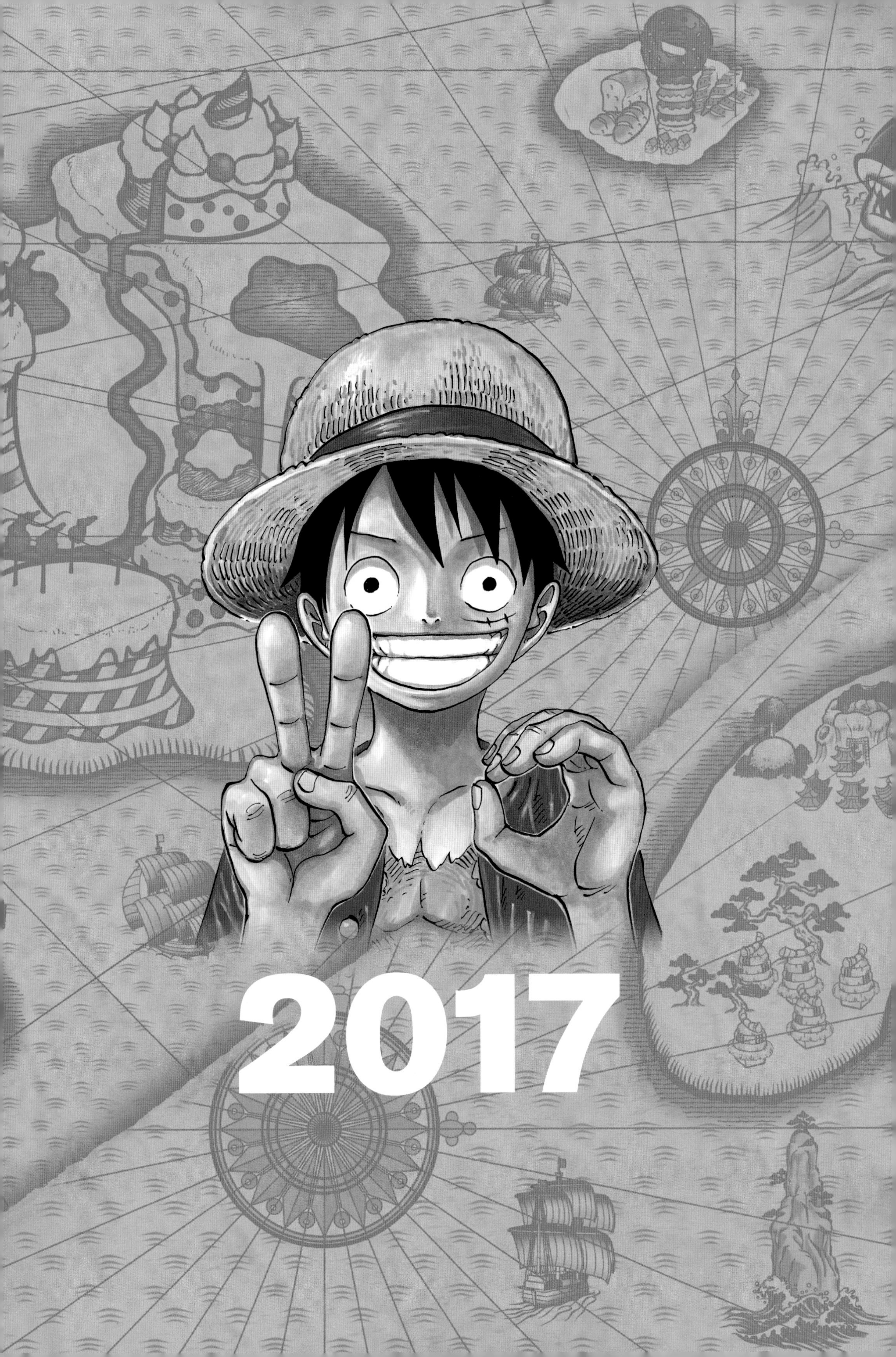
2017

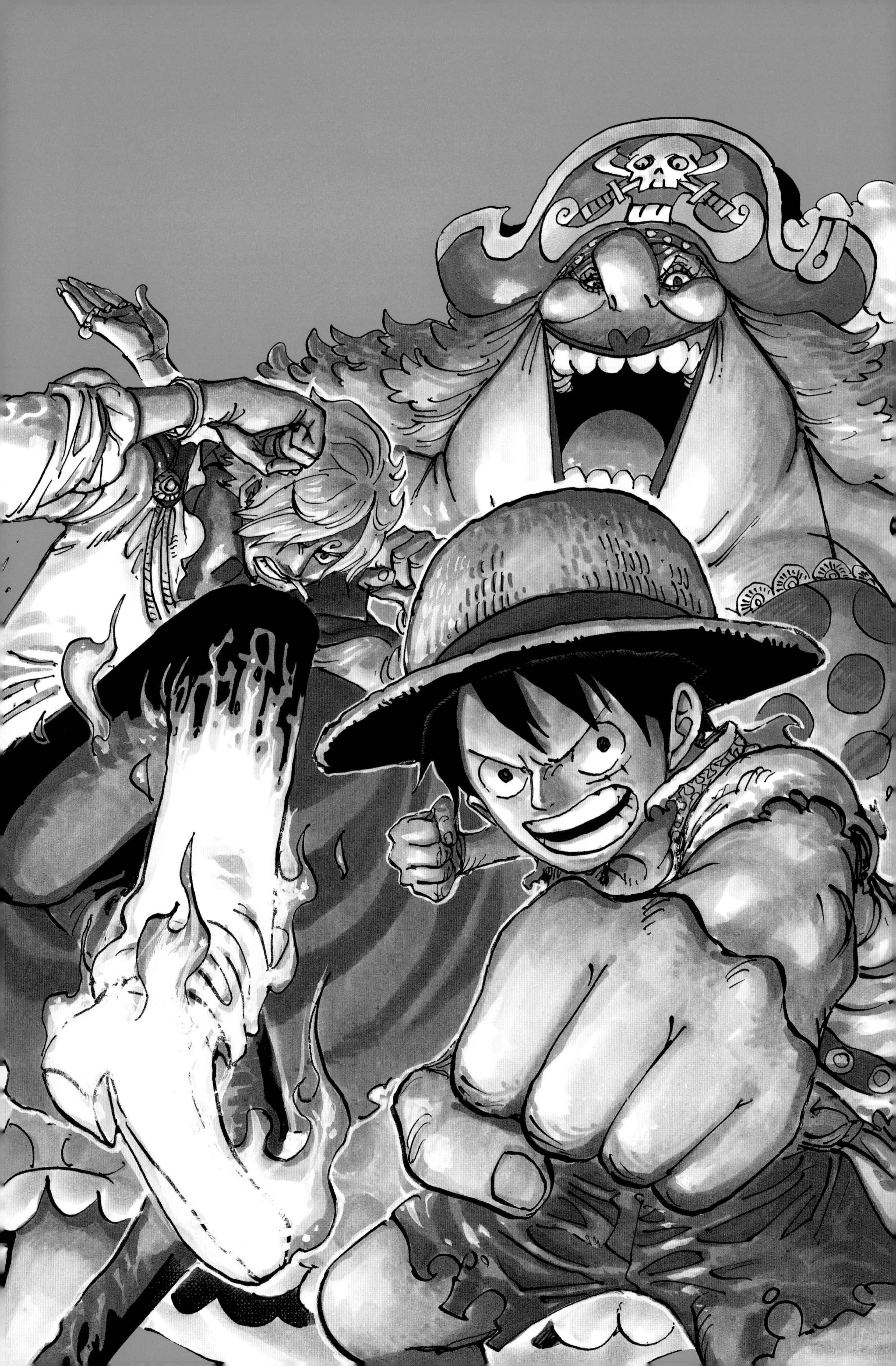

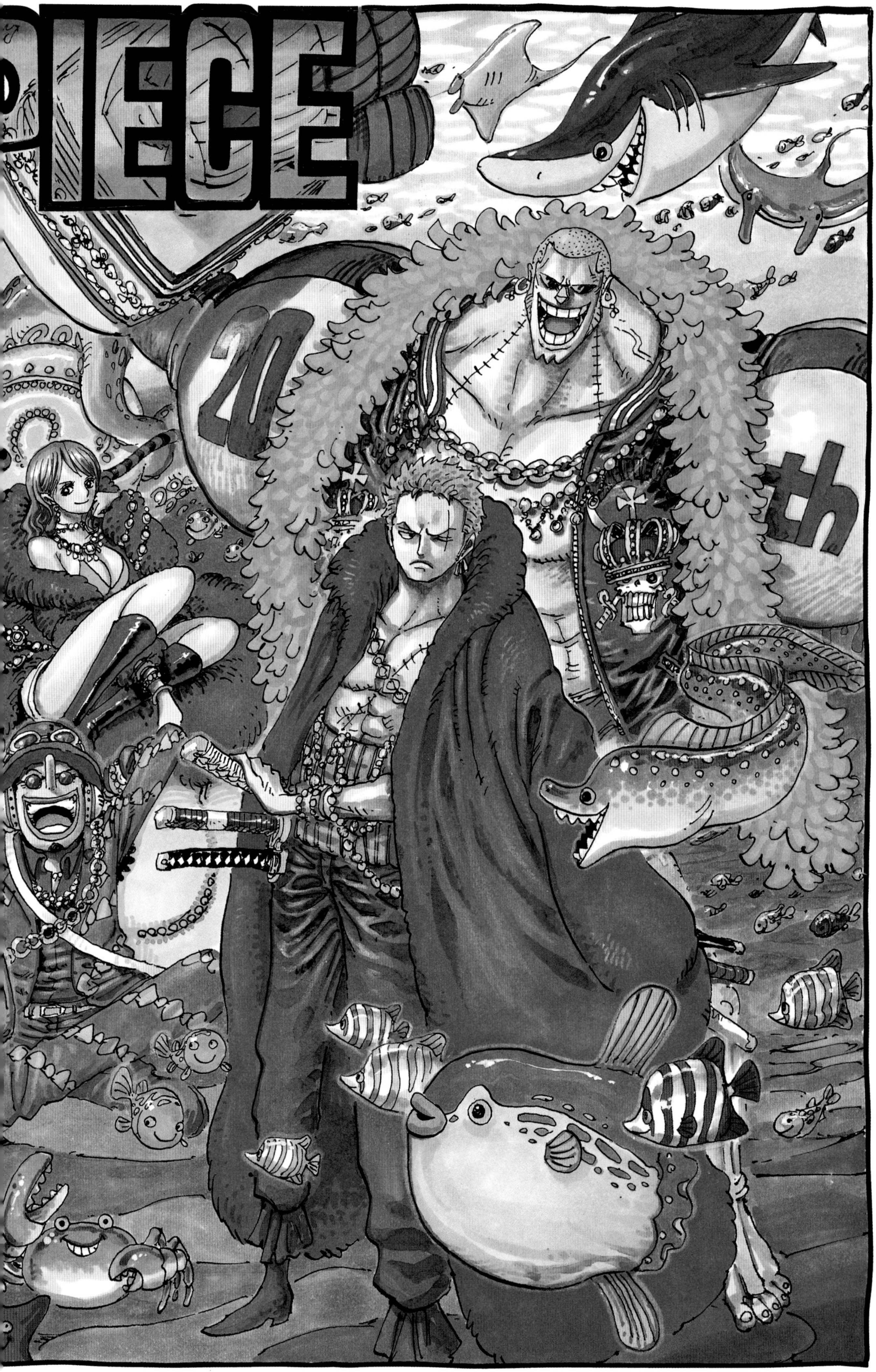
PIECE
20

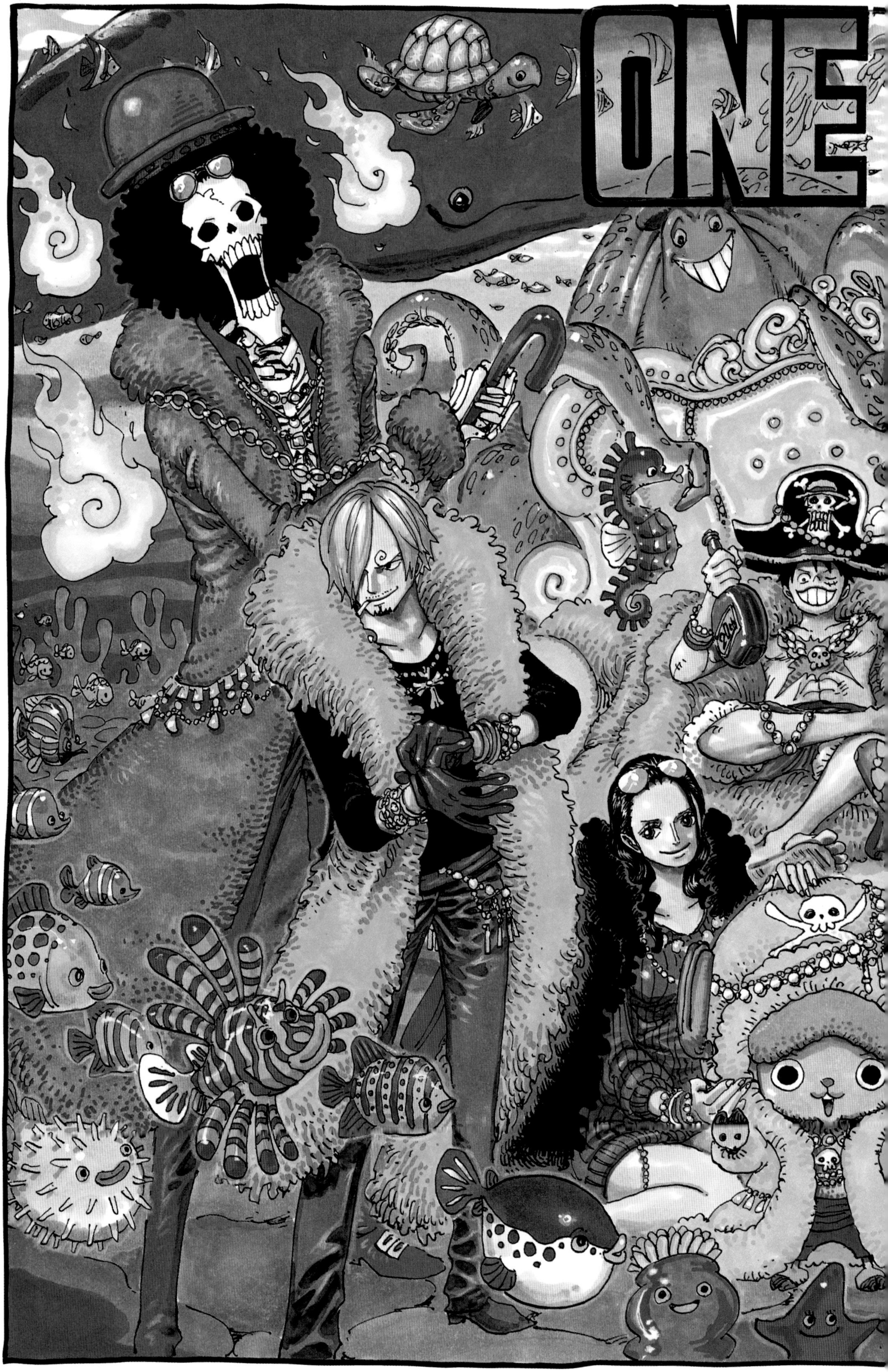
ONE

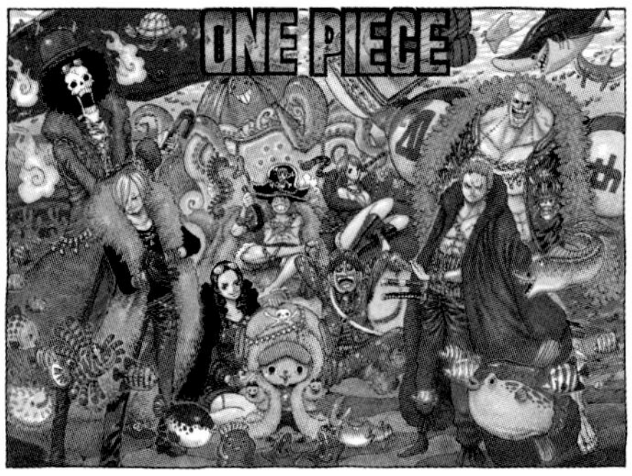
ONE PIECE

Comments P.226–227

My editor wanted some special outfits to get people excited about the twentieth anniversary of the series. They were going to be made into figures too. I thought, "I'll draw outfits so fancy, even the figure modelers won't know what to do!" The end result was that they were super-awesome figures. Never underestimate a professional.

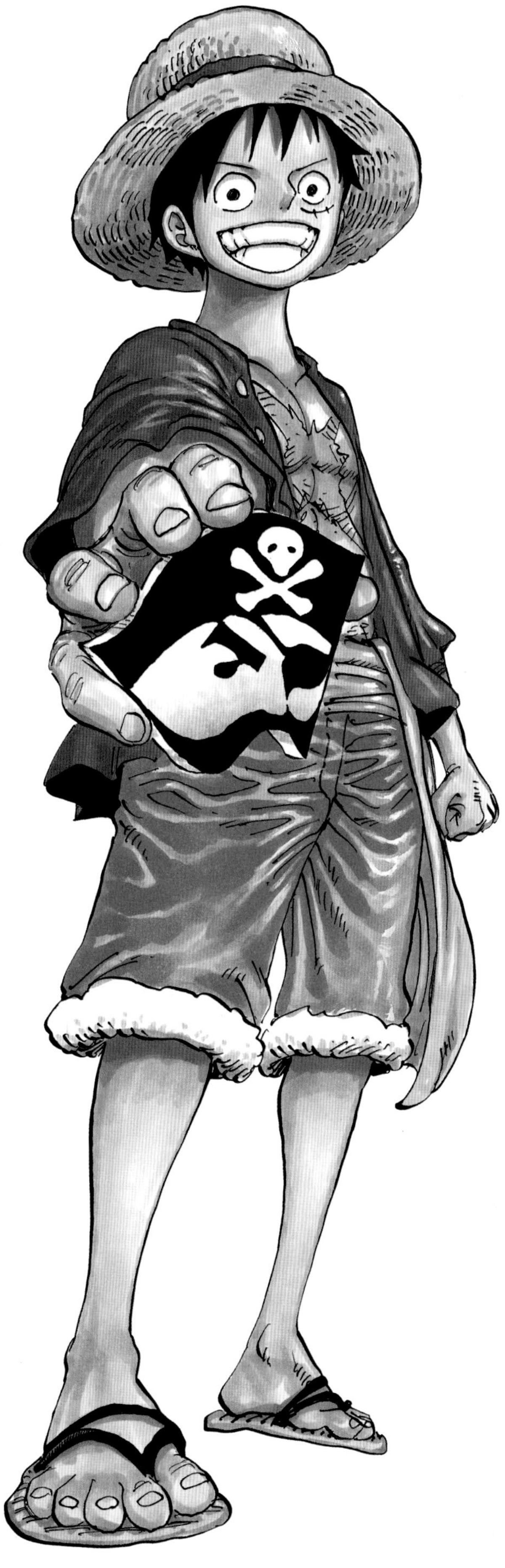

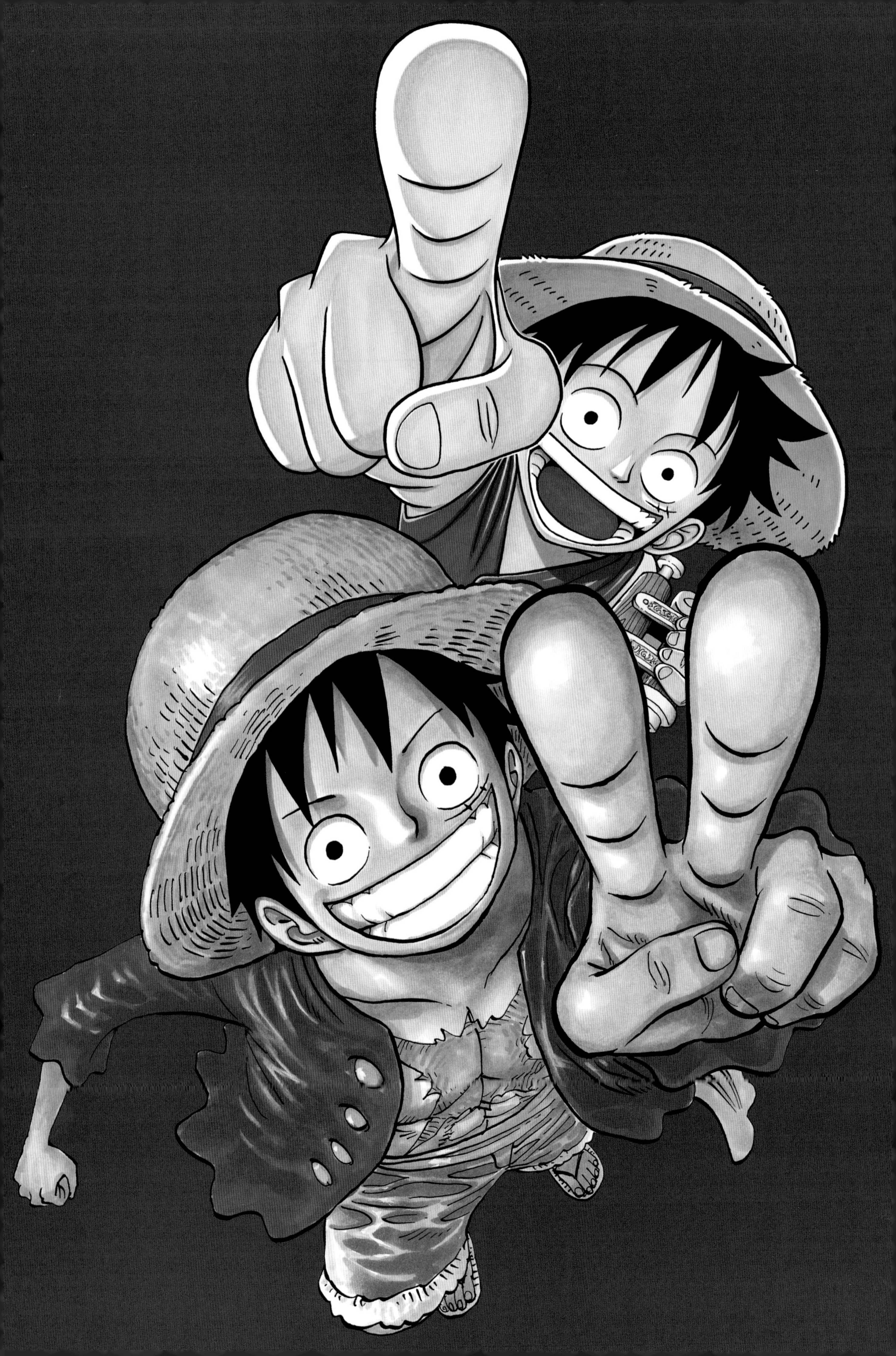

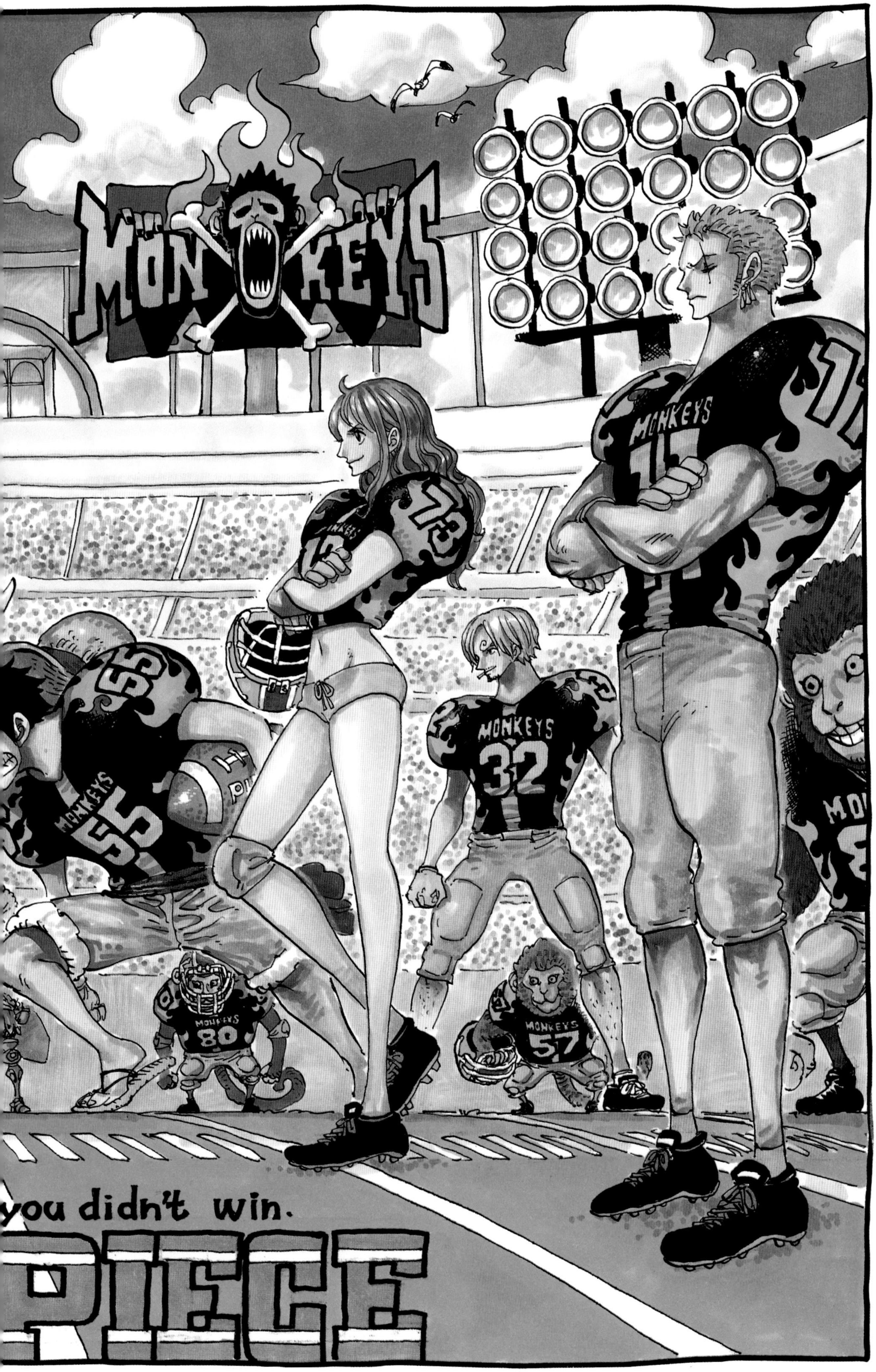
MONKEYS
MONKEYS
MONKEYS
MONKEYS
MONKEYS
MONKEYS
MONKEYS
you didn't win.
PIECE

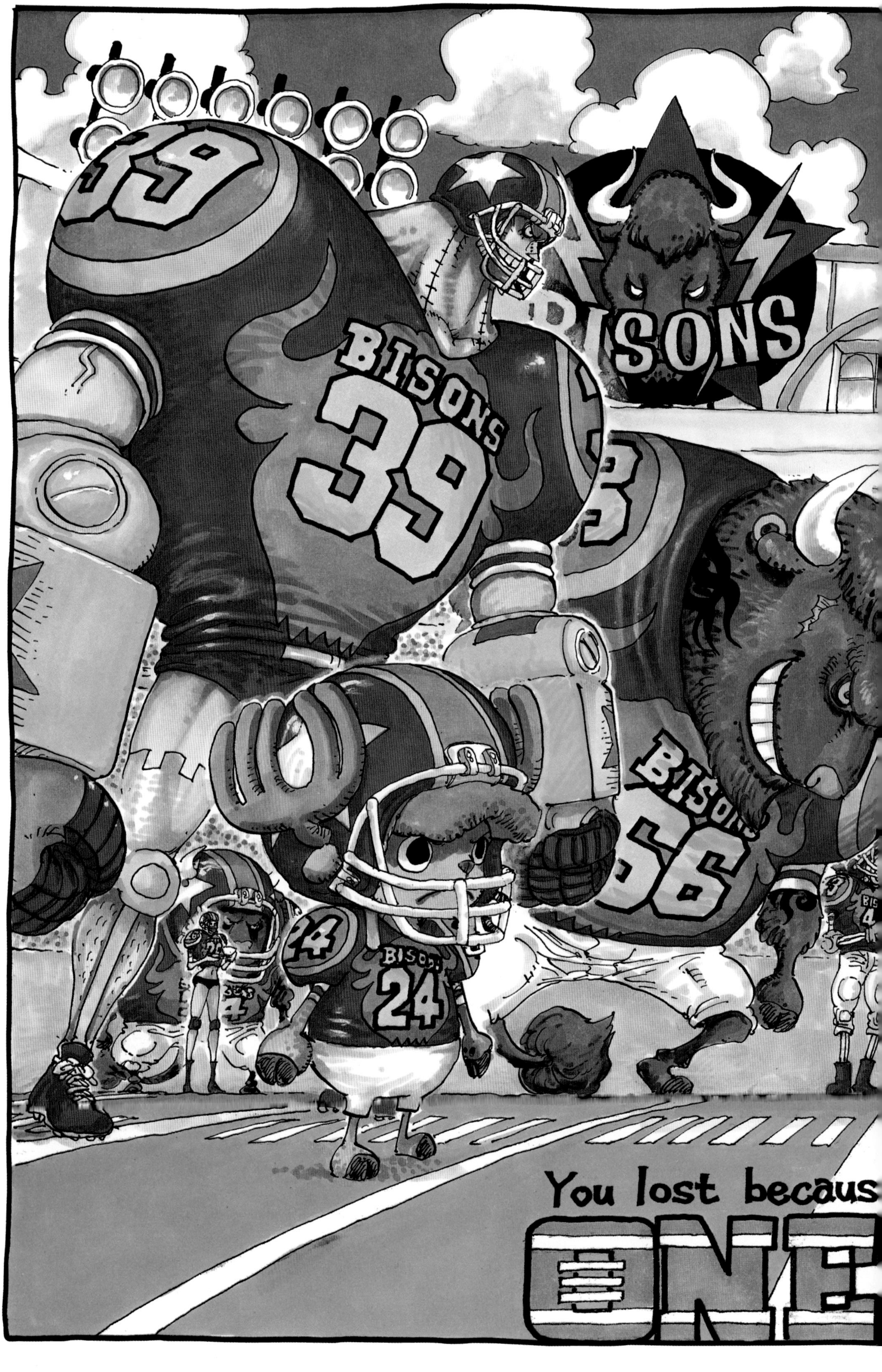
BISONS
BISONS 39
BISONS 24
BISONS 56
You lost becaus
ONE

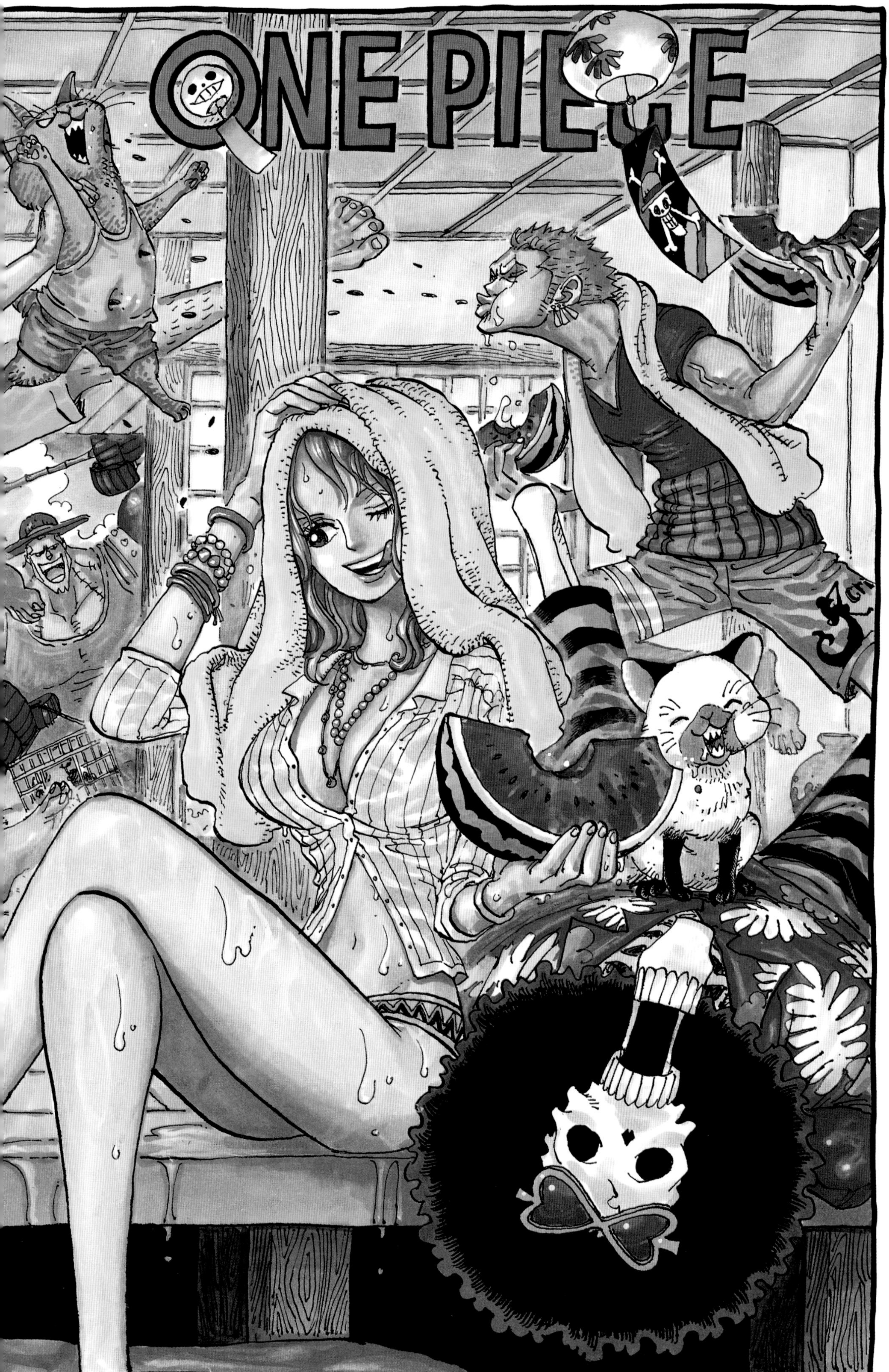

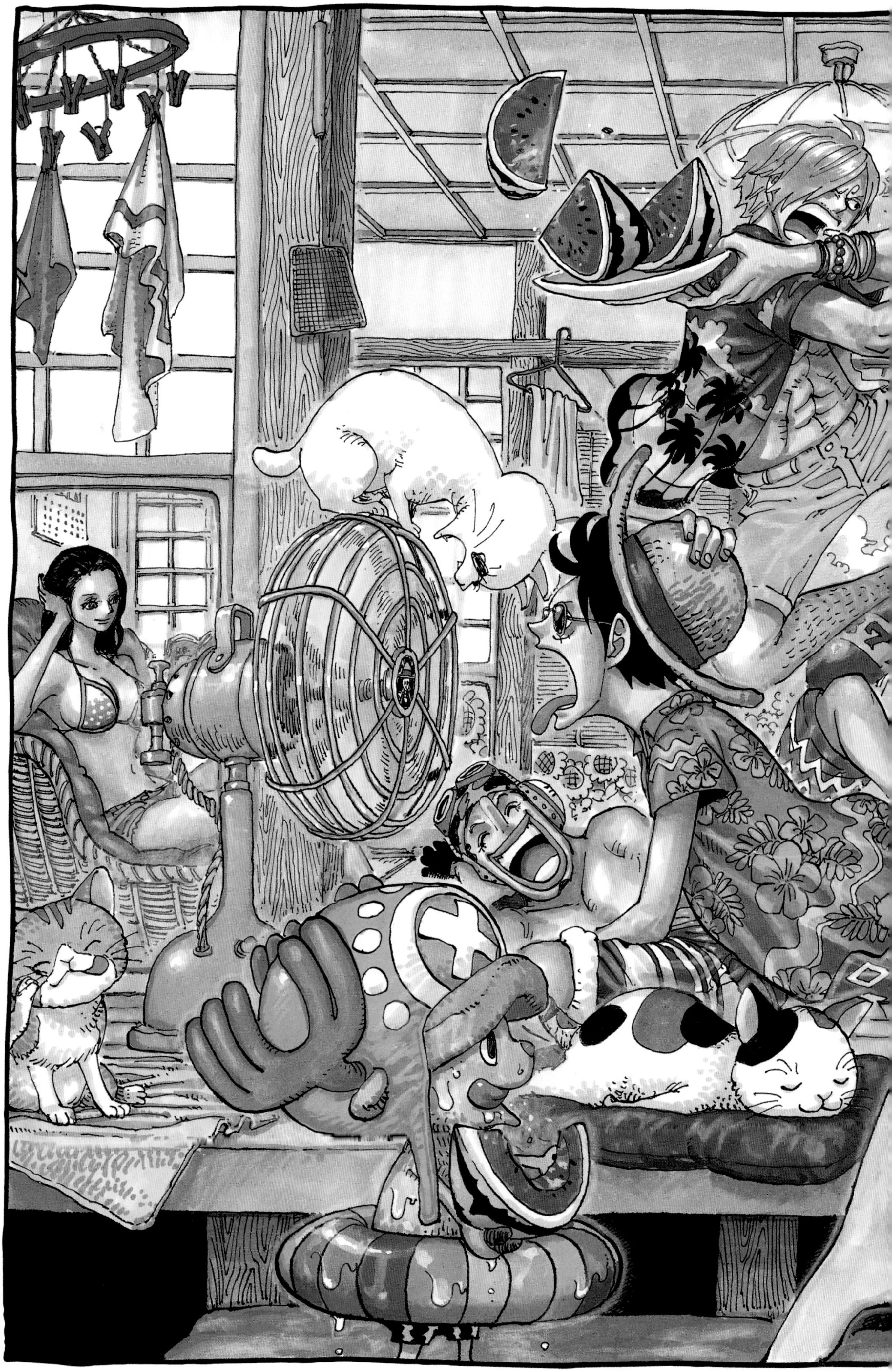

THANK YOU

ONE PIECE 20th

FOR ALL STAFF

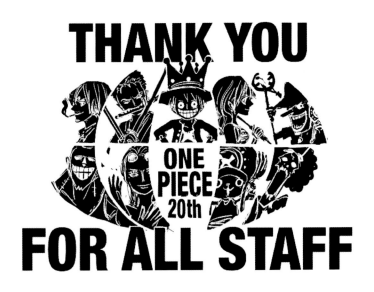

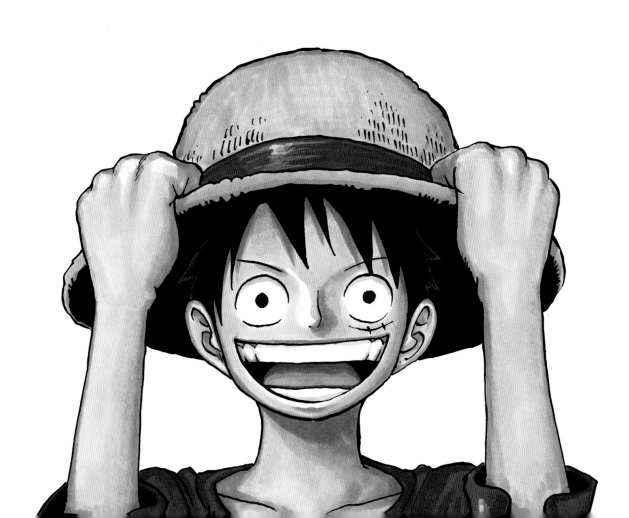

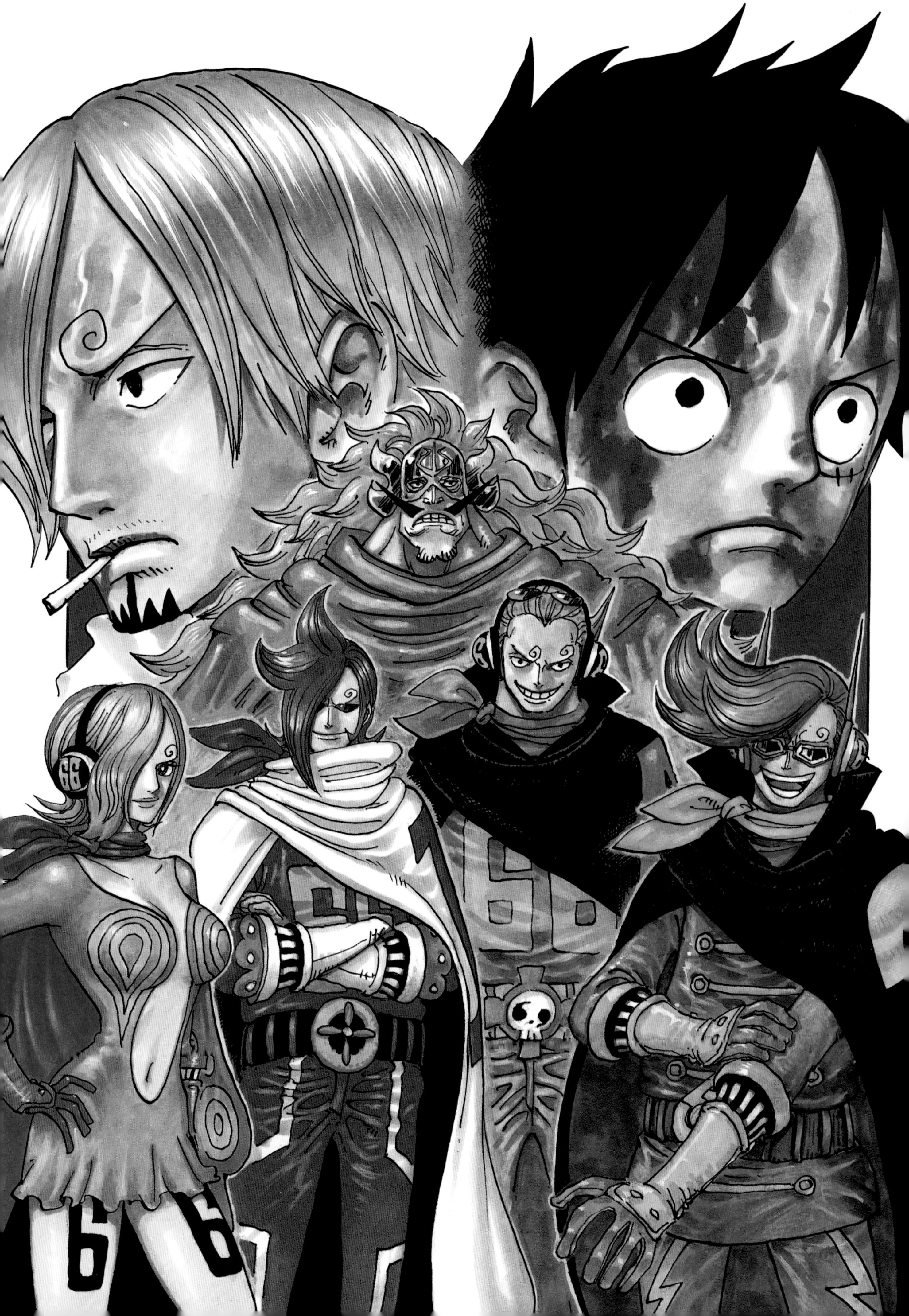

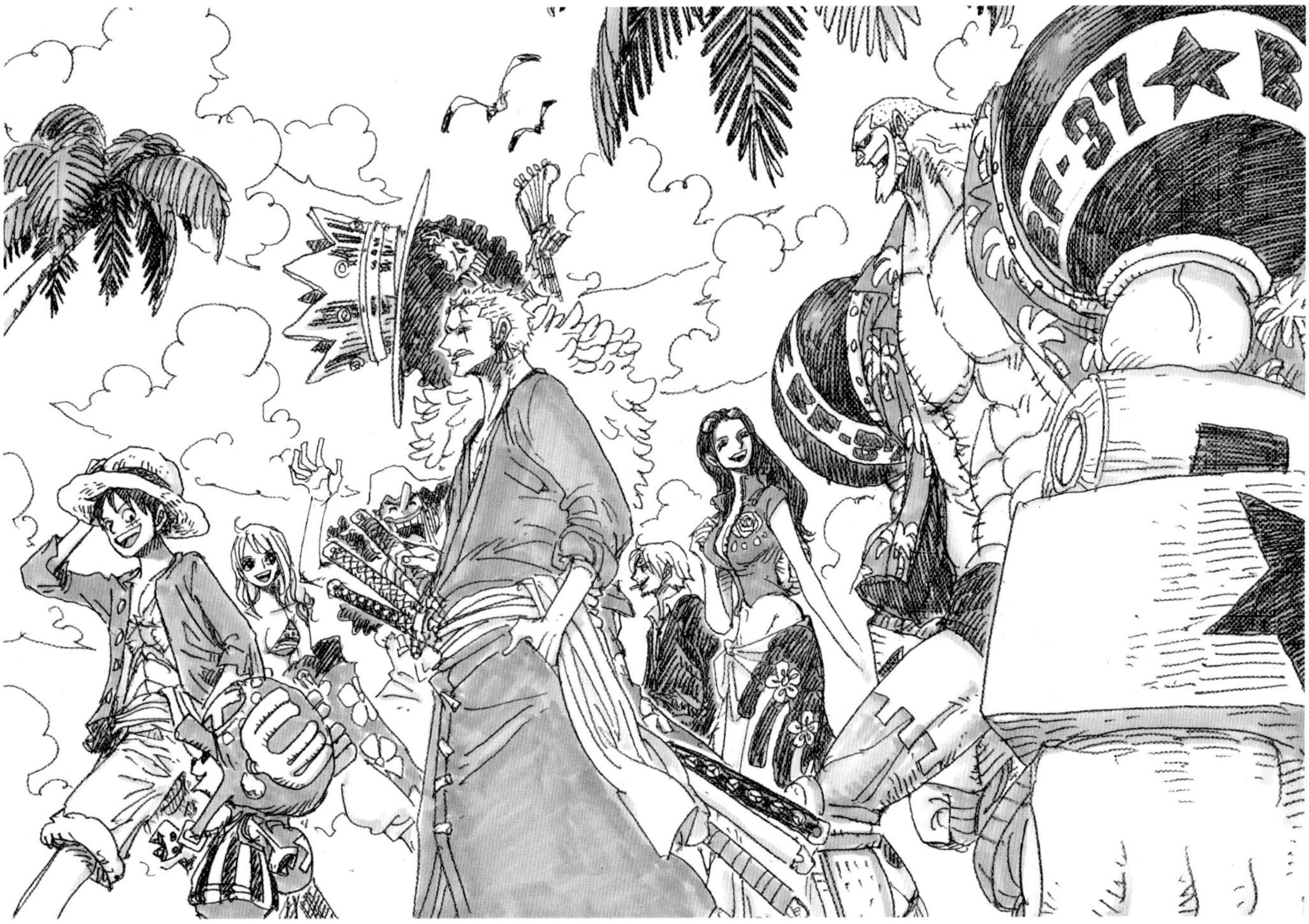
BF-37★B

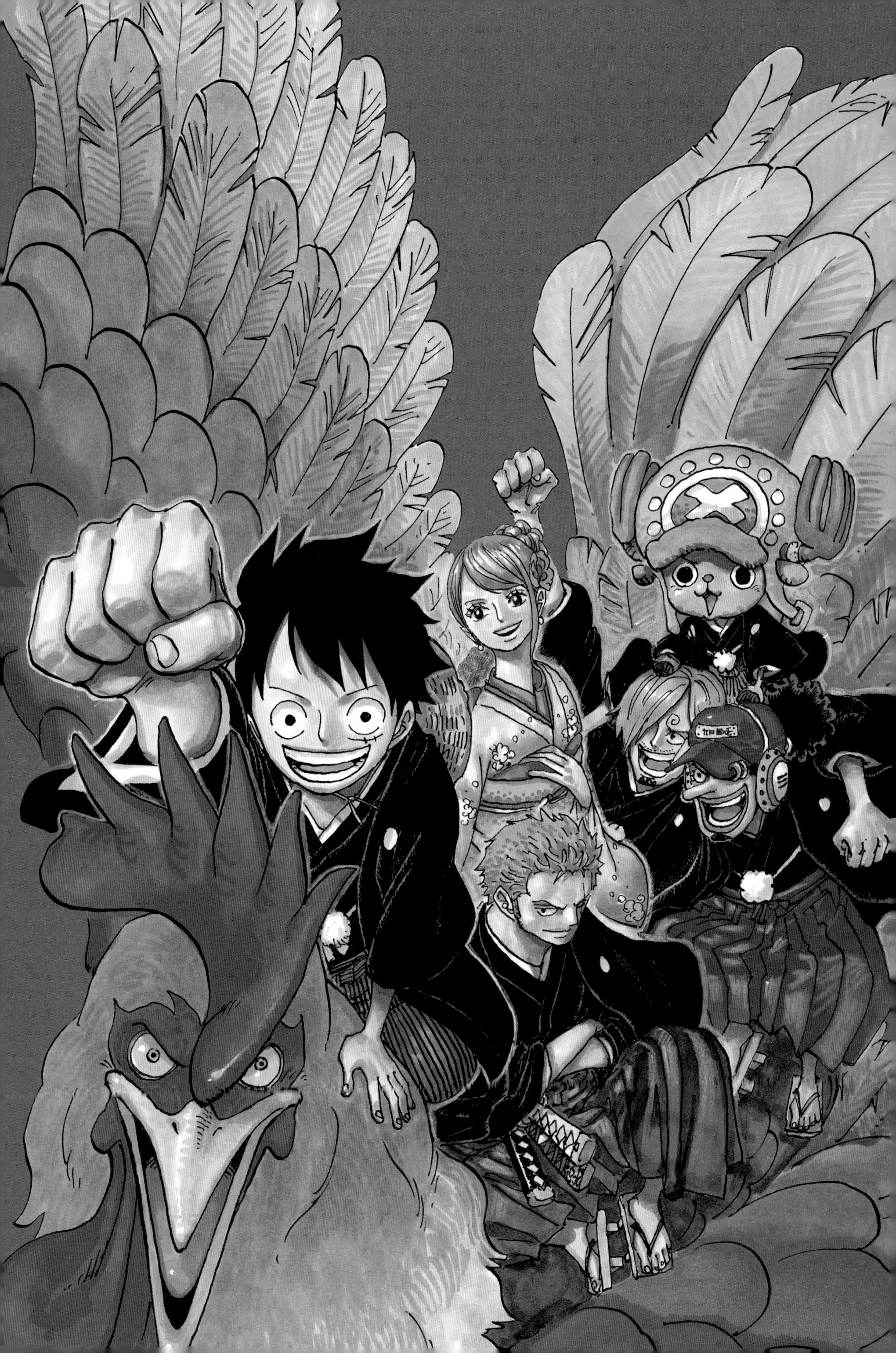

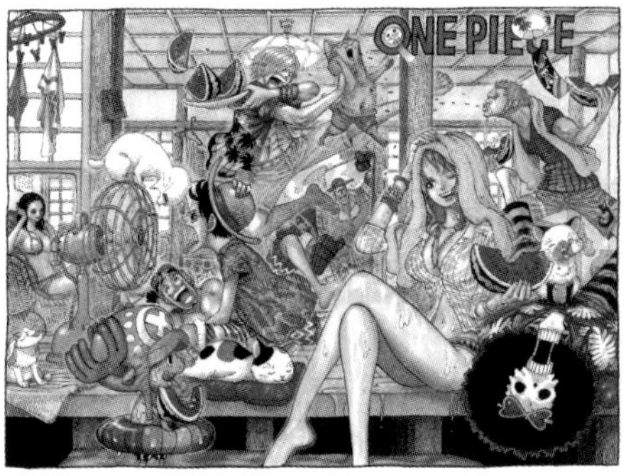
ONE PIECE

Comments P.232–233

Is it old-fashioned to stand in front of a fan and go, "Aaaaah"? Is it old-fashioned to do a watermelon-seed machine gun? The duty of an artist is to depict the culture of a time, just like they did with *ukiyo-e*.

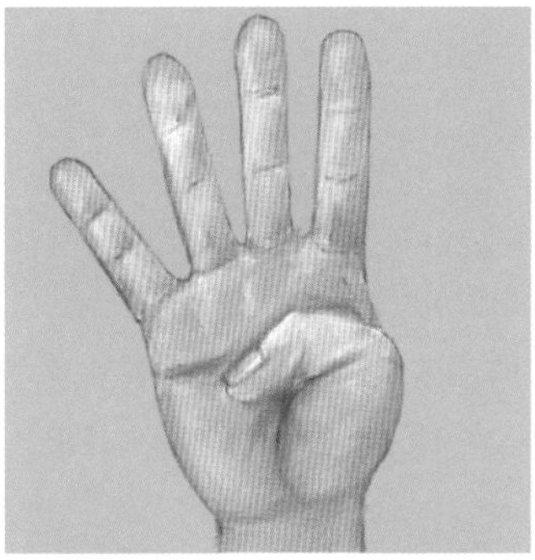

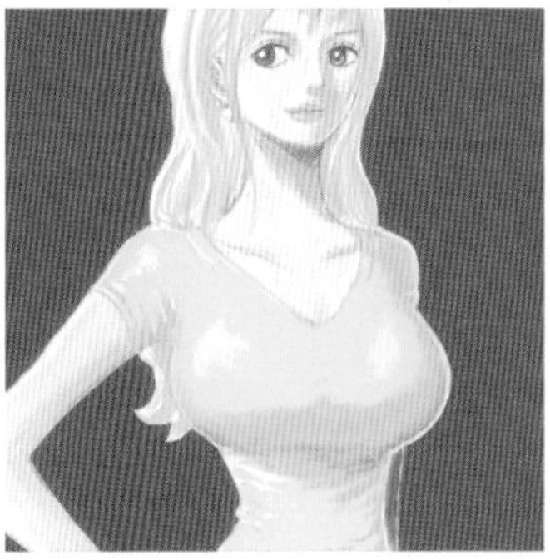

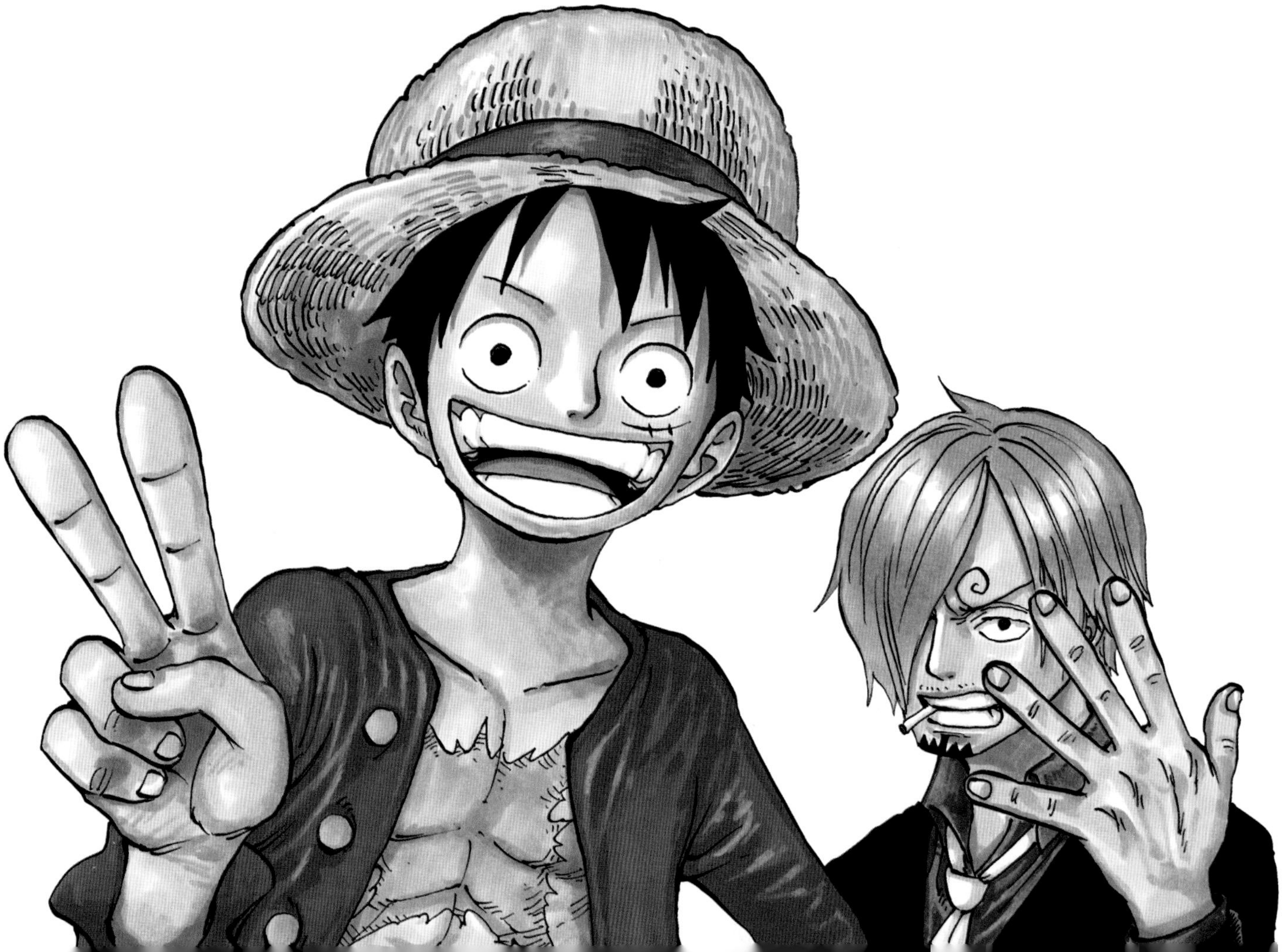

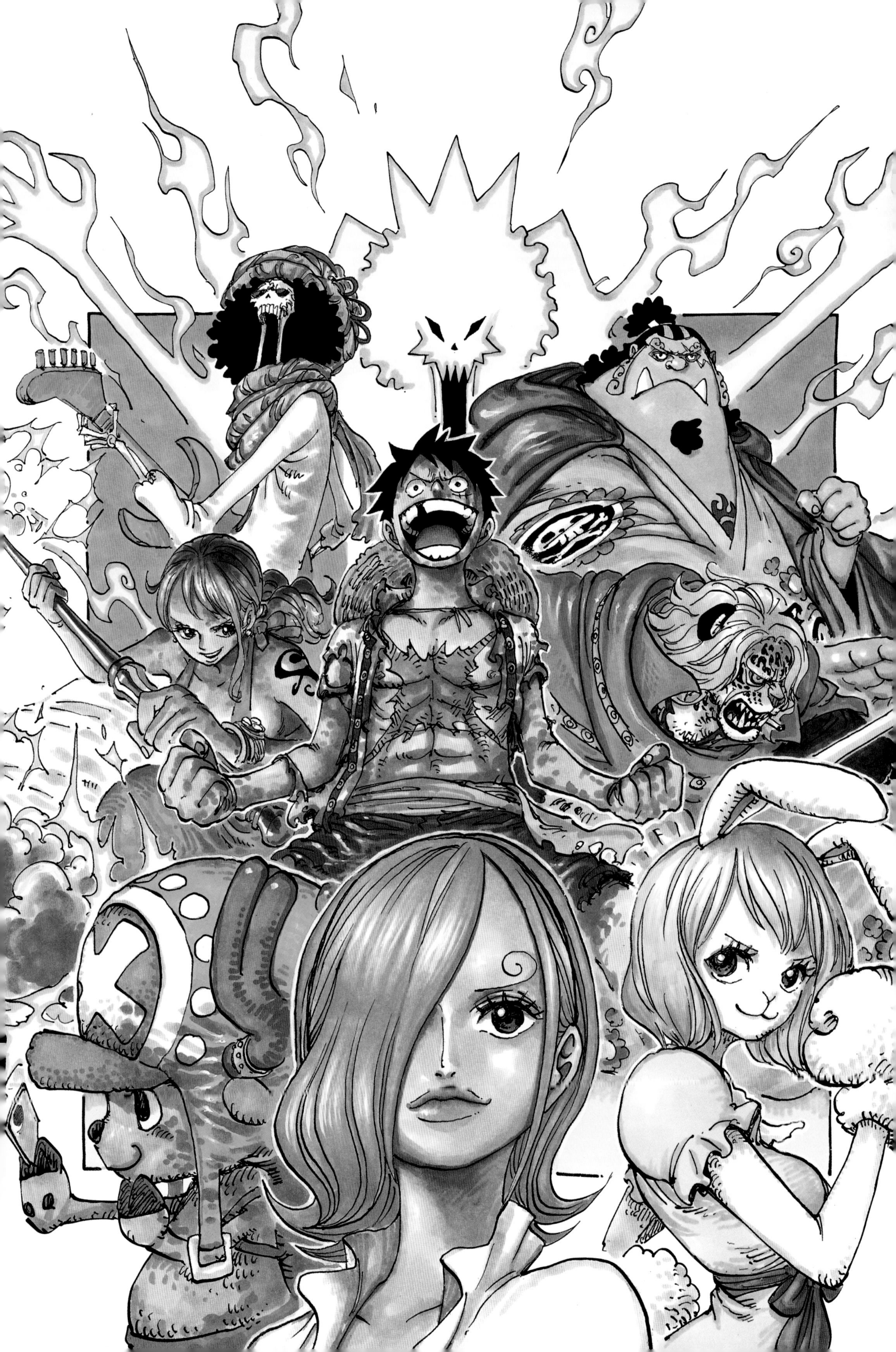

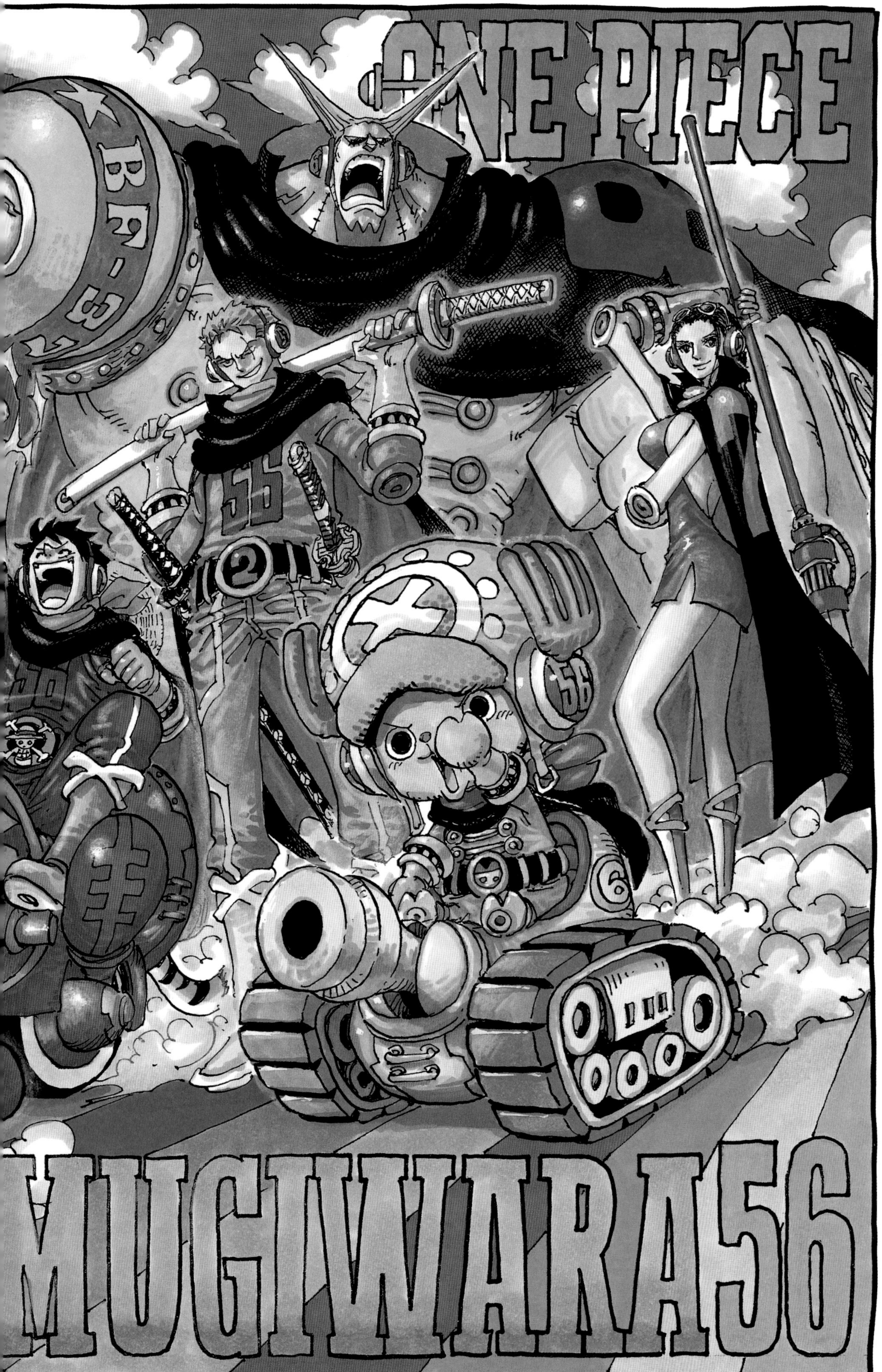
ONE PIECE
BF-37
MUGIWARA56

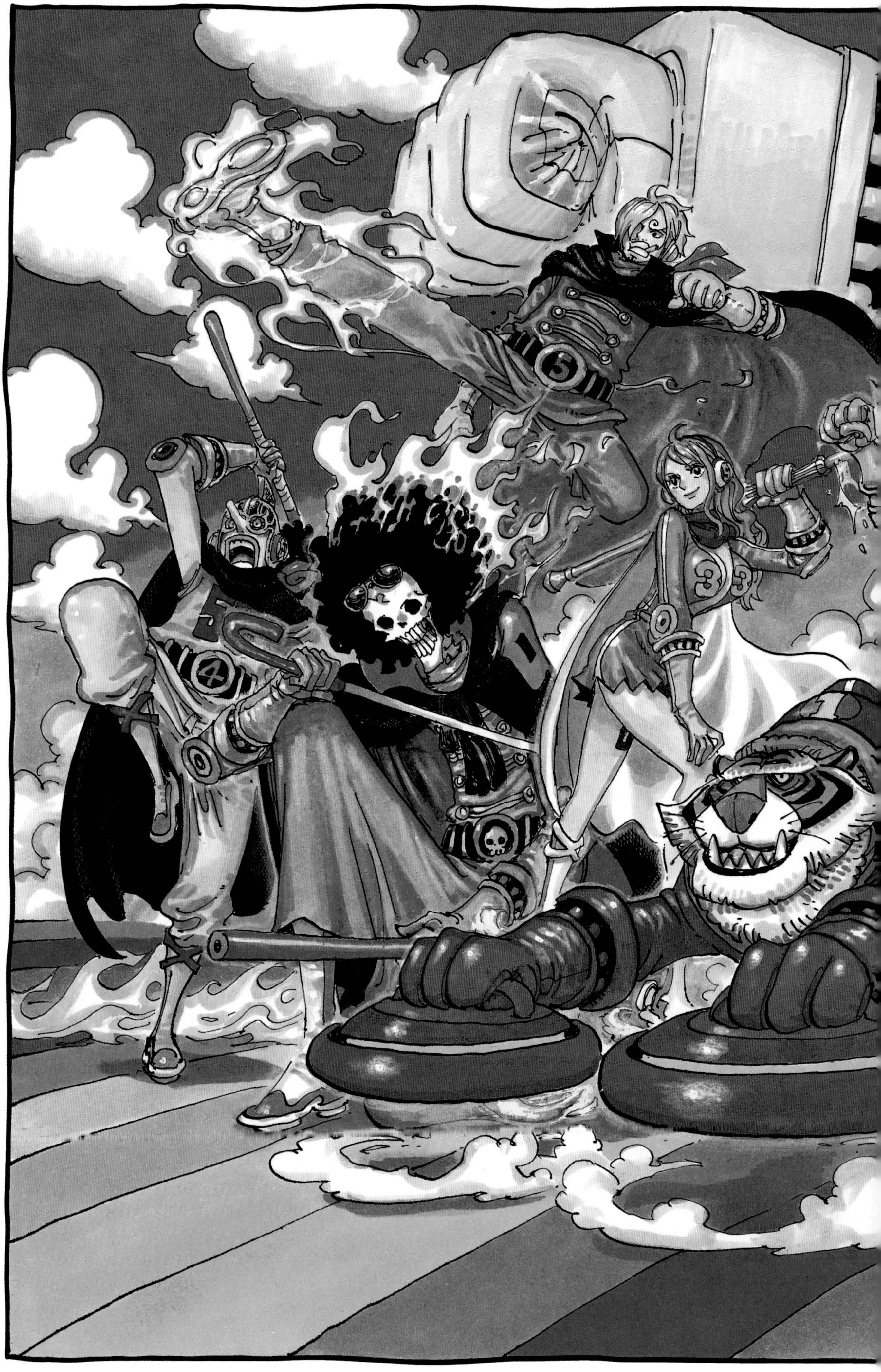

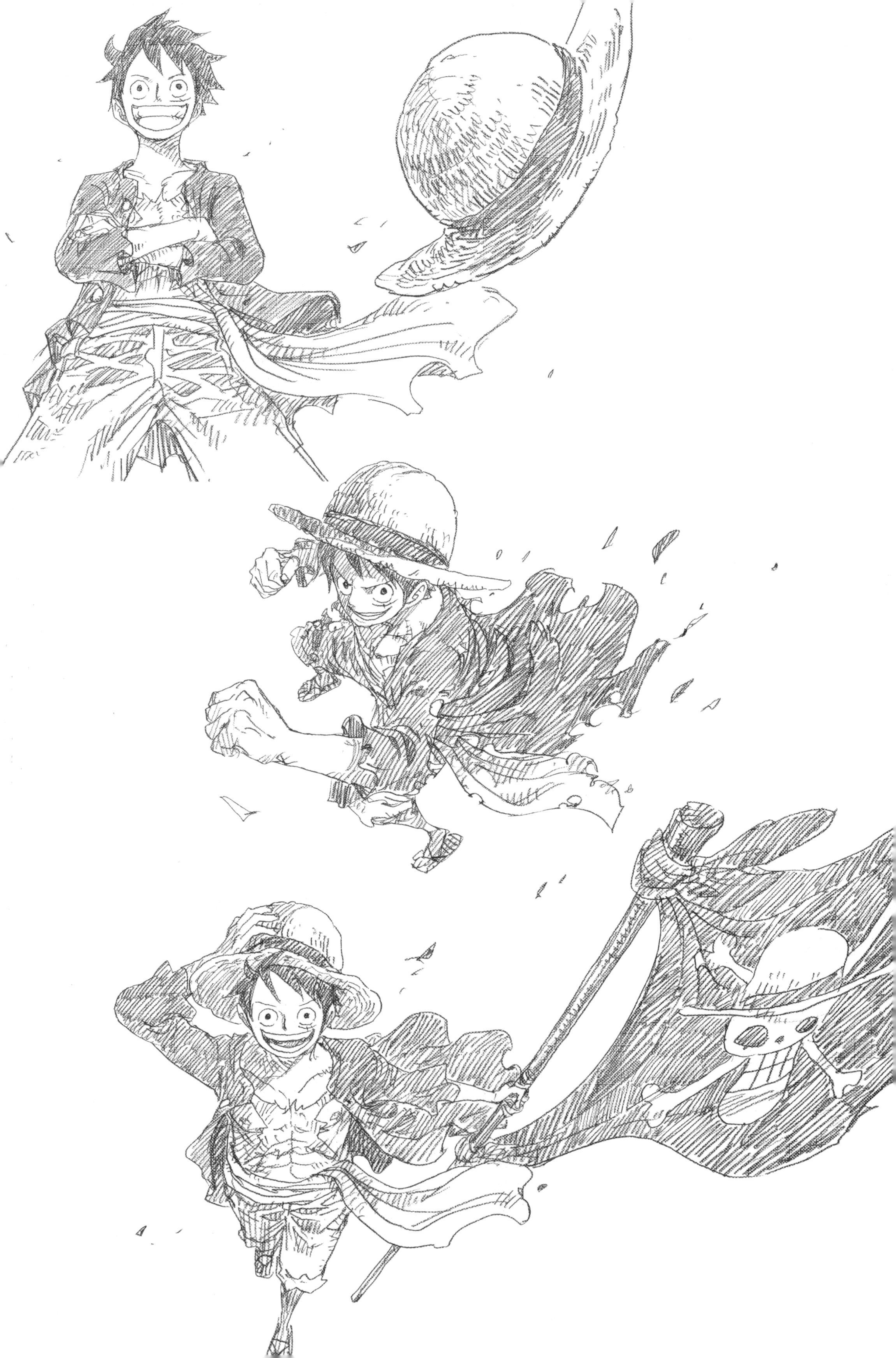

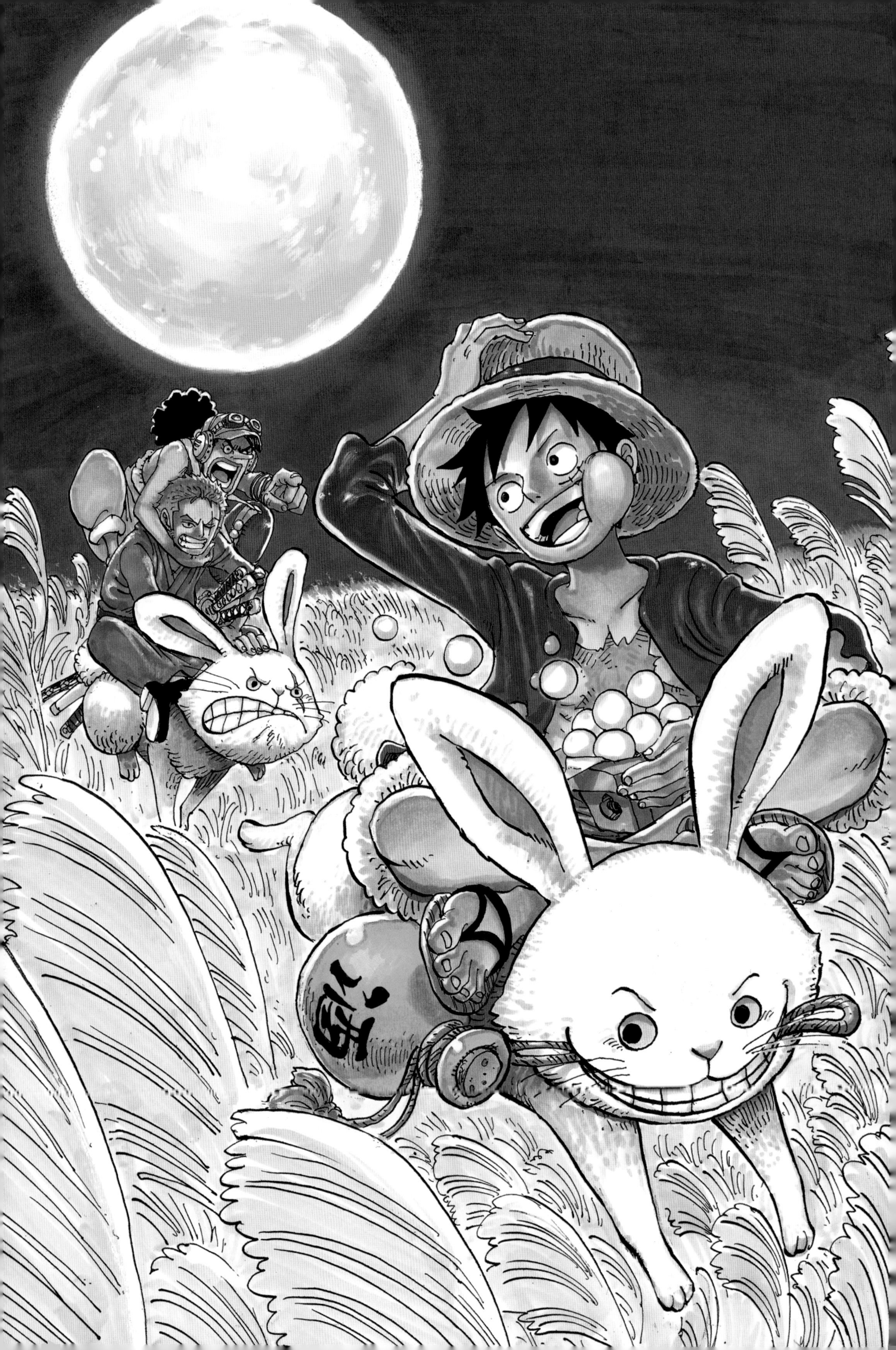
酒

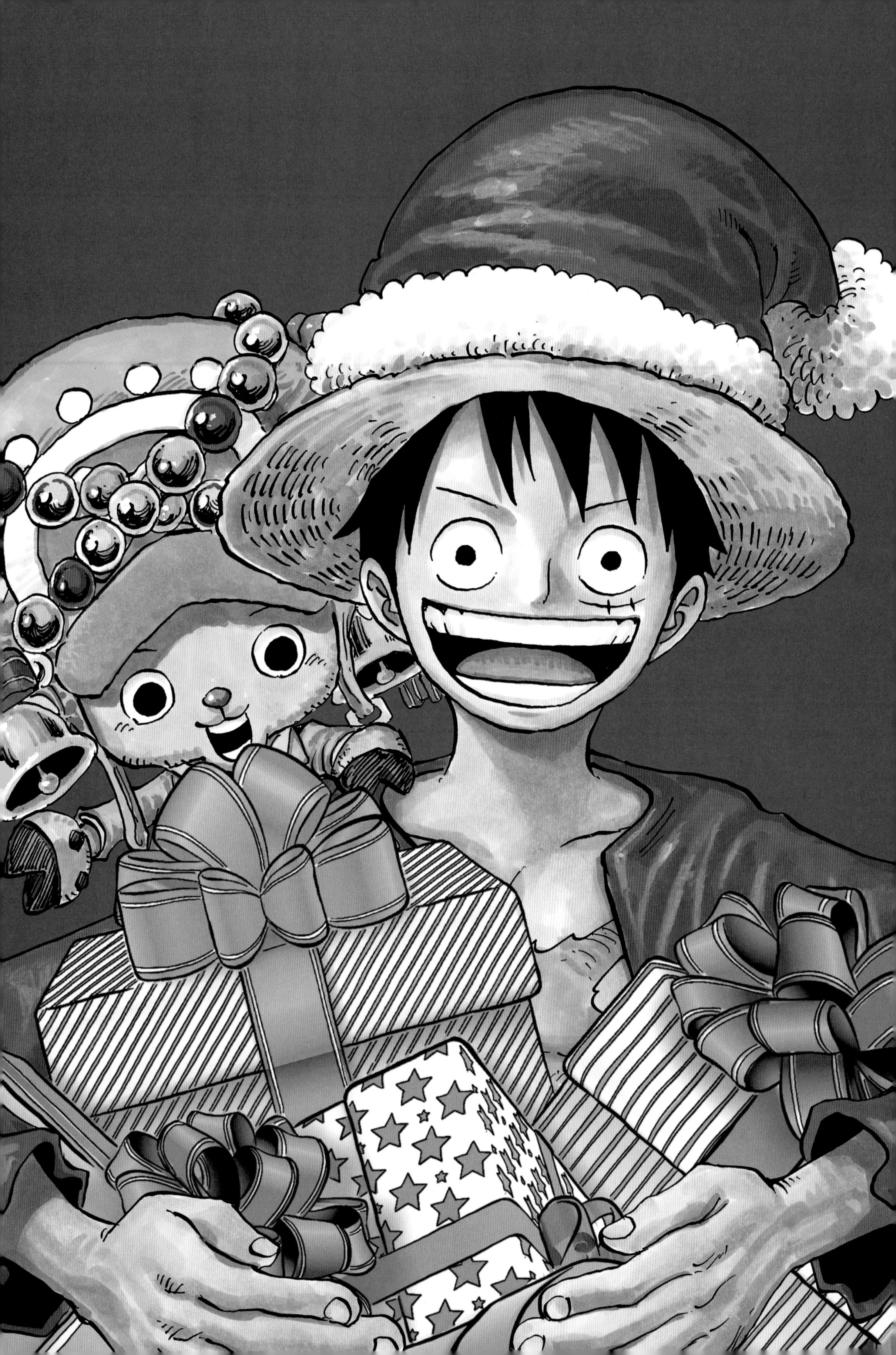

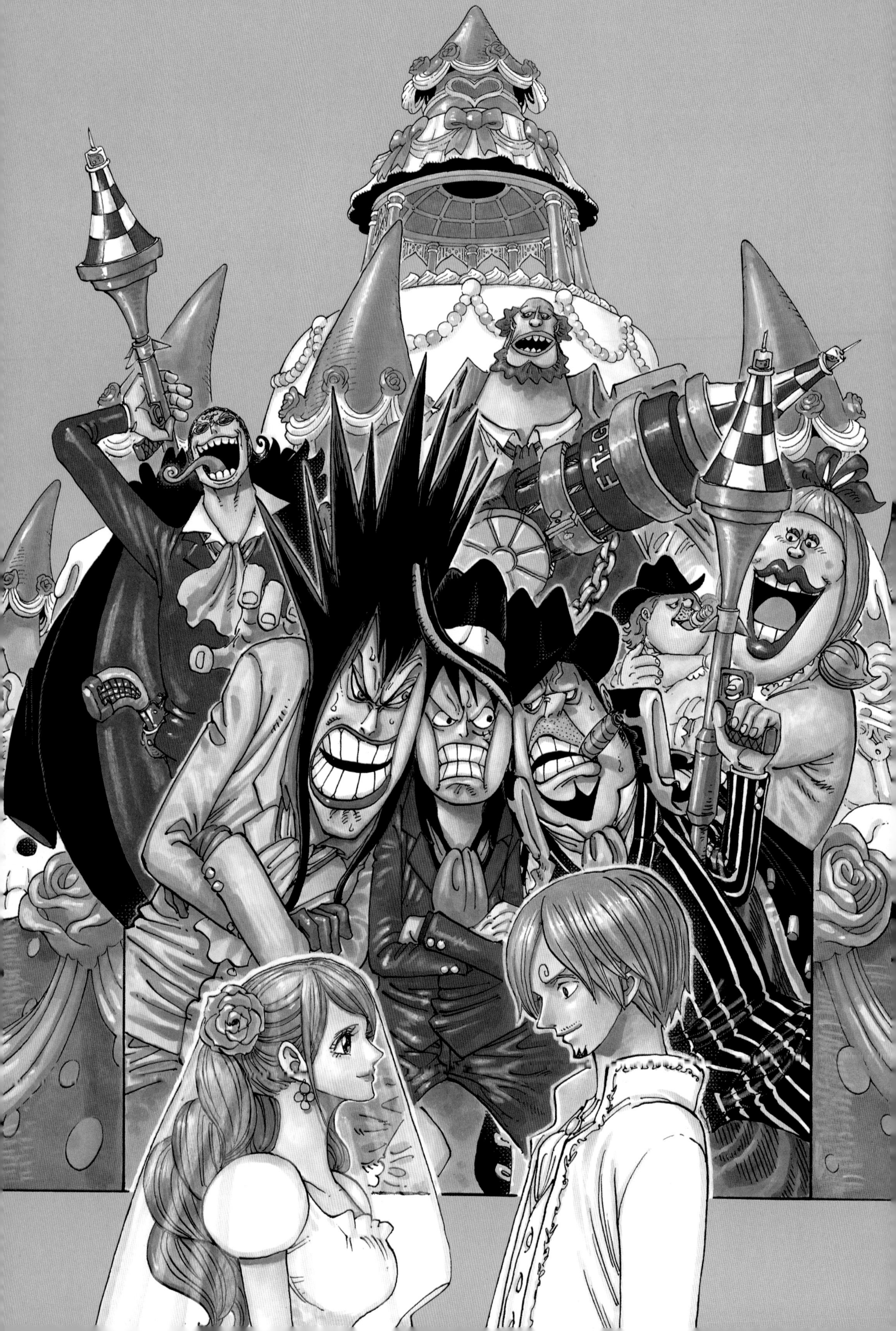

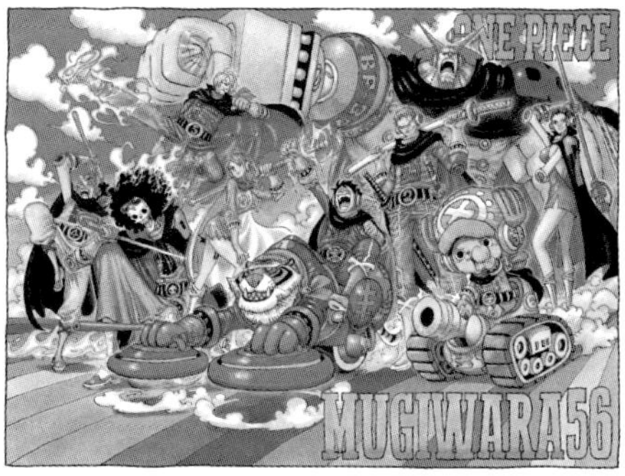
ONE PIECE
MUGIWARA56

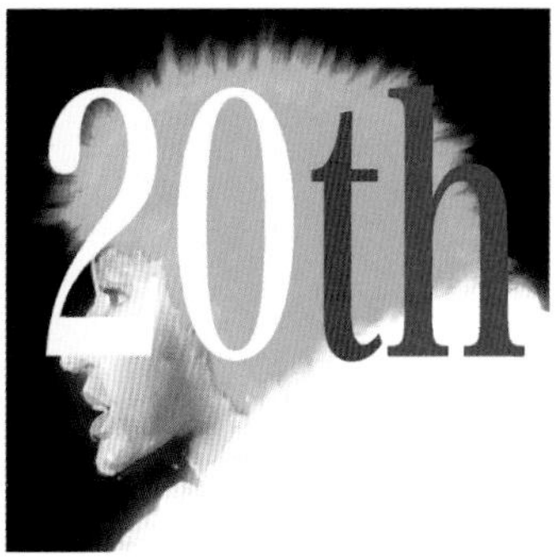
20th

Comments P.240–241

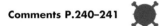

Every boy loves sentai heroes! Adults like them quite a lot too. You guys are just kids, you know that? And so is the guy drawing them.

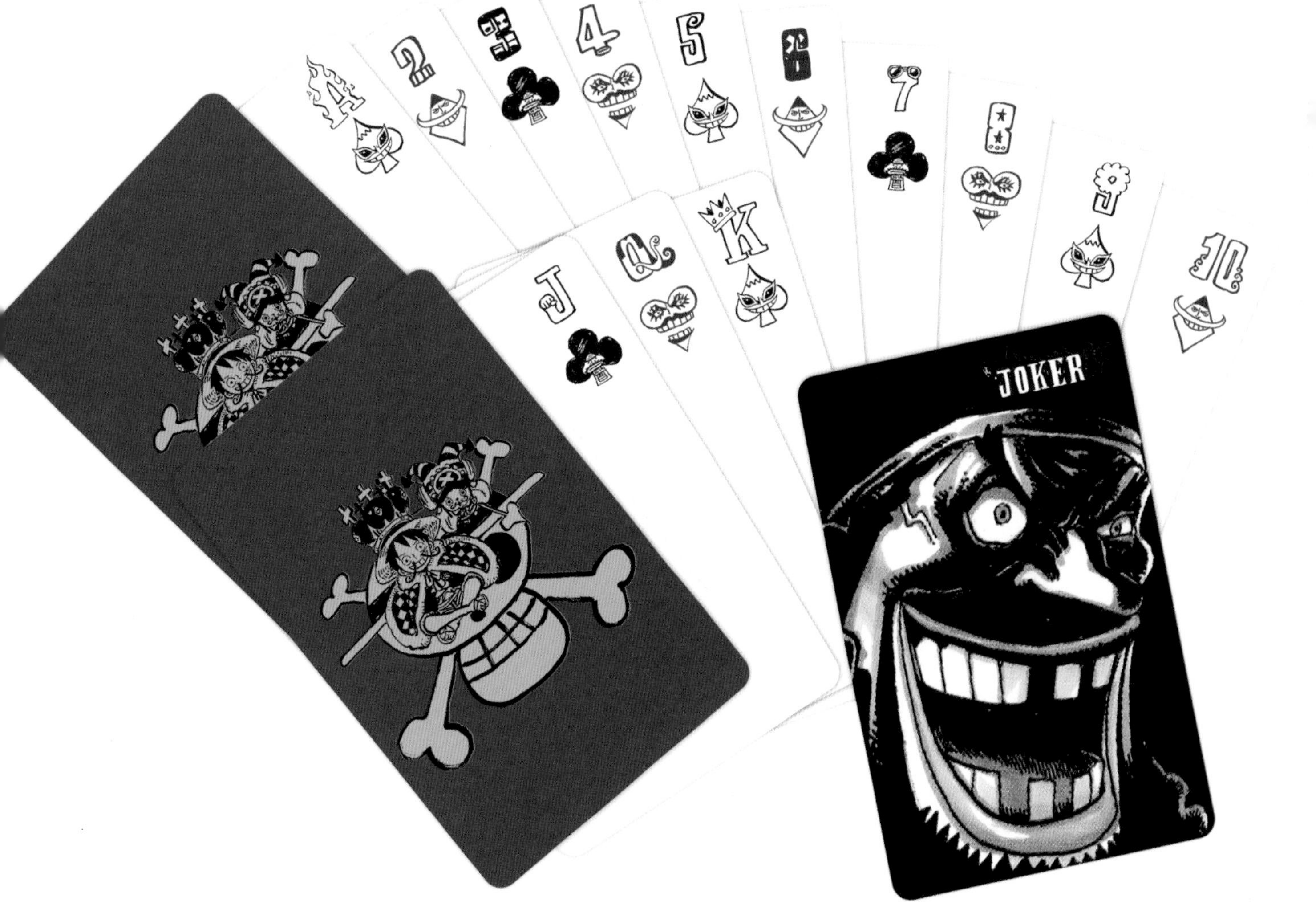
A
2
3
4
5
6
7
8
9
10
J
Q
K
JOKER

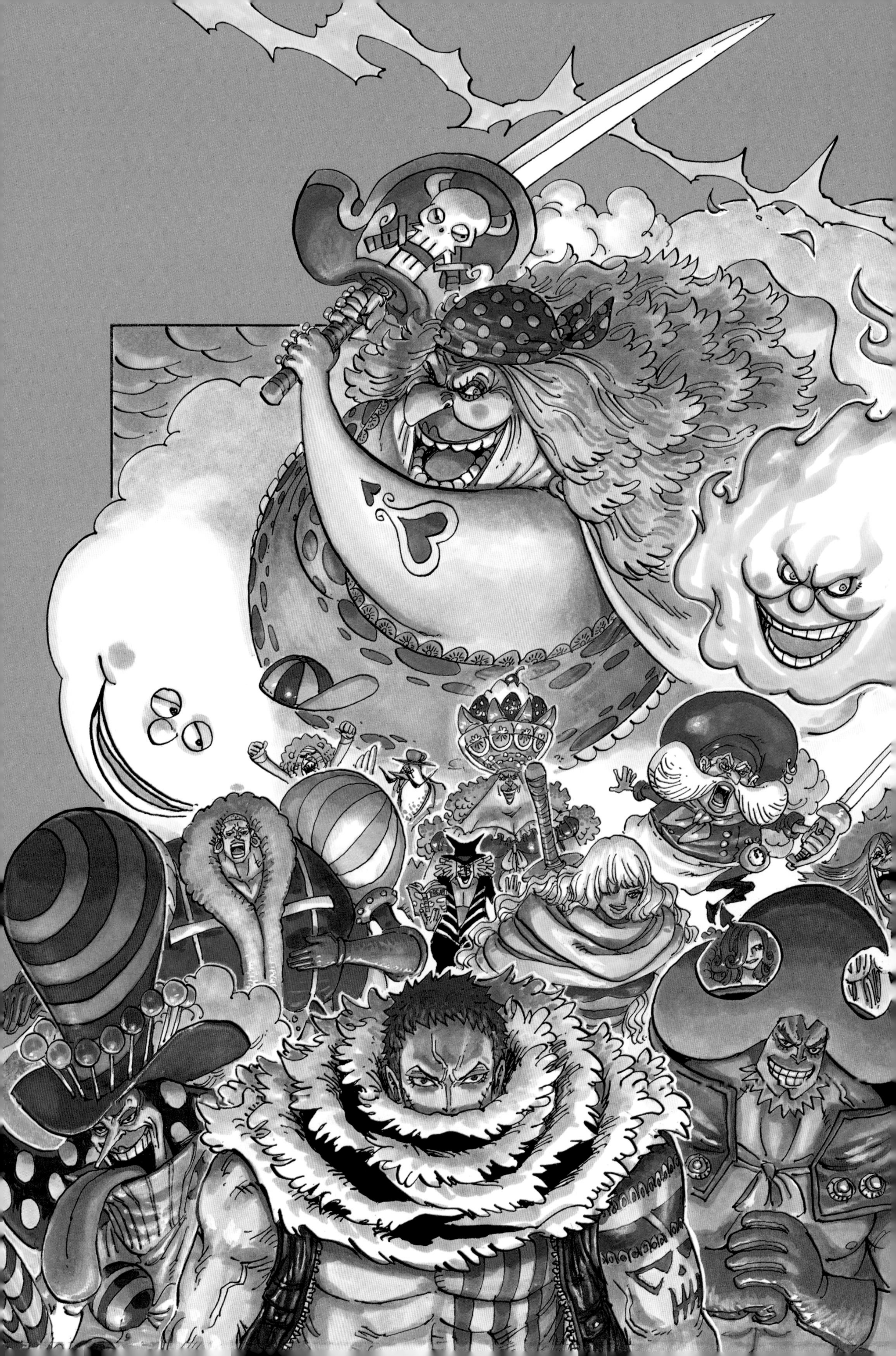

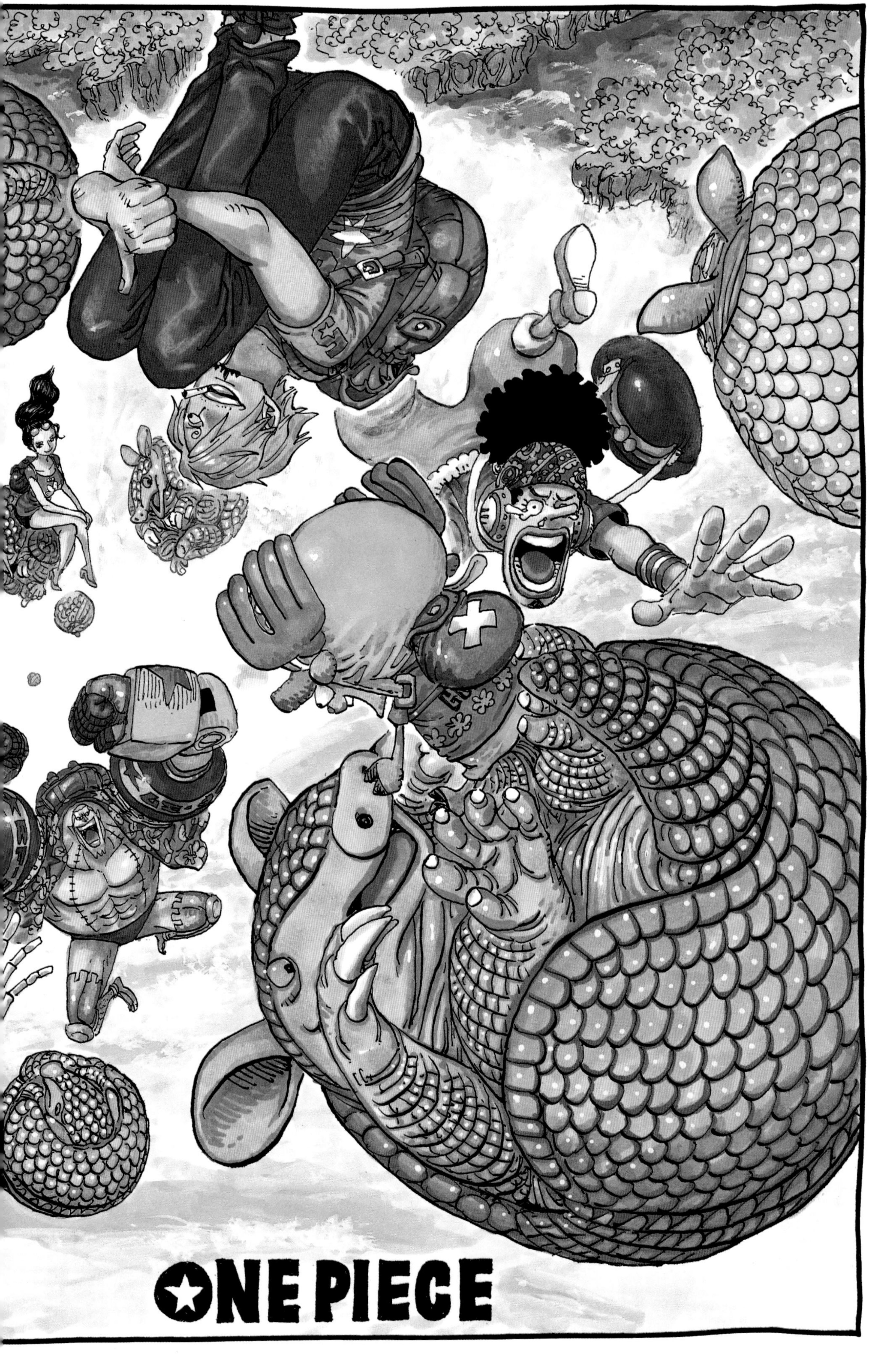
ONE PIECE

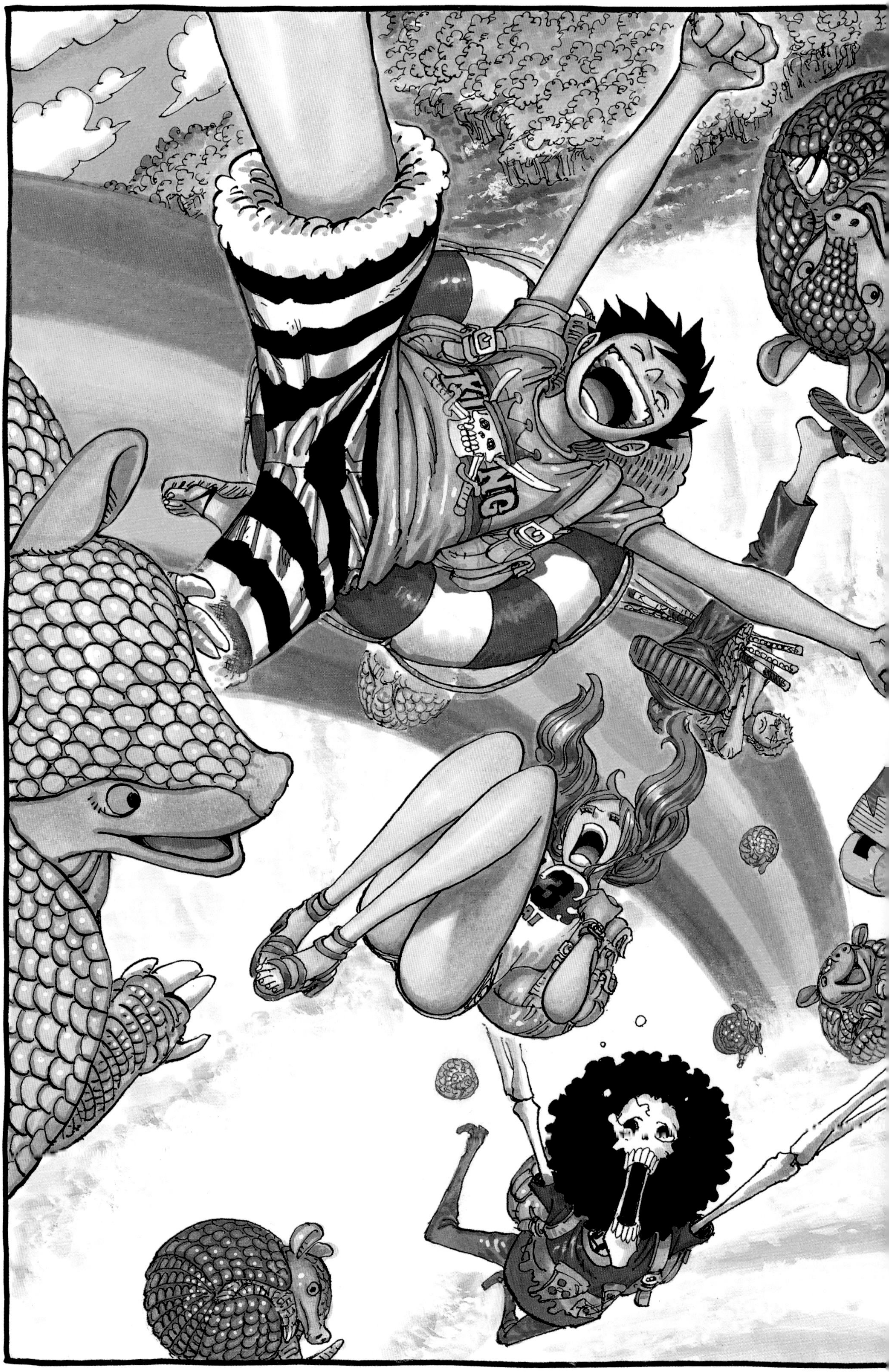

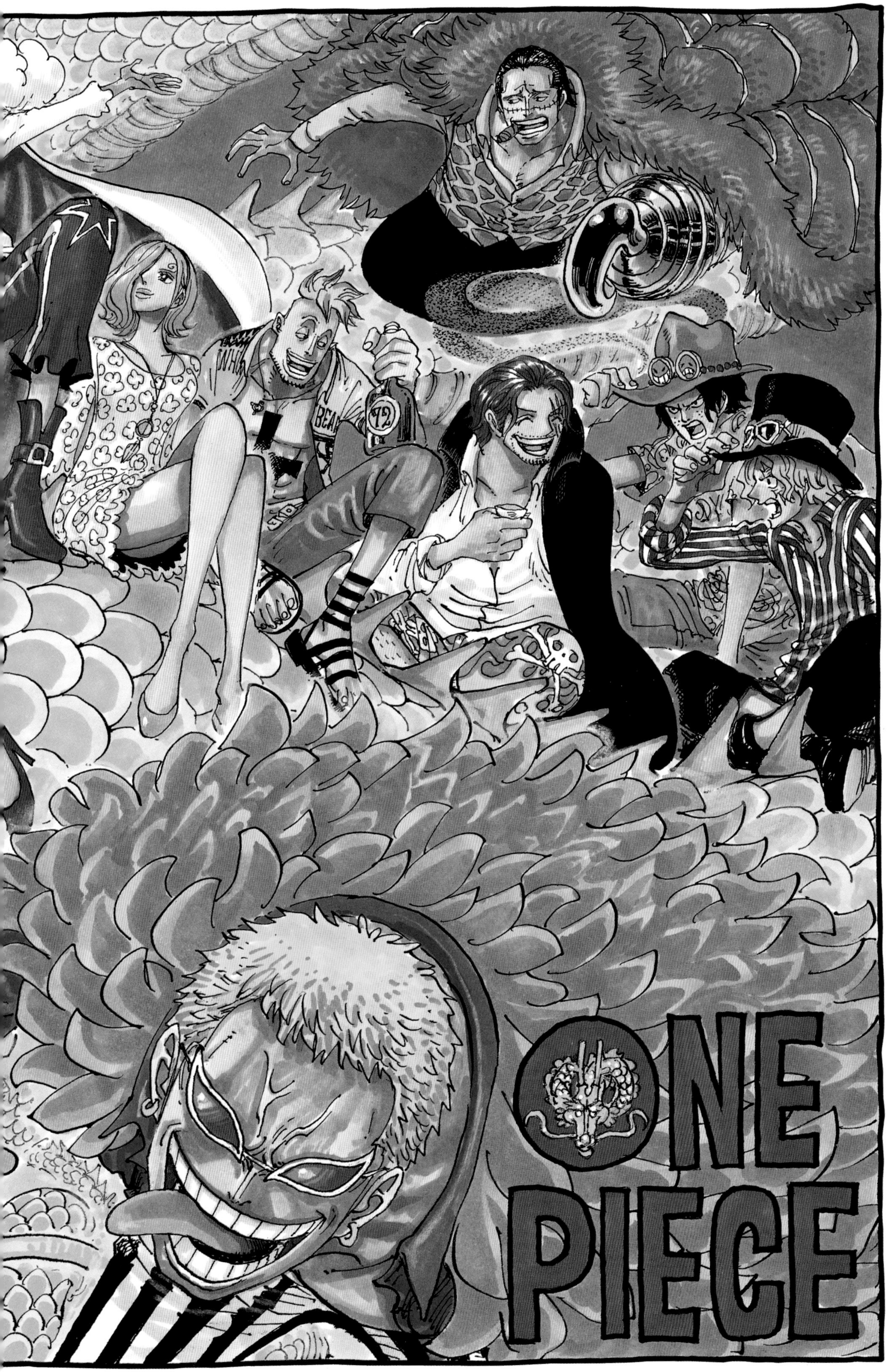
ONE PIECE

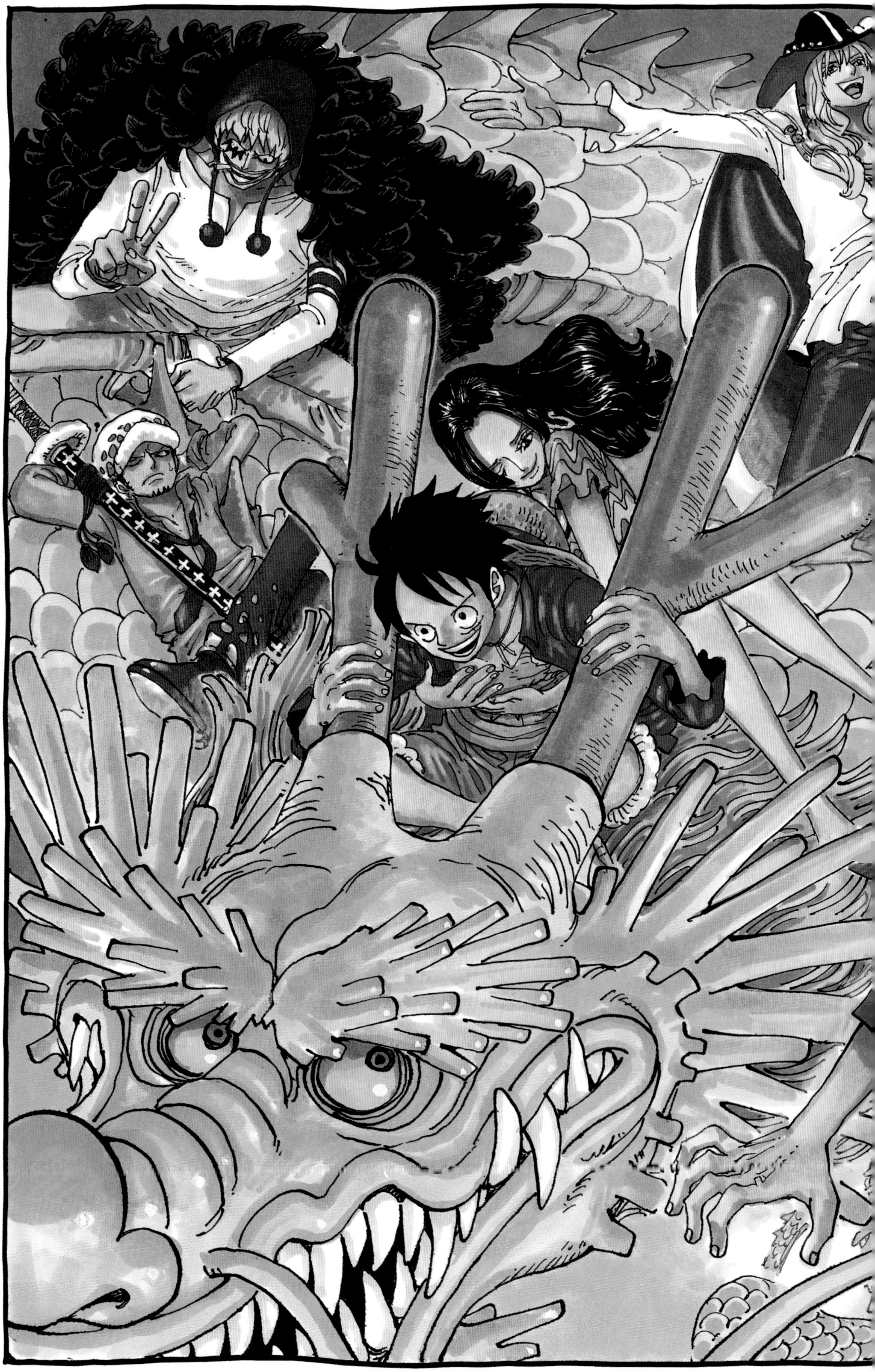

ONE PIECE WORLD SEEKER

An action-adventure game set on the mysterious Prison Island. In this game, you can explore a large, wide-open island with the freedom to choose your own adventure.

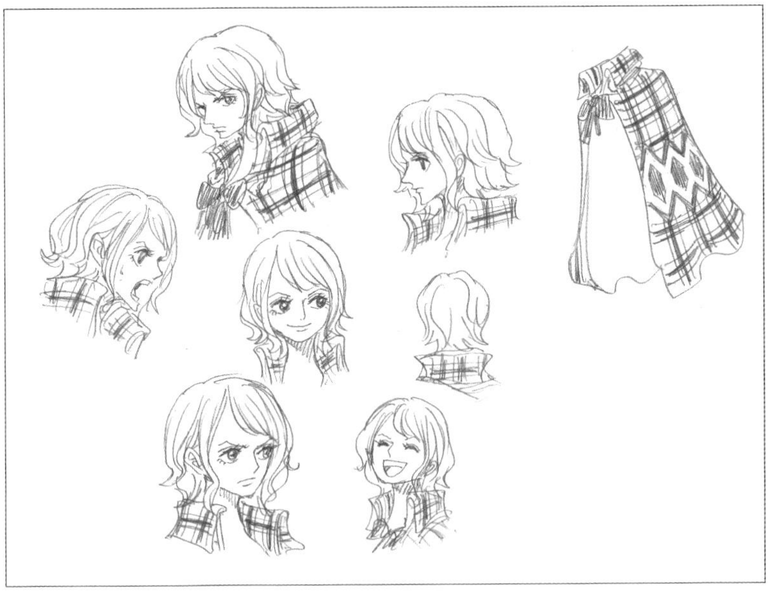

JEANNE

The leader of the anti-Navy faction opposed to Isaac. She fights to take back their island and restore it to its original beauty as "Jewel Island."

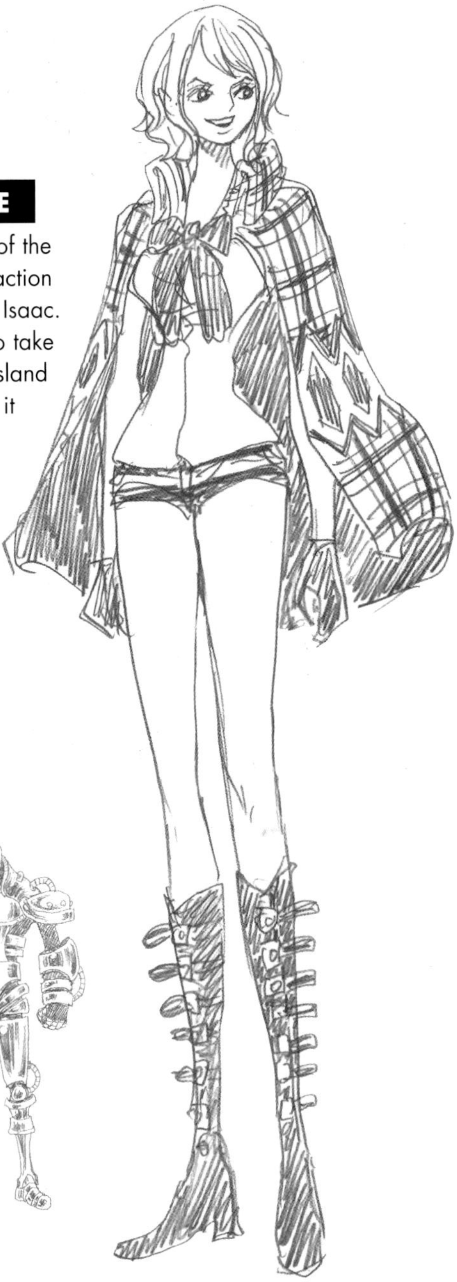

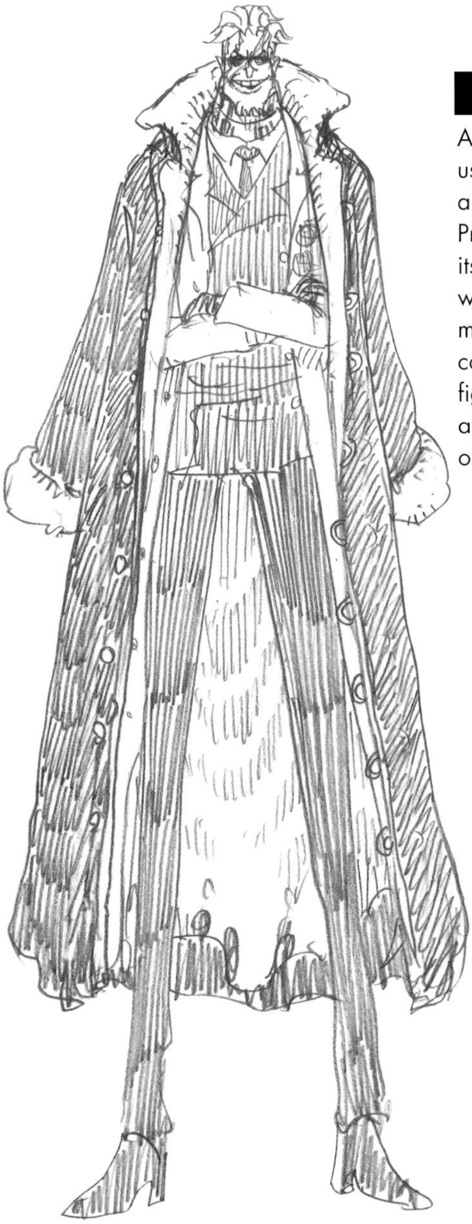

ISAAC

A scientist who used his incredible abilities to revitalize Prison Island after its devastation in a war. He builds a mammoth prison and commands the Navy, fighting personally in a suit of battle armor of his own design.

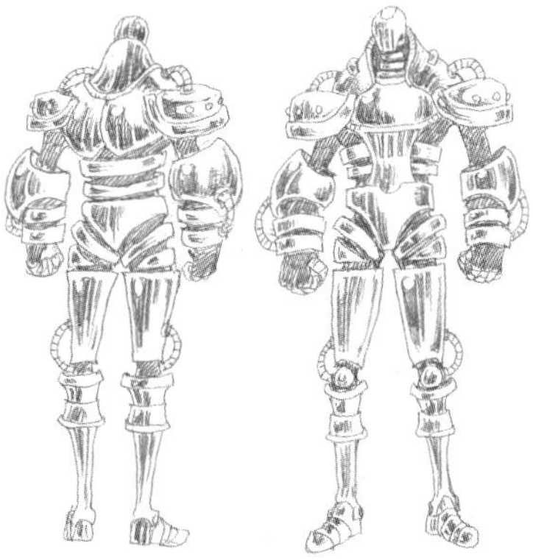

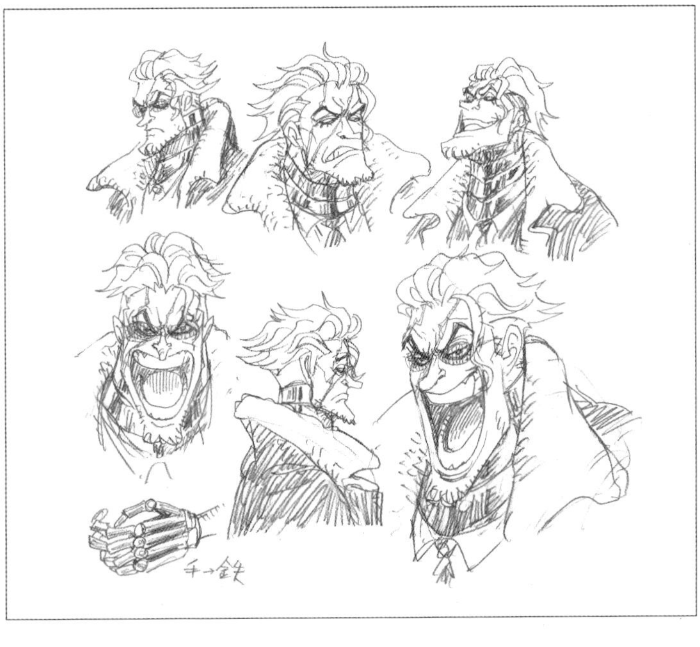
手→鉄

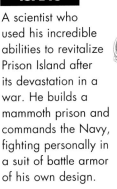

TOKYO ONE PIECE TOWER

Design sketches for original characters appearing in *One Piece Live Attraction 3: Phantom,* which ran from April 2017 to April 2019.

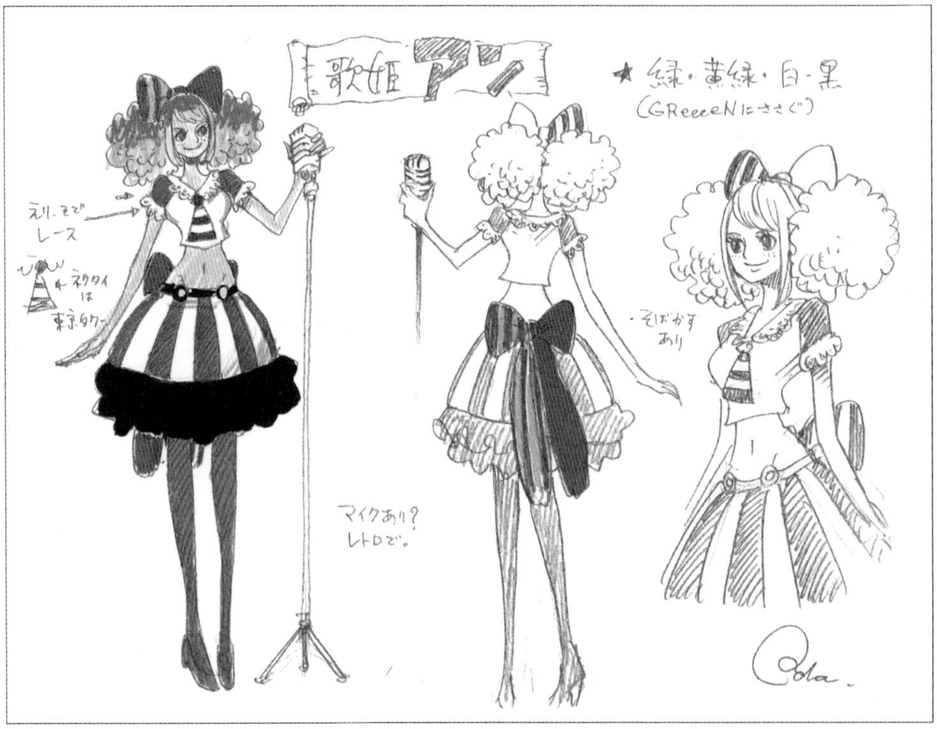
歌姫アン
★緑・黄緑・白・黒
(GReeeeNにささぐ)
マイクあり?
レトロで。
Oda

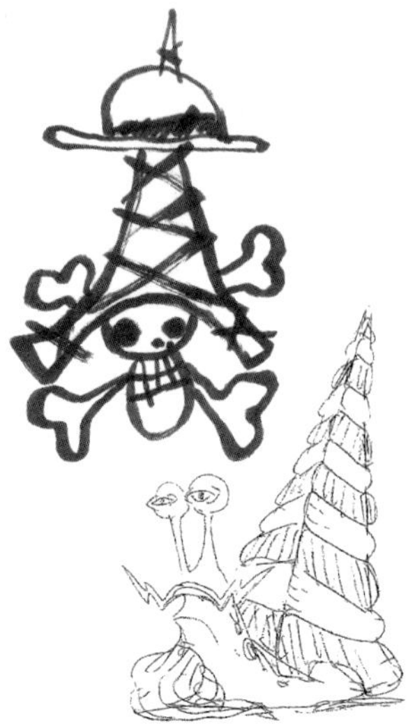

Sketches of the elder Tongari transponder snail from Tongari Island in Luffy's territory, and an icon mixing Tokyo Tower with the Straw Hat logo.

ANN THE DIVA

A singer from Tongari Island with the Vision-Vision Fruit, capable of producing illusions of whatever she has touched. She also appeared as a guest of the Pirates Festival in *One Piece: Stampede*.

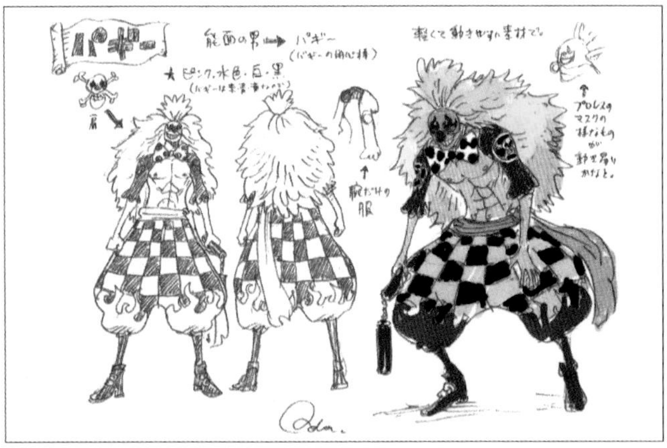
パギー
Oda

PUGGY

One of the toughest fighters in the pirate temp agency, "Buggy's Delivery." His bounty is 200 million berries, and he's said to be Buggy's primary apprentice.

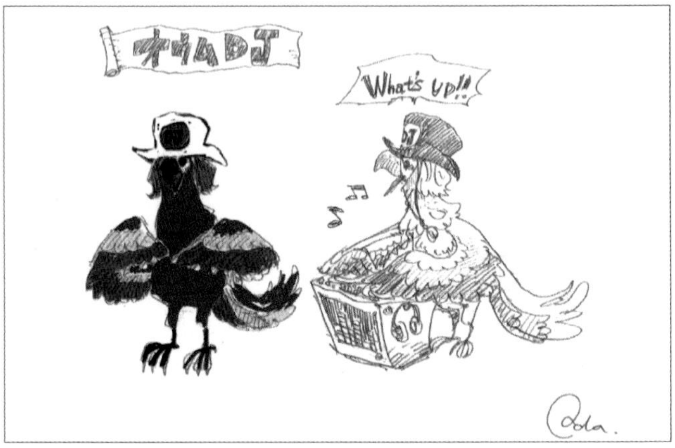
オウムDJ
What's up!!
Oda

DJ PARROT

A parrot who works as a DJ at a club on Tongari Island. Eiichiro Oda had a sudden burst of inspiration and added him to the set of cast designs.

With the opening of the park, Eiichiro Oda designed a number of different uniforms and props that can be worn by the crew.

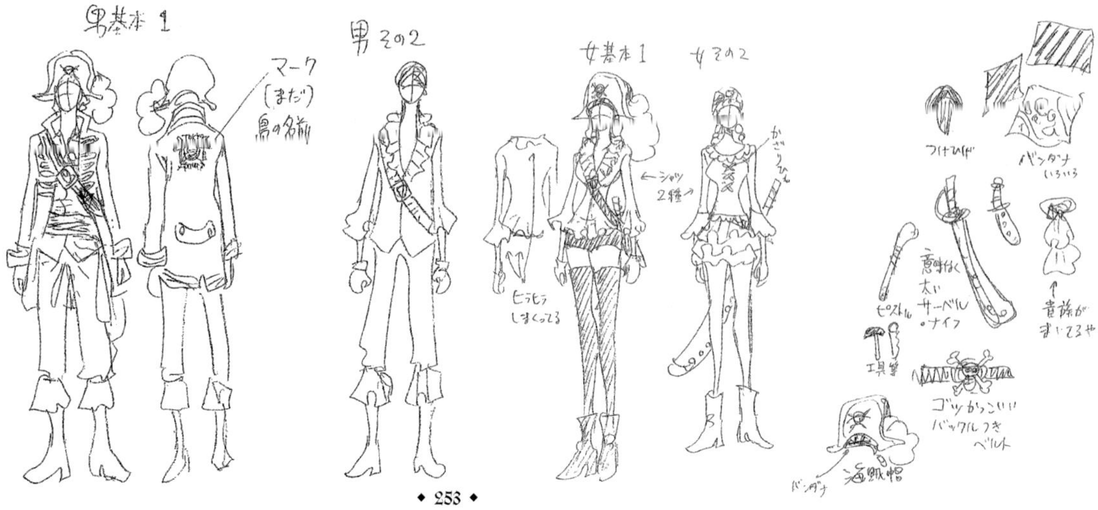
男基本1
男その2
女基本1
女その2

ONE PIECE: ACE'S STORY

A two-volume novel series that tells the story of how Ace went to sea, found friends with whom to form the Spade Pirates with, and eventually joined the Whitebeard Pirates.

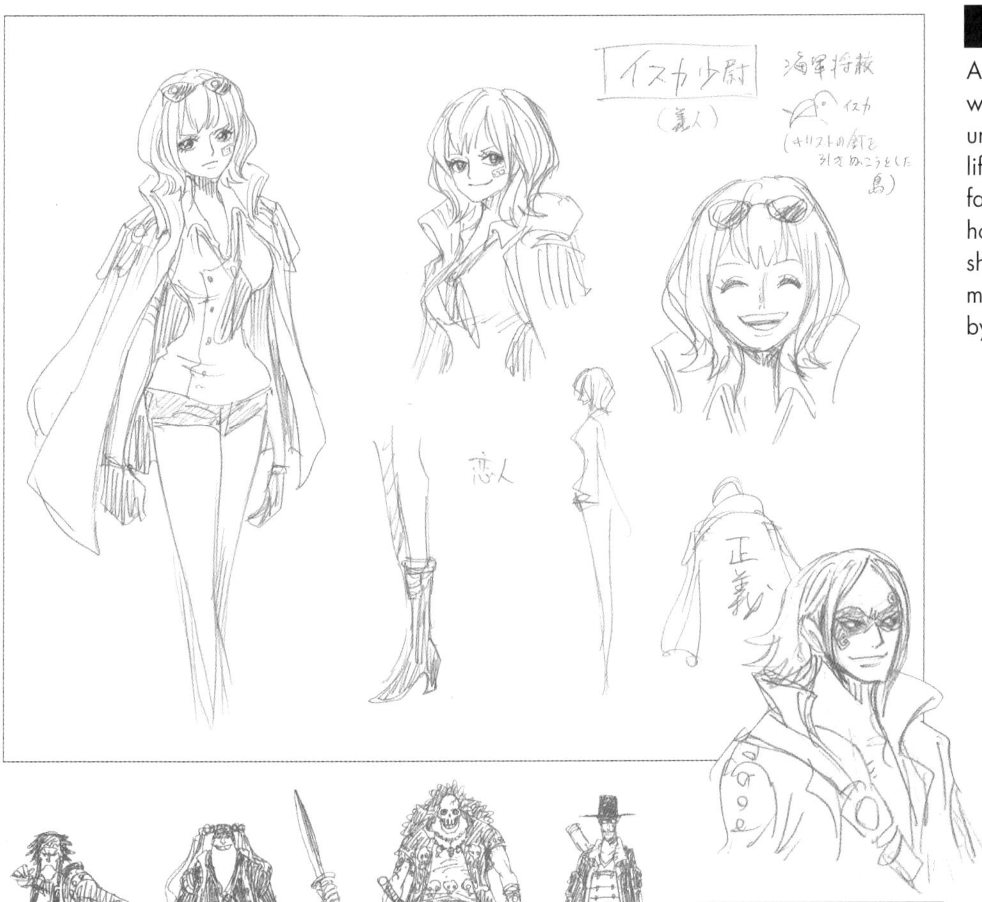
イスカ少尉
海軍将校
恋人
正義

ENSIGN ISUKA

A Naval officer who burns with passion to arrest Ace, until, one day, he saves her life. Because she lost her family in a house fire, she is traumatized by fire.

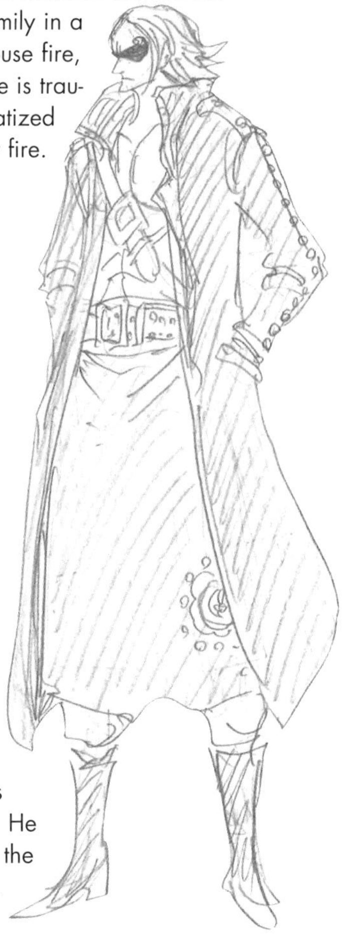

MASKED DEUCE

First to join Ace. Duece is his alias; real name is unknown. He wears a mask, and not even the Navy knows his true identity.

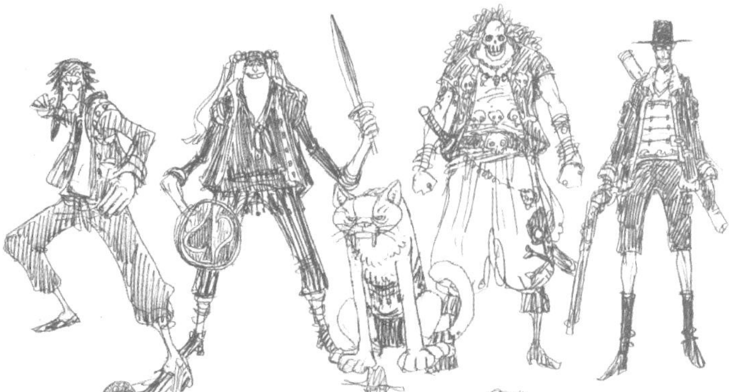

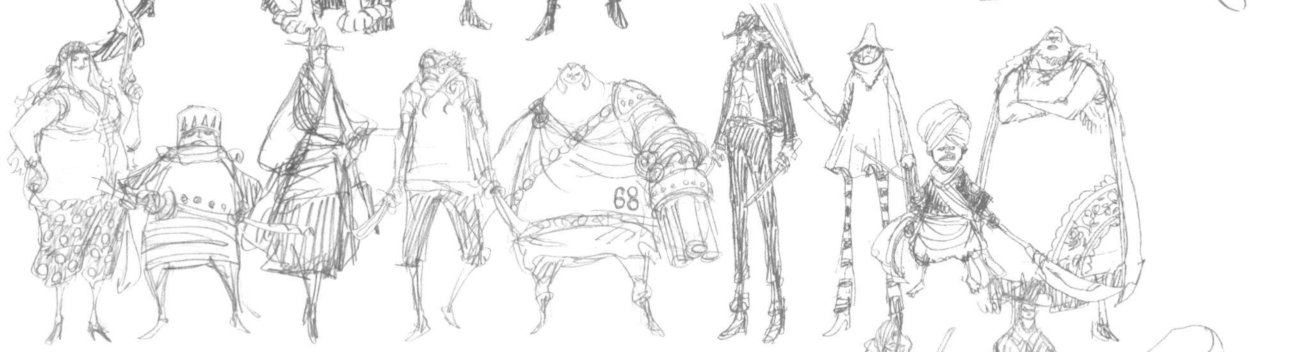
68

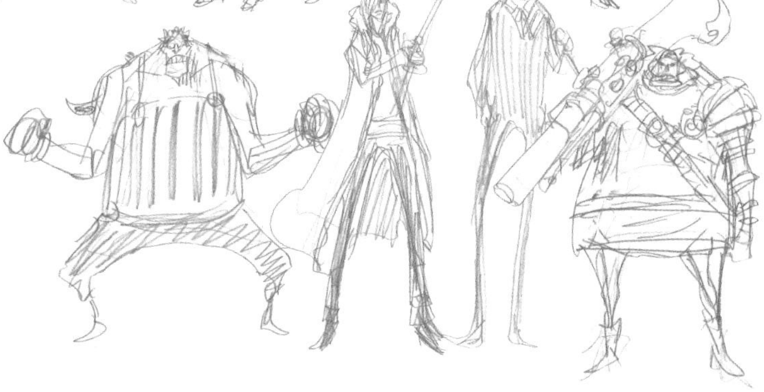

SPADE PIRATES

Comprised of a variety of folks, from longarms to fish-men. They join Ace in taking shelter under Whitebeard's wing, and later risked their lives fighting to save Ace during the Paramount War.

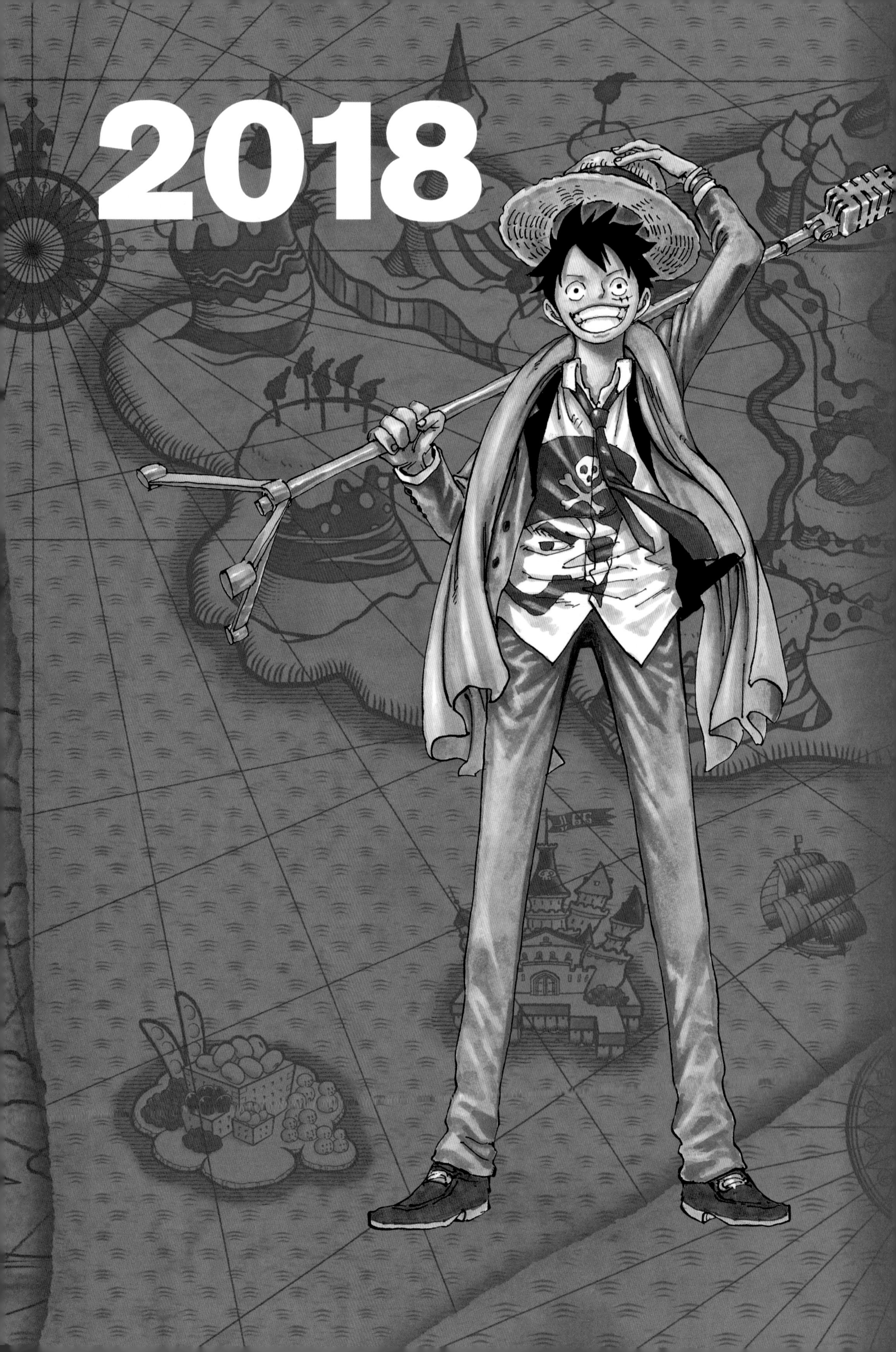
2018

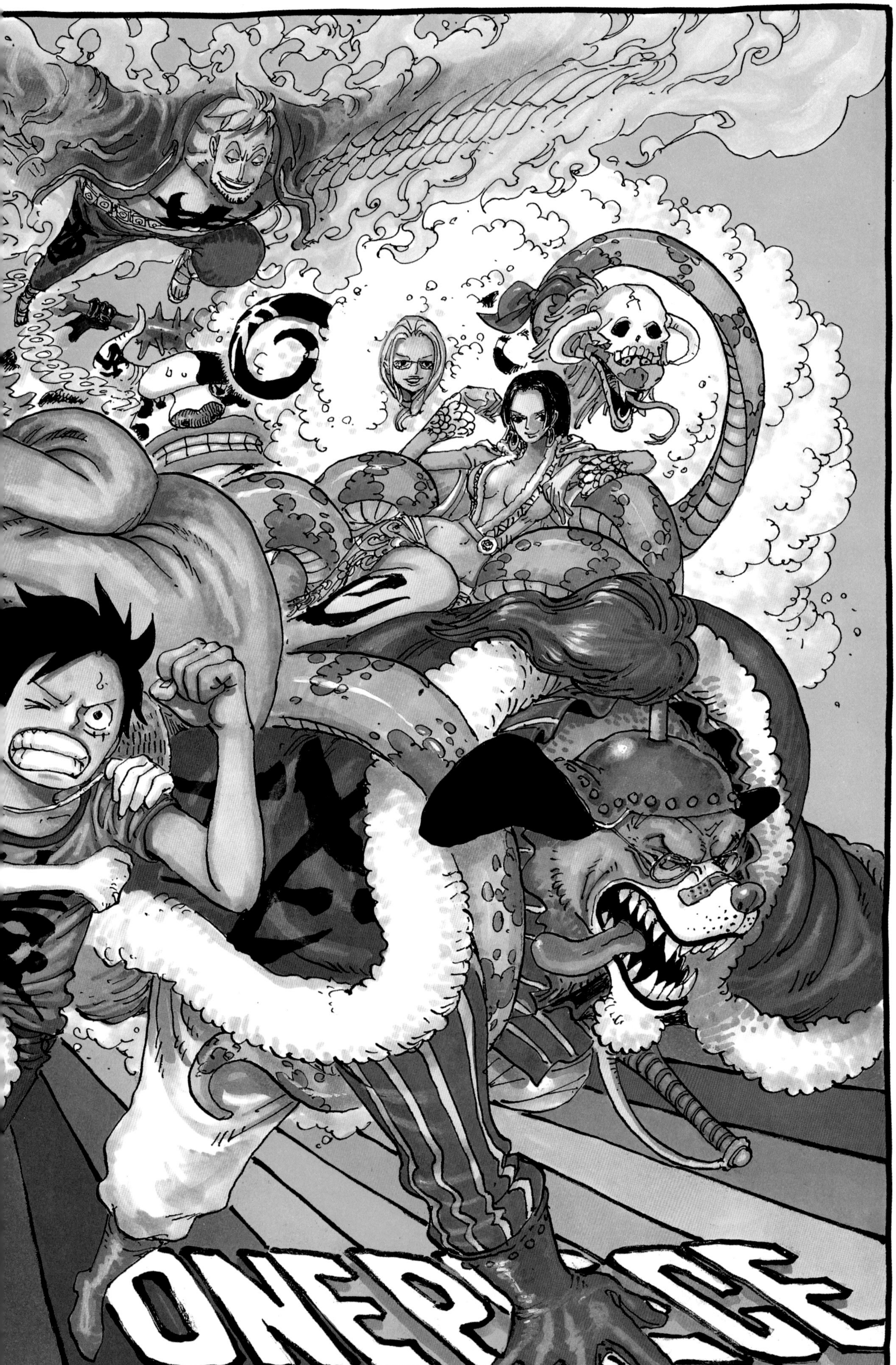

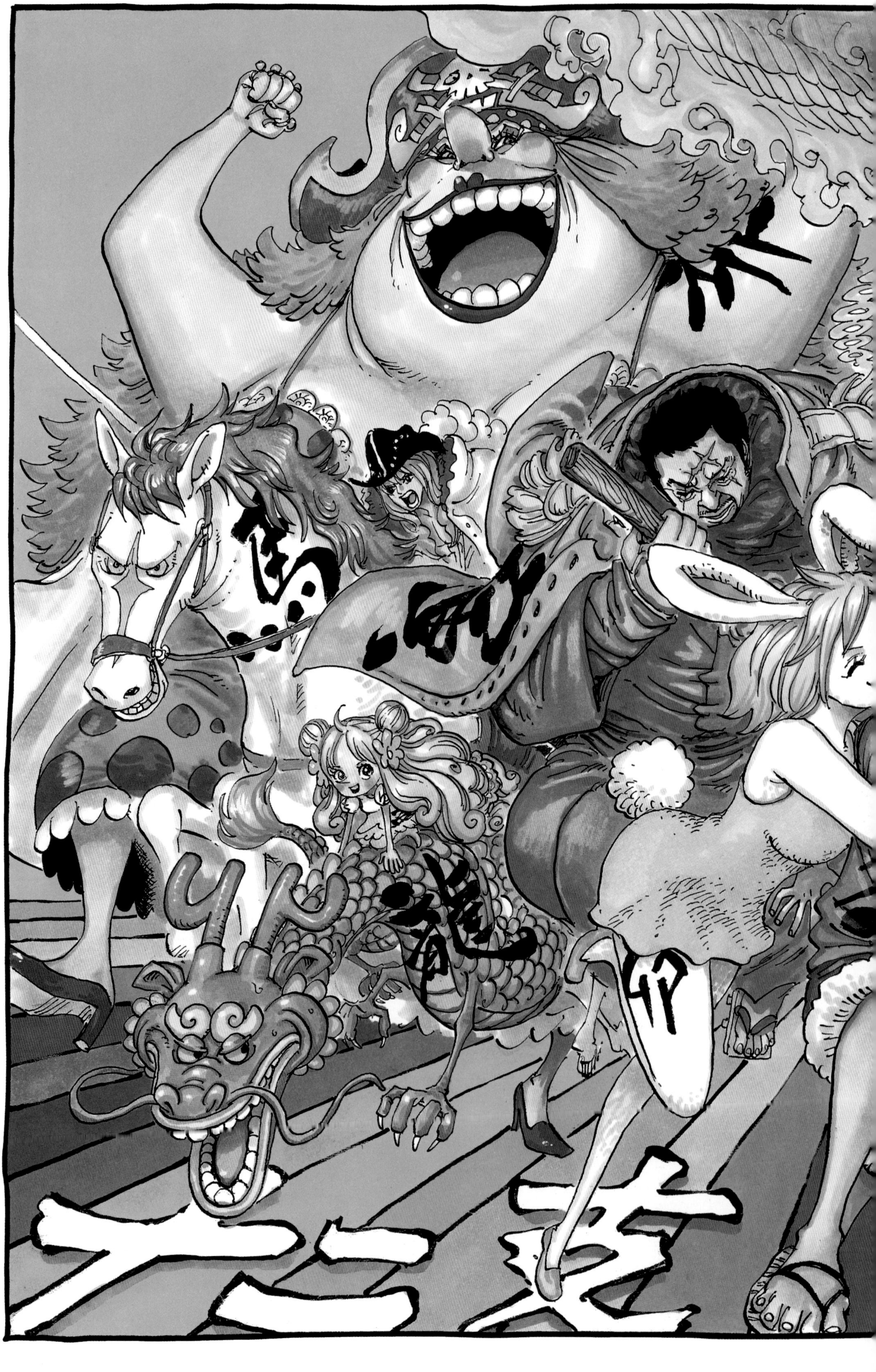
龍

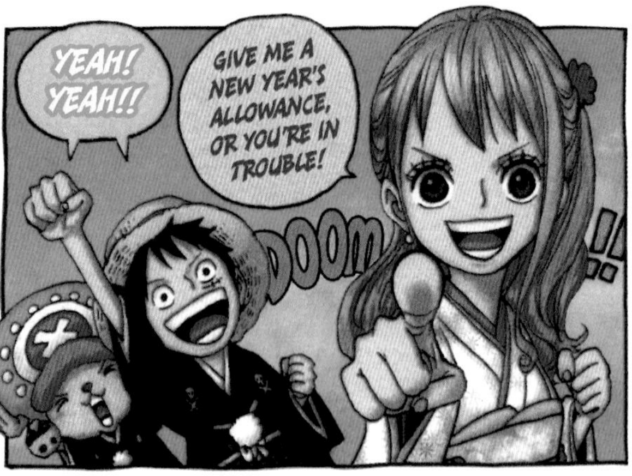
GIVE ME A NEW YEAR'S ALLOWANCE, OR YOU'RE IN TROUBLE!
DOOM
YEAH! YEAH!!

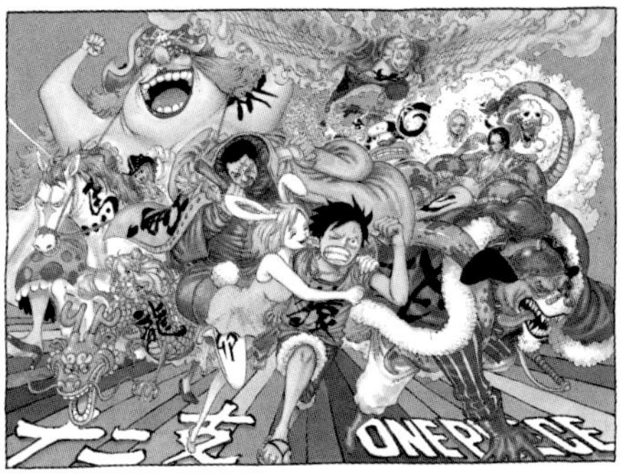

Comments P.256–257

Representing each of the Chinese Zodiac animals with a character! The toughest ones to choose were rat and boar. I selected Mansherry because the Japanese name of her fruit sounds like a mouse (*chiu-chiu*). And for the boar... that's it! Gotta be her! The barelling, berserk Big Mom!

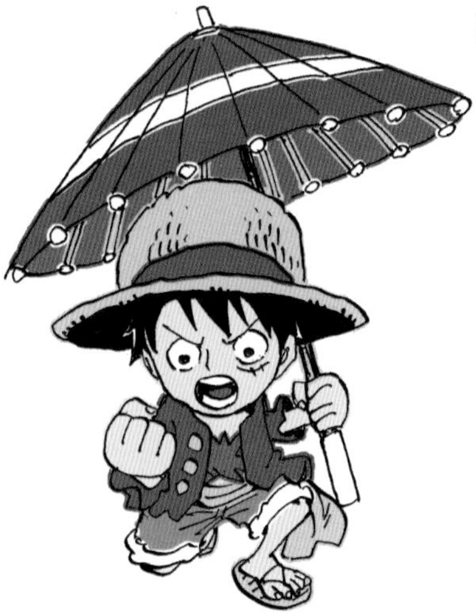

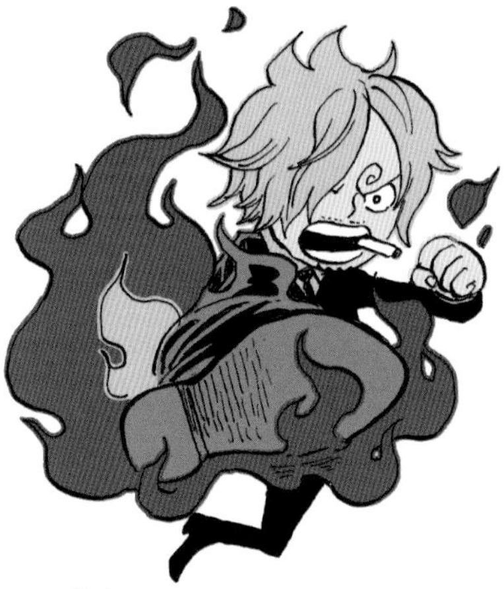

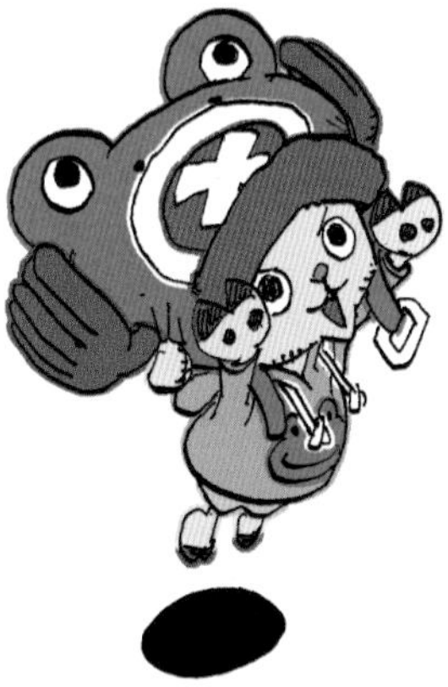

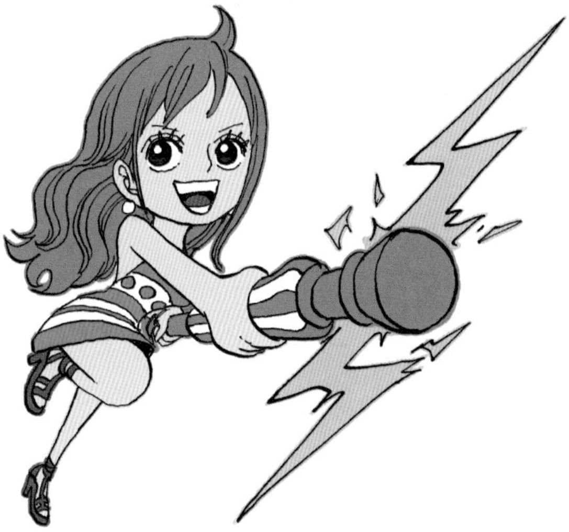

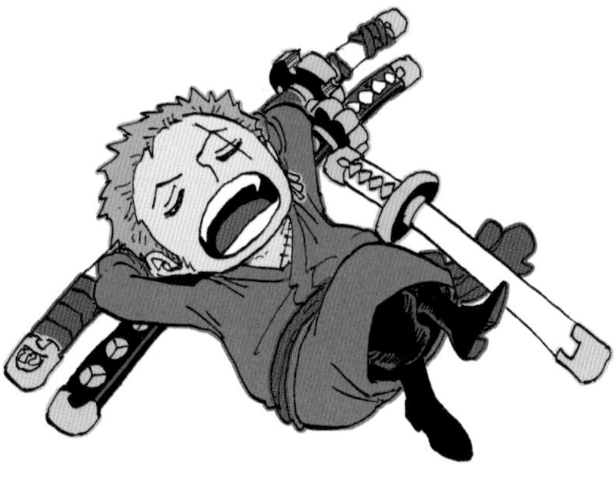

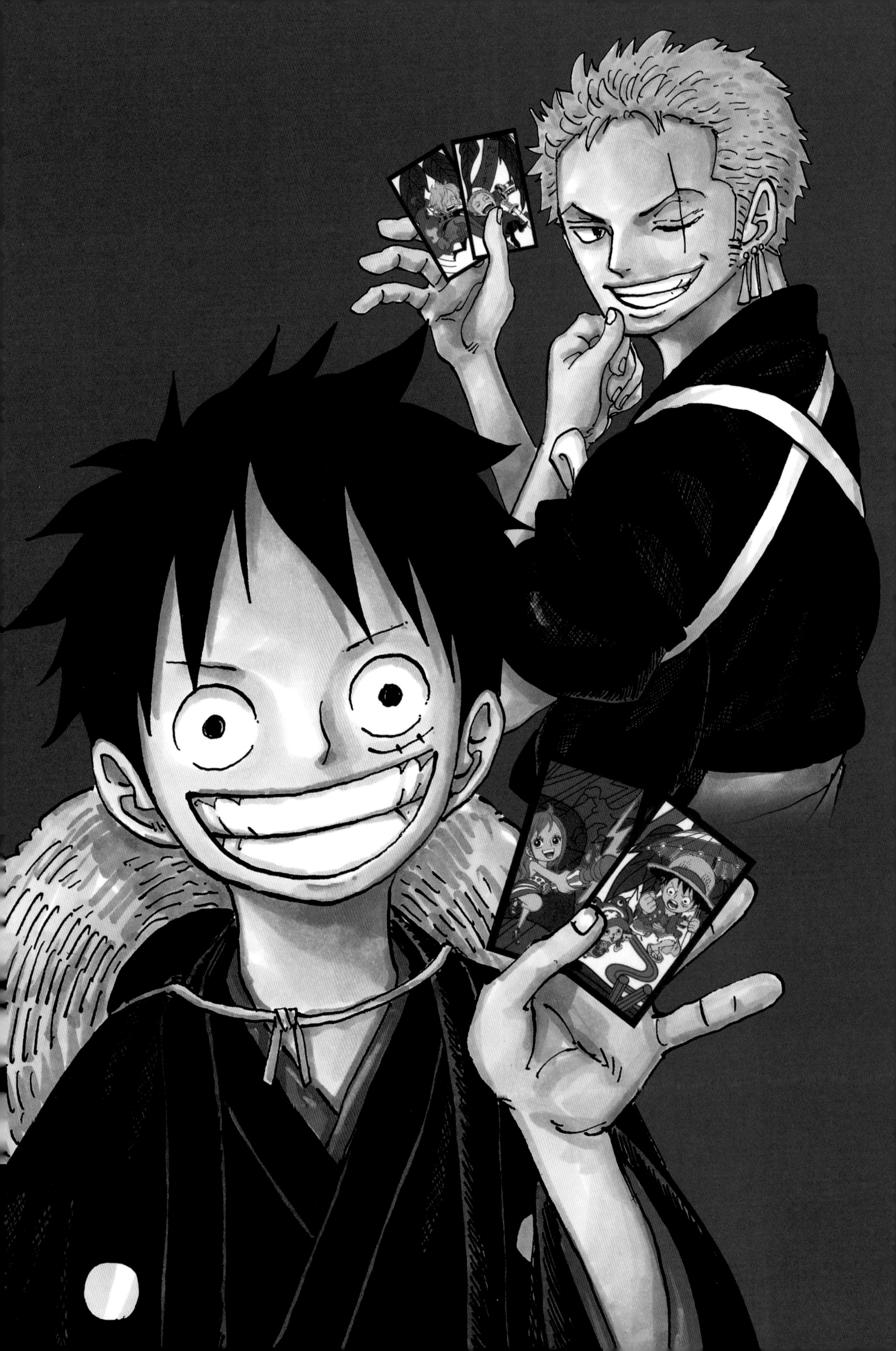

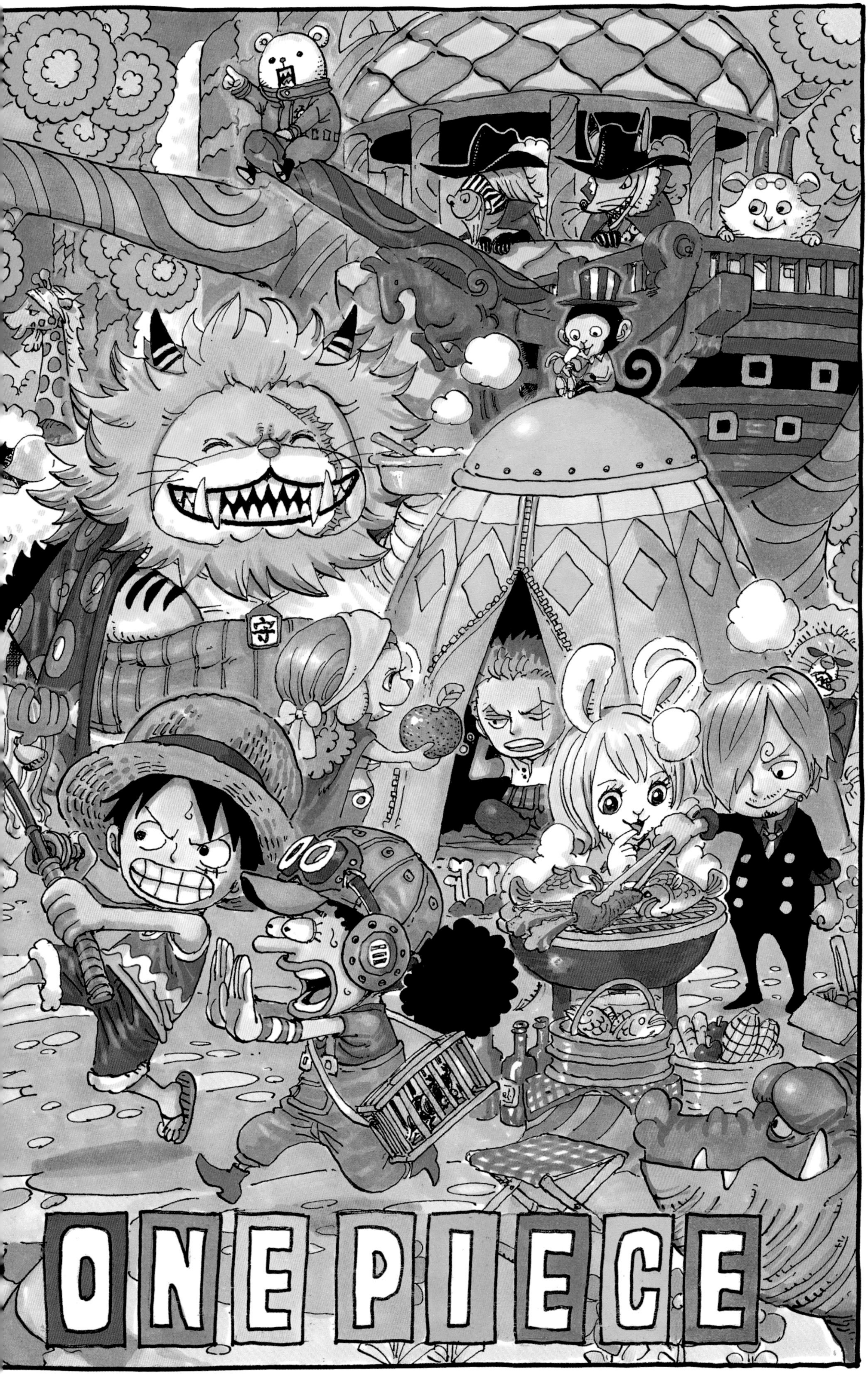
ONE PIECE

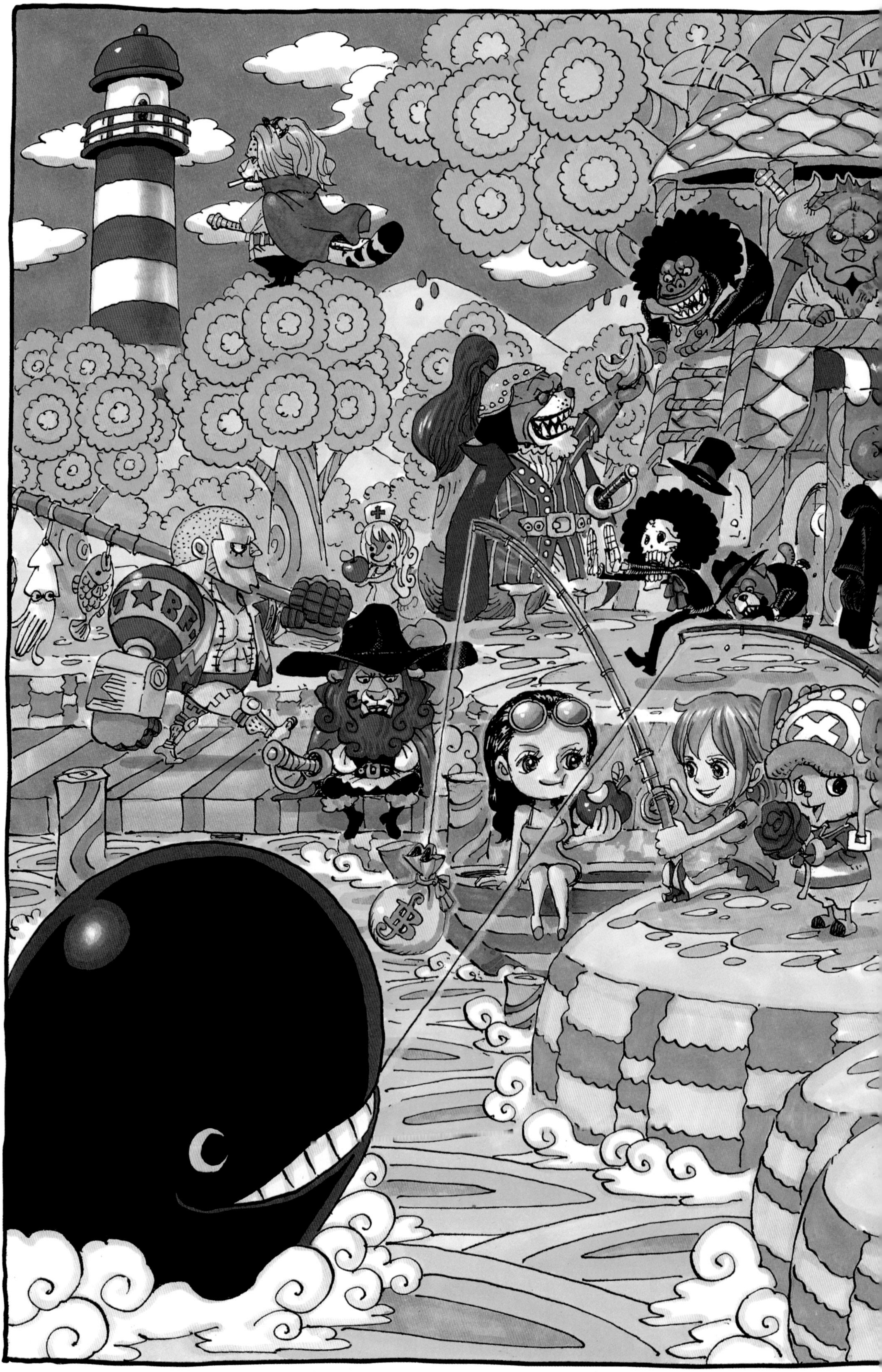

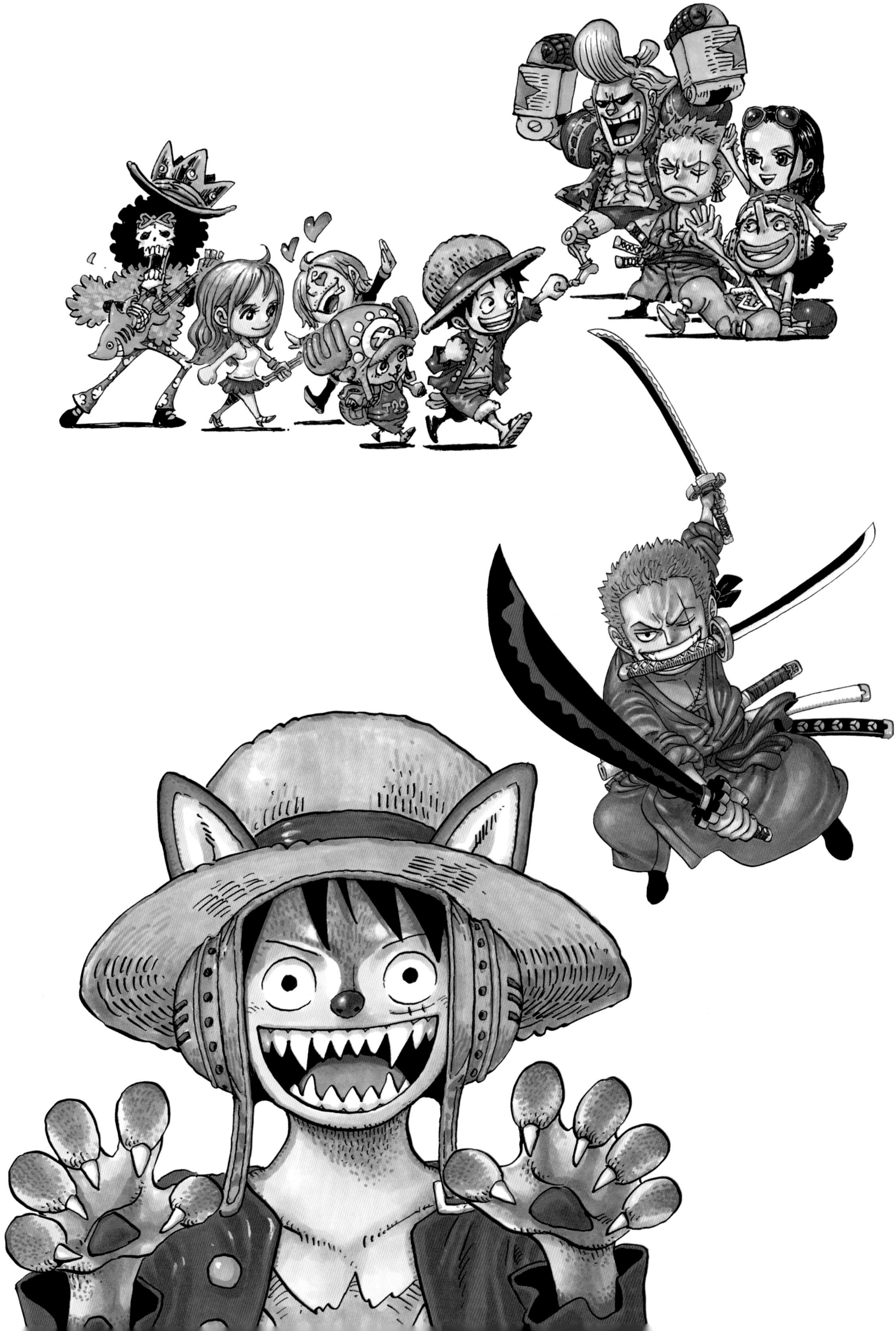

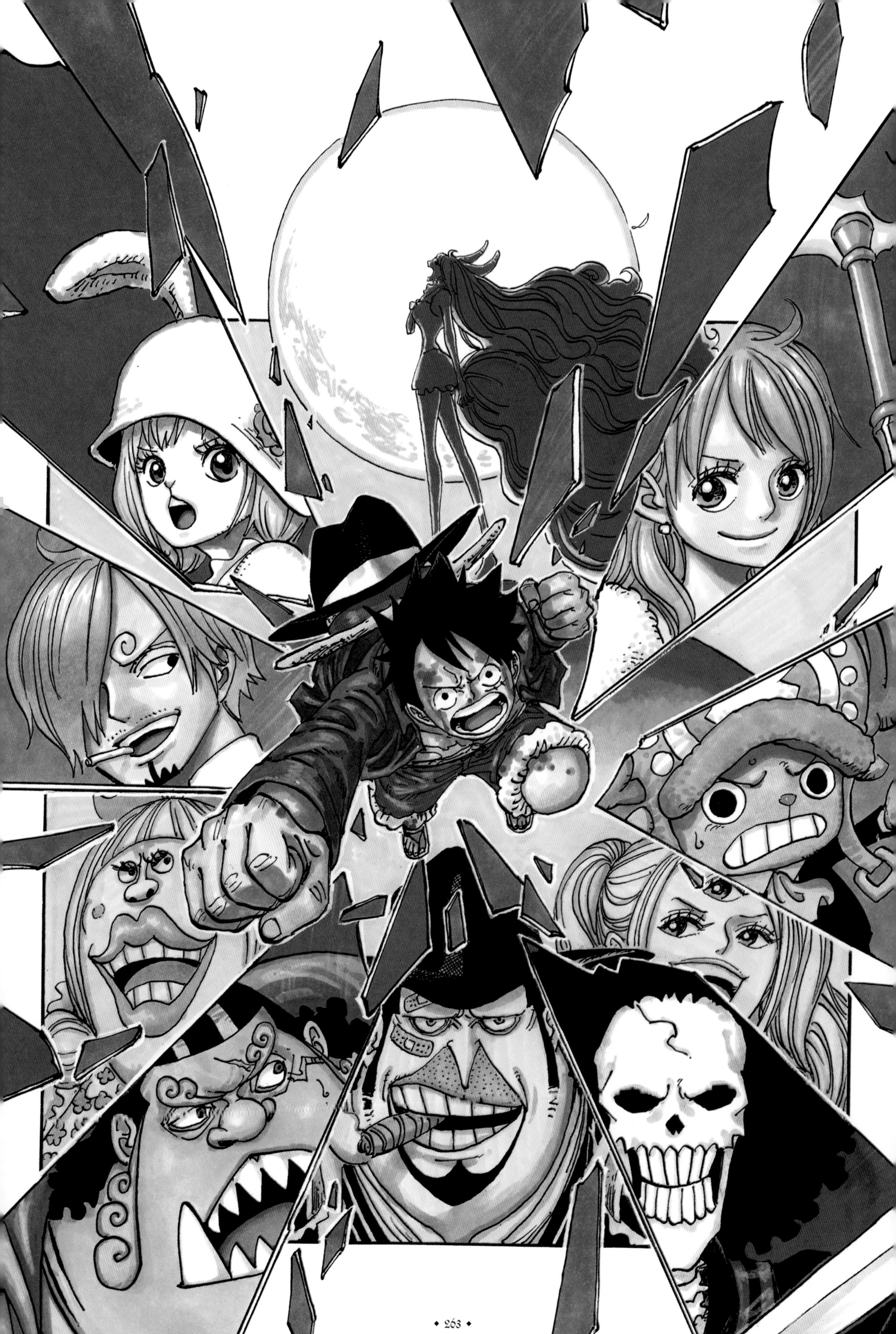

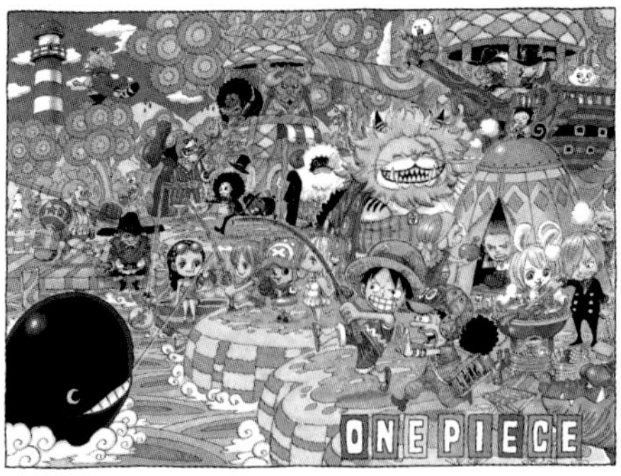
ONE PIECE

Comments P.260–261

I've always loved the *Animal Crossing* games. A new one had just come out around this time, and I realized, "Hey, I have a village full of animals too!" So I recreated it with minks.

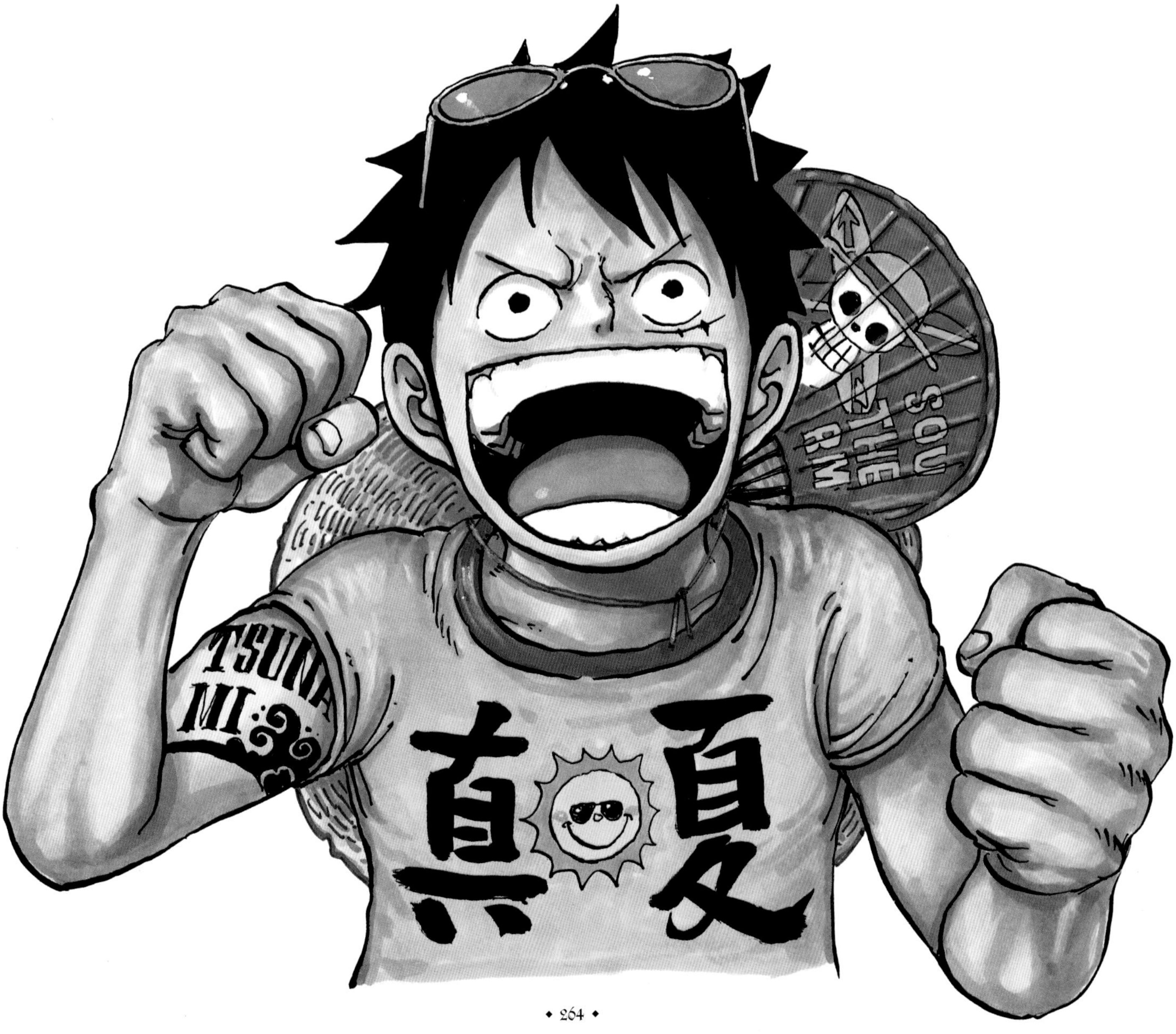
TSUNA
MI
真夏

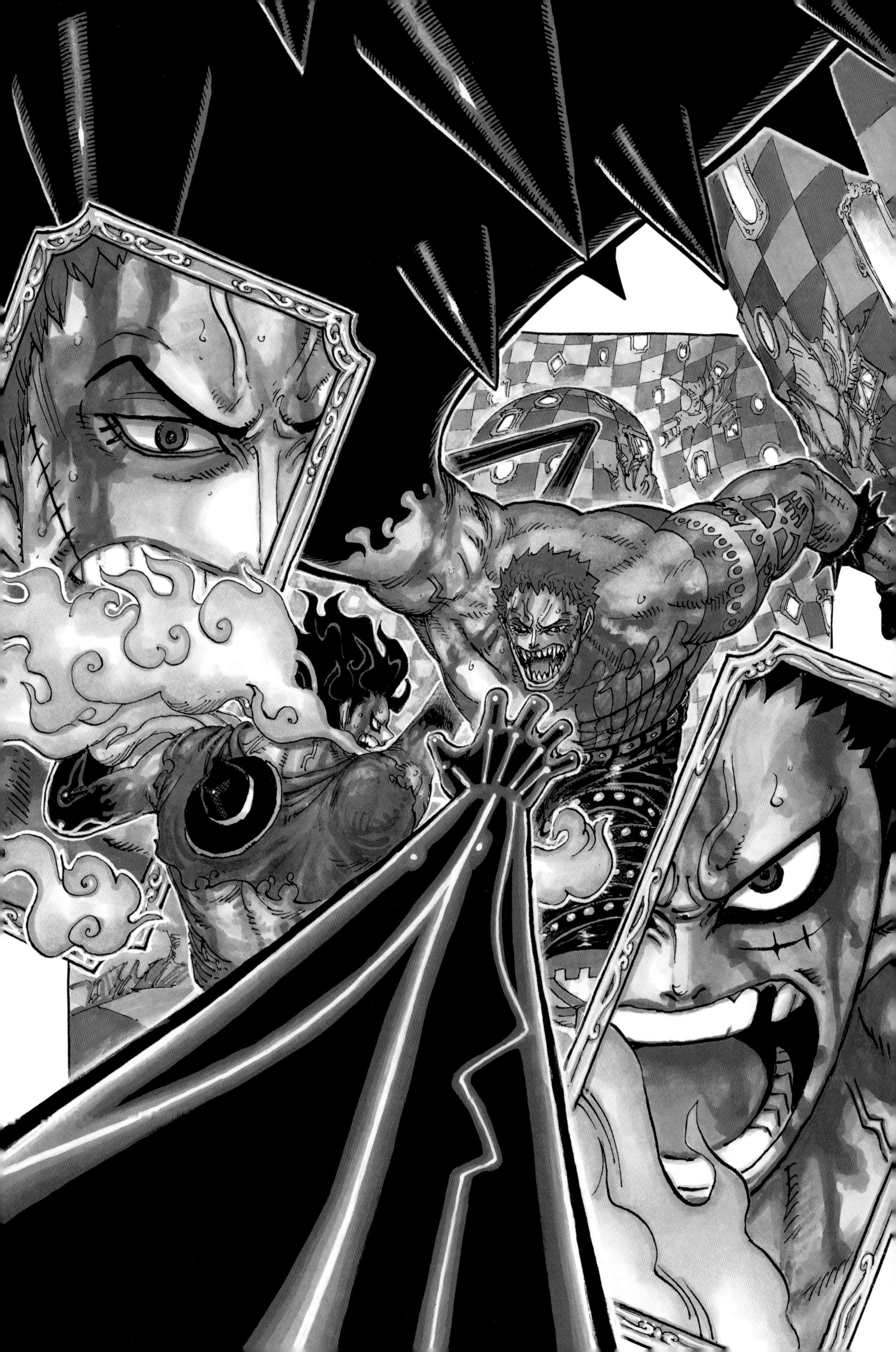

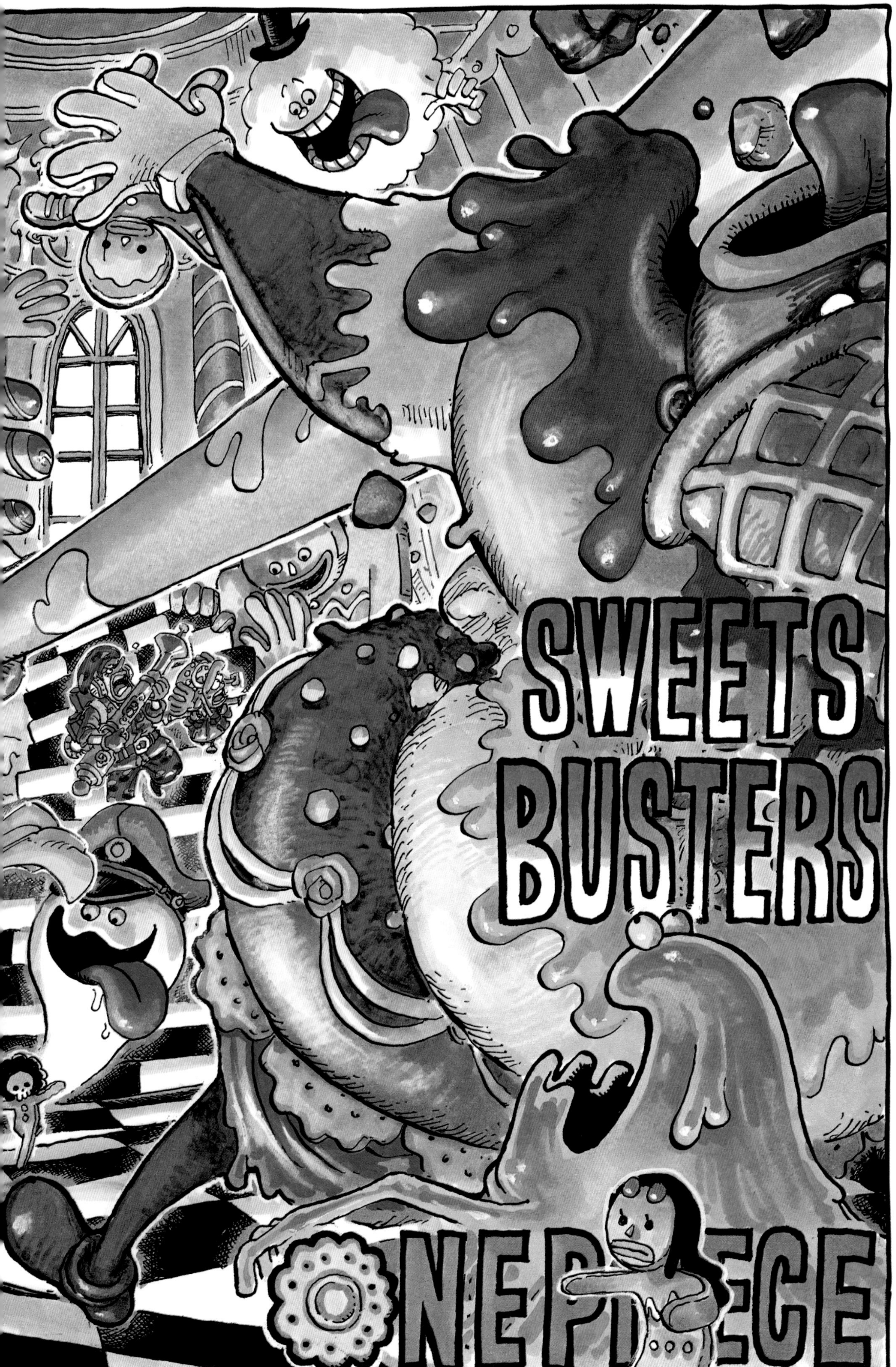
SWEETS BUSTERS
ONE PIECE

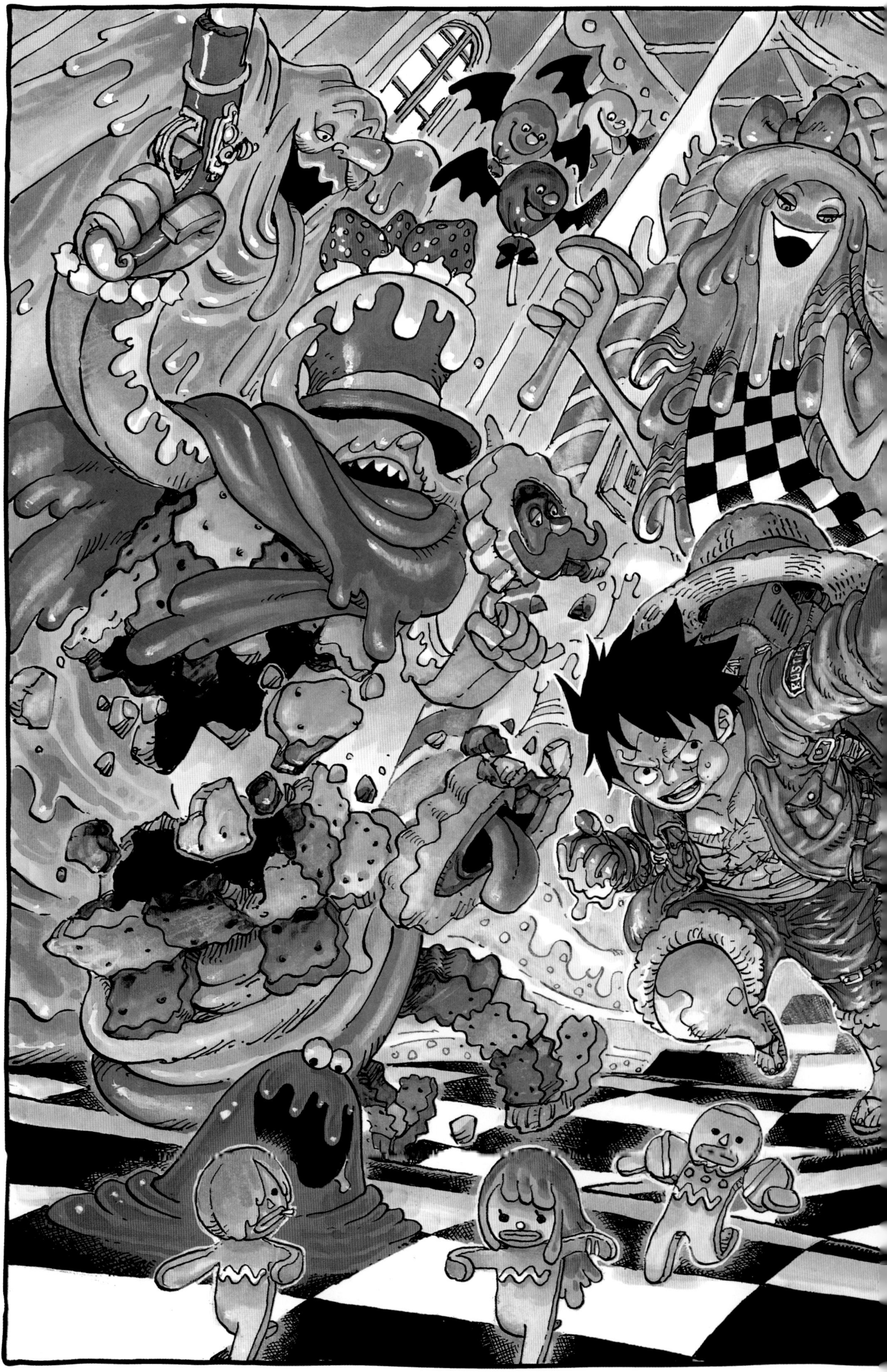

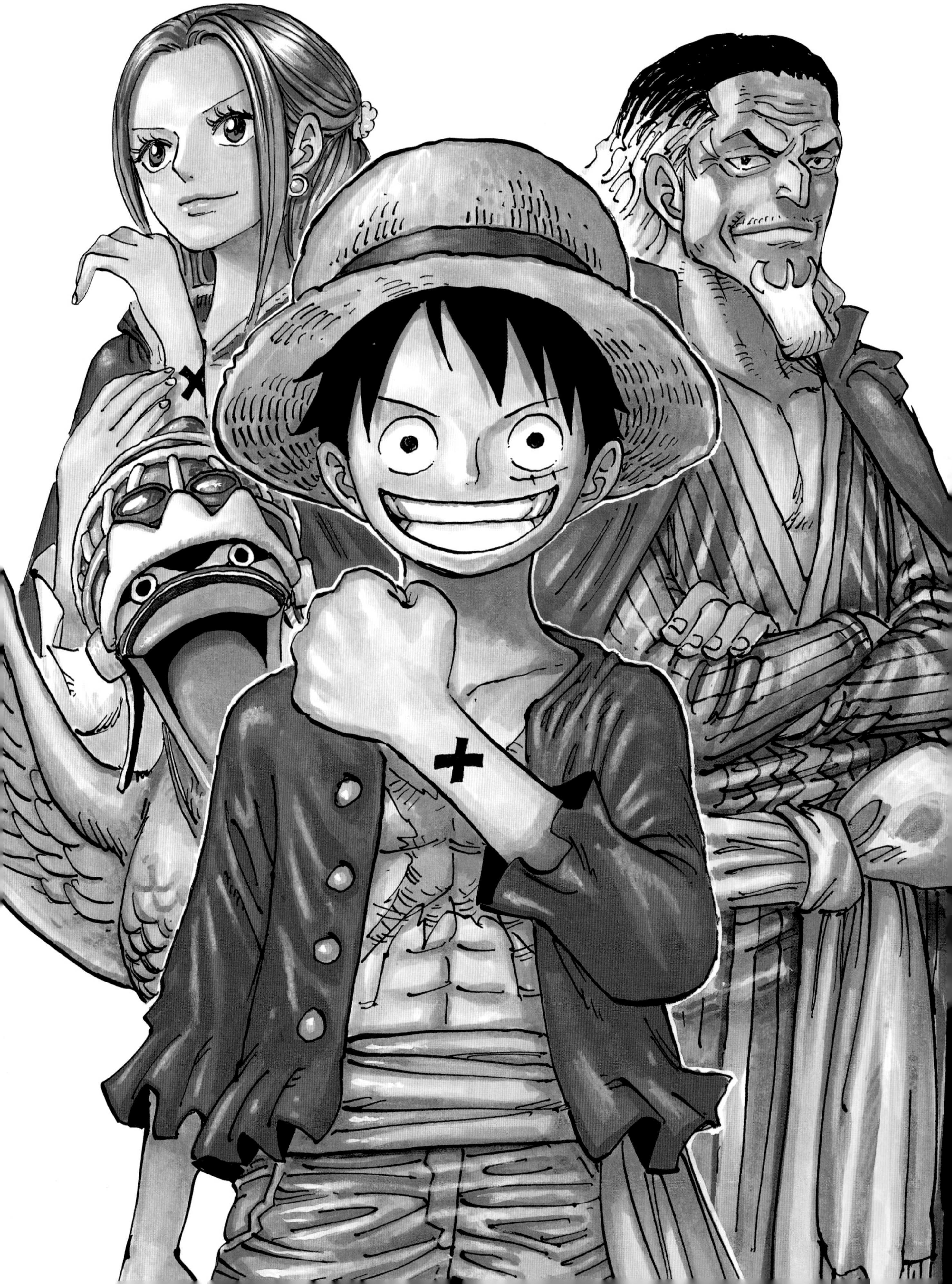

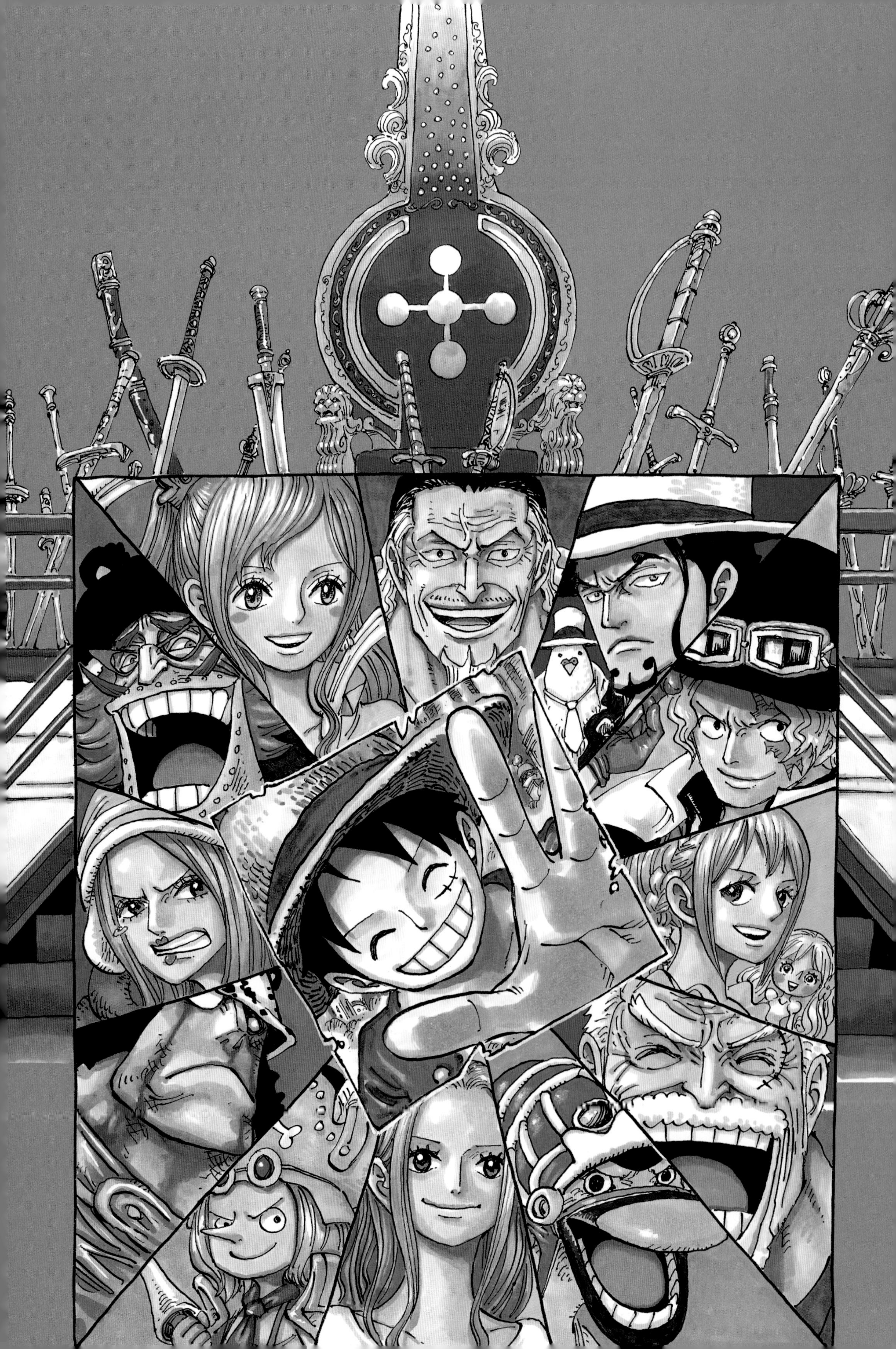

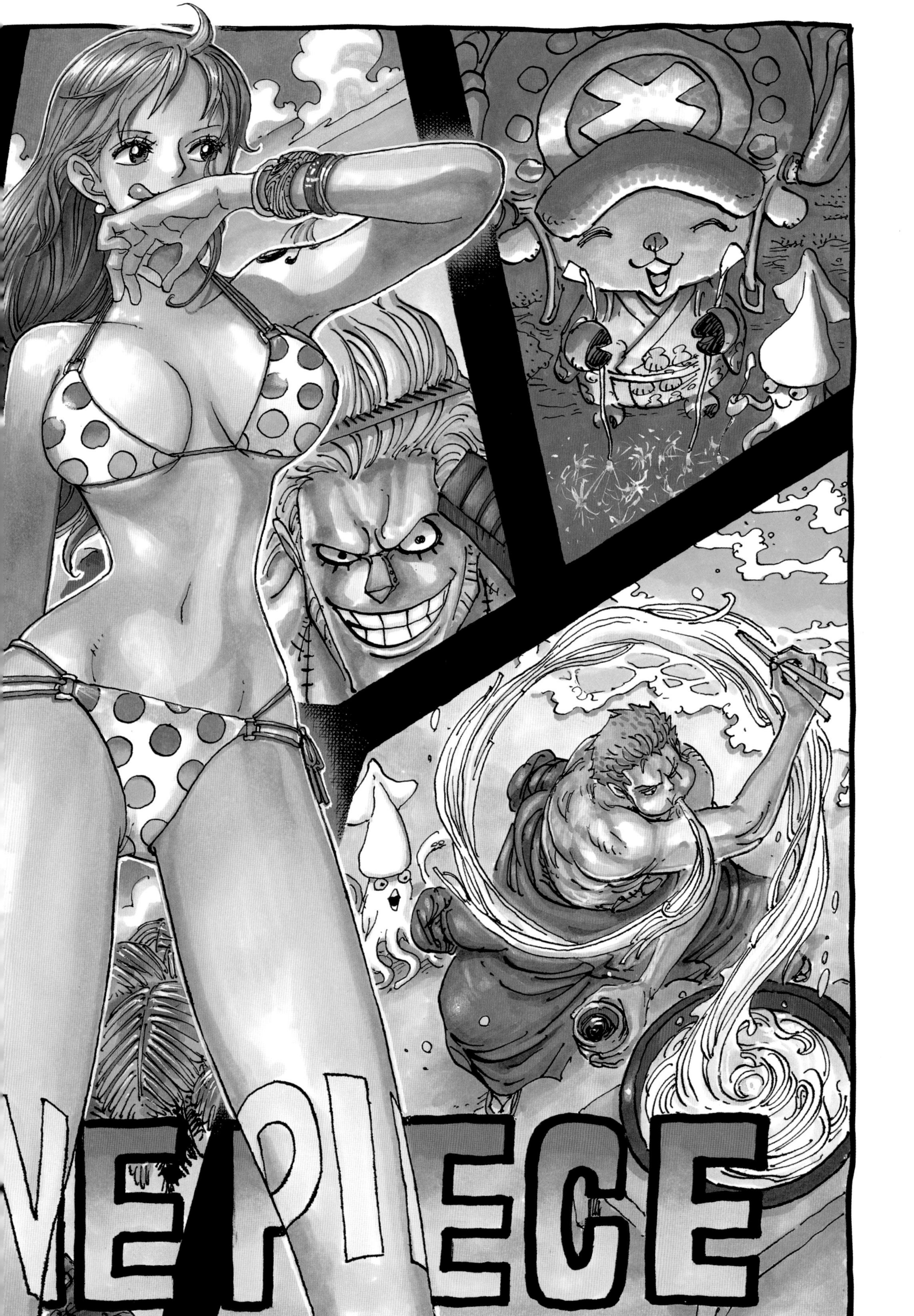

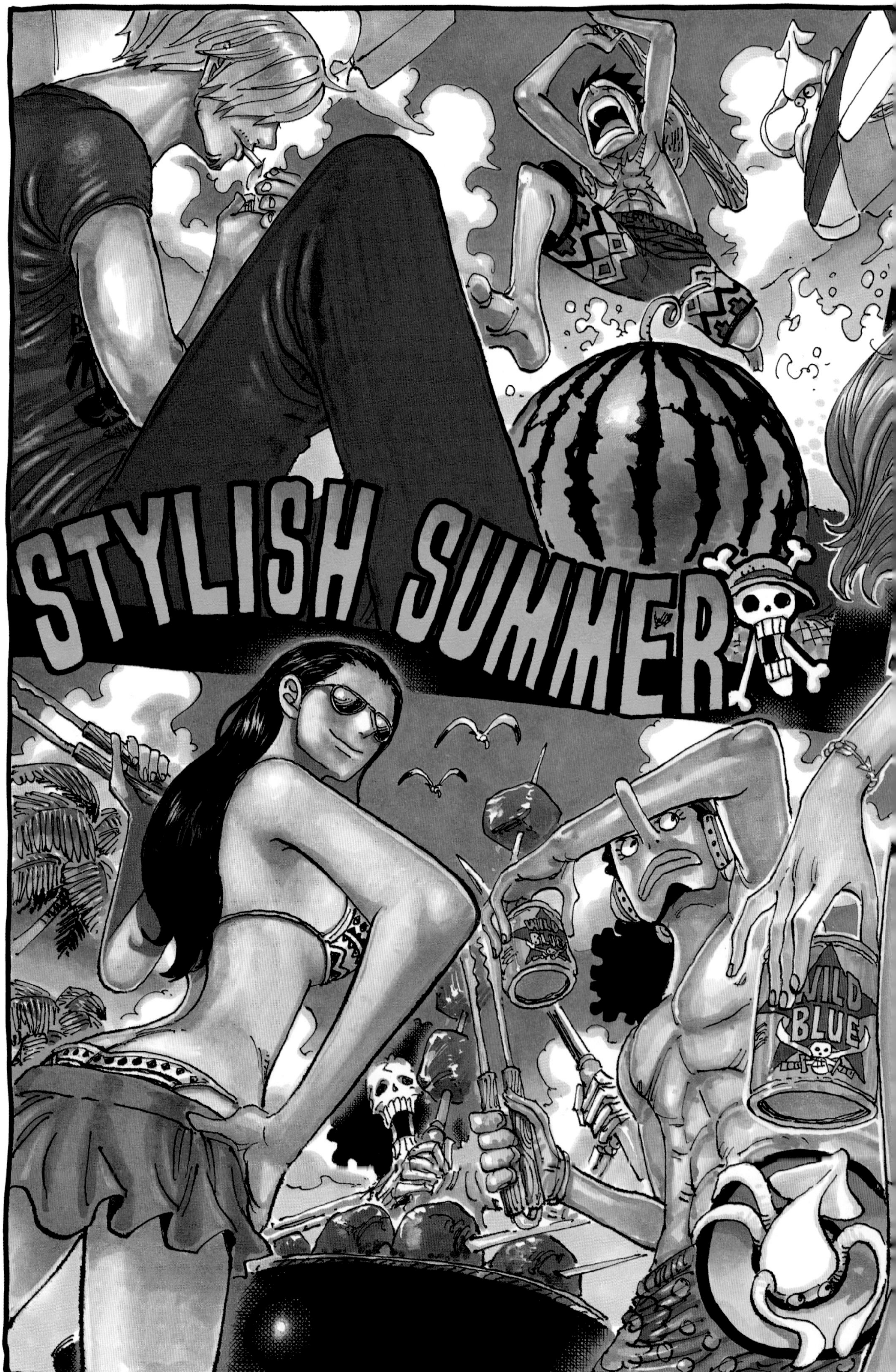
STYLISH SUMMER
WILD BLUE
WILD BLUE

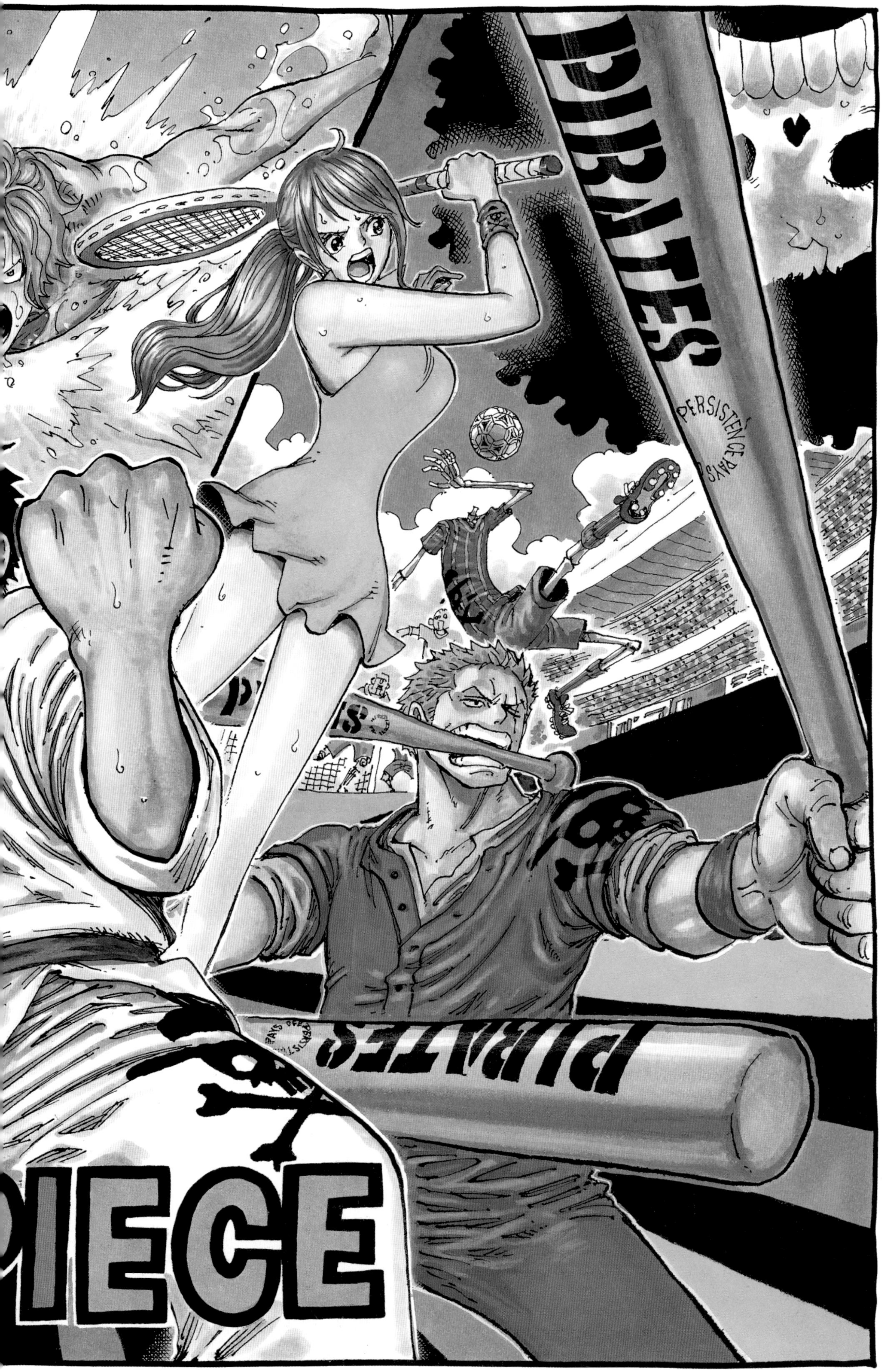
PIRATES
PERSISTENCE PAYS
PIECE

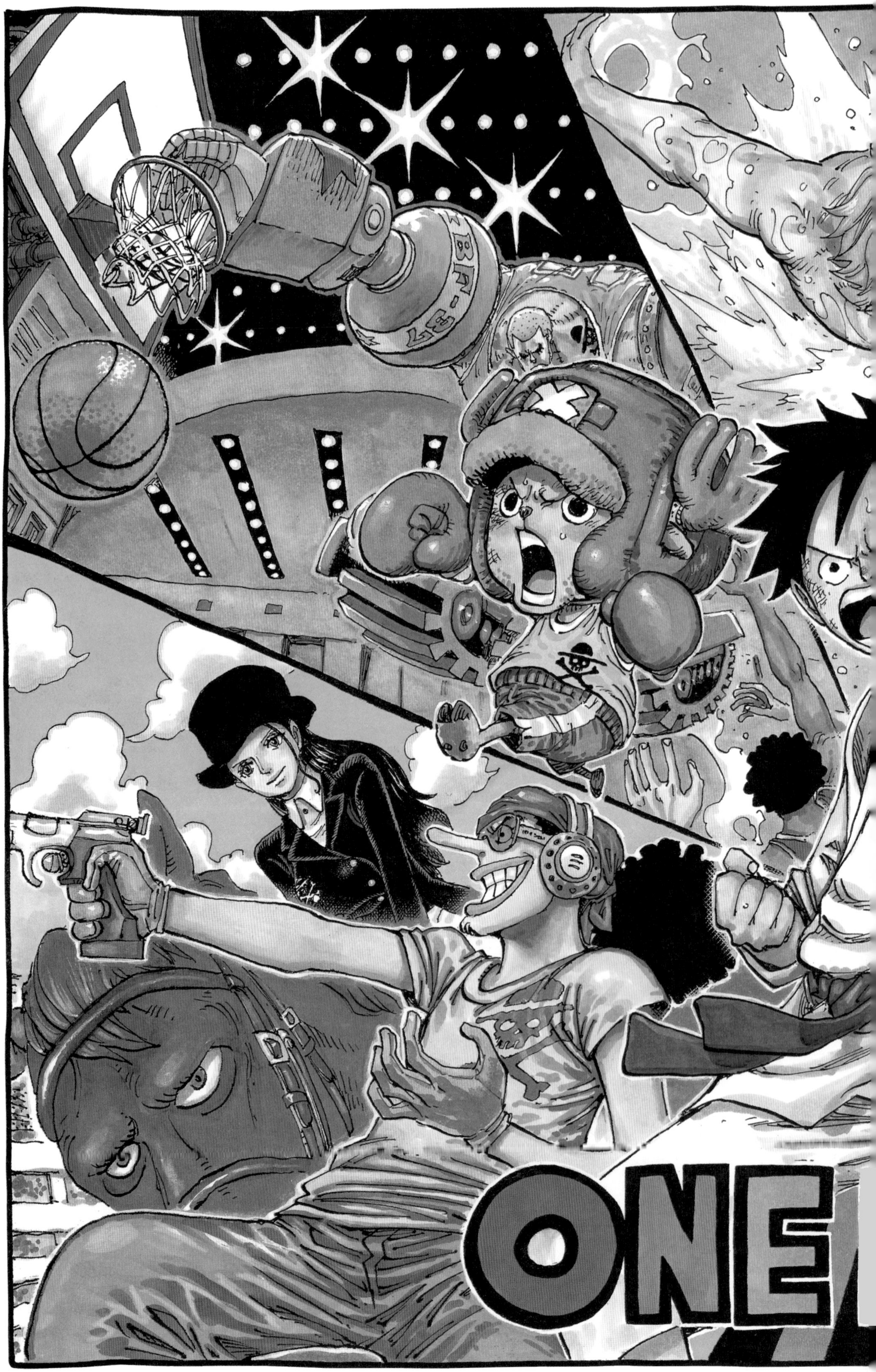
ONE

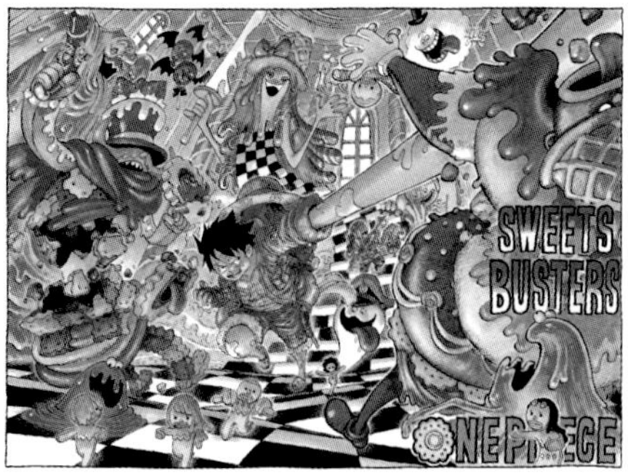
SWEETS
BUSTERS

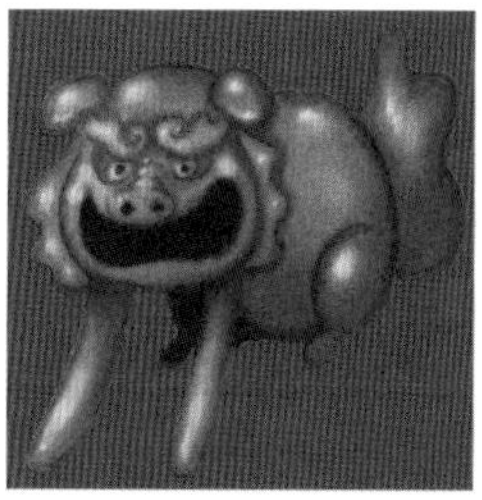

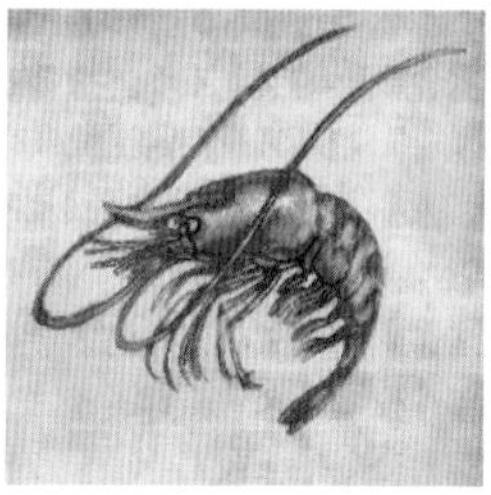

Comments P.266–267

My darling daughter baked me some delicious cookies.
Me: Look, I drew them.
Daughter: Hmm...
Apparently it wasn't a good likeness.

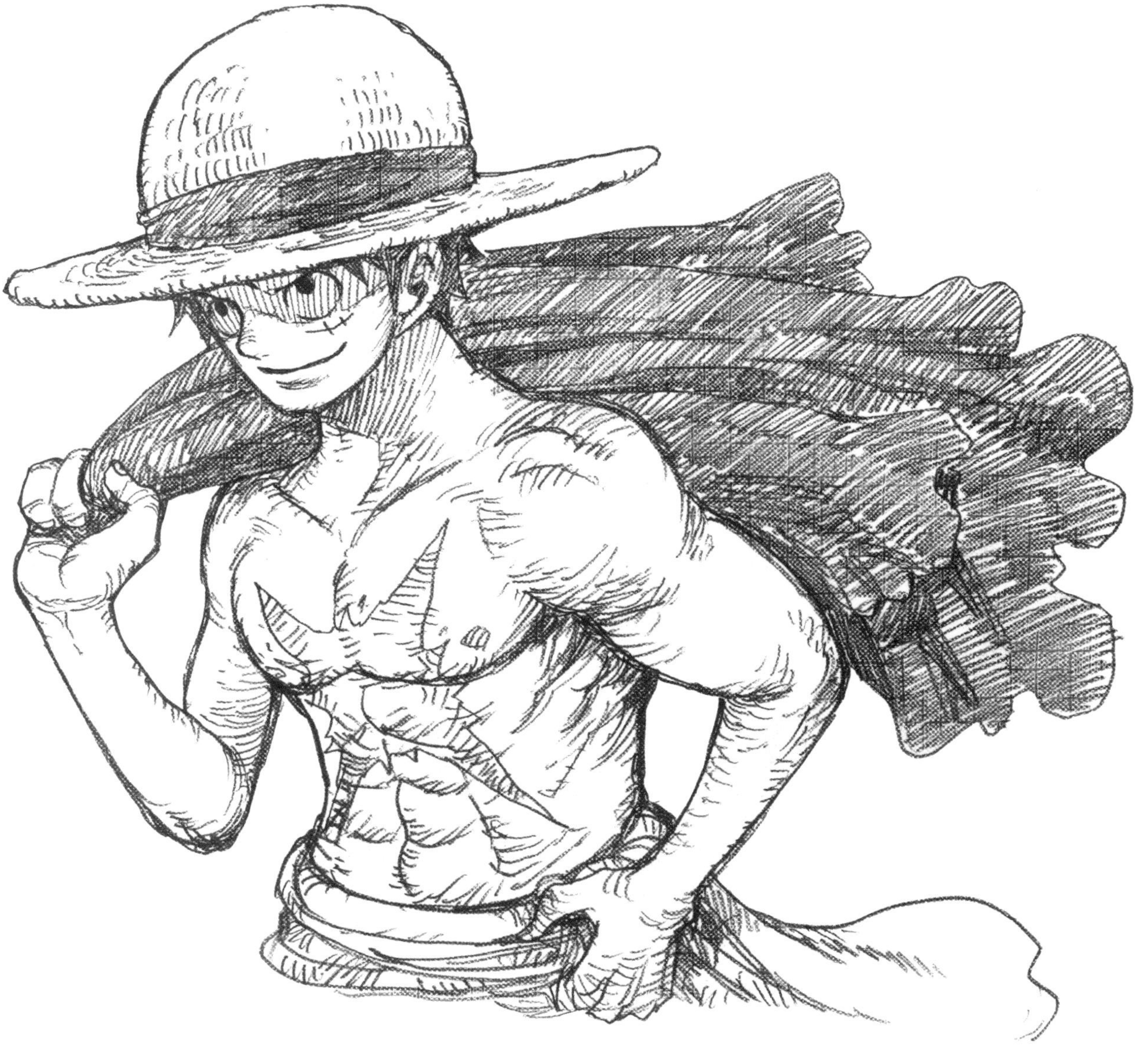

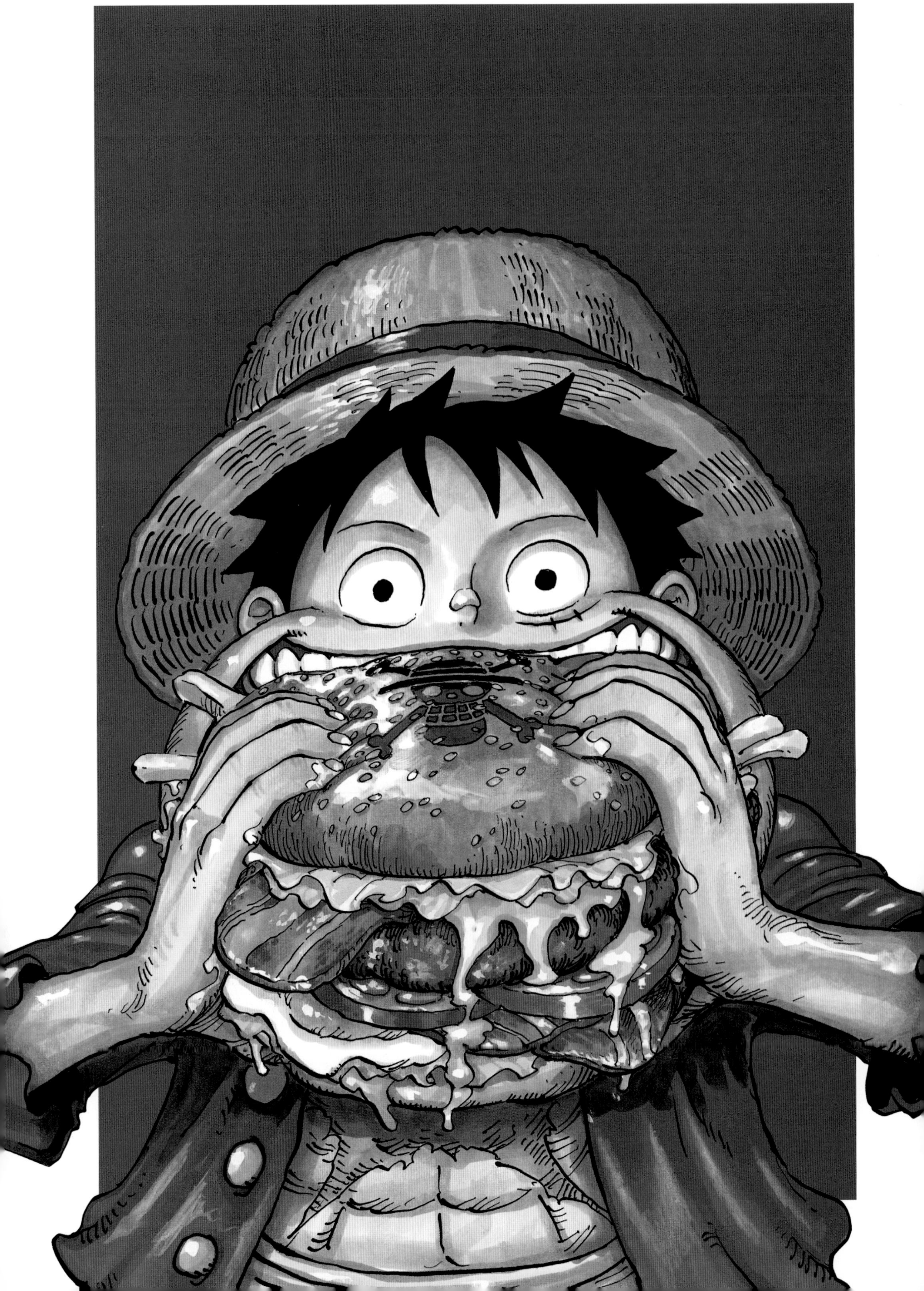

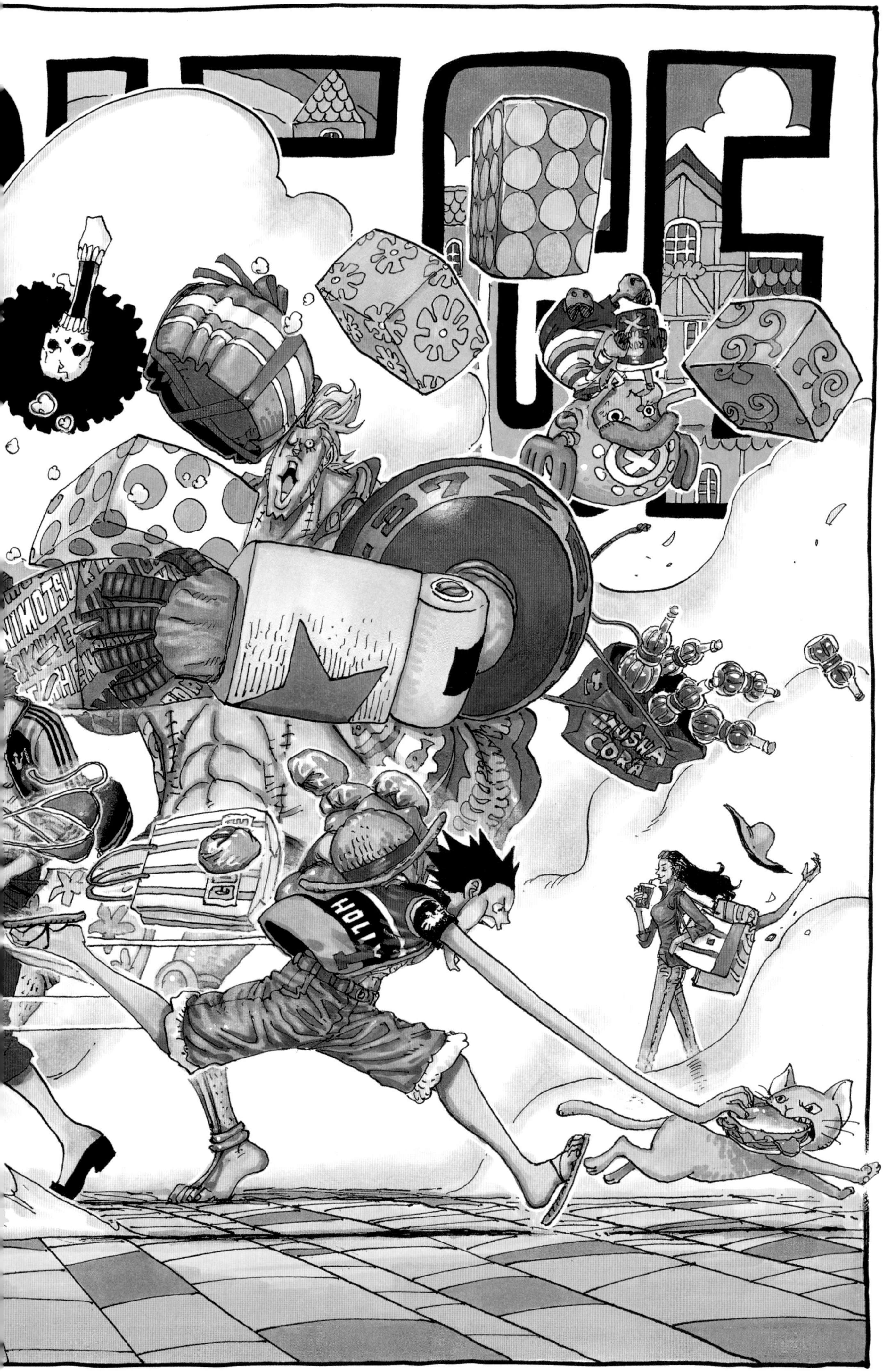
NIMOTSU
MUSHA
CORA
HOLLY

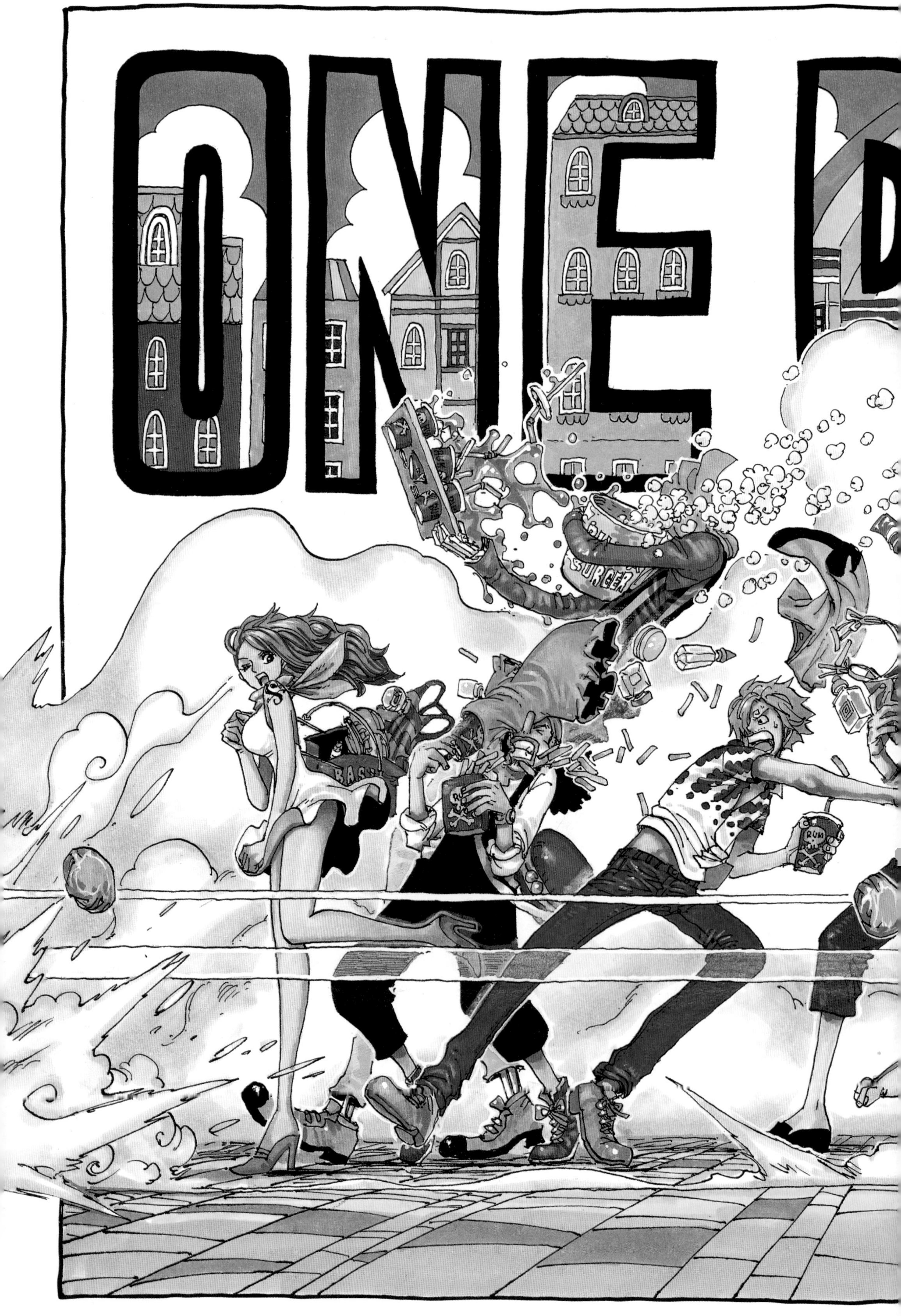
ONE
BURGER
RUM

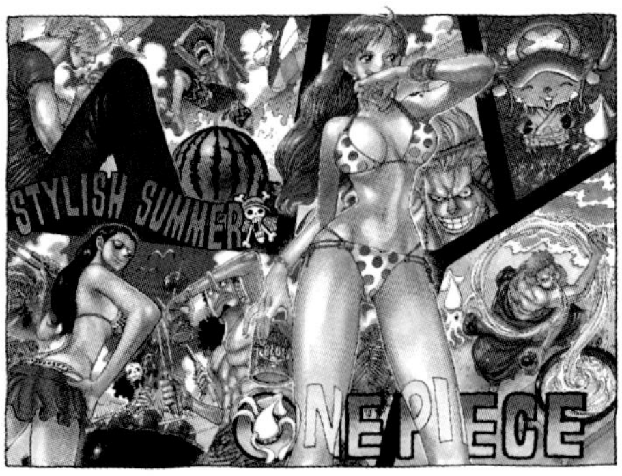
STYLISH SUMMER
ONE PIECE

Comments P.270–271

I always want to draw bathing suits, and so I do it at least once a year! Usopp's showing off too hard. Zolo's slurping those noodles and not even bothering with the dipping broth in his hand. Who cares about guys on the beach?!

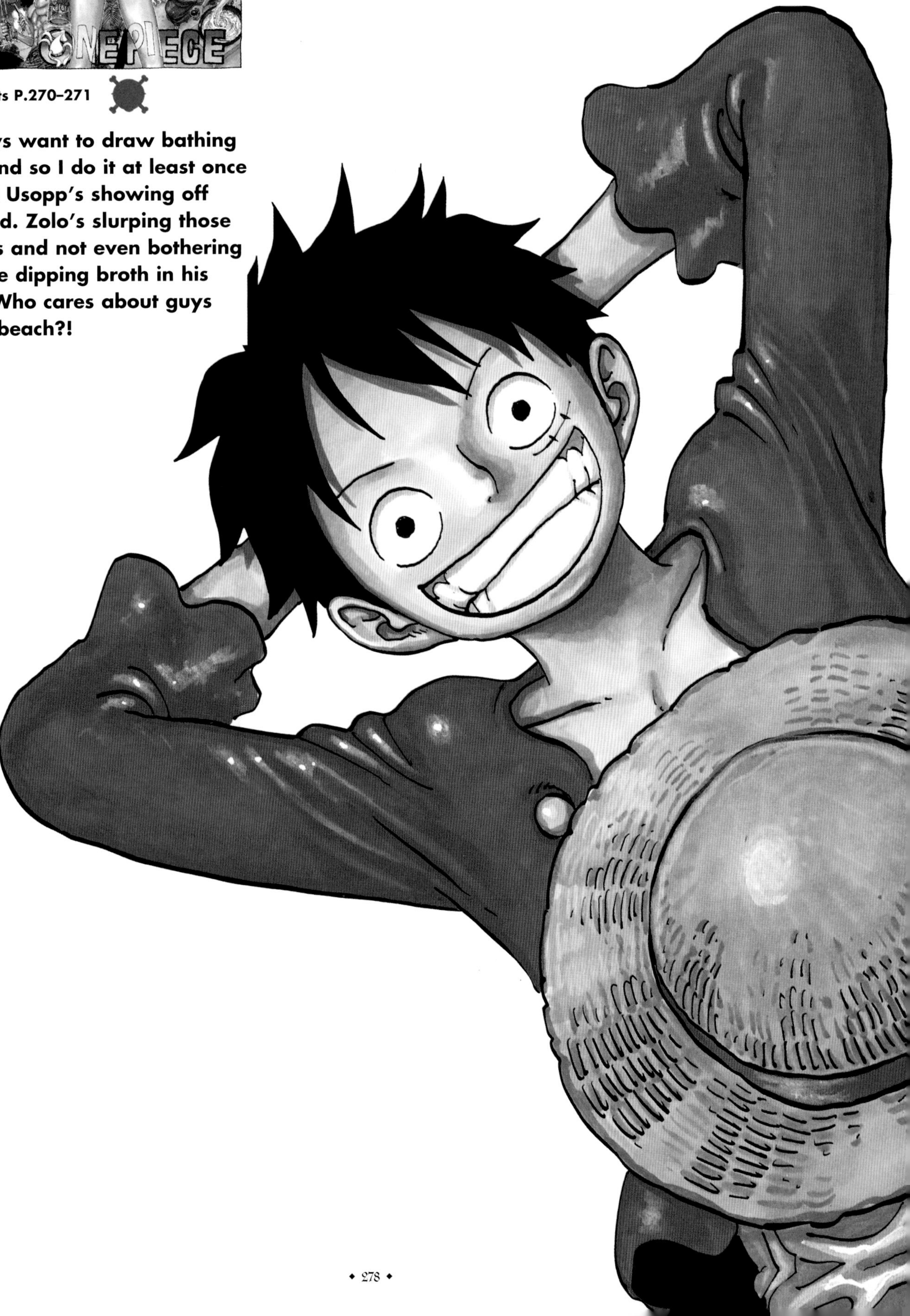

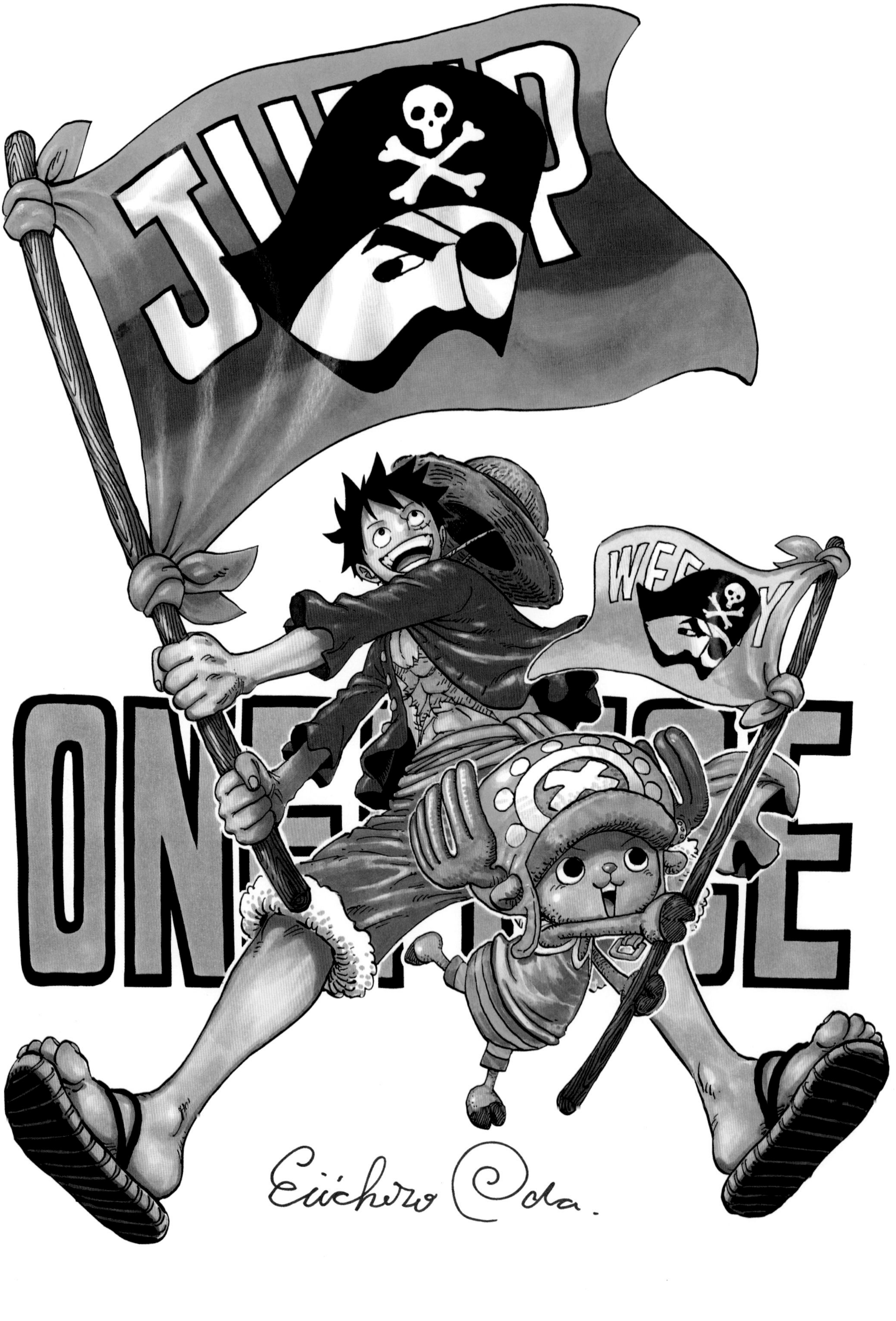
Eiichiro Oda.

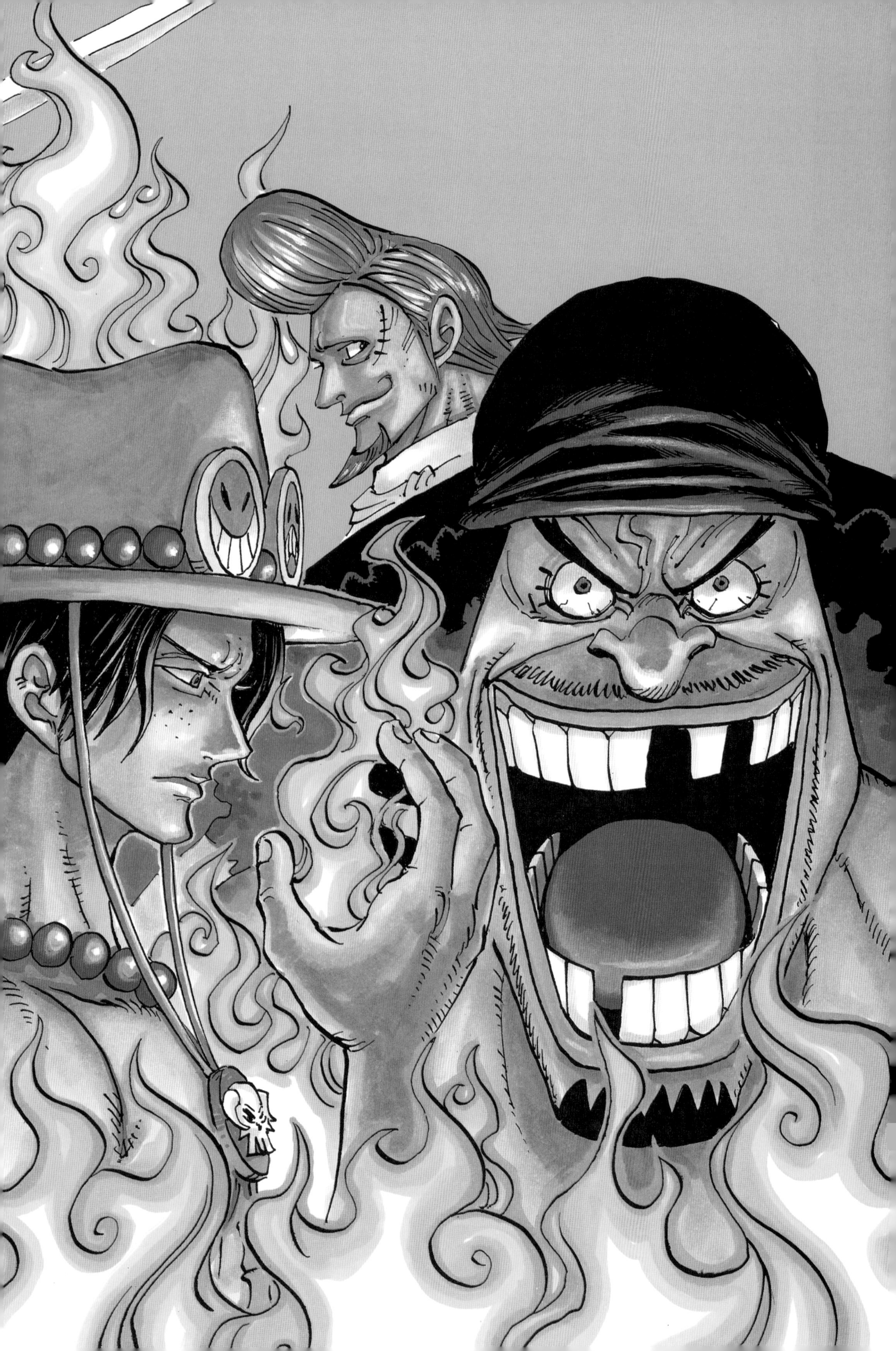

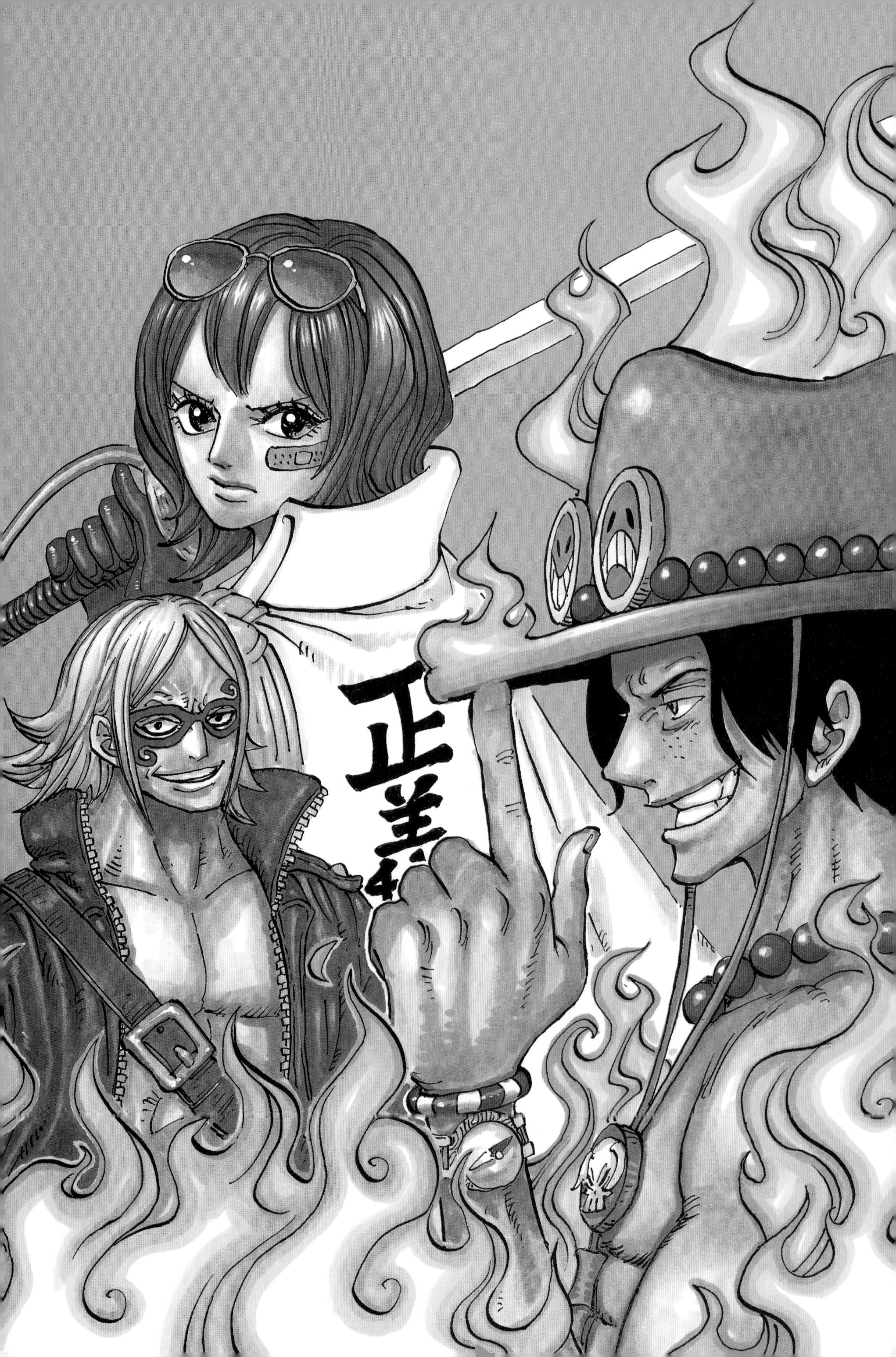

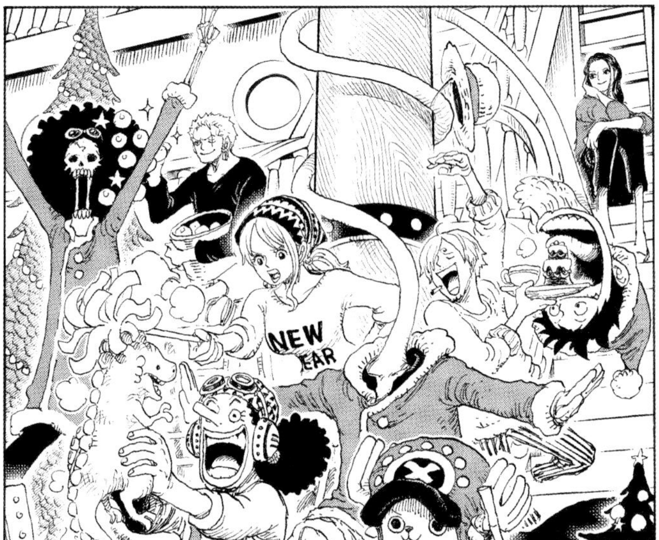
NEW
EAR
OLLY
MUG
PIRATES

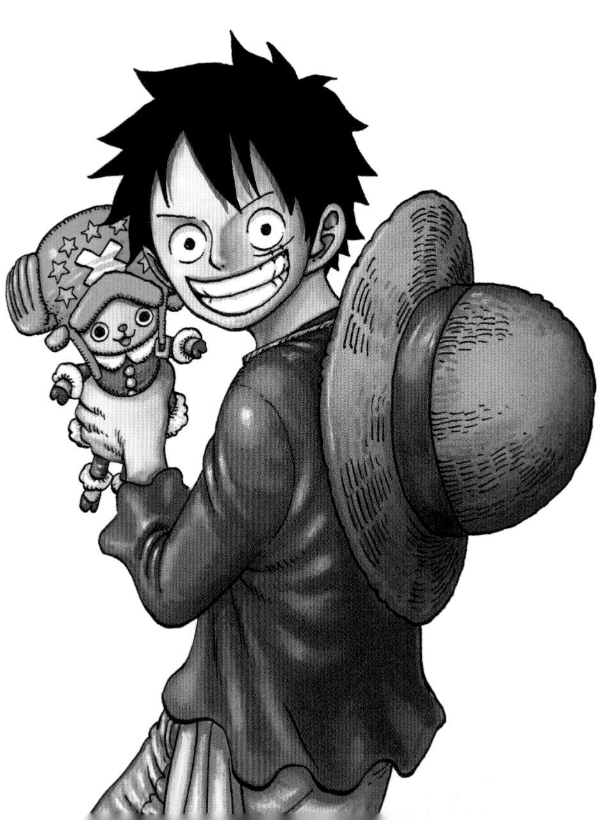

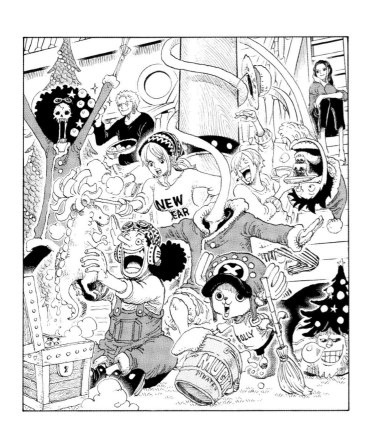

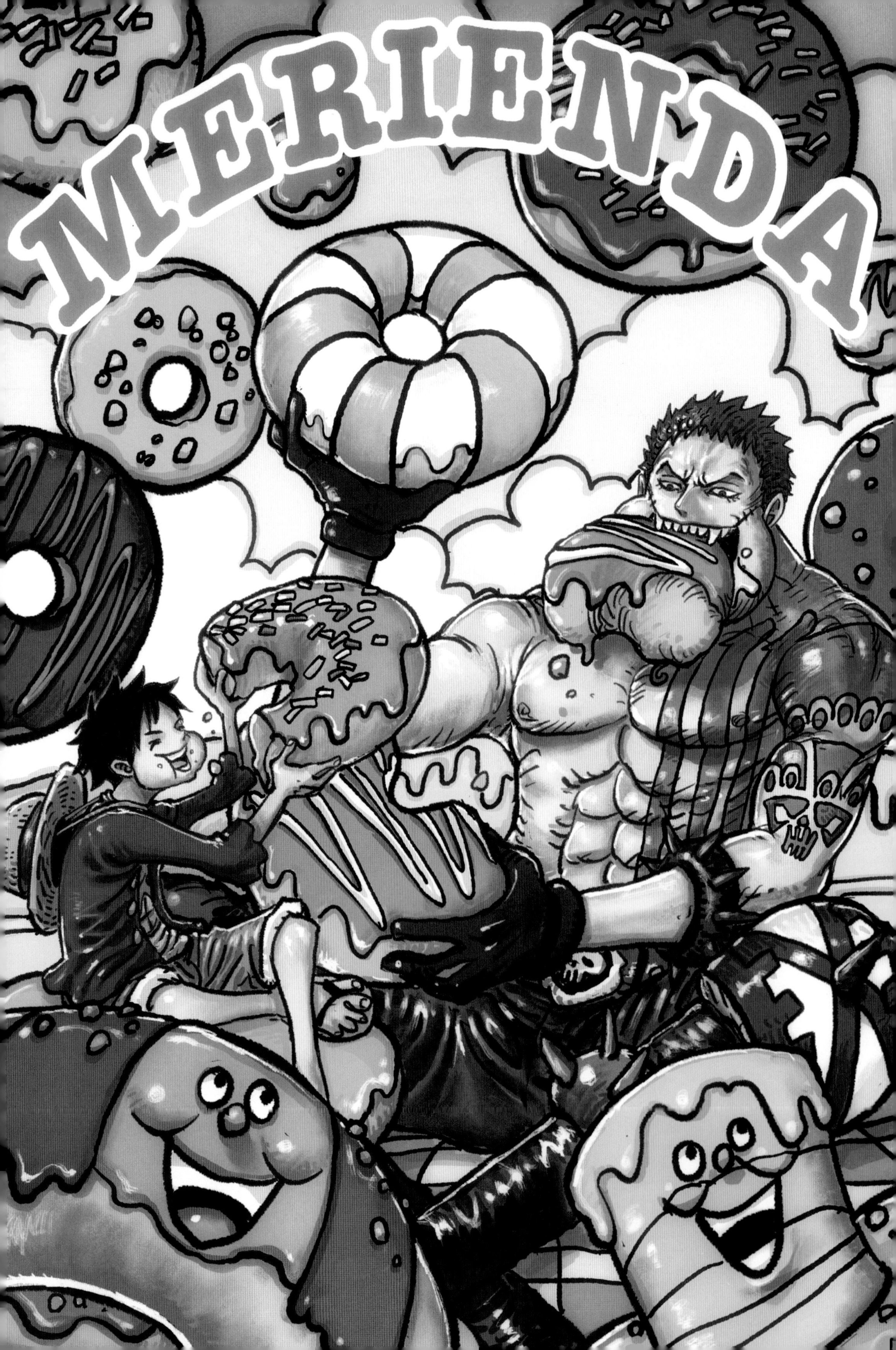
MERIENDA

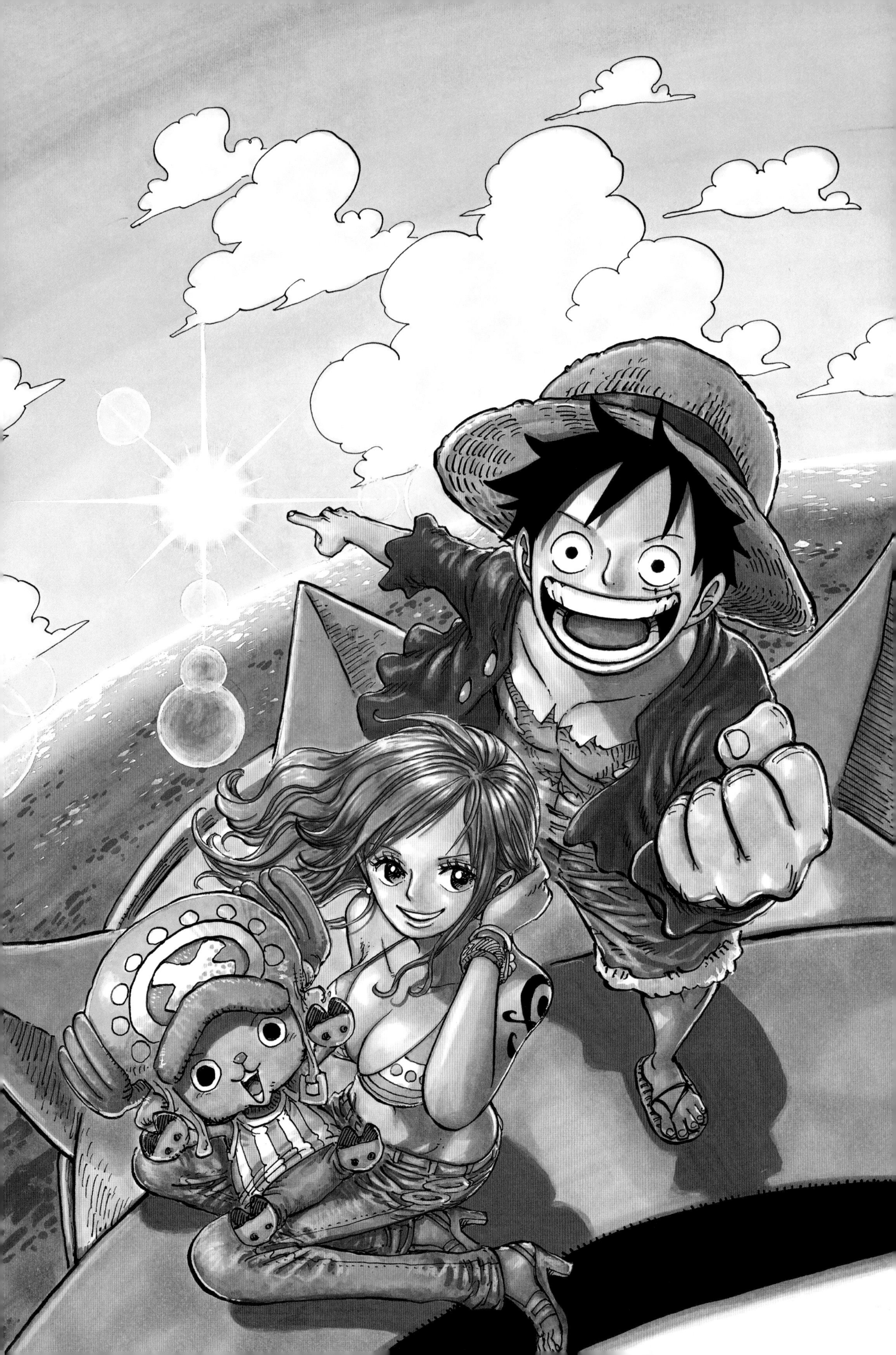

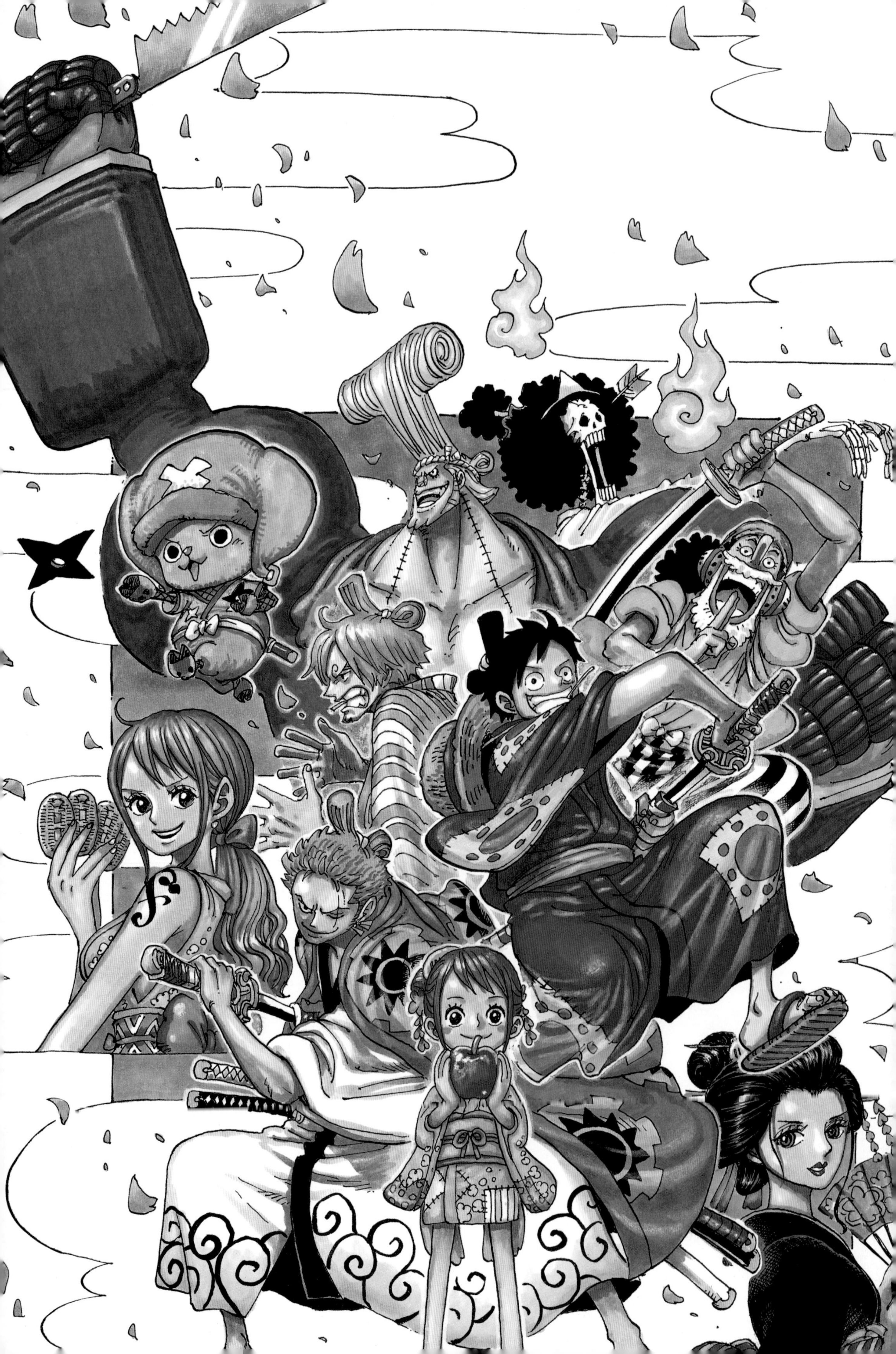

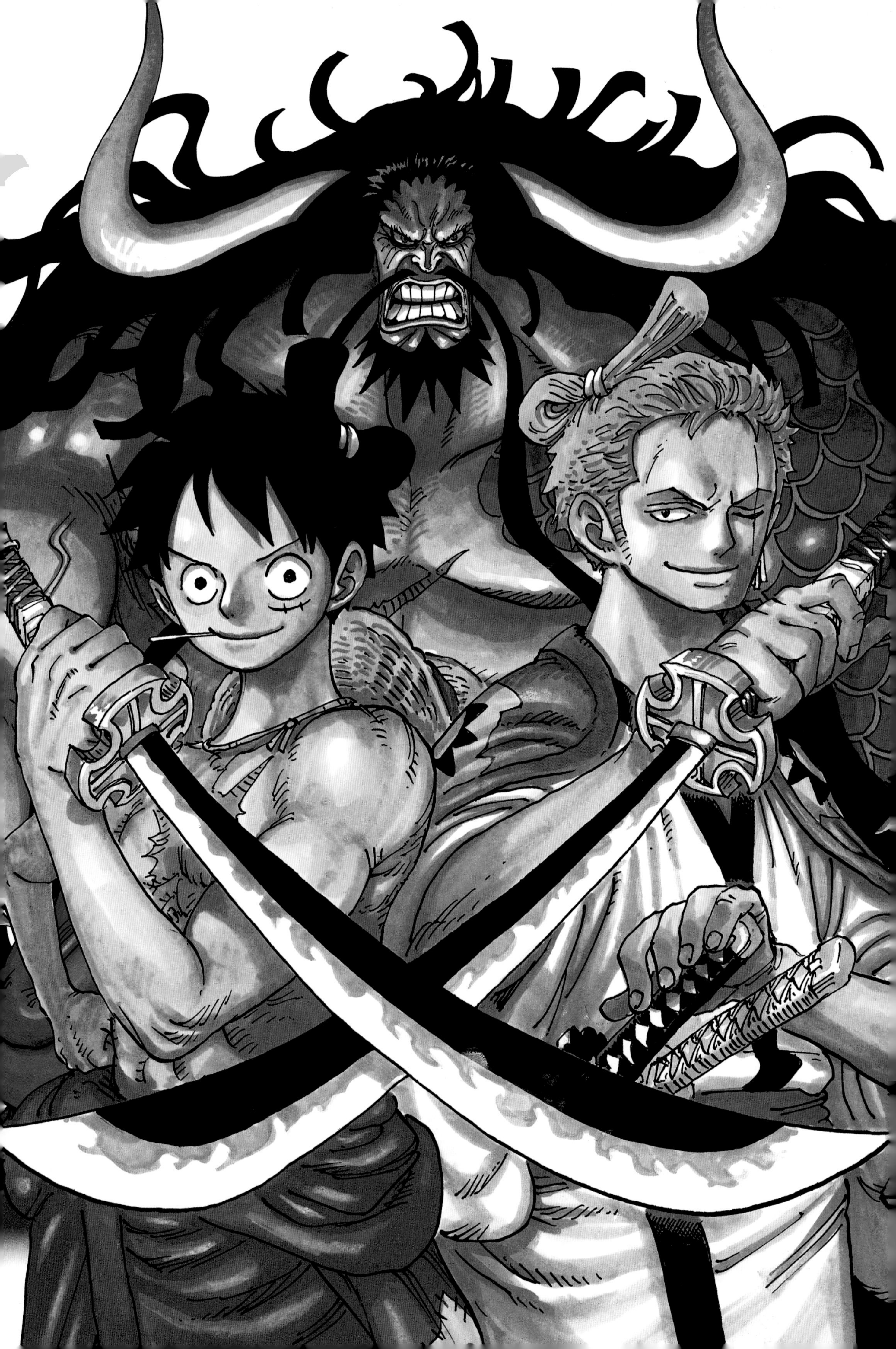

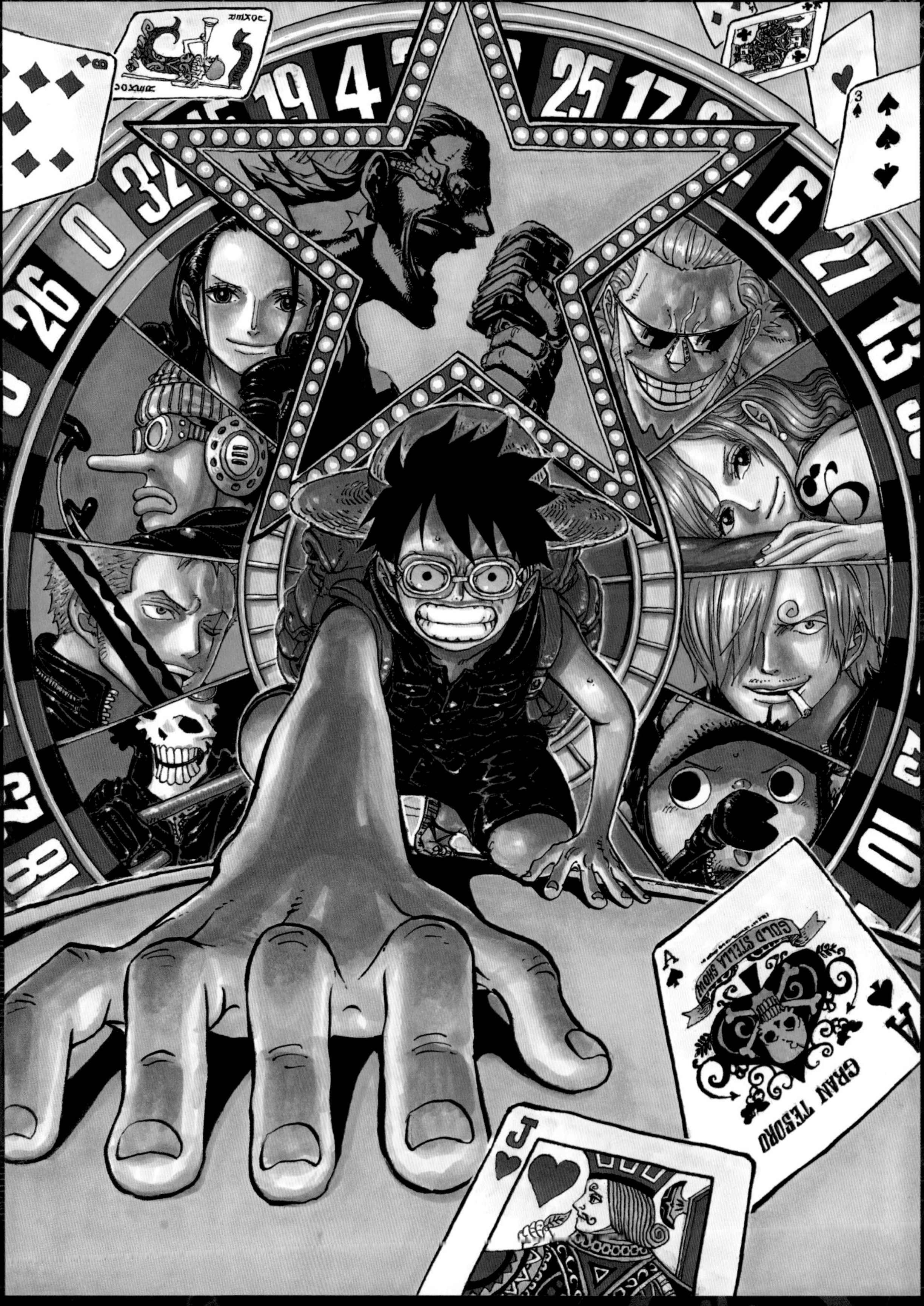
GOLD STELLA SHOW
GRAN TESORO

MOVIE

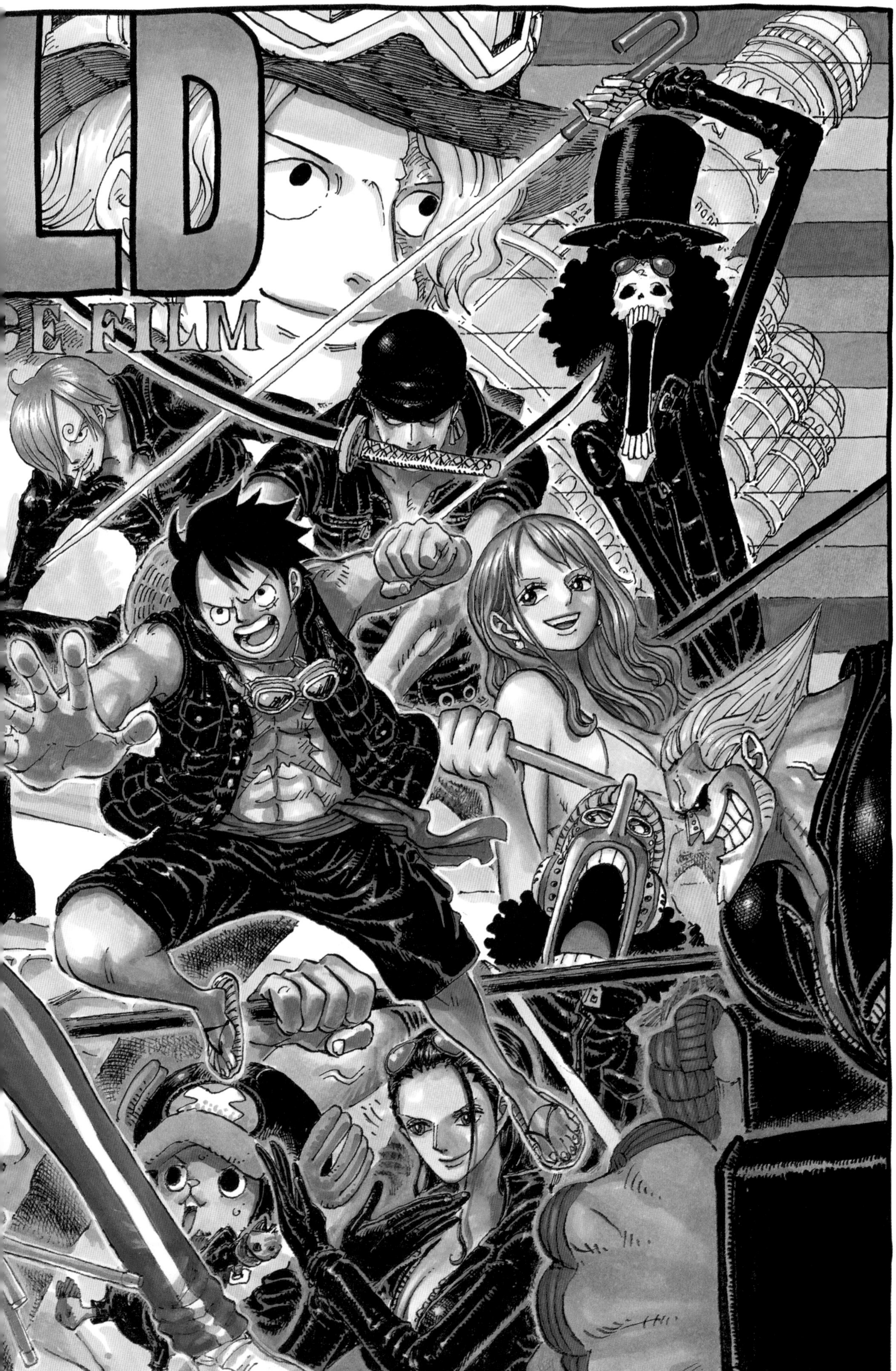
LD
E FILM

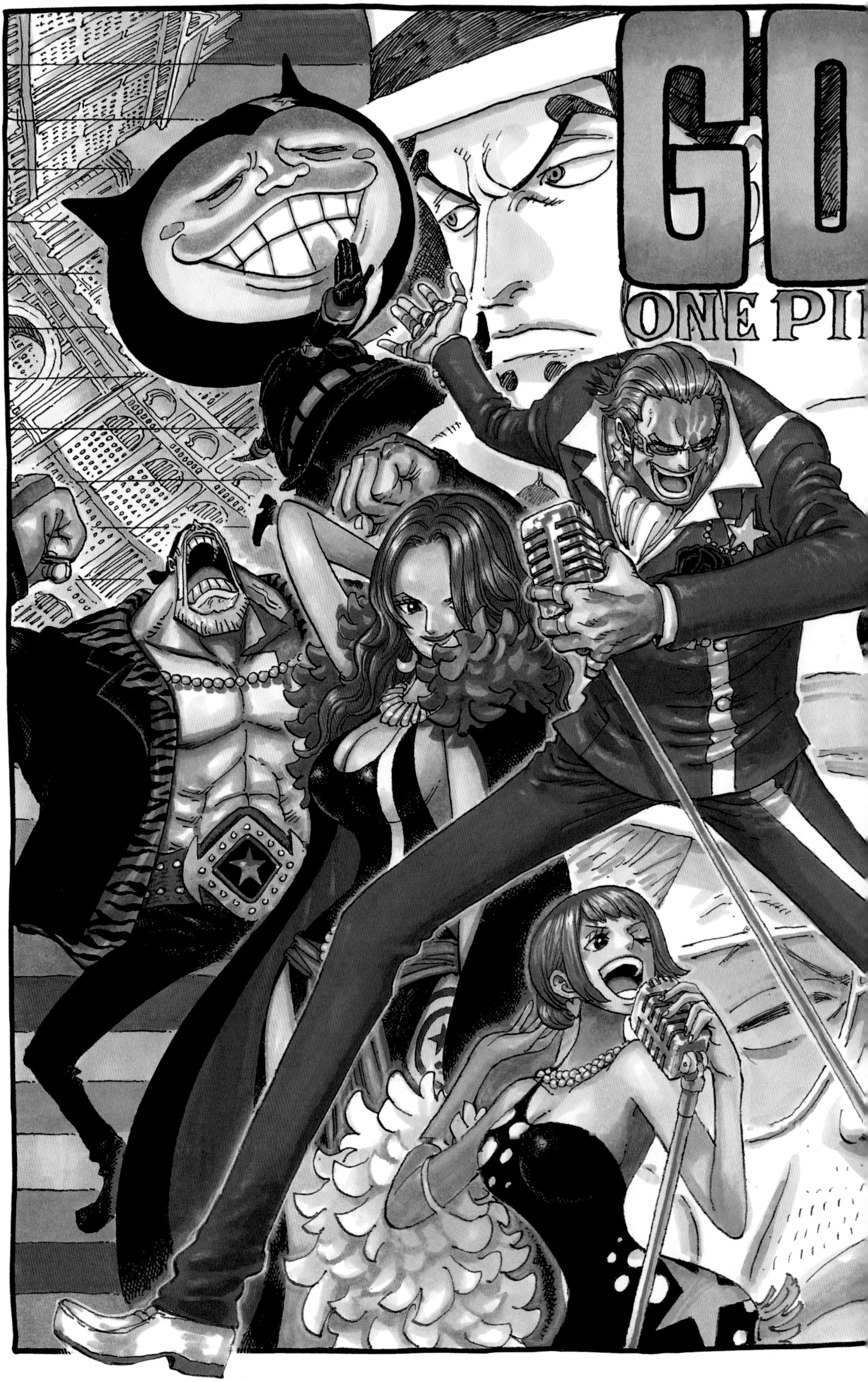
GO
ONE PI

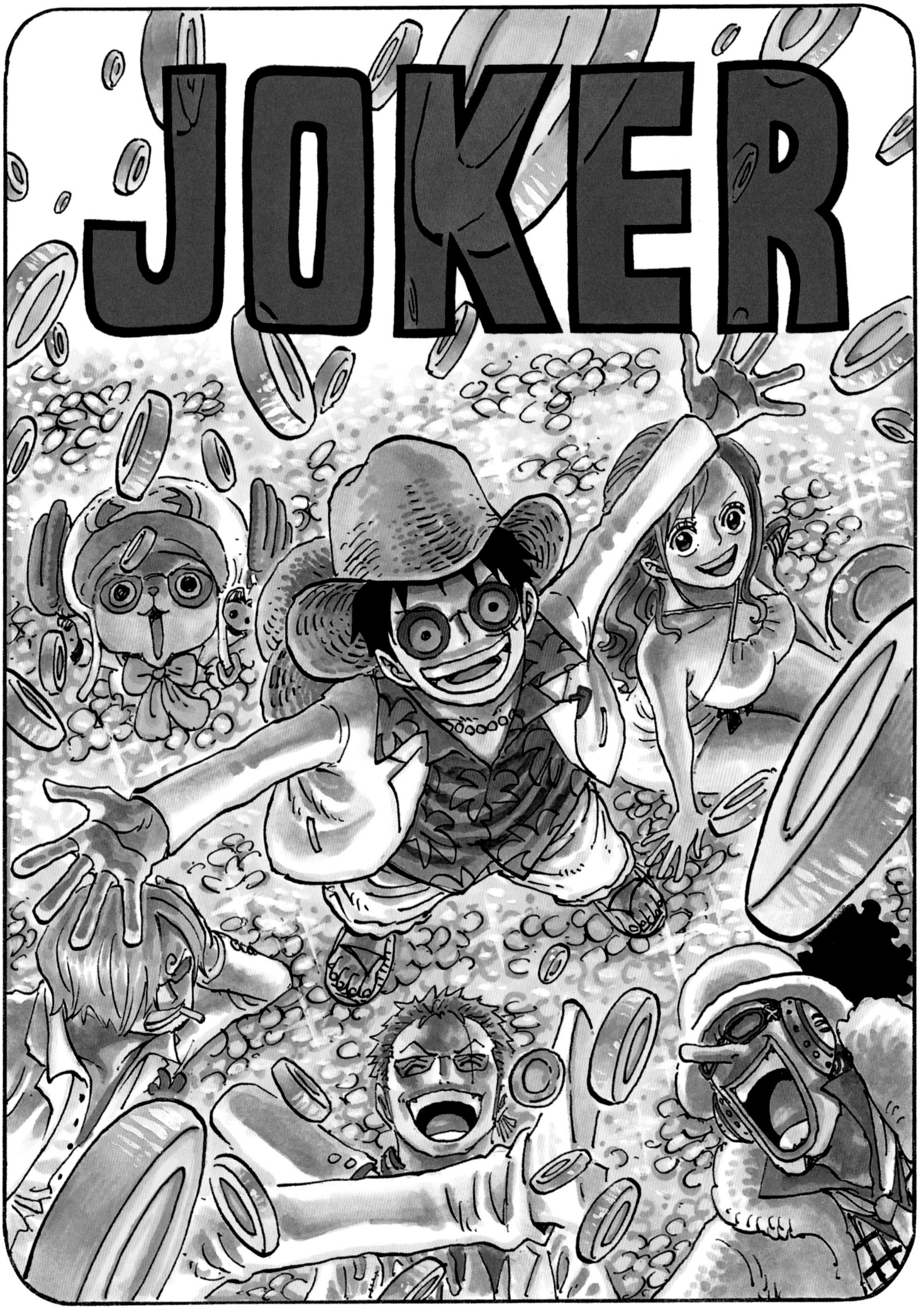
JOKER

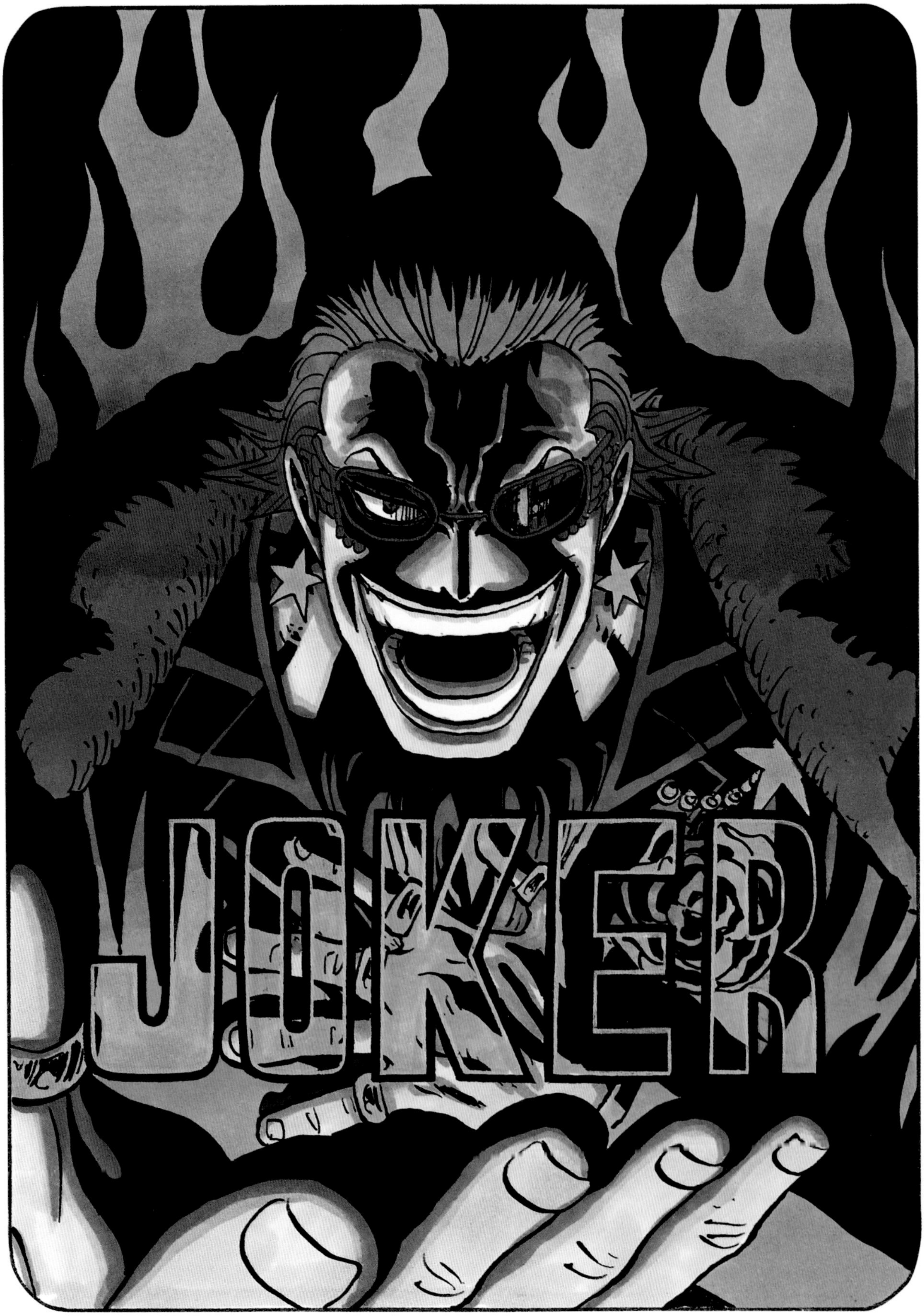
JOKER

GRAND TESORO
GOLD STELLA SHOW
Lack of money is the root of all evil.

IT'S ENTERTAINMENT!
GOLD
ONE PIECE FILM
GREAT HIT THANKS!!
Eiichiro Oda!!

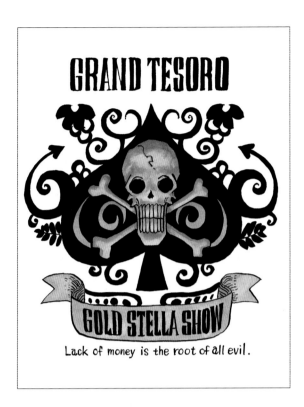

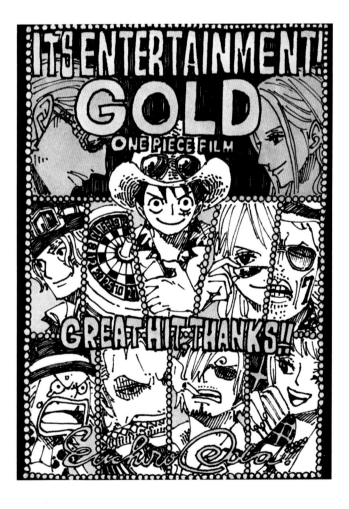

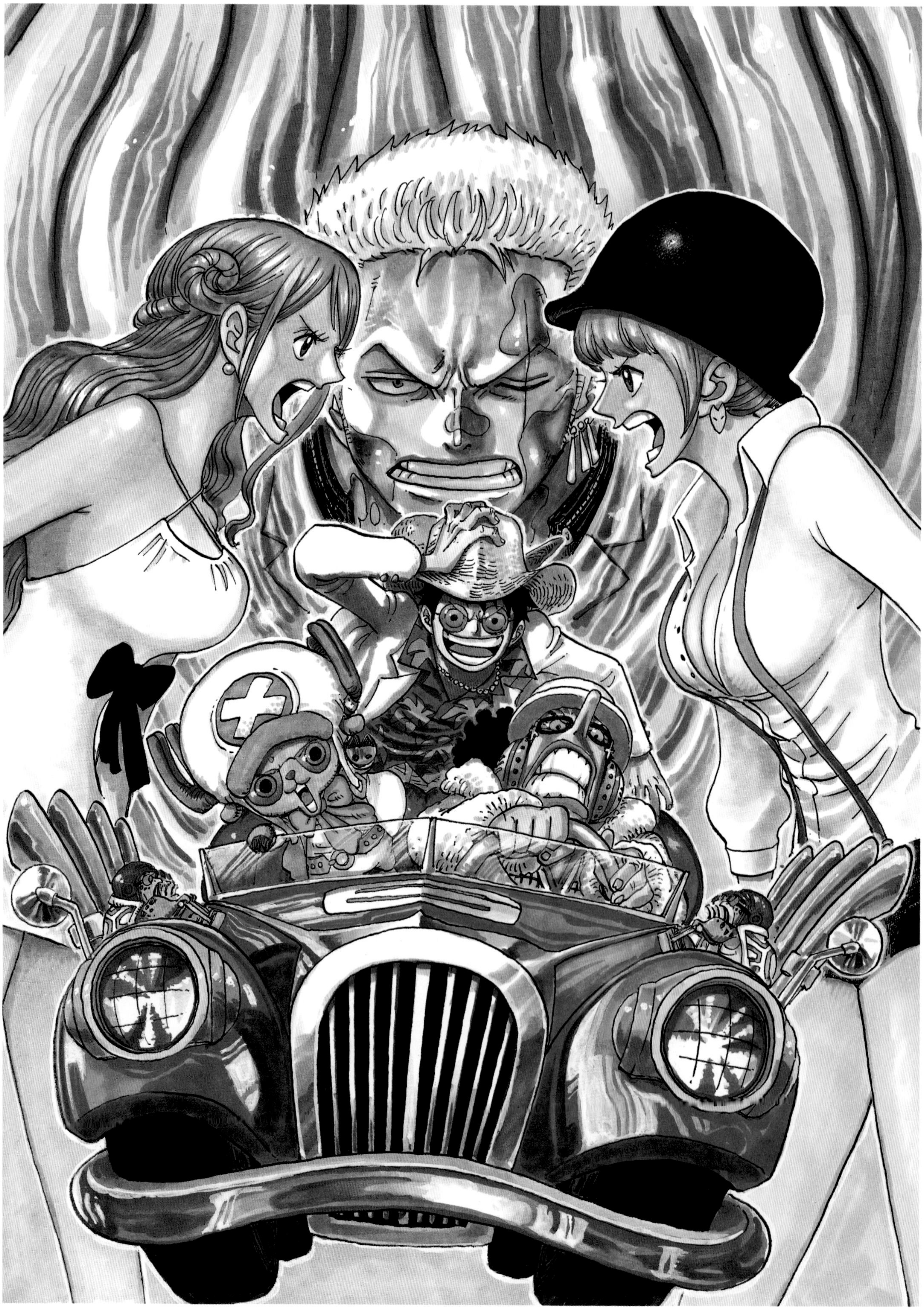

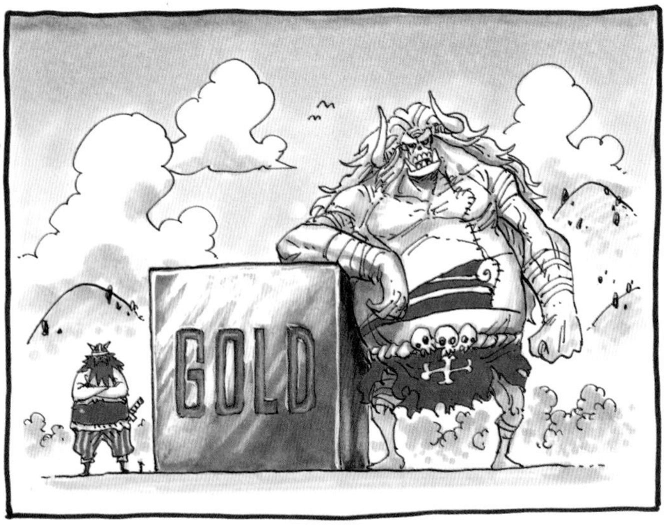
GOLD

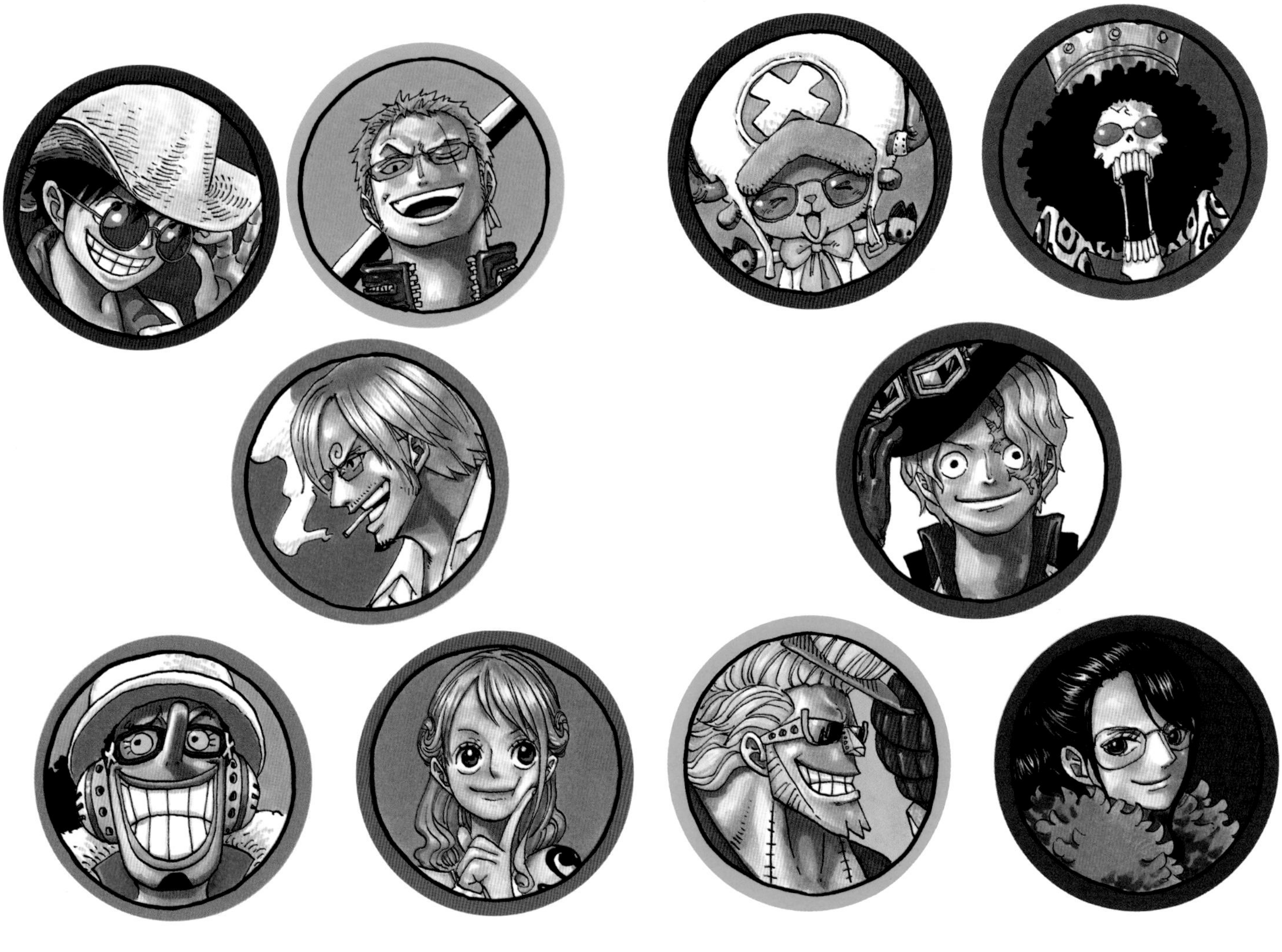

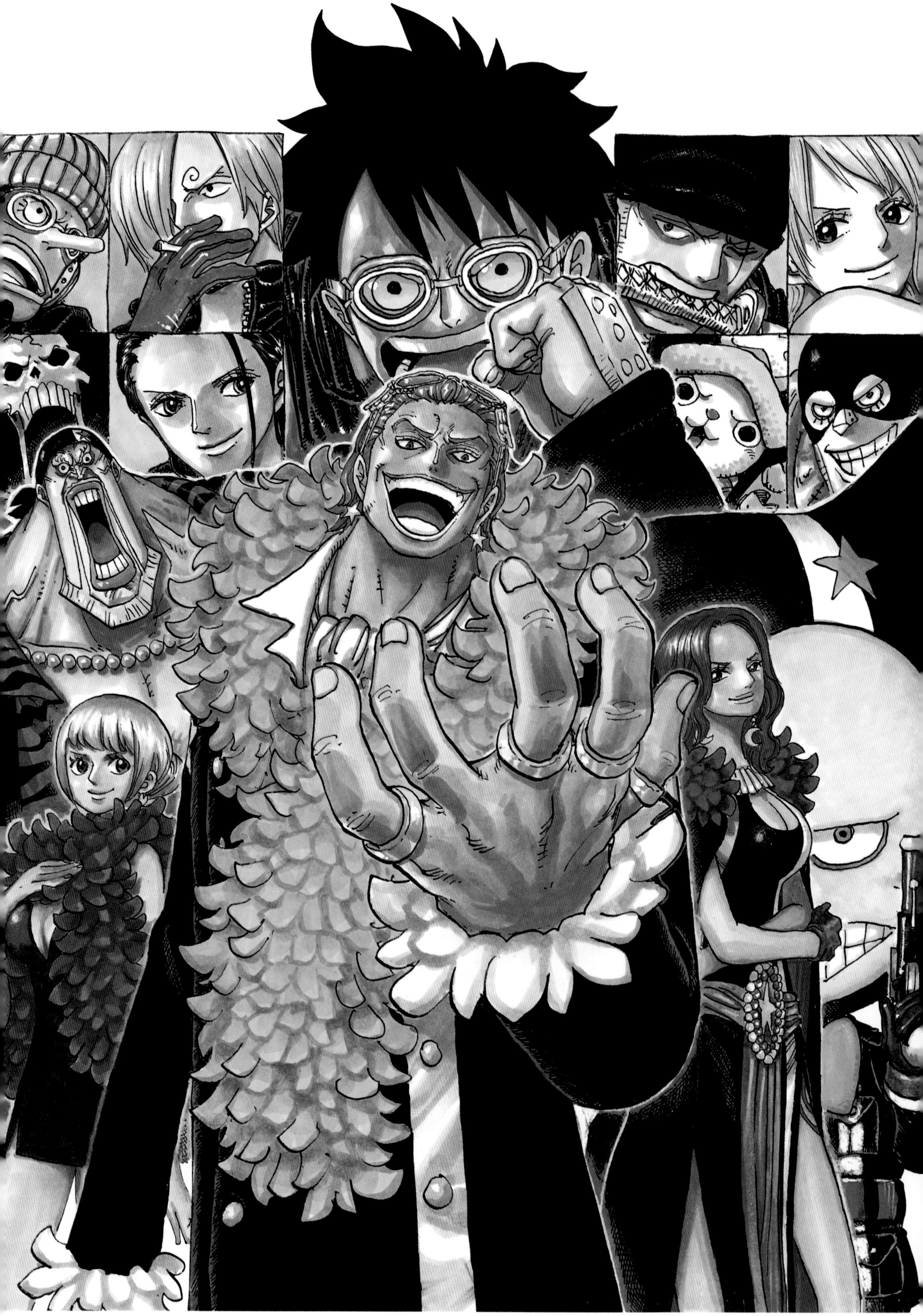

ONE PIECE 20th × KYOTO

STRAW HAT TRAVELS IN KYOTO ~A DIFFERENT LAND OF WANO~

An exhibition that ran in Kyoto during October 7–22, 2017. There was a stamp rally involving several locations in the city, and Daikaku-ji Temple held two exhibits: *One Piece Art Nue Daikaku-ji* and *The Beast, the Princess, and the Flower of Promise.*

TORATSUGU

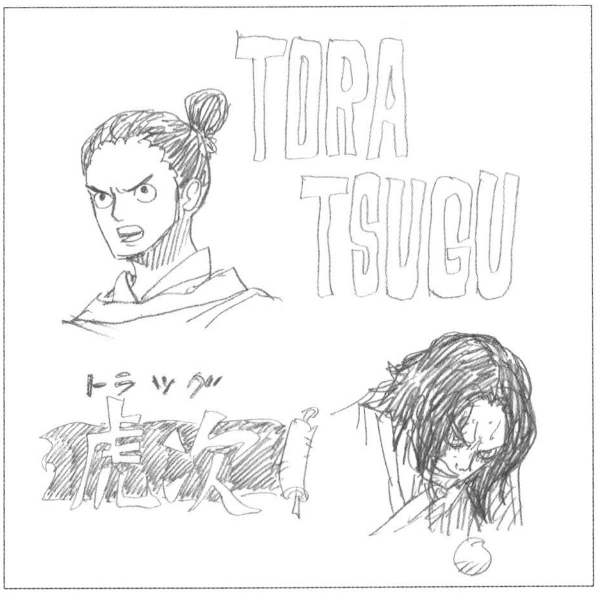
TORA
TSUGU
トラツグ
虎次

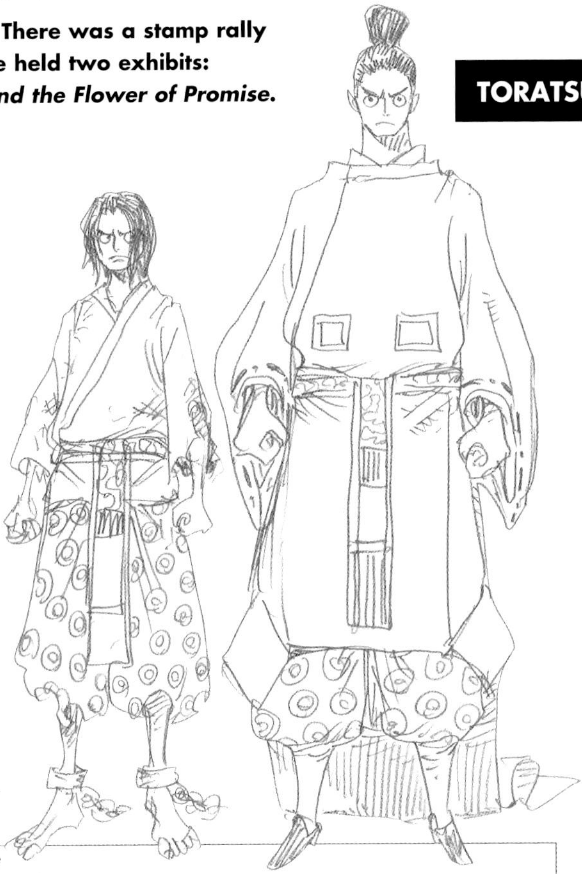

A master of flower arrangement for the Hitaki Clan. Childhood friends with Kikuhime. He gets thrown in jail on suspicion of killing Hitaki, but escapes, and in the process, accidentally eats a Devil Fruit.

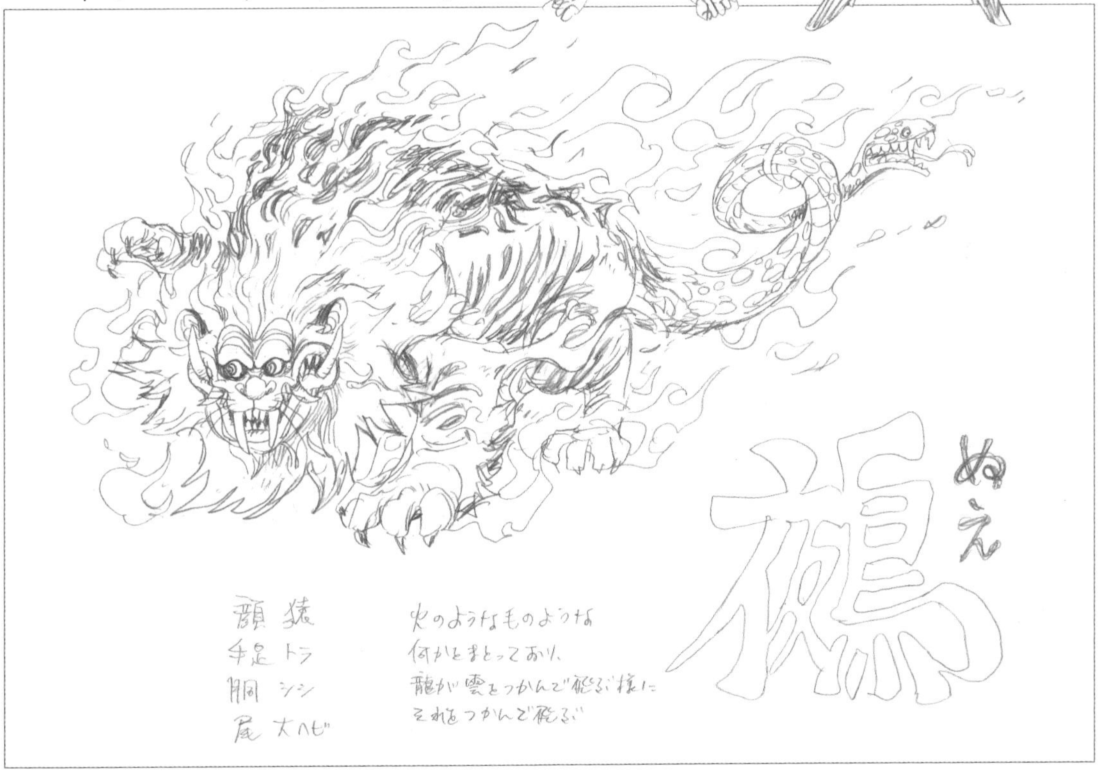
ぬえ
鵺
顔 猿
手足 トラ
胴 シシ
尾 大ヘビ

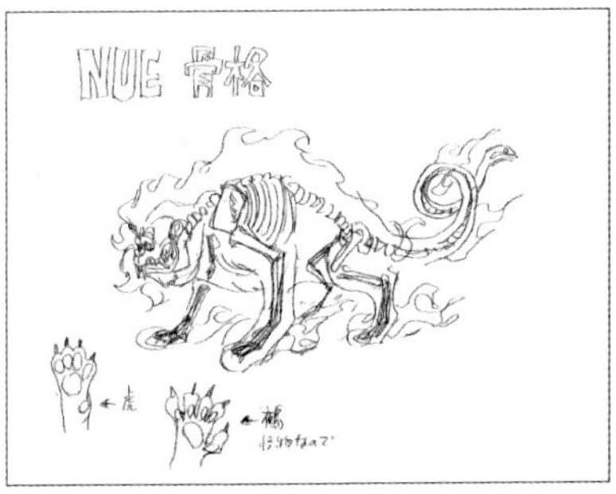
NUE 骨格

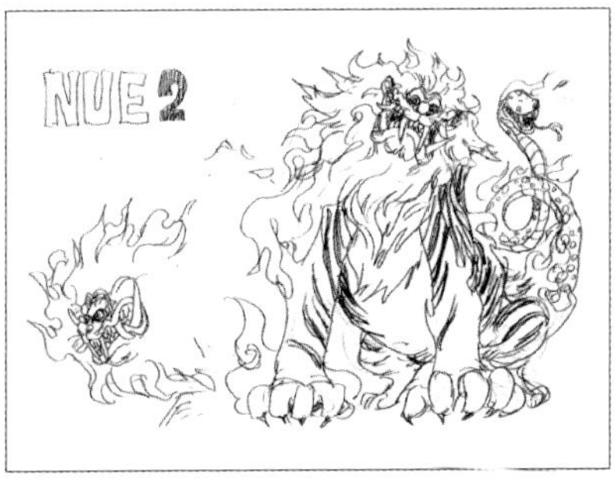
NUE 2

NUE

A freakish creature with the face of a monkey, the limbs of a tiger, the body of a lion, and the tail of a serpent! Could it possibly be a mythical Zoan type? The design sketches include fine details like skeletal structure.

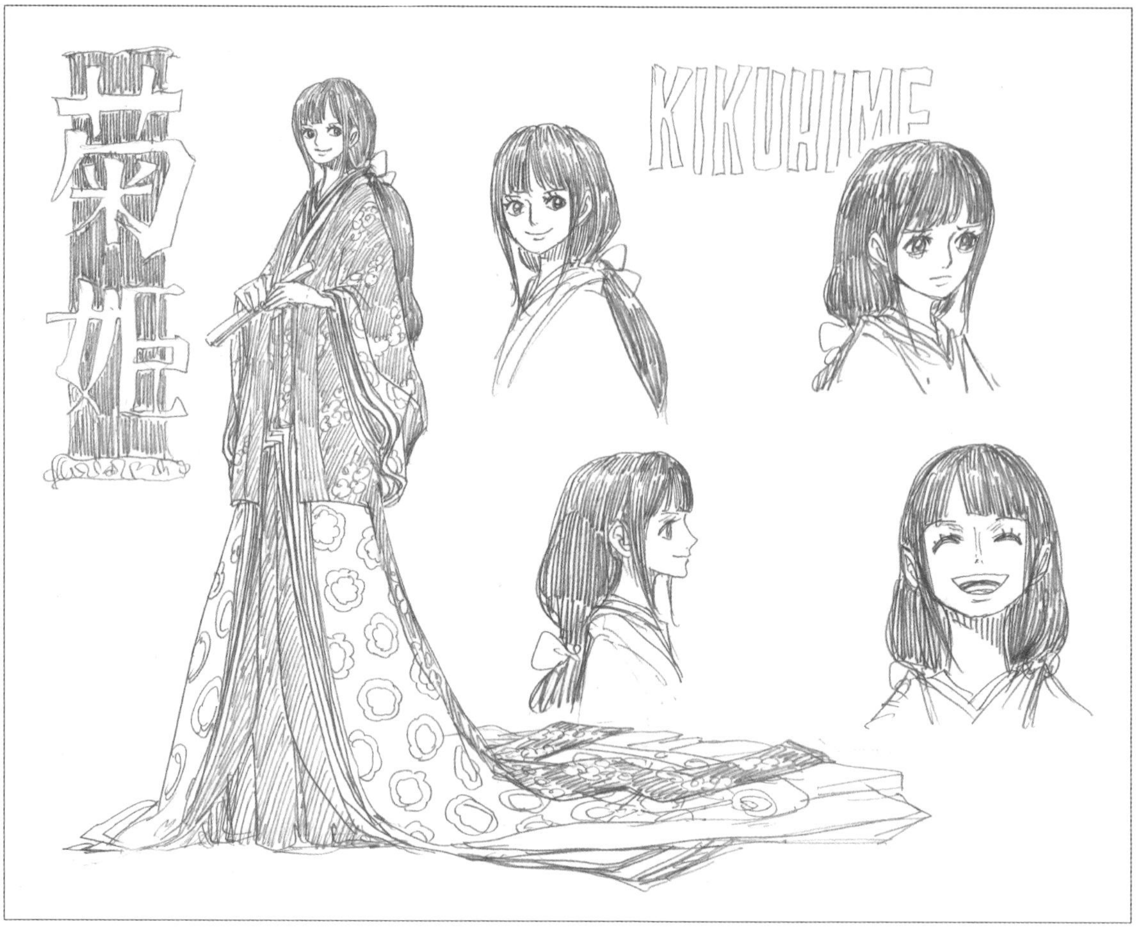

KIKUHIME

KIKUHIME

A beautiful princess. She and Toratsugu share a bond, but she must follow her family's arranged betrothal. However, during her wedding to Prince Lark, she is kidnapped by the Nue.

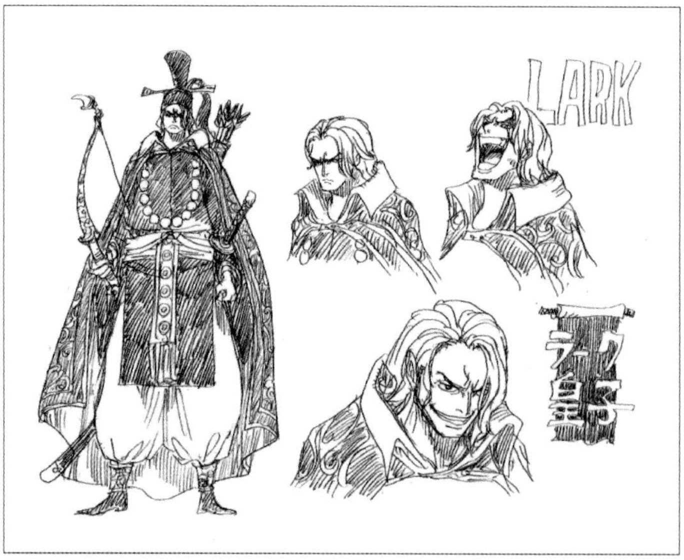

LARK

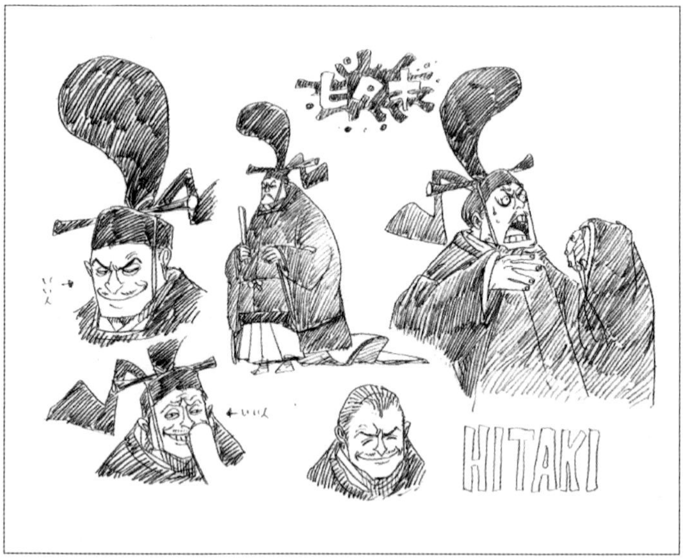

HITAKI

PRINCE LARK

Prince of a neighboring kingdom. He asks the Straw Hats to vanquish the Nue to recover his kidnapped bride. But what is he really after...?!

HITAKI

Daimyo in charge of Yo, in the Land of Wano. He marries off his beloved daughter Kikuhime for military aid, but is killed by a mysterious figure later.

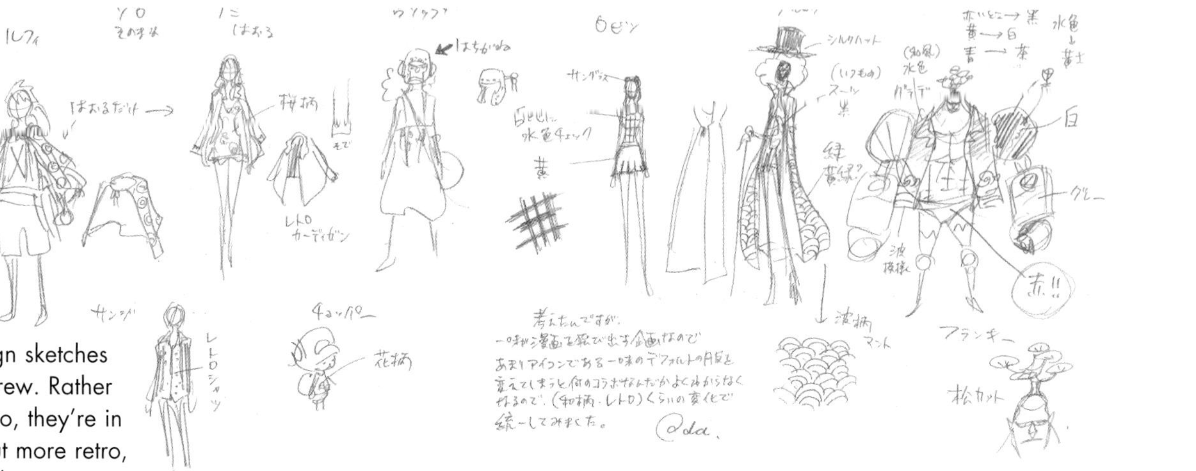

There are also design sketches for the Straw Hat Crew. Rather than wearing kimono, they're in their usual styles, but more retro, or with Japanese-style patterns.

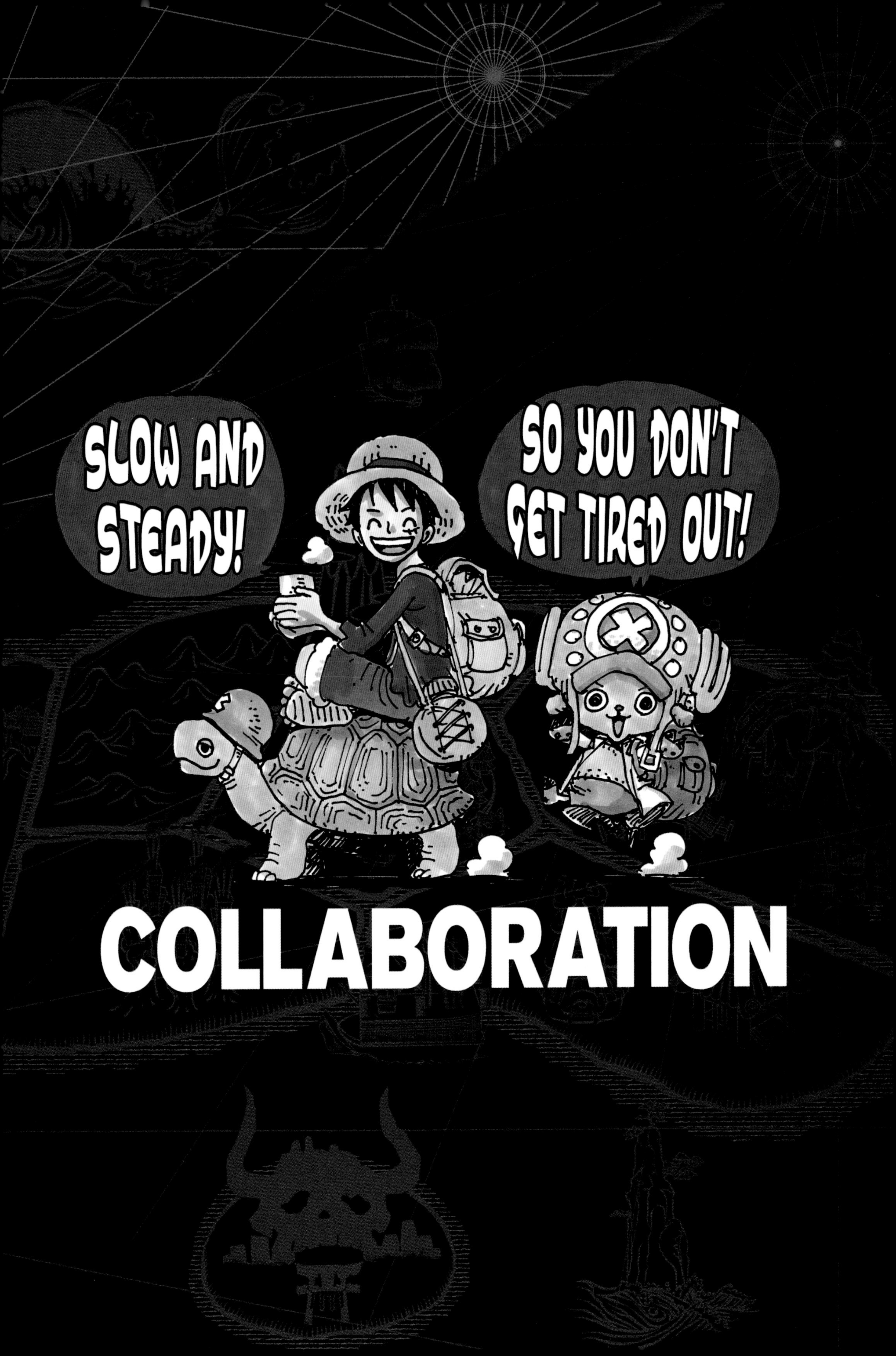
SLOW AND STEADY!
SO YOU DON'T GET TIRED OUT!
COLLABORATION

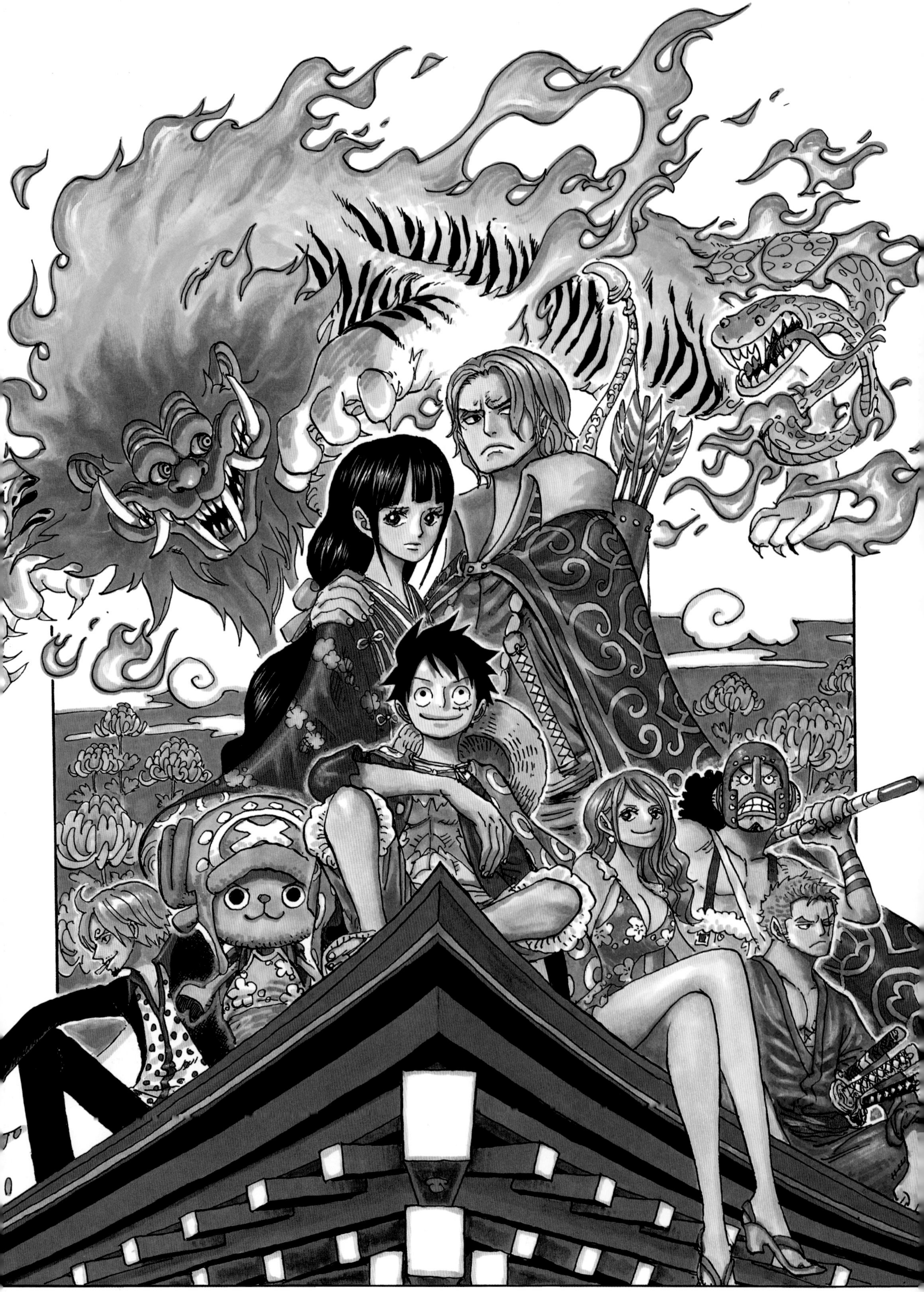

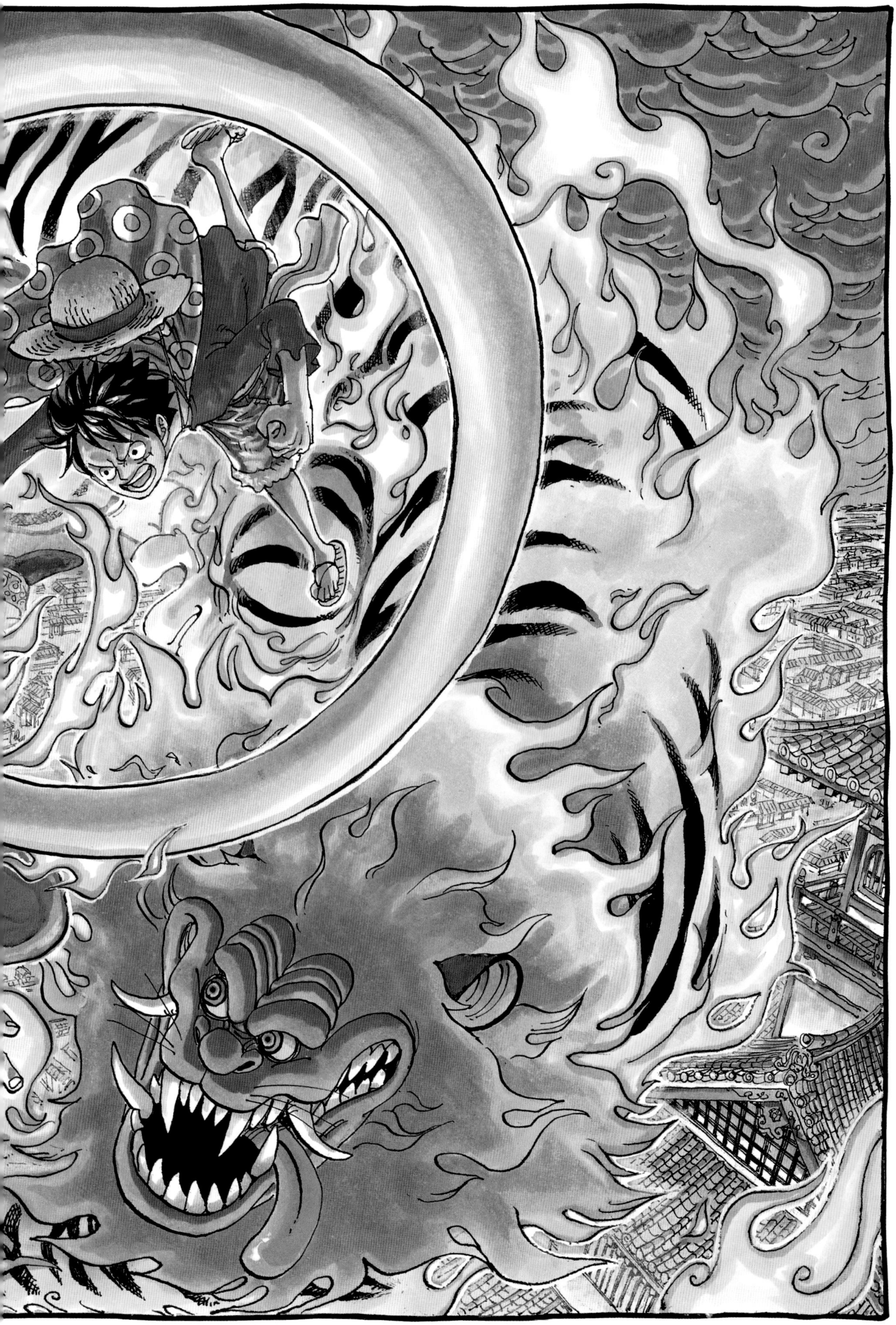

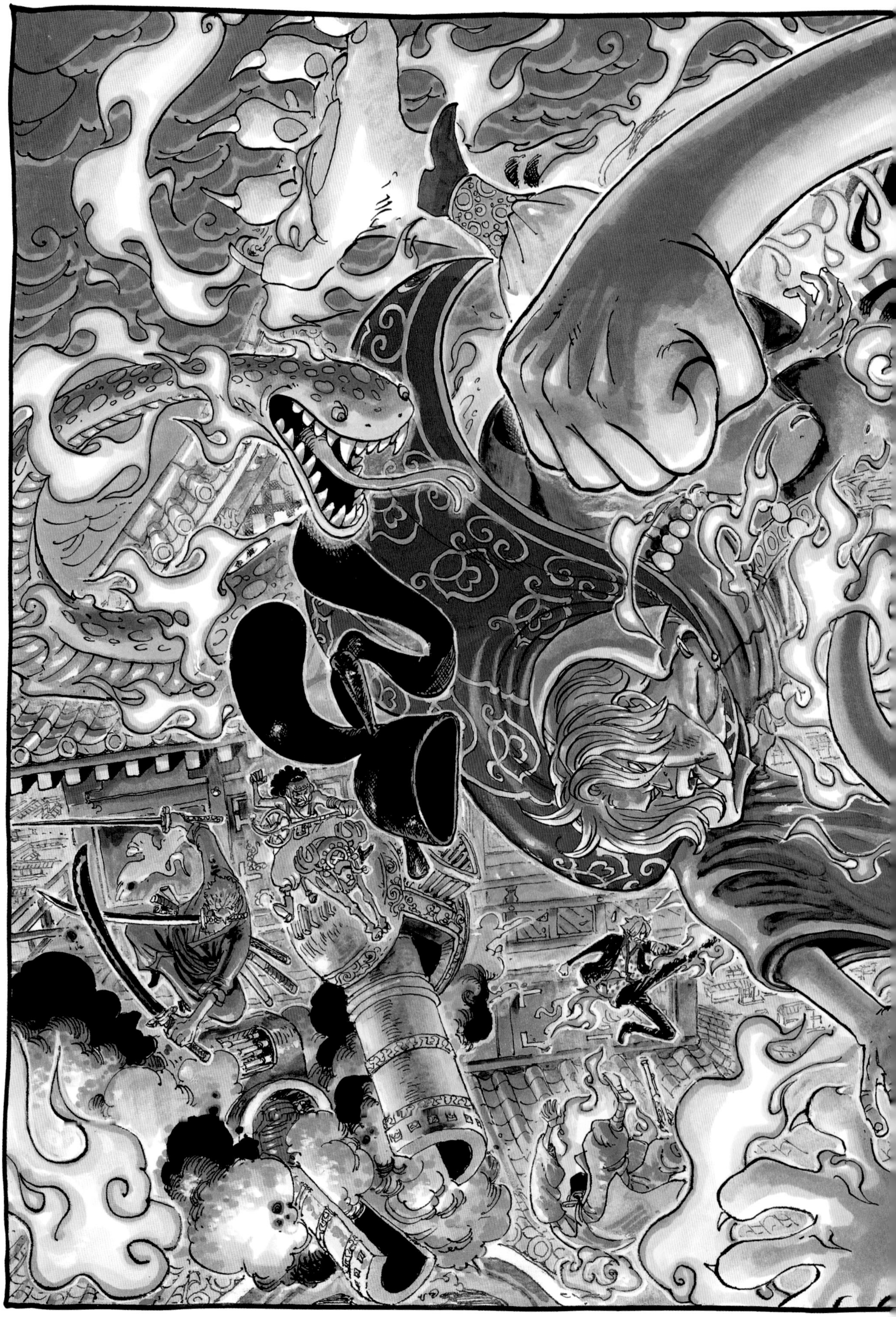

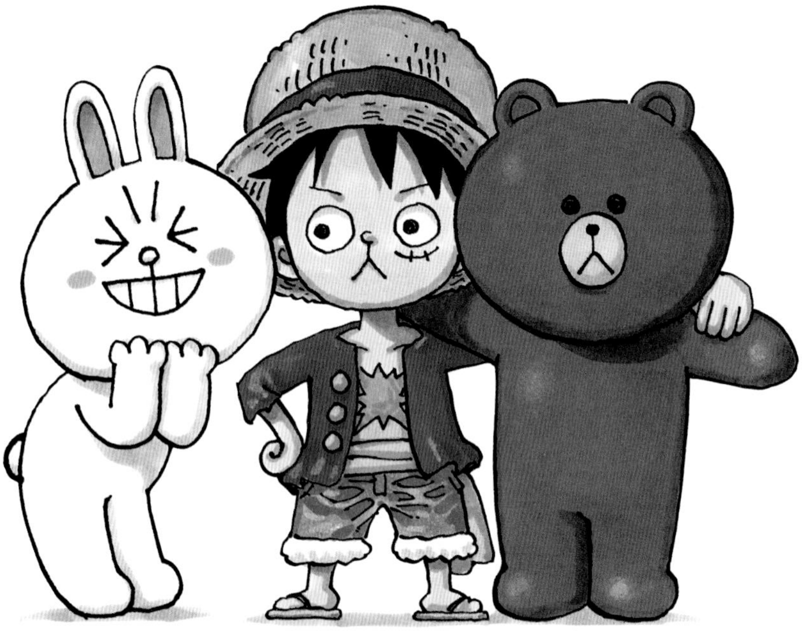

Eiichiro Oda.

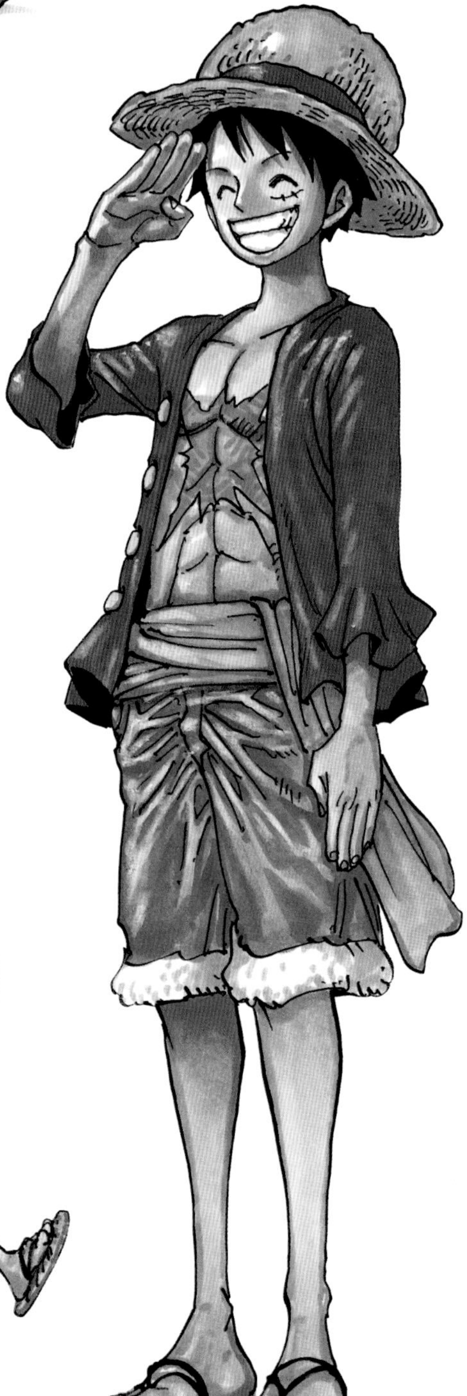

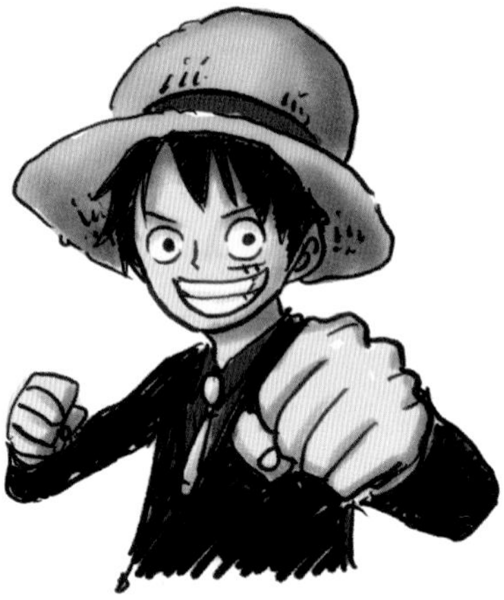

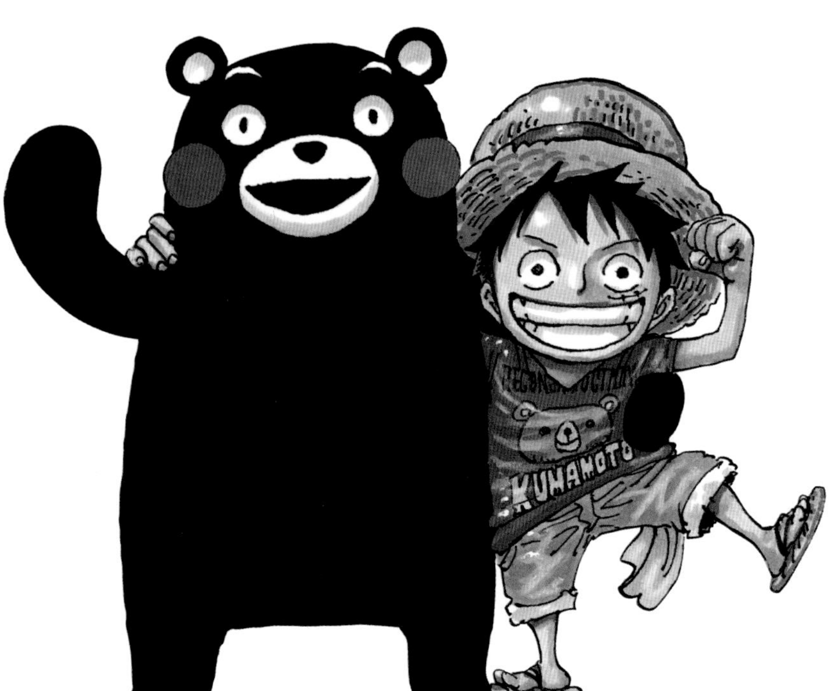
KUMAMOTO

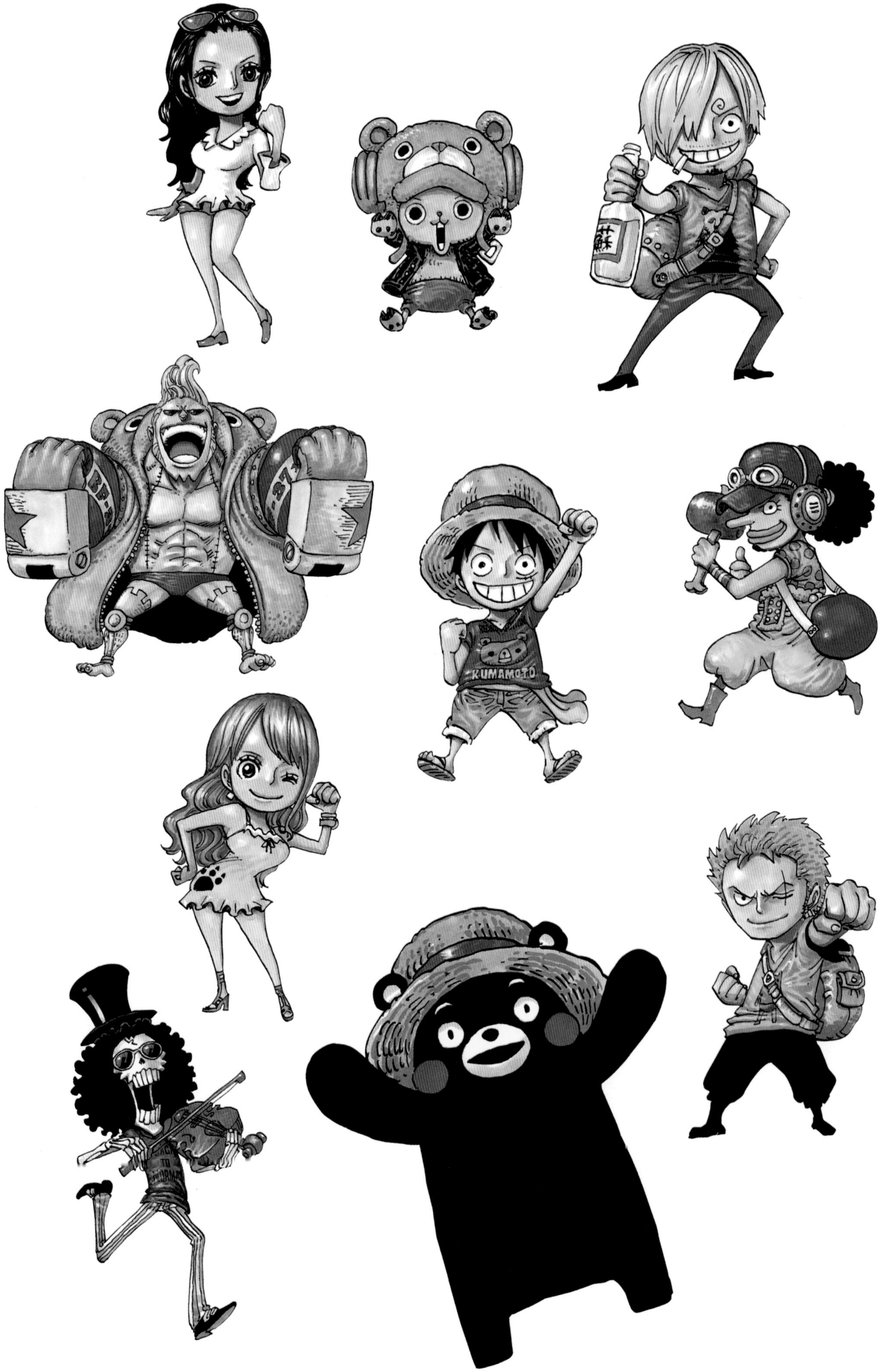
KUMAMOTO

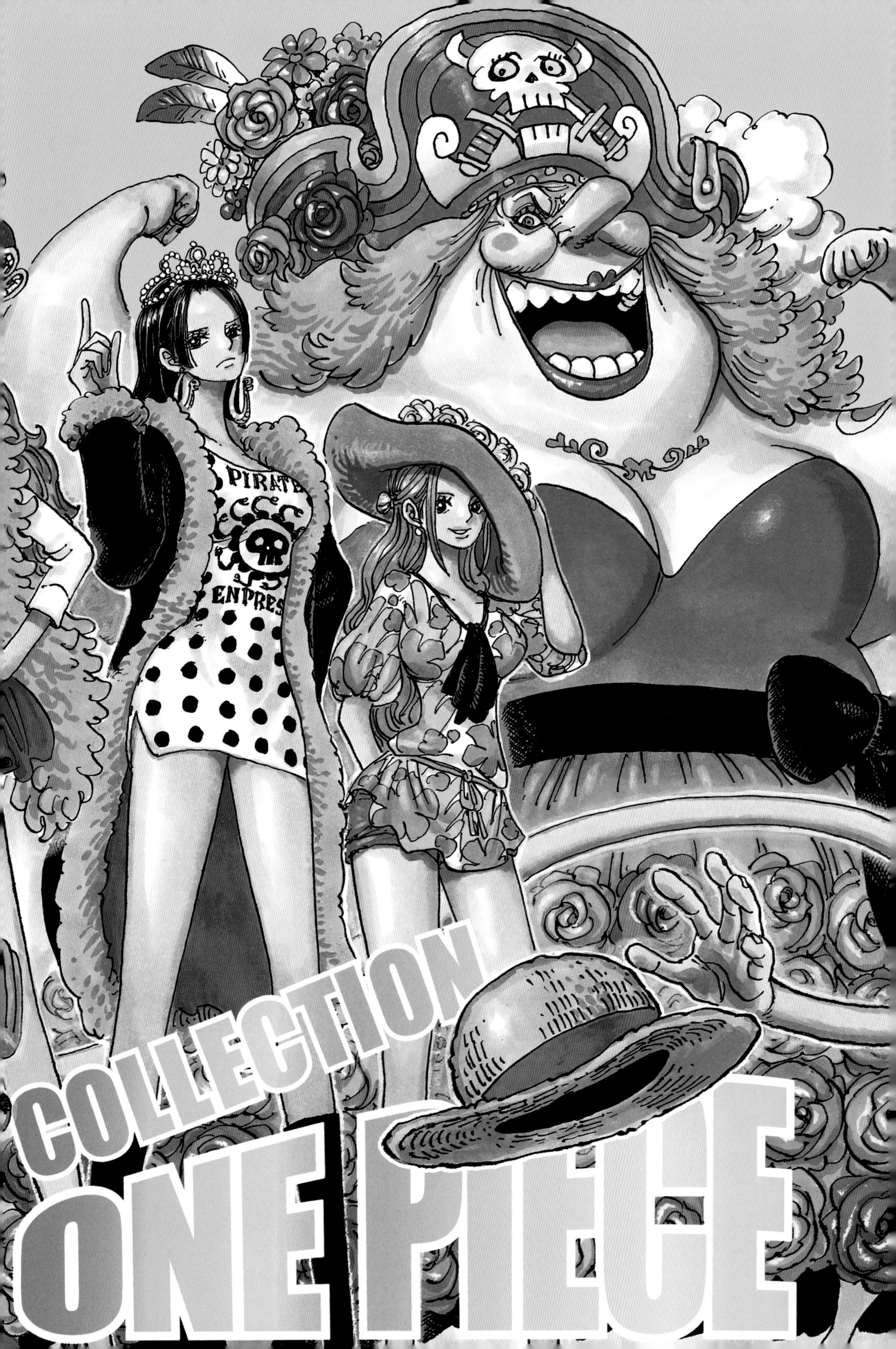
PIRATE
ENPRES
COLLECTION
ONE PIECE

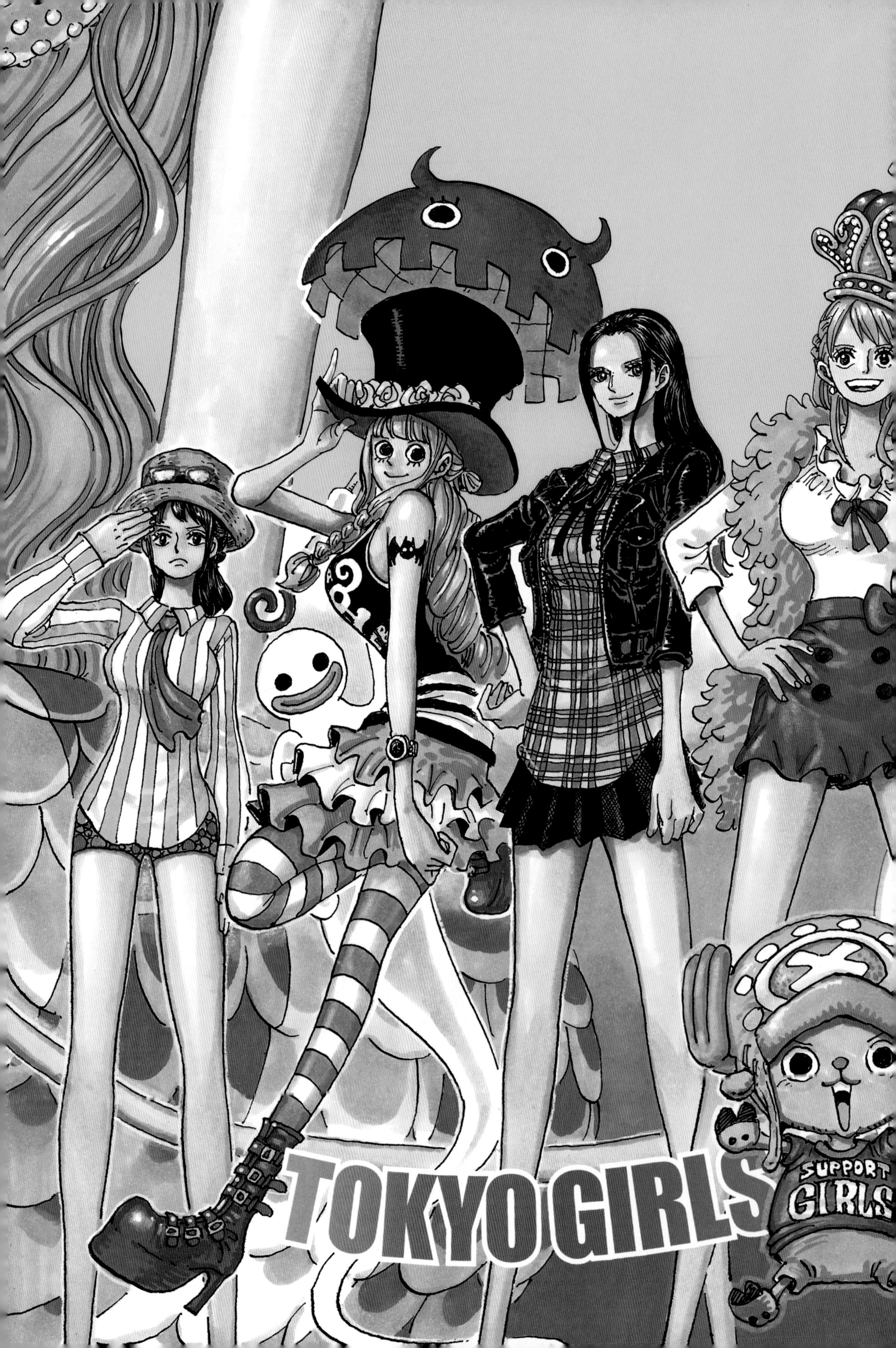
TOKYO GIRLS
SUPPORT
GIRLS

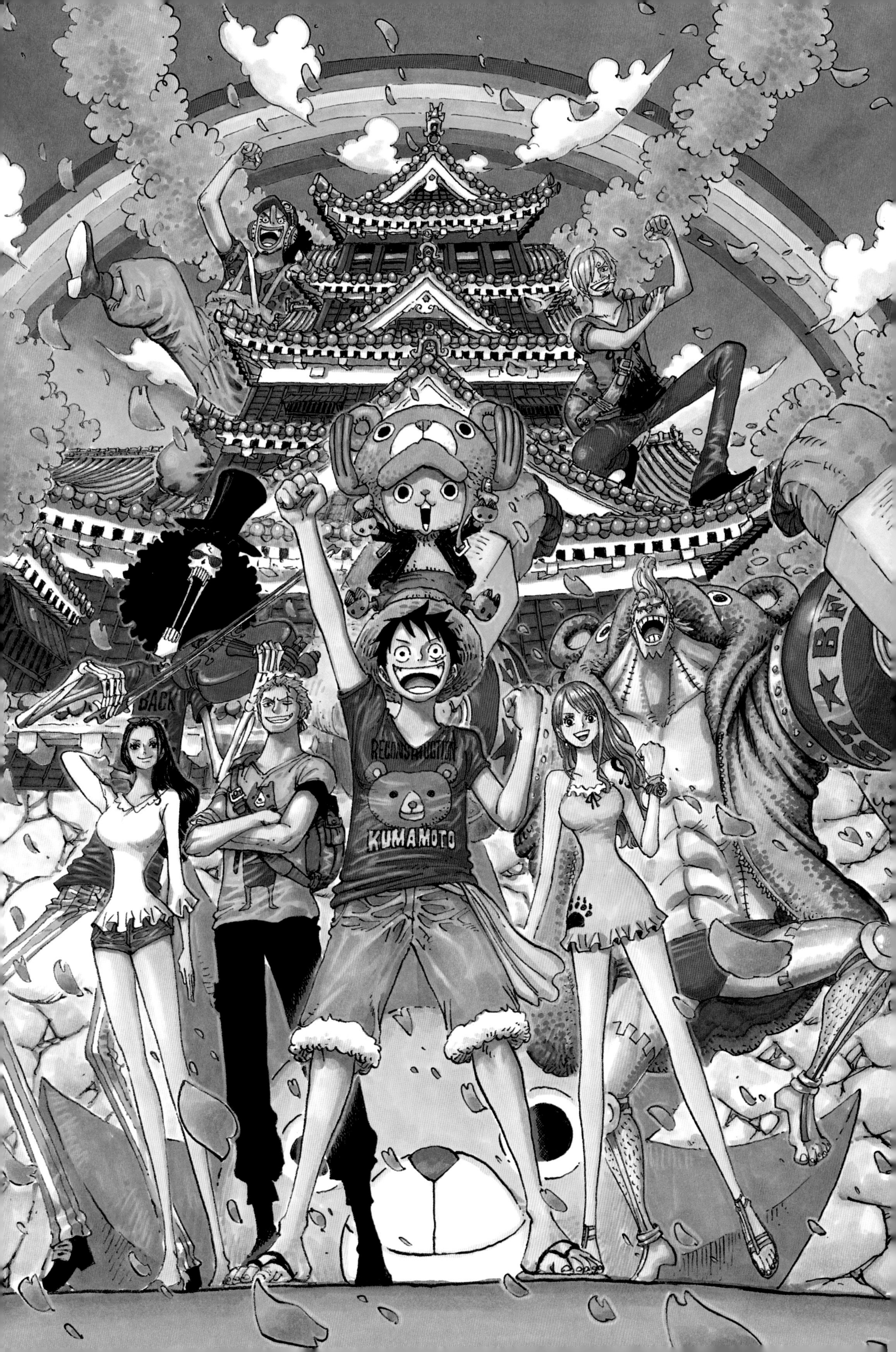
BACK
RECONSTRUCTION
KUMAMOTO

AUTHOR'S COMMENT
2016 ～ 2018

When I was in early elementary school, I entered a prefectural art contest and won the top award: "Special Selection." The theme of the contest was "future dreams," so I drew myself riding on a gigantic stag beetle. Its eyes were shining as it flew through the city at night. It was totally awesome. When I stood on stage proudly receiving my award, I saw the other winning entries on the wall, and I was stunned.

Everyone else had drawn things like,
"Myself as an office worker."
"Myself as a nurse."
"Myself as a police officer."

Was that the point?! Once I realized the theme, I felt embarrassed of my mistake. But all of the adults smiled and praised my drawing.

Nowadays I remember their smiles more than I do my embarrassment. Well, I haven't grown up at all, and now I've put out my ninth book of color illustrations!

Thank you for all of your support!!

Eiichiro Oda.

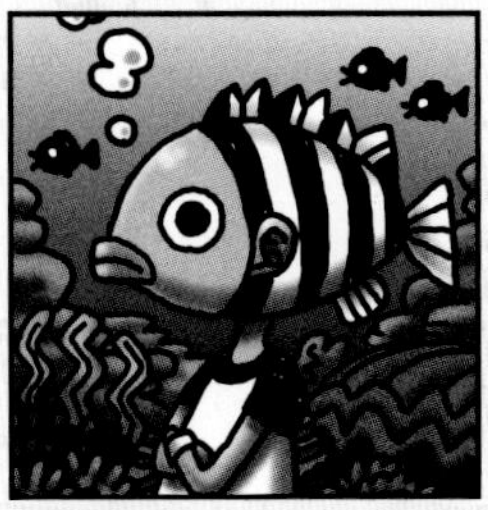

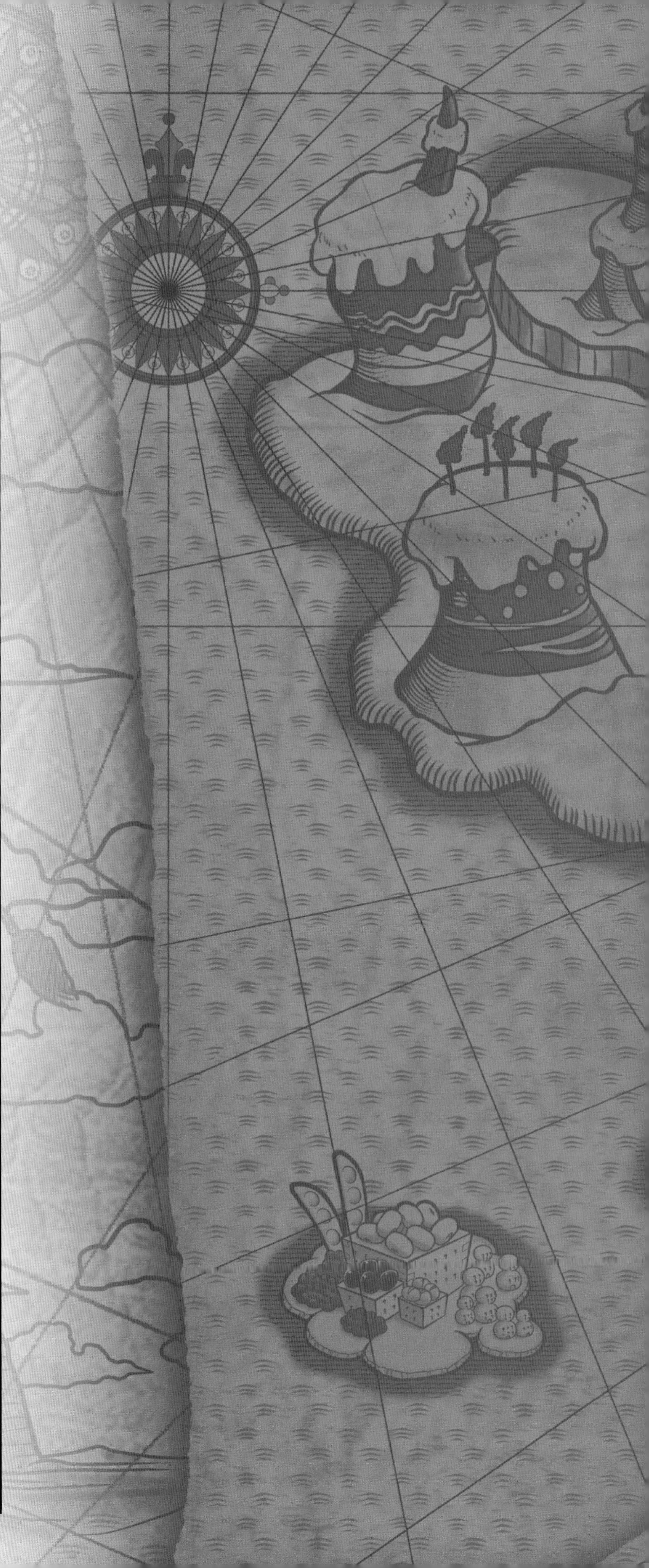

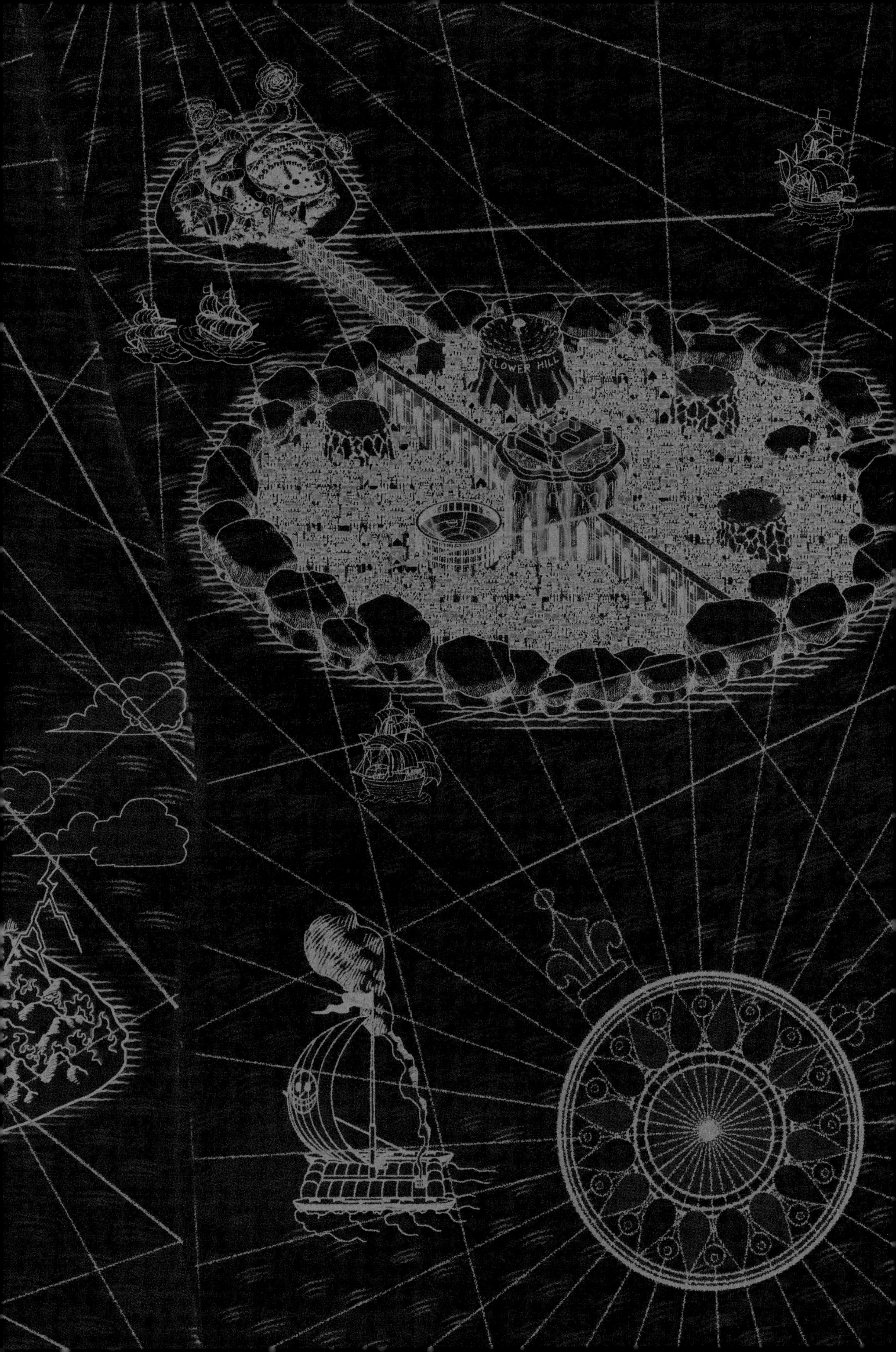
FLOWER HILL

A passion for manga that unites teacher and student!

MONOCHROME TALK

A conversation between Eiichiro Oda and the manga artist he considers his mentor, Masaya Tokuhiro! We'll hear Tokuhiro Sensei describe his pupil as a young artist brimming with ambition to be great. Eiichiro Oda says he "learned much and absorbed many things." What exactly was the professional spirit he inherited from his mentor?!

徳弘正也

MASAYA TOKUHIRO
EIICHIRO ODA

尾田栄一郎

««« READ THIS WAY

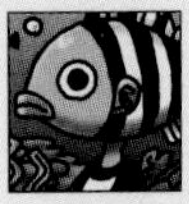

"All of us who worked as your assistants really look up to you."

ODA

MODERATOR: This time, we've invited Oda Sensei's mentor, Masaya Tokuhiro Sensei, for a little chat!

ODA: It's so good to see you again after all this time. I think it's been about twenty years since we last met in person. You really haven't changed since then.

TOKUHIRO: I haven't changed at all.

ODA: We were exchanging some emails after this interview was arranged, and you said the most awful thing. [*laughs*] You said, "Because you were my assistant, the only thing people want to talk about with me now is *One Piece* this, *One Piece* that. It sucks!" [*laughs*]

TOKUHIRO: When I go to the gym, they try to ask me things about you. Nobody actually wants to talk to me anymore.

ODA: I'm very sorry about that. But you know, you could just tell them, "I taught him everything he knows." You've always been the kind of person who says everything he thinks, whether good or bad. It's why people trust you.

TOKUHIRO: Oh, that's not true.

ODA: It is! All of us who worked as your assistants really look up to you.

TOKUHIRO: Well, the only pupils of mine who made it as manga artists were Mitsuyoshi[1] and you. It's a tough business to thrive in.

ODA: Mitsuyoshi was really good. Watching him work would take my breath away. And he's an even better artist now than back then. He was telling me that he wanted to see you again too.

TOKUHIRO: The only thing we exchange these days is traditional New Year's cards. But former students all sent me cards every year for nearly two decades, and they tell me everything they're up to. It's nice to hear the stories.

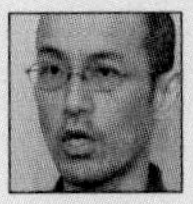

"The first time we met... Oda, you were still just a kid."

TOKUHIRO

MODERATOR: Do you remember the first time you two met?

TOKUHIRO: I remember it. Oda, you were still just a kid.

ODA: I was nineteen. I'd quit after my first year of college, and freshly arrived into Tokyo.

MODERATOR: So the first thing you did after coming to Tokyo was work for Tokuhiro Sensei as an assistant?

ODA: No, the first month I was an assistant for Kaitani Sensei[2], and then my editor Mr. Kushima[3] asked if I wanted to work with Tokuhiro Sensei next.

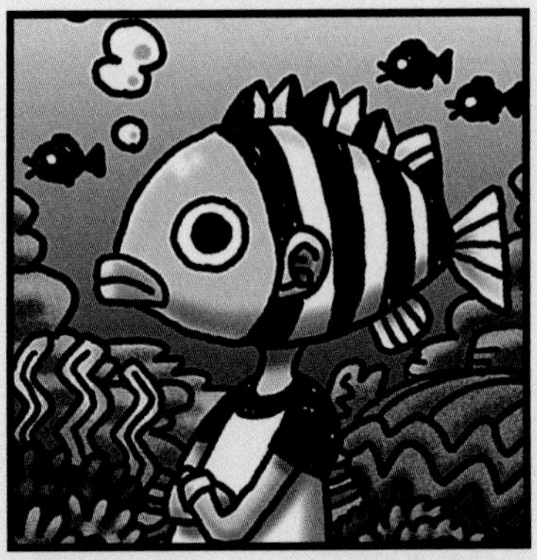

"There's something that's been weighing on my mind for nearly twenty years."

EIICHIRO ODA

V.S. EIICHIRO ODA

FOOTNOTES

1. Kenji Mitsuyoshi, a former assistant of Tokuhiro Sensei and currently the artist in the manga team Ark Performance. Known for series like *Arpeggio of Blue Steel* and *Mobile Suit Gundam MSV-R: The Return of Johnny Ridden.*

2. Shinobu Kaitani. Artist of *Sommelier*, *One Outs*, *Liar Game*, and others.

3. The editor for Oda Sensei before he started *One Piece*. He was a tough but enthusiastic teacher whose sternness concealed a core of love. He helped found the cornerstone of what would go on to become *One Piece*.

4. Nobuhiro Watsuki. Artist of *Rurouni Kenshin*, *Buso Renkin*, *Embalming*, and others.

ODA: That's true, I guess. The problem is, I remember some really rude things I said to you back then. I said, "The way you draw muscle is incredible! I want to be as good as you at it," but even though I was already learning by your example, I said something like, "I can't just copy *your* style, Sensei." Just so people understand where I was mentally... Back then, I thought that people who worked as assistants and let the style of that studio change their own art style were uncool. I didn't respect them, especially because I saw so many of them. But you were very gentle with me. You didn't get angry, you just said, "Look at this and practice," and handed me a book of bodybuilders.

TOKUHIRO: I don't remember that at all. [*laughs*]

ODA: I still have that book.

TOKUHIRO: How interesting. I agree with you, though. If you copy your teacher, you're just mimicking them.

ODA: That's right.

TOKUHIRO: Do you remember coming to ask me for advice about your own manga?

ODA: I did?! What did I ask?

TOKUHIRO: You said, "My editor says I'm cutting my panels too diagonally, so they're hard to read. What should I do?" I said, "Your editor is an amateur, so you should do it the way you want."

ODA: Oh, I remember that now! I never went back and fixed that. I still break up my panels the same way.

TOKUHIRO: That was the right answer.

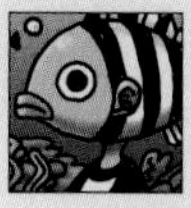

"It was so much fun working at your studio."
ODA

TOKUHIRO: From my perspective at the time, you were like the one raw kid among everyone else.

ODA: You and all the other assistants were much older, so I'm sure I seemed even younger because of that.

TOKUHIRO: You had fun at our place though, right?

ODA: It was so much fun.

TOKUHIRO: After each chapter, we'd all go out for sushi, or to an *izakaya* for drinks. Me and one other person would drink, and you and one other person couldn't drink, so you'd eat sushi or sashimi or whatever.

ODA: I remember that too. It was something to look forward to every week.

TOKUHIRO: You were the most cheerful person. The mood maker of the group. After you stopped doing assistant work, did you start *One Piece* right away?

ODA: No, I had a little bit of a gap before it started.

TOKUHIRO: But you already had the structure for *One Piece* in your mind while you were an assistant.

ODA: Well, I do remember that I talked a very big game. [*laughs*]

TOKUHIRO: There was a used bookstore near the studio at the time. We went there together once, and you bought a used copy of a manga about pirates. I could tell you were already preparing to achieve the ambitions you had in mind. And it all worked out, so that's got to feel pretty good.

TOKUHIRO: That's right, Kushima was my editor at the time.

ODA: When editors are working with new artists and want to give them some professional experience, they send them to be assistants for the other manga artist they're working with. That's the very first step for any new artist. There's so, so much you can learn in that workplace, especially if it's a big established artist. But they usually have their own dedicated assistants, so it's hard to find a slot where you can fit in. So it was really lucky for me that I was able to get into your studio so quickly, Sensei.

TOKUHIRO: And after you were done at my place, you went to Watsuki's[4], right?

ODA: Yes. After the end of *King of the Jungle Tar-chan*[5] I went to Watsuki Sensei's studio[6]. Then you called me back to say, "I'm starting a new series," so I went back and helped through the end of *Watery Friend Kappaman*[7].

TOKUHIRO: So you spent the most time with me.

ODA: That's true, and I learned so much from you. I'd like to talk about this more later, but when the assistants come to the studio to work, the pencil work has already been done. So tracing your pencils to draw the background, I realized what a huge difference in expression there was between your work and mine. At the time, I didn't even understand basic ideas like, you can draw closer details thicker and distant details thinner. I learned so much on that job.

TOKUHIRO: Still, you could already do it all.

ODA: Not in the least! At Watsuki Sensei's place, they said, "You've already got the fundamentals down," but that was only because I had learned so much at your studio.

TOKUHIRO: So Watsuki was your great mentor and Kaitani was your early mentor. I guess that makes me...your boob mentor.

ODA: You're not my boob mentor. You're my *great* boob mentor. [*laughs*]

6. At Watsuki Sensei's workplace, Oda Sensei met and became friends with fellow artists Hiroyuki Takei, Mikio Ito, Gin Shinga, and Shinya Suzuki.

7. A series that ran in *Weekly Shonen Jump* from 1995–1996. It's the story of Kawataro, a half-human, half-kappa hero who fights against aliens known as "monsters" and traditional *yokai*.

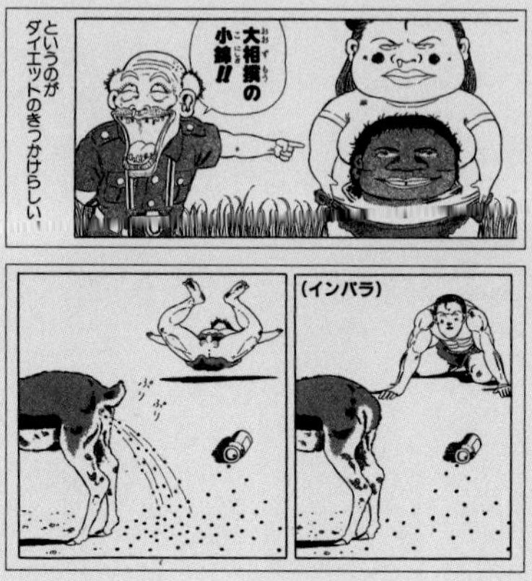
大相撲の小錦!!
というのがダイエットのきっかけらしい
(インパラ)
ぷり
ぷり

FOOTNOTES

5. A series that ran in *Weekly Shonen Jump* from 1988–1990. After that, it changed titles to *New King of the Jungle Tar-chan* and ran until 1995. The original series was a short-form comedy series with seven pages each chapter, but in the newer series the page count was expanded and it became more story-based. The powerful combat scenes won it acclaim from readers. It was made into a TV anime series in 1993. Oda Sensei says, "There are two scenes I really loved from this series. One was when Jane wears a T-shirt of Michael Jackson, but it stretches until he looks like the sumo wrestler Konishiki. The other was when he spills a bottle of pills, and then an impala poops on top of them. Later, he scoops the pills back into the bottle, but doesn't realize it's fuller than it was before. I thought it was genius."

ODA: A long time ago, you were talking about how "There are only a few different story patterns in the world." That was shocking to me. I was like, that can't be true. But as I've gotten older, I've come to understand what you meant by that. There are as many stories as stars in the sky, but only a few definitive ones that delight people. In preparation for this discussion, I went back and reread a lot of your work...and I still think the one that influenced me the most was *Ken-chan Chako-chan*[13].

TOKUHIRO: It's surprising how many people like that one.

ODA: Every single chapter is like its own movie, and they're all classics, even now. It's unbelievable to me that you were drawing that at the same time as *Tar-chan*.

TOKUHIRO: After *Tafel Anatomiko*[14] ended, I was drawing that one while waiting for my next weekly series. But you're right, I was working on it at the same time as *Tar-chan* later.

ODA: I can't switch between two things in my head that way. At the time, I bought *Ken-Chako* as a reader, particularly for the pervy parts. But once I read it, I got into the story construction, and it's just fascinating. The camera work is intriguing, and I used it as a major reference when starting *One Piece*. I was like, "This is it!" I was amazed that you could send the camera directly into the drama and have it capture and depict emotion that way. Wow, I'm just full of praise today. [*laughs*]

TOKUHIRO: You think so?

ODA: I know so. And that's because you're such a movie buff.

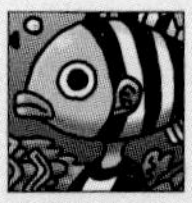

"This one panel is what created the *One Piece* of today."
ODA

switched to ballpoint pens called Hi-Tecs, 0.3 and 0.2 width. It made my callus[10] disappear.

ODA: No matter what I do, I can never get a callus. My hands are too squishy. I know I'm putting them through incredible strain, but I never feel it on my skin. [*laughs*]

MODERATOR: Tokuhiro Sensei, you're known for drawing muscular characters, of course, but also sexy women. How do you draw their breasts, in particular?

TOKUHIRO: Once my hand went bad, around the time of *Fugu-Man*[11], I started using a ruler. You know those rulers with all the different-sized circles on the inside? I'd set that down and draw the curves. By the end of *Vampire*[12] my control was just pitiful, so I had to make the change.

ODA: But the boobs are incredible when you see them on the finished page. His women are so sexy.

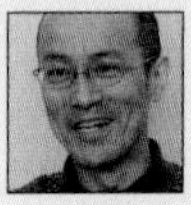

"Movies are the source of my ideas."
TOKUHIRO

ODA: Do you ever pick up issues of *Jump* to see what's going on these days?

TOKUHIRO: I almost never read manga. If you read manga to draw manga, you're not going to make anything good. So I watch movies that people say are classics. That was how you got the hint to start on *One Piece*, wasn't it? I know about that. [*laughs*]

ODA: [*laughs*] I'll admit that when I'm creating manga, I get a lot of inspiration from movies.

TOKUHIRO: If you go back to the beginning, *Kyoshiro* was just *Romeo and Juliet*. You only need a moment. Just one little spark of inspiration that seems cool to you, and that can be the next great idea for your manga.

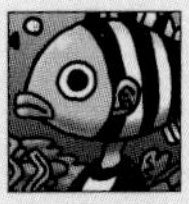

"I've always kept those words close to my heart."
ODA

ODA: The most surprising thing about working at your studio, though, was that the pencils were already done when we came in to work. All I had to do was trace the background. Nobody does that.

TOKUHIRO: In *Komon-sama*[8] there are group fight scenes, and I drew all of them. You see little characters the size of a grain of rice. I drew 'em too. [*laughs*]

ODA: I understand that desire.

TOKUHIRO: It's the smaller characters that you *don't* want anyone else to draw, right?

ODA: Exactly. I don't want to leave a single detail up to someone else.

OKUHIRO: The smaller something is, the more different it feels when another person draws it. The smaller it is, the more you want to draw it. How much do you draw on your own, Oda?

ODA: I draw everything that's alive. Also, anything that's moving, like the waves and the clouds. I've carried on your will, Tokuhiro Sensei.

TOKUHIRO: I feel like the editors think I'm the guy who will teach kids lessons by showing them what *not* to do.

ODA: That's not true! At the time I said something like, "It's amazing how so much of your character is contained in the smallest details," and you told me, "If you pack the detail in, people will notice." I've always kept those words close to my heart.

TOKUHIRO: Yes, and that's why I ended up with tendonitis. When I was drawing *Kyoshiro*[9] I couldn't get a proper grip, and I couldn't draw circles. So I couldn't use a G-pen anymore, and

V.S. EIICHIRO ODA

10. When you grip a pen for long periods of time, a bump of hardened skin develops on the side of the finger and along joints. Among manga artists, this is basically the sign of a professional.

11. A manga serialized in *Super Jump* from 2008 to 2010. A researcher named Toranosuke Takeda undergoes genetic reconstructive surgery, and turns into a fugu-man with toxic properties. Suddenly, women find him irresistible, but it is very difficult for him to safely come into physical contact with anyone.

9. The full title is *Kyoshiro 2030*, serialized in *Super Jump* from 1997 to 2004. A near future hard sci-fi series about a post-WWIII Japan under a stifling micro-management system. Protagonist Kyoshiro meets a woman named Shino through a virtual machine, and sets off on a dangerous journey to meet her in person. Will the ever find each other...?!

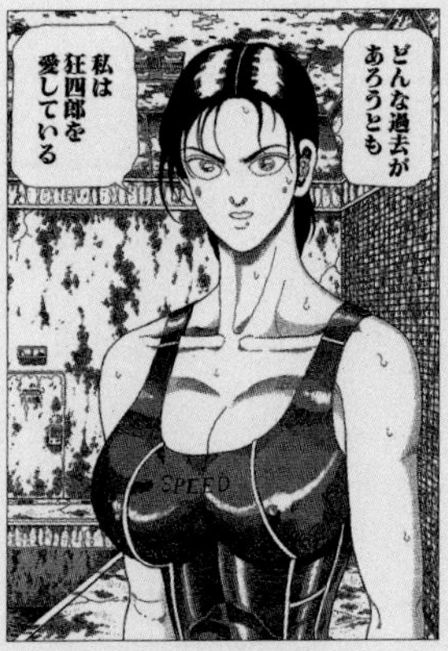
どんな過去があろうとも
私は狂四郎を愛している
SPEED

FOOTNOTES

8. The full title is *Komon-sama: The Melancholy of Suke-san*, serialized in *Grand Jump* from 2013 to 2015. It is a comedy manga about the eccentric and elderly Mitsukuni Mito, who hires the young ronin Shinnosuke, nicknamed "Suke," to be his bodyguard. Instead of asking his assistants to draw the background figures in the battle scenes or the many dogs in the kennel scenes, Tokuhiro Sensei draws them himself.

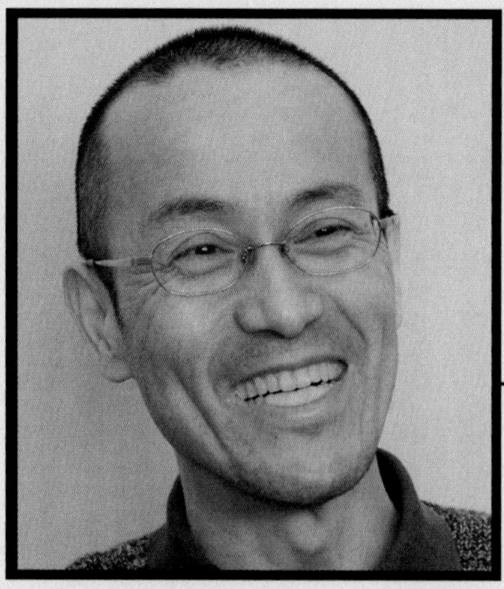

“In that case, I forgive you today. [*laughs*]”

MASAYA TOKUHIRO

PROFILE: Born in Kochi Prefecture, 1959. Received a runner-up prize for the 17th Akatsuka Award in 1982. Debuted in *Weekly Shonen Jump* with *Shape Up Ran* in 1983. His 1988 series *King of the Jungle Tar-chan* and its follow-up *New King of the Jungle Tar-chan* were made into an animated TV series. In the late 1990s, he transitioned to seinen manga aimed at an older audience, and drew titles such as *Kyoshiro 2030, Showa Immortal Legend Vampire, Fugu-man, Komon-sama: The Melancholy of Suke-san, A Lively Dog Makes the Best Husband*, and *Mokkori Hanbei*.

TOKUHIRO: I'm just glad to hear that, whether it's true or not.

ODA: It's absolutely true.

TOKUHIRO: You do keep up with sending me holiday gifts every year, I'll admit. [*laughs*]

ODA: I'll send them my entire life. [*laughs*]

And I felt such terrible regret—how could I have done that to such an important scene in such a precious story to you? And I was never able to say that before...

TOKUHIRO: In that case, I forgive you today. [*laughs*]

ODA: Thank you. I finally got that off my chest... Anyway, I changed a lot after that day. I would draw different facial outlines and practice making them all different styles. I think it was thanks to this one panel that the *One Piece* of today exists.

TOKUHIRO: There are people who reflect on their mistakes and try to improve on them, and there are people who don't. You did that, Oda. Ordinary people don't. When you realized it was a problem, you chose the path that lead you to sucess rather than failure.

ODA: To me, the fact that you accepted my work on that panel is something I'm grateful for, and it's also a huge turning point for me. Then again, I've really taken that lesson off the deep end. I might be going too far with it now. But this was the moment you taught me that it's important to see your characters as silhouettes.

ODA: Okay, maybe I should finally bring this up... There's something that's always weighed on my mind. Do you remember this panel?

TOKUHIRO: Ah, that's the one you drew[15], wasn't it?

ODA: It was a panel that you put a lot of trust in me to draw, and I was delighted to do it. But when I saw the finished product, you asked me, "What, isn't it good enough?" In the end, you used it, but when I saw it in the pages of *Jump* later, a nasty shiver ran down my back. The faces of all the people were the same shape.

TOKUHIRO: When you're doing a crowd scene and the faces are tiny, you have to distort the sizes to make them different.

ODA: I remember exactly what I was doing when I was drawing it. And the outline was the same for every single person.

TOKUHIRO: Then they're all going to look the same. [*laughs*]

ODA: And that's what I was doing in all of my manga to that point. I realized that I wasn't distinguishing their silhouettes from each other.

FOOTNOTES

12. A pair of series titled *Showa Immortal Legend Vampire* and *Near Future Immortal Legend Vampire*, serialized in *Super Jump* from 2005 to 2006, and 2006 to 2008. It's the story of Maria, an immortal vampire, and Shohei Honda, a boy with psychic powers who loves her. The two have to fight off the secret organization Bhikkhuni Club that seeks the power of immortality, and the Maria Society led by Atsuhiko Jumonji. According to Tokuhiro Sensei, "*Vampire*'s greatest rival was *Kyoshiro*. It was very difficult to surpass my past self."

13. The full title is *Fundoshi Detectives Ken-chan Chako-chan*, serialized in *Super Jump* from 1986 to 1990. A detective story about the gay veteran Jiro Kenzaki (Ken-chan) and the enthusiastic rookie Shiro Chaya (Chako-chan). The first seinen manga from Tokuhiro Sensei

14. A manga serialized in *Weekly Shonen Jump* in 1986. A comedy series about Tomiko Kameda, a doctor's daughter, and Kuya Tendo, a Buddhist priest's son.

15. A panel from the final volume of *New King of the Jungle Tar-chan*. Tokuhiro Sensei asked his assistant at the time, Oda Sensei, to draw a scene featuring people from all over the world. Tokuhiro Sensei never let his assistants draw background characters, so it was a rare and prestigious opportunity which Oda Sensei took very seriously. He later said, "It's always weighed on me that I handed back this panel without recognizing the major flaw in the way I drew it."

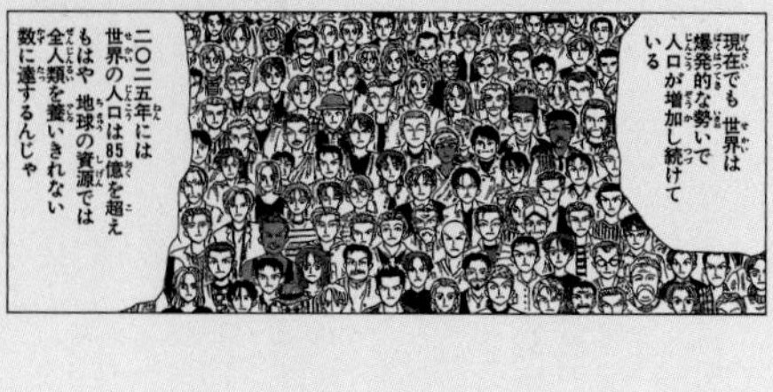
現在でも 世界は爆発的な勢いで人口が増加し続けている
二〇二五年には世界の人口は85億を超えもはや 地球の資源では全人類を養いきれない数に達するんじゃ

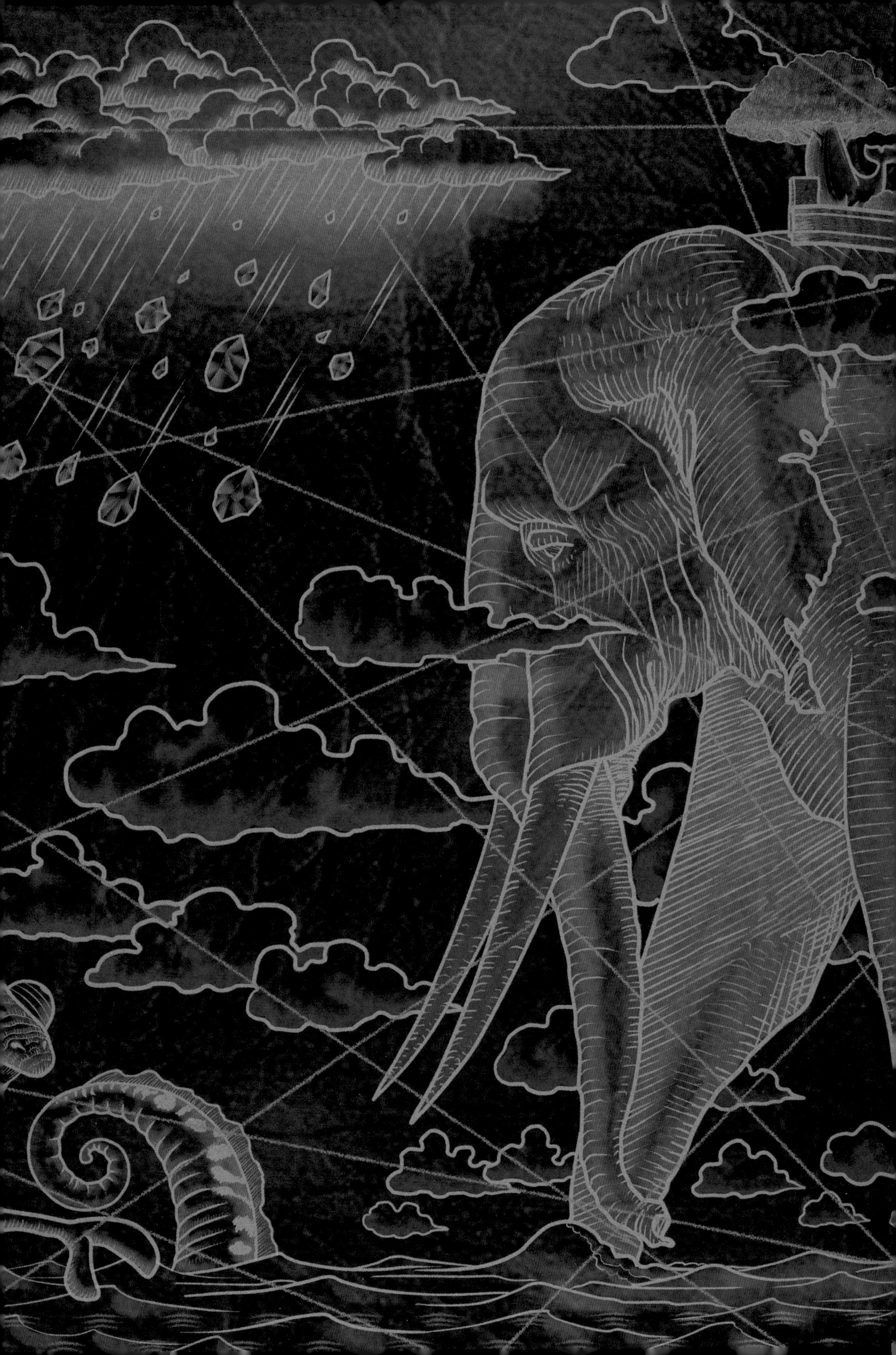

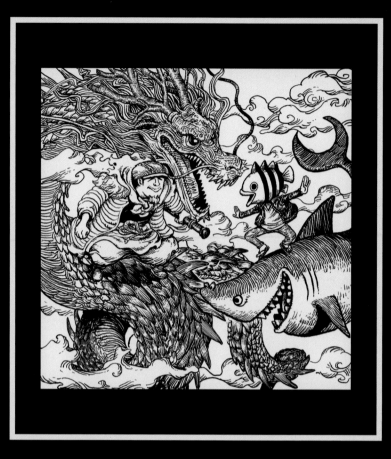

Put your soul into each line!! A meeting between two men who live through art!

MONOCHROME TALK

It's a conversation between Eiichiro Oda and Katsuya
Terada, who drew an illustration for *One Piece: Ace's Story*!
Read on as two artists who put their souls into drawing find
their thoughts synchronized across boundaries, between
manga and illustration, analog and digital!

寺田 克也
KATSUYA TERADA
EIICHIRO ODA
尾田栄一郎

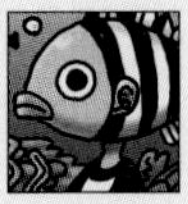

"He can describe characters and stories simply through visuals."
ODA

MODERATOR: Today our guest is Katsuya Terada Sensei, who drew an illustration in collaboration with our Ace novel!

ODA: Thank you so much for coming! I felt intimidated on the way here, because your art is just so phenomenal. Your collaboration artbook with Kim Jung Gi[1] blew me away.

TERADA: Oh, please. You can be intimidated by Kim if you want, but there's no need for that with me!

ODA: No, it's true! I think anyone who does art would be intimidated by the name Katsuya Terada. [*laughs*] I'm really happy we have the chance to sit down and have a nice conversation.

MODERATOR: Oda Sensei, tell us what appeals to you about Terada Sensei's art.

ODA: I think the most impressive thing is the way he can describe characters and stories simply through visuals. In manga, you can build things up with dialogue and story flow, but in his case, he tells you just as much without those things. And most of all, you can tell simply from looking at it that he's really enjoying the creation of it. His art makes *me* excited to draw.

TERADA: Thank you. [*bows*] I think of myself as half manga artist, half illustrator. But the manga artist part is my dominant leg, if that makes sense. That's why I want to create art that tells a story, that has characterization. Like, I can't draw someone's face if I don't know what they're thinking.

MODERATOR: When you did the Ace illustration[2], what part of Ace struck you as being the coolest?

TERADA: I would say...his face! He always looks great, no matter the situation. Basically, I took a bird's-eye view of all of those faces, compared them to the varieties of handsome faces I can create, and came up with that piece. I guess you could compare the mental process I used to casting a film.

ODA: Oh, I see. Thank you so much for that awesome illustration!

MODERATOR: Terada Sensei, can you tell us what you like about Oda Sensei's art?

TERADA: I'm just going to be bold and ask straight up, are you a child of the Akira Toriyama[3] generation?

ODA: Yes [*firmly*].

TERADA: Everyone grows up within the influences of the great artists who came before them, and the bigger that influence is, the harder it is to escape it. But within that system, you've always had your own worldview and perspective. And that's why it's not an imitation of Toriyama. Which is incredible. When you're switching between doing manga and illustration work, does your process or your approach change at all?

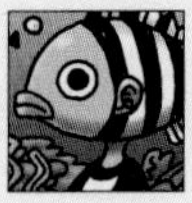

"I treat illustrations and manga the same way."
ODA

ODA: It doesn't. I treat illustrations and manga the same way, which is to say that I want to express the emotions and actions of the characters. Like I'm just slicing out a single moment of time where those things are visible. But I feel like I've long since finished drawing all the things I wanted to draw. That's the biggest hurdle for me now. Do you ever get bored, Mr. Terada?

TERADA: [*Instantly*] Yes! All the time! I want to draw things I've never drawn before, and find lines I've never found before. That's always on my mind. But even within the same motif, sometimes the second time around, you can do things you couldn't do the first time. Maybe you can draw a piece that surpasses what you drew before. So if you put your hopes on that, it might help you enjoy the process more.

ODA: That's a good point! I agree. What illustrators and manga artist influenced you when you were younger?

TERADA: I really loved the man who drew the *Tarzan* covers for the Hayakawa SF line, whose name was Motoichiro Takebe[4], and a French comic artist named Moebius[5]. I took a ton of influence from them.

ODA: Ooh. And Katsuhiro Otomo[6] really loved Moebius too, didn't he?

TERADA: Right. In terms of generations, you're probably more of a grandchild of their influence, but when I came across them at age fifteen, it was instantaneous. I'd collect back issues of imported magazines and pore over them. The text was in French, so I had no idea what was happening in the story. But the art was so incredible, I could imagine it was something grand and epic. Then a Japanese translation came out later, and it wasn't at all what I expected it to be. [*laughs*]

ODA: Like a misleading movie trailer.

TERADA: But it's like that for weekly manga too, isn't it? You get the readers' expectations up, then you give them something that's beyond what they imagined and hoped for. It's an amazing feat to do that consistently for such a long period of time.

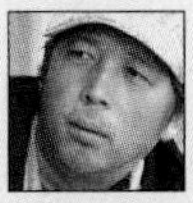

"Manga is the highest conceptual form of entertainment."
TERADA

V.S. EIICHIRO ODA

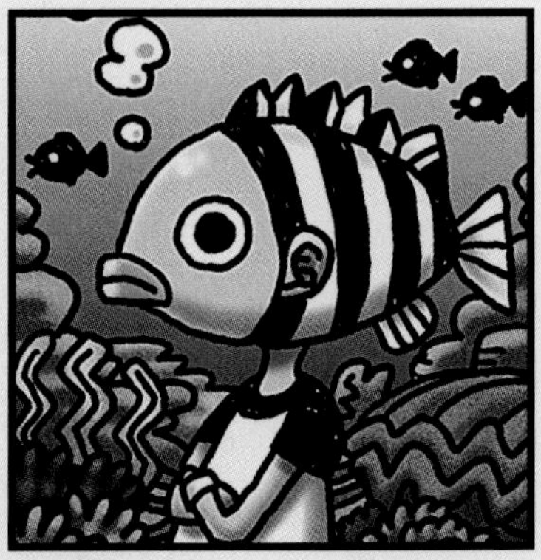

"Just looking at Mr. Terada's art, you can tell that he's really enjoying the creation of it. His art makes me excited to draw."

EIICHIRO ODA

"I finally found a brush that feels right."

EIICHIRO ODA

TERADA: Just the 6B pencil that comes with it. I fine tune the strength as I go, that's it.

ODA: I thought you must have had your own original brush settings... I've gotten really into collecting different brush tools lately.

TERADA: I guess you can just try out different things and use the ones that suit your look the best.

ODA: I finally found a brush that feels right to me. I've been drawing on paper my whole career, but recently I've started getting into the habit of doing digital pieces for the various extra things *Jump* wants from me. It really feels like the digital tools are at a point where you can't tell the difference between digital art and ink on paper. I really enjoy the time lapse[13] feature too.

TERADA: That's great. It's surprisingly easy to make things that look way more laborious than they are. [*laughs*]

TERADA: To me, manga is the highest conceptual form of entertainment. It's like, whatever you can say about movies, one single person drew this manga for you! Ever since I was a boy, I wanted to make a living drawing. I ended up taking the path of an illustrator, but in my mind, I'm half manga artist. I just haven't ever gotten past the stage of manga "rookie," that's all. [*laughs*]

ODA: I think I understand why your art has so much character and story to it now.

TERADA: As a kid, you never had any doubts about wanting to be a manga artist, did you?

ODA: That's right.

TERADA: I figured as much. Those are the type of people who end up actually becoming artists or manga artists.

ODA: I was hoping to pick your brain about working digitally today. What software do you use?

TERADA: I used to use *Painter*[11], but now I use *Procreate*[12]. Now that you can draw anywhere as long as you have an iPad Pro, it's made working while overseas so much easier.

ODA: And what brushes?

TERADA: I started reading *Jump* in third grade. The stories at the time were stuff like *Mazinger Z*[7], *Dr. Toilet*[8], *Manga Drifters*[9]. Tezuka Sensei drew for them too. When did you start reading?

ODA: The same, third grade. *Dragon Ball* hadn't started yet. It was all *Kinnikuman*, *Fist of the North Star*, and *Captain Tsubasa*.

MODERATOR: Terada Sensei, I understand you were an assistant to Masakazu Katsura Sensei during the *Wingman*[10] days.

TERADA: He was an upperclassman at my vocational school. We're still in touch. I came to Tokyo to attend an art school, and I met Katsura at a new students welcoming party. He was dancing around in a *tokusatsu* hero costume, but the costume itself was incredibly high quality. I asked him, "Who made that?" And he said, "I did." I was amazed.

ODA: So he already loved superheroes back then.

TERADA: That's how I met him, and then I assisted him just once at the start of his series. It was my job to erase the pencil, and I'd scrunch up the paper doing it. [*laughs*] That was the first time I saw a pro manga artist at work. I met Mr. Toriyama through Katsura too.

ODA: Oh! That's interesting.

FOOTNOTES

1. An artist born in South Korea in 1975, the same year as Oda Sensei. He started as a comic artist, until footage of his live drawing exhibition at an event went viral and brought work offers from all over the world. He's also done a live drawing with Terada Sensei. Has a tremendous technique, capable of producing balanced, detailed art without any sketching underneath. Terada Sensei told us, "He has an excellent grasp of the three-dimensional structure of objects. He'll understand the shape and workings of a car engine, for example, and can use that practical knowledge to draw it. When he gets going, it's such a trance-inducing experience that people will stand there and watch, and never leave to do something else. His live drawings are fascinating. And he's still got room to grow with his single pieces that aren't done live, so I'm excited to see where he goes next."

2. An illustration done for the first installment of *One Piece: Ace's Story*, which ran in *One Piece Magazine, Vol. 1*, for the twentieth anniversary of *One Piece* in July 2017. After Terada Sensei, there were pieces done by Kinu Nishimura Sensei and Kazuya Takahashi Sensei.

3. A legendary manga artist, known for his series *Dr. Slump* and *Dragon Ball*. He switched to doing art digitally in the latter half of the 1990s. Apparently, he's visited Terada Sensei's workplace before.

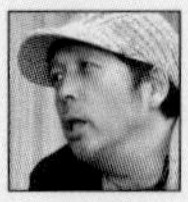

"If you use digital tools to make the process easier, your art's going to feel flat."
TERADA

ODA: When did you start working digitally?

TERADA: When I was doing *The Monkey King*[14]. The first chapter was done with Liquitex[15] and Copics, and I switched to digital with the second chapter.

ODA: Drawing your color pages with digital tools is so standardized now, it's hard to stand out. Yet you really have your own color and style.

TERADA: If you use digital tools to make the process easier, your art's going to feel flat. So most art, when I look at it, I think, "It's lacking flavor." But some people are good at it. When Toriyama switched to doing digital, it was still his art. I think you need to look at them as tools. Work digitally, but always have that thought in your head that you can do the same thing analog.

MODERATOR: With digital art, you can keep fixing and changing things indefinitely. It must be difficult to reach the part where you think, "It's done!"

TERADA: In my case, I usually decide on my palette first—my blue will be this shade of blue, and so on—and I don't stray from that until I'm done. Because if you start thinking, "Well, I could use red instead," you're going to create too many possibilities, and you get stuck in the swamp of choice.

MODERATOR: What about you, Oda Sensei?

ODA: When I do color work on paper, there's a physical limit to how much color changing you can do, so I don't have to worry about it.

TERADA: You don't think about switching over to digital?

ODA: I've decided that I'll draw the *One Piece* manga and its color pages with pen and paper until the end. I think that's what the readers want too.

TERADA: But the art supplies are drying up, bit by bit. What will you do if they stop selling Copic markers?

ODA: That would be bad. [*laughs*]

TERADA: It might only be theoretical at this point, but you should consider the possibility that you might want to switch to digital for physical reasons. Drawing lines with a pen does require physical strength.

ODA: I've started wondering about that. How many years can I keep working with all of my strength like this? The reason I went ahead with the live-action *One Piece* show[16] is because I thought this was the last moment I could do it. A few years from now, I won't have the stamina to have tough conversations with production people overseas and perform quality checks. So I thought, "Now's the time!" Do you think about a decade in the future, or have goals for yourself?

TERADA: A decade from now...? No idea! But I want to be fit enough to keep drawing, and to not have my art weaken. I want to keep drawing forever. I'm fifty-four now. In the Edo period, I'd be retired already, and in the Warring States period, I'd be long dead. [*laughs*] I'm grateful I was born in a time when I can live long, and I want to draw until it's time to go. My goal is to surpass Hokusai Katsushika[17] then! Staying healthy is the most important thing.

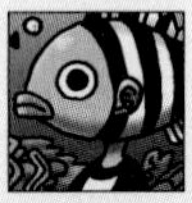

"When you're busy, that's when you enter the invincible zone."
ODA

MODERATOR: Since you're both here, we might as well ask: how do you get better at art?

TERADA: Simple—keep drawing! But everyone always gets upset when you tell them that's the answer. [*laughs*]

ODA: They always want to hear about some special trick, or the perfect tool you can buy that will make it all work.

TERADA: When I was a kid, I thought there was a shortcut to getting better too...but there wasn't.

ODA: I think it can be hard to keep drawing when you're a kid too. If you go to school and take art classes, they scrape away all the freewheeling ideas you have, and the unique touches that are your own.

TERADA: I went to an art class when I was a little boy, and it wasn't very much fun. But the thing is, art is 80 to 90 percent reason and logic. It's that last part after that where your uniqueness comes out. But the unique part has to go on top of the foundation of skills, like being able to draw a proper curve or a straight line. So first things first, draw a lot. I'd say the majority of people who *want* to get good at art don't even do that.

ODA: Uh-huh. I know how important it is to keep your hands busy. It's when you're busiest that you'll draw the best lines. When you haven't slept in a long time, that's when you enter the "invincible zone." [*laughs*]

TERADA: You really should sleep! [*laughs*] I've always been completely useless without sleep, even when I was young, so that's never been a problem for me. One time I was trying not to fall asleep and accidentally wrote the numeral 5 as the kanji for seven. That freaked me out.

ODA: I once suddenly realized that I was drawing boobs on Luffy. [*laughs*] Speaking of that, the girls you draw are so sexy and cute. Are there any specific people you use as a motif? Like, any celebrities or whoever.

FOOTNOTES

4. An illustrator who drew the covers for many science fiction novels in the 1960s and 1970s. He's also known for drawing the illustrations of the original Japanese edition of *Faithful Elephants.*

5. Comic artist born in France, 1938. His bold, visionary style had a large influence on the world of Japanese manga.

6. Manga artist and film director, born in Miyagi Prefecture, 1954. He is known for his detailed and vivid science fiction manga, like *Domu* and *Akira.* He got into animation directing with the animated feature film of *Akira.* He got to know Terada Sensei through animation work, and they released a book together about bicycling.

7. A manga by Go Nagai, serialized beginning in 1972. It had an animated TV series running at the same time, and its imposing "Chogokin" action figures were a huge hit. One of the cornerstones of giant robot anime.

8. A comedy manga by Kazuyoshi Torii, that began serialization in 1970. Wildly successful with young children at the time due to its procession of dirty humor and poop jokes. Terada Sensei says, "I'll never forget the chapter about holding back your poop for an entire year, until it finally comes out and shoots you through the clouds into outer space."

9. A manga by Yuya Enomoto that began serialization in 1970. It ran for over five years, which was quite long at the time. A comedy manga based on the real-life comedy group The Drifters, who were popular on TV at the time.

10. Masakazu Katsura's debut serialized manga, that began serialization in 1984. The middle schooler Kenta Hirono, who idolizes heroes, turns into the superhero Wingman one day, and must fight enemies coming to invade the third dimension. It serves as the root of what Katsura Sensei would be known for: pretty girls and superheroes.

ODA: I completely agree.

MODERATOR: Lastly, a final message for each other!

ODA: I'll go first. Like I mentioned earlier, seeing your art really just makes *me* want to draw. I hope you're able to continue forever, without getting tired of it!

TERADA: You said you'll "keep on drawing *One Piece* like always," but the truth is, things change. You can't stop that. And I'm really looking forward to that change. You struggle with different things as you go, and get even better. I love watching artists evolve over time, and it's a real treat to get to see that process unfolding. I really want to see you draw something that isn't *One Piece* too, something that isn't even recognizably Eiichiro Oda! So please, stay healthy. [*laughs*]

MODERATOR: So is observing women key to drawing them?

TERADA: That's true of everything, really. And you might examine a lot of women's faces, but you don't really commit them to memory. We're drawing this art for entertainment purposes, so we want to draw beautiful women, of course. But if you're not very clear about what the standards of that beauty are, you'll end up a bit out of focus. Things like makeup styles change so quickly. If you're focusing on the wrong things, you'll end up drawing makeup rather than the actual faces of the women.

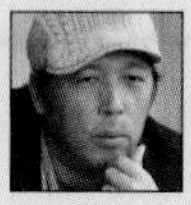

"I really want to see you draw something that isn't *One Piece* too."

TERADA

TERADA: There's no specific person or model that I prefer to use as inspiration. There are faces I like. And that's a different thing than what I would look for in a partner. I guess when I'm drawing, I tend to go for cool looks rather than desirable ones.

ODA: So if a women who looked exactly like one of your drawings said, "Please marry me," what would you do?

TERADA: I'd...probably consider it. [*laughs*] Are your favorite looks and the looks you draw the same thing, then?

ODA: Yes, they're the same.

TERADA: Well, you see, I started drawing women once I started getting jobs drawing the covers of erotic magazines. Until then, I didn't really draw them very much. So it became a major theme with me back then that I'd try to draw a different face each time.

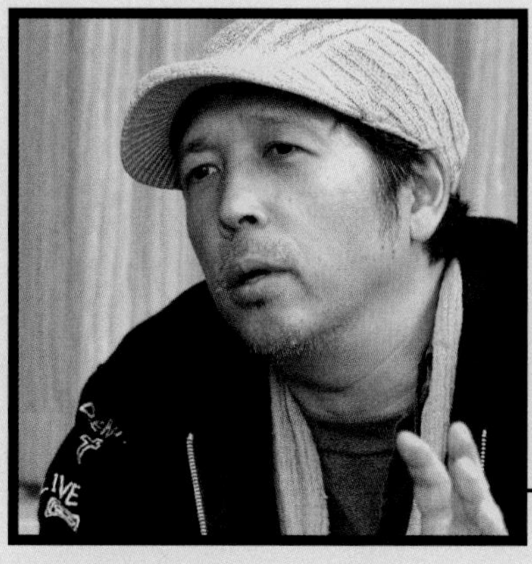

"Despite thinking you'll always do things the same way, you'll change. I'm looking forward to how you change, and what new things will result."

KATSUYA TERADA

PROFILE: Born in Okayama Prefecture, 1963. Started doing illustration jobs while he was in vocational school, and continued on as a professional after graduation. Famous for being an international pioneer of digital illustration and manga production. Aside from books like *Katsuya Terada Everything*, *Katsuya Terada RakugaKing*, and *Katsuya Terada's Last 10 Years*, he also does art exhibits domestically and abroad. Recently he has started producing tableware with his artwork on it. He's engaged in a variety of creative projects, such as drawing the manga *The Monkey King* and doing creature design for *Kamen Rider W*.

K A T S U Y A T E R A D A

FOOTNOTES

11. A digital art and painting program created by Corel. One of the premier pieces of software for creating art in a digital environment. It is most often used with a tablet device to make digital art creation possible using the same methodology and feeling as drawing by hand. Terada Sensei wrote a book called *Painter Bon!* that describes and demonstrates his process using these tools.

12. A program for creating digital art using an iPad. Oda Sensei uses this program. Terada Sensei draws in this program using a stylus called an Apple Pencil. He says that many of his current illustrations are done this way.

13. A software feature that records and saves the status of the artwork over time, allowing you to view its process, frame by frame, until it's finished. It allows you to see exactly how a piece of art was made. Oda Sensei used this feature to make a video in collaboration with Yasutaka Nakata on the *One Piece* official website in 2016. See the URL below.

14. A full-color manga based on *Journey to the West (Saiyuki)*, serialized in *Ultra Jump* starting in 1995. After a while, the publication switched to black and white, but it was updated into full-color form when it was collected into graphic novels.

15. A brand of water-based acrylic paints developed in America in the 1950s. Because it has the benefits of both water and oil-based paint, it is easy to use, and was a favorite of painters in the 1960s such as Andy Warhol. Since then, it's become a standard art supply. Some manga artists use it in their color art when they want to create a painterly look and texture.

16. An American live-action adaptation of *One Piece* was announced in September 2017, handled by Tomorrow Studios, producers of *Prison Break* and other shows.

17. An *ukiyo-e* painter from the late Edo Period. He painted using over thirty pen names, and was active into his eighties.

***One Piece* official website - https://one-piece.com**

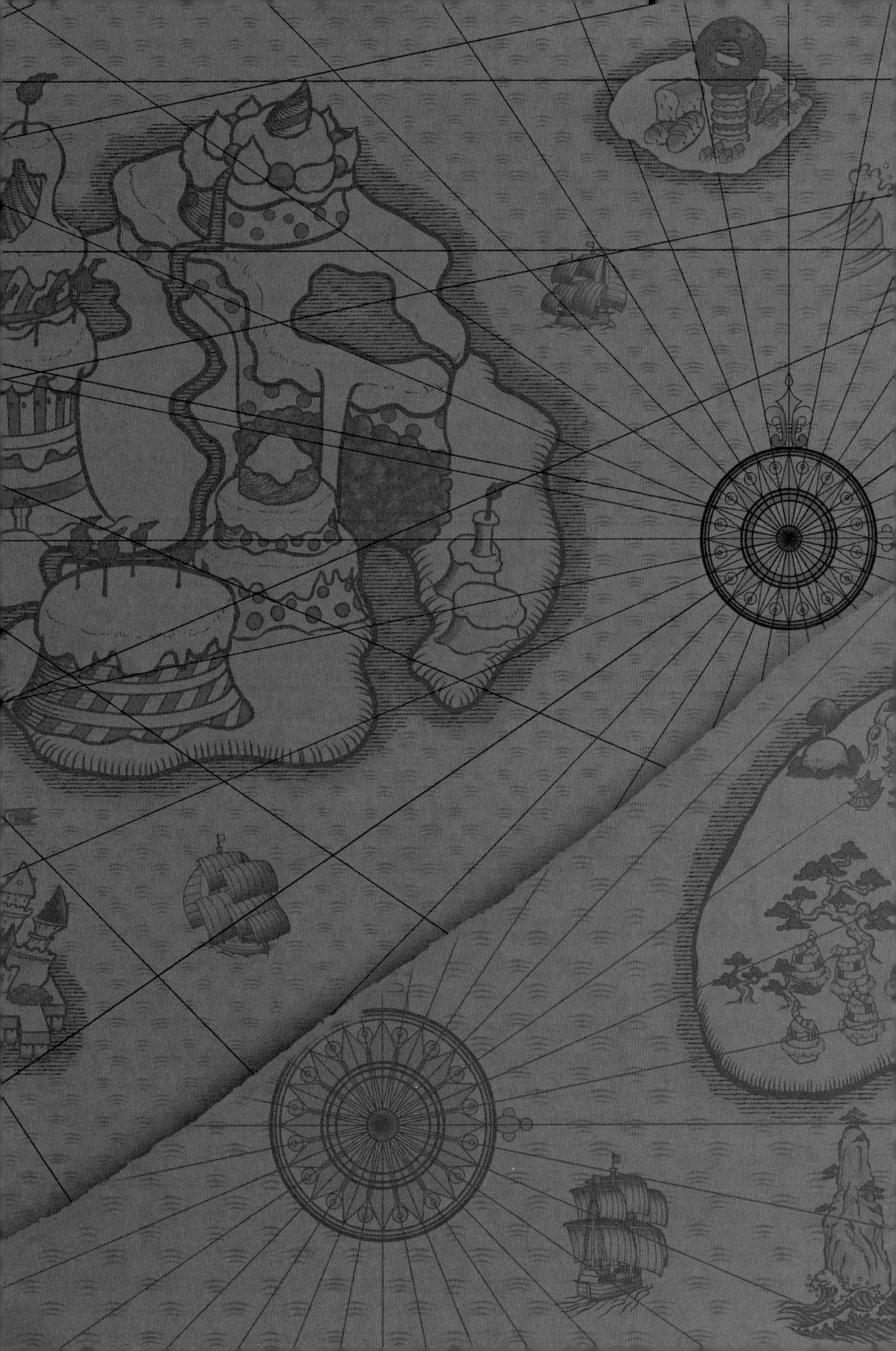

The two men behind a dream collaboration speak about the life of drawing manga!

MONOCHROME TALK

Following the "Hungry Days" crossover commercial series with Nissin's Cup Noodle, we sit down with Eisaku Kubonouchi! In addition to behind-the-scenes details of creating the commercials, we'll get to hear what these two men who have given their lives to manga have to say!

窪之内英策

EISAKU KUBONOUCHI
EIICHIRO ODA

尾田栄一郎

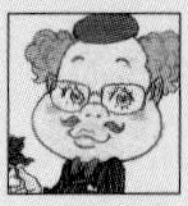

"My first thought was, 'Oh crap, I can't touch this one!'"

KUBONOUCHI

MODERATOR: We're sitting down today with Eisaku Kubonouchi Sensei, who handled the character design for the Nissin Cup Noodle/*One Piece* "Hungry Days" commercial series.

KUBONOUCHI: Thank you for having me.

ODA: It's a pleasure.

MODERATOR: First of all, can we have your thoughts on the finished commercials?

KUBONOUCHI: There wasn't much time to do these, so there was a lot of patience and persistence on the part of the animation staff and directors, and the quality is very high across the bar. I think everyone did a great job.

ODA: All I can say is that I love them. When I heard about the commercial offer, I went back to reread your *Tsurumoku Bachelors' Dorm*[1] series, and reminisced a lot.

MODERATOR: When the collaboration was finalized, what was your impression of *One Piece*, Kubonouchi Sensei?

KUBONOUCHI: To be perfectly honest with you, I hardly ever read manga. I hardly ever watch anime. But of course, I did know about *One Piece*, and the general worldview and vibe that it has. I'd just never actually read it. So when I got the commercial offer, I kind of panicked. I thought, "Can I really draw this?" *One Piece* is still very much an ongoing affair, and it's the best-selling manga in the entire world. So my first thought was, "Oh crap, I can't touch this one!"

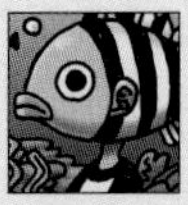

"I come up with the character forms based on various childhood memories."

ODA

ODA: I love creating characters. And I love designing characters. But I make so many of them that I have trouble giving them clear roles after that.

KUBONOUCHI: Do you draw up design documents while you're working on the series?

ODA: I don't do proper design sheets. I just whip up some rough sketches, and usually finalize them when I'm first drawing them in the manga.

KUBONOUCHI: Does that mean you're just memorizing the form and details of the character as you go?

ODA: No, I don't memorize them. Over time, I'll remember the main characters I have constantly in action, but when there's a whole bunch of characters doing stuff at once, I'll go back to the rough sketches and materials to refresh my memory.

KUBONOUCHI: I guess that makes sense, when you have so many characters to deal with.

ODA: Whenever I draw them from memory, thinking I've got it down right, that's when things go wrong. I'll forget about scars on faces or bodies, stuff like that. It happens so often, it's easier just to check from the start.

KUBONOUCHI: Ahh, interesting. I was noticing that the outline of *One Piece* characters tends to be either human or monster in style, and the monster-type characters often have a *Tetsujin 28*[2] outline. Do you like that sort of silhouette?

ODA: I come up with the character forms based on various childhood memories.

KUBONOUCHI: I see. It's a bit old-fashioned, in a way, that you've got so many characters with that kind of silhouette to them. As I was drawing up the characters, I kept noticing that. "Oh, he must like this look."

ODA: There are a bunch. I think you're probably correct about that.

KUBONOUCHI: Really? Overall, there's just such a great variety that it was really fun to work on characters with such different physiques. Especially the most extreme monster-type ones.

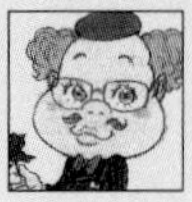

"There's a big difference between people who can sketch skeletal structure and those who can't."

KUBONOUCHI

ODA: You guys drew so much, to the point that you can't tell how much is the animators and how much is you, right?

KUBONOUCHI: That's right. Basically, the director always wanted more retakes. [*laughs*]

ODA: That sounds really rough...

KUBONOUCHI: The production company was straining under the workload as it was, but I gave instructions as detailed as I possibly could. If the animated art is too different from my own style, then it's like, "Why am I even doing the character design?" I feel like animators are too locked into contemporary anime styles, so designs tend to get converted into that look. I call it "anime laundering." They just can't help but redraw things into a style they're more comfortable with. And then there's no point to having me design them, so it's like, "Why not just draw them in a typical *moé* anime style, then?" So I drew as many characters as I could and did my best to explain the details to the animators, so that my presence had a purpose. I did as much of the rough drawing before the key animation as possible. In the Vivi-centric commercial, the animators just couldn't get her downcast expression to look like my art, and the director ordered lots of retakes. That one came down to the wire.

ODA: So the director and animators were really focused, then. They wanted to do whatever it took to incorporate your art.

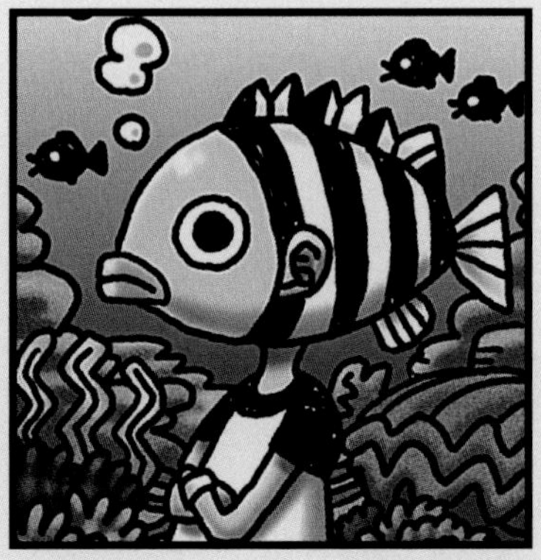

"I love creating characters. And I love designing characters. But I make so many of them that I have trouble giving them clear roles after that."

EIICHIRO ODA

V.S. EIICHIRO ODA

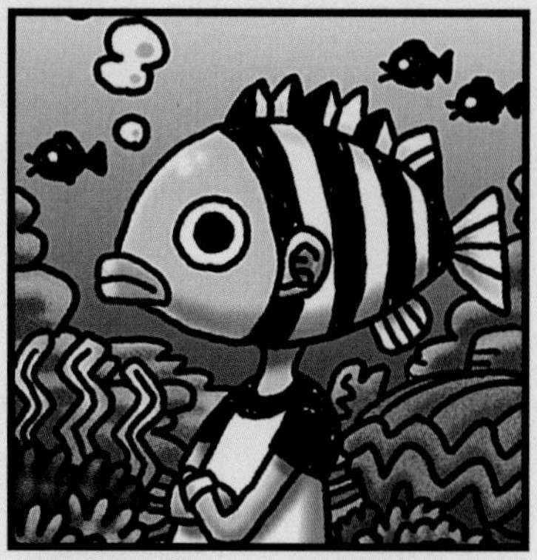

“Whatever is involved in the presentation affects the story, so I have to draw it myself.”

EIICHIRO ODA

ODA: I figure, I just have to keep doing it this way.

ODA: When I read *Tsurumoku Bachelors' Dorm*, I thought, “The guy who drew this must have lived through so much romance.”

KUBONOUCHI: Actually, not at all. I went to an all-boys technical high school, so girls were, like, in a completely different world. When we opened up the campus for the culture festival and the girls came in, I remember being really nervous. So I didn't really have the same kind of youth experience lots of other people did. And then I got a manga series when I was 21, and was basically living entirely in my studio from that point on.

ODA: I see. Once I started my series, I realized that I couldn't have anyone around me.

KUBONOUCHI: Yeah, I definitely get that. In my case, I'm drawing cute girls and beautiful women because I never got to experience those bittersweet things when I was young, so I have a stronger longing for them. Even now, at my age.

ODA: Like, you want to get that youth back?

KUBONOUCHI: Yeah, I'm like, “I still want to experience love!” That's creepy when you're in your fifties. [*laughs*] Anyway, that's a kind of creative drive I have. So when I'm riding on the train or whatever, and I see a beautiful woman, I don't do anything, but I just watch, and let my imagination come up with various scenarios.

ODA: So you make your romantic stories through imagination? Not personal experience?

KUBONOUCHI: If I based it on personal experience, my story would be over in three volumes. [*laughs*] Basically, I just imagine, if that were my younger self in that situation, what would I have done? Let's say that I spot a girl and a boy walking together. And the boy's just a little bit ahead, and she's holding on to the sleeve of his shirt. That's enough to make me think about the story. Like, what's going on there? Did she start holding his sleeve from the beginning? Or is she holding the sleeve because she's not able to hold his hand yet? I'll envision different scenarios and romanticize them in my mind like a weirdo in the corner. [*laughs*]

ODA: My staff wanted to help once, and asked, “Why can't we draw the snow?” So I tested them and said, “Go on and draw it, then.” But it was still different than what I wanted to express. So I was like, “See the difference?” and they said, “Oh, I get it now...”

KUBONOUCHI: Exactly. That's the dilemma.

ODA: And depending on the individual panel, the way the snow or rain is falling might depend on how I'm feeling at that moment, or has to reflect the way the characters are feeling. It's a subtle thing. Maybe most of the readers wouldn't even notice it...

KUBONOUCHI: No, they will, they will! I'm sure they do.

ODA: Do you think so?

KUBONOUCHI: I was that way too. I'd let them draw the minimum necessary amount of background detail, but then I'd go in and smudge it up, draw extra shadows, and so on.

ODA: Your are very particular about the backgrounds.

KUBONOUCHI: I did all of the moving parts myself. And when I had my assistants do the speed lines, and it wasn't right, I'd just do that myself too. I wanted to do as much of it as possible, so when I saw the volumes of *One Piece*, I knew, “Oh, man, Oda's going through so much trouble to do this.” I can't believe you've done this weekly for twenty years.

ODA: That's right. It's a ton of work, but I told the readers, “I draw everything that moves, even the snow and rain,” so I can't break that promise now.

KUBONOUCHI: Oh, it's a promise, is it? [*laughs*]

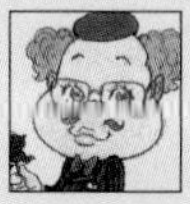

“I usually put those situations into the story by imagining, what would I be doing if that were me?”

KUBONOUCHI

KUBONOUCHI: I think so.

ODA: And that's got to be difficult when you're talking about characters with skeletal structures that have no precedent.

KUBONOUCHI: My art looks like it would be easy to mimic, but from what people tell me, it's surprisingly hard. Outside of these commercials, I've done character design on anime a number of times before, and it always causes trouble for the animators.

ODA: In what way?

KUBONOUCHI: Let's see. I have a unique way of using the lines themselves, and I use a lot of negative space. Apparently you can't really do the same thing with anime.

ODA: I see. So there are manga techniques you can't use in anime...

KUBONOUCHI: In anime you can't really vary the line weight the same way. Also, lots of animators don't actually sketch out the facial structure and stuff first. In my case, I'm envisioning that before I draw, so differences often arise from that. When you're doing distorting poses like looking up or looking down, there's a difference between people who can sketch skeletal structure and those who can't. I think that's a big part of it.

KUBONOUCHI: I've been thinking all along as I read the volumes of *One Piece* that you must put a lot of work into that.

ODA: I draw everything that moves.

KUBONOUCHI: Even the little things in the backgrounds, and the smudges, and so on?

ODA: That's right. Things that affect the presentation affect the story, so if I had someone else doing the movement of the wind or the angle of the snow, it's going to turn into something a bit different than what I'm thinking of.

KUBONOUCHI: Because it *will* be different.

KUBONOUCHI: I think your line work has incredible flavor to it. There are shapes that might feel incredibly out-of-date if they were drawn just the tiniest bit differently, but you bring them such a zest. I've felt that many times while using your art as a reference for these commercials. I think you've incorporated some more extreme styles from past generations that kids these days aren't familiar with, and it allows you to produce all of these varied characters that are still unified by the "Oda touch." It's why it feels so cohesive overall. You have characters with such distinct and different visual values when you distill them down, and yet you can have them all in the same image and none of them feel out of place. That's how strong your style is.

ODA: Thank you. I will say that cohesiveness is something I'm very conscious about. I wonder about how other artists handle different-looking characters. In a manga sense, it's more fun to have a wild and wacky variety, but I'm really careful not to ever come away thinking, "This is a character that came out of a different manga." Although I don't consciously know how exactly I'm doing that adjustment.

KUBONOUCHI: So then you're probably doing it unconsciously.

ODA: You suppose? I do adjust the balance of the character until I feel like they fit.

KUBONOUCHI: Whether consciously or not, you have the ability to do it. So you can have a new character next to an old character, and there are no weird discrepancies between them. Because whatever rules you have that govern your style have been consistent throughout. I bet your readers intuitively pick up on that. It's the flavor the series has. I think *One Piece* is remarkably well done in that respect.

ODA: Thank you. As for you, I feel like you've got a kind of painterly sense to you, but I don't know where it comes from. Would you say you're influenced by pop art?

KUBONOUCHI: Oh, yes. I've been influenced by that stuff since I was young. But I also love *ukiyo-e*.

ODA: Really? You do?

KUBONOUCHI: I just love Hokusai Katsushika[4] and Hiroshige Utagawa[5].

ODA: I'm surprised by that. But it's definitely true that they're incredible.

KUBONOUCHI: I especially love Hiroshige, and the way he constructs his visuals is actually very pop for the time. Hokusai is more the type who wants to overwhelm you and blow you away, but Hiroshige's very gentle, very pop, very fashionable.

ODA: When I read other manga or watch movies, I don't cry. It's really difficult to cry. So I can't submit a chapter until I'm able to get myself into the headspace to cry, for whatever the reason—even if it's just because I'm exhausted from lack of sleep. If I can't make myself cry, how can I expect the readers to? I'll think, "There's still something missing," and keep redrawing it.

KUBONOUCHI: That's phenomenal.

ODA: When I have a really great image in my mind, but it's just not coming together right on the page, that's when I really spend time on the storyboards. That's the real hump. Once I've got my storyboards, I only have to draw them. I'm pretty confident in how quickly I draw, so even if there's no time, I'll say, "No, I can make it." It's coming up with the story stuff that's the tough part. I'm not necessarily waiting for inspiration to strike—but it does take time.

KUBONOUCHI: I think I and many other artists are the same way, in that we think, if we're crying as we draw, so will the readers. There's a way that we share emotions through paper and art, and if you're just drawing on the surface level, they'll see through it. If you're thinking, "Oh, this'll make 'em weep," they won't care. Instead, they'll cry if you're thinking, "This is where *I'll* cry!!" And when you're thinking, "This is so funny!" that's when they'll crack up. It all comes down to how much you're lying to the paper in front of you. I think not lying to your art and your manga is the most fundamental tool for success in this business.

ODA: I get that.

KUBONOUCHI: It's really incredible. I could feel just what kind of emotion you were using to draw these big character moments, just from the touch of your pen. It's why I had to work so hard to capture it.

ODA: Thank you very much. I'm glad to hear that.

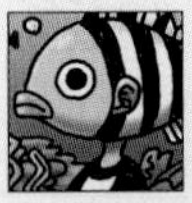

"I think you've got a universal style that never gets old."
ODA

KUBONOUCHI: I'd say that you've got a taste that's been built up since your early childhood, that manifests in these kinds of old-fashioned physical forms and silhouettes that are scattered among all the many characters you create, and they all add up into one cohesive visual design and style that is entirely yours.

ODA: Thank you.

KUBONOUCHI: Do you use a G-pen to ink your pages?

ODA: Yes, G-pen.

KUBONOUCHI: You've got a particular feel with it.

ODA: Do I? I wouldn't really know.

ODA: While I was reading *Tsurumoku Bachelors' Dorm*, I was thinking to myself, the romantic balance of all the characters is so incredible. You can manipulate this character in this way and have them fall in love. And it's so natural, and doesn't feel cynical. I thought, "How does someone so young write this so well?"

KUBONOUCHI: At the time, I was just twenty-two or twenty-three. It basically just comes down to love for the characters. Even when I created characters with a kind of twisted sense of love, like Reiko Shiratorizawa[3]...

ODA: It's amazing that even her journey feels earned.

KUBONOUCHI: For her, well, this was back in the days of the economic bubble in Japan, and I saw a girl like her at a pub.

ODA: Really! [*laughs*]

KUBONOUCHI: Yes. This was a really long time ago. I heard someone going on and on, saying, "The thing about love is," in the way that all the characters talked in the youthful romantic dramas that were popular at the time. I looked over and saw this girl who had a really distinctive facial shape, and I thought, "*You're* the love expert?" Back then, I thought the attitudes in the bubble period were really distasteful, so Reiko Shiratorizawa was a kind of ironic response to that. But the more I drew her, the more I thought, "Actually, she's kind of sweet." And I realized that if I treated her like a weirdo and gave her a misfortunate ending, it would be leaving the readers with a bad aftertaste. So partway through the story, I thought, "I have to give her a happy ending." I knew I was going to pair her up with Sugimoto, the handsome guy.

ODA: So you were figuring it out as you went.

KUBONOUCHI: I tinkered with the finer details as I went, to make sure it led to the scene I wanted in the end.

ODA: I think a normal artist would think, this character's a joke, they can only ever be a joke. But you managed to give her a real, fulfilling romance that the readers can appreciate and accept! You can only do that if you have real love for your characters.

KUBONOUCHI: Yes, exactly. It all comes down to loving your characters. I think it's the same way for you too. When I see your scenes that have a real emotional punch to them, I think, "Oh, he must have been crying as he drew this."

ODA: I cry when I draw them.

KUBONOUCHI: I knew it. You can really feel it. Like in the scene when Robin's crying.

> “If we’re crying as we draw, so will the readers. There’s a way that we share emotions through art, and if you’re just drawing on the surface level, they’ll see through it.”

EISAKU KUBONOUCHI

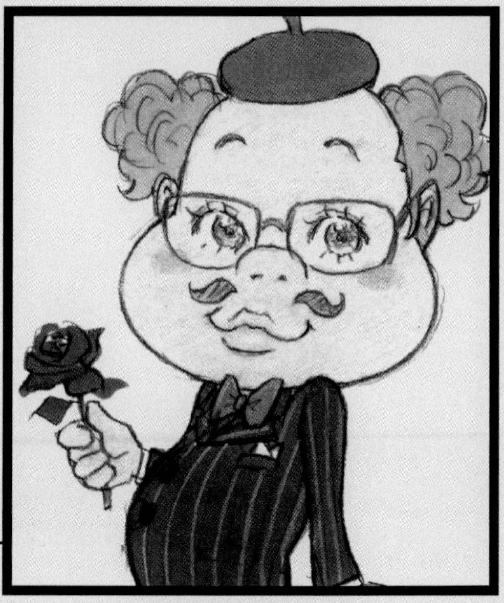

PROFILE: His most famous manga series, *Tsurumoku Bachelors’ Dorm* and *Chocolat*, are beloved worldwide, with international translations and film/live action adaptations. Currently works primarily in illustration and design. His beautiful and lively characters, typically drawn with color pencils and markers, have captured the hearts of readers of all ages, but especially young women.

ODA: It’s really impressive to me that you can look at art that old and describe it as “pop.” I’ve never seen things that way, although I will get blown away, of course. I went to a Hiroshige exhibit once, and I was actually a little crushed on the way home. He was just too good.

KUBONOUCHI: Yes. That linework is immaculate. In that sense, I think he’s in exclusive territory on a worldwide level.

ODA: But you saw it as pop art and didn’t feel crushed by his skill. I suppose that’s just the eye that you have for it.

KUBONOUCHI: Go back and look at *The Fifty-Three Stations of the Tokaido*. It’s so pop.

ODA: Really? [*laughs*] Your sense for artwork is really something else, Kubonouchi Sensei. *Tsurumoku Bachelors’ Dorm* might be an old manga by this point, but it’s still well worth reading now. I think you’ve got a universal style that never gets old.

KUBONOUCHI: Thank you.

ODA: I think that’s how you still resonate with young people today at your age. You’ve got a timeless sense of artistry.

KUBONOUCHI: Thank you. Wow, I’m so embarrassed. [*laughs*]

KUBONOUCHI: Well...this was really great, getting to sit down and talk with you like this. One of my oldest friends is a stylist, and they’ve been reading *Weekly Shonen Jump* for forever. About 20 years ago, they said to me, “You should see this new series, *One Piece*, it’s just fantastic.” I still remember that. Normally I’d just shrug it off and forget about it, but I still remember that conversation today.

ODA: The things people say are important. The things that travel furthest are the words of your friends.

KUBONOUCHI: That’s true. Sometimes the most casual words from someone close to you have the greatest element of truth to them. I’ve heard so many great stories today, now I can go back home to the country and brag to my friend about them. [*laughs*] I’m sure they’ll be very excited.

ODA: Thank you. I had fun, too.

FOOTNOTES

1. *Tsurumoku Bachelors’ Dorm* is a manga by Eisaku Kubonouchi that ran in *Big Comic Spirits* (published by Shogakukan) from 1988–1991. It’s a romantic comedy about Shota Miyagawa, a new employee at Tsurumoku Furniture, and the other residents of the bachelors’ dorm he lives in. A live action movie was made in 1991.

2. *Tetsujin 28* (*Gigantor*) is a robot that appears in the *Tetsujin 28* manga series by Mitsuteru Yokoyama, which ran from 1956–1966. The protagonist Shotaro Kaneda manipulates a robot via remote control. The story was turned into an animated TV series, a tokusatsu TV series, and an animated movie.

3. Reiko Shiratorizawa is the daughter of the Shiratorizawa Conglomerate in *Tsurumoku Bachelors’ Dorm*. She has a sultry manner but an extremely bizarre face, and often shows up in unexpected situations to drag away the handsome Sugimoto, the object of her affections.

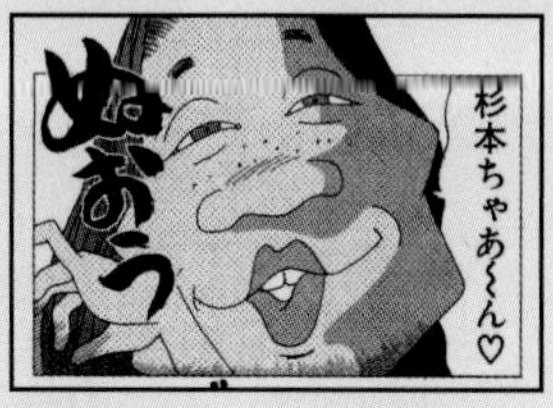
杉本ちゃあ～ん♡

4. Katsushika Hokusai was an ukiyo-e painter representative of the arts in the late Edo period. He is renowned worldwide for his many famous works, such as *Thirty-Six Views of Mount Fuji* and *Hokusai Manga*. He was an eager and prolific artist who created over thirty thousand works in his life. His influence on later artists was profound.

5. Utagawa Hiroshige was an ukiyo-e artist at the end of the Edo period. His most famous works are *The Fifty-Three Stations of the Tokaido* and *One Hundred Famous Views of Edo*. He was especially known for his woodblock depictions of nature. His pieces were prized in Europe, and very influential to painters like Van Gogh and Monet.

One Piece official website - https://one-piece.com

INDEX

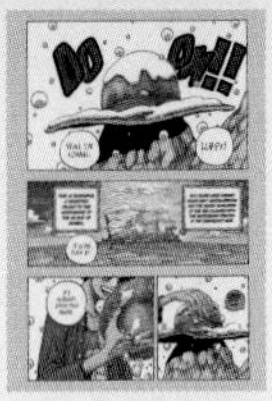
Page 5: *Weekly Shonen Jump*, 2010, Issue 44

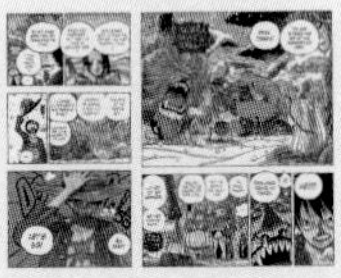
Page 6: *Weekly Shonen Jump*, 2010, Issue 44

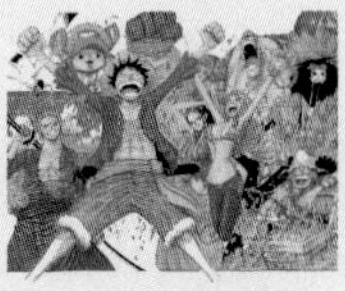
Page 9: *Weekly Shonen Jump*, 2010, Issue 44

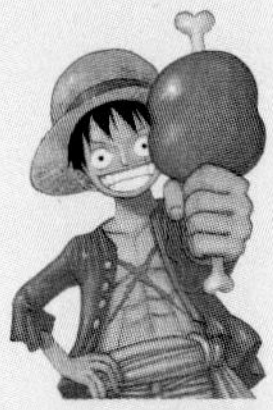
Page 10: *Weekly Shonen Jump*, 2011, Combined Issues 3 & 4 Cover

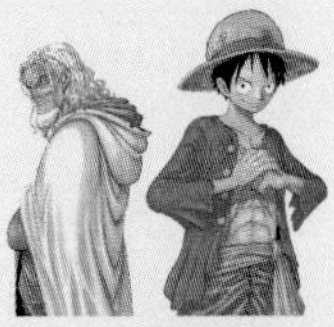
Page 11: *Weekly Shonen Jump*, 2010, Issue 44 Cover

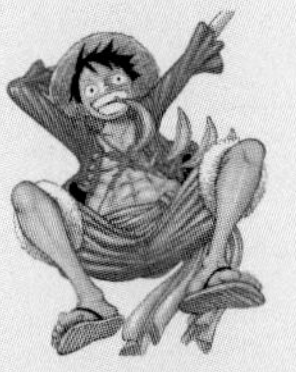
Page 12: *Weekly Shonen Jump*, 2010, Issue 50 Cover

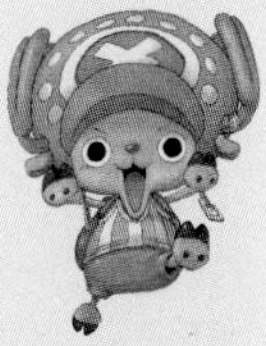
Page 13: *Weekly Shonen Jump* Special Extra Publication *Saikyo Jump* Cover

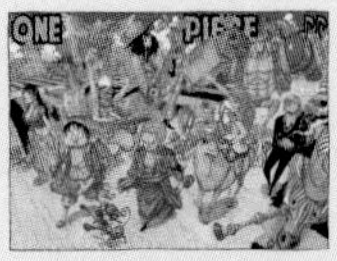
Page 14: *Weekly Shonen Jump*, 2010, Issue 50

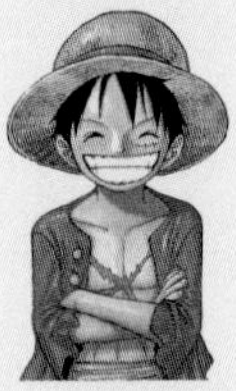
Page 16: *Weekly Shonen Jump*, 2011, Combined Issues 20 & 21 Cover

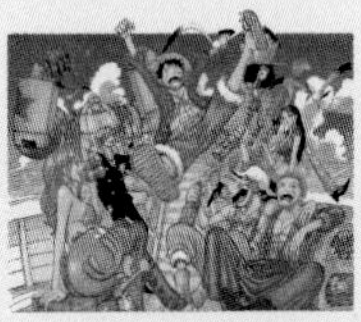
Page 17: Graphic Novel Volume 61 Cover

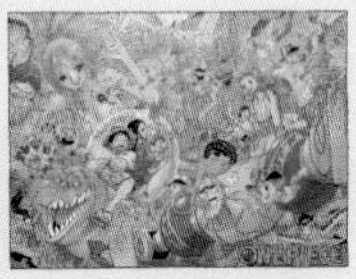
Page 18: *Weekly Shonen Jump*, 2011, Combined Issues 35 & 36

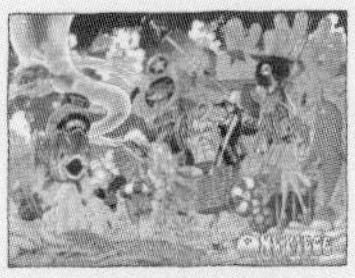
Page 20: *Weekly Shonen Jump*, 2011, Issue 45

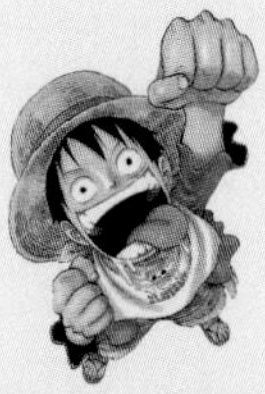
Page 22: *Weekly Shonen Jump*, 2011, Issue 45 Cover

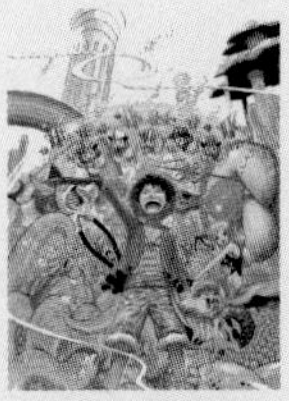
Page 23: Graphic Novel Volume 62 Cover

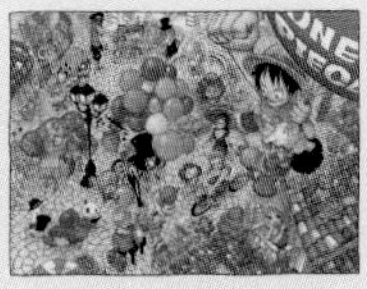
Page 24: *Weekly Shonen Jump*, 2011, Issue 16

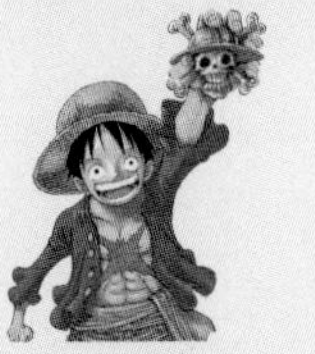
Page 26: *Weekly Shonen Jump*, 2012, Combined Issues 3 & 4 Cover

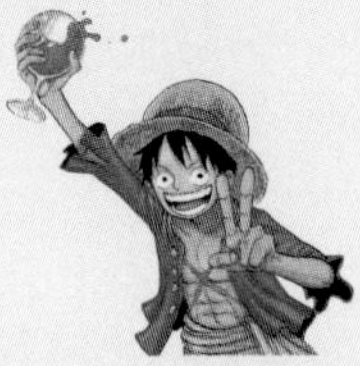
Page 26: *Weekly Shonen Jump*, 2011, Issue 17, "Eat an Actual Devil Fruit!!"

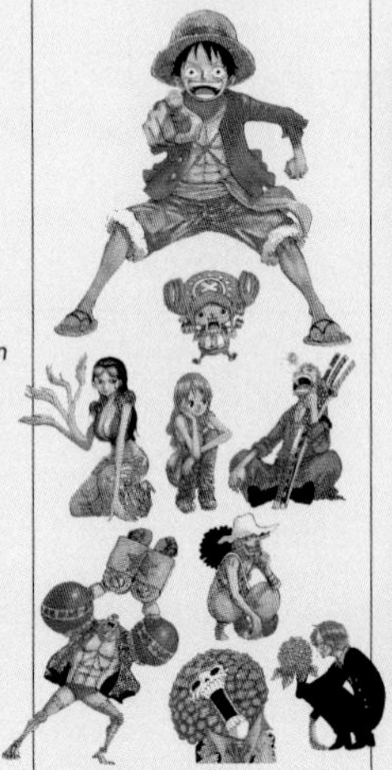
Page 27: *Weekly Shonen Jump*, 2011, Issue 25 Cover

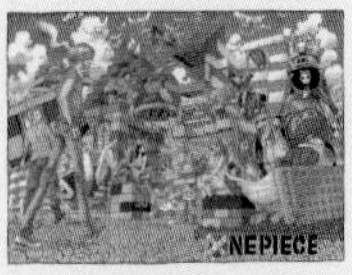
Page 28: *Weekly Shonen Jump*, 2011, Combined Issues 20 & 21

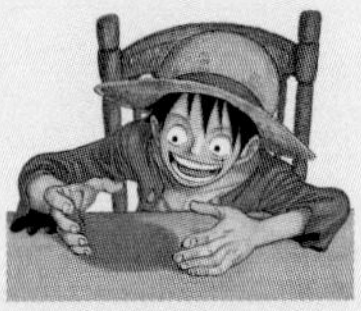
Page 30: *Weekly Shonen Jump*, 2011, Issue 9 Cover

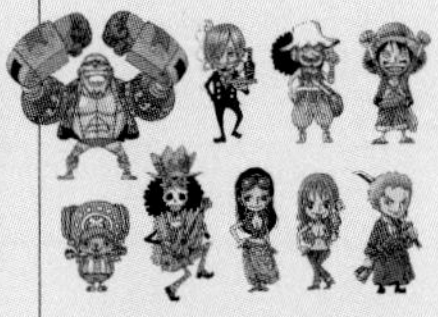
Page 30: *Weekly Shonen Jump*, 2011, Issue 9, Straw Hats Together!! *Thousand Sunny* Premium Papercraft

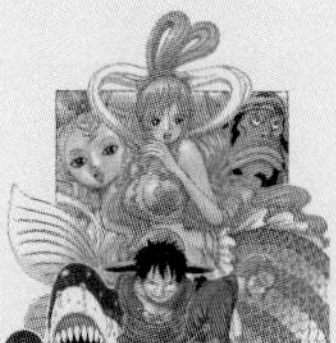
Page 31: Graphic Novel Volume 63 Cover

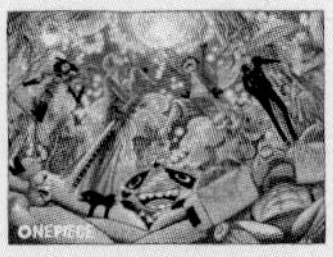
Page 32: *Weekly Shonen Jump*, 2011, Combined Issues 5 & 6

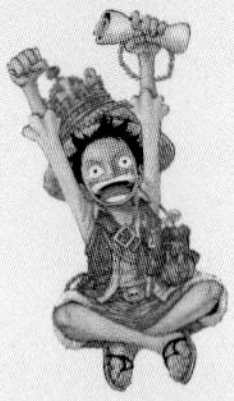
Page 34: *Weekly Shonen Jump*, 2011, Combined Issues 35 & 36 Cover

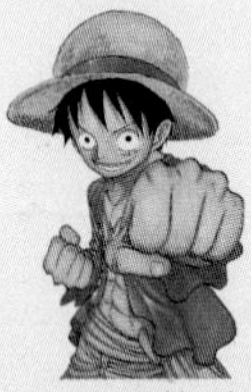
Page 34: *Weekly Shonen Jump*, 2011, Combined Issues 5 & 6 Cover

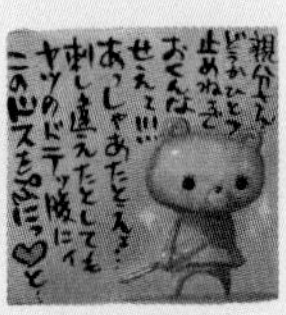
Page 34: Graphic Novel Volume 61 Artist Illustration

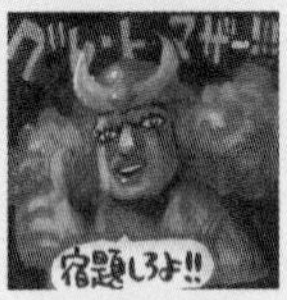
Page 34: Graphic Novel Volume 62 Artist Illustration

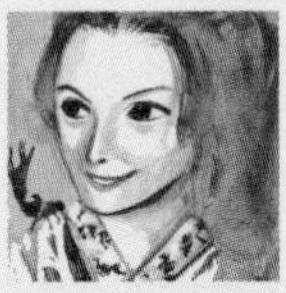
Page 34: Graphic Novel Volume 63 Artist Illustration

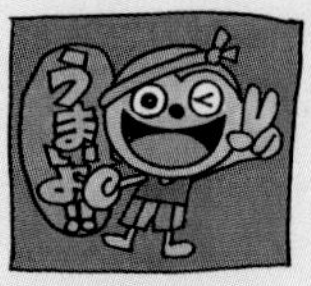
Page 34: Graphic Novel Volume 64 Artist Illustration

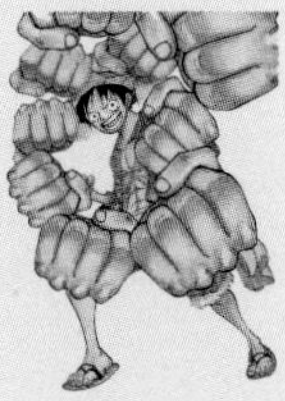
Page 35: *Weekly Shonen Jump*, 2011, Issue 16 Cover

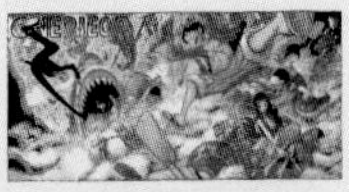
Page 36: *Weekly Shonen Jump*, 2011, Issue 9

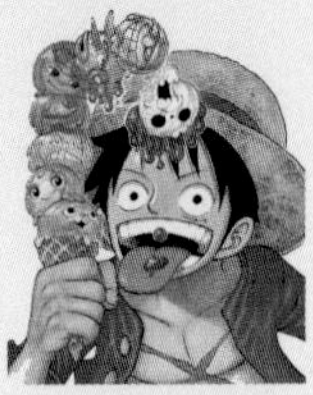
Page 38: *Weekly Shonen Jump*, 2011, Issue 28 Cover

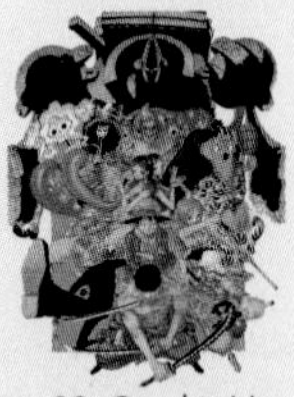
Page 39: Graphic Novel *Volume 64* Cover

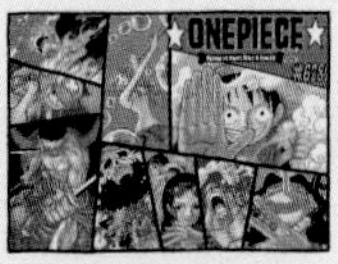
Page 40: *Weekly Shonen Jump*, 2011, Issue 28

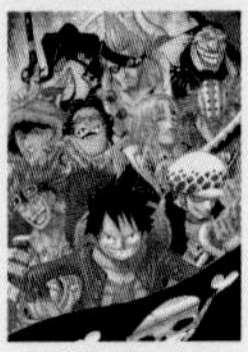
Page 42: *Weekly Shonen Jump*, *2011*, Issue 41, Catchphrase Grand Prix

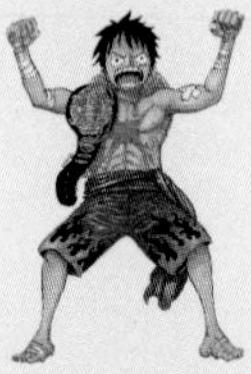
Page 49: *Weekly Shonen Jump*, 2012, Combined Issues 21 & 22 Cover

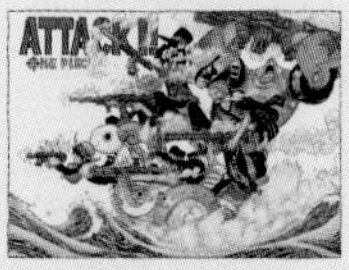
Page 50: *Weekly Shonen Jump*, 2012, Combined Issues 21 & 22

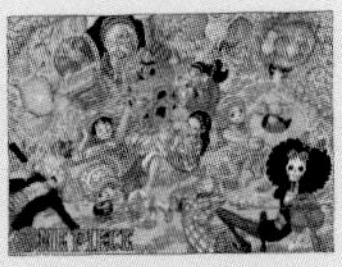
Page 52: *Weekly Shonen Jump*, 2012, Issue 16

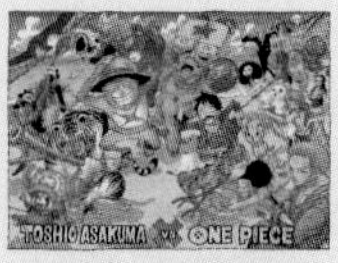
Page 54: *Weekly Shonen Jump*, 2012, Combined Issues 5 & 6

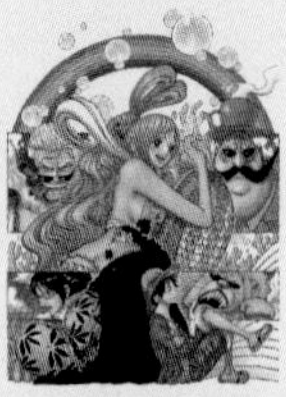
Page 56: Graphic Novel Volume 66 Cover

Page 57: Graphic Novel Volume 65 Cover

Page 58: *Weekly Shonen Jump*, 2012, Issue 47

Page 60: *Weekly Shonen Jump*, 2012, Combined Issues 36 & 37

Page 62: Graphic Novel Volume 67 Cover

Page 63: Graphic Novel Volume 68 Cover

Page 64: *Weekly Shonen Jump*, 2013, Issue 3

Page 94: *Saikyo Jump*, 2012, January Issue

Page 94: Wish Mark Bookmark

Page 95: *Katsura Taizen* © Masakazu Katsura

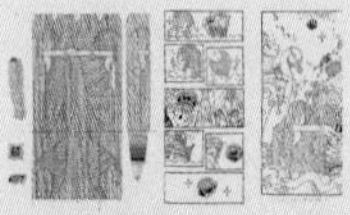

Page 96: *New York Times* and *China Times* Newspaper Advertisements

Page 98: *Takuya Kimura & Men's Non-No Endless*

Page 93: *Jirocho Sangoku-shi Collection 1* DVD Package

Page 93: *Jirocho Sangoku-shi Collection 2* DVD Package

Page 93: *Jirocho Sangoku-shi Collection 3* DVD Package

Page 94: S. T. Dupont *Sleeping Mermaid Collection*

Page 94: *Weekly Shonen Jump*, 2013, Issue 17

Page 87: *Eiichiro Oda Presents: One Piece Ten Gallery x Video x Experience* Osaka Location Main Visual

Page 89: *Eiichiro Oda Presents: One Piece Ten Gallery x Video x Experience*

Page 89: *Eiichiro Oda Presents: One Piece Ten Gallery x Video x Experience* Taiwan Location Main Visual

Page 90: *Eiichiro Oda Presents: One Piece Ten Gallery x Video x Experience*

Page 92: Jump Festa 2013

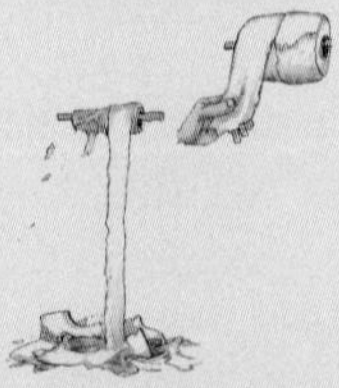

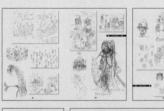

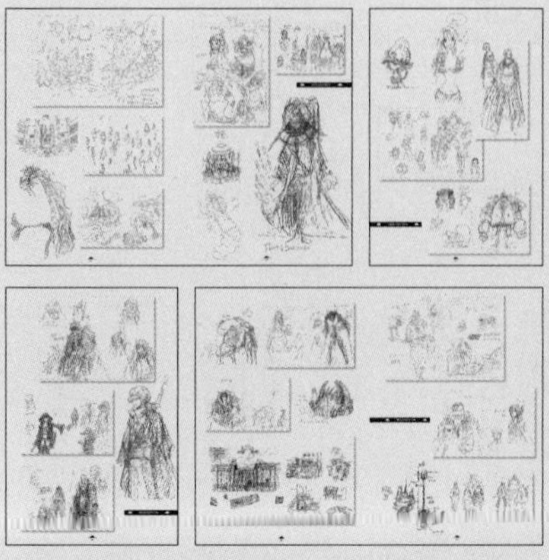

Pages 43-48: A selection of Mr. Oda's concept sketches.

Front Poster: *Weekly Shonen Jump*, 2013, Issue 2

Page 78: *Weekly Shonen Jump*, 2013, Issue 13

Page 80: Graphic Novel *Volume 1000* Golden Treasure Chest

Page 81: *One Piece Film Z* Poster

Page 82: *One Piece Film Z* Theatrical Bonus, *One Piece Film Adventure Island Dice* Game

Page 83: *One Piece Film: Z* Poster

Page 84: *Weekly Shonen Jump*, 2013, Issue 3 Cover

Page 85: *Weekly Shonen Jump*, 2013, Issue 2 Cover

Page 86: *Eiichiro Oda Presents: One Piece Ten Gallery x Video x Experience* Tokyo Location Main Visual

Page 70: *Weekly Shonen Jump*, 2013, Combined Issues 4 & 5

Page 72: *Weekly Shonen Jump*, 2013, Combined Issues 4 & 5 Cover

Page 73: *Weekly Shonen Jump*, 2013, Combined Issues 6 & 7 Cover

Page 74: Graphic Novel Volume 69 Cover

Page 75: Graphic Novel Volume 70 Cover

Page 76: Graphic Novel Volume 69 Artist Illustration

Page 76: Graphic Novel Volume 70 Artist Illustration

Page 77: *Weekly Shonen Jump*, 2013, Issue 13

Page 66: *One Piece: Pirate Recipes* Cover

Page 68: Graphic Novel Volume 65 Artist Illustration

Page 68: Graphic Novel Volume 66 Artist Illustration

Page 68: Graphic Novel Volume 67 Artist Illustration

Page 68: Graphic Novel Volume 68 Artist Illustration

Page 68: Graphic Novel Volume 1000 Artist Illustration

Page 68: *Weekly Shonen Jump*, 2012, Combined Issues 5 & 6 Cover

Page 69: *Weekly Shonen Jump*, 2012, Issue 47 Cover

Page 142: *Weekly Shonen Jump*, 2015, Combined Issues 4 & 5

Page 134: Crossing Japan! OPJ47 Cruise Local T-Shirt Reader Vote Contest

Page 123: *Jump Next*, Spring 2013 Issue Cover

Page 118: *Weekly Shonen Jump*, 2013, Combined Issues 22 & 23 Cover

Page 111: Graphic Novel Volume 72 Cover

Page 144: *Weekly Shonen Jump*, 2015, Combined Issues 4 & 5 Cover

Page 134: *Weekly Shonen Jump*, 2014, Combined Issues 37 & 38 Cover

Page 124: *Weekly Shonen Jump*, 2013, Issue 28

Page 118: *Weekly Shonen Jump*, 2013, Combined Issues 22 & 23

Page 112: *Weekly Shonen Jump*, 2013, Combined Issues 37 & 38

Page 101: *Weekly Shonen Jump*, 2013, Issue 33 Cover

Page 144: Graphic Novel Volume 73 Artist Illustration

Page 135: Graphic Novel Volume 75 Cover

Page 126: *Weekly Shonen Jump*, 2014, Issue 16 Cover

Page 119: *Weekly Shonen Jump*, 2013, Issue 49 Cover

Page 114: *Weekly Shonen Jump*, 2014, Combined Issues 4 & 5, Jump Stars Christmas!!

Page 102: *Weekly Shonen Jump*, 2013, Issue 49

Page 144: Graphic Novel Volume 74 Artist Illustration

Page 136: *Weekly Shonen Jump*, 2014, Combined Issues 22 & 23

Page 127: Graphic Novel Volume 73 Cover

Page 114: Graphic Novel Volume 71 Artist Illustration

Page 104: *Weekly Shonen Jump*, 2013, Combined Issues 22 & 23

Page 144: Graphic Novel Volume 75 Artist Illustration

Page 138: *Weekly Shonen Jump*, 2014, Issue 47

Page 128: *Weekly Shonen Jump*, 2014, Combined Issues 6 & 7

Page 114: Graphic Novel Volume 72 Artist Illustration

Page 106: *Weekly Shonen Jump*, 2013, Issue 18 Cover

Page 144: Graphic Novel Volume 76 Artist Illustration

Page 140: *Weekly Shonen Jump*, 2014, Combined Issues 6 & 7 Cover

Page 130: *Weekly Shonen Jump*, 2014, Issue 30 Cover

Page 120: *Weekly Shonen Jump*, 2013, Issue 46 Cover

Page 114: Crossing Japan! OPJ47 Cruise Bookstore Promotion

Page 107: Graphic Novel Volume 71 Cover

Page 144: *Weekly Shonen Jump*, 2014, Issue 19 Cover

Page 140: *Weekly Shonen Jump*, 2014, Combined Issues 22 & 23 Cover

Page 131: Graphic Novel Volume 74 Cover

Page 122: *Weekly Shonen Jump*, 2014, Combined Issues 4 & 5 Cover

Page 115: *Weekly Shonen Jump*, 2013, Combined Issues 37 & 38 Cover

Page 108: *Weekly Shonen Jump*, 2013, Issue 18

Page 145: *Weekly Shonen Jump*, 2014, Issue 47 Cover

Page 141: Graphic Novel Volume 76 Cover

Page 132: *Weekly Shonen Jump*, 2014, Issue 16

Page 122: *Jump LIVE*, "Lub-Dub ★ Sexy Summer Swimsuits

Page 116: *Weekly Shonen Jump*, 2013, Issue 46

Page 110: *Weekly Shonen Jump*, 2013, Issue 28 Cover

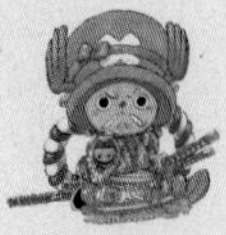

Page 193: *Super Kabuki II: One Piece*

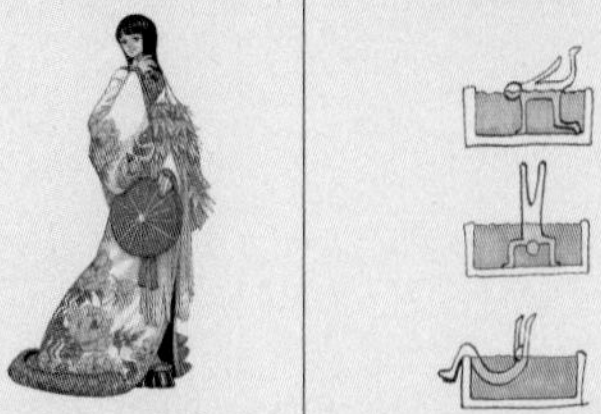

Page 194: *Super Kabuki II: One Piece*

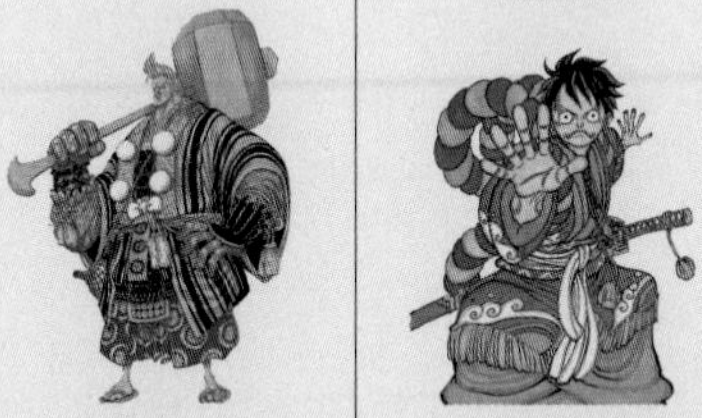

Page 195: *Super Kabuki II: One Piece*

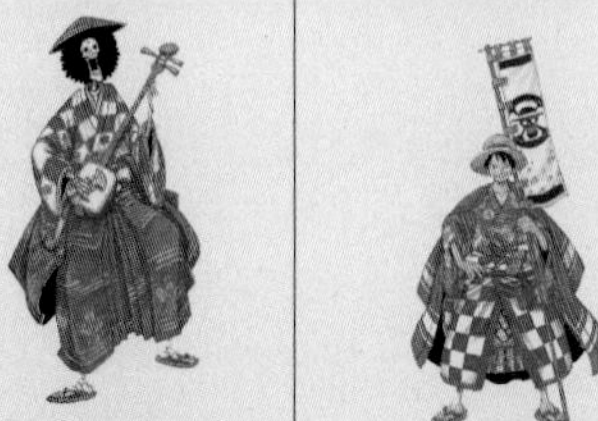

Page 196: *Super Kabuki II: One Piece*

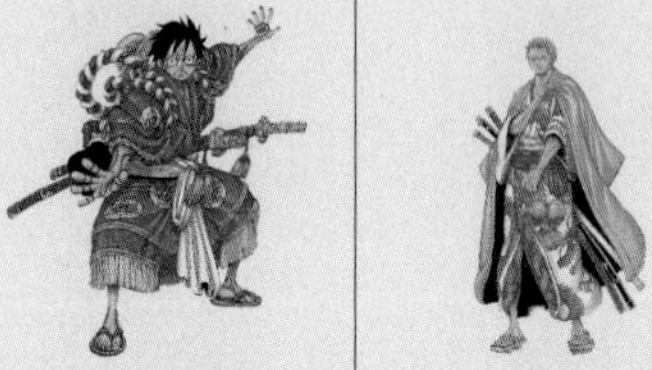

Page 197: *Super Kabuki II: One Piece*

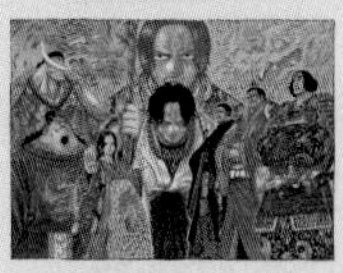

Page 198: *Super Kabuki II: One Piece*

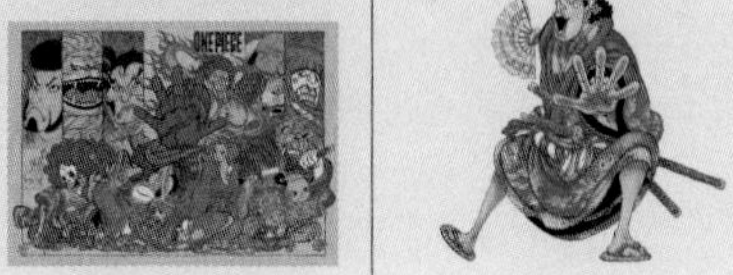

Page 200: *Weekly Shonen Jump*, 2016, Issue 18

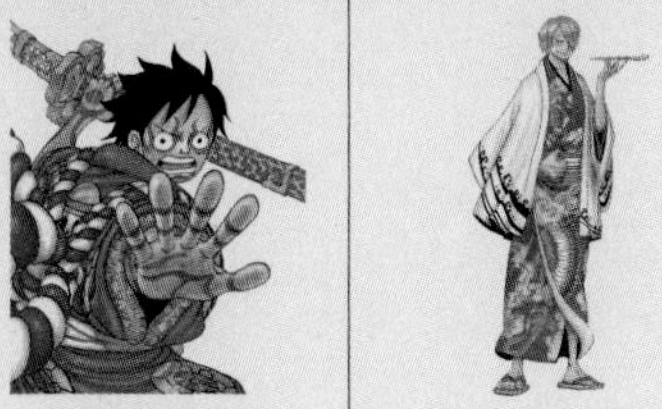

Page 202: *Weekly Shonen Jump*, 2015, Issue 45 Cover

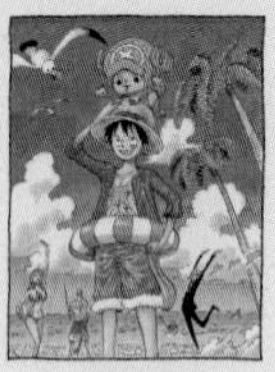

Page 186: *Jump-ryu! Vol. 3*, Eiichiro Oda Art Replica

Page 186: Graphic Novel Volume 81 Artist Illustration

Page 187: *Weekly Shonen Jump*, 2015, Combined Issues 6 & 7 Cover

Page 188: *Super Kabuki II: One Piece*

Page 189: *Super Kabuki II: One Piece*

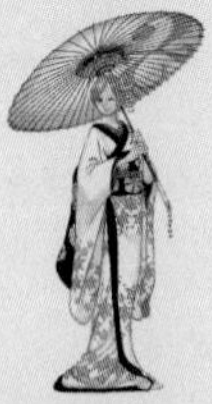

Page 190: *Super Kabuki II: One Piece*

Page 191: *Super Kabuki II: One Piece*

Page 192: *Super Kabuki II: One Piece*

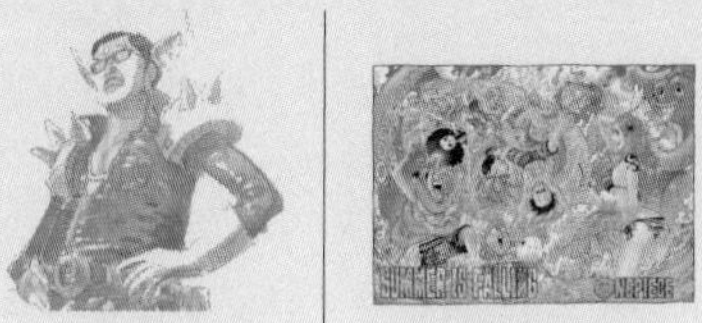

Page 178: Graphic Novel Volume 78 Artist Illustration

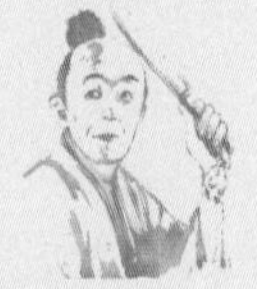

Page 178: Graphic Novel Volume 79 Artist Illustration

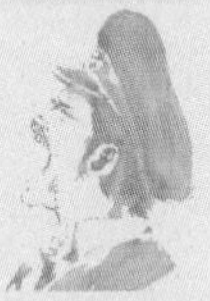

Page 178: Graphic Novel Volume 80 Artist Illustration

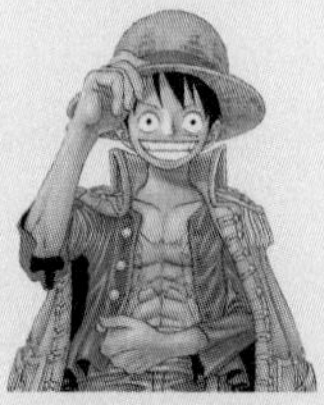

Page 179: *Weekly Shonen Jump*, 2015, Issue 30 Cover

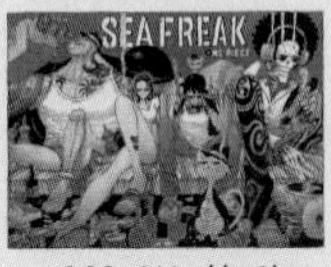
SEAFREAK

Page 180: *Weekly Shonen Jump*, 2016, Issue 1

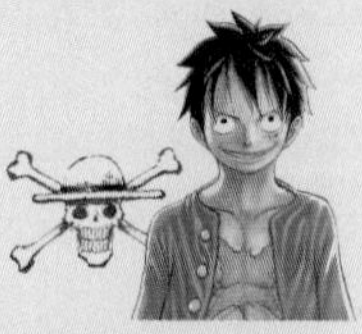

Page 182: *Weekly Shonen Jump*, 2016, Issue 13 Cover

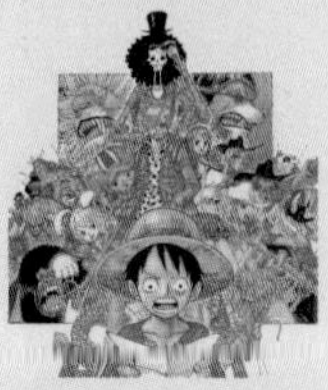

Page 183: Graphic Novel Volume 81 Cover

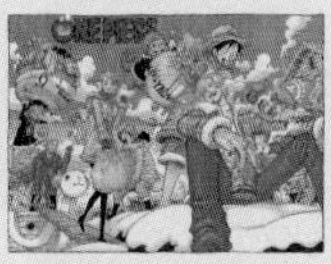

Page 184: *Weekly Shonen Jump*, 2016, Combined Issues 5 & 6

Page 168: *Weekly Shonen Jump*, 2015, Combined Issues 37 & 38

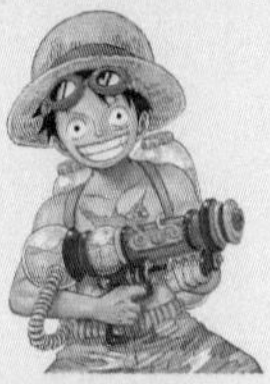

Page 170: *Weekly Shonen Jump*, 2015, Combined Issues 37 & 38 Cover

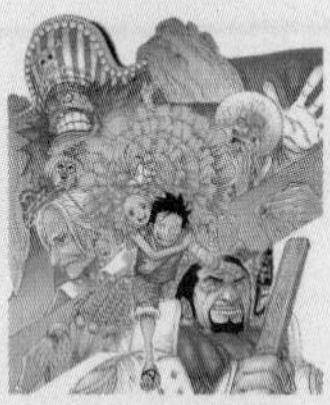

Page 171: Graphic Novel Volume 80 Cover

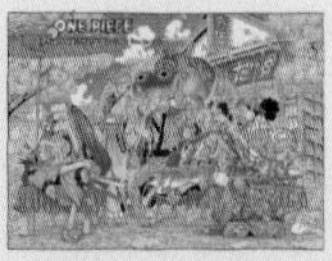

Page 172: *Weekly Shonen Jump*, 2015, Issue 45

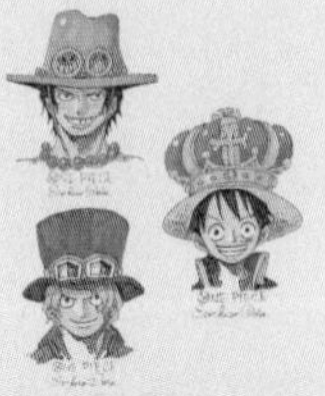

Page 174: Shueisha 2015 Summer Comiket Pins

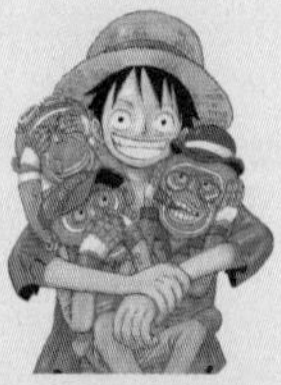

Page 175: *Weekly Shonen Jump*, 2016, Issue 1 Cover

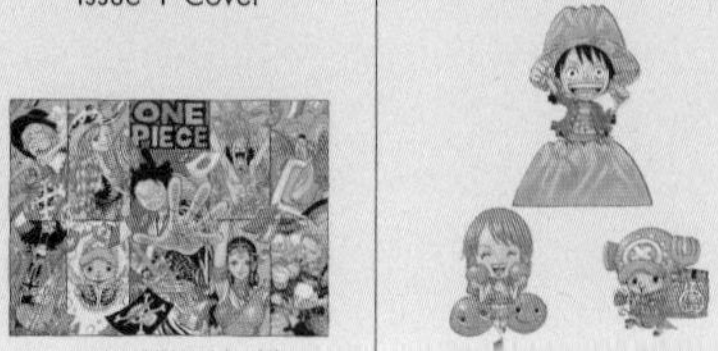
ONE PIECE

Page 176: *Weekly Shonen Jump*, 2015, Issue 30

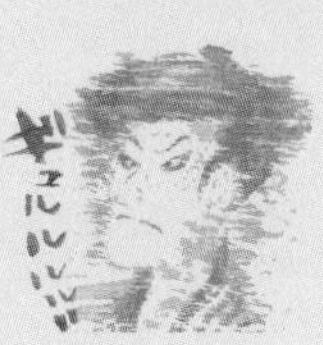

Page 178: Graphic Novel Volume 77 Artist Illustration

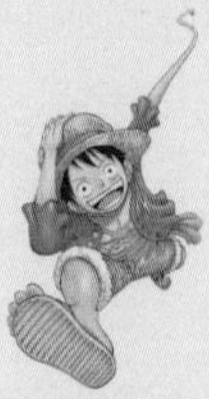

Page 160: *Weekly Shonen Jump*, 2015, Issue 15 Cover

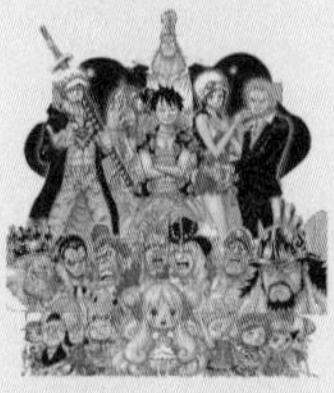

Page 161: Graphic Novel Volume 78 Cover

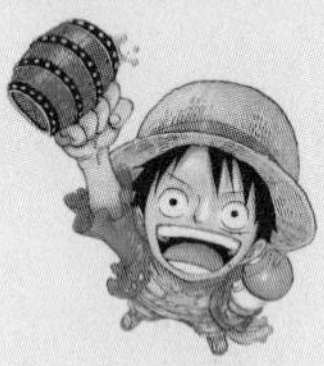

Page 162: *Weekly Shonen Jump*, 2015, Issue 19 Cover

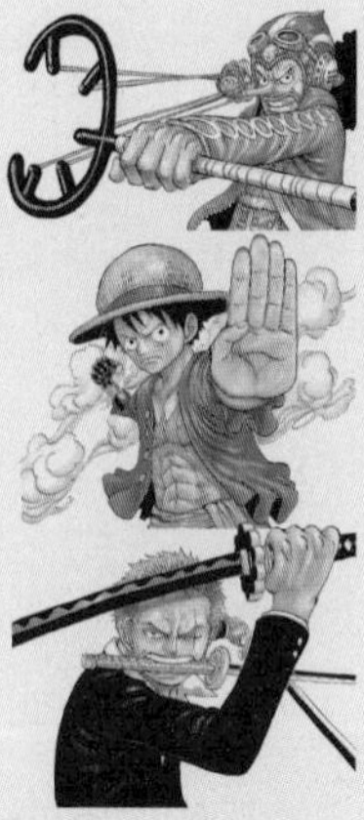

Page 163: *Weekly Shonen Jump*, 2015, Issue 10 Cover

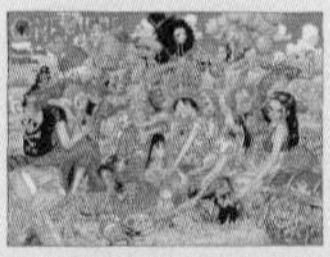

Page 164: *Weekly Shonen Jump*, 2015, Combined Issues 22 & 23

Page 166: *Weekly Shonen Jump*, 2015, Combined Issues 22 & 23, Deluxe Special Jump Map of Japan Poster

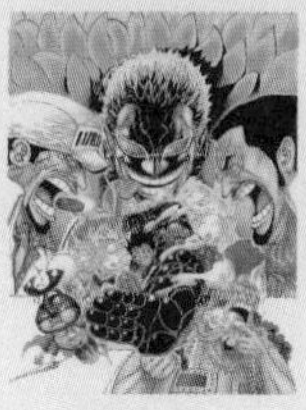

Page 167: Graphic Novel *Volume 79* Cover

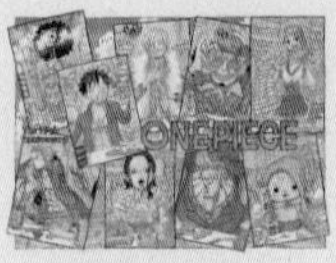

Page 146: *Weekly Shonen Jump*, 2014, Combined Issues 37 & 38

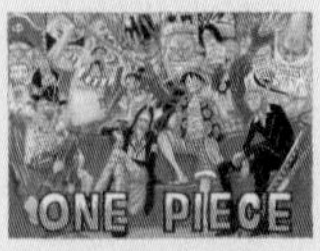
ONE PIECE

Page 148: *Weekly Shonen Jump*, 2014, Issue 30

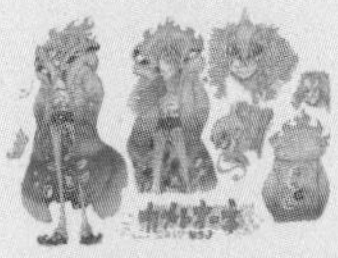

Page 150: *Universal Studios Japan One Piece Premier Show 2012*, Chameleone Design Sketches

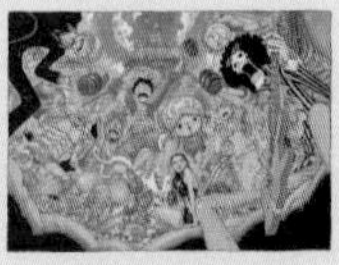

Page 152: *Tokyo One Piece Tower* Grand Opening Visual

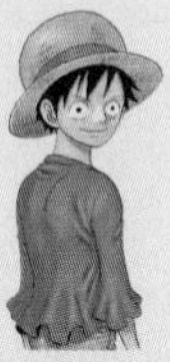

Page 154: *Weekly Shonen Jump*, 2015, Combined Issues 22 & 23 Cover

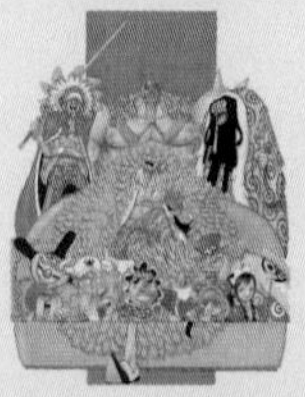

Page 155: Graphic Novel *Volume 77* Cover

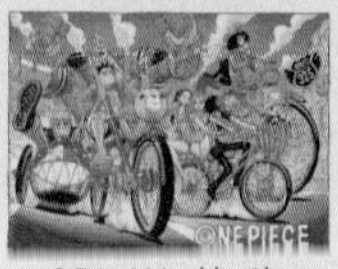

Page 156: *Weekly Shonen Jump*, 2015, Issue 10

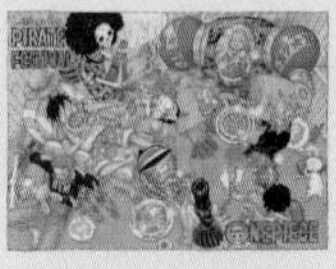

Page 158: *Weekly Shonen Jump*, 2015, Issue 15

INDEX CONT'D

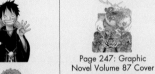

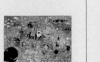

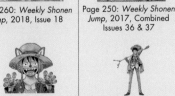

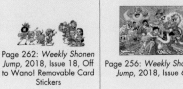

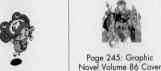

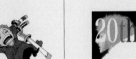

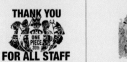

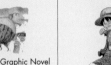

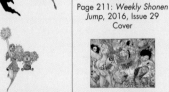

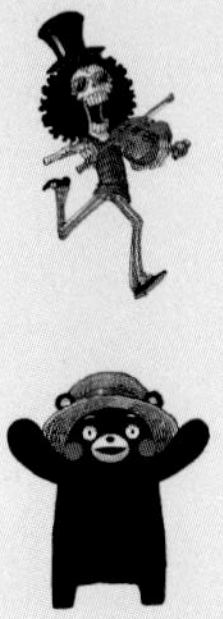

Page 302: *One Piece* Kumamoto Rebuilding Project

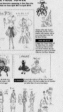

Page 304: *TGC Kumamoto 2019 by* Tokyo Girls Collection Special Collaboration Visual (*Weekly Shonen Jump*, 2019, Issue 47)

Page 306: *One Piece* Kumamoto Rebuilding Project Key Visual (*Weekly Shonen Jump*, 2016, Issue 47)

Pages 252–254/296–297: A selection from Mr. Oda's concept sketches.

Back Poster: *One Piece Magazine* Vol. 1, Vol. 2, Vol. 3 Poster

Page 295: *Weekly Shonen Jump*, 2016, Issue 34 Cover

SLOW AND STEADY!
SO YOU DON'T GET TIRED OUT!

Page 298: Graphic Novel Volume 82 Rear Cover

Page 299: Straw Hat Travels in Kyoto ~A Different Land of Wano~ Main Visual

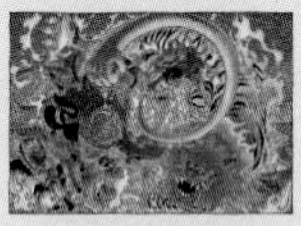

Page 300: Straw Hat Travels in Kyoto ~A Different Land of Wano~ Nue Exhibit

Page 302: *Weekly Shonen Jump*, 2016, Issue 52

Page 302: *One Piece* 20th Anniversary LINE x One Piece

Page 302: Message to New Adults, Kumamoto Prefecture 2018 Coming-of-Age Ceremony

Page 286: *Weekly Shonen Jump*, 2018, Issue 47 Cover

Page 287: *One Piece Film Gold* Poster (*Weekly Shonen Jump*, 2016, Issue 13)

Page 288: *Weekly Shonen Jump*, 2016, Issue 29

JOKER

Page 290: *One Piece Film Gold* Theatrical Giveaway All-Star Gold Cards

Page 291: *One Piece Film Gold* Theatrical Giveaway All-Star Gold Cards

GRAND TESORO

Page 292: *One Piece Film Gold* Theatrical Giveaway All-Star Gold Cards

ENTERTAINMENT
GOLD

Page 292: *One Piece Film Gold* Theatrical Giveaway 15 Cast Member Signed Card Illustration by Eiichiro Oda

Page 293: *Weekly Shonen Jump*, 2016, Issue 33 Cover

Page 294: *One Piece Film Gold* Theatrical Giveaway, *Volume 777*

Page 294: *One Piece Film Gold* Ticket Pre-order Bonus Casino Chips

Page 274: Graphic Novel Volume 91 Artist Illustration

Page 275: *Weekly Shonen Jump*, 2018, Issue 40 Cover

ONE PIECE

Page 276: *Weekly Shonen Jump*, 2018, Issue 33

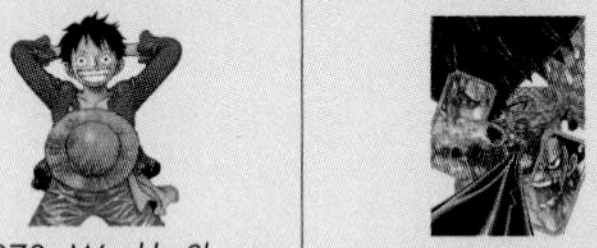

Page 278: *Weekly Shonen Jump*, 2018, Issue 34 Cover

Page 279: *Weekly Shonen Jump 50th Anniversary Exhibit*, Vol. 3

Page 280: *One Piece: Ace's Story*, Volume 1 & Volume 2 Cover

Page 282: *Weekly Shonen Jump*, 2019, Combined Issues 4 & 5 Cover

Page 282: *Weekly Shonen Jump*, 2019, Combined Issues 4 & 5, All-New Jump Character Holiday Special Collection

Page 283: *One Piece Magazine* Vol. 4, Dream Illustration

Page 284: *Weekly Shonen Jump*, 2018, Issue 18 Cover

Page 285: Graphic Novel Volume 91 Cover

Page 262: *Saikyo Jump*, 2018, May Issue Cover

Page 263: Graphic Novel Volume 88 Cover

Page 264: *Weekly Shonen Jump*, 2018, Combined Issues 36 & 37 Cover

Page 265: Graphic Novel Volume 89 Cover

Page 266: *Weekly Shonen Jump*, 2018, Combined Issues 21 & 22

Page 268: *Weekly Shonen Jump*, 2018, Issue 23 Cover

Page 269: Graphic Novel Volume 90 Cover

Page 270: *Weekly Shonen Jump*, 2018, Issue 40

Page 272: *Weekly Shonen Jump*, 2018, Issue 34

Page 274: *One Piece Magazine* Vol. 4 Cover

Page 274: Graphic Novel Volume 90 Artist Illustration

EIICHIRO ODA PROFILE

Born in Kumamoto City in Kumamoto Prefecture, Japan, on January 1st, 1975. In 1992, as a high school student, he applied to Shueisha *Weekly Shonen Jump*'s 44th Tezuka Awards and won the honorable mention prize with Wanted. In 1993, receives the secondary prize in the 104th Hop Step Award for *Ikki Yako*. After presenting numerous short story manga in Jump magazine, starts the serialization of *One Piece* in 1997, which continues to this day.

List of comic book publications:

One Piece serialized in *Shonen Jump Magazine*
One Piece Manga Editions
Color Walk Art Books

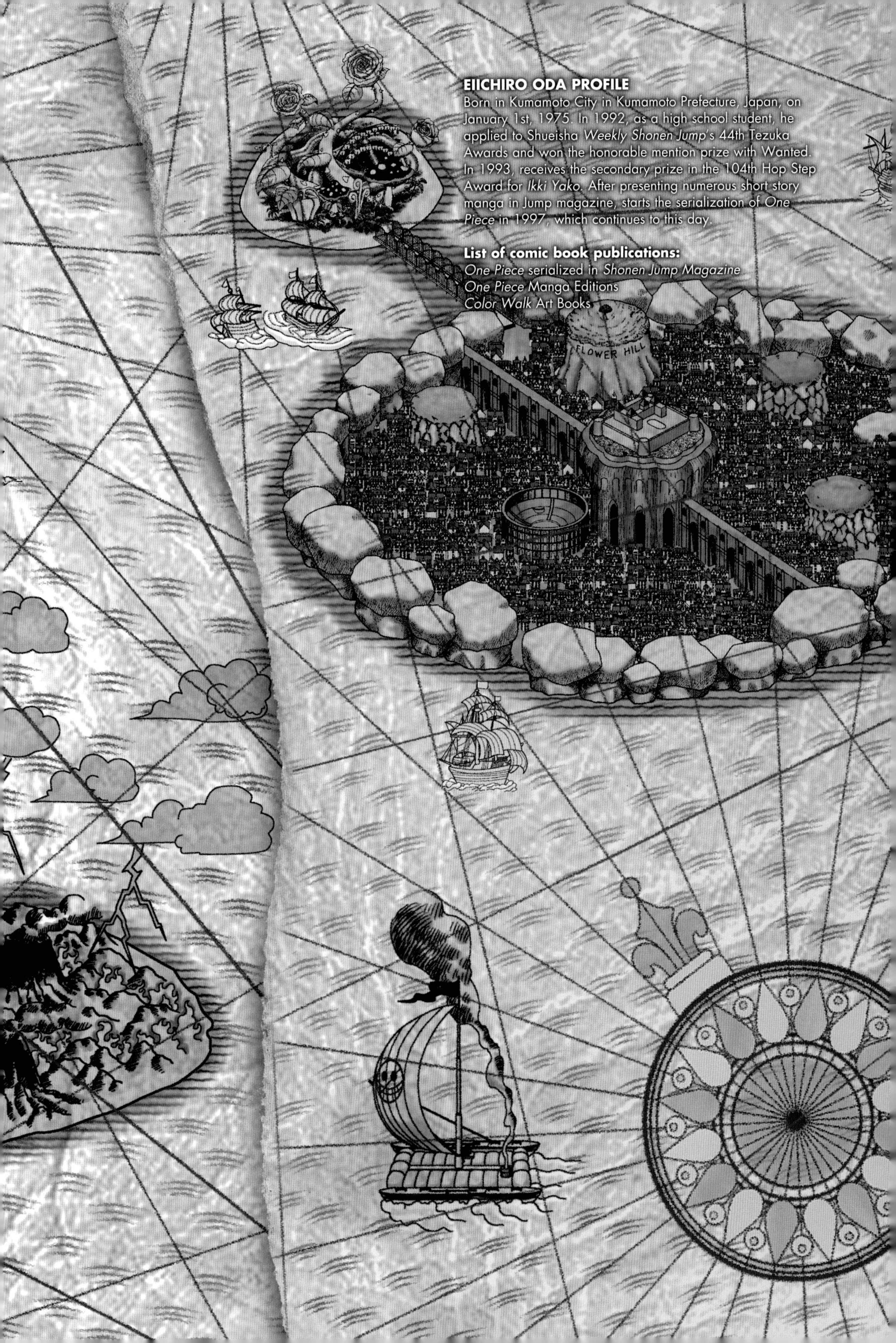
FLOWER HILL

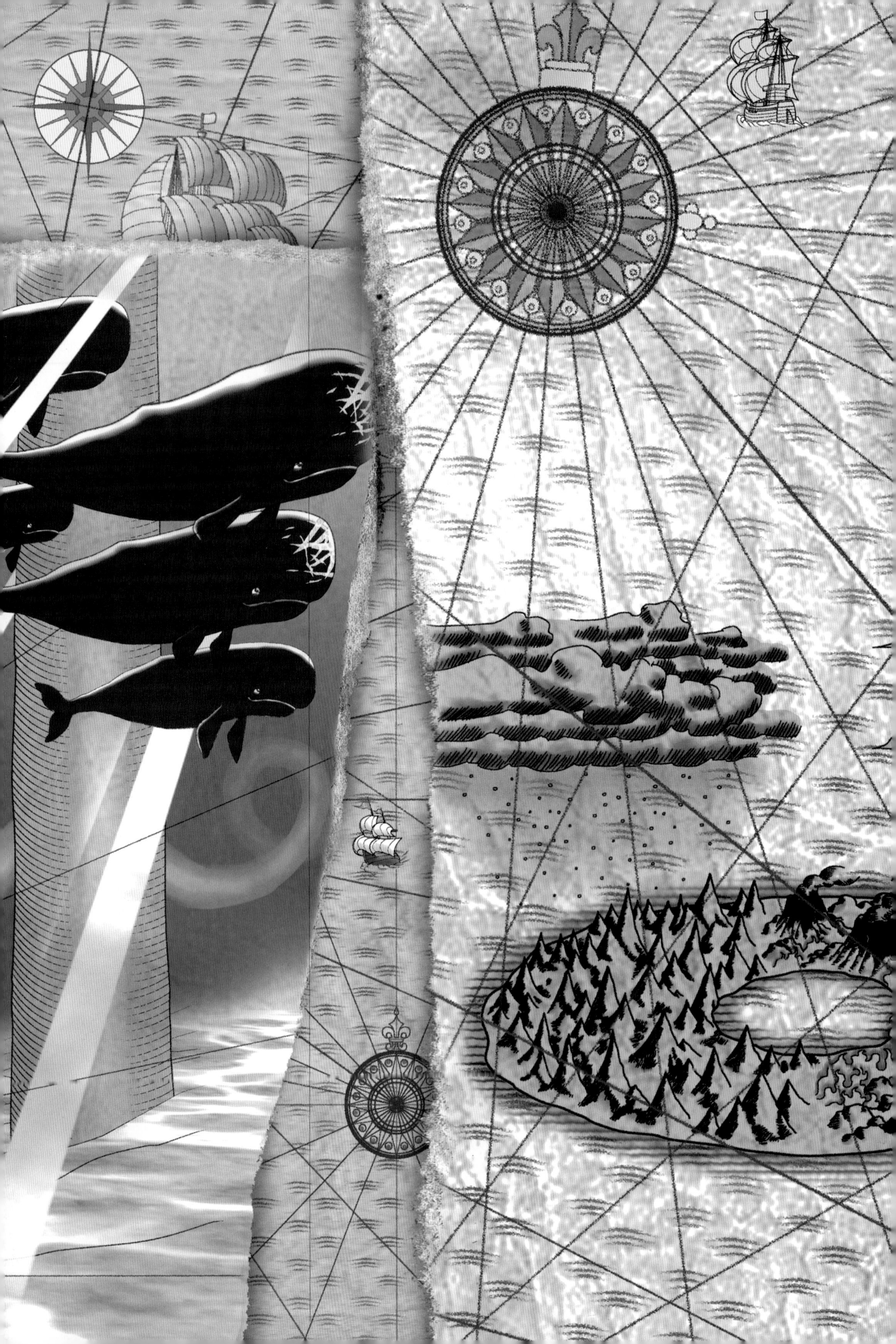

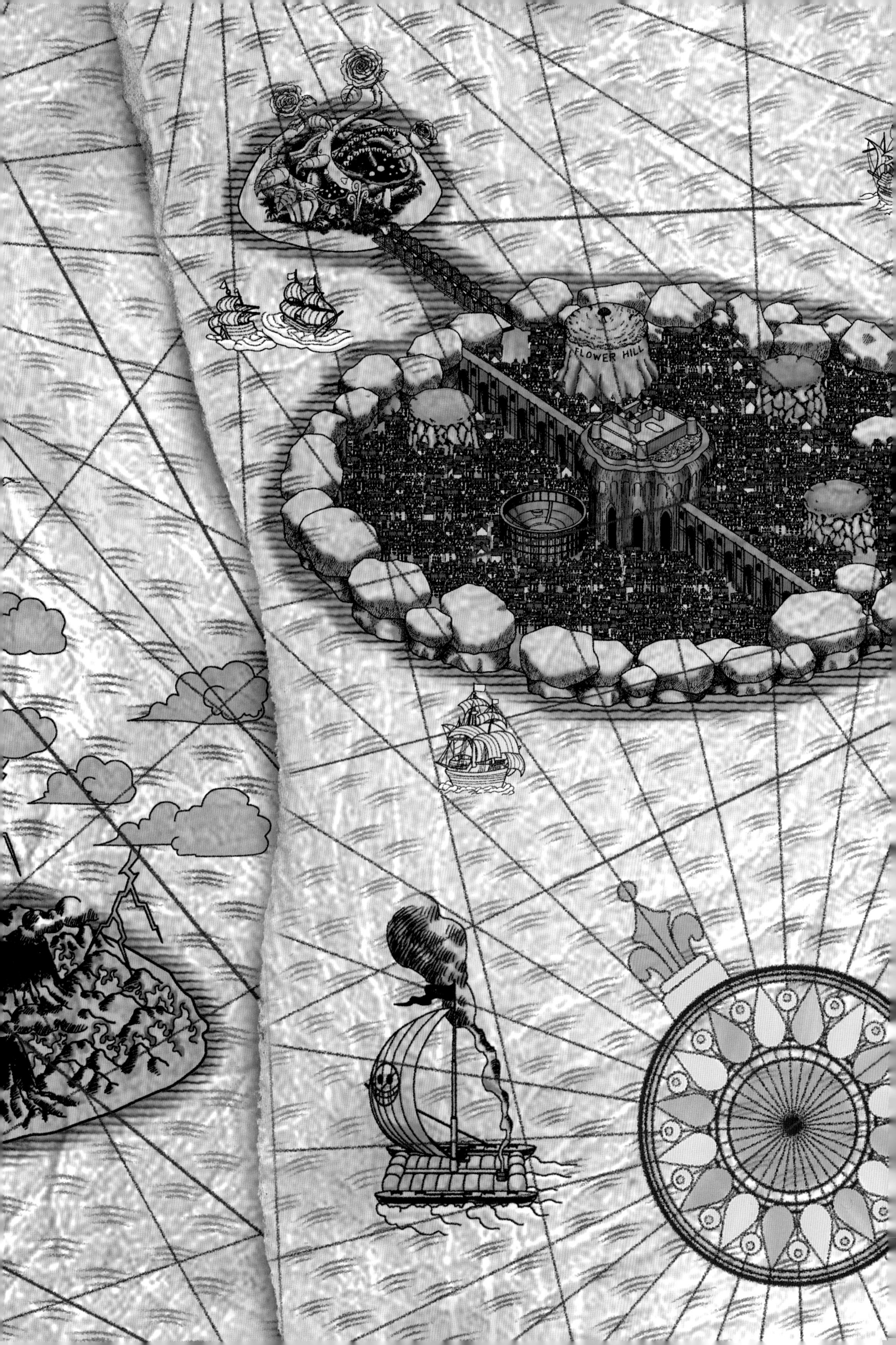
FLOWER HILL

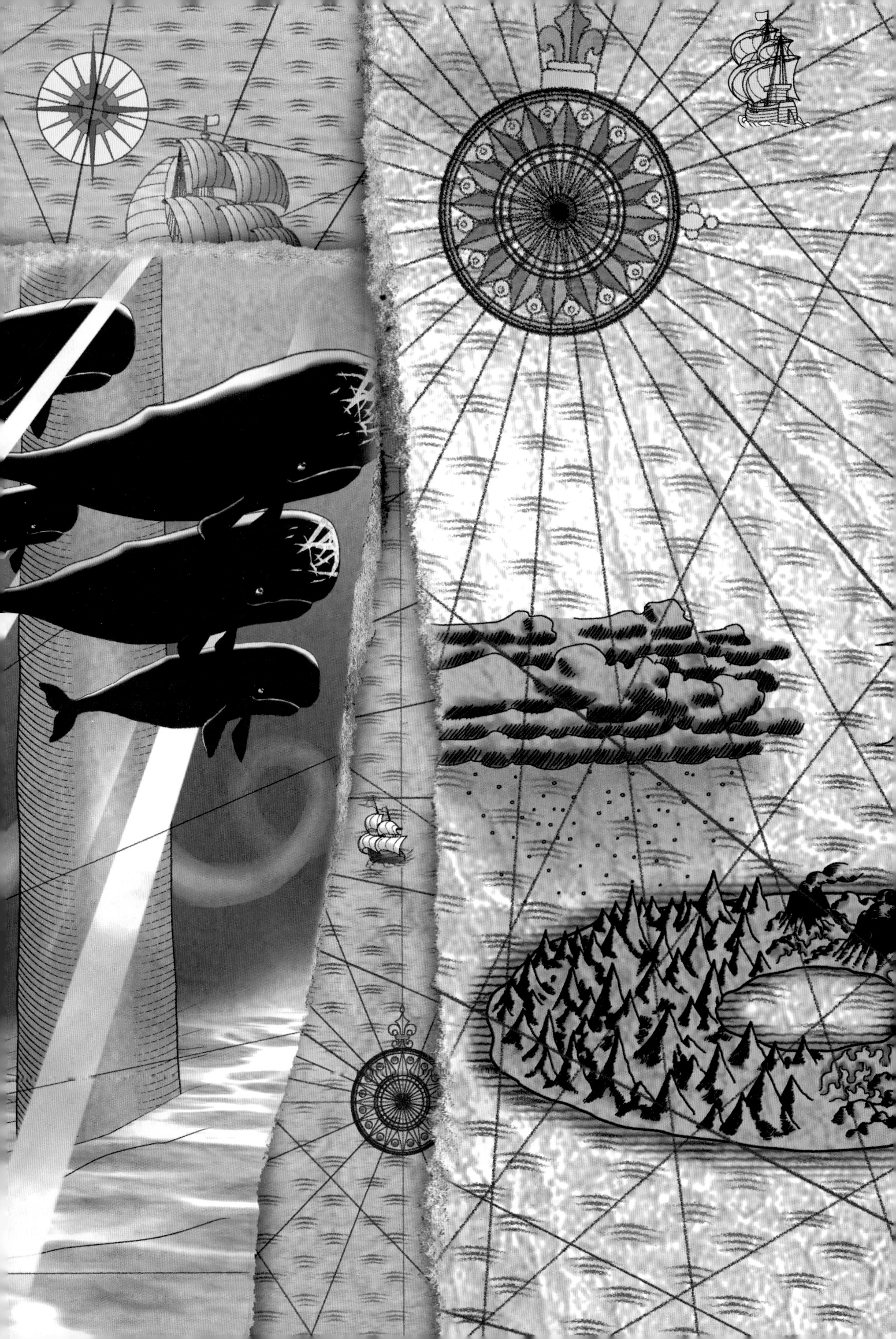

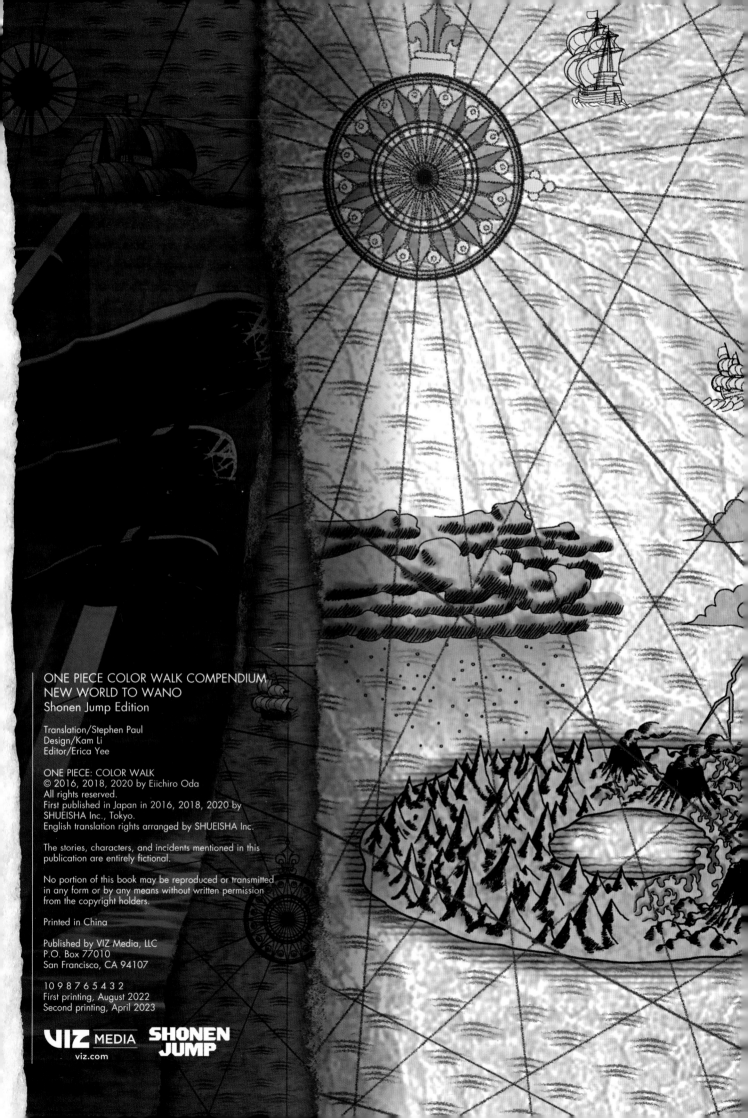

ONE PIECE COLOR WALK COMPENDIUM
NEW WORLD TO WANO
Shonen Jump Edition

Translation/Stephen Paul
Design/Kam Li
Editor/Erica Yee

ONE PIECE: COLOR WALK
© 2016, 2018, 2020 by Eiichiro Oda
All rights reserved.
First published in Japan in 2016, 2018, 2020 by
SHUEISHA Inc., Tokyo.
English translation rights arranged by SHUEISHA Inc.

Printed in China

Published by VIZ MEDIA, LLC
P.O. Box 77010
San Francisco, CA 94107

10 9 8 7 6 5 4 3 2
First printing, August 2022
Second printing, April 2023

VIZ MEDIA   SHONEN JUMP
viz.com

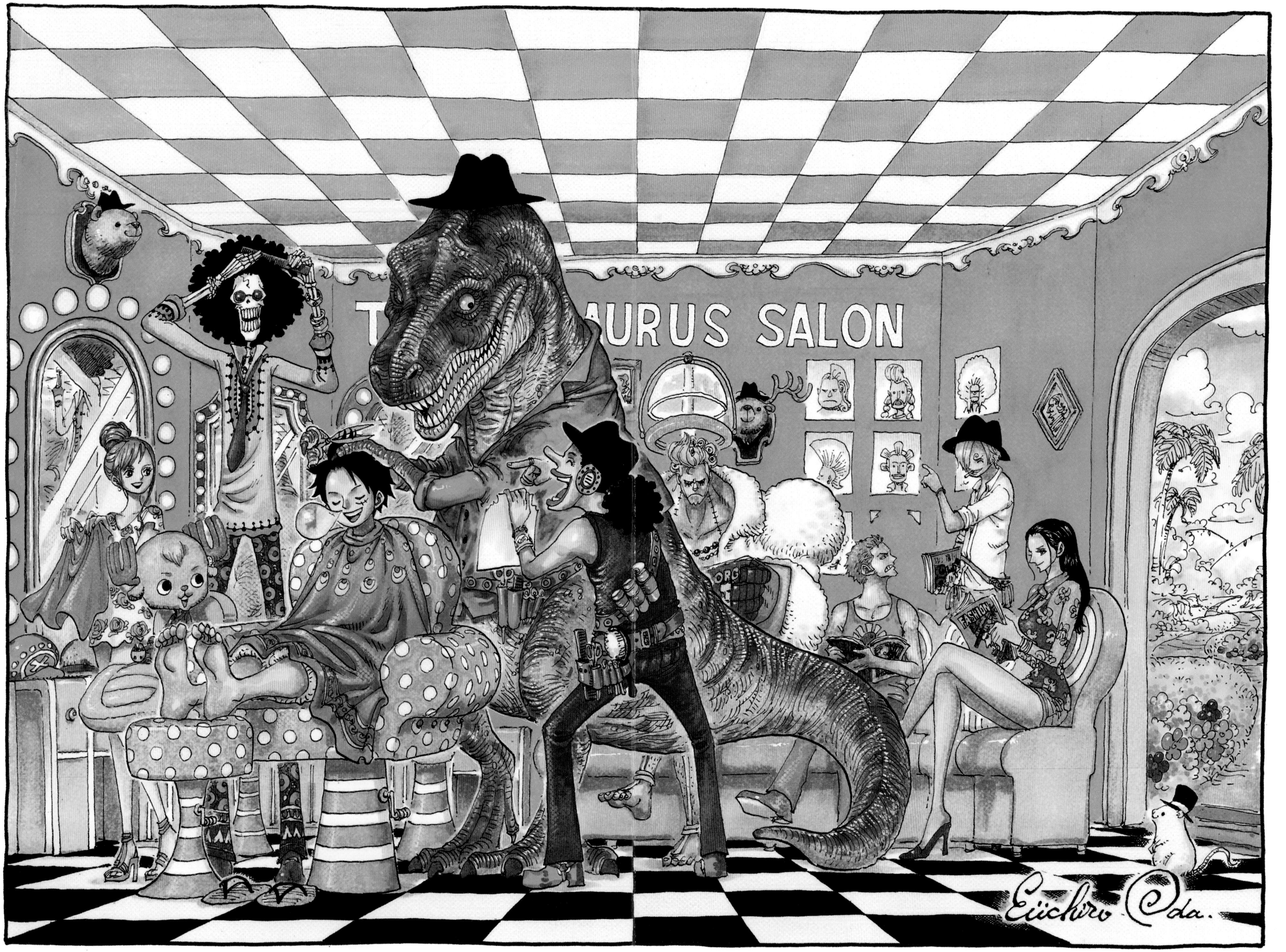
T
AURUS SALON
FASHION
Eiichiro Oda.

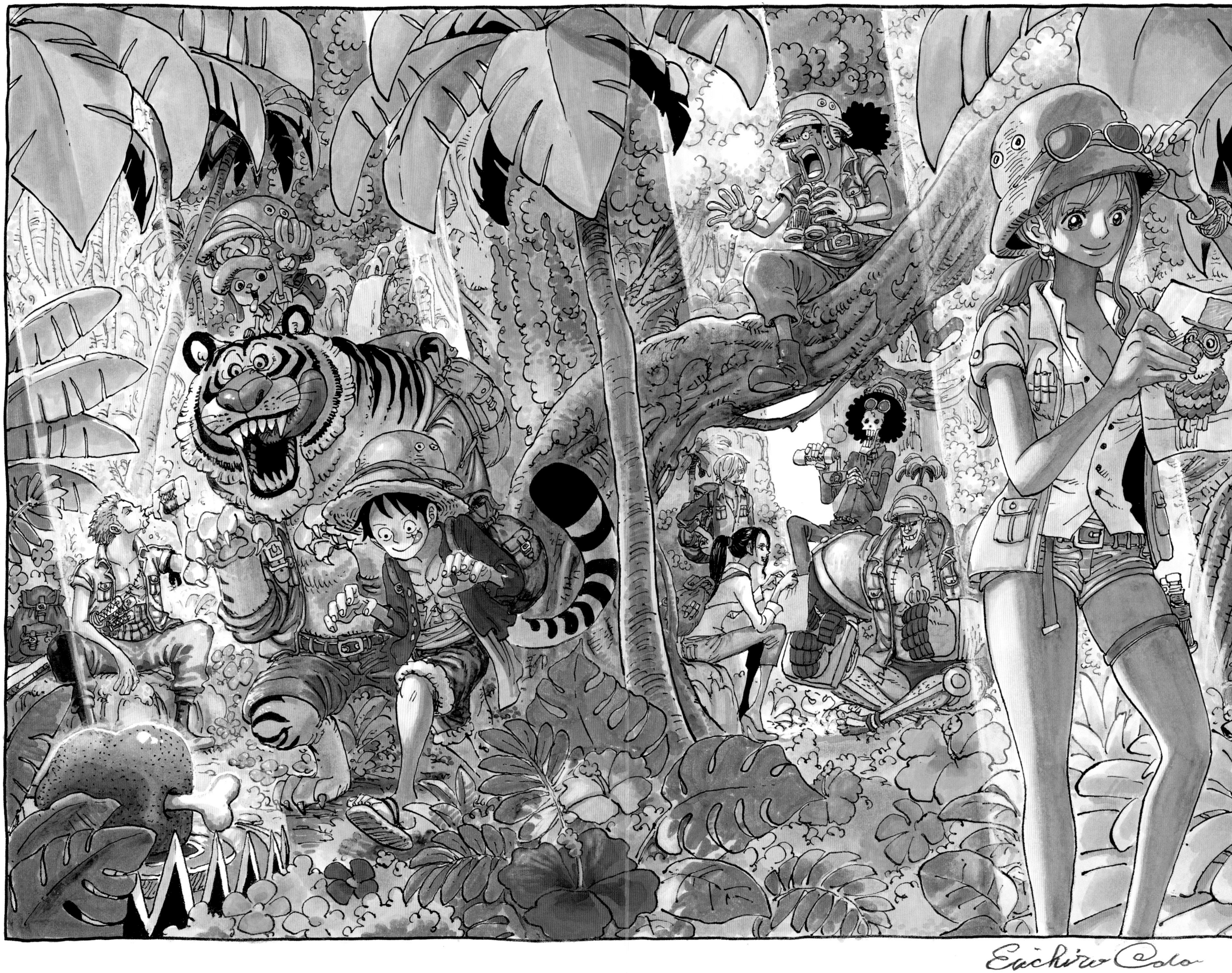

Eiichiro Oda